Prosperity and Plunder

In the Catholic countries of seventeenth- and early eighteenth-century Europe, communities of monks and nuns were growing in number and wealth. By 1750 there were at least 25,000 communities containing at least 350,000 inmates. They constructed vast buildings, dominated education and played a large part in the practice and patronage of learning, music and the arts. They also fulfilled an amazing variety of political, economic and social roles, notably in providing career opportunities for women. Yet many accounts of the period ignore them altogether.

   Prosperity and Plunder recovers this forgotten dimension of European history, assesses the importance of monasteries across Catholic Europe and compares their position in different countries. It goes on to explain the almost complete destruction of the monasteries between 1750 and 1815 by reforming rulers, 'Enlightenment' and the French Revolution, and asks how much society gained and lost in the process.

DEREK BEALES FBA, Litt. D, is Professor Emeritus of Modern History, University of Cambridge, and a Fellow of Sidney Sussex College. His publications include *England and Italy, 1859–60* (1961), *From Castlereagh to Gladstone, 1815–1885* (1969), *The Risorgimento and the Unification of Italy* (1981) and *Joseph II: In the Shadow of Maria Theresa, 1741–1780* (1987).

Joseph Gerstmeyer, view of Melk abbey from the Danube, 1845

Prosperity and Plunder

European Catholic Monasteries in the Age of Revolution, 1650–1815

DEREK BEALES

PUBLISHED BY THE PRESS SYNDICATE OF THE UNIVERSITY OF CAMBRIDGE
The Pitt Building, Trumpington Street, Cambridge, United Kingdom

CAMBRIDGE UNIVERSITY PRESS
The Edinburgh Building, Cambridge, CB2 2RU, UK
40 West 20th Street, New York, NY 10011–4211, USA
477 Williamstown Road, Port Melbourne, VIC 3207, Australia
Ruiz de Alarcón 13, 28014 Madrid, Spain
Dock House, The Waterfront, Cape Town 8001, South Africa

http://www.cambridge.org

© Derek Beales 2003

This book is in copyright. Subject to statutory exception
and to the provisions of relevant collective licensing agreements,
no reproduction of any part may take place without
the written permission of Cambridge University Press.

First published 2003

Printed in the United Kingdom at the University Press, Cambridge

Typeface Quadraat 10.5/15 pt.   *System* LaTeX 2_ε [TB]

A catalogue record for this book is available from the British Library

Library of Congress Cataloguing in Publication data

ISBN 0 521 59090 6 hardback

FOR SALLY,
WITH LOVE AND GRATITUDE

Dialogue on Soldiers and Monks

A: Isn't it dreadful to reflect that we have more monks than soldiers?

B: What you mean to say is that there are far more soldiers than monks.

A: No, no, more monks than soldiers.

B: You may be right about one or two countries of Europe. But in Europe overall? If the peasant sees his crops destroyed by slugs and mice, what does he think is dreadful about it? that there are more slugs than mice? or that there are so many slugs and mice?

A: That I don't understand.

B: Because you don't want to. What then are soldiers?

A: Protectors of the state.

B: And monks pillars of the Church.

A: Confound your Church!

B: Confound your state!

A: Are you dreaming? The state! The state! The state guarantees happiness to every single member in this life.

B: The Church promises everyone salvation after this life.

A: Promises!

B: Idiot!

(G.E. Lessing, c. 1778)

CONTENTS

List of illustrations	page ix
Preface	xv
List of abbreviations	xviii
Introduction	1

PART I   AT THE BRIM OF PROSPERITY

1	The Counter-Reformation and the monasteries	27
2	The great monasteries of the German Catholic lands	39
3	France	84
4	Spain and Portugal	112
5	Italy	126

PART II   PATTERNS OF MONASTIC REFORM

6	The suppression of the Jesuits	143
7	France: the *commission des réguliers*	169
8	The Austrian Monarchy: the Josephist solution	179

PART III   THE TIME OF REVOLUTION

9	The Revolution in France	231
10	The impact of the Revolution outside France	270
	Conclusion	291

Notes	316
Bibliographical essay	359
Index	371

ILLUSTRATIONS

COLOUR PLATES

Frontispiece   Joseph Gerstmeyer, view of Melk abbey from the Danube, 1845. Photo © Stift Melk, Austria

Between pages 174 and 175

1 P.A. de Machy, *Louis XV laying the foundation stone of the church of the abbey of Ste-Geneviève* (detail), Paris, 6 September 1764. Musée Carnavalet. Photo © Centre des monuments nationaux, Paris
2 Turkish bed, c. 1707. © Augustiner-Chorherrenstift St Florian, Austria
3 The Kaisersaal or Marmorsaal, Melk abbey. Photo © Stift Melk, Austria
4 Grand staircase of Göttweig abbey, Lower Austria. Photo from the abbey of Göttweig
5 The pilgrimage church of Vierzehnheiligen. Photo from the Franziskanerkloster, Vierzehnheiligen, Germany
6 The church of the Cistercian abbey of Stams, Tyrol, Austria. Photo © Gregor F. Peda, Kunstverlag Peda, Passau
7 Interior of the library of the Benedictine abbey of St Gall, Switzerland. Photo © Stiftsbibliothek St Gallen
8 The pergola gallery of the cloister of Santa Chiara, Naples, Italy. Photo © Archivio dell'arte Luciano Pedicini, Naples

LIST OF ILLUSTRATIONS

9 Detail of the *sagrario* of the charterhouse of Granada, Spain. Photo © Institut Amatller d'Art Hispanic, Barcelona

BLACK AND WHITE ILLUSTRATIONS

1 Engraving of the Carthusian abbey of Villefranche-de-Rouergue, southern France. Photo © Centre des monuments nationaux, Paris — *page* 20
2 View of the abbey of Melk from the Danube. Photo © Bildarchiv Foto Marburg — 42
3 Two views of a monastic cell of c. 1700 in the former Premonstratensian abbey, Verdun, eastern France. The Conway Library, Courtauld Institute of Art, London — 53
4 Benedikt Prill, ink drawing c. 1750 of the proposed design for Klosterneuburg. Stiftsmuseum, Stift Klosterneuburg, Lower Austria — 55
5 Arcaded fishponds at the Benedictine abbey of Kremsmünster, Upper Austria. Photo © Bildarchiv Foto Marburg — 56
6 The observatory and museum building at Kremsmünster. Photo © Bildarchiv Foto Marburg — 57
7 Plan of the old Benedictine abbey church at Ottobeuren, Germany, superimposed upon the new — 63
8 Ottobeuren abbey, theatre interior. Photo © Bildarchiv Foto Marburg — 64
9 Engraving of Joseph Gabler's organ in the Benedictine abbey of Weingarten, Germany. Cambridge University Library — 67
10 Aerial photograph of the monastery of St Blasien. Photo © Verlag Revellio GmbH, Villingen — 70
11 Design by F.J. Salzmann, c. 1770, for the organ screen in the new abbey church of St Blasien. Generallandesarchiv, Karlsruhe, Germany — 71
12 Painting by Dominikus Zimmermann (detail) of the procession carrying the relic of the Scourged Saviour to the new pilgrimage church of Die Wies, Germany. Photo from the Wieskirche. — 79
13 Cartoon by Joseph Anton Koch of 'monks at table', 1793. Kupferstich-Kabinett der Staatlichen Kunstsammlungen Dresden — 82

LIST OF ILLUSTRATIONS

14	Main courtyard of the abbey of Prémontré, France. The Conway Library, Courtauld Institute of Art, University of London	91
15	Engravings of the abbey of Bec, Normandy, photo © Centre des monuments nationaux	92
16	Hubert Robert, *Les cygnes de Saint-Antoine-les-Champs*. Private collection	102
17	General view of the Escorial, near Madrid, from a sixteenth-century print. Cambridge University Library	119
18	Grand staircase of the nunnery of Las Descalzas Reales, Madrid. Photo © Patrimonio Nacional, Madrid	120
19	General view of the palace-monastery of Mafra, Portugal. Photo Elo-Publicidade, Mafra	123
20	Cistercian monks harvesting in the fields under the protection of the Virgin and St Bernard, Alcobaça, Portugal. Photo Elo-Publicidade, Mafra	124
21	Pietro Longhi, *The Convent Visit*. Museo Civico Correr, Venice, photo © Fratelli Alinari, Florence	133
22	The great cloister of the Carthusian abbey of San Martino, Naples. Photo © Fratelli Alinari, Florence	136
23	The basilica of Superga, near Turin: painting, school of Pannini, in the Palazzo Reale, Turin	137
24	Nave interior of the neo-classical cathedral of Subiaco, Italy. Photo © Fratelli Alinari, Florence	138
25	Satirical depiction of the Jesuits' expulsion from Lisbon, 1762. Photo © The Houghton Library, Harvard University	152
26	Façade of the Franciscan church of San Francisco el Grande, Madrid. Photo © Patrimonio Nacional, Madrid	158
27	Pietro Longhi, *La frateria di Venezia*. Fondazione Querini Stampalia, Venice	188
28	Engraving illustrating the impact of Joseph II's reforms (author's collection)	198
29	Façade of the philosophical library of the Premonstratensian monastery of Strahov, Prague. Photo © Bildarchiv Foto Marburg	204
30	The refectory of the Benedictine archabbey of Pannonhalma, Hungary	206
31	Late eighteenth-century print of the 'Nouvelle Place Royale', Brussels. Photo Bibliothèque Royale de Belgique	220

32	Engraving showing monks chasing out Joseph II's troops, 1789. Photo © Direktion der Museen der Stadt Wien (Historisches Museum)	224
33	Depiction of the sacking of the convent of St-Lazare, 1789. © Photothèque des musées de la ville de Paris (Musée Carnavalet)	244
34	Jacques-Louis David, *The Tennis Court Oath*. Photo © Centre des monuments nationaux, Paris (Château of Versailles)	246
35	Caricature showing a peasant woman supporting a noblewoman and a nun, 1789. © Photothèque des musées de la ville de Paris (Musée Carnavalet)	248
36	Caricature of the French clergy being forced to surrender their property, 1789–90. © Photothèque des musées de la ville de Paris (Musée Carnavalet)	249
37	The French abbey of Cluny (a) before its destruction during the French revolution and (b) in the process of being destroyed c. 1810, from contemporary illustrations.	266
38	The Benedictine abbey of Einsiedeln, Switzerland. Graphische Sammlung, Stiftsbibliothek, Einsiedeln	279
39	*Der Entschädigungs-Baum* ('The Compensation Tree') by F.L. Neubauer, 1803. Germanisches Nationalmuseum Nürnberg	287
40	I.S. Dürr, The secularisation of the Cistercian monastery of Salem, Germany, 1804. Photo © Generallandesarchiv Karlsruhe, Germany	288
41	Watercolour cartoon satirising secularisation in Bavaria, 1803. Museen der Stadt Nürnberg	290

MAPS

1	Austrian monasteries	44
2	Monasteries of S. Germany and Tyrol	61
3	Belgian monasteries	211
4	Swiss monasteries	277

FIGURE

1	Numbers of monks and novices at Melk abbey, 1684–1990	47

List of Illustrations

TABLES

1	The capital value of Melk's resources	43
2	Percentage of Melk's income from various sources	43
3	The monastic timetable	50
4	The monastic day as reformed by Joseph II	200
5	Monasticism in Lower Austria and Hungary compared	207

PREFACE

This book is a much expanded version of the Birkbeck Lectures in Ecclesiastical History which I gave in the Michaelmas Term 1993 under the title *Lazy Monks and Philosophic Spoilers*. I have retained the lecture form in which it was originally conceived.

I owe profound thanks to the Master and Fellows of Trinity College for inviting me to give these lectures. In so honouring me they presented me with a glorious opportunity to study more deeply a subject which had long fascinated me. I am further indebted to the College for its great generosity in making me a grant that has enabled me to include coloured illustrations in the book. Among the Fellows of Trinity the late Dr Robert Robson and Dr Boyd Hilton lent unstinting support, and Professor Roger Paulin presided graciously over the lectures.

The founder of the Birkbeck Lectures, Mrs Anna Margaret Mednyanszky, was the daughter of George Birkbeck, creator of the Mechanics' Institutes that offered part-time education to working men in nineteenth-century Britain, and half-sister of William Lloyd Birkbeck, Fellow of Trinity and F.W. Maitland's predecessor as Downing Professor of the Laws of England. She published a book entitled *Rural and Historical Gleanings from Central Europe* (1854). When I had cut the pages of the University Library's copy, I discovered it to be a passionate defence of Hungary, especially Protestant Hungary, for which her husband, Colonel Mednyanszky, had fought against the Austrian oppressor in and after the 1848 Revolution. It is unlikely that she and her family would have relished courses of lectures on Counter-Reformation Catholicism. But her book does contain one favourable reference to an abbey, the Benedictine abbey of Tihány on lake Balaton, where she tells us the abbot dispensed truly Hungarian hospitality even to English Protestants. In saying this she provides evidence for several of the arguments I shall be putting forward.

Since my interest in this subject has caused surprise, I should perhaps try to explain it. It was fired at first by the inspiration and example of the late Brother Peter, OSF, who while I was at Bishop's Stortford College introduced me to the Dorset house of the Anglican Franciscans. A less direct but continuing influence has been my passion for Baroque organs and their music, nurtured for more than fifty years by the late Mr Bertram Bayford. Another friend made at school, Mr Roger Peers, has ever since fostered my interest and delight in architecture and music. As an undergraduate I heard the spellbinding lectures of the late Dom David Knowles on medieval monasticism and the late Sir Nikolaus Pevsner on German and Austrian Baroque.

Many members of my College have helped to develop my interest. The late Dr R.C. Smail taught me most of what I know about medieval Christendom. The charisma of the late Dr Royston Lambert communicated to me some of his enthusiasm for Baroque, as for so many aspects of the arts. I have never forgotten an essay written for me in or around 1958 by Mr Fred Murphy, in which he argued powerfully that historians (including myself) exaggerated the importance of the handful of early Jesuits and neglected the impact of the larger cohort of later centuries. My first slides of German Baroque monasteries were given me by Professor Stanford E. Lehmberg; my first visit to any of them, in 1962, was made in the company of Dr John Reid; they and Mr Martin Thorpe have continued to encourage my work in this field. Professor Tim Blanning has shared with me over the last forty years his profound knowledge of eighteenth-century Europe, and by his kindness in reading and commenting on the typescript of the book has much improved it. I have profited from Dr Christopher Page's learning and enthusiasm, while Professor Barry Nisbet made me aware of Lessing's wonderfully apt *Dialogue on Soldiers and Monks*, and he and Mr Tom Wyatt have given me invaluable help with translation from German and French. I owe a special debt to the wisdom and friendship of two former Fellows, Professor Simon Dixon and Dr Benjamin Thompson, and three Visiting Fellows, Professor Carlo Capra, the late Rev. Professor Donal Kerr and Professor Hagen Schulze.

The Rev. Professor Owen Chadwick has encouraged me personally and through his *The Popes and European Revolution*, by far the best book in English on the Catholicism of Europe in the eighteenth century. I have benefited enormously from Professor Peter Dickson's work and advice, though I hasten to absolve him from any responsibility for my use of statistics. As this book turned into a comparative study, I incurred many further debts, so many over such a long period that it is difficult to include everyone. But I owe particular thanks to Dr Nigel Aston; Professor Éva Balázs; Professor Robert Baldick; Lady de Bellaigue;

Professor Wim Blockmans; Mr R.P. Blows; Miss Brenda Bolton; Professor David Brading; Mr Robin Briggs; Professor Christopher Brooke; Mgr Charles Burns; Dr Richard Butterwick; Dr Melissa Calaresu; Dr Frans Ciappara; Professor H. Coppens; Mr James Day; Dr Guy Dejongh; Professor J.A. Downie; Professor Eamon Duffy; Professor Robert Evans; Dr Andreas Fahrmeir; Dr Giovanna Farrell-Vinay; Mag. Elisabeth Fattinger; Professor Dermot Fenlon; Dr J.L. Fuchs; Professor Antonio García y García; Professor Elisabeth Garms-Cornides; the late Mr E.E.Y. Hales; Dr Ian Harris; Dr Tim Hochstrasser; Dr Éva Hoós; Professor Olwen Hufton; Dr Maurizio Isabella; Dom Philip Jebb; Professor Harm Klueting; Dr Éva Knapp; Professor Domokos Kosáry; Dr Elisabeth Kovács; Dr Ferdinand Kramer; Dr David Laven; Dr Mary Laven; Dr Albert Lavigne; Dr Helen Ledbury; Dr Mark Ledbury; Dr Peter Linehan; Father Umberto dell'Orto; Dr Jon Parry; Professor László Péter; Professor Brian Pullan; Dr James Raven; Professor Jan Roegiers; the late Dr John Rosselli; Dr Ulinka Rublack; Professor David Sacks; Professor Eda Sagarra; Professor Hamish Scott; Dr Peter Shore; Dr István Szijártó; Dr Stephen Taylor; the late Dr Christiane Thomas; Professor István György Tóth; the Marquis de Trazegnies; Dr Gabor Tüskés; Dr L.C. Van Dyck; Dr Márta Velladics; Professor Peter Wende; and Dr Christopher Wright. Many of those named have generously given me copies of their books and articles.

I should like to acknowledge the ready help I have received from many archivists and librarians at the National Archives and Royal Library in Brussels, the National Archives and the National Library in Budapest, the University Library in Cambridge, the University Library of Ghent, the British Library in London, the Archivio segreto vaticano and the Biblioteca apostolica vaticana in Rome, the British School at Rome, the Haus-, Hof- und Staatsarchiv and the National Library in Vienna and the abbeys of Bec, Downside, Melk, Pannonhalma, St Florian, St Gall and Tongerlo.

I gratefully acknowledge the permission of Her Majesty Queen Elizabeth II to use material from the Royal Archives at Windsor. I record with gratitude that my travels to libraries and archives were assisted by grants from the British Academy, Cambridge University and Sidney Sussex College, Cambridge.

Mr William Davies of Cambridge University Press has not only shown remarkable patience but has also taken a great interest in the book, giving most generously of his time and expertise in obtaining the photographs.

My greatest debt is recorded in the dedication. My wife Sally made the project possible, entering into my enthusiasm, driving me to numerous French, Swiss, German, Austrian, Italian and Czech monasteries, joining me in visits to many more, particularly in Spain, and giving me support in countless other ways.

LIST OF ABBREVIATIONS

AHY	Austrian History Yearbook
AP	Archives parlementaires
ASVNV	Archivio segreto vaticano, Nunziatura Vienna
BL	British Library, London
DIP	Dizionario degli Istituti di Perfezione, ed. G. Pelliccia and G. Rocca (Rome, 1973–)
FRA	Fontes rerum austriacarum
HHSA	Haus-, Hof- und Staatsarchiv, Vienna
HJ	Historical Journal
MIÖG	Mitteilungen des Instituts für österreichische Geschichtsforschung
MÖSA	Mitteilungen des österreichischen Staatsarchivs
TRHS	Transactions of the Royal Historical Society
ZBL	Zeitschrift für bayerische Landesgeschichte

INTRODUCTION

THE IMPORTANCE OF MONASTERIES IN EUROPE OF THE *ANCIEN RÉGIME*

For most historians of modern Europe my subject might as well not exist. Whereas in every history of the European Middle Ages monasteries play a principal role, the great majority of books on later periods ignore monks and nuns altogether – except perhaps for the Jesuits. This is true not only of general surveys but even of some distinguished works specifically concerned with church history. On page 259 of the *Oxford Illustrated History of Christianity* Patrick Collinson tells us that 'in Luther's perception the mass and all other devotions were "works" with a false motivation. There was no longer any rationale for monasticism.' After this, apart from a few mentions of the Jesuits, the authors, as if taking their cue from Luther, make no further direct reference to any monasteries or religious Orders in Europe until page 587, which is concerned with the period since the Second World War.[1]

Leaving aside for the moment the question of its rationale, I shall look first at the sheer scale of early modern monasticism. During the Reformation, of course, monasteries virtually disappeared from countries where Protestantism became the official religion. As for the lands in which Catholicism maintained itself or recovered its position, a commonly held view is encapsulated in C.H. Lawrence's justly respected work on *Medieval Monasticism*. He acknowledges that in these areas the institution survived. But even there, he declares:

because associations devoted to the celebration of liturgical ritual no longer met the religious demands of society or provided convenient homes for its surplus children, and because the number of monastic establishments vastly exceeded the needs of those few who had a personal vocation to the ascetical life, social and economic support fell away; the number of monasteries dwindled, and monastic property was transferred to other purposes.[2]

The truth is utterly different. In the countries where the Reformation did not succeed, monasteries not merely survived; they increased and flourished anew. Old Orders were reformed and prospered again; new Orders were founded, with aims somewhat different from the old, and grew mightily. This was true of France, the southern Netherlands, Spain, Portugal, Italy, southern Germany, Poland, parts of Switzerland and the vast lands of the Austrian Monarchy in central and eastern Europe. In most of these areas numbers of monks and nuns reached a peak in the second or third quarter of the eighteenth century. By around 1750 Catholic Europe boasted well over 15,000 monasteries for men and at least 10,000 nunneries – using those terms in the broadest sense.[3] These houses belonged to dozens of distinct Orders. In a cycle of mid-eighteenth-century paintings that decorate the walls of the abbot's antechamber in the Cistercian monastery at Schöntal in Franconia, 302 different types of clerical dress are depicted, most of them specific to a particular Order of monks or nuns; and its coverage was certainly incomplete.[4]

Around 1750 there were in the whole of Catholic Europe at least 350,000 inmates of monasteries out of a total population of less than a hundred million, a proportion of rather more than 1 in 300. They were not evenly spread, but their presence was everywhere evident and felt. In Spain and Italy nearly 1 person in 100 was a monk or nun of some sort; in exceptional places like the papal states the proportion was nearer 1 in 50. In France it was only about 1 in 300, near the average level for Catholic Europe, but even there, just before the Revolution, the agricultural writer Arthur Young complained: 'I search for good farmers, and run my head at every turn against monks.'[5] In fact these ratios of monks and nuns to total population, high though they seem by modern standards, give a misleadingly low impression of the strength of monasticism. Since in this period scarcely half of those who were born reached adulthood, and since the great majority of monks and nuns were adults, a more meaningful ratio is that of all monks and nuns to all adults. To arrive at that, the proportions already given need to be roughly doubled. Special circumstances could produce ratios so high as to be scarcely believable. The most extreme that I have come across is this: in seventeenth-century Florence the ratio of nuns to married women reached 102:100, more than double what it had been a century earlier.[6]

Two further numerical comparisons highlight the differences between early modern and modern society. In most Catholic countries there were in the eighteenth century many more monks than nuns, though in France – and at least in parts of Italy – it was the other way round. And in most, if not all, Catholic countries monks and nuns, taken together, formed the majority of all clergy.

The illustrations in this book depict some of the grandest monastery buildings, but they cannot begin to do justice to the monastic presence as a whole. In many dioceses the cathedral was rivalled in scale and opulence by several abbeys, which had usually been exempted for most or all purposes from the jurisdiction of the bishop.[7] Parish churches were generally unimpressive, much less grand than monastic churches that commonly served a mere handful of monks or nuns. From most parts of the countryside some monastic complex could be seen, often dominant on a hill. In towns of any size there were sure to be several forbidding conventual façades louring over the modest dwellings of ordinary citizens. Lisbon possessed in the mid-eighteenth century about fifty houses, one third of which were for women.[8] If that sounds like an extreme case, it pales into insignificance beside Paris, which is said by one authority to have had fifty-eight houses of monks and well over a hundred of nuns, while Naples broke all records with more than a hundred monasteries for males and nearly a hundred for females.[9] To mention a monastery conjures up for most people an image of splendid rural isolation, but by the eighteenth century monasticism in Catholic Europe was predominantly urban.

Monasteries were believed to be enormously rich, and extravagant estimates of their wealth were current – for example, that they owned over half of all land in Bavaria and in Naples.[10] To calculate the correct figures on the basis of the surviving information is always difficult and sometimes impossible, but it is clear that these very high estimates are exaggerated. Still, it is accepted that in Bavaria the greater monasteries were lords to 28 per cent of all peasants, which means that monasteries as a whole controlled an even higher proportion; and in Lower Austria, the province that includes Vienna, monasteries owned roughly 20 per cent of all land. In both cases their share was half of all church property.[11] In some areas the percentage of monastic land was much lower. In the different regions of France the proportion of land held in 1789 by the Church as a whole varied from 40 per cent in some regions to less than 1 per cent in others, and it is a reasonable guess that the average holding of monasteries was greater than 5 per cent, but not much greater. It is generally believed that a quarter of the immensely valuable land in Paris belonged to monasteries. So, across Catholic Europe, the Orders must have owned on average somewhere near 10 per cent of all the land, which was about half of all the Church's land.[12] This is a very substantial proportion, quite enough to account for the belief of contemporaries that monasteries, taken as a whole, were very rich. By way of comparison, the National Trust even now owns little more than 1 per cent of the land of England, Wales and Northern Ireland.[13]

In addition to owning land, many monasteries, especially of the old Orders, had the right to levy tithe, which was in origin and principle a tax of 10 per cent, payable in kind by the producer on all the products of agriculture for the support of the parish priest. In a good proportion of parishes all or part of the tithe had been granted to monasteries or other ecclesiastical corporations, which had a duty to pay for the parish priest but could keep the surplus for themselves. The yield of tithe to monasteries was often even greater than the revenue from their own land.[14]

Among monasteries, however, and as between Orders, there was immense variation in wealth.[15] Most of the really well-endowed houses belonged to the old Orders which had been founded by 1150, chiefly the Benedictines, Cistercians, Augustinians, Premonstratensians and Carthusians. Later houses, including the very large number possessed by the Orders deriving from the Franciscans, founded in the thirteenth century, were originally in principle propertyless and 'mendicant', and they remained in general relatively poor, in many cases genuinely impoverished; and in some of these Orders the monks still begged for their living. But the richer monasteries, taken together, were landowners on the grand scale, lords to millions of peasants. They possessed farms and forests, which they sometimes managed themselves and sometimes leased out; they developed suburbs; they made and sold beer, wine and liqueurs; they acted virtually as banks; in fact they were involved in commercial and industrial enterprises of almost every kind. They were major employers of labour. If, as seems probable, a majority of monks became priests, the remainder took only minor orders. These, assisted in certain Orders by lay brothers and sisters, undertook some worldly and menial tasks. But many houses also employed numerous servants. All this support enabled the 'choir monks', especially the priests among them, and most nuns to devote themselves to higher things. An army of builders and craftsmen was required to construct and maintain their buildings. In seeking to make their churches and their services beautiful and splendid, they acted as major patrons of the visual arts and of music.

Monasteries continued to fulfil their ancient duties of hospitality and charity. Many of them, especially those in remote places, acted as virtual hotels. In addition to employing many people – usually more than was strictly necessary – they distributed food and alms to the poor and needy, and were known to be especially generous to those affected by natural calamities. This indiscriminate charity was criticised by reformers and economists, but it is clear that many individuals, and whole villages in the neighbourhood of richer monasteries, survived only through these doles.[16]

Most monasteries were largely freed by law from the control of the ordinary church authorities and had valuable secular privileges too: these included exemption from some taxation, and jurisdiction over their inmates and over the inhabitants of their lands. Many of the abbots of the greater houses – and even, mainly in Germany, a few abbesses – had seats in the assemblies or 'Estates' of their provinces; and in the First or ecclesiastical Estate they often outnumbered the bishops.[17] The lands of many of the major monasteries within the Holy Roman Empire formed virtually independent principalities, ruled by their abbots or abbesses.[18] Further, most monastic Orders were international or supranational, their individual houses being in certain matters subject to authorities based outside their own countries, not only to the pope but also in some cases to a presiding abbot or to a 'general', perhaps located in Rome. This position still seemed natural enough in the Empire, with its hundreds of political units holding widely scattered lands, but appeared increasingly anomalous in the compact absolute monarchies that dominated most of Catholic Europe.

The rationale of monasticism remained essentially the desire or call to remove oneself from many of the ordinary cares and preoccupations of the world, taking vows – in most Orders lifelong vows – originally of poverty, chastity and obedience, in order to give oneself wholly to the service of God. This service always included prayer, meditation and worship, and helping to run the relevant institutions. According to the aims of particular Orders, it might also involve preaching, teaching, pastoral work and missionary activity; charity and the care of the sick, the old, the mad, the crippled and the deaf and dumb; music, scholarship and the copying and illumination of manuscripts; or even, in the case of the military Orders, taking up arms on behalf of the Church.

It was rare for an Order or even an individual house to have forgotten this rationale completely. But monasteries were so numerous, and in many cases so long established, so well endowed and so firmly rooted in their localities and in contemporary society, that they had come to fulfil social functions that had little to do with that rationale. Monastic property and wealth were seen by most Catholics as a part of the natural order, as was the monastic life itself. They offered various kinds of opportunity to society at large. If a family enabled a son to become a monk, or a daughter a nun, especially in a wealthy house, it was opening to them what was often their only chance of education, status, security, responsibility and a degree of comfort for life. To do this usually required the provision of a dowry for a nun and a corresponding down payment for a monk. A bookish or musical boy or girl, even of very humble origin, might be welcome in a major monastery, and to enter one might be their only way of using their particular gifts. The family strategies of the nobility often depended on sending younger sons into monasteries, especially if they were scholarly or physically weak, and – even more important – providing for surplus daughters by placing them in nunneries. A Dominican, protesting to Philip II of Spain against a proposal to sell church lands to augment the royal treasury, declared that

[nuns,] who form a very large part of the Spanish nobility, will be particularly affected... The great lords and all men of note, since they can marry off only one in four or six of their daughters because of excessive dowries, have no other remedy but, out of necessity, to place the others in monasteries; and the founders of these convents, with this idea in mind, worked to endow and enrich them so that poverty does not lead [the nuns] into wickedness or to live in despair and misery. To provide them with secure revenues that they can easily collect, they have been given lands and serfs.[19]

This practice, though more general in Spain and Italy than elsewhere, was accepted as normal in every Catholic country. At a lower social level, the life of the mendicant monk, committed to celibacy but guaranteed a roof over his head and legally protected as a member of the clergy, might well seem preferable to the ordinary fate of a penniless city youth; and, where the mendicant Orders were strong, especially in Italy, they could be seen as agents of poor relief or social control not only because of their work for people outside their houses but also because they admitted into their ranks men and women who would otherwise probably be unemployed and disaffected.[20]

The social gulf between the propertied and the mendicant Orders was highlighted by a Victorian Anglican clergyman called Hobart Seymour in his book *A Pilgrimage to Rome*, published in 1848. He was strongly anti-Catholic, and he was writing after the end of my period. But he was unusual in having made it his business to visit a variety of monasteries – and in having studied both at Trinity College, Dublin, and Oxford – and his acute observations would have applied with little alteration in the eighteenth century:

The hotels and boarding houses of London and Paris [he declares] do not present a more perfect system of gradation than the convents and monasteries of Italy... Some... are well and richly endowed;... are supplied with many comforts, and... admit only a superior class of persons as members, with the exception of a few laymen of the lower classes, who are admitted on the express understanding of their being servants to the others; acting as porters, cooks, messengers, &c. In convents of this class, the mode of life is not unlike that of some members of our English universities. Having nothing to do, they live in their apartments, dine together, gossip with one another, attend the prescribed number of services at chapel... Some [monks], whose inclinations lead them to study,... have proved themselves among the most intellectual, learned, and able men of the age. Some, whose tendencies are towards religion,... devote themselves to the acquisition of religious knowledge, and political intrigue... Others devote themselves to the amusement of the passing hour...

There are other [monasteries] which are exclusively appropriated to the inferior orders of life. These are chiefly Franciscans and Capuchins, whose appearance is familiar to every one who has visited any part of Italy. Their coarse brown dresses, their shaven crowns, their wooden-sandaled feet, their cord, their rosary, the shaven face of one order, and long beards of the other, are familiar to every eye; while the filth of their persons and the odour of their clothes are no less familiar to every traveller.

I was conducted through one of the convents of these men... It contained at the time no less than *one hundred and seventy monks!*... The dirt and stench of [their] little rooms, equalled only by a squalid garret in St Giles' in London, exceeds any possible description... It was a sort of overgrown alms-house, a sort of union poor-house, the inmates of which were not the sick and the infirm and the aged, as in England; but the strong, the active, the healthy, and the able-bodied of the population, who ought to have been compelled to labour for their support.[21]

Mendicants necessarily spent much time outside their houses. But monks of most other Orders – and some nuns – also took a much greater part than is generally realised in religious and secular life outside the monastery walls. Monks quite frequently achieved the highest positions in the Church. The eighteenth-century frescoes in the refectory of the Benedictine abbey of Pannonhalma in Hungary claim that the Order had produced 15,000 bishops, 7,000 archbishops, 200 cardinals and 52 popes.[22] Of the eighteenth-century popes Benedict XIII (1724–30) was a Dominican, Clement XIV (1769–74) a Franciscan and Pius VII, elected in 1800, a Benedictine. Many instances will be given in the course of this book of monks and nuns involved in a rich variety of apparently secular pursuits. But the most influential of all the social roles of monks and nuns was in education. Above the primary level, the colleges and universities of Catholic countries were dominated by monks.[23]

So, in the mid-eighteenth century, monasteries had immense, though largely forgotten, importance not just within the Church but also in the economic, social, political, artistic, intellectual and educational life of all parts of Catholic Europe.

THE ASSAULT ON THE MONASTERIES

By 1812 the situation was utterly different. Virtually no monasteries or nunneries survived in France, Germany, Belgium or in northern and central Italy. In Switzerland, Poland, southern Italy and much of Spain only a small number remained. On the other hand, in the Austrian Empire only about a third had been suppressed, while in Sicily, Portugal and the rest of Spain they had hardly been touched.[24] In most cases the lands and possessions of the suppressed houses had been confiscated by governments and sold off; and their buildings had been commandeered or vandalised. The surviving monks and nuns from these houses were mostly scattered, many in exile. While some had found congenial employment as parish clergy or in education, others were struggling to survive, on inadequate pensions if they were lucky. Given the previous influence of the Orders, this was a revolution – not only in religious and ecclesiastical history but also in the history of education and of society at large.

At government level the serious assault on the Orders had begun in the 1750s, when the rulers of Portugal set about destroying the Jesuits. By 1773 the movement against them had spread to all Catholic Powers, and pope Clement XIV concluded that it was necessary in the wider interests of the Church to suppress the Order.[25] Meanwhile, Catholic states were turning their attention to other Orders. Louis XV established in 1766 a *commission des réguliers* which led to the abolition of hundreds of monasteries, but among the reforming rulers the most prominent was the emperor Joseph II, who during the 1780s dissolved about a third of the more than 2,000 houses in the Austrian Monarchy.[26] Then in the early months of the French Revolution the National Assembly seized all church lands and abolished all monastic Orders and vows. Between 1794 and 1812 the armies and diplomacy of the Revolution and Napoleon saw to the extension of these drastic measures to the southern Netherlands, Germany, most of Italy and Switzerland and parts of Spain. The partitions of Poland between 1772 and 1795 led to substantial suppressions there.[27] In most countries revival followed the Restoration in 1815, but it had hardly been imaginable during the previous fifty years.

Though all Catholic countries shared some elements of this story, there were enormous differences between the experiences of individual states and regions. As we shall see, the situation of monasteries in *ancien régime* France was in many respects peculiar, but so in varying degrees was their position in every country, whether Belgium, Spain, Portugal, Italy, Germany, Switzerland, the Austrian Monarchy or Poland.[28] The chronology of decay, suppression and revival varied. Sometimes completely contradictory trends were at work in neighbouring countries. For example, two months after the nationalisation of all monastic land in France in 1789 some of the greater Belgian houses organised and funded the forces that drove Joseph II's army from their provinces.[29] The composition and status of the clergy, and of the monks and nuns among them, varied from region to region, as did the social balance between sympathy with monasticism and hostility to it. These variations have both reflected and shaped the character of localities and nations, and deserve study in this connexion as well as for church history. To take two obvious examples, one of the defining characteristics of modern France is that its thousands of monasteries were all dissolved between 1790 and 1793, and that most of them were destroyed, vandalised or converted to other purposes, so that their traces are often lost or barely discernible.[30] Modern Austria, on the other hand, is visually dominated and still influenced by its great abbeys which, unusually, despite or because of the policies of Joseph II, escaped suppression in the late eighteenth and early nineteenth centuries, many of them boasting a continuous existence from the Dark Ages to the present day, except for the Nazi years.[31]

These are the phenomena that I wish to highlight, to explore and in some degree to explain in this book. I wish I could take the story beyond 1815, into the period of astonishing Catholic revival. But, as will become apparent, the story down to the end of the Napoleonic regime is by itself a very big subject indeed, more than enough for full scholarly treatment in a set of lectures or a short book. My justification for taking it and treating it in this cavalier way is that even in Catholic countries – and still more in Britain – it has been neglected, often literally ignored, not only by general historians but also by historians of religion. I hope both to encourage more historians to study it and to persuade a wider readership of its interest and importance. This is not a question of drawing attention to a quaint survival or a picturesque backwater. It is more like bringing to the surface 'a submerged Continent'.[32] In eighteenth- and nineteenth-century Catholic Europe monks, nuns and their monasteries really mattered in the life of society; and they, and the institution of monasticism itself, were the object of continuous interest and fierce controversy. It is a grave distortion of history to leave them out of it.

THE DIFFICULTIES OF THE SUBJECT

Why has this distortion occurred? The most general aspect of the problem is that for many modern historians religion has little or no meaning, and so they find it difficult or impossible to believe that anyone can ever have been genuinely actuated by a religious motive. Faced with ostensibly religious activity, they ignore it, underplay it or seek a secular explanation for it. Here are some examples. The great Tudor historian, Geoffrey Elton, was unable to accept that resentment at the dissolution of the monasteries could really have been, as the rebels claimed it was, a principal motive in the revolt against Henry VIII's government in 1536 which is known as the Pilgrimage of Grace. Many historians of the English Civil War and of England in the age of the industrial revolution have seen religious movements and disputes as merely the reflexion of economic and social divisions. French historians have carried out vast quantities of often valuable research into the origins and course of the Revolution as though it was simply a question of class struggle, rising prices and population pressure, neglecting or diminishing the role of individuals, politics and ideas, and especially of churches and religion. Most of these writers have accepted a more or less diluted version of Marxism, which claims to supply a materialist explanation of cultural, intellectual and religious manifestations. Put crudely, as Marx himself put it, 'religion is the opium of the people', and churches are simply an aspect of feudal or capitalist oppression. The specific examples just given are all instances where, recently, some historians have set out to redress the balance, insisting that religion must be taken seriously if the story is to be properly understood. But it remains difficult to win acceptance for such arguments.[33]

Perhaps the most extreme cases of blind ignoring of religious and ecclesiastical issues, and particularly of monasteries, are to be found in certain economic histories. These matters are hardly mentioned, for example, in the post-medieval volumes of the *Fontana Economic History of Europe*. Even more astonishingly, they hardly surface in a collection on Castilian economic decline in the seventeenth century.[34] This silence no doubt owes something to the reluctance of contemporary scholars to indulge in anything that smacks of denominational bickering, though it probably owes more to the discredit into which debates about 'religion and the rise of capitalism' have fallen among historians. But it is not necessary to assume that the peculiar twist given to these debates by their main promoters, Weber and Tawney, is the only possible approach. They were chiefly interested in the question whether the Protestant, especially the Calvinist, ethic encouraged entrepreneurship, innovation and hard work, and therefore, ultimately, industrialisation. The fact that discussion of these topics has run into the sands should not preclude argument about other aspects of the relationship between religion and economic growth. All European countries had churches which owned large amounts of land, but those that became Protestant must have contained on average substantially less church land than Catholic states, and many of them contained *no* monastic land.[35] It must surely be worthwhile for historians to consider whether the Church behaved differently from other landlords, in particular whether monasteries acted differently from other ecclesiastical lords, and also whether, as Enlightened reformers believed, the restriction of the land market by the inalienability of church land – a restriction inevitably of greater weight in Catholic than Protestant countries – seriously limited or distorted economic development. The Catholic Church glorified celibacy, the Protestant Churches did not. Although all Catholic clergy were debarred from marriage, and so it was not only monks but also secular priests who remained unmarried, the institutional celibacy of women was virtually confined to nuns. These restrictions on population growth must be of some significance, even if critical reformers exaggerated their impact. Again, the vast growth in bequests for the provision of Masses to be said for the souls of the dead, creating what has been dubbed a veritable 'industry' in the case of early modern Spain,[36] and helping to pay for the increase in numbers of monks, had no parallel in Protestant countries. This development cannot have been of no economic consequence. Those historians at the London School of Economics who, when I offered as a lecture subject the European monasteries of the eighteenth century, declared it inappropriate to an institution dedicated to economics and political science, were revealing a shameful lack of knowledge and understanding.

In most Catholic countries the study of religion is bedevilled by the long history of bitter antagonism between the Church and the secular state going back well before the revolutionary period, a history which has made it peculiarly difficult to treat religious issues impartially, especially since it has led to a physical separation between avowedly Catholic universities and self-consciously secular universities. In Belgium, for instance, the ancient Catholic University of Louvain, which still possesses halls of residence for student monks of several religious Orders, was deliberately challenged in the early nineteenth century by the Free University of Brussels, founded by Freemasons.[37] While Catholic institutions have fostered voluminous but often uncritical studies in church history, the lay or secular institutions have either ignored it or scoffed at it. Christian Hermann, author of a fine book on the Spanish Church of the *ancien régime*, tells us that at the now laicised Sorbonne – where in the sixteenth century Ignatius Loyola, the founder of the Jesuits, had won his intellectual spurs – he could attend classes on everything except two subjects he was to need most particularly in his research, canon law and theology.[38] This situation helps to explain why Le Roy Ladurie in his standard work on *The Ancien Regime* mentions no monks other than Jesuits and ignores the reforming *commission des réguliers* altogether; why François Furet, writing the semi-official bicentenary history of the Revolution, gave only the barest mention to monasteries; and why, in the *Critical Dictionary of the French Revolution* which he and

Mona Ozouf published at the same time, there is a long entry on the short-lived experiment in 'Dechristianisation' while monks are dismissed in a sentence.[39]

Despite this pervasive secularism, recent French historiography prides itself on having created a 'new religious history'.[40] But by this term is generally meant the study of 'popular religion', the religion (or superstition) of laymen and laywomen, and of 'religious sociology', that is, the social significance of the ministering church. These are subjects into which monasteries do not fit well – though they fit better than many of the works of this school would suggest.[41]

Stress on the pastoral and the parish, associated with disdain for monasticism, is not confined to modern French historiography. It was one of the main emphases not only of the Reformation but even, initially at least, of the Counter-Reformation. A report commissioned in 1536 by the pope recommended the suppression of the unreformed Franciscan and Augustinian Orders, because their scandalous corruption threatened to demoralise the secular clergy and bring the Church and the world to ruin.[42] The Council of Trent, summoned in 1542 to address the challenge of the Reformation, though less radical in its approach, gave priority to increasing the number and effectiveness of parish clergy, and sought to curb and purify traditional monasticism.[43] In present-day religious discussion in every denomination, pastoral work far outweighs in immediacy the original monastic preoccupations of prayer, contemplation, meditation and worship. Since all history is in a sense contemporary history, this current concern is another part of the explanation for the neglect of monasticism by historians of modern Europe.

Those writing in the English historical tradition, steeped as it is in Protestantism, have perhaps more justification for such neglect than the historians of Catholic countries. Students of Elizabethan, Stuart and Hanoverian Britain have little reason to trouble themselves with monasteries. From a British standpoint they are seen as essentially medieval institutions, to be honoured for having preserved civilisation and learning through the Dark Ages, but to be condemned as irredeemably outdated, bloated and corrupt by the sixteenth century. Even for many modern English Catholic historians eighteenth-century monasticism seems alien. I once tried to discuss it with the greatest of them, David Knowles, but I was soon made aware that, apart from the work of the pioneering Benedictine historians of the French Congregation of St-Maur, he found it uncongenial. The monks he admired, whether in the Middle Ages or in the twentieth century, were those who strictly kept the rule, not the often lax, worldly, wealthy, lazy monks of the *ancien régime*;[44] and his attitude seems to be shared by the great majority both of monastic historians and of contemporary monks and nuns in Britain. They would rather gaze on bare, ruined, Gothic choirs – now looking misleadingly austere – than on continuously active houses resplendent in sumptuous Baroque. In so far as these monasteries have been studied in Britain, it has been chiefly by aesthetes and historians of art.[45]

In certain conspicuous cases the reluctance of Anglophone historians to consider Continental monasticism has clearly weakened their work. J.C.D. Clark, for example, argued in his controversial *English Society 1688–1832* that eighteenth-century England was much more like a Continental *ancien régime* than had been appreciated, since it was a 'confessional state' in which the Church of England had a role similar to that of the Roman Catholic Church in France. Neither he nor his critics made the rather important point that in the century before 1789 France contained many thousands of monasteries, while Britain possessed none. In his recent edition of Burke's *Reflections on the Revolution in France* he reveals the same blindness to the significance of French monasteries and their suppression. Arno Mayer strikingly demonstrated *The Persistence of the Ancien Regime* into the twentieth century, citing the continuing importance of monarchy, aristocracy, military and Church, especially in Germany and eastern Europe; but he did not so much as allude to monasteries, whose survival as a political and social force in the lands of the Austro-Hungarian Monarchy and in Russia would have lent powerful support to his argument.[46]

Moreover, it is not quite true that monasteries had no significance in the history of Britain after the Reformation. Catholic families continued to send their sons and daughters to be educated in monasteries based on the Continent, and a good many of these children stayed on and took vows, some of the monks later returning to Britain on mission. In the early seventeenth century Mary Ward, from north Yorkshire, founded a pioneering and controversial Order of nuns, known as 'the English Ladies'.[47] During James II's brief reign a few monks established themselves again in England, the Jesuits among them contributing greatly by their sinister reputation to the animosity felt towards the king. But even among Anglicans respect was sometimes shown for the monastic ideal: a quasi-monastic community was established at Little Gidding in the early seventeenth century, and the great Chelsea Hospital for veterans founded in the 1680s was thought of as a 'Coledge or Monastrie' and was intended to have rules 'in every respect as strict as in any religious convent'.[48]

And there is one paradoxical way in which British historians may be said to have a special *entrée* to the monastic history of the *ancien régime*. The nearest thing to monasteries in the England of the eighteenth century were the Colleges of Oxford and Cambridge. In a few cases they were direct descendants of monasteries, in all cases they were based on the monastic model.[49] As Gibbon said of his own

College, Magdalen, Oxford, it 'is esteemed one of the largest and most wealthy of our Academical corporations, which may be compared to the Benedictine Abbeys of Catholic countries.'

Our Colleges [he went on] are supposed to be schools of science as well as of education: nor is it unreasonable to expect that a body of litterary men, addicted to a life of celibacy, exempt from the care of their own subsistence, and amply provided with books, should devote their leisure to the prosecution of study, and that some effects of their studies should be manifested to the World. The shelves of their library groan under the weight of the Benedictine folios, of the editions of the fathers, and the Collections of the middle ages, which have issued from the single Abbey of St. Germain des Préz at Paris... If I enquire into the manufactures of the monks at Magdalen, if I extend the enquiry to the other Colleges of Oxford and Cambridge, a silent blush, or a scornful frown, will be the only reply.[50]

These Colleges, though reformed, retain to this day vestiges of their monastic origins, as do few other academic institutions anywhere in the world. In some respects eighteenth-century Continental monasteries resembled modern Oxbridge Colleges – at least before the advent of co-residence – more closely than they resemble twentieth-century monasteries.

I must not go too far in stressing the previous neglect of my subject. Among British ecclesiastical historians two have conspicuously contributed to it, the greatest of their generation, Owen Chadwick and John McManners. I depend heavily on Chadwick's *The Popes and European Revolution*, and am conscious that I cannot match its extraordinary range and spiritual awareness. McManners's account of the Church in eighteenth-century Angers and his recent monumental *Church and Society in Eighteenth-Century France* bring out the role of the monasteries with skill, charm and unparalleled learning.[51] Among other British historians of Europe, T.C.W. Blanning, P.G.M. Dickson and R.J.W. Evans are far from forgetting monks – or nuns.[52] Moreover, the emergence of the genre of women's history has led to a revival of the study of nuns, as exemplified in J.A.K. McNamara's *Sisters in Arms: Catholic Nuns through Two Millennia* and works such as *The Dévotes: Women and Church in Seventeenth-Century France* by Elizabeth Rapley and Olwen Hufton's *Women and the Limits of Citizenship in the French Revolution*.[53] On the one hand, women are seen to have been virtually forced by social convention into harsh seclusion in nunneries. On the other hand, it is evident that life in a nunnery could be agreeable and enabled some women to engage in activities from which they would have been debarred in the world: study, writing, music, administration, teaching, nursing and other social work. So rapidly has this branch of study burgeoned that, in comparison with nuns, monks seem almost to have become neglected.

There are other signs that the history of monasteries may be making a comeback. During the last few years, for example, many Austrian and south German monasteries have attained their nine-hundredth, thousandth, eleven-hundredth, twelve-hundreth anniversaries – in 1996 the Benedictine abbey of St Peter's in Salzburg reached its thirteen-hundredth. These occasions have led to the mounting of splendid exhibitions and the publication of lavish scholarly catalogues which have illuminated more than just the history of the institution concerned.[54] An exhibition of 1991 in the suppressed abbey of Benediktbeuren, with the title 'Glory and Demise of the Monasteries of Bavaria', yielded a particularly valuable catalogue.[55] In 1992 appeared two important volumes edited by Mario Rosa on *Clergy and Society in Modern Italy* and *Clergy and Society in Contemporary Italy*. In these titles 'modern' means 'early modern' and 'contemporary' means nineteenth and twentieth century. In the introduction we read:

It cannot fail to strike the reader... [how much space has been here] assigned to the Orders, regular congregations and religious institutes. Two motives determined this choice: on the one hand, their objective importance...; on the other hand, the fact that this aspect... has remained... at the margins of national historical research, essentially entrusted to the specialist historians of the individual religious Orders.[56]

It is beginning to be realised in relation to the monasteries that, in the words of Christian Hermann, 'The history of the Church is too important to the history of Europe to be left to clergy and pious laymen.'[57]

Several more or less independent developments suggest a general revival of interest in the subject. Within the last few years a number of guidebooks have been published listing active monastic houses across Europe which are accessible to the public.[58] A new appreciation of plainsong has enabled many monasteries to market recordings of their singing, so that some record shops have taken to advertising 'Monks (and Nuns) of the Month'. Excavations at the splendid Baroque abbey of Altenburg in Austria have uncovered some of the replaced medieval buildings, making it possible to create a museum which celebrates a new field of scholarship, 'monastic archaeology'. In addition, the exhibition contains a section called 'Kloster for Kids'.

All that said, there is no denying that the study of monks, nuns and monasteries presents the contemporary historian with terrible difficulties. The *raison d'être* of these institutions was to serve God, first and foremost by prayer and worship, to which all monks and nuns devoted much of their time, and some nearly all of their time. They did so not with a view to obtaining credit or benefits in this world during their lifetime but to securing for themselves and for others eternal life in the next world after death. I have met Austrians who regret that Joseph II suppressed so many monasteries, although he spared more than half of those in his dominions. But relatively few people nowadays, even among Christians, sympathise with the fundamental aim and approach of monasteries. Society at the beginning of the twenty-first century is overwhelmingly against poverty, chastity and obedience, indeed against vows altogether, especially lifelong vows, and concentrates on improving and exploiting this world. Even some Catholics regard the monastic life with suspicion, particularly as it was practised in the eighteenth century. The wealth of the monasteries seems offensive, and some of their purposes, like fighting the infidel, seem wholly inappropriate. Many of their activities, though in themselves laudable, seem religiously neutral: some of the music, scholarship, education, manual work and charitable endeavour. But the fact has to be faced that at the time they were done 'to the greater glory of God' and to illustrate, glorify, impose and spread the doctrines, practices and power of Catholic Christianity.

How is the secular-minded historian of eighteenth-century Europe to deal with these genuinely serious problems of comprehension and interpretation? First and obviously, he cannot begin to evaluate the success of prayer and worship, meditation and mysticism, or any other monastic activity in so far as it was directed to securing benefits in the next world. In other words, he cannot apply to these institutions the test by which they perhaps deserved and would certainly have wished to be judged. On the other hand, one of his main duties is to report, so far as the sources permit, the huge extent of this activity; and the chief point he has to make is precisely that it did bulk so large, and hence rendered Catholic countries in the eighteenth century so different from Protestant countries of the time and from the society of the twenty-first century virtually everywhere. He may well find aspects of the Catholic piety of the period difficult to stomach. He knows that some monks and nuns were virtually forced or inveigled into the cloister. Perhaps they were offered to a monastery by their parents at the age of five or six and sent to an enclosed monastic school where they might grow up without the least idea of what went on in the world. We are told of three such girls for whom after some years their brother arranged a few outside visits.

On one of these excursions the girls had the misfortune to encounter a herd of cattle on the way to be slaughtered. In the cloister they had never seen such big animals. Terrified, they begged their guide to take them back as quickly as possible. 'That's the world,' they said, 'oh how hideous it is!' They quickly offered themselves to become Carmelites. Marie de Jésus became prioress of Châtillon in 1700 . . . Magdeleine de St Joseph prioress of Compiègne in 1728.[59]

The words and symbolism of the service at which vows were taken, at once simulating a marriage and echoing a funeral, could be tolerable only to the initiated and inured. In Chapter 3 I quote a disturbing description of such an occasion when the nun-to-be was manifestly ill and reluctant to proceed.[60] It is impossible to expect that more than a fraction of such large numbers of monks and nuns would have lived up to their professions, and it was notorious that many did not. But the historian's aim must be to describe them as they were in society as it was, and to evaluate their earthly activities mainly within that historical frame of reference.

VARIETIES OF CATHOLIC MONASTICISM, AND DEFINITION OF TERMS

It is time I said something more specific about the nature and diversity of monasticism and the related problems of analysis and terminology. The Church of my period officially divided clergy into 'secular' clergy or 'seculars', 'living in the world', and 'regular' clergy or 'regulars', whose essential distinguishing feature in principle was that they lived under the provisions of a 'rule', which usually meant that they had joined a religious Order or similar organisation. It generally, but not invariably, also meant that they had 'taken vows' of poverty, chastity and obedience – obedience to the rule and to their superiors – and that they lived together in communities. But the development of monasticism has been punctuated by a bewildering series of diverse initiatives from below, which the church authorities could only partially regulate and which have defied categorisation. When the Council of Trent legislated on the subject of regulars in December 1563, it took account of the diversity achieved up to that time by spelling out that its decrees applied to

> all cloisters and monasteries, colleges and houses of every type of monks and regulars together with all kinds of holy women and widows..., and by whatever name they are called, under whatever rule or constitutions, and under guardianship, governance or whatever kind of subjection or connection or dependent relationship to any sort of Order, of mendicants or non-mendicants or of other regular monks or canons of any kind.[61]

I intend to adopt this authoritative and gloriously inclusive definition, which is so broad that it can embrace the numerous initatives of more recent centuries. However, I shall restrict myself almost entirely to those regulars who were located in Europe, at the cost of omitting the immensely important work of monks and nuns overseas, though I recognise that it is impossible to ignore the extra-European dimension altogether, especially in relation to the fall of the Jesuits. I shall also concentrate on Catholic monasticism, to the virtual exclusion of the Orthodox and therefore of Russia and most of the Balkans.

The Council of Trent's definition is convenient and sensible precisely because it accepts that the differences between the various organisations falling within it are immense. To complicate matters further, nearly all the terms involved are used in varying ways. For example, a distinction was and is generally made between 'abbeys' and other monasteries, the abbeys being the grander houses of the old Orders, sometimes defined as those whose only superior is the pope. Sometimes 'monasteries' and 'abbeys' are used only for houses of men. 'Convents' may be used as a generic term for all houses but is commonly confined to houses for women. There is additional risk of confusion arising in the translation of such terms. In most languages the word nearest to the English 'convent' denotes any kind of monastery, with no suggestion that a nunnery is meant. In Italian 'monasterio' is the word that can be general in its application but carries with it a whiff of the nunnery. German – or, nowadays, the German of Austria and Switzerland – has the unique usage of *Stift*, which basically means 'foundation', but connotes the well-endowed abbeys of the old Orders that dominated the life of their locality and had a role in the Estates of their province.[62] 'Cloister' has three meanings in English, like its equivalents in many other languages: the rectangular covered way within a monastery (or other building); the whole monastery; and the seclusion or 'enclosure' enforced in a monastery or monasteries. This multiplicity of meaning causes confusion, enhanced by the fact that in German and Italian the equivalent of 'cloister' is the commonest word for a single monastery, whereas in English and other languages it is relatively rare in this sense. To try to get round these difficulties, I shall use 'monasteries', unless I specify otherwise, to mean all houses of all kinds of regulars of either sex, but I shall use 'monastery' only to mean a house for men. I shall avoid using 'convent' and 'cloister' to denote a monastery of any kind, and I shall generally use 'nunnery' for a house of women.

At least as thorny are the issues raised by the use of 'Order'. Many monastic bodies are not properly called Orders: the Jesuits, for example, are a 'Society' or 'Company'. It is common to distinguish 'Orders' and 'Congregations', the latter generally having less stringent vows and rules. These terms reflect the variety of organisations concerned. But I shall normally use the term 'Orders', as is commonly done, to describe all the institutions that fall within the Council of Trent's generous definition.[63]

It is perhaps worth drawing attention to three further terms which can cause much confusion. 'Abbot' is not so straightforward a word for the head of a monastery as it might appear to be. Real perplexity is caused by the fact that in French the word for abbot, *abbé*, had become by the eighteenth century 'an honorific form of address for canons, curés, and all other ecclesiastics short of the rank of bishop'.[64] Hence men like Condillac, Diderot, Morellet and Raynal who had embarked on a church career but soon abandoned it, and had become strongly anticlerical, were still liable to be called *abbé*. Even the most scholarly historians trip up over this usage. J.F. Bosher wrote in his *French Revolution*: 'At least nine abbots wrote articles for the *Encyclopédie*.' Actually, at least twenty-three *abbés* did so, but none of them was an abbot.[65] A similar usage exists in other Romance languages. I shall use the word 'abbot' only for the head of a monastery.

Another term that risks causing genuine difficulty is 'religious', meaning 'regular' – or a type of regular, as in the title of David Knowles's second volume on medieval English monasticism, *The Religious Orders* (as opposed to *The Monastic Orders* of volume 1). This goes with the still more confusing ancient sense of 'religio' to mean a single Order. I shall avoid these usages.

Thirdly and most confusingly, 'congregation' has five relevant senses. It first has the best-known meaning, 'the group gathered for a church service'. Secondly, it can mean a non-monastic religious brotherhood. Thirdly, it refers, as explained above, to communities more loosely organised than those of the old Orders. Fourthly, it is the usual term for a grouping of monasteries within an Order, such as the Congregation of St-Maur formed by some of the French Benedictine monasteries in the seventeenth century. I shall normally employ the word only in this sense. Finally, it is the name for a committee or commission set up by the Vatican, of which the most relevant example is the Congregation of Bishops and Regulars, set up in the seventeenth century.

The only way to explain the variety of Orders is historically.[66] By the mid-eighteenth century four main types of Orders existed, including in each case segregated institutions for men and for women.

1. The Orders of monks and nuns living under strict vows according to the sixth-century Rule of St Benedict or its derivatives: principally Benedictines of various types, and Cistercians, an offshoot dating from the eleventh century. They laid stress on prayer, contemplation, meditation and participation by the whole community in the full range of (originally) seven daily choral services or 'offices'. The rule also prescribed manual work, but in many houses this had been delegated to lay brothers and/or servants long before the eighteenth century. To these should be added the Carthusians, founded in the late eleventh century, one of the Orders in which monks lived virtually as hermits in separate little houses, joining together

INTRODUCTION

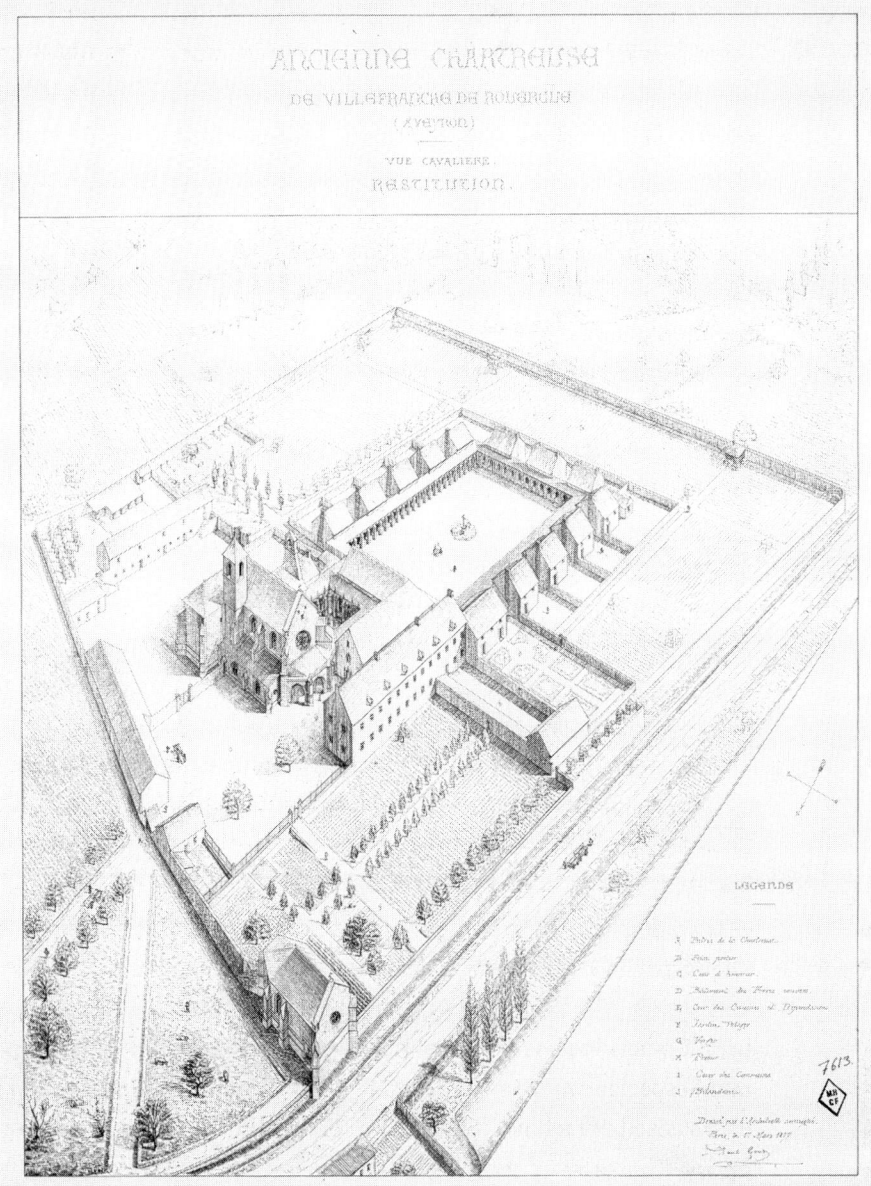

ILL. 1 Engraving of the Carthusian abbey of Villefranche-de-Rouergue, southern France

almost only for worship – which explains why the French word for bungalow is 'chartreuse' (Ill. 1). All these Orders are commonly called 'contemplative', but only the Carthusians can be said to have been almost exclusively contemplative. Many of the houses of these early Orders, especially of the Cistercians, were deliberately located in remote and inhospitable places.

2. Orders of 'regular canons' who were less strictly cloistered and, if priests, often worked in parishes: the most widespread were Augustinian and Premonstratensian canons, the latter founded in the twelfth century at Prémontré near Laon in France. Their rule derives from St Augustine.

These two types of Order were originally and in principle agglomerations of individual houses. The monk or nun joined a particular house, not an Order. The head of the house, called abbot/abbess or prior/prioress or, in the case of the canons, often 'provost', was elected for life and, though required to consult the monks/nuns gathered in 'chapter' on certain questions, had monarchical and spiritual power over the community and had an ecclesiastical status close to a bishop's. (In the case of nunneries, of course, the abbess lacked the priestly power of the abbot.) It is true that by the eighteenth century most of the houses of these Orders had joined together in 'congregations', but the arrangement still left individual houses a high degree of autonomy.

These were the old Orders which, having accumulated substantial endowments over many centuries, possessed nearly all the grandest monastic estates and buildings in the eighteenth century.

(A small group of Orders mainly dating from the twelfth century has to be regarded as inherently different from all others, namely, the military Orders. It was the special purpose of these Orders to supply knights to fight the infidel, or to rescue and ransom prisoners and slaves, and they also ran hospitals to look after the sick and wounded. Some of these organisations, such as the Trinitarians and the Teutonic Knights, became very wealthy and survived into the eighteenth century despite the fact that their aims had by then become more or less obsolete.)

3. Then, in the early thirteenth century, were created the Orders of mendicant or begging friars, Dominicans founded by St Dominic and Franciscans founded by St Francis, whose purpose was to go out into the world and minister to laymen, especially in towns. They were ready to work as or with parish priests and emphasised preaching and missions. They did not follow the elaborate pattern of worship of the older monasteries. The Dominicans and Franciscans were both founded explicitly as Orders, under the central direction of generals, and the heads of individual houses had only short tenure and limited power. But a friar still joined a particular house rather than the Order. Originally their founders insisted that their houses, as well as the individual inmates, should be poor and that the friars should support themselves by begging, but before long most of their communities grew closer to the pattern of the older Orders, living in established houses and holding property. The Franciscan Order was subject to many internal disputes leading to schisms and to the foundation of a range of Orders, strict and less strict,

which all maintained their Franciscan inspiration. Of these offshoots the most important were the relatively strict Capuchins, dating from the early sixteenth century. In eighteenth-century Europe Franciscans of some kind were almost everywhere the most numerous group of monks, and among them the Capuchins were the largest single Order.[67]

4. At the time of the Counter-Reformation were founded Orders (or congregations) of 'regular clerics', and companies of priests, usually with the duty of performing some specific task in the world, who dropped the requirement to meet for frequent worship and in some cases took less stringent or 'simple' vows. The most famous were the Jesuits, devoted to missionary work in Europe and outside, who in fact made an additional vow of absolute obedience to the pope. But others, both of men and women, concerned themselves with education or, like those inspired by St François de Sales and St Vincent de Paul, ministered to the sick and the down-and-out. By the eighteenth century, especially in France, there was a considerable number of what can loosely be called Orders, especially for women, in which only simple vows were taken and the members lived uncloistered, usually working as teachers and nurses. The list of such organisations was to grow enormously during the nineteenth century.

I shall sometimes have to refer to the technical distinctions between mendicants and non-mendicants, between monks, canons, friars and regular clerics (and their female equivalents). But I shall usually call all these persons monks and nuns, justifying this practice from the quoted words of the Council of Trent – and encouraged by the work of medievalists who have shown that the much-canvassed differences between monks, canons and friars were always in fact blurred.[68]

I have divided up my account of eighteenth-century European Catholic monasticism by country. This seems to me to reveal significant variations within the institution; and such a division is in any case unavoidable when reform and secularisation is discussed, given the decisive role of the state. But of course such a framework has drawbacks: political boundaries were much less rigid and also less straightforward then than now; to proceed country by country makes some repetition unavoidable and also risks underplaying the features of monasticism that were common everywhere. In order to avoid repeating myself more than is necessary, I give my only full account of the monastic day in reference to Melk abbey in the section on Austria in Chapter 1, but it applied with minor variations to most monasteries of the old Orders everywhere; and much of what I say about the estates of Melk applied more or less to all wealthy houses. When I quote the graphic account of Mlle de Rastignac's profession in Chapter 3, I am providing my only description of this rite, but of course it was performed from time to time in every house of the major Orders, though usually in less harrowing circumstances. My aim is to illustrate not only the varieties of monasticism but also those elements in it which were common to most or all of the countries of Catholic Europe; and, unless I state that a practice is peculiar to one country or area, it should be assumed that it could be paralleled elsewhere.

PART I

AT THE BRIM OF PROSPERITY

CHAPTER 1

THE COUNTER-REFORMATION AND THE MONASTERIES

It was in the middle years of the eighteenth century that the Counter-Reformation reached its apogee. This statement may well astonish, since most historians have located the movement squarely in the sixteenth century, with perhaps an extension into the early seventeenth when the Austrian Habsburg emperors, inspired by the Jesuits, sought to recover Germany for Catholicism in the Thirty Years War. The Peace of Westphalia terminated that war in 1648 by ratifying the political division of Germany on denominational lines. This settlement has been taken to mark both the end of serious religious conflict on the Continent and the general acceptance that Catholicism could hope for no further gains. One notable historian, A.G. Dickens, 'considered the Counter Reformation, properly so called, to have terminated around the middle of the seventeenth century, a time of spiritual cooling and many non-Catholic trends'.[1] But in fact, during the course of the next century, most of one large country, Hungary, was to be won back to Rome by a combination of force and proselytisation, and much of another, Poland, chiefly by missionary effort.[2] After the revocation of the Edict of Nantes in 1685 Protestants were persecuted and then driven out of France. Among lesser states that followed suit was the prince-archbishopric of Salzburg, which expelled all Protestants in 1731. Of the major rulers who became Catholics, two, Christina of Sweden and James II of England and VII of Scotland, lost their thrones as a result, but a third, Augustus of Saxony, thereby secured election as king of Poland in 1697. It was calculated that a total of fifty-one German princes converted from Protestantism to Catholicism during the seventeenth and eighteenth centuries. Under the Treaty of Westphalia the subjects of a German ruler who changed his religion could retain theirs, but they inevitably suffered a loss of status and influence, and often worse.[3] Until after the middle of the eighteenth century Protestants had reason to fear that intolerant Catholicism was still militant and still gaining ground.[4]

Contrariwise, many historians date 'the crisis of the European mind' to the years between 1680 and 1715, when the works of geniuses such as Newton, Locke, Shaftesbury, Bayle, Fontenelle and Leibniz revolutionised our understanding of the universe and of ourselves, thus opening the way to the Enlightenment, a movement that embraced attitudes hostile to Catholicism and even to Christianity itself.[5] Most Enlightened writers were enemies of monasticism, and in any explanation of its *débâcle* during the revolutionary period their attacks must figure prominently. But it took much longer than historians have generally allowed for 'the crisis of the European mind' and the Enlightenment to make a significant impression on Catholic Europe. Many indicators suggest that, long after 1715, Catholicism, far from being in retreat, was still strengthening its hold on the people of many countries. Until at least the middle of the century a high proportion of Catholics' wills, in some areas the majority, stipulated that Masses should be said for the testators' souls.[6] Though the *proportion* of theological and religious works among new publications was certainly declining overall throughout the century, there was a notable increase in the *total* number of such works that were published.[7] It has been found that, in the libraries accumulated by nobles in western France, the proportion of religious books actually *grew* until around the middle of the eighteenth century.[8] More surprisingly still, when in 1778–9 a relaxation of government controls in France led to a flood of reprints of works by dead authors, of over two million copies produced no less than 63.1 per cent were religious. Hence it is possible for the new French school of religious history to claim of France that 'it was in the eighteenth century that the piety of the Catholic Reformation won the day, through the weight of books of hours, psalters, prayer books and lives of saints', and, going even further, that this was the time when France was at its most Catholic – indeed that the eighteenth century should be seen as 'the truly Christian century'.[9] It was a period of massive missionary effort within countries already officially Catholic, for example in France, Bavaria and Italy.[10] Throughout Catholic Europe during most of the century laymen and lay women of all classes, literally in their millions, continued to join in religious brotherhoods under priestly supervision, of which the most famous were those associated with the Jesuits. These organisations had varying emphases but mostly had more than one of the following objects: prayer, religious observances, processions and pilgrimages, religious education, poor relief, care of the sick and aged, and providing for funerals.[11] Pilgrimages to the sites of miracles and holy relics grew ever more popular, and the number of such places increased as 'tree, rock, spring, hill and cave were brought into relation with the Catholic faith'. Nearly all were connected with the cult of the Virgin Mary. At Mariazell, the principal shrine in Austria, 120,000 to 150,000 people arrived annually in the seventeenth century, 188,000 in 1725 and 373,000 in the jubilee year 1753.[12] But, at least at first glance, the most telling indication that Catholic Reform reached its peak as late as the mid-eighteenth century is the evidence that the proportion of secular priests to population reached its highest known level at roughly that date not only in France, but also in Spain and Italy.[13]

Even those historians who contend that Catholicism was still advancing in the first half of the eighteenth century rarely extend the claim to monasteries and the regular clergy. But in fact they too – monks, nuns and their houses – were still, overall, increasing in numbers. The most striking gain was made by the various Franciscan Orders, among which the Capuchins grew from about 22,000 brothers in 1650 to nearly 33,000 in 1754. In many countries the number of regular clergy, like the number of seculars, peaked around the middle of the eighteenth century. In Poland the number of both male and female monasteries increased by a third between 1700 and 1773, and in the admittedly special case of Hungary the number of monasteries almost doubled between 1700 and 1773.[14] It is certain of course that monastic wealth was still growing, both because land was increasing in value and because property once acquired by the Church could not in general be alienated.[15]

These monastic advances are manifestly, in a crude sense, advances of Catholicism and also of the Counter-Reformation. But it is a question whether the Counter-Reformation ought to be understood as including every apparently successful Catholic activity, or only those developments that fit into a particular programme of reform, especially that of the Council of Trent. Some historians distinguish between the Counter-Reformation directed against Protestantism and a more spontaneous movement perhaps called the 'Catholic Reformation'.[16] Whatever terminology is adopted, it is impossible to treat every aspect of monastic expansion as part of a movement of reform. But, to put it at its lowest, no monastery in this period of spiritual renewal could be immune to reforming influences.

During the acute phase of the Reformation Benedictines, Cistercians, Augustinians and Premonstratensians, despite their wealth and political standing, suffered a serious decline even in the countries where monasteries were not suppressed by Protestant rulers. Houses located in the areas that were ravaged by wars of religion were inevitably affected, especially in parts of France during the second half of the sixteenth century and in most of Belgium and the German lands for over a hundred years before the Peace of Westphalia in 1648. Monasteries were assailed, often physically, by the Protestantism that was at times dominant even in what now seem the most unlikely places, such as Austria, Bohemia, Belgium and Provence. But the old Orders were not simply victims of violence; many of their houses were simply abandoned. They had lost much of their appeal even to loyal Catholics.

On the one hand, reformers were uncomfortable with the relaxation of the original rules which had been permitted in almost all the old Orders. What has been written of the Benedictine monks of Westminster abbey in the early sixteenth century applied very widely:

[They] ate flesh-meat almost as frequently as their equals in secular society; as many of them as possible made use of private chambers, in preference to sleeping in the common dormitory; and they moved in and out of the monastery quite freely. They allowed themselves substantial wages, or personal incomes... They employed professional cantors to sing their services, and schoolmasters to teach in their schools. Already, in fact, there was a pragmatic resemblance between the community at Westminster and a collegiate establishment.[17]

The Cistercians had long ceased to live in the wilderness and to keep their churches unadorned. As for the Franciscans, those branches which had abandoned their original insistence on poverty were held by many reformers to have entirely lost their justification.[18]

On the other hand, as we saw in the Introduction, many of the leaders of the Catholic Reform movement of the sixteenth century, intent above all on increasing the numbers and effectiveness of parish clergy and filling parish churches, mounted a more fundamental critique of traditional monasticism. Monasteries, however strict and observant, were seen as obstructing these aims because they isolated their priestly inmates from the world, took worshippers out of parish churches and escaped the supervision of bishops, as also did the private chapels of the aristocracy and, in many cases, even the brotherhoods that financed Masses for their members at special times and in special buildings. Many Catholic reformers throughout our period were torn between the conflicting aims of restoring the older Orders to their original purity and challenging their very *raison d'être*.[19]

However, by the time the Council of Trent came to discuss these matters in 1563, monasticism, condemned by Luther and suppressed by all Protestant rulers, had become accepted as one of the indispensable defining elements of Catholicism. A Church that maintained belief in purgatory and in the value of praying to saints and of saying Masses for the dead, and glorified chastity and celibacy, necessarily accepted the rationale of monasticism. Though some popes, Catholic rulers and bishops wished to reform the Orders drastically and to take away much of their independence and wealth, it had become impossible to take truly radical measures against them. In its decrees of 1563 the Council of Trent stressed the need for monasteries to adhere to the rules of their Order, insisted that they group themselves into congregations, and encouraged the bishops to inspect them. It recalled monks and nuns to their vows of chastity, poverty and obedience, totally forbade them to own land as individuals and allowed them the use of other property only with the permission of their superiors and only if it included 'nothing superfluous' – though 'they were not to be denied anything that may be necessary'. The age at which binding vows could be validly taken was fixed at sixteen for both men and women.[20] But that was as far as the Council dared go. The sternest 'reform', in fact, was imposed two years later, by the new pope Pius V, when he decreed in his bull *Circa pastoralis* that all nunneries must henceforth be strictly enclosed.[21]

Moreover, far from reducing the number and influence of monks and nuns, broadly defined, the promoters of the Counter-Reformation created new Orders, principally the Jesuits and Capuchins, which not only attracted the faithful away from parish churches but introduced new rivalries among the regular clergy, especially over control of education. The Jesuits indeed amounted almost to a new hierarchy under direct papal control, in competition with all the Church's traditional authorities. The monastic ideal, applauded by the Church, commanded widespread respect and there was no shortage of vocations. Many men preferred to become members of a religious community, probably based in a town, to working in isolation as a parish priest, especially in the countryside. Archbishops and bishops were generally under the thumb of the secular rulers who effectively appointed them. Most parish clergy were admitted to lack both zeal and education, and many of them were appointed by lay lords who might be Protestants or at least hostile to the new piety. There was virtually no provision for the education of parish clergy until the Council of Trent required each bishop to set up a seminary for priests, and this decree was ignored in many dioceses for decades, in some for centuries. The geography of dioceses and parishes, largely fixed in a distant past, did not meet current needs, yet was enshrined in law and had created so many vested interests that it was very difficult to modify. All these constraints monasteries could ignore. Houses of the old Orders had the wealth, and could therefore recruit the personnel, to contribute in various ways to education and the cure of souls. But much the most speedy and effective way of providing zealous and educated clergy for pastoral work was to establish a brand new Order which would create its own seminaries and whose members, bound by a vow of obedience, could be ordered to areas where there was a particular need for them.

In the seventeenth century renewed attempts were made to reform traditional monasticism. Cardinal Richelieu, the ruthless minister of Louis XIII, building on the work of cardinal de La Rochefoucauld, had plans to get rid of all old Orders in France that would not reform themselves. Richelieu was in a unique position to realise these plans since he had caused himself to be appointed abbot of at least seventeen monasteries and prior of a few more, and was head of the three greatest of the ancient Orders by virtue of being abbot of Cluny (Benedictine), Cîteaux (Cistercian) and Prémontré (Premonstratensian). But he died in 1642 before he could carry through his programme. In John Elliott's words the monasteries then staged 'a virtual . . . insurrection', almost like the nobles' *Fronde*, and the old Orders in France were safe – and in a sense prospered – for another century.[22]

In Italy, however, Innocent X decreed in 1652 the biggest reform and purge of monasteries there before the late eighteenth century, suppressing a quarter of the peninsula's 6,000 male houses – in principle, all those that had fewer than twelve monks. But this, too, evoked a strong reaction, and he was forced to re-establish at least a third of the houses he had condemned, lowering his criterion of acceptable size to six monks.[23]

Traditional monasticism therefore still seemed to be secure, even sacrosanct, in Catholic countries during the seventeenth and most of the eighteenth centuries, apparently little affected either by the schemes of church reformers or by the growth of state power and consciousness. As the numerous conversions of princes show, Catholicism had come to be regarded as the natural support of absolutism. In return, rulers whose dynasties had stood out against Protestantism felt committed to maintaining the ethos and institutions of the old religion – or at least dared not risk assailing them. Many Catholic monarchs and statesmen believed that monasteries, monks and nuns were too numerous, that they diverted scarce resources from activities more useful to the state and that they ought to be curbed. The nobilities of Catholic states regularly complained that the Church was steadily buying up their estates. In a few special cases such pious kings as Philip II and Louis XIV succeeded in acting on these views: Philip seized some monastic property to help pay for his wars against heretic Powers; Louis reduced certain monasteries' privileges.[24] But in general rulers accepted the

Church's teaching that the ascetic impulse was a laudable, perhaps the highest, manifestation of the Christian life, acknowledged that individuals were entitled to give themselves and their property to monasteries and recognised that that property, like all the Church's land and goods, was held in perpetuity, in 'mortmain'. They conceded to monasteries and their members, as to all clergy, at least partial exemption from ordinary taxation. They acquiesced in the position that they had few rights over monasteries, and further that many houses were wholly or largely outside the jurisdiction of the bishop of their diocese, owing obedience in ecclesiastical matters instead to authorities that were often based outside the lay ruler's territories: to superiors and generals, to congregations and, in some cases, only to the pope.

Protestant rulers, of course, had reaped great financial benefit, at least in the short term, by the dissolution of monasteries and the appropriation of their lands – though Henry VIII was exceptional in diverting almost all the proceeds to secular uses. But Catholic rulers derived practical advantages of other kinds from the continuing existence of rich old monasteries. Although the Council of Trent had decreed that all communities should be free to elect their heads, many elections were in fact heavily influenced or determined by the secular government. A practice existed, though frowned on by the Council, whereby the ruler appointed a 'commendatory' abbot, perhaps a bishop, perhaps a lay statesman or nobleman, even a foreign prince, who might have little or nothing to do with the community but would enjoy a good proportion of the house's revenues and could, if he wished, reside in the abbot's often opulent lodgings. The religious side of the monastery would then be overseen by an elected prior deploying a much reduced budget. This practice was widespread in Italy, and still more in France, where in the eighteenth century the king, having acquired from the pope the right to appoint to most senior church benefices, nominated commendatory abbots to more than a thousand major houses of monks. This patronage was naturally of great value to the monarch.[25] In Austria and Bohemia the great monasteries of the old Orders, as the dominant element in the First Estate, were deliberately raised up by the Habsburgs in the sixteenth and early seventeenth centuries as a counterpoise to the then largely Protestant nobility. There were moments in Bavarian history when Protestantism was so strong among the nobility that the ruler needed the prelates of the First Estate to defeat it.[26] The richer monasteries also made themselves useful to governments by lending substantial sums to the Crown at reasonable rates of interest, fulfilling some of the functions of banks and offering exceptionally good security.[27] So, although Catholic rulers commonly imposed certain restrictions on monasteries' recruitment and property and on their activities in the world, and monitored, manipulated and frustrated abbatial elections, they did not seriously contemplate the drastic action against the old Orders that had accompanied the Protestant Reformation – not, at any rate, until the second half of the eighteenth century.

Rome too had to show great restraint in its dealings with monasteries, even those nominally under its direct jurisdiction. The Congregation of Bishops and Regulars, a permanent commission of cardinals, established in the seventeenth century, had some power to oversee monastic life, though only in Italy.[28] But the Vatican's fundamental attitude was – and ultimately had to be – that the Orders were spontaneous growths, representing successive renewals of the Church. Historically, popes had at first looked askance both at the brand of monasticism promoted by St Francis and at that invented by St Ignatius Loyola, but had come round to accepting them as manifestations of the workings of the Holy Spirit, though needing to be regulated and moderated. In the less spiritual eighteenth century new Orders were few but the story was the same. The Redemptorists, founded by Alfonso Liguori in the kingdom of Naples in 1732 to conduct rural missions, were approved by the Vatican, but only after some years of reluctance and under strong pressure from below. The same happened with the new devotions surrounding the Stations of the Cross and the Sacred Heart, which the new Orders promoted.[29] More generally, the pope's freedom of action was subject to the severest political constraints. Many of the cardinals were in effect appointed by secular rulers rather than by the pope. In most countries his authority in spiritual matters was recognised only with strict limitations, and any attempt to assert his normally latent claims to temporal power over states other than his own evoked a violent reaction compounded of fury and derision. The doctrine of papal infallibility, maintained by popes and some of the Catholic hierarchy, especially the Jesuits, was accepted by few others. Catholic rulers commonly ignored or suppressed the pronouncements of the Vatican. Some of the major Catholic governments of Europe – France, Austria, Venice – refused for long periods even to publish the decrees of the Council of Trent, and when the publication was allowed in Spain it was accompanied by a reassertion of royal power over the Church.[30] Hence it was only in Italy that Innocent X could hope to impose a reform of the monasteries, and even there the resistance he met from other rulers in the peninsula forced him to abandon half his scheme.[31] Elsewhere papal attempts to interfere with local Orders and monasteries usually rallied rulers in their defence. Even if popes sometimes regretted it, rather more than half of all Catholic clergy were regulars, many of them belonging to old Orders that had not been thoroughly reformed, many of them virtually beyond Rome's control, and many of them none the less more effective and reformist than the average secular. The Vatican had to live with this situation and make the best of it.

These conditions, on the one hand fostering monastic independence and creativity but on the other hand permitting abuses to flourish and blocking even the most obviously desirable reforms, prevailed in every Catholic country until well after the middle of the eighteenth century. But the spirit of the Catholic Reformers lived on, and there were always elements within the Church which deplored at least some aspects of monasticism. In the late seventeenth and eighteenth centuries the most significant of the critical tendencies was 'Jansenism'.[32] I can only present its exceedingly complicated story in a crudely simplified form. Originally Jansenists were followers of Cornelius Jansen, professor at the University of Louvain in Belgium and then bishop of Ypres, whose book called *Augustinus* was published in 1640, two years after his death. It glorified the theological stance of St Augustine, which placed greater emphasis than did most of the Fathers of the Church on the depravity of Man. Taken to its extreme, this line of argument led to the view that only the arbitrary grace of God could save him, and hence that faith was the way to salvation and works were valueless. This was Protestantism, and it is no accident that Luther had been an Augustinian friar, steeped in the writings of the Father from whom his Order claimed to derive its inspiration. With these doctrines often went demands for simpler worship, plainer buildings, access to the vernacular Bible, stricter personal morality, better parochial care and fewer and more observant monks and nuns. These attitudes became quite fashionable in the France of Louis XIV, where they were particularly associated with the Cistercian nunnery of Port-Royal des Champs near Paris. They soon became entangled in a complex and endless web of intellectual, political and ecclesiastical disputes. Within the Church the principal enemies of the Jansenist tendency were the Jesuits, determined to assert the superiority of their own theological teaching, which had become notable not only for its emphasis on the merit of works but also for its cultivation of 'casuistry' or 'probabilism', a mode of argumentation designed to create subtle justifications for a wide range of actions which at first sight breached morality and Christian teaching. Towards the end of his long reign Louis XIV came to see the nuns of Port Royal and their male sympathisers as, like the Huguenots, a threat to the unity of Church and state, and in 1709 evicted them. Not content with that striking exercise of absolute power, in the following year he had the buildings of the nunnery demolished. In 1713 pope Clement XI, urged on by the Jesuits and the ageing Louis XIV, condemned in his bull *Unigenitus* 101 'Jansenist' propositions from a book by Quesnel known as the *Réflexions morales*. These reflections were attached by Quesnel to his French translation of the New Testament, and some of the condemned passages came word for word from Augustine's own writings.

By this pronouncement the pope was outlawing opinions which were widespread in the Church and had hitherto been held to fall within the range of acceptable theology. Few modern writers, however orthodox, doubt that the bull was a grave error: its new, narrow doctrinal position was unsustainable and in the long run its adoption seriously weakened the papacy and the Church. A small group of Jansenists left the Church and formed a schismatic body, the Old Catholics. Other sympathisers conformed outwardly, but none the less worked more or less secretly to promote Jansenist ideas – and almost any critic of any aspect of papal policy or of the Jesuits was now liable to be called a Jansenist, especially by the Jesuits and their allies. The ramifications of the dispute were immense. It led, for example, to renewed questioning of papal authority and demands for the calling of a general council of the Church. It provoked such bitter debates that in many Catholic countries the ruler forbade further discussion of it. In France the solidarity and partisanship of the Jansenists enabled them, though in a minority, almost to dominate the *parlements*, the courts that ratified government decrees, and so to conduct a campaign against Bourbon absolutism which played a large part in precipitating the Revolution of 1789. The controversy is especially important to us because it was, among other things, a dispute between monastic Orders: the papal condemnation naturally gave great offence to those that took their inspiration from St Augustine. Ultimately, the Jesuits' success in obtaining the bull *Unigenitus* evoked a backlash, in which other Orders played a prominent part. But in the short run – for a little more than a generation – the pope's support for the Jesuits' line contributed to enhance their influence in politics and education as well as in the Church, and to facilitate the triumph of the Baroque piety and the artistic display associated with them.

By the 1740s, however, Jansenists were receiving powerful support from the writings of Lodovico Antonio Muratori (1672–1750), the polymath librarian of the duke of Modena. Nowadays famous as the ground-breaking editor of Italy's medieval documents, he was then better known for his *Treatise on Christian Charity* (1723) and his *On Well-Ordered Christian Devotion* (1747). Particularly in the last decade of his long life he dedicated himself to stating the case for internal reform of the Church. This mild scholar-priest, friend of pope Benedict XIV (1740–58), argued for changes such as the use of the vernacular in services. He declared that there were far too many clergy overall. As for monks and nuns, he complained of the factions created within the Church by the rivalry between religious Orders and by their overweening power, wrote of the Benedictine scholars of southern Germany as 'sunk in the darkness of barbarity', applauded only those Orders that like the Capuchins retained their original spirit, was quite ready to see other Orders suppressed, and urged that the secular clergy – at least those who fulfilled their pastoral role – should be strengthened and accorded higher respect. He hoped that Benedict XIV would legislate in this spirit, which he saw as reviving the programme of the Council of Trent.[33] In practice, Benedict's monastic reforms were very modest. In any case, as we shall see, and as Muratori sometimes recognised, many of the houses of the old Orders, partly as a result of pressure from outside, but also partly through renewal from within, had themselves become promoters of Catholic Reform, improving their discipline, forming congregations, fostering scholarship, participating in the modernisation of theology and, where their rules permitted, engaging in charitable and parochial work.[34] Even so, it seems in retrospect that this was the last opportunity that the Roman Catholic Church had in the eighteenth century to embark on serious reform under a respected pope in a relatively favourable climate. For, by the time Benedict died in 1758, the first rumblings were to be heard of the mental and political earthquake that was to shake the institution to its foundations, as Jansenism in a broad sense joined forces with absolutism, Enlightenment and eventually Revolution against it. Most ominously, Portugal had already launched the campaign which was to bring down the Jesuits.[35]

In 1763 a new challenge was thrown down to the papacy. A book was published by 'Febronius' – the easily penetrated pseudonym of Hontheim, suffragan bishop of the elector-archbishop of Trier – called *Of the State of the Church*, in which he argued that secular rulers, and especially prince-bishops, had the right and duty to reform the Church in their territories. This publication fitted into a campaign by the German ecclesiastical electors to arrogate to themselves many of the prerogatives claimed by the pope. A prince who was also an archbishop could make a special case, but Febronius's work was well received by many lay Catholic rulers who wished to curb the privileges of the Church and carry through ecclesiastical reforms on their own authority. The fact that the pope had proved unable to bring about significant changes strengthened the argument. Though Rome acted with unusual speed to condemn the book, this only enhanced its fame. In discussing the state of the Church Febronius maintained that monasteries were too numerous, that disputes between the different Orders did serious harm and that monasticism needed to be cleansed and curbed.[36]

I shall describe in Parts II and III how these various strands combined to destroy most of Europe's monasteries. In the next four chapters I shall be talking of the period before that convulsion, and of more or less traditional monasticism continuing to flourish down to the 1780s and beyond, even while the ground was beginning to move. As Chateaubriand wrote of the Napoleonic Empire, 'at the brim of prosperity, people hear only the strains of the dream that is passing away.'[37]

CHAPTER 2

THE GREAT MONASTERIES OF THE GERMAN CATHOLIC LANDS

In this chapter I shall concentrate on the area in which there occurred during the late seventeenth and early eighteenth centuries the most spectacular efflorescence of the monasteries, especially of the old Orders, in the whole of Europe: the so-called German Catholic lands, namely, south Germany, Switzerland, Austria and Bohemia. Throughout this large region the landscape is dominated to this day by abbeys that were lavishly rebuilt during these years. Elsewhere the period saw much monastic building, but not on this colossal scale and not in the version of Baroque – merging into Rococo – that is characteristic of this area, more exuberant, playful, colourful and curvaceous than the French and Italian brands.[1] From this standpoint these diverse lands seem to constitute a unit. Moreover, the monasteries of this area included the most politically independent to be found in Europe, many of the richest, some of the most observant and reformist, and a number of those that made the greatest contribution to learning. It is here, more than anywhere else in Europe, that the old Orders truly flourished in the eighteenth century.

In the first century of the Counter-Reformation the most conspicuous development of monasticism in the region, as elsewhere, had been the advance of the Jesuits, called in by almost every authority – rulers, bishops and other Orders – to revitalise Catholicism and reconvert the people to it. They had been given charge of nearly all universities and many high schools; they controlled theological teaching and censorship; and they supplied virtually all royal confessors. They and other new Orders like the Capuchins, aided admittedly by political and military repression, played a major role in re-Catholicising most parts of the region by the late seventeenth century.[2] It was as a by-product or result of this process that, between the early 1600s and the 1770s – and especially between the 1680s and the 1750s – the great majority of the churches in the area were rebuilt or refurbished. The new emphases of Counter-Reformation piety required that the high altar and the nearby tabernacle of the sacrament be theatrically decorated and visible to the mass of the congregation, that large numbers of communicants could easily approach the high altar, that numerous altars should be provided in sidechapels, that the pulpit should be so placed that the preacher could speak to the congregation effectively and that confessional boxes should be available in which individuals could make their confession anonymously.[3] Gothic churches divided up by screens would not do. Indeed no church interior now seemed acceptable unless it was essentially a hall-church, Baroque or Rococo in its ornament and decoration, peopled with statues of saints and prophets, home to a goodly number of well-displayed relics of saints, festooned with dramatic frescoes and stuccoes, brightly painted and ablaze with gold, and furnished with one or more organs (cf. Plate 6). Externally, domes – often in the 'onion' shape peculiar to the region – replaced Romanesque towers and Gothic spires.[4] It is comparatively easy to see why these statements should apply to churches of the Jesuits and of other Orders associated with the Counter-Reformation, and to the parish churches which their missions targeted. What is more surprising is that nearly all the most magnificent examples of this process are those built or refurbished by monasteries of the old Orders, which in the sixteenth century had seemed moribund.

To give a crude economic explanation of this building boom is not too difficult. Certainly it could not have been afforded until the Thirty Years War had been brought to an end and the economy of the lands it had ravaged had been given a chance to recover. During the war the population of Germany fell, at a minimum, by a third, and possibly by even more.[5] Of course the impact of the conflict was fitful and uneven, and in some areas later upheavals were at least as damaging: in the eastern regions of Austria the last incursions of the Turks, culminating in the siege of Vienna in 1683, brought a further period of devastation, especially in and around the capital itself. But, in general, the period of greater stability and comparative peace that followed the Thirty Years War enabled the population to rise again, which naturally went with higher agricultural employment and production.

The most obvious beneficiaries were rulers who had the power to levy taxes, and landowners who could exact labour and dues from their peasants. Renewed prosperity was less evident in the German cities that had been so flourishing at the time of the Reformation. Generally speaking, it was only cities where rulers resided and held their Courts which participated in the boom. But, at least down to the

1730s, landed incomes in the region tended to rise in real terms, and monasteries of the old Orders, with their large estates and their right to tithes and other dues, were conspicuous among the gainers.[6]

More will be said later of these aspects of the story. But the undoubted improvement in the state of the region's economy, though a necessary condition for the architectural bonanza, is by no means a sufficient explanation for it. No doubt many monastic houses had been able to do very little to maintain and improve their buildings for more than a century, and some of them may well have become so dilapidated that they needed drastic restoration or replacement – which is what some abbots claimed when pressing their chapters to approve ambitious plans.[7] But there was evidently much more to it than that. As recovery proceeded after the Peace of Westphalia, a sense of security and triumph emerged, now that the region, once apparently on the verge of falling to Protestantism, at last seemed safe for Catholicism. A further wave of relief and rejoicing followed when the Turks, seen for so long as a threat to German Christendom, were driven back from Vienna in 1683, and the euphoria was renewed as they were progressively expelled from Hungary over the next forty years. The same feelings help to account for the rapid and lavish rebuilding of the secular palaces of Vienna at the same period. But these points still leave it unexplained how the old Orders could take the leading role in celebrating the triumph of the Counter-Reformation.[8]

I shall now take some examples of notable individual houses, intending to convey with the aid of illustrations an impression of the ostentation and quality of the great monasteries' architecture, to help explain their efflorescence in this period, and also to give some insight into their way of life.

AUSTRIA AND BOHEMIA

MELK

I begin with Austrian and Bohemian houses, and first of all with Melk, which I shall describe in detail because it was of more than local importance, has rich archives, has been especially fortunate in its historians and has displayed unusual openness about its finances.[9] Every great abbey had certain customs peculiar to itself, and Melk was exceptional in its wealth and standing, but much of its history and practice applies more or less to many other houses of the old Orders in the region, and its way of life resembles in essentials that of all monasteries influenced by the Rule of St Benedict.

ILL. 2 View of the abbey of Melk from the Danube

Melk is perhaps the grandest of all Benedictine abbeys, built on a bluff overlooking the Danube about fifty miles above Vienna. Its scale and its stunning position are brought out in the frontispiece and in Ill. 2. Founded by the Babenberg ruler of Austria in the late eleventh century, on the site of his former castle, Melk always ranked among the greatest houses of the region, and in the eighteenth century was one of the two richest in Lower Austria, with over 7,000 subjects in 1695 and a revenue of 44,000 florins per annum in 1751, that is, almost exactly 1 per cent of the revenue of the entire province of Lower Austria. In the latter year a return made to the government classified and valued the capital resources of Melk and its parishes as shown in Table 1.[10]

This table shows the enormous importance to the monastery of rents and tithe, the considerable scale of peasant or feudal services and dues, and the overwhelming predominance of agricultural activities on its lands and in producing

Table 1 *The capital value of Melk's resources*

	Florins	% of total
Cultivated land	38,225	4.4
Pasture land	3,367	0.4
Vineyards	5,792	0.7
Woodland etc.	8,195	0.9
Naturalrobot (services in kind)	84,560	9.6
Cash	3,565	0.4
Tolls	423	0.1
Hunting rights etc.	2,014	0.2
Licences	2,448	0.3
Ungeld (other payments)	3,692	0.4
Mills	1,560	0.2
Domestic service	27,453	3.1
Rents	76,501	8.7
Services in money	8,863	1.0
Corn for rent and tithes	438,965	50.0
Wine for rent and tithes	170,134	19.4
Livestock tithe	1,444	0.2
TOTAL	877,201	100

Table 2 *Percentage of Melk's income from various sources*

Agriculture	Vineyards	Cattle	Woods	Rents	Lordship	Services/Taxes	Other
39.5	29.6	3.7	3.9	9.1	1.4	11.3	1.5

its income. A return made half a century later categorises the income of the abbey on a different and perhaps more revealing basis (see Table 2).

The first point that leaps to the eye from these figures is the value of the vine crop, mainly from the notable wine-producing district of the Danube valley known as the Wachau, a good part of which was owned by Melk. The second is the relatively high proportion of 'rents', which include mortgages, deriving partly from the suburban extension of Vienna on to the abbey's lands.

In the eighteenth century the number of monks hovered around the high figure of seventy, most of them priests (see Fig. 1, p. 47). This was a far cry from its situation in 1564 when, beleaguered by both Turks and Reformers, Melk had a mere ten inmates, only three of them priests. By the end of the sixteenth century, supported

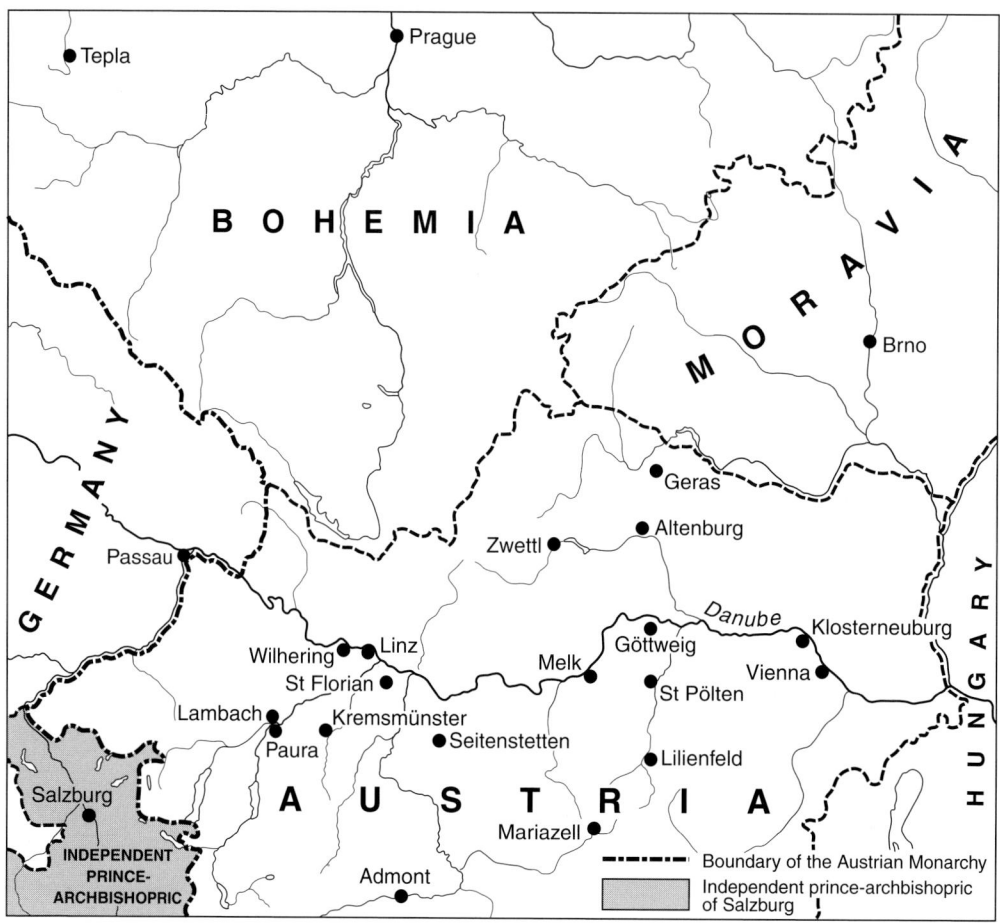

MAP 1 Austrian monasteries

by the Habsburg rulers of Austria, and with its monks replenished from south Germany, it was recovering under abbot Caspar Hoffmann (1587–1623) its discipline, prestige, numbers and prosperity. In 1625 the pope approved the establishment under its aegis of a congregation of the major Austrian Benedictine abbeys, an initiative self-consciously recalling the first 'Melk Reform' of the fifteenth century. This development greatly increased the level of interchange and co-operation between these monasteries and provided a mechanism by which a delinquent house could be brought back into line. Another feature of the reform was that, in place of paid seculars or laymen, monks were put back in charge of the house's administration.[11] Melk did not cease to be a fortress when it became a monastery: it was strengthened and garrisoned in wartime down to the nineteenth century, and the abbot himself organised the defence of the district against the Turks in

1683.[12] Like all the larger monastic houses of the German lands, it was obliged to provide itself with a suite of apartments designated for the emperor's use, which were also available for the monastery's formal occasions. It was the first staging-post on any journey up the Danube from Vienna to Germany, and the abbey's imperial suite was often occupied by Austrian monarchs, as it was to be by the pope in 1782 and on two occasions by Napoleon.[13]

Melk's political pre-eminence was guaranteed when its abbot was confirmed in 1631 as the president of the First Estate in the Estates of Lower Austria, and therefore a permanent member of the small standing committee of the Estates, which conducted the business between the full sessions.[14] The diocesan map of the region had been drawn long before the political, and nearly every part of the Austrian duchies belonged to a diocese whose cathedral lay outside Habsburg territory. So the First Estate of all of them consisted of abbots rather than bishops – in the case of Lower Austria, twenty-six abbots (or provosts). In so far as bishops were represented, they often ranked among the nobles, the Second Estate. The main business of the Estates was to grant and collect taxes for the ruler. Maria Theresa's great administrative reform of 1749 took away the right of most of the provincial Estates to deny revenue, but there was still room for argument about the level of taxation, and they remained responsible for distributing the burden among the landowners and for collecting the money. The abbey whose head was president of the First Estate could therefore expect to gain financial advantage as well as prestige. The Estates were also normally consulted about projected major reforms that would affect them, for example over the reform of labour services. It was naturally in wartime that the financial business was heaviest, and it seems that in emergencies the senior abbot in a province could find himself acting as a full-time minister of state. The most striking instance I have come across concerned abbot Markus Egle of Wilten, president of the First Estate of the Tyrol. During the French wars he had his bed permanently made up in the Estates' building in Innsbruck, so that in an emergency he could at once go there and help take decisions about the defence of the province. His devotion to duty was the less surprising since Bavaria was threatening to annex the province and then impose its policy of suppressing all monasteries, which duly happened in 1807, though the occupation lasted only a few years.[15] But even the normal duties of the abbot of Melk as president of the First Estate, and his religious and political role at Court, meant that he resided for much of the time in the Melkerhof, the monastery's large administrative centre in Vienna, leaving the prior to manage the day-to-day affairs of the abbey. Austrian rulers in their turn were especially interested in getting these houses to elect as abbots trusty persons who would manage the business of the Estates efficiently. Sometimes abbots were offered other official posts. Abbot Dietmayr, the promoter of the Baroque rebuilding of Melk, became in 1706 rector of Vienna University, but he refused the highly flattering offer of the emperor Charles VI to send him as ambassador to Poland in 1720, preferring to 'stay in the Austrian paradise'.[16] He was not the only abbot to be given such opportunities: his contemporary Gottfried Bessel, abbot of Göttweig, took on many diplomatic missions on behalf of the emperor and the elector of Mainz, Lothar Franz von Schönborn, whose chaplain he had been.[17]

In the late sixteenth century Melk and other Benedictine abbeys in the German lands assumed a new – or significantly enhanced – responsibility which greatly altered their character. From the beginning these houses had owned parishes and appointed clergy to preside over them, but these had usually been secular clergy; the monks, except for the abbot, had normally remained immured in the cloister, engaged in the traditional duties of prayer and contemplation, worship, learning and the education of prospective monks. Now, with the encouragement of the government, it became normal practice to appoint monks as vicars of its parishes. The initial justifications were the acute shortage and low quality of secular priests and the need to combat the Protestantism espoused by many nobles in the region, but the practice grew steadily even after the crisis had passed. The result, as can be seen from Fig. 1, was that in the eighteenth century a third or even more of the monks of Melk were engaged in parochial work outside the monastery, visiting it only occasionally. The community inevitably lost something of its cohesion, though it gained by not having to pay secular vicars in its parishes, by providing occupation for its monks, by enhancing its direct influence on its estates and by the abbot taking over the supervision of parish work from the bishop. The practice incidentally made it important for the abbey to try, just as lay owners and rulers did, to consolidate its hitherto scattered estates into a coherent bloc.[18] Among the old Orders the Premonstratensians and Augustinians had always supplied some parish priests, but they expanded this provision during the period of the Counter-Reformation, and its extension to the Benedictines and Cistercians ensured that in this region they were all deeply involved in 'useful' parochial work, thus refuting one of the main criticisms brought against them in the age of the Reformation and the Counter-Reformation. No study appears to exist of this phenomenon, which seems as natural to modern Austrians as it seems surprising to others.[19]

A related aspect of the reform of monastic discipline consisted in improving the education of the monks, to qualify them to become parish priests as well as scholars and contemplatives. Each major monastery made itself into a seminary, and at any one time several monks held office as teachers, though some novices

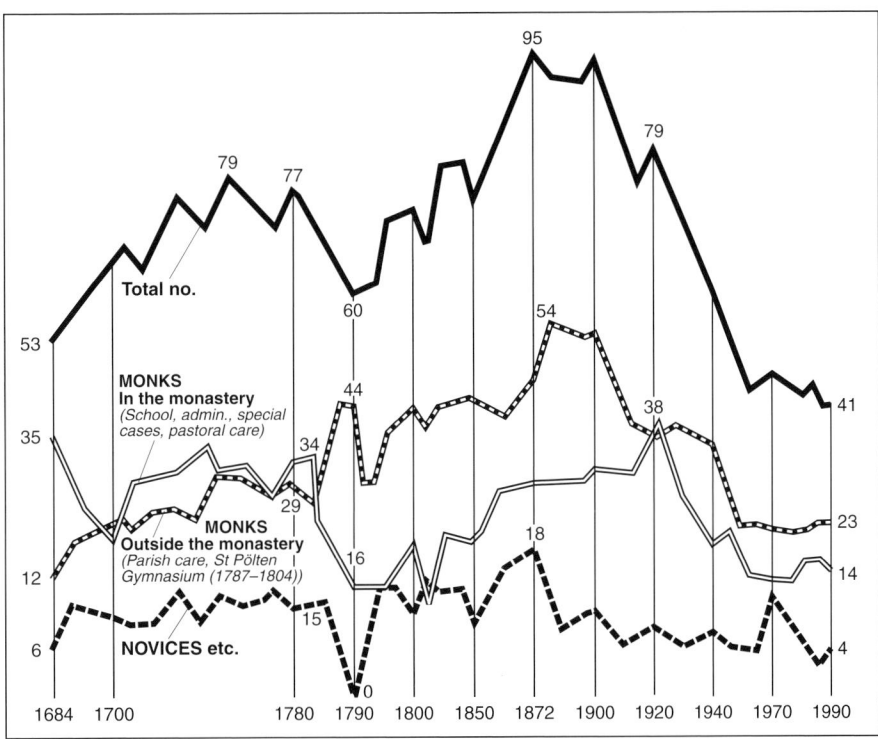

FIGURE 1 Numbers of monks and novices at Melk abbey, 1684–1990

received part of their education in universities. Such seminaries vied with, and generally surpassed in quality, those which some bishops had created. Schooling was also commonly provided for boys of the neighbourhood. This educational provision removed still more monks from the unadulterated routine of prayer, worship, contemplation and scholarship.[20]

It is against this background that the rebuilding of Melk has to be seen. Little was left of the original early medieval buildings by the time of the Reformation, a new church having been built in 1428. During the seventeenth century the monastery was modified piecemeal to meet the demands for new liturgical practices in the church and higher standards of comfort in the living quarters. Then in 1700, after the ravages of the Turkish siege of 1683 had been repaired, and the abbey's finances re-established, Berthold Dietmayr, the son of a monastic official at the charterhouse of Gaming, was elected abbot at the age of thirty. He proved to be a man of exceptional vision and drive. Having been in charge of the abbey's administration in the Melkerhof, he had seen the beginnings of the aristocratic rebuilding of Vienna. Immediately on becoming abbot, he persuaded the chapter that structural weaknesses made it necessary to rebuild the church, a task which in 1702 the abbey gave to the architect Jakob Prandtauer, under the abbot's direction. Dietmayr further argued that, by changing the plan of the whole complex in such a way as to isolate the imperial apartments and the administration of its estates from the monks' quarters, the tranquillity of the cloister would be restored. This concern is easily understandable, since well over a thousand distinguished guests arrived each year, many of them with a large retinue, to take advantage of the abbey's duty of hospitality. By 1711 the project had developed 'imperceptibly' into a complete rebuilding of the monastery. Like many other such schemes of the period, most of which were left unfinished, it totally rejects the standard medieval layout of a monastery and replaces it with a symmetrical design that ignores the traditional orientation, a design perhaps deriving ultimately from Philip II's vast palace monastery of the Escorial in Spain (Ill. 17).[21] The result of Dietmayr's planning and management is one of the great architectural masterpieces of the world, often compared with Durham cathedral. The south front of the abbey is 362 metres and sixty-four bays long, the extreme example of the Baroque passion for immense repetitive façades. A list of the various structures with their completion dates further emphasises the scale of the operation and the speed with which it was carried through: the summer sacristy 1701, built first in order to provide a temporary church; the dome of the new church 1712; the prelature or abbot's lodgings 1713; the prior's house 1714; the church 1715; the west part of the south wing and the imperial staircase 1716; the west wing of the monastic court 1717; the Kolomanisaal – St Koloman or Colman was an Irish saint whose relics the abbey possessed, making it a pilgrimage site – and the refectory underneath 1718; the tower and north bastion 1718; the north and east wing of the abbot's court 1723; the east part of the south wing and the Kaisersaal or Marmorsaal 1726 (see Plate 3); the north wing of the monastic court 1728; the library 1730. After the death of Prandtauer in 1726 his nephew Joseph Munggenast followed him as architect. The interiors took longer to complete: the church organ, for example, was not built until 1731–2, and the frescoes by Johann Michael Rottmayr and others were finished later still. A serious fire in 1738 made much repair necessary. Then in the 1740s an elegant garden was landscaped, partly on top of the fortifications. The total cost ran to 725,000 florins, yet the entire sum was paid out of income.[22]

Why – and with what justification – did the abbey spend these huge sums to create such a grandiose palace? Not all the monks approved at first, and some of them later staged a 'rebellion' which the abbot faced down with the backing of the Court. In general he kept the support of the majority by proceeding step by step. Motives that seem straightforwardly secular were obviously of major importance. The obligation to receive the emperor and other grandees was held to require the abbey to provide them with elaborate accommodation. The abbot, working politically with the greatest nobles of the realm, felt the need to compete with them in the grandeur of his residences and the splendour of his hospitality, especially to the imperial family, and in overawing the thousands of subjects to whom he was the secular lord. There was also a strong element of competition between the great monasteries. One object of the scheme was to separate administration and hospitality from contemplation and worship – in a sense to keep the secular apart from the religious – but the two were not in general felt to be distinct spheres. Rather they interpenetrated and reinforced each other, or even seemed to be one. It was to the glory of God, His church and the Benedictine Order that the abbot should be able to vie with lay rulers, and that the architecture, furniture and decoration of the monastery should be of a quality to impress the grandest visitors. Moreover, lavish display, especially in the abbey church, redounded to the glory of God, who deserved to receive at least as much honour as earthly princes. It was equally to the glory of the ruler of the Monarchy that the abbey which his predecessors had founded and endowed, and which assisted his government, should prosper and be imposing. Further, it was the goal of contemporary aesthetic theory to achieve what has come to be called a *Gesamtkunstwerk*, a complex in which all the arts – principally architecture, sculpture, painting, music and theatre – were mobilised to create a unified whole. A deliberate theatricality was to be seen in the brilliant exploitation of the site to engineer stunning views of the abbey from the river (see Frontispiece) and of the valley from the monastery, and also in the employment of the greatest stage designer of the age, Giuseppe Galli-Bibiena, to erect boxes for distinguished visitors in the church. As for the decorative scheme,

What subtlety [wrote Germain Bazin in his book *The Baroque*] there is in the symbolic design of the monastery of Melk, a sacred triangle formed by the marble hall (Marmorsaal), the library and the church. In the marble hall, *Hercules heroicus*, once chosen as an emblem by the emperors Nero and Commodus, symbolises the prince, or excellence in the human sphere; in the library *Hercules Christianus*, adopted in the Renaissance as a speaking resemblance of Christ, signifies that this excellence can only reside in Christian perfection, which the prince must possess. The 'mental fight' – the psychomachy – which is the theme of the Marmorsaal, and the celebration of divine wisdom which is the theme of the library, are united in the sanctuary where the triumph of the Church Militant is symbolised by the martyr apostles Peter and Paul, the two athletes of the faith who constitute the Christian Pillars of Hercules.[23]

What went on in this palace of a monastery? The core activity was worship, the observance of the canonical 'hours'. The timetable of the offices and meals can

Table 3 *The monastic timetable*

		Weekdays and Semi-double Feasts	Sundays and Double Feasts
4.00 a.m.	Matins	chanted	3.30 chanted
	Lauds	chanted	chanted
5.00–5.30	Meditation or spiritual reading		
6.00	Prime	said	chanted
	Low Masses	said	said
9.00	Terce	chanted	chanted
9.15	High Mass	chanted	polyphonic
	Sext	said	said
10.30	Midday meal		
11.15	None	said	said
	Rosary	said	said
11.30–14.15 p.m.	Two hours communal recreation followed by silence for 3/4 hour		
3.00	Vespers	chanted	polyphonic
5.15	Dinner followed by recreation		
7.00	Compline	chanted	chanted (polyphonic antiphon)
8.00	To bed		

be reconstructed roughly as shown in Table 3. 'Most of the Offices', says Robert Freeman, 'were held in the abbey church...After lunch None was read in the refectory...In winter the morning and evening Offices (Matins, Lauds, Prime, Vespers and Compline) were celebrated in the heated winter choir room.'

This timetable draws attention to many issues. First, it was in principle the duty of all resident monks to attend all the offices, and it seems that down to 1786 this rule was in general observed at Melk, as in most German and Austrian houses of the old Orders.[24]

Secondly, there were a great many feast-days, some of them peculiar to Melk – but other monasteries would have their own special observances – on which not only the services, but also the meals, would be unusually elaborate. It was one of the stereotypes of criticism of monks in general that they were gluttonous and bibulous (Ill. 13). Although in all respectable houses they were subject to certain restrictions, sometimes fasted and must generally have behaved with moderation, in the wealthier monasteries they had many opportunities to enjoy large quantities of good food and wine. All notable Austrian monasteries had acquired vineyards in favoured spots like the Wachau or south Tyrol, in many cases far distant from the house. As with other indices, the production of wine grew markedly between the mid-seventeenth and the eighteenth century. The peak was commonly the 1770s, partly because the competition of beer seems then to have become more serious. Some of the very large amounts of wine produced was marketed, some was sold in the house's taverns, but most was disposed of within the monasteries themselves. At Melk in the eighteenth century the cellars contained more than 20,000 *Eimer*, that is, rather more than a million litres, worth by the end of the century more than 50,000 florins. At one point Göttweig was storing almost twice as much. If the celebration of Masses required a considerable supply, much more was consumed at meals. Hierarchy was strictly observed: at the abbot's table *Prälatenwein* was drunk, the monks had *Conventwein*, lesser persons made do with inferior vintages.

The abbot of [the Premonstratensian foundation of] Geras used in 1735 (with not many guests)... a daily average of 1 Maß (about 1 1/2 litres) per person. In 1763, for abbot, monks and guests, per person per day, an average of about 2 Maß was served. The chief clerk [*Amtsschreiber*] was allowed 1 Maß daily, the students received 2 *Seidel* [a *Seidel* was roughly a pint].

It can hardly cause surprise that there were said to be monasteries, such as Schäftlarn in Bavaria, where 'an excessive thirst' prevailed for 150 years, leading to drunken disorders and attempted suicides.[25]

Thirdly, at least at Melk – and many other houses were similarly equipped – there was a large musical establishment to maintain the quality of the services. A *Regens chori*, who was a monk, presided over a lay organist, a *Thurnermeister* in charge of a band of trumpeters and drummers, a number of professional vocalists and instrumentalists, and a dozen or more choirboys. They performed in the church, which sometimes meant that elaborate unrelated music went on simultaneously with a said Mass; and they were required to play at most meals, during the Carnival festivities, for the abbot and for guests, in processions, at the theatre and at the important annual ceremony when all monks were bled. Much music was composed, and more bought or copied, and many instruments purchased, to make all this possible. In the years 1771–80, for example, perhaps the peak decade in this respect, eighty-three symphonies and seventy-three Masses were acquired, together with many other religious and secular works. Hence the collections of music surviving at monasteries such as Melk are fundamental sources for the history of music. The abbey's musicians had regular contacts with those of other monasteries and with the musical world of Vienna. Among those employed at Melk the most famous was Johann Georg Albrechtsberger (1736–1809), who, having been born in Klosterneuburg and first trained in the monastery there, became a choirboy at Melk, then an organist in Hungary and Vienna, made friends with

Haydn, returned to Melk as organist in 1759, resigned in 1765 to work in Vienna but repeatedly came back to play the organ at the abbey. Much of the music he composed was written for Melk. He became organist of St Stephen's cathedral, Vienna, in 1793, Mozart having worked with him and been happy to take the post of his deputy. Most notable of all perhaps, he taught Beethoven.

Mention of the theatre in reference to a monastery may seem odd. But in fact many plays, oratorios and operas were performed at Melk, mainly in connexion with the school, which followed the Jesuits' practice of using drama as an educational tool. More elaborate entertainments were mounted for the visits of great personages or for the celebration of landmarks in the careers of the abbot, prior and monks. Although at Melk there was no building specifically designed as a theatre, performances took place at various times in nine different rooms. The playwrights and directors – and even the choreographers of the ballets – were all drawn from the monastery. The texts were rigorously censored, but none the less the variety was considerable, ranging from hearty German comedies through dramatisation of Bible stories in Latin to serious German plays and cantatas.[26]

A more continuous concern of the monastery was study, as an aid to preaching and teaching and as a preparation for scholarly writings. New catalogues were compiled of the books, manuscripts and archives in the abbey's possession. Among the monks of the early eighteenth century several, especially the brothers Bernhard and Hieronymus Pez, acquired a European reputation for their work on early manuscripts relating to the history of Melk and to German and Austrian monastic history. This activity was paralleled in many of the great houses. The library ranked second only to the church in monasteries of the old Orders, and the building of a spacious, lavishly decorated room to house their books was invariably part of their rebuilding programmes. Melk's was particularly fine, and is designed to hold an unusually large number of volumes – the monastery, like several others, possessed more than were to be found in Wren's great library at Trinity College, Cambridge – leaving much less wall space for ornamentation than in some examples.[27]

So far as what may be called the private life of the monks is concerned, the monks had individual cells or rooms, no doubt of the type that has survived at the Premonstratensian abbey at Verdun in eastern France, where the sleeping area could be curtained off, leaving an elegant sitting-room (Ill. 3). At Melk stoves had been installed in the cells for the first time in the late seventeenth century; previously, the only heated room available to the ordinary monks had been the study room.[28] For further details of monastic life I draw on information from other houses, which probably in most cases applied also to Melk. Monks were

(a)

(b)

ILL. 3 Two views of a monastic cell of c. 1700 in the Premonstratensian abbey, Verdun, eastern France, now the Préfecture

allowed 'pocket money' and relatively small possessions, for example books, snuff and snuff boxes, coffee and coffee machines etc. They could take annual holidays away from the monastery and they might be permitted to travel for scholarly or religious purposes. In the monastery they would enjoy brief periods of recreation when they could play chess, cards, billiards, skittles.[29] But, despite all this, and though they lived and worshipped amid the splendour of Prandtauer's architecture and Troger's frescoes, their lives were tightly regulated and comparatively austere. Anyone who has visited one of these monasteries in a central European winter will testify to the hardship involved in attending services in their largely unheated churches. While many winter functions were held elsewhere, on major occasions the great church would naturally be used.

OTHER AUSTRIAN AND BOHEMIAN HOUSES

Much of what I have said about the rebuilding and development of Melk applies in a general way to many major German and Austrian houses. I shall refer to other Austrian monasteries chiefly to illustrate hitherto unmentioned aspects of monastic life. Melk's nearest rival in Lower Austria, **Klosterneuburg**, also on the Danube, an Augustinian foundation of 1133 by margrave Leopold III of Babenberg, canonised as St Leopold, had long been the goal of regular pilgrimages by Austrian rulers. In 1730, at the height of his power, Charles VI, who disliked his half-finished palace of Schönbrunn near Vienna and had spent his twenties in Spain as claimant to its throne, decided to turn Klosterneuburg into a palace-monastery on the model of the Escorial. The gigantic plan, by Donato Felice d'Allio, was to multiply the already numerous buildings, suppress the surviving Gothic structures, create four vast courts and adorn them with nine domes, each topped by an imperial crown (Ill. 4). Only a quarter of this colossal scheme had been completed when Charles died in 1740, having in the meantime suffered a series of defeats in war and lost immense territories in Italy and the Balkans. His heiress, Maria Theresa, whose brand of piety was less traditional and ostentatious, faced with a desperate international situation and its financial implications, soon stopped work on the project, though there was a brief attempt to revive it as late as 1776. Nothing could better illustrate than this scheme the continuing hold of the monastic ideal on the minds of Catholic rulers in the first half of the eighteenth century. The same ambition on the part of John V of Portugal had led to the creation – by a German architect – of the palace-monastery of Mafra, begun in 1717 and largely completed by 1730 (Ill. 19).[30]

ILL. 4 Benedikt Prill, ink drawing c. 1750 of the proposed design for Klosterneuburg (never completed) being blessed by St Leopold

A feature common to many of the great *Stifte* is a grand processional staircase leading to the imperial suite. Melk's is less impressive than a number of others, of which perhaps the finest is at **Göttweig**, another Benedictine monastery in Lower Austria, for which Lucas Hildebrandt prepared the monumental rebuilding scheme during the rule of abbot Bessel, only part of which was completed (Plate 4).[31]

Of the monasteries of Upper Austria, Benedictine **Kremsmünster**, founded by a duke of Bavaria in the late eighth century, was pre-eminent. Its abbot was president of the Estates of its province, and it was nearly twice as rich as Melk with an annual revenue of over 76,000 florins.[32] It too was rebuilt during the Baroque period, though the process started earlier, took almost a century and produced a less unified result than in the case of Melk. Three of its attributes deserve particular mention. First, it preserves the most elegant imaginable fishponds, originally designed by Carlo Antonio Carlone in the 1690s, the apotheosis

ILL. 5 Arcaded fishponds at the Benedictine abbey of Kremsmünster, Upper Austria, by C.A. Carlone, 1690–2

of an amenity that all monasteries needed if their inmates were to observe without undue hardship the regulations requiring abstention from meat on numerous days during the Church's year (Ill. 5). Secondly, in 1744 Maria Theresa approved the foundation there of an academy for nobles, at which the whole range of subjects needed by courtiers, politicians and administrators was taught, including French, German, architecture, experimental science, Wolffian philosophy, up-to-date political theory, history and geography, together with dancing and riding. The abbey became known as an enemy of the scholastic philosophy that was still, somewhat unfairly, associated with the Jesuits, and for teaching the merits of religious toleration.[33] One of its educational tools, thirdly, was a 'mathematical tower' such as was planned but never built at Melk. This extraordinary structure (Ill. 6), begun in 1748, has eight or nine stories, according to how they are counted. The lower ones contained a 'universal museum', including various collections of objects such as paintings, geological and botanical specimens, stuffed

ILL. 6 The observatory and museum building at Kremsmünster, 1748–59

birds and animals, antiquities, coins and scientific instruments. Next to the top is an observatory with a telescope. The highest storey, nearest to God, is given over to a chapel. Collections of specimens were a common feature of monasteries as of royal and noble palaces, and extensive picture galleries dating from this period are still to be found in Austrian houses such as St Florian (Plate 2), Seitenstetten and the Schottenstift in Vienna; but the building at Kremsmünster offers exceptional evidence of the level of 'Catholic Enlightenment' attained in some houses.[34]

To continue this highly selective tour into Bohemia, the most conspicuous of the old Orders there was the Premonstratensian. It boasted two especially prominent monasteries. The first, **Strahov**, a royal foundation next to the castle in Prague, had built a fine 'theological' library (including a museum) after suffering damage from Swedish forces during the Thirty Years War, and became known as anti-Jesuit in its teaching. It added new monastic quarters in the eighteenth and was, unusually, to develop further, as we shall see, in the 1780s under Joseph II. The second, **Tepl** or **Tepla**, is special in a number of ways. It elected a noble abbot, count Trauttmansdorff, in 1767, who lived in his detached mansion, seldom attended the abbey church and firmly believed that it was his duty to play the *grand seigneur*, so much so that the monks' devotions were disturbed by the sound of his festive music and the noise of his shooting parties. He fostered another noble academy at which a range of subjects and approaches similar to Kremsmünster's was taught. In retrospect, however, his most remarkable contribution was to begin the development of the springs on the abbey's property into what became in the nineteenth century the fabulous spa of Marienbad.[35]

In the lands of the Austrian Monarchy the seismic shift of attitude towards monasticism in the second half of the eighteenth century is so bound up with the action of the state and with 'Josephism' that I shall deal with it under that heading in Chapter 8. I now move on to discussing southern Germany, where the story is significantly different.

CATHOLIC GERMANY

About a third of the inhabitants of what is now Germany were Catholics, living mainly in the south and west of the country, overwhelmingly in states ruled by Catholics.[36] The sumptuous rebuilding of the great monasteries in these territories had many characteristics in common with that of their Austrian and Bohemian associates. But in Germany the boom peaked slightly later and continued into the 1770s: hence there are more examples of Rococo style than in Austria, and even a few neo-classical schemes. This chronological difference is partly explained by political factors. The main rulers, apart from Joseph II who possessed scattered lands in southern Germany, showed little enthusiasm for monastic reform. Bavaria, the principal state, was still vigorously encouraging Jesuit missions down to the suppression of the Order and, while Joseph was closing hundreds of monasteries, brought itself to abolish only six, all on quite special grounds.[37] Further, the exceptional independence of some of the great German monasteries enabled them to cultivate Catholic Enlightenment more spontaneously and over a longer period than was possible in the abbeys of the Monarchy. So it is appropriate to pursue here the history of the south German houses right down to the end of the eighteenth century.

In order to make the situation comprehensible, it is necessary to say something about the history and structure of the Holy Roman Empire.[38] In the early Middle Ages many of the major German monasteries had formed part of the large group of ecclesiastical institutions, including also bishoprics, to which the early emperors had given land and privileges in return for support against troublesome secular princes, support which originally included the provision of troops and the duty to house the emperor and his suite on his remorseless journeys through his far-flung empire.[39] Between the tenth century and the Reformation the emperor gradually lost power to the princes nominally subordinate to him, and the more successful among them managed to form substantial, virtually independent territories. Most of these states or principalities were ruled by laymen: the most important examples were the Palatinate, Saxony and Brandenburg, whose rulers were among the seven original electors of the emperor, and Bavaria, which became an electorate in the seventeenth century. But some of these sizable territories were in the hands of ecclesiastics, of whom the most powerful were the archbishops of Mainz, Cologne and Trier, who were also electors. Although the Reformation reduced the number of ecclesiastical states, by the eighteenth century there remained altogether more than twenty prince-bishoprics within the Empire, nearly all of them Catholic, including the three electorates. Over thirty imperial abbeys, mostly in southern Germany, had the same technical status: they qualified as *reichsunmittelbar*, that is, they owed allegiance to the emperor but to no other secular ruler. As late as 1792 the heads of ten of these abbeys had seats in the Imperial Diet (*Reichstag*), a further twenty-three monastic prelates from Swabia had one vote between them, and another vote was shared by seventeen monastic prelates from the Rhineland. Many were represented too in the assemblies of the relevant imperial 'circles'.[40] According to one authority 'the sixty-five ecclesiastical rulers' controlled 'fourteen per cent of the total land area and approximately twelve per cent of the [Empire's] population, ... perhaps three and a half million subjects'.[41] Though no monastery had succeeded in amassing territories comparable in scale with those of the greater prince-bishops and secular rulers, several of them had put together landholdings comparable in size to those of the lesser prince-bishops – one of them, Fulda, was actually converted into a bishopric in 1752;[42] and the others could rival the lesser independent lay princes. The largest was the anomalous imperial abbey of St Gall, located in Switzerland which had ceased to be part of the Empire in 1648, whose abbot ruled more than 1,000 square kilometres and roughly 100,000 subjects. It actually provided a contingent of soldiers to its ally Louis XIV, and was itself involved in a war from 1712 to 1718 to maintain its control over the largely Protestant territory of Toggenburg. Although the abbot and his monks were for a time refugees from their monastery, they were in the end victorious, preserving even their right to conscript the inhabitants into their army.[43] But by this time such behaviour was altogether exceptional in monastic states, and the fact that most of them had virtually no defence expenditure made it much easier for them to finance elaborate building schemes. But in other respects the abbots and abbesses of these imperial monasteries, however small their territories, behaved exactly like minor secular princes: they kept an ostentatious Court, built lavishly, claimed to be absolute rulers and, assisted by officials, issued laws, maintained order and dispensed justice, promoted public works, conducted diplomacy and made treaties.[44]

Except for the papal state itself, states ruled by clergy had disappeared everywhere else in Europe, and they were regarded generally as anachronistic. But the Treaty of Westphalia, the settlement that in 1648 had ended the religious wars in Germany, had frozen not only the religious map of Germany but also its political map, the constitution of the Empire and the constitutions of the individual states. This was done both in the interests of future stability within Germany and in order to prevent the emergence of a strong power in the centre of Europe. The Treaty left the Catholics with a majority among the electors and in other imperial bodies which depended on the existence of the major ecclesiastical states. Not only they but also the independent abbeys were regarded as intrinsic to the constitution of the Empire. In turn, the ecclesiastical states were the most devoted to the maintenance of the *Reich*.

To illustrate the situation, I shall take some examples of monasteries that by 1700 were, or were striving to become, *reichsunmittelbar*. I take first the Benedictine abbey of **Kempten**, which dated back to the eighth century and was unquestionably in that category. It had the largest territory of any monastic state except St Gall, with a population of nearly 40,000, and its lands were also unusually compact, except that it did not control the original town of Kempten, an imperial free city separated from it only by walls. In decay at the time of the Reformation, the abbey was one of the very few remaining in Germany whose monks had to be of noble birth. It was reformed under Jesuit influence at the end of the sixteenth century but was then gleefully destroyed by the Swedes, assisted by the citizens of old Kempten, during the Thirty Years War. Hence its rebuilding began early, in 1651, with Michael Beer and Giovanni Serro as its architects, in a thoroughly Italianate style. This monastic state is one of the few to have been studied by a notable modern historian, namely Peter Blickle.[45] Most writers on monasteries are themselves monks or closely associated with them, treat the aims of these institutions with reverent respect and take their benevolence for granted. It is almost an axiom, based on contemporaries' comments, that the inhabitants of ecclesiastical states were unusually prosperous and contented.[46] Blickle endorses the importance of studying the *Kleinstaat*, the small state, and allows it certain special merits – in the particular case of Kempten that it fostered music and that its peasants, though bound to serve the monastery, were able to participate in village government. But he also records repeated disputes between serfs and the

THE GREAT MONASTERIES OF THE GERMAN CATHOLIC LANDS

MAP 2 Monasteries of S. Germany and Tyrol

abbey, in which imperial commissions, to which subjects could appeal against oppression by their rulers, upheld some of the peasants' complaints. As at St Gall, the old town seized the opportunity of the Reformation to defy the abbey and turn Protestant, and managed to remain so even while the Counter-Reformation was triumphing around it. The abbey of Kempten was exceptionally rich, with an income approaching 200,000 florins a year. Yet it has been pronounced 'as good as worthless' in its scholarship;[47] it was always appealing to the emperor to help it keep out of its lands the pilgrims or beggars who came to the neighbouring monastery of Weingarten twice a year for customary doles; and it was the abbot of Kempten's court that ordered the last execution of a witch in the Empire, as late as 1775.[48] When the abbey was dissolved in 1803 it was heavily in debt. Kempten is one monastic state whose elimination it is particularly difficult to regret.

I turn to a lesser house, Cistercian **Schöntal** in the Main valley, built inside a many-towered wall like a castle. It had been declared *reichsunmittelbar* in the early fifteenth century, but at the end of the century it was subordinated to the prince-archbishop of Mainz whose territory surrounded it. During the Reformation the house was abandoned. Reoccupied in the 1630s, its community set about rehabilitating it and trying to re-establish its position as an imperial abbey. In 1683 it elected one of its number, Benedict Knittel, of humble origin and from a nearby village, to be abbot at the age of thirty-three. The election was held the day after the death of his predecessor, with the necessary high clergy hastily summoned to confirm it, so that the archbishop of Mainz should have no time to intervene and assert the rights he claimed. Knittel, as though he was an emperor, took as his device Hercules brandishing his club. During his reign of forty-nine years he put in hand the rebuilding of the monastery, which was explicitly intended to underline its claims to independence. As architect he brought in Johann Leonhard Dientzenhofer, who had already worked at other Cistercian houses. First the new living quarters and the new library were built. It then took thirty years to finish the new church; and the new residence for the abbot, designed to impress by its grandeur, could not be begun until after Knittel's death. It was presumably lack of funds that made it impossible to proceed faster, though the abbey's annual income of 80,000 florins put it among the wealthier houses. At any rate Knittel managed the financing well enough that he left his successor virtually no debt, by dint of selling off some land. Striking though the finished building is, it did not bring the desired recognition of imperial status.

Abbot Knittel was a minor figure in the literary culture of Catholic Germany. He published books on the history of his abbey, but his speciality was the production of pious and/or topical poems in Latin, German or a mixture of the two, and he excelled in composing chronograms, mostly Latin tags in which the highlighted Ms, Ds, Cs, Xs, Vs and Is added up to the date of the year. At the least provocation he would fire one off to grandee or emperor, and he supplied one for the door of every monk's cell. His literary skills were also displayed in inscriptions all over the church and monastery proclaiming the Catholic faith and its triumph. Like most abbots he did his best to encourage pilgrims to a local shrine, which brought income to the monastery, and he enjoyed hunting and shooting on the abbey's lands. More unusually, he created a zoo. But, if a trifle eccentric, he was a serious scholar and an effective ruler under whom the abbey had a reputation for good discipline.[49]

Many Baroque schemes amounted to little more than drastic refurbishments of medieval or Renaissance buildings which left their basic structure intact. Others, like Schöntal's, involved rebuilding but on the existing plan. In a few cases such as **Ottobeuren**, a Benedictine house in Swabia, the entire monastery was rebuilt,

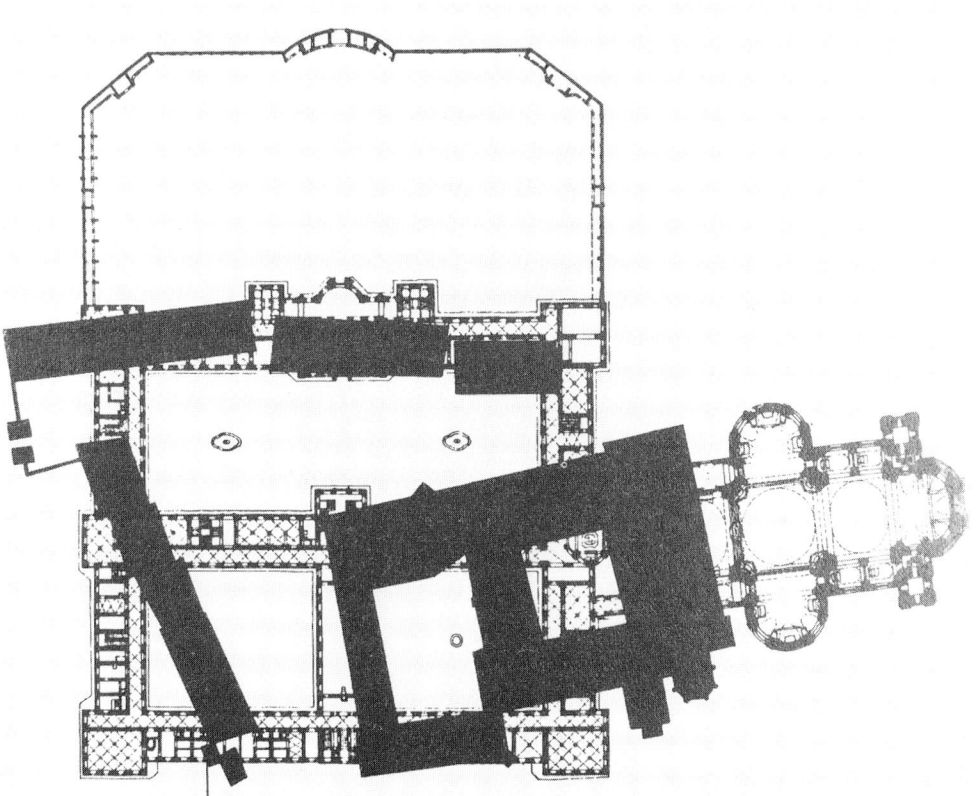

ILL. 7 Plan of the old Benedictine abbey church at Ottobeuren, Germany, superimposed upon the new, plan adapted from W. Braunfels, *Monasteries of Western Europe* (1972)

ILL. 8 Ottobeuren abbey, theatre interior by Johann Michael Fischer, 1724–5

in this case on a new orientation and on a new plan of the Escorial type. It thus became one of the grandest of all abbeys (Ill. 7).[50]

Ottobeuren had previously possessed quaint but rather humble buildings. It had lost its *reichsunmittelbar* status in the fourteenth century and had suffered badly during the Reformation and the Thirty Years War. But in 1710 a new abbot was elected, Rupert Ness, the son of a coppersmith of Wangen, about a hundred kilometres from the abbey. Soon after his election he succeeded in re-establishing the position of the abbey as *reichsunmittelbar* at a cost of 30,000 florins, and so became (subject to a measure of control by the monks in chapter) unquestioned ruler of its principality of about 300 square kilometres and 10,000 inhabitants. The achievement of independence was the signal for the acceptance of a master plan to rebuild the whole monastery. Various architects were consulted, but the abbot and his monks, especially the prior, had the major part in settling the ultimate design. One of its aims, as at Melk, was to separate the abbatial and administrative blocks, known as 'the Court', from the monastery proper. The work began with the monastic quarters (1711–15) and buildings such as the library (1715–17), the theatre with its particularly elaborate machinery (1724–5) (Ill. 8) and the grand imperial reception hall (*Kaisersaal*) (1723–6). After this extremely rapid progress things moved at a slower pace, and at one point the chapter refused to go ahead with the scheme until the financial position improved. But the rebuilding of the administrative block was well under way by the time Abbot Ness died in 1740, and his successor completed the scheme with J.M. Fischer's immense domed church (1737–66), just too late for the celebration of the abbey's millennium in 1764. The church alone had cost 550,000 florins.

The story of the construction is fully documented and has been well studied. Abbot Ness embodied the Catholic Baroque's identification of artistic splendour both with the assertion of the abbey's standing in the world and with the advancement of religion. He was criticised even by the Benedictine abbot of Neresheim in 1724 for 'going grossly and inadmissibly beyond the bounds of *religious modesty*'. This was his reply:

My intention is no other than to build such a house of God as is fitting for the Holy Order and the abbey in honour of the Holy Trinity, to whom alone I have dedicated it. I have imagined that I would acquire merit in the eyes of God and men, . . . but I must do without the praise of men and expect it only from the Good Lord . . . In any case most of it, thank God! is already built. I cannot break off now, and must go on for the honour of God, God willing. If God gives me grace to build the church too, I shall exert myself to build a rare temple to the Holy Trinity, beside which the conventual buildings shall be nothing.[51]

The new quarters for the monks certainly brought a vast improvement in amenity. Their 'open and beautiful view to the east, their neat division of every cell into a room and an alcove, and in general their great convenience seemed to every elderly inmate who remembered the old narrow, wooden, dark cells to have transported him into a new, open world.'[52] The abbot brought water down from a spring to the abbey's baths, and there were outlying houses to which monks could go for a change of air.

A special contribution of Ottobeuren had been the principal part played by its abbot in assembling the consortium of Benedictine houses that made possible the foundation of the University of Salzburg in 1617. This institution, self-consciously non-Jesuit, was based in the seventh- (or perhaps even sixth-) century Benedictine abbey of St Peter in the independent prince-archbishopric of Salzburg and drew professors and students mainly from Switzerland, Swabia, Bavaria and Upper Austria. Ottobeuren continued to supply teachers to the university, and six of its later abbots had studied there.[53] In addition, the abbey ran a school for the novices and a *Gymnasium* for the locality.

Weingarten, also in Swabia, vies architecturally with Ottobeuren. Here the decision to rebuild was taken under abbot Sebastian Hyller, at almost the same time as at Ottobeuren. Abbot Hyller came from a nearby village and, like all the later abbots of Weingarten, was a graduate of Salzburg. The abbey encountered difficulties over its rebuilding plans because it was not yet recognised as *reichsunmittelbar*. Since the Austrian authorities claimed that the site of the conventual buildings was their territory, the new church was built first, between 1715 and 1725, on the site of the old one which unquestionably belonged to the abbey. Several architects were involved at one stage or another in the design and construction of this vast edifice, the largest post-medieval church in Germany, supposedly capable of holding a congregation of 12,000. The total cost of the church was over 250,000 florins.

Only in 1740, under another abbot, did Weingarten achieve *reichsunmittelbar* status, at considerable expense. This gave it lordship over about 400 square kilometres and 11,000 inhabitants.[54] The scheme to replace the rest of the buildings was at once put in hand. Although not quite the richest of the monasteries of Germany, Weingarten was determined to build everything on the largest scale. The capacity of the wine-cellars, for example, exceeded 1,000,000 litres. Weingarten's income was rather larger than Ottobeuren's, perhaps second only to Kempten's, but an abbot had to resign in 1745 because the monastery had incurred too great debts; and, though the work was resumed soon afterwards, one section of the scheme was never completed.[55]

It was not simply for ostentation that the abbey church of Weingarten was built on such a huge scale. It possesses a relic of the Holy Blood of Christ, given to it in 1094, and this has made it the focus of perhaps the largest pilgrimage in Germany, which is still annually attended by thousands of people on foot accompanied by over 1,800 on horseback. A pilgrimage of this magnitude, of course, brought immense profit to the abbey. The scale of the church necessitated the building of an exceptionally large organ at the west end which, both because of its size and its design, is of special significance. The builder, Joseph Gabler, agreed in his contract of 1737 that it would take six years to build, cost 6,000 florins, have sixty stops and 6,666 pipes; that it would be built round six windows and have six double wind-chests, and that the case would be in six double parts. What is more, a committee of six persons would make the detailed arrangements. This religious

ILL. 9 Engraving of Joseph Gabler's great baroque organ in the Benedictine abbey of Weingarten, Germany, completed 1750, from Dom Bedos, *L'art du facteur des orgues* (1756–70)

arithmetic was extended to a later contract for the monks' organ in the choir, which was to have two keyboards, twenty-two stops and 2,222 pipes. Other quasi-theological features of the west-end organ were that one set of stops was supposed to include examples of all the works of Creation, and another set represented the instruments described in the book of Daniel, chapter III, 'the cornet, flute, harp, sackbut, psaltery and dulcimer'. The organist could actuate two sets of drums and bells of two types, which are made visible in the fantastic design of the case. There is no obvious biblical warrant for the nightingale and the two cuckoo stops. The presence of this array of special effects, hardly paralleled until the days of cinema organs, had presumably the mundane though unmentioned justification that they would help to entertain vast congregations of pilgrims as they milled round the church. This must also explain why, despite great technical difficulties, the builder made it possible for the organist, as he played in the west-end gallery, to look straight down the huge church to the high altar. The instrument was at last completed in 1750. By then the builder had provided a few more stops than sixty and rather more pipes than 6,666, but the latter number has always been the official figure. His miscalculation of the cost was more dramatic. In the end it came to 32,000 florins (Ill. 9).[56]

The mental world in which abbots Knittel and Ness planned their buildings and Gabler his organs was still that of the Baroque and the Counter-Reformation, barely touched by the Enlightenment. But the great shift of Catholic opinion that began around 1750 showed itself in south Germany as in every other region. From the 1740s the University of Salzburg, despite strong internal opposition, became a centre for the dissemination of the reforming anti-Baroque Catholicism associated with the writings of Muratori. Partly because of a European reaction against the expulsion of the Protestants from Salzburg in 1731–2, a movement for religious toleration began to spread through the Catholic Church in Germany. Long-standing beliefs, such as that in witchcraft, were being abandoned by intelligent Catholics in Germany as elsewhere.[57] There was a falling-off in bequests to monasteries, as the institutions themselves came under attack as useless or worse – sinister, unnatural, despotic, obsurantist. The crowd of new devotions introduced in the Middle Ages and especially during the Counter-Reformation, and the whole Baroque conception of using sumptuous art in the service of religion, were losing their appeal.[58] The abbot of **Neresheim**'s criticism of his brother's ostentation at Ottobeuren was becoming orthodoxy – though ironically, his own abbey church was lavishly rebuilt after 1750 under a successor. The progress of this work too was encouraged by the house's achievement of *reichsunmittelbar* status in 1764. However, the approach to worship embodied in the new church was utterly different from that at Ottobeuren, despite the fact that their construction dates overlapped:

> The key... is the word 'explanation'. Neresheim is no longer intended to be *theatrum sacrum*, and also not dramatized architecture, but an explanation. When one enters this space one should not be carried away, but made to understand. But this is not intellectual understanding; it manifests itself rather as 'enlightened presence'.[59]

Monks and monasteries, then, shared in many of the tendencies of the late eighteenth century. Nowhere is this better shown than by the history of the Benedictine abbey of **St Blasien** in the Black Forest and its remarkable abbot, Martin Gerbert. He was born nearby in 1720, not into the humblest of local families but certainly not into a noble one. Soon after he entered the abbey, it achieved princely status, though in a roundabout way. The house lay in Austrian territory and was therefore subordinate, but had acquired the adjacent principality of Bondorf which was *reichsunmittelbar*, and in 1746 the abbot was made a prince. This oddity brings to attention the fact that, as with everything about the *Reich*, the complexities and varieties of *Reichsunmittelbarkeit* were infinite. In 1764 Gerbert was elected abbot, and he held the office until his death in 1793. Like Muratori he was a polymath the scale of whose output and activity is hard to credit. He wrote many theological works of a moderately progressive character. He wrote a history of the Black Forest and accounts of the early Habsburgs, who had sprung from this area. He travelled to Rome and elsewhere and published an account of the journey. So far as scholarship was concerned, he gave space in his abbey to the compilers of the *Monumenta Germaniae Historica*, the German equivalent of Muratori's work for Italy and the Maurists' work for France. But his most extraordinary achievement, which puts him into world class in this particular sphere, was to make the first major collection of works of music and musical theory from the Middle Ages. He ranks with Burney and Hawkins for England and Martini for Italy as the first great musical historian of Germany – but the others, as Burney remarked, had no principality to rule. Gerbert became famous in that capacity too, especially for his road-building, no mean undertaking in that mountainous land of bitter weather. He also took up modern Catholic ideas of education, founded schools and introduced a new catechism.[60] He became an effective politician in the Empire and was skilful enough to persuade Maria Theresa to exempt his monastery from her legislation of 1771 raising the age of profession, on the ground that it would suffer from the competition of the surrounding houses that were not subject to her rule.[61] Perhaps it helped that he had craftily collected the bones of old Habsburgs to add to its already considerable collection and built a crypt to house them.

In 1768, as has happened quite frequently to this monastery hewn out of the forest, most of the abbey burned down. That meant not only that Gerbert had to do much of his musicological work over again, but also that he had to have the abbey rebuilt. He decided to do so on a vast scale and in the French neo-classical style, with P.M. Ixnard as his architect. It is quite often asserted that the spirit of neo-classical architecture is inimical to the *ancien régime* and chimes in with the spirit of the French Revolution, and perhaps even of the bourgeoisie and of democracy. But, as we shall see, one of the greatest monuments of neo-classical architecture in France, taken over by the revolutionaries as their Pantheon, was built by Louis XV in fulfilment of a vow for the abbey of Ste-Geneviève, starting in the 1760s (Plate 1).[62] Gerbert's design for St Blasien has been represented as 'an attempt at enlightened and rational order, which is quite illusory...It no longer aspires to be the *Civitas Dei* on earth.'[63] However that may be, it shows no lack of confidence in the future of his monastery and its Order. The dome of its church, when built, is said to have been the third largest of any European Christian church (Ill. 10). It is certainly true that the nature of the piety it was designed to serve was very different from what had been normal in the first half of the eighteenth century. The interior was inspired by Gerbert's belief that 'In a house of God there

ILL. 10 Aerial photograph of the monastery of St Blasien as rebuilt by Ixnard from 1768

ILL. 11 Design by F.J. Salzman, c. 1770, for the screen incorporating the organ built by J.A. Silbermann, 1772–5, in the new abbey church of St Blasien

should be nothing which distracts, nothing which interferes with devotion... no senseless frills, no decorative overloading, no crossing arches.' A striking novelty in the design, which underlines the point, is that the worshipper's eye was drawn not so much by the high altar as by the sumptuous organ placed on a screen (Ill. 11).[64]

The stylistically revolutionary building and the abbot's learning and benevolent rule were admired almost uncritically by Nicolai, the editor of the Protestant and Enlightened *Allgemeine deutsche Bibliothek* of Berlin, who paid a visit in 1781 and came away charmed.[65] At the same time the house improved its reputation for piety and discipline, and when it was suppressed in the 1800s it still had the very large number of 100 monks. St Blasien shows that in the very late eighteenth century, under a notable abbot, a monastery could still flourish mightily, could still be abreast of many aspects of European religious and cultural development and could, it seems, observe its rule, satisfy its subjects and win the admiration of the lay world.

Nicolai was not the only outsider to visit St Blasien. Another aspect of these abbeys' growing openness was that they now received visits from tourists, a number of whom have left accounts. Georg Wilhelm Zapf from Augsburg, evidently a Protestant, published in 1786 a description of his tour of 1781 through Swabia and Switzerland. He was especially impressed with Weingarten, where the prior conducted the services 'majestically' and where his entertainment was 'in no way princely but quite simple'. He admired Gerbert for his benevolent work as a ruler, for his liturgical reforms and as a historian: 'when he gets on to his favourite subject, he is like a rushing stream that sweeps all before it'. Commentators seldom refer to the observances of the monks, but it is commonly stated that they no longer followed many of the precepts of the rule: that, for example, they ate much more, and much more meat, than had been laid down; that they no longer observed strict silence; and that the obligation to attend seven offices had been reduced to five or fewer.[66] Some of this is clearly true for many houses. Gerbert certainly shared the view, widespread in his Order, that St Benedict's original requirement of manual work was no longer appropriate and that monks should instead concentrate on scholarship and pastoral care. Zapf, however, by contrast, regards them as much too observant: he complains that monks have to sing too many offices, which tires them and interrupts their studies. He tells us that he was made to endure a silent meal at St Blasien, and Gerbert laughed at his impatience, saying the rule had to be observed. While Zapf concluded that there remained monasteries 'where it is still like night', in many others he found encouragement of enlightened learning, and he declared: 'Tolerance is preached everywhere in our times, and it reigns even in monasteries and is shown to every Protestant. I found no difference between the two religions in zeal, for everyone strove equally hard to offer love and friendship in a sympathetic way'.[67]

A traveller from a very different background was Father Hauntinger, a monk of **St Gall** who was sent by his abbot in 1784 to accompany a monk of Neresheim, Beda Pracher, back to his monastery, calling at many other houses on the way.[68] The abbot of Neresheim was Swiss and a cousin of the abbot of St Gall, and Pracher had been seconded to pass on Neresheim's up-to-date educational expertise. This included the establishment of a *Normalschule*, or teachers' training college, in 1782, deriving from the principles of abbot Ignaz Felbiger of the Augustinian monastery of Sagan in Silesia, who had reorganised Catholic popular education for Frederick the Great and had gone on to do the same for Joseph II in the Austrian Monarchy.[69] Hauntinger, though only twenty-eight, was already St Gall's librarian, having been trained by monks who had had contacts with the Maurists and St Blasien. The library's wealth of ancient manuscripts and early printed books remains a marvel to this day, since it survived the period of secularisations almost intact. In the 1780s there were many houses which could approach its holdings, but St Gall's were already known to be especially remarkable, and recent abbots had expanded them, as Hauntinger himself was to do. The magnificent Baroque library of the monastery had been designed by Peter Thumb for abbot Gugger in 1758, though the furnishings were still being completed in Hauntinger's period, and Gugger had dedicated it, grandly and ecumenically, 'to the learned world' (Plate 7). During his journey Hauntinger investigated as much as he could the libraries of the monasteries that he visited. These libraries, most of which had been lavishly rebuilt, he found well stocked with certain types of book. But, especially in the first half of the century, there had been monasteries, like Neresheim for example, where the abbot would not admit the writings of Protestants and *philosophes*. Hauntinger was shocked by the fact that, in the particularly beautiful library of Schussenried, there were triumphant statues of prophets and evangelists lining one side, and on the other, in order to depict 'freethinking, false politics, erroneous teaching', statues of writers such as Luther, Calvin, Machiavelli, Voltaire and Rousseau. By the 1780s many monasteries had come to place great emphasis on the disinterested pursuit of learning, almost to the exclusion of their other purposes, and the young librarian of St Gall thought that a library should be open to all students, and that religious disputes should be banished from it.

Such eirenic attitudes had entered Neresheim too with a change of abbots, and by the time Hauntinger visited it it had become the seat of a remarkably radical set of monkish reformers, associated with the eccentric Catholic convert, duke Karl Eugen of Württemberg. Pracher himself favoured the abolition of private Masses and of Mass priests, candles, incense, Catholic vestments and the use of Latin. He left his Order in 1788, as three years later did the more famous Neresheim monk, Werkmeister, who had come to reject binding monastic vows and wished to marry. Hauntinger notes that some of the monasteries he visited were in the van of progress in other ways, boasting impressive collections of objects of scientific interest; and in the very year of his journey, 1784, Ottobeuren staged the first balloon ascents in the region.

Tempting though it is to concentrate on the abbeys that had or claimed *reichsunmittelbar* status and therefore ranked among the richest and grandest, it has to be remembered that they were only a small minority of all monasteries and that most houses, including some that were wealthy and powerful, were undoubtedly subordinate to some lay or ecclesiastical prince. This was true, for example, of many significant monasteries in Bavaria. In Altbayern, the core of Bavarian territory, seventy monasteries had the right to representation in the Estates. Among them one or two, like Polling and Tegernsee, had vast buildings and libraries second only to St Gall's.[70] By the 1780s, however, it was impossible not to fear for the future of these institutions. The Jesuits had gone; Joseph II was suppressing some entire Orders and many individual monasteries in the Austrian Monarchy; and a few were being shut down even in Bavaria and in the prince-archbishopric of Mainz, where Schöntal was among those threatened.[71] As we shall see in later chapters, published attacks on monasticism were now frequent and increasingly virulent.[72]

It is one of the novelties of the late eighteenth century that some monks are to be found keeping diaries or writing accounts of monastic life, almost in the style of laymen describing their lives or observing an eccentric social scene. Such behaviour was not only forbidden but almost unimaginable in earlier periods, from which the only surviving autobiographies of monks are spiritual odysseys. One of this new class of documents, an anonymous monk's memoir, makes it possible, with the aid of more formal records, to give a final example from among the Benedictine monasteries of the German lands showing how unhappy and intolerant such a house could become under a bad abbot, and how obstinate in the old ways it could remain right down into the first years of the nineteenth century.

Lambspring or **Lamspringe**, in the territory of the bishop of Hildesheim in north Germany, was one of the small number of monasteries on the Continent which catered more or less exclusively for British and Irish Catholics who wished to be monks (or nuns) during the centuries when this was impossible or very difficult in their own countries.[73] Founded as a nunnery in the ninth century, it became in 1542 a Protestant female community. Having been recovered for Catholicism in the Thirty Years War, it was assigned to English monks, who arrived in 1643. Hence most of its records, now kept at Downside abbey, are in English. Though not one of the richest houses in Germany, it was the richest in Hildesheim, and it carried through an elaborate building programme between 1670 and 1731, incurring heavy debts.

In the eighteenth century it attracted an average of two or three novices a year and a number of students (nineteen in 1730), nearly all from England, some in each category aristocratic in origin. The fact that its inmates mostly came from overseas created special difficulties, but far more unsettling was the expectation that most of the monks would be sent to their homeland for lengthy periods on mission.

A few quotations from 'The Book of Cloathing Novices', though they admittedly concern unusual cases, will highlight the abbey's recruitment problems:

Henry Kalmus tooke ye habit aft^r Vesperas by ye name of Laurence. But proved a dissembling Cheate to ye surprize of all . . . September ye 20th 1724.

The Honourable Edmund Darmes tooke ye habit immediately after Vesperas and retained his own name. But proved to be of too weak a constitution to goe on. April ye 9th 1725.

Pitt Copsey came July 1727, cloathed 31 May 32 but ran away, returned hither distracted was afterwards put into a maddhouse at Turnay in Flanders where in 1757 he continu'd raving madd.

. . . one James Compton an Ex Jesuit from Liege was admitted to ye habit Nov. 1773 by ye name of Jerome & after almost finishing his Noviceship & earnestly petitioning for his Profession here, was by ye President Mr Fisher & his Secretary Mr Cowley Prior of St Edmunds at the visit Jul: ye 21st 1774 taken to St Edmunds & professd, this proceeding appear'd wonderful and unwarrantable to all here. He apostatizd 1782.[74]

In 1762 Maurus Heatley was elected abbot of Lambspring. This, as the anonymous chronicler records,[75] was a moment when the monastery's debts had been increased by his predecessor's 'splendid way of living' and by the ravages of 'two armies in the neighbourhood' during the Seven Years War. Heatley set about paying off the debt, but his early popularity waned as it became apparent that he could not 'bear opposition of any kind'. If he could not reduce his opponent to submission,

the Mission was generally the ultimate remedy: the consequence was, he had a convent of tame passive Religious. His presence among them inspired fear, but in his chapters he struck terror, especially the last ten years [1792–1802], when his imprisonment and arbitrary treatment of Maurus Chaplin seemed to stamp a sanction of unlimited and self-willed authority on all his proceedings.

Maurus Chaplin, returning from Mission, was accused of 'nightly elopements', 'bad company' and 'excessive drinking'. 'It appears that he provided himself with a cricket bat and threatened "to make use of it against the Prior; and that for the abbot he had something else, a pistol should do the business."' Clapped in the abbey's prison, he escaped after two years, was brought back, flogged and imprisoned again.

In the late 1790s, while the French revolutionary wars were disrupting relations with Britain, a dispute was developing between the abbot and the president of the

English Benedictine Congregation, the abbot insisting that he had absolute authority despite a long history of visitations and involvement by the congregation. Heatley had his party among the monks who rowed with his opponents about every conceivable aspect of the abbey's life. The abbot, for example, was accused of serving 'uneatable' cheese – although he declared it was edible, he withheld cheese thereafter, asserting that the rule only permitted, and did not require, it to be served. The dissidents complained of this as well as of graver matters to the president of the congregation. Heatley got into disputes about the endowments and scholarships; and he put off students who wished to come, pleading shortage of funds and the desperately uncertain political position of the monastery. Eventually, during the period of peace in 1801–2, the president of the congregation, Bede Brewer, came to make a visitation, contrived to release Chaplin but was met with intransigence from the abbot. The president then admonished the abbot on three counts and suspended him. The abbot summoned his council to challenge one of the counts against him and questioned the minutes, overriding the monk who was secretary, Harsnep. Thereafter we are told that the meetings became slanging-matches, and there is a long gap in the council minute book.[76] The abbot insisted that the rule must be obeyed. 'I suppose,' replied a monk, 'you mean your Will, my Lord.' The abbot said yes. By this time the bishops of Hildesheim and Paderborn and sundry abbots were involved. Then suddenly Heatley, now over eighty, surrendered, and his suspension was approved by the general chapter in London. Thus, says the memoirist, was won 'an auspicious victory over monastic tyranny'. But within weeks Prussia occupied the bishopric, a few days later Heatley died and in the following year the abbey, like most others remaining in Germany, was suppressed.

CONCLUSIONS

To begin with, it is possible to make certain generalisations about German, particularly imperial, abbeys. First, it is obvious how important in the building history of many of them was their campaign for recognition as *reichsunmittelbar* and, especially, success in attaining it. This is true also of a number of monasteries I have not so far mentioned, for example St Emmeram in Regensburg, which won independence in 1731, and was immediately refurbished in the Baroque manner. Secondly, the fact that several monastery-states enhanced their independence during the eighteenth century is evidence of how much prestige and influence they could still wield. By this criterion at least, monasteries were more powerful within the Empire in the 1780s than they had been in the 1700s.[77]

Their obsession with securing *Reichsunmittelbarkeit* was not a mere question of prestige and politics. They could hope for economic as well as legal advantage from it, and the acquisition of this status made it easier for them to undertake large building schemes. We saw that the abbey of Kempten was sometimes pulled up short in its dealings with its peasants by imperial intervention. But this could happen only rarely: the courts of the Empire moved with legendary deliberation, and to mount a case before them required large resources of money, patience and obstinacy. By contrast, abbeys that were not *reichsunmittelbar* owed allegiance to a ruler whose Court was nearby and who had the authority and opportunity to enquire more briskly into their proceedings. They would need permission from him to expand their buildings and they did not, as independent abbeys did, possess the sovereign right to levy taxes on their subjects without passing any of the proceeds on to a superior. These limitations did not of course prevent many abbeys that lacked sovereign status from building, but they made the operation more difficult. Hartmut Zückert has shown that such abbeys, like Schwarzach, could face effective opposition from their peasants. He further argues that the campaigns for *Reichsunmittelbarkeit* can reasonably be seen as part of a broader 'feudal' or absolutist reaction that involved ecclesiastical princes emulating secular grandees in making higher demands on their subjects in services and taxes with a view to asserting their sovereign status, enhancing their lifestyle and executing vast building programmes. In creating their splendid architectural ensembles some monasteries received grants or, more usually, loans from rulers. They borrowed money on the security of their property. They appealed to other clergy, as well as to ordinary people, for contributions. But, even in a time of relative peace and prosperity, these methods, together with ordinary revenue, would hardly have sufficed to make possible schemes on the scale of Ottobeuren or Weingarten. Many cases can be found of peasants complaining of the extra burdens imposed on them, in the name of religion and obedience, to further such projects: increases in the amount of forced labour required, and of taxes levied; longer, more onerous journeys to collect building materials or to transport the wine that might help pay for them or grease a powerful palm; enclosure of land previously believed to be common; in the case of Ottobeuren, a reduction in the hospitality of the abbey which had hitherto fed half the inhabitants of the little town. It is easy to write that a building was paid for out of income, which was growing. But of that growth a significant part often came from enhanced dues and services exacted from peasants. Ordinary subjects cared for the village or other local community, the *Gemeinde*, in the affairs of which they could participate and from which they could derive tangible benefit, and for their parish church, but often resented calls from the abbot to contribute more to the glorification of his already wealthy monastery.[78]

Much of this applies in Austria too, though there the abbots were not in the strict sense princes and the abbeys had to pay more attention to the secular power. On the other hand, the benefits that a rebuilding scheme could bring to the monastery's subjects are also evident across the whole region. It would of course create employment, much of it paid. Sometimes an abbey would also renovate parish churches and offer other compensations to the workforce. Moreover, the monasteries were associated with popular culture in ways that aristocratic palace-building could not be. It is striking that nearly all the dynamic abbots I have mentioned – indeed, a high proportion of the abbots of the monasteries in the German lands – were genuinely elected by the monks and were non-noble, usually from the locality and often of humble origin. This represents a remarkable exception to the aristocratic dominance of state and Church in eighteenth-century Europe. Almost all Catholic bishops in the German lands, as in most other countries, were nobles, especially prince-bishops, when they were not royal; and the canons of many cathedrals and collegiate churches had also to be nobles. But in most of the German and Austrian abbeys the career was open to talent: in this way a man could rise from the status of peasant to the status of prince of the Empire.[79] This fact is one of many pointers to the close relationship between these abbeys and the society around them. It cannot of course be maintained that all was sweetness and light between monks and their neighbours, certainly not if the latter were Protestant and sometimes not if an abbey pressed its economic demands too far. But the Baroque monasteries were built and ornamented in a style that was designed to appeal to ordinary Catholics as well as to the educated, and there are many ways in which the monks and their subjects collaborated together. The Benedictines in particular helped to foster the religious brotherhoods of the area, in which some monks, including the abbot of Ottobeuren himself, joined with secular clergy, laymen and lay women.[80] Village miracle plays, of which Oberammergau's is a spectacular survival, were encouraged and assisted by Jesuits and other Orders. Oberammergau was the seat of the Court of the Benedictine abbot of Ettal.[81] Visually, the most striking evidence of interaction between monks and people is provided by pilgrimage churches. They included some of the most original and intoxicating of all the religious buildings of the age: Stadl-Paura in Upper Austria, basically triangular in honour of the Trinity, with three equal altars each with its reredos and organ; the similar Kappel on the German–Bohemian border; the oval palaces of light at Birnau by Lake Constance, Steinhausen and Die Wies

THE GREAT MONASTERIES OF THE GERMAN CATHOLIC LANDS

ILL. 12 Painting by Dominikus Zimmermann (detail) showing the procession carrying the relic of the Scourged Saviour to the new pilgrimage church of Die Wies, Germany, 1750

in Bavaria, and, most astonishing of all, Vierzehnheiligen in Franconia, built by Balthasar Neumann in honour, for once, not of Mary but of the fourteen helpers in time of need, its interior a luminous vision in pastel (Plate 5). All of these architectural *tours de force* – and centres of popular piety – were built by monasteries: Stadl-Paura by Benedictine Lambach; Kappel by Cistercian Waldsassen; Birnau by Cistercian Salem; Steinhausen by Premonstratensian Schussenried; Die Wies by Premonstratensian Steingaden; and Vierzehnheiligen by Cistercian Langheim. Three of the last four date from as late as the 1740s, and in the case of Die Wies the pilgrimage itself had begun only in 1738.[82]

The houses of the old Orders were further linked with the people of their neighbourhood by the fact that they sent out their monks to be priests in the parishes they owned. Although this practice is especially associated with Austria, it was also followed, if to a lesser extent, by many of the German houses. Thereby the monasteries almost turned the distinction between secular and regular clergy on its head.[83] For, while many of these abbeys' monks were acting as parish priests, a good proportion of the secular clergy were chaplains to noble families or to brotherhoods, schoolteachers, or even further removed from parochial duty. This state of affairs puts into perspective the statistics mentioned above which show that the ratio of seculars to population was at its highest in most, if not all, Catholic countries around 1750. Since the number and revenue of parishes had scarcely changed in many areas, the rise in the number of seculars did not greatly increase the number of clergy actually engaged in parochial work.[84] It was claimed, probably with truth in some cases, that regulars were keeping seculars out of parish benefices. But this could be persuasively justified:

> The abbot [Gerbert of St Blasien] argued that it was impractical and counterproductive to send priests to isolated and impoverished villages. 'Clergymen sent to such villages would not last long without suffering a collapse, without becoming completely helpless, or without becoming themselves completely uncivilized'. He also specifically asked that the village of Menzenschwand continue to be served by a priest coming from St. Blasien, an hour and a half away, because the place was perched between two mountains, and was so unhealthy, 'that the majority of the inhabitants become imbeciles'.[85]

As well as being closely involved in the popular culture of Catholic south Germany, the monasteries dominated its elite culture. In so far as Bavaria took part in the Enlightenment in the 1750s and 1760s, it was largely through monastic writings, and monks formed an important element in the Bavarian Academy, founded in 1759.[86] The Jesuits were of course important in scholarship, for example in mathematics, and dominant in education. But before and especially after the suppression of the Society in 1773, as the cases of St Blasien and Neresheim prove, some monasteries of the old Orders were in the van of Enlightenment, religiously tolerant, educationally progressive and theologically radical. Catholic critics of Jesuit education had, with much exaggeration, accused them of continuing to purvey the scholasticism of St Thomas Aquinas. In fact Jesuit philosophers were working towards a new modernised theology, a project which was carried forward late in the century by writers from other Orders who published manuals of theology that drew on Kant and never cited St Thomas.[87] In the Austrian lands as well as in south Germany monasteries led a surge of historical and antiquarian scholarship which was their chief contribution to learning in this age. The musical activity of the German houses was as notable as that of the Austrian.[88] Indeed Mozart's C minor Mass was too elaborate to be performed in the Austria of Joseph II, and was written for the Benedictine house of St Peter's in the prince-archbishopric of Salzburg, where one of the composer's friends, Dominikus Hagenauer, was a monk and was soon to become the abbot.[89]

In their capacity as secular rulers many abbots practised enlightened absolutism. There were few reforms in that spirit which cannot be paralleled from monastic states, even the suppression of lesser monasteries. Road-building and utilitarian improvements were especially common features of prince-abbots' rule, and they had to concern themselves with filling the educational gap left by the suppression of the Jesuits. Neresheim even abolished, like Joseph II, the traditional indiscriminate alms-giving and food distribution of the monastery as harmful to the morality of the poor and damaging to the progress of the economy, establishing instead a general poor relief institution on rational lines.[90] This kind of modernisation did not of course commend monasteries to those to whom they had previously supplied food and other comforts in the old-fashioned casual way. Enlightenment, theological, economic or political, had much less popular support than the Baroque.

I have deliberately highlighted the Enlightened aspects of late eighteenth-century German monasticism, since I believe it to be important to appreciate that it could adapt remarkably well to the tendencies of the period. But, although certain houses won approval from progressive persons such as Nicolai, much educated opinion in the German Catholic lands, especially but not only among laymen, was evidently turning away from the institution altogether. Though the bitter hostility of some *philosophes* to Catholicism met with little sympathy in Germany, even there monasteries and nunneries were increasingly seen as at least useless and perhaps pernicious. Even a monk of St Blasien could write to Nicolai in 1784: 'We monks are now the object of general hatred, and this jaundiced century makes fun of us in the most wretched fashion. It is enough to be a monk to be seen as the most contemptible creature on God's earth.' Monks were commonly represented in caricatures as idle, greedy, fat and ugly (Ill. 13).[91] The monasteries' rapprochement with Enlightenment won them few friends among the elite, essentially because even the moderately progressive came to regard the institution as fundamentally flawed.

While the numbers of Austrian monasteries and monks have been established with unusual precision, it is hard to arrive at overall totals for southern Germany, where political authority was so fragmented. In the Austrian duchies barely five hundred houses served about seven million people.[92] When it came to suppressing

ILL. 13 Cartoon by Joseph Anton Koch of 'monks at table', 1793

all the surviving houses of south Germany in 1802, there too the grand total, for a population of similar size, seems to have reached about six hundred. These, as we shall see, are tiny figures, even allowing for differences in prosperity and population size, compared with those for the other major Catholic countries, although it appears to be the case that German monasteries had an unusually high complement of inmates.[93] And in all other countries, too, the numbers of mendicant houses and of nunneries were proportionally higher and the numbers of male houses of the old Orders proportionally lower than was usually the case in the German lands. On the other hand, available figures show that the monasteries of this region owned a substantially greater percentage of the total land area than their brother-houses in other countries. In the city of Cologne they owned a good third; in Bavaria 28 per cent of the peasantry lived on monastic property; in Lower Austria the monasteries had something like 20 per cent of the land.[94] The average wealth of German and Austrian houses of the old Orders must therefore have been exceptional.

Österreich Klösterreich is an old saying, which is normally taken to mean 'Austria, rich in monasteries' but could be translated as 'Austria, the monasteries' empire'.

Exaggerated though of course this formulation is, it draws attention to an important fact not just about Austria but about the German Catholic lands as a whole. While their monasteries, monks and nuns were markedly less numerous than those of other Catholic countries of western and southern Europe, in the religious, political, social, intellectual and cultural life of their region they played an altogether exceptional role.

CHAPTER 3

FRANCE

In the German Catholic lands, as we have seen, a high proportion of the major monastic buildings erected in the seventeenth and eighteenth centuries still survive. Many of them, especially in Austria, form part of functioning monasteries that have a virtually unbroken history since the early Middle Ages and are accepted to this day as public institutions of wide-ranging importance in their localities and beyond. Their activities are by no means limited to the strictly religious sphere. They run notable schools, which teach not only academic subjects and music but also practical skills such as cookery and, in the case of the Cistercian house of Stams, skiing. People who have visited these regions and some of these houses will readily accept that long after the Reformation many monastic communities, especially of the old Orders, possessed not only formidable and growing wealth and power but also remarkable vitality and the respect of most of the population.

Visitors to France confront a totally different situation. Many of the great houses have disappeared altogether, lie in ruins or are unrecognisable because they have been adapted for secular use. Very few are now working monasteries, and even they have suffered long periods of dereliction and exile. Ever since 1789 they have been regarded as alien to the country's revolutionary and republican traditions. For most modern French men and women the monasteries of the *ancien régime* are perished as though they had never been.

It is true that numerous studies have been published on aspects of French monastic history in the early modern centuries, but they are usually confined to particular Orders or localities and have made minimal impact on general historical writing about the period. No French work begins to match in overall coverage Joan

Evans's astonishing book of 1964 on *Monastic Architecture in France from the Renaissance to the Revolution*, largely ignored by British historians because it is on architecture, and unread by most French historians both because it is about architecture and because it is in English. Yet this work is based on visits she made in the difficult conditions of the years immediately after the Second World War to hundreds of former monasteries of 'Orders living under vows' through the length and breadth of France, taking and obtaining photographs of their surviving buildings from the early modern period. She could not help the fact that the 822 photos she published from the 1950s and earlier are dimly black and white. Here at least, by looking at her record of what survives and reading her fundamental introductory chapters, it is possible to form some idea of what has been lost, and of the wealth and importance of the Orders in France in the early modern centuries.[1] In 1998 another British historian, John McManners, brought out an account of *Church and Society in Eighteenth-Century France* which far surpasses anything previously written on the subject in any language and incorporates a masterly survey of the monasticism of the *ancien régime*.[2] It will clearly take some years for this monumental book to exert its due influence on general historians. But it is evident from these two pioneering works, taken together, that, once the veil interposed by revolutionary vandalism, republican hostility and historians' neglect is drawn aside, monks, nuns and monasteries are seen to have played as significant a role in France as they did in other Catholic countries during the eighteenth century. This is not to say that they were significant in exactly the same ways as elsewhere for, as we shall see, the position of the Orders in France was in many ways exceptional.

Compared with many other countries, the statistics for eighteenth-century French monasteries seem at first sight remarkably full and secure, based as they are on state enquiries, first by the *commission des réguliers* in and after 1766, then by the revolutionary governments from 1789 onwards and finally on material collected when compensation and revival were being considered after the Restoration. Virtually every authority on the subject cites the *commission*'s figures for 1768, 2,972 houses of monks containing 26,674 monks, and later figures showing that these numbers had fallen drastically by the time of the Revolution. The only statistic more treacherous than a dubious estimate is a secure one. Most scholars have realised that the figures for monks in 1768 exclude the recently expelled Jesuits and that they do not give a fair indication of the position around 1750. The most sophisticated student of the subject, Bernard Plongeron, has shown that these and other figures omit lay brothers and have other small defects, but even he has not challenged them more fundamentally.[3] To my knowledge only one historian, Léon Lecestre in 1902, has pointed out – and no one seems to have followed him – that the *commission*'s figures, even if reliable so far as they go, have the serious limitation that they ignore several relatively new Orders for men of major and growing importance, for the simple reason that it was not instructed to enquire into them.[4] It follows that there must have been in the middle of the century well over 3,000 male houses with over 30,000 inmates. Information on nunneries and nuns is much less complete, partly because the *commission* did not deal with them at all, but it is generally reckoned that there were about 5,000 female houses containing about 55,000 female regulars. This makes France unique in possessing so many more nuns than monks. These estimates yield rough ratios of about 1 regular to 300 in the population as a whole, or about 1 monk to 400 males and 1 nun to 200 females.

As elsewhere, there were in France more regular than secular clergy. However, because of the highly unusual preponderance of nuns over monks in France, there were actually many fewer *monks* than secular clergy in France. Even so there were more monks in France, both absolutely and in relation to population, than in the entire Austrian Monarchy, though only half as many as in Italy or Spain, with their smaller populations.[5]

THE OLD ORDERS

The grandest French monasteries were as wealthy and prestigious as any country's. They included the mother-houses of the Carthusian, Cistercian and Premonstratensian Orders and of the Cluniac branch of the Benedictines – namely the Grande Chartreuse, Cîteaux, Prémontré and Cluny – all of which continued to exert influence on their hundreds of daughter-houses across Catholic Europe, not just in France. The major abbey churches vied with cathedrals in scale and opulence, and Cluny's, the largest church in Christendom until St Peter's, Rome, was rebuilt in the sixteenth century, remained by far the biggest in France (Ill. 37(a), p. 266).[6] The figures of monastery incomes given in the sources vary considerably, partly because they relate to different dates and define income in different ways, but also because so little work has been done on the subject. But it appears that in Paris the Benedictine abbey of St-Germain-des-Prés, which practically controlled the area of two modern *arrondissements* on the south bank of the Seine, was often regarded as the richest of all and is certainly the best studied, had an annual income of 225,000 livres in 1789, and the nearby abbey of Ste-Geneviève not much less. In Lorraine, which became part of France only in 1766, the nunnery of Remiremont, whose abbess was a princess of the Holy Roman Empire, disposed of 300,000 livres annually; and the Augustinian double monastery of Fontevraud in Anjou, often headed by a member of the royal family, of a similar sum.[7] These are figures markedly higher than those attained by the richest Austrian abbeys, Melk and Kremsmünster, and bear comparison with the revenues of the monastic principalities of southern Germany.[8] As everywhere, the distribution of monastic wealth was extremely uneven: such huge incomes were of course rare, the average income was very much lower, and many houses, especially of the more recently founded Orders, were mean and impoverished. If a small number contained more than a hundred monks or nuns, hundreds of them mustered fewer than ten. In addition, there was very great variation from region to region. In parts of France, especially the north-east, the Church as a whole owned a proportion of the land almost as high as anywhere in Europe, perhaps 40 per cent in Flanders, and there monasteries were numerous. Hence English travellers to the Continent at once encountered French monasticism at its most imposing. Thomas Bentley in 1776 noticed no châteaux between Calais and Paris, 'but magnificent abbeys and churches everywhere, especially in Artois, which seems to be the paradise of the monks'. In this region were to be found such hugely rich houses as the abbeys of St-Vaast in Arras and St-Ouen at Rouen. The towns, especially Paris, were bulging with monasteries. In Alsace and Lorraine also the Church was rich in land, but in parts of the west and centre it was poor – in the extraordinary case of Béarn virtually landless. Hence a reasonable guess at the average percentage ownership of all land by monasteries is 5 per cent or a little more.[9]

Monasteries – at least those of the older, 'endowed' type – were inevitably entangled in the 'feudal' or 'seigneurial' system of the *ancien régime*. Like lay lords they exacted a variety of dues and taxes and, in certain areas where such arrangements survived, relied on the unpaid labour of 'serfs'. By far the most important tax they levied was tithe, which, taking the country as a whole, contributed more to the monasteries' revenue even than their own landholdings: about 120 million livres from tithes compared with about 80 million from land. Tithes had been assigned to non-parochial institutions in about a third of France, and most of the greater monasteries were entitled to receive them from all or part of one or more parishes. In return the monasteries commonly provided the parishes with priests, usually by appointing a vicar and paying him a low stipend, the *congrue*, fixed by the government. In some cases, however, as with the Premonstratensians in 600 parishes and many other regular canons, the monks themselves did the duty.[10]

Houses with substantial landholdings were of course heavily engaged in agriculture, especially wine-growing, and many were involved in a wide range of other economic activities, such as renting out urban property, running a forge, a factory or even a spa. Granted reasonably good management, a monastery's revenue from land was virtually certain to grow during the eighteenth century, since population was rising and agricultural techniques were improving. Some houses apparently achieved astounding increases: three Benedictine monasteries in Metz are said to have raised their incomes between 1766 and 1789 respectively from 25,000 to 63,000 livres, from 24,000 to 65,000 and from 16,000 to 50,000.[11] Monasteries behaved in most respects just as lay landlords did – with these great differences, first, that most church land could never be alienated and, secondly, that monastic communities very rarely died out and by virtue of their continuity of management could be (though they were not always) more far-sighted and consistent than lay seigneuries that were subject to the caprices of death and incapacity. Quite a number of France's agricultural improvers were in fact monks, such as Dom Leronge, author of *Principles of the Cultivator*. Among the publications of the economic theorists known as the physiocrats – advocates of the free market and 'the single tax' on land, seen as the only productive resource – few were more widely read than the *Ephémérides du citoyen*, a periodical founded in 1762 by monks of the Augustinian abbey of Chancelade in Périgord.[12] Many of the wines produced on monastic estates were famous for their high quality, and one monk, Dom Pierre Pérignon, bursar of the abbey of Hautvillers, earned the special gratitude of posterity by making technical innovations that led to the creation of modern champagne.[13] When Arthur Young said that, searching for good farmers in France, he kept running up against monks, he perhaps did not realise that he was paying a compliment to the regular clergy. Edmund Burke was more direct: 'I have got more information, upon a curious and interesting branch of husbandry, in one short conversation with a Carthusian monk, than I have derived from all the Bank directors I have ever conversed with.'[14]

The Orders, understood in a broad sense, had played an essential part in the triumphs of the Counter-Reformation in France. No doubt the old Orders were less effective than the new and, in so far as they were effective, owed much to the influence of the new, especially the Jesuits. But at least in some places it was only an ancient monastic house which had held out against advancing Protestantism and thereby provided the rock on which a revived Catholicism could be founded. As in Germany, it was older Orders rather than the Jesuits that fostered the ever growing numbers of pilgrimages, while the Jesuits played the largest role in the expansion of confraternities.[15]

In certain other, sometimes potentially conflicting, ways the old Orders showed that they had the capacity to renew themselves. To begin with, in the first half of the seventeenth century, partly under the impulsion of Richelieu, some of them tightened their discipline and observance, and groups of their houses joined in reformed congregations, of which the most famous was the Benedictine Congregation of St-Maur, founded in 1618 and ultimately embracing 180 French Benedictine monasteries.[16] What this tranquil-sounding development might mean can be seen from the case of the once rich and prestigious house of Montmajour near Arles. Its monks refused to accept the new organisation, asking instead that the monastery should be secularised, until the archbishop of Arles was authorised in 1638 to use force to impose the reform. After the Maurists took over they had themselves to face the threat of armed attack. They were required to provide the former monks with pensions out of the abbey's revenues, ensuring a long period of financial difficulty which prevented them from starting on necessary rebuilding until 1703.[17]

Secondly, without the nunnery of Port-Royal, its determined abbess, Angélique Arnauld, her numerous relations and the house's connexions, Jansenism might never have developed from a theological tendency into the embattled party it became in the last decades of the seventeenth century. Later, in the early part of Louis XV's reign, after the papacy had condemned it and the government had declared war on it, some of the greatest abbeys, among them St-Germain-des-Prés, and many nunneries helped to keep its spirit alive in the Church. The Abbaye-aux-Bois, an aristocratic Cistercian nunnery in the capital, was still tainted with Jansenism in the late 1770s, and the archbishop of Paris, having seen its library, ordered the theological bookcases to be sealed up. But he was overstepping his rights, and an appeal to the abbot of Clairvaux, the superior of the Order, led to the removal of the seals – followed by a large gift of Bordeaux wine from the abbot to the nunnery.[18]

Thirdly, the Cistercian Order gave birth to a 'reform', effectively to a new Order. In the late 1650s Armand-Jean de Rancé, commendatory abbot of several abbeys, underwent a kind of conversion experience which led him to give up all his abbeys except the Cistercian house of La Trappe in Normandy, of which he became the regular abbot. There he set about restoring what he saw as the ancient rule of the Order, making his Trappists famous for their strictness, especially for their observance of silence. This example inspired a number of other houses to adopt his practice and form a strict congregation of Cistercians.[19]

Fourthly, at almost the same time the monks of St-Germain-des-Prés, the greatest house of the Benedictine congregation of St-Maur, were taking up the systematic study of the many ancient manuscripts to be found in their own splendid library and in others accessible to them. Initially their aims included vindicating the authenticity of their Order's saints, miracles, relics and their own charters. But, particularly after they were joined by Jean Mabillon in 1664, their vision broadened. The first volume of their *Acta sanctorum* (The Deeds of the Saints of the Order of Saint Benedict) appeared in 1668; Mabillon's edition of St Bernard's correspondence soon followed; and in 1681 was published *De Re Diplomatica*, a path-breaking study of how charters and early documents should be authenticated and appraised. Mabillon, humble, mild, pious and obedient though he was, was determined to pursue scholarship and historical truth for their own sake, refusing, for example, to accept as genuine the large quantities of bones then being excavated in the Roman catacombs and exported by the papacy as relics of ancient martyrs.[20] David Knowles described in a beguiling essay how Mabillon and Rancé engaged in a pamphlet war, Rancé presenting 'the Trappist practice of extreme austerity, perpetual silence and mute, unlearned docility as the only defensible version of the Benedictine ideal', Mabillon demonstrating that learning had always held an honoured place in the Order's work. In the end the controversy between them was brought to an end by Mabillon visiting La Trappe and charming Rancé – into silence. It was a crucial moment not only in monastic history but for the development of all historical studies when Mabillon wrote that the historian

must present as certain things certain, as false things false, and as doubtful, things doubtful; he must not seek to hide facts that tell for or against either party to an issue. Piety and truth must never be considered as separable, for honest and genuine piety will never come into conflict with truth.[21]

One monastery could not be entirely responsible for such a breakthrough; many houses contributed to the work that is particularly associated with St-Germain. In any case the Maurists were consciously emulating another compilation of *Acta sanctorum* made by the Jesuits in Belgium to a plan by Jean Bolland, the first volumes of which had appeared in 1643. But St-Germain was an exceptionally wealthy, prestigious and well-located house and it made scholarship its speciality, improving on the methods of the Bollandists. Its monks travelled France in search of material; in 1713 they built a new library to house their growing collections, and by 1789 they had produced more than two hundred substantial volumes. As the remark of Gibbon quoted in the Introduction showed, they acquired an immense European reputation for learning, and helped to inspire the work of German and Italian scholars such as Gerbert and Muratori – and of Gibbon himself. In all these respects the monks of France may be said to have set in train movements that influenced their brothers across Catholic Europe and, in some cases, a wider circle still. All this amounts to a major contribution by monks to the development of critical history associated with the Enlightenment.

As emerges strongly from the Abbé Prévost's career and from his classic novel, *Manon Lescaut* (1731), a young man of scholarly bent without any family money had virtually no option but to enter a monastery if he wanted to make a respectable scholarly career. Prévost himself tried two Orders, the Jesuits and the Maurists, but could not stay the course. By way of Protestantism and enforced exile, he eventually made his way as a free-lance writer, producing, as well as his famously shocking novel, both scholarly tomes that the Maurists might have applauded and translations of the novels of Richardson into French.

Though monks and nuns of the old Orders probably grew in number during the early decades of the eighteenth century, from about 1740 decline set in – though, remarkably, their recruitment rose again in the 1780s.[22] As in other countries, monks' and nuns' quarters and conditions became markedly more comfortable. The cells of the Premonstratensian abbey of Verdun, unaltered since about 1700, appear typical (Ill. 3). They resemble Oxbridge Fellows' sets of rooms from the same period, or guest bedrooms in secular mansions. If they appear unsuitably luxurious, it should be remembered that the permission for regulars to live and work in heated cells had a serious justification: the pursuit of scholarship required it, and even in monasteries the practice of piety was now much more a matter for each individual in private than it had been in the early Middle Ages. However, the pocket money that, contrary to the spirit of their rules, monks and nuns were paid or allowed to keep enabled them to furnish their apartments more agreeably than was easy to justify, given their vow of poverty. To take just one case among thousands, a Premonstratensian, Father Broutier, was found in 1790

ILL. 14 Main courtyard of the abbey of Prémontré, France, detail from an early nineteenth-century engraving

ILL. 15(a) Engravings of the abbey of Bec, Normandy, (a) before the Revolution and (b) after its partial destruction

to have acquired – out of his own savings, he said – a full suite of furniture, a harpsichord, a pipe-organ and two stills.[23] Most of the great houses built grand new quarters, of which many survive, though nearly always converted to other uses. Among the most impressive are those of the historic houses of Cluny, Cîteaux, Clairvaux, Prémontré, Bec and Fontevraud, and especially the twin monasteries for men and women at Caen, generally regarded as the masterpiece of the best of the many Benedictine architects, Dom Guillaume de la Tremblaye.[24] The contrast with the past could be stark: behind the splendid seventeenth- and eighteenth-century buildings of Maurist Brantôme, overlooking elegantly landscaped canals, are still to be seen the dank cells hewn out of the rock in which monks had lived since Carolingian times.[25] A few notable libraries were built, as at St-Germain and Ste-Geneviève in Paris. Old Gothic churches were remodelled to meet the new liturgical demands and adjust to changing taste, especially by the removal of screens that separated the laity from the clergy – though it is also true that some monasteries lovingly preserved many Gothic buildings, rebuilt others following Huguenot vandalism and even added to them in matching style.[26] Among the

ILL. 15(b) (cont.)

finer Baroque churches of the age of Louis XIV, St-Sulpice in Paris was built for a parish under the control of St-Germain and was largely paid for by the abbey.[27] The Church in general, and monasteries in particular, remained among the principal employers of labour, and especially of architects. Here is just one instance: the young Jean-Baptiste Kléber, soon to become famous as a revolutionary general, working as an architect in Alsace from 1784 to 1792, carried out major alterations to several churches including the Capuchins' in Strasbourg, to the abbey of Lure and to both the buildings and the gardens of the nunnery of Masevaux.[28]

This relative luxury did not mean that communal religious observances had lapsed. Monks and nuns in general continued to say or sing at least the main offices, and much money and effort was spent on maintaining and improving their musical establishments, of which the most expensive item was often an enlarged organ. The author of the classic textbook on *The Art of the Organ Builder* (1766–8) was Dom Bédos of the abbey of Ste-Croix in Bordeaux.[29] Nor does it appear that life in the monasteries was becoming more scandalous – probably the contrary. But there remained, as we shall see, many houses with significant revenues and sizable buildings which contained only a handful of monks who showed no particular spirituality and performed no obvious good works.

So the monasteries of France carried out a building progamme on a scale comparable to that seen in the German lands, though more steadily and over a longer period.[30] But it had a markedly different character. France saw hardly any complete rebuilds of monasteries, virtually no imitations of the Escorial plan and the construction of remarkably few new monastic churches. Further, French monastic architecture, though often stylish and imposing, not to say grandiose, was lacking in many of the qualities of Catholic buildings in other countries, their experimentalism, their colour, their prodigality with sculptured and painted images, their *naïveté* and their success in expressing apparently spontaneous emotions of joy, wonder, reverence and fear. In the words of Germain Bazin,

Nowhere does one feel greater coldness than in French churches of the seventeenth century. Their architecture may well arouse admiration, but it scarcely moves to prayer...I incline to think that in contemporary monastic architecture the purely domestic buildings surpass the churches in beauty...In these churches one senses as nowhere else how far French Catholicism is permeated by the spirit of asceticism. Religion in seventeenth- and eighteenth-century France was completely internalised and mistrusted all outward expression.[31]

One may question the absoluteness of Bazin's verdict. After all, the colour and ornaments of the surviving churches were mostly removed during the Revolution; and French monks and nuns were often enough criticised for lack of asceticism. But there is no denying the general truth of his architectural comparison between France and other Catholic countries.

Even in this field, however, a French monastery led the way for the Continent as a whole. In 1744 Louis XV, gravely ill, made a vow that, if he recovered, he would build a long-needed new church for the abbey of Ste-Geneviève. This promise was improbable enough during the decade in which the early volumes of the *Encyclopédie* were being compiled in France. It seems especially bizarre coming from its maker, who for most of his reign was excluded by the Church from Communion and from touching for the king's evil because he would not give up his mistresses.[32] But he was also a rather superstitious believer, and the promise was kept. In 1755 the government allocated lottery money to the project and selected the architect, Jacques-Germain Soufflot. His architectural ideas were revolutionary. They resembled those of Marc-Antoine Laugier, a Jesuit who in 1753 had published a provocative and influential *Essay on Architecture* in which he condemned virtually all early modern buildings, including Versailles and St Peter's as well as St-Sulpice and the residential blocs at Prémontré (Ill. 14). He loathed almost all the props of Baroque and Rococo: pilasters, pillars, arcades, cartouches, broken pediments, twisted capitals, tormented sculptures and shell motifs. He imagined a new church architecture – for it was in churches, he thought, that architects could really spread themselves – that would be 'simple', 'natural', 'delicate', lofty as a Gothic cathedral yet pure as a Greek temple. Free-standing columns would adorn exteriors and porches as they would divide nave and aisles; apses would be replaced by square ends; and all fussy ornament would be banished.[33]

The new church of Ste-Geneviève, as it rose slowly and fitfully during the last decades of the *ancien régime*, was revealed as a vast basilica recalling the early Christian churches of Rome and Ravenna in its use of columns rather than arcades, but resembling still more the Roman temple at Nîmes, where Laugier had gone to college – except that it was deliberately much higher, and crowned by a dome similar to that of St Paul's in London. It was centrally planned so that the reliquary of Ste-Geneviève could be placed in the middle and the crowd of worshippers could circulate around it. Laugier's book and Soufflot's building between them established a new ideal of a church building, whose influence can be seen, for example, in Ixnard's work, already described, at St Blasien (Plate 1, Ill. 10).[34]

As the most striking early statement of neo-classicism, the church of Ste-Geneviève became during the Revolution the Panthéon, the place where the heroes of the Enlightenment, the Revolution and the Republic were to be honoured without benefit of religion. It is typical of the historiography of eighteenth-century France that, though the fact that this innovative building was intended as a church is usually acknowledged, its monastic context is almost never mentioned. Wolfgang Herrmann, for example, in his admirable *Laugier and Eighteenth Century French Theory*,[35] while devoting many pages to the church, does not refer to the fact that it was monastic. Some art historians even go so far as to write of the neo-classical style as essentially progressive, as imbued with the spirit of Enlightenment and even of Revolution.³⁶ To sustain this view they have to ignore the role of the *bête noire* of the Enlightenment, the monasteries, in promoting the neo-classical style, together with the fact that a Jesuit was one of its principal theorists. It is true that the buildings from which the Revolution was run and the new French state created were mostly classical, including some important neo-classical examples. But the revolutionary regimes built few of them. They had no need to. Once they had abolished the Orders, they found themselves with thousands of vast, regular, well-built, up-to-date edifices on their hands which had been constructed by monasteries as administrative and residential quarters. Those that escaped destruction and vandalism they commandeered, and it is in buildings originally monastic that are to be found a high proportion of the hospitals, asylums, town halls, prefectures, *lycées*, museums, hotels, factories, studs, barracks and prisons of modern France. Ironically, the office buildings of successive French Republics have breathed the spirit of monasticism.³⁷

The French regular clergy of the old Orders possessed, partly because of their land and wealth, political and social power that was in many ways comparable to that of their brethren and sisters in the German lands. In a few provincial Estates heads of monastic houses still had the dominant position in the First Estate: in Artois, for example, it consisted of two bishops, fourteen deputies from chapters and eighteen abbots; in Brittany it contained nine bishops, nine chapter deputies and forty abbots; and in Burgundy five bishops and twenty-two deans were outmatched by twenty abbots and seventy-two priors.³⁸ Major monasteries, even though cloistered and of contemplative Orders, filled a conspicuous public role. The bustling outer court of a great house, especially in a town, full in daytime of tenants, petitioners, tradesmen, beggars and sightseers, contrasted sharply with the quiet of the inner cloister; and the duties of some monks – as preachers, confessors, parish priests and scholars, bursars and farm managers – frequently took them out of the monastery altogether. Monasteries often possessed relics of saints, which the faithful came to venerate, incidentally contributing to the houses' coffers. Some at least of their devotions were commonly open to the public. The abbey of St-Germain seized the opportunity of notable deaths and events to mount elaborate ceremonies that would be attended by royalty, ambassadors, ministers and nobility, summoned by its notoriously clangorous bells.³⁹ Many houses ran pilgrimages and hosted traditional processions which attracted large numbers both of participants and observers. To give Parisian examples, every seven years on 1 May the monks of St-Denis and the inhabitants of the seven neighbouring parishes marched with drums beating to the nunnery of Montmartre. After High Mass, the two abbeys distributed bread, fish pâté, butter and eggs to all the marchers. On rare occasions of national grief or rejoicing – the last was in 1725 – the reliquary of Ste-Geneviève was paraded through the streets to Notre-Dame, escorted by the archbishop, the cathedral canons, monks, numerous other clergy, the magistrates of the *parlement* and the city officials, perhaps the king himself.[40] Several houses had standing connexions with the monarchy. It was in the rich abbey of St-Denis that the Bourbon kings were buried and Masses were regularly said for their souls. In 1726 Louis, duke of Orleans, son of the Regent for the child Louis XV, 'renounced the world' and withdrew to Ste-Geneviève, where he had an elegant house specially built for him, wrote theological works and collected books, medals and natural curiosities.[41] The last two he bequeathed to the abbey, greatly augmenting its already significant museum. A number of female royals entered nunneries such as the Cistercian Abbaye-aux-Bois in Paris, Remiremont and Fontevraud, where four of Louis XV's daughters were sent in infancy to receive what proved to be a very poor education.[42]

As everywhere in Catholic Europe, parents, especially nobles, included in their calculations for the future of their children the possibility of their entering monasteries. In the case of sons, the eldest would succeed to the family properties, others could with luck earn a living in the army or as lawyers, but one or more of the younger, perhaps studious and frail, would be destined for the Church. If the greatest rewards that the Church could offer in wealth and position went to the aristocrats who became bishops, to take vows in a well-endowed monastery promised a disciplined but secure and comfortable existence, with much higher life expectancy than outside the cloister.

The eight monks of the Cistercian abbey of Pereigne in 1789 had two cooks, a baker, two porters, a brazier, a gardener, two cowherds, a boy to look after the guest-house, three women (housekeeper, sewing-maid and dairy maid) and an archivist with legal qualifications. At this time the Grande Chartreuse had a hundred monks and three hundred servants.[43]

A Premonstratensian, Louis Parent d'Estany, expelled from St-Martin at Laon by the Revolution, wrote: 'The majority of the individuals who make up the endowed Orders come from respectable families and entered for genuine motives ... into a state where they thought they were certain of spending the rest of their days honourably provided for in gentlemanly ease.' He had given up his property to his brothers and felt he had denied himself the prospect of jobs as good as they obtained. Another Premonstratensian, Hervé-Julien Le Sage, wrote: 'I looked on every field that the monastery possessed as the sacred and inviolable guarantee of my means of subsistence until my last breath.'[44] The phrase has almost the ring of Newman's nostalgia in his autobiography for the snapdragon on the walls of Trinity College, Oxford.

So far as girls of good family were concerned, if parents could not marry them off – perhaps for lack of a dowry or because they were otherwise unattractive – the natural thing for them to do was to become nuns. The dowry would be cheaper than for a bride, and most nuns led a secure and relatively comfortable life offering the possibility, otherwise rare for women in that period, of filling administrative offices and doing rewarding work outside their families.[45] Further, the only education available to girls outside the home was provided by nunneries: hence many well-off girls spent their childhood years in schools run by such institutions. Some of the pupils, under the influence of their teachers, took their vows and became nuns at or soon after the canonical age of profession, sixteen (eighteen after 1768). Others left to get married. Some stayed on for many years awaiting a suitor.

As with most aspects of the monastic life, there was one pattern for the rich, and another for the poorer. The rich have naturally left the better records. Helen Massalska, a member of one of the two greatest families of Lithuania, who in 1779 was to marry Charles prince de Ligne, son and heir of the celebrated writer and general, wrote a classic account of her education in the Abbaye-aux-Bois, which makes it possible to paint an unusually detailed and lively picture of the nunnery. She was sent to board there in 1771 at the age of eight when her uncle, the archbishop of Vilnius, exiled from Poland, brought her to Paris. Her memoir, written in her teens, together with the biography she attracted, provides a full and lively picture of an experience which, with allowances made for her and the nunnery's exceptional wealth and social standing, was widely shared.

In the words of her biographer,

All the ladies charged with the boarders' education belonged to the highest nobility, the pupils themselves bore the greatest names of the kingdom and, strangely enough, their education combined training in the most bourgeois domestic duties with lessons intended to prepare them for the ways of high society.

Music, dancing and painting were cultivated with great care. The abbey possessed a fine theatre, many stage sets and costumes of the utmost elegance. Molé and Larive taught the boarders declamation and reading aloud; the ballets were directed by Noverre, Philippe and Dauberval, principal dancers of the opera. All the teachers came from outside the abbey, except for [those of] botany and natural history.[46]

The domestic training, however, was given by nuns.

At this time the abbey had 73 nuns, 8 novices, 177 boarders and 104 *sœurs converses*, i.e. sisters whose role was to run the material side of the foundation.

There were four confessors. In the year 1778–9 the abbey spent more than 61,000 livres on domestic provision, 45,000 of which went on food and wine and 5,000 to wood merchants, presumably for heating. The confessors cost 950 in total, the organist 200, Holy Week sermons and music 246, doctors and surgeons 500, maids over 2,000, journals, gazettes and books approaching 1,000.

These 177 well-bred and carefully supervised girls sometimes behaved in ways reminiscent of St Trinian's. During a midnight feast in her dormitory Helen, aged eight, having just eaten a great deal of pâté and had a powder, insisted on sampling some cider. Whether as a result or not, she was next day taken off to the infirmary, where she nearly died of a putrid fever and had to stay for two months. It was now decided that she should be given a private room, a maid, a chambermaid and a nurse. 'I was assigned', she wrote, 'four louis a month pocket money . . . My banker, M. Torton, received orders from my uncle to supply me with up to thirty thousand louis a year, if necessary.' On this prodigious allowance, she had a highly successful school career, performing equally well at history and dancing, for example in *Orpheus and Eurydice*, and at acting parts in some of Corneille's plays and in Racine's *Athalie* and *Esther*. The abbey had a custom like that of the boy bishop, under which twice a year the girls elected from among their number an abbess and other officials, who were allowed to take over the adults' duties for a day. On at least one occasion Helen was chosen to be abbess. Her domestic training began with service in the abbess's splendid mansion. Then she went on to the sacristy, 'the repository of every story and all the news, [where] people abounded the whole day'. The main interest of work in the library was humouring the eccentricities of the nun in charge, who got up late and used to say: 'I didn't take a vow not to sleep to my heart's content.'

Helen's memoir gives glimpses too of the darker side of monastic life. The present abbess was thought to be kind and fair, but one of her predecessors was remembered as having been so tyrannical – imposing severe corporal punishments and prison sentences – that the Regent had removed her. Many nuns evidently had a genuine vocation, and many novices took their vows, or 'professed', cheerfully. But not all. Helen gave an account of a reluctant profession which deserves quoting extensively for several reasons: first because it describes so vividly a ceremony which with necessary variations was experienced by most monks and nuns; secondly because this particular rite was so anguished; thirdly, because the account deserves comparison with passages in Diderot's *La religieuse*, written in the 1760s though not published until 1796; and fourthly, because the lengthy extract from Helen's description given in J.K. Macnamara's *Sisters in Arms* has been edited, without any indication of the omissions, in such a way as to purge it of its disturbing features:

For two years there had been in the novitiate a young woman called Mlle de Rastignac, who was twenty. She seemed to be in a deep depression, was always ill and spent more time in the infirmary than out of it. She had already put on the habit. Her profession had been twice arranged and then put off because she fell ill... Two or three times she was sent back into the world among her family, but to no avail. It was finally decided to go ahead with her profession, and it was said that, although she was very ill and could hardly stand, she desired to take her vows.

On the day of her profession, the church was filled by all the Hauteforts in the world, since she was their close relation. Mlle de Guignes carried her candle and acted as her sponsor, the comte d'Hautefort was her knight. She was very pretty. At first she was in the outer church on a prie-dieu in a gown of white crepe embroidered in silver and covered with diamonds. She stood up very well to the abbé Marolle's sermon, in which he told her that it was a great merit in God's eyes to renounce the world when one was cut out to be adored there and to charm and adorn it. It seemed that he took pleasure in painting in glowing colours all that she was about to abandon. But she kept her composure.

After the sermon the comte d'Hautefort took her by the hand and conducted her to the entrance of the enclosure. As soon as she had passed through, the door was shut behind her with a great bang and noisily bolted, for this is a courtesy never omitted on such occasions. We all noticed that this had a terrible effect on her and she paled very visibly. She went into the courtyard more dead than alive. They were still saying that this was because she was ill, but it seemed to us that her mind was suffering more than her body. When she reached the choir screen, it was closed so that she could be undressed. Then they hastened to remove her worldly ornaments. She had long blonde hair. When it was loosened, we all wanted to cry out to stop them cutting it, and all the boarders muttered 'What a shame!' At the moment when the novice mistress put the scissors to it, she shuddered. The hair was put on a great silver dish, where it looked ravishing. Then they reclothed her in the habit of the Order, put on her veil and a circlet of white roses. Finally they opened the screen and presented her to the priest, who blessed her.

Then they brought near the screen a chair, on which Mme the abbess sat, with her crucifer and chaplainess on either side. Mlle de Rastignac knelt before her and put her hands between hers. The formula for taking vows is: 'Between your hands, Madame, I make a vow to God of poverty, humility, obedience, chastity and perpetual enclosure, according to the rule of St Benedict, observance of St Bernard, Order of Cîteaux, filiation of Clairvaux.' She was so weak that she could hardly keep kneeling... [The novice mistress] spelled out the vow one word at a time, and she repeated it. When she had made her vow of obedience and the vow of chastity was reached, she paused for so long that all the boarders, who had wept a great deal, could now hardly stop themselves wanting to laugh. At last, after looking all round, as if to see whether any help was forthcoming, the mistress went up to her and said: 'Come on, courage, my child. Complete your sacrifice!' She sighed deeply as she said the words 'chastity and perpetual enclosure', letting her head fall on Mme the abbess's knees. It was clear she had fainted, so they took her to the sacristy.

The custom is that she must go and embrace the knees of all the nuns after her profession, and then embrace the boarders. We were told that she was not in a fit state for that, and that she would emerge only to prostrate herself in the middle of the choir. Nothing moved me more than when she appeared at the sacristy door, pale as death, with a glazed look, supported by two nuns. Mlle de Guignes, who was carrying her candle, was trembling so much that she could scarcely walk. Mme Ste-Magdeleine – for this was the name Mlle de Rastignac had taken – proceeded to the middle of the choir where they helped her to prostrate herself. They stretched the funeral cloth over her and sang the *Miserere* of Lalande, in which we joined, and the *Dies irae* and the *Libera* of the Cordeliers, which is superb music. The whole thing lasted an hour and a half, because the prayers for the dead are said over them to remind them that they are dead to the world.

That same evening, as she had a fever, they put her in the infirmary, where she stayed for six weeks . . . She remains in a state of dejection which everyone is concerned about and seeks to dispel by trying to make her life pleasant.[47]

This unfortunate nun was evidently the victim of family pressure – though perhaps exerted for less discreditable reasons than in the case of Diderot's heroine, who was offered up as a sacrifice to atone for her mother's adultery. It was unquestionably contrary to the Church's law to force novices to take vows, and we are told that her confessor had been opposed to her becoming a nun. But in the final stages the authorities of the nunnery are seen to have propelled Mlle de Rastignac towards her profession. Helen and her friends clearly regard this as distressing but also exceptional.

It was not only young girls of good family in need of education who were given lodging by such monasteries and thereby offered refuge or social opportunities. Some houses had been especially founded for widows. Wealthy women involved in scandalous affairs or unhappy marriages might betake themselves, or be sent by the king or by their relations, to a nunnery. This was the tactic used by Louis XV, under the orders of his confessor, to disembarrass himself of his mistress, Mme du Barry, as he neared death.[48] Grand houses of canonesses like Remiremont took in a good many ladies in similar situations. It was possible too for well-connected

ILL. 16 Hubert Robert, *Les cygnes de Saint-Antoine-les-Champs*, commissioned by Madame Geoffrin

ladies to rent rooms in nunneries where they could live permanently or have a second home, entertain, conduct affairs and run a salon, as the marquise du Deffand did in her apartment at St Joseph's and Mme Geoffrin at St-Antoine-des-Champs. Both of these brilliant ladies received many *philosophes* in their monastic lodgings, men such as D'Alembert, Diderot, Turgot, Marmontel and archbishop Loménie de Brienne. In 1781 Mme Geoffrin had some charming if idealised pictures painted by Hubert Robert of her life among the nuns and novices (Ill. 16).[49]

The monasteries of the old Orders, it must by now be evident, were integrated to a remarkable degree and in numerous, sometimes paradoxical ways into the aristocratic society of the *ancien régime*. But in order to understand the full extent of this involvement it is necessary to place the monasteries in the context of the special relationship between the king and the French Church as a whole. By the Concordat of Bologna of 1516 the pope had confirmed the surrender of most of his powers over the Church in France to the king. The latter now had the absolute right, as against Rome, to appoint all the bishops and many of the other clergy of France, including numerous abbots and abbesses, to tax the Church, to decide all appeals from its courts and to ignore any papal decrees he disliked. These prerogatives were not much wider than those possessed by the king of Spain in his lands, especially after the Concordat of 1753, but they far exceeded those of Italian and German rulers, even including the ruler of the Austrian Monarchy.

Despite these arrangements, however, the French Church still possessed a high degree of autonomy and considerable political power. It was unique in having a General Assembly of the Clergy, founded in 1561 as part of a contract in which the king guaranteed the autonomy and privileges of the Church while the clergy acknowledged his right to tax them. The Assembly was normally summoned every five years and negotiated with the king appropriate levels of tax on church property. It could also discuss religious and related issues with considerable freedom. This arrangement greatly reduced the scope of effective royal absolutism.[50] As in Spain, but in sharp contrast with the Austrian Monarchy, French churchmen were still considered suitable ministers of the Crown. Three of the most notable first ministers of the eighteenth century were cardinal Dubois during the Regency after Louis XIV's death, cardinal Fleury from 1726 to 1743 and cardinal Loménie de Brienne in the last days of the *ancien régime*.[51]

Moreover, Louis XV and Louis XVI seldom tried to impose radical measures of any kind against strong opposition and, when they did try, lacked the determination to carry them through. In practice, royal power was generally exercised in the interests of maintaining the position of the aristocracy. The treatment of the

Church is a prime example of both these points. Faced with the debts incurred during the War of the Austrian Succession, Louis XV appeared in 1749–51 to be ready to impose a new tax, the *vingtième*, on the Church as on the nobility. He would thus have breached the Church's taxation privileges, to the delight of *philosophes* like Voltaire. But, in the face of a massive campaign on the part of the clergy the king backed down, though he had succeeded in imposing tougher control on gifts of land to ecclesiastical institutions in mortmain.[52] Virtually every French bishop of the eighteenth century was of noble birth, and so were the great majority of the abbots and abbesses of the greater monasteries. The king had made the upper ranks of the Church into a vast system of outdoor relief for the aristocracy and had thereby apparently bound together the interests of the First and the Second Estate.

The impact of this policy on monasteries was far worse even than it was on the episcopate. For, whereas aristocratic bishops had to be ordained clergymen and were expected to carry out the pastoral and administrative duties of bishops, the noble commendatory abbots and abbesses were usually chosen without the least regard to their suitability as directors of the religious activities of their houses. This practice, already briefly mentioned, needs fuller explanation.

Most ancient monasteries throughout Europe had exemption from royal as well as episcopal control; and, in so far as they were subordinate to anyone, it was to their Orders and congregations and to the pope. After the Concordat, however, those of France were in most respects subordinate to the king and not to the pope. In many Catholic countries, especially in the German lands, monasteries genuinely elected their abbots. This remained true of lesser houses in France and of some greater houses, but the heads of four-fifths of the major houses, those classed as *abbayes* (of men and women), were not only appointed by the king but appointed *in commendam*, which meant that they were not monks or nuns and that they were debarred from acting as regular abbots or abbesses, though they drew a good proportion of the revenues of their house, legally a third, commonly much more. The arrangement applied to the huge number of at least 815 *abbayes* and 280 priories.[53] Those appointed were commonly (for abbeys of men) bishops and Court chaplains, who at least were ordained; but some were princes or princesses of the blood, ministers of the Crown or their relatives, in a few cases foreign princes, quite often lay aristocrats. Occasionally, like Rancé or Angélique Arnauld, they turned into genuine spiritual leaders and became regular abbots or abbesses. But for the most part they sapped the wealth and injured the reputation of their houses. It was often a case of 'To them that hath shall be given.' McManners details the classical example of an unspiritual aristocrat waxing rich on ecclesiastical funds..., Louis de Bourbon Condé,... son of the prince de Condé and Mlle Nantes, daughter of Louis XIV and Mme de Montespan. With such a lineage, bulls for abbatial appointments rained on his once-tonsured locks – Bec, Saint-Claude, Marmoutier, Saint-Nicolas-des-Champs, and two others by the age of 13, and one more to top up at the age of 23. He surrendered three of these when the immense revenues of Saint-Germain-des-Prés came to him in 1737. Rumour had it that he now had 300,000 livres a year, though in fact he had more than double this. Authorized by the Pope to bear arms without renouncing his benefices, he played the general in the French armies... His harem in Paris was principally recruited from the Opéra... The nearest he came to performing an ecclesiastical function was to build a marble mausoleum for his pet monkey McCarthy.[54]

To mount a defence of appointments like Condé's, and of other scarcely less scandalous cases, would be difficult indeed. But overall the king's use of *commendes* could be defended, at least in its social context. In the first place, it was maintained with some plausibility that unworldly monks and nuns needed the help of well-placed commendators to further the worldly interests of their houses. Secondly, it was pretty well agreed by French kings and statesmen that monasteries were too numerous, and many of them far richer than they needed to be to fulfil their aims. Thirdly, they were under-taxed. Here was a huge source of wealth which the Concordat, through the system of *commendes*, enabled the king to tap for purposes useful to Church and state. Some bishoprics yielded an inadequate income, and it was not unreasonable to supplement it by milking a rich abbey, perhaps by making the bishop its abbot or by giving him a pension out of its revenues. Furthermore, the king had insufficient money to fund his foreign policy and to pay his ministers adequate salaries. One established royal recourse was the sale of offices, now being practised on a large scale: let candidates buy posts, active or sinecure, and see what income they could get by exploiting them.[55] The *commende* was similarly used to augment the salaries of ministers and reward the king's relatives and favourites, including some foreign princes and princesses. Beyond this select group of commendators were assorted noblemen, whose appointments could also be defended from within the thought-world of the *ancien régime*. Birth conferred merit, aristocracy had to be preserved, yet nobles were often too poor to live up to their station. Hence it was deemed a positive benefit to the monarchy, to society at large and therefore to the Church, to help keep aristocracy afloat. The same kind of thinking is to be found, together with a desire to create employment, behind Colbert's decree of 1666 ordering the monasteries to spend their revenues not on their churches, but on building and repairing their abbots' and abbesses' lodgings, their cloisters and the monks' or nuns' residential and administrative quarters – a decree which helps to account for the small number of monastic churches built in the eighteenth century.[56] The official attitude was that all these measures tended to make monastic property more useful to society than it would be if controlled solely by the monks and used for strictly monastic purposes. But, notwithstanding all these more or less persuasive arguments, which recall English justifications of rotten boroughs and 'virtual representation', it cannot be denied that the practice of commendation implied contempt for the monastic life and rule, especially that of the old Orders. Not only was much of their revenue thereby diverted to the support of laymen and secular clergy, but a commendator could also exploit for his own purposes his abbey's patronage, perhaps controlling the admission of monks and nuns, appointments to offices within the monastery and the selection of priests for its parishes. The system went far to diminish the influence of the monastic element in the Church which elsewhere, if not usually dominant, was of greater importance not only in religious development and ecclesiastical affairs but even in secular politics than it was allowed to be in France.

In other ways too the government and society of the *ancien régime* discriminated against the regular as compared with the secular clergy. Though in a few of the French provinces abbots were well represented in the First Estate, most *pays* had lost their Estates altogether. In any case, many of the abbots who sat in the surviving Estates must have been commendatory. In the Estates-General of 1614, the last time it had met, regular clergy amounted to only 10 per cent of the First Estate.[57] Remarkably, they were unrepresented in the General Assembly of the Clergy.[58] Unlike in other Catholic countries, French regulars virtually never became bishops. Whereas in Bavaria monks dominated the new Academy, in France they were not allowed to be elected to the Académie des Sciences and the Académie des Inscriptions. Yet a few French monks became Fellows of the Royal Society.[59] Politically and in some ways socially, traditional monasticism was in a weaker position in France than in other Catholic countries.

THE NEW ORDERS

The opposite was true, however, so far as the new Orders were concerned. They, and especially those for women, were uniquely successful in France. To start with male Orders, the Franciscans must count as 'old' in the sense that they were founded in the early thirteenth century. But they appear 'new' in several other senses: first, that from the start they rejected the purely contemplative, cloistered life in favour of activity in the world; secondly, that they lacked the vast properties and privileges of the early medieval Orders; and thirdly, that in the fifteenth and sixteenth centuries the Order broke up into a group of five Orders which, while acknowledging their common origin, had separate, in some ways rival organisations. Of these the unreformed element, known as the Conventuals, were hardly represented in France. In 1517 the reformed 'Observants' became distinct and in France were called **Cordeliers**. They had in the mid-eighteenth century about 250 French houses, of which some had acquired social cachet and considerable revenues, most notably their main house in Paris, patronised by successive kings, with an income of 45,000 livres a year, an impressive library and an immense church famous for its sermons and its music. So large and strategically placed was its site that under Louis XVI an elaborate scheme was promoted by the reforming minister, Necker, to transfer the friars to another church, in order to make way for various public buildings, a barracks, a prison and an archive. But after several years of dispute the king rescinded his previous eviction order – one of the last victories of monasticism under the old regime. However, the Observant Order in general was not highly respected: 'once the apostles of poverty, they had come to stand for wealth, influence and privilege, not always wisely or unselfishly used'[60]. Another reformed branch dating from the sixteenth century were the **Recollects**, *Récollets* in French, so called because they emphasised 'recollection', by which was meant 'retreat, withdrawal for spiritual exercises'. They had over a hundred houses. The **Minims**, dating from the fifteenth century, also supposed to be reformed, were notorious for never eating meat. Their tally was 150 houses. But, as elsewhere in Europe, the **Capuchins**, dating from 1528, were pre-eminent among the Franciscans of France, with 420 houses. If 'Capuchin' was commonly used as a virtual synonym for 'naïve', 'ignorant' and 'superstitious' or 'dishevelled' and 'dirty', the Order none the less commanded widespread respect for having maintained its strict discipline and adhered more closely than any other branch to St Francis's original intentions. Poverty was genuinely enforced: the Order's funds really came from begging, and a monk might not be allowed to have even a watch in his room or about his person. Fasting was ordained for many days of the year, and self-flagellation was prescribed three times a week throughout the year and more often in Holy Week. The Order was known too for its pastoral work, its missions, its members' selfless ministry to the sick, including plague victims, and for various forms of public service such as establishing fire-brigades. The total number of Capuchin houses in France hardly changed after the 1660s and the complement of monks seems to have declined slowly in the early decades of the eighteenth century, but there was a marked increase of new professions in the 1740s and so the peak may well have been reached around 1750.[61]

Of the Orders that were founded from scratch in the sixteenth century, the most influential by far were the Jesuits. Like the Capuchins, their great period of growth in France was the first half of the seventeenth century, when many of their Colleges were built, impressive compositions of three courts with a church at the centre. In 1640 they had 90 Colleges, and in 1763 104. Of those remaining, the grandest, built 'regardless of expense' by command of Henry IV, is at La Flèche in the Loire valley.[62] In the seventeenth century the Jesuits were exceedingly effective promoters of the Counter-Reformation in France, and almost until their expulsion from France in 1764 they seemed to be winning their battle with Jansenism. As controversialists, preachers, missionaries and educators they acquired an immense reputation. Among their achievements was the creation of a centrally organised network of brotherhoods or congregations involving monks and laymen of all classes.[63] The Jesuits' social prestige and the quality of their teaching ensured that they received a high proportion of the ablest and best-connected boys to train in their Colleges, which served as the principal secondary schools of the day. Most French princes and princesses had Jesuit confessors.

It was at La Flèche in its early days that perhaps their greatest pupil, the philosopher René Descartes, was educated. His teachers had clearly helped to inspire his intellectual rigour and, to some extent, his readiness to question received wisdom. He repaid them by providing the Order and the Church with a philosophical system that, though at first condemned, was soon found easy to baptise as a new rational theology. Having reached by reasoning the position that nothing in the physical world could be proved to exist outside people's consciousness, he then argued that, because he (and others) could think, they must exist, from which he claimed it followed that God must exist, and hence other things too. The Jesuits were the most conspicuous defenders of religious orthodoxy, but their rationalism, their critical spirit and their awareness of modern developments in philosophy and science – and their adoption of a Cartesian theology – seem in the long run to have prepared minds for the advance of the Enlightenment.[64] Their socially prestigious Collège de Louis-le-Grand in Paris had Voltaire among its pupils, and in the early decades of the eighteenth century some of its staff belonged to an able and enlightened group of Jesuit writers who formed part of the salon culture of the Capital.[65] At least until the 1750s, Voltaire made a point of expressing his debt to the Order's teaching, as in an open letter of 1746 to the principal of his old college of Louis-le-Grand:

Nothing will blot out in my heart the memory of father Porée, who is equally dear to all who studied under him. No man ever made study and virtue more agreeable... I know that he has successors worthy of him. In short, what did I see during the seven years I spent in [the Jesuits'] house? The most laborious of lives, the most frugal, the most orderly. All their time was divided between the care they lavished on us and the practice of their austere profession. I declare that among the thousands of men educated by them like me, not one will contradict me. This is why I never cease to be astonished that they can be accused of teaching a corrupting morality.[66]

On the other hand, they clung obstinately to Cartesian metaphysics against Newton's discoveries and the empiricism associated with them; and, by the middle of the eighteenth century, they were coming to seem obcurantist. In the 1750s the *Mémoires de Trévoux*, their mouthpiece, bitterly attacked the successive volumes of the *Encyclopédie* as they appeared. Their criticism focussed on the work's extensive plagiarism as much as on its unorthodoxy, and it was generally suspected that part of their animus against it stemmed from jealousy that the project had been entrusted to the hands of raffish *philosophes* rather than to their own respectable scholars. There was even a moment in 1752 when it seemed that the Jesuits might after all be put in charge of the work by the Court. But in the event the *Encyclopédie* was allowed to continue on its original basis. Despite this controversy, Jesuits' 'relations with the *philosophes* were by no means severed'[67] even though they had certainly been damaged.

Their educational work was supplemented by that of other Orders such as the Oratorians and the Congregation of Christian Doctrine, founded in 1592, which had respectively twenty-six and twenty-nine colleges around 1760. In total the three Orders then had about 48,000 students. The Brothers of the Christian Schools, founded by Jean-Baptiste de la Salle in 1680 specifically to educate poorer boys, ran elementary schools in 79 towns in 1750, and in 116 by 1790.[68]

One of the most important activities of such Orders was the running of the diocesan seminaries which had been gradually established all over France during the seventeenth and eighteenth centuries. Around 1760 153 of these institutions existed, of which 60 were directed by the Lazarists, 32 by the Jesuits, 20 by the Sulpicians, 14 each by the Oratorians and the Doctrinaires, and 13 by the Eudistes. The mere catalogue brings out the number of such Orders. But what is most striking about the list is its demonstration that, when bishops wished to improve the quality of parish clergy, they found it natural and even necessary to turn to monks – though to monks of new, unenclosed Orders – to carry out the task. No better example could be given of the close interaction between the regular and secular clergy, or of the integral role of monks in the life of the Church as a whole.[69]

Still greater expansion was achieved by Orders dedicated to the education of girls. In the sixteenth century, as was described in the Introduction, the papacy and the Council of Trent had allowed the development of new kinds of Orders for men such as the Jesuits and the Oratorians, who worked in the world rather than in the cloister and, in the case of the Oratorians, had no formal rule of life and even included some laymen. For nuns, however, the official attitude was shown in the bull of 1566 imposing on them the strictest enclosure and barring the way for women to adopt the looser forms of organisation recently approved for men.[70] Yet it was clear that there was a widespread desire among pious women to form such institutions and to bind themselves to do religious and charitable work without committing themselves to a lifetime of claustration. There was also a widespread lay demand for education of girls, which few people thought it appropriate to satisfy other than in a religious and female context.

Early attempts by women to obtain papal approval for uncloistered foundations failed. In two very important cases those involved were reluctantly obliged to adopt a traditional monastic life. The Ursulines, founded in 1535 as a society without vows or houses, had by 1612 become a strict enclosed Order with this purpose. Introduced in France in 1596, they came to be thought of as the feminine branch of the Jesuits, and had at least 350 monasteries and 9,000 nuns by 1789. Another Order active in female education, though not originally intended for that purpose, was the Visitandines, that is, communities of the Visitation, founded by Jeanne de Chantal under the guidance of St François de Sales in 1610 and, after episcopal pressure, turned into a regular order in 1616. The papacy had been slow to approve these Orders, even though the prestige of women in the Church had been greatly enhanced by the impact on other Orders, of both sexes, of the saintliness, writings and reforms of the Spanish Carmelite nun, St Theresa of Avila (1515–82). But the effect of these new foundations, as Elizabeth Rapley has put it, was that 'The Gallican church was prised open, to admit women into its inner life.'[71]

Whereas the Ursulines and the Visitandines usually required a dowry from postulants and were in consequence largely aristocratic, once these Orders had made the breakthrough, many organisations of a similar type but of a less socially exclusive character were founded. In 1633–4 Louise Marillac and St Vincent de Paul devised another scheme for an Order of women who would be halfway between nuns and laity, the *Filles de la Charité* or Sisters of Charity. St Vincent wrote: 'They have for monastery only the houses of the sick and the house where the superior lives, for cell a rented room, for chapel the parish church, for cloister obedience, and for veil holy modesty.' Their aims included the education of the poor, but they came to be chiefly concerned with treating and caring for the sick. They transformed nursing and made French hospitals the best in the world in the eighteenth century, famously providing Florence Nightingale with her model as late as the Crimean War. In 1788 they had 451 houses and 4350 sisters.[72] Other similar foundations followed – so many that they cannot easily be listed and few of them have been studied. McManners lists seven new sisterhoods founded between 1703 and 1762.[73]

After the middle of the eighteenth century almost every French cloistered Order of monks and nuns declined in strength, at least until the 1780s. This even applied to the Ursulines and the Visitandines. But the more loosely organised Orders for women continued to grow rapidly, and to some extent they had inspired similar male Orders, including the Brothers of the Christian Schools. These developments – unique to France, at least in their scale – are dramatically reflected in the fact that, of the hundred or more houses for women existing in Paris when the Revolution began, the vast majority had been founded in the seventeenth and eighteenth centuries.[74] France of the *ancien régime* is remembered above all for its anti-Catholic Enlightenment, pouring scorn on a decaying Church and especially on its moribund monasteries. But, whatever was moribund about the monasticism of the period, it was not the female teaching and nursing congregations, which the *philosophes* themselves applauded.[75] These Orders, despite their suppression during the Revolution, were to prove one of the most notable legacies of the old regime to the nineteenth century.[76]

CHAPTER 4

SPAIN AND PORTUGAL

It has become fashionable to emphasise the singularity – the *Sonderweg* – of German history. Robert Tombs has applied the same concept to France.[1] But it has even greater appropriateness to the history of the Iberian peninsula. Hence, no doubt, the relative neglect of the subject in other countries and the reluctance of many of those who work in the field to place it in a broader European context. Most general histories of art and architecture, for example, give only very limited coverage to the glories of Spain and Portugal.[2] Whereas many scholars straddle the Rhine and the Alps, the Pyrenees seem almost as effective a barrier to historical understanding as the Urals.

The first and fundamental singularity of Iberian history[3] is that Muslim rulers conquered almost the whole peninsula in the eighth century and retained control of much of the centre and south for many hundreds of years. The main theme of medieval Iberian history has in consequence been seen as the struggle of the indigenous Christian population to 'reconquer' the peninsula – re-establishing Catholicism has been equated with restoring native rule. In reality, the *Reconquista* was a very long, complex and fitful struggle, partly because the Christians were for centuries divided between several small kingdoms and principalities which quarrelled with each other almost as much as with the Muslims. While Portugal established itself relatively early as a distinct Atlantic-orientated state and completed its reconquest in the mid-thirteenth century, it was not until 1469 that the marriage of the future king Ferdinand of Aragon and queen Isabella of Castile made possible the unification of Spain, and only in 1492 that they ejected the 'Moors' from their last stronghold on the mainland, Granada. Christian fervour and proselytisation had been integral to the process of reconquest, which in its later stages was blessed by the popes as a continuation of the Crusades. Especially as new territories were conquered, lavish donations were made by the Christian rulers to the Church.

Even these devout countries, however, had not been unaffected by the laxity and corruption endemic in the late medieval Church. But in Spain the last stages of the *Reconquista* were accompanied by a movement for church reform, strongly encouraged by Ferdinand and Isabella and carried through by their chief minister, cardinal Jiménes de Cisneros, archbishop of Toledo. He attempted to improve the education of the clergy and in particular their knowledge of the Bible, and began to clean up the worst abuses to be found among monks and nuns. Though Portugal experienced no comparable movement in this period, it followed the example of Spain in campaigning more vigorously to root out heresy. In 1478 Ferdinand founded the Spanish Inquisition for this purpose and to strengthen royal power, and Portugal obtained papal permission to follow suit in 1536. The heretics in question were Muslims – or Jews, whom both the Catholic and the Muslim states had previously tolerated. It came to seem virtually impossible to be a Portuguese or a Spaniard and not to be a Catholic. More than that, even though both countries insisted by the sixteenth century that Muslims and Jews must either go into exile or be converted to Christianity, those who stayed and were converted, called *conversos* in Spain and 'New Catholics' in Portugal, were treated as second-class citizens, lacking 'purity of blood', and the two Inquisitions harassed and persecuted them until late in the eighteenth century. Many Orders and monasteries made regulations excluding them from becoming monks and nuns.[4]

The nature of the *Reconquista*, together with these reforms, ensured that Protestantism, although the merest hint of its appearance evoked hysterical fear in the two countries, in fact hardly surfaced there at all, except among foreign visitors. Spain and Portugal suffered no civil wars of religion between Catholics and Protestants such as devastated parts of France and much of Germany in the sixteenth and seventeenth centuries. Even compared with the Italian peninsula, the Iberian was relatively free of both war and religious discord between 1492 and 1800. It is true that in the second half of the sixteenth century Spain, having already achieved its own partial Catholic Reformation, became the unquestioned leader of what elsewhere looked like the Counter-Reformation, that it largely inspired the decrees of the Council of Trent and that it worked and fought for the next hundred years to annihilate Protestantism in Britain, France, the Netherlands and Germany. The Netherlands, of course, were united with Spain in the early sixteenth century, and so the growth of Protestantism there became an internal problem from the point of view of the Madrid government. The costs of this further crusade, and its ultimate failure outside the southern Netherlands and parts of Germany, help to explain the domestic unrest of the mid-seventeenth century in the peninsula and had much to do with Spain's decline as a Power. But Catholicism remained unchallenged in both Spain and Portugal.

This peculiar trajectory of Spanish and Portuguese church history was naturally reflected in the history of monasticism.[5] As the peninsula was recovered for Catholicism, parishes were of course created or newly endowed to reinvigorate the faith of the Christian population. But much more conspicuous was the foundation of hundreds of monasteries. In the words of Pedro Palacio,

Monasteries ... contributed to consolidate the *Reconquista*, brought under cultivation barren or abandoned lands, thus collaborating in a veritable internal colonisation. They built bridges, roads and hospitals, offered security and maintenance in return for work, and their wealth reached untold levels thanks to donations and privileges granted by kings and nobles. Monarchs spent long periods in these abbeys and convents, ... giving rise to a hybrid of palace and monastery, ... a permanent singularity in the habits of our monarchs which eventually culminated in the Escorial experience.[6]

Monasticism seems to have had exceptional prestige at all levels of society in Spain and Portugal, almost until the end of the eighteenth century. A bevy of Habsburg archduchesses and grand ladies withdrew to royal nunneries in the sixteenth and seventeenth centuries, followed by princesses of the new Bourbon dynasty in the eighteenth.[7] Many Spanish bishops were drawn from the Orders, including the great Jiménes, an Observant Franciscan. While 200 of Castile's eighteenth-century bishops came from the ranks of the secular clergy, 85 were regulars.[8]

Part of the explanation for the readiness to found monasteries and for the respect in which monks were held is that the secular clergy of the late medieval and early modern periods were often uneducated and loose-living, whereas most monks received serious training from their Orders and observed their rules of conduct. Further, although there were amply enough seculars to staff them, many parishes in fact lacked a priest. It was evidently more attractive to most seculars to take a post in some cathedral or collegiate church, to act as a nobleman's, a college's or a confraternity's chaplain, to pick up casual fees for conducting services, or to work in a university – in all these cases probably living in a town – than to accept a cure of souls in a remote and impoverished village. 'In many places,' Philip III was told in 1603, 'there are no preachers and confessors for want of monasteries.'[9]

Among the Orders the Dominicans, the various types of Franciscans and later the Jesuits were the most important of those which engaged in pastoral work, although some parishes were, despite prohibitions, manned by Benedictines and Cistercians. An originally contemplative Order virtually unknown outside Spain and Portugal, the Hieronymites, founded in the fourteenth century, which by the sixteenth century had become immensely rich and prestigious, had broadened its activities to include education and scholarship. It occupied in Spain the great Marian sanctuary of Guadelupe, Yuste (where Charles V retired and died) and the Escorial, and in Portugal the former Benedictine house of Belém.[10]

For a donor, and for a concerned churchman, to found a monastery was a great deal simpler, legally and socially, than to establish a new parish. It also held out for the founder the comforting prospect of vast numbers of Masses being said for his and his family's souls. The assault of the Counter-Reformation Church on what it saw as superstitious and pagan rites concerning the dead, together with the high mortality, epidemics and population decline of the early seventeenth century, appear to have multiplied by many times the demand for such Masses during that period.[11]

These considerations applied elsewhere than in Spain and Portugal, at least until the diocesan seminaries envisaged by the Council of Trent became general and raised the standards of the parish clergy. But in the peninsula the spread of such seminaries was slow, and their teaching poor, as compared with France. Moreover, Spanish and Portuguese history had created a peculiar balance and distribution among the monastic Orders and in the Church as a whole, to such a degree that historians speak of two distinct Spains, northern and southern.[12] Since it was only in the north of both countries that Christians had exercised political control during the early Middle Ages, it was only there that a dense network of parishes was created and great Benedictine, Cistercian, Augustinian and Carthusian houses were founded in that period; and only a very few such institutions, including an important group of Carthusian houses, were later created in the south. On the other hand, both countries were uniquely well endowed with military Orders, some of them peculiar to the region, which played a large part in the reconquest and were granted substantial lands, mostly in the centre of the peninsula. But these Orders lost much of their *raison d'être* as the Muslim states in north Africa declined and after the great naval victory over the Turks achieved mainly by a Spanish fleet at Lepanto in 1571. Most of their wealth was siphoned off by the rulers to provide valuable sinecures to the royal and noble families, while their humbler members devoted themselves to hospital care. So, when it came to supplying the reconquered southern districts with monasteries, it was the newer Orders, Dominicans, Franciscans of various kinds and later Jesuits, which inevitably predominated. The Dominicans and Jesuits, of course, had both been founded by Spaniards and retained something of the character of Spanish Orders. Though, as everywhere, the largest group of regulars belonged to one or other of the Franciscan branches, the Dominicans remained exceptionally strong and well endowed in Spain and Portugal, often dominating the Inquisition and rivalling the Jesuits as missionaries and educators. If we look for an analogy in other countries to the sumptuous architecture of a Dominican house such as San Esteban in Salamanca, it is to be found in grand Benedictine monasteries rather than mendicant houses. Inmates of San Esteban contributed largely to the impressive scholarship of the University of Salamanca during its most creative phase in the sixteenth century, including men of the calibre of Francisco de Vitoria, 'the founder of international law', and Domingo de Soto, physical scientist, as well as to missionary work in Spain and America, and as bishops both in Spain and overseas. Except perhaps in the north, the same peculiarities of Iberian history ensured that Spanish and Portuguese foundations were to an unusual extent concentrated in towns, not only because economic development in the sixteenth and early seventeenth centuries caused spectacular urban growth but also because in many regions no or very few houses of the rurally based Benedictine and Cistercian Orders existed.[13]

It was in 1492, the very year when Granada fell, that Columbus set sail, under the auspices of queen Isabella, on his voyage that led to the discovery of America. Portugal had already begun establishing colonies on the African coast and on the nearer Atlantic islands. But after the great discovery the conquest, exploitation and conversion of Central and South America, shared by treaty between Spain and Portugal from 1494, became virtually a continuation of the *Reconquista* with its 'holy mission'. I have deliberately excluded this vast and momentous process from study in this book, except in so far as it affected European monasteries – but this it did very greatly. The imperial crusade required the training of missionaries in large numbers, which at first took place mainly in the home countries. It was monks who were needed, and so monasteries and their seminaries flourished. The new crusade brought vast wealth to Portugal and to Spain, especially to Lisbon and to Seville, which was granted the monopoly of Spanish trade to 'the Indies'. Of this wealth much was donated to the Church and made possible the building, refurbishing and maintenance of numerous monasteries, again with emphasis on the Orders that undertook education and pastoral work.

As a result of all these tendencies, large numbers of monasteries came to exist in the major towns of Spain and Portugal. Lisbon, we have seen, had at least fifty in the mid-eighteenth century. At the end of the seventeenth century Valladolid, capital of Spain until the reign of Philip II, though it had sixteen parishes, boasted forty-six monasteries. Toledo, now a decaying city of 20,000 inhabitants subsisting on the tithes and rents paid to its ecclesiastical institutions, contained, as well as its fabulously rich cathedral, twenty-seven parishes and thirty-nine monasteries. The new capital, Madrid, relatively short of parishes, possessed in 1759 fifty-seven religious houses. Seville was served by twenty-eight parishes and at least sixty-four monasteries.[14] In some parts of Catholic Europe monastic numbers fell markedly in the age of Enlightenment and of enlightened absolutism, and the French Revolution and Napoleon suppressed all monasteries. But in Spain and Portugal, though these movements had an impact, their effect on monasteries was remarkably limited – further evidence of the singularity of the peninsula's history.

Houses for men predominated in both Spain and Portugal, as we shall see, and at this stage in Spanish and Portuguese history it was only monks who could take part in parochial work and in the imperial adventure. Nuns, even more than in other countries, were strictly enclosed, especially in the sixteenth and seventeenth centuries. But among nunneries there were institutions in which upper-class families could place daughters for education and maintenance in comfortable conditions until, after or instead of marriage. Even in the late eighteenth century, though, it proved very difficult to obtain acceptance for the new brand of female Orders that in France staffed the hospitals.[15]

Inevitably, the history of religious, including monastic, art and architecture also has a peculiar trajectory in Spain and Portugal. In France it was the seventeenth century that saw the greatest development, in the German lands the late seventeenth and early eighteenth centuries. In both regions some of what had been built in the sixteenth century and earlier succumbed or suffered in the wars of religion. But in Spain and Portugal the sixteenth century was the golden age both of economic expansion and of Catholic zeal, continuing, at least in Spain, well into the seventeenth century. Decay or a slackening of advance ensued, followed by economic, if not religious, revival in the eighteenth century. What has been lost from these centuries was more often deliberately revamped by builders than wantonly destroyed in war. Admittedly, the earthquake of 1755, most devastating in Lisbon but affecting much of Portugal and part of Spain, ruined many significant buildings. But, though a considerable number of Iberian churches were despoiled by the armies of Napoleon and by Spanish liberals and republicans in the nineteenth and twentieth centuries, the resulting toll does not begin to match the losses suffered in the rest of Catholic Europe from the activities of French revolutionaries and the two World Wars. Hence religious buildings in late Gothic, Renaissance and Mannerist styles, as locally interpreted, figure more prominently in Spain and Portugal than elsewhere, and Baroque is relatively less pervasive than in the German lands. Still, many striking Baroque complexes exist in the peninsula, such as the charterhouse in Granada, Our Lady of Guadalupe and the palace-monastery of Mafra in Portugal; and Baroque church decoration, furniture and statuary clearly won the same popular affection as in Italy and the German lands. Indeed, in both Spain and Portugal the elaboration of some examples – known in Spain as 'Churrigueresque' – outdoes even those of south Germany.[16] None is more overwhelming than the sacristy and *sagrario* of the Granada charterhouse, which has shocked many observers by the contrast between its extravagance and the austerity of the Carthusian rule. Indeed such display was denounced in one visitation as 'lust of the eyes, a stumbling-block for souls and the devil's disease [pride] in Israel' (Plate 9).[17]

I have so far treated Spain and Portugal more or less as one. Their history certainly has many similarities, but they have always been rivals and often enemies. Although Philip II of Spain became king of Portugal by hereditary succession in 1580, a revolt in 1640, followed by a protracted war, broke the union for ever, reducing the influence of each country on the other. Their national cultures are now regarded as quite distinct.

SPAIN

Spain in the early modern period was united by its dynasty, its religion and little else. Dynasty and religion were indissolubly linked. With papal collaboration, the monarchs had more complete control over the Church than over the nobility: they effectively appointed many of the higher clergy and, through the Inquisition, exerted great influence over religious practice, censorship and public morality. The pope accorded them virtual dictatorship over the Church in their colonies, thus indirectly enhancing their power at home. Since the rulers' wealth enabled them to commission many churches, including numerous grand monasteries, they had a considerable impact on the style both of the buildings and of the worship conducted in them.

It is Philip II's Escorial that symbolises this influence (Ill. 17). Built between 1563 and 1584 at a cost of six million ducats, it included within an immense rectangle of walls an elaborate monastery for Hieronymites with a vast church, a huge royal palace, government offices, a gruesome mausoleum, eight organs, a major picture gallery and a magnificent library. Lifesize statues of Philip and

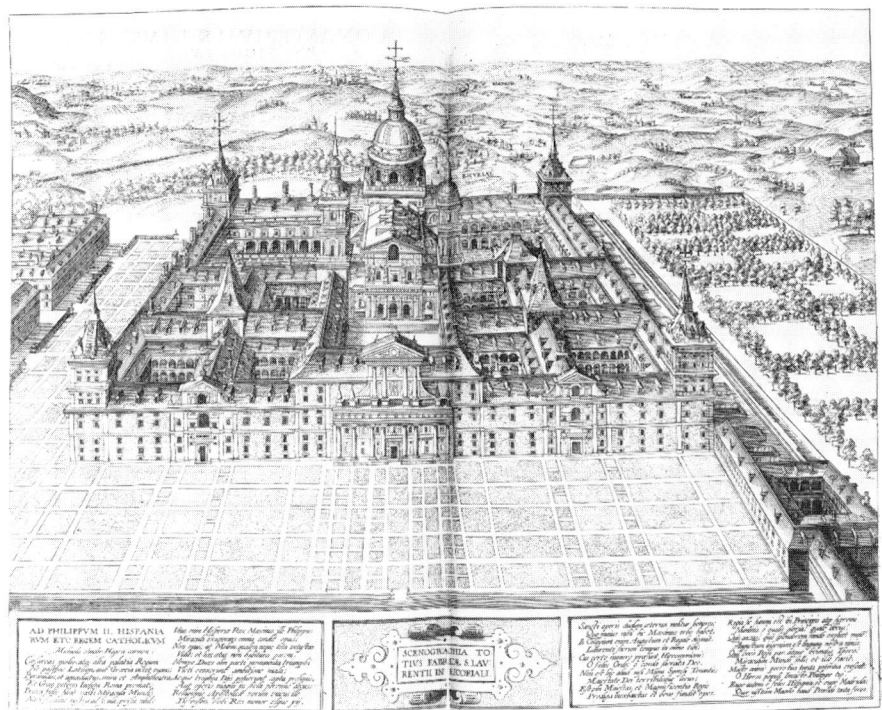

ILL. 17 General view of the Escorial, near Madrid, built 1563–84, from G. Braun and F. Hogenburg, *Civitates orbis terrarum* (1572–)

his father Charles V kneel in prayer, looking towards the high altar of the great church. The king's apartments had been so designed that he could hear and see Mass from his bed. Built in sombre grey granite, the palace is constructed in the austerest classical style, virtually unornamented. There is no doubt that the example of a completely symmetrical palace-monastery, ignoring the traditional medieval layout, influenced many of the building schemes of major German and Austrian houses, that the idea of removing the king and the government to a purpose-built palace influenced Louis XIV's Versailles and that the complex inspired the eighteenth-century Portuguese attempt to outshine it at Mafra. But it is questionable whether it had much effect on the planning of ordinary monasteries, for which its scheme was inappropriate in plan as well as scale. On the other hand, for perhaps a hundred years the austere style of the Escorial was emulated in some Spanish churches. But its purity evidently alienated most Spaniards, who preferred highly ornamented churches, whether Gothic, the brand of Renaissance known as 'Plateresque', Mannerist or Churrigueresque. It resembles other Spanish religious buildings, however, in conveying an intensity of Catholic conviction that is hard to parallel in other countries.[18]

ILL. 18 Grand staircase of the nunnery of Las Descalzas Reales, Madrid, founded 1559, showing portraits of benefactresses and archangels dating from 1684

Spain is recognised as the heartland of Christian mysticism, and in the sixteenth century produced perhaps the two greatest of all mystical writers, St Teresa of Avila and St John of the Cross, whose works describe their meditations, and the agony and fervour of their search for union with the divine. Similar attitudes pervade the visual arts. Just as El Greco's paintings, most famously *The Burial of Count Orgaz*, bring together life on earth and the afterlife into a continuum, so on the staircase wall of the Madrid nunnery of Las Descalzas Reales – staffed by the Order that St Teresa reformed – portraits of the archduchesses who entered it associate unembarrassedly with likenesses of archangels (Ill. 18). During his Spanish travels in the 1780s William Beckford was shown the most prized relic kept at the Escorial, a large feather from the wing of the archangel Gabriel.[19] Spanish statues of the suffering Christ or of bleeding martyrs exhibit a special raw realism, positively demanding the empathy of the monk or nun praying before them. At least in the richer monasteries their inmates are confronted at every turn by altars, images, relics and coffins, all costly, many beautiful, most spelling out some awful warning. To a modern visitor such an ambience seems suffocating and to have required so continuously high a level of religious fervour as to be insupportable. But it is impossible to doubt that, at least for some of the donors, artists and inmates, the fervour was there.

Against this background it is hardly surprising that monasteries grew in number, wealth and population. The following list shows how many of the more than three hundred monasteries of the 'kingdom of Seville' in the south were founded in each of the early modern centuries:

fifteenth-century monastic foundations	41
sixteenth-century	169
seventeenth-century	90
eighteenth-century	11[20]

In 1591 it is estimated that the Spanish population of under ten million included, as well as 40,599 seculars, 50,486 regulars, almost exactly divided between men and women. Official figures for 1747, which do not include colleges and hospitals, put the number of seculars at over 66,000, of monks at over 65,000 and of nuns at over 32,000. These totals represent a distinctly higher proportion of the whole population than those for 1591, for all regulars almost 1 in 100 and for monks alone 1 in 150. If to the numbers of actual monks and nuns are added lay brothers, assistants and servants, the full monastic population surpasses 100,000; and if, instead of the proportion of regulars to the whole population, the proportion of regulars to all adults were to be calculated, then it might reach 1 in 50. Most of this very large increase over 150 years no doubt occurred in the seventeenth century but, except in the case of the old landed Orders, it seems that numbers continued to grow down to and even after 1750. The total number of houses in 1787 was just over 2,000 for men, just over 1,000 for women, figures which correspond to an average complement of about thirty, far higher than in France. As for their property, the entire Church is thought to have owned almost 14 per cent of the land of Spain, with varied proportions in different areas, but including a much higher proportion, 24 per cent, of the cultivable land.[21] The regular clergy probably owned about 5 per cent of rural land, which would again imply a higher proportion of the good land; but they also possessed immense numbers of houses in towns and drew rent from numerous leases. The old Orders depended much more heavily on rural land, the newer on urban. On top of all that, the regulars received tithes which, as in other countries, yielded an amount comparable to their income from land. All these types of property increased markedly in value and return in the first half of the eighteenth century – in the kingdom of Seville at least, more than doubled, easily outpacing inflation – enabling monasteries to buy ever more properties and afford substantial rebuilding programmes.[22] But, though such gains benefited the monasteries, it was often alleged that they harmed others. An official appointed by Charles III to look after the interests of the common people wrote:

A town over which a wealthy religious corporation . . . has gained control falls in a few years into the deepest misery. For, being more influential than all their townsmen, today they buy up the fields, tomorrow the vineyards, later the houses, and finally all real property, until they have forced once useful subjects down to the miserable level of beggars.[23]

The Rev. Joseph Townsend, rector of Pewsey, who published an account of his travels through Spain in 1786–7, repeatedly referred to the swarms of beggars which the monasteries encouraged by giving them doles, and to the ill effects of 'this superabundance of the drones'.[24]

PORTUGAL

To define the difference in spirit between Spain and Portugal, and particularly between Spanish and Portuguese Catholicism, is far from easy. Though Portugal is less diverse than Spain, there are still marked variations between north, centre and south. But it is widely agreed that, compared with the Spaniards, the Portuguese were less sympathetic to mysticism and to austerity. Portugal's buildings, according to Lees-Milne, 'whether clerical or lay, are genial and gay'.[25] Building in a pure style influenced by the Escorial ceased soon after the end of Spanish rule in 1640, to be replaced by a local brand of Baroque, highly ornamented, eclectic and playful.

Reform in the spirit of the Counter-Reformation came rather late to Portugal but was affecting even the Benedictines well before the end of the sixteenth century.[26] Between 1550 and 1668, taking all Orders together, 166 new houses were set up, chiefly by Franciscans, Jesuits, Carmelites and a local Order, the Arrábidos. The period from 1668 to the mid-eighteenth century saw almost another 90 founded. It is believed, though, that by 1750, as in some other countries, the old Orders were declining in numbers and that thereafter the grand total of regulars stagnated and then began to fall.[27]

Portugal, of course, had no pretensions to dominate Europe or become the standard-bearer of the Counter-Reformation. In fact 'Portugal without Brazil was an insignificant Power.' Soon after the re-establishment of Portuguese

ILL. 19 General view of the palace-monastery of Mafra, Portugal, begun in 1717 and occupied from its consecration in 1730

independence from Spain in the second half of the seventeenth century, a rich source of gold was discovered in Brazil, bringing great wealth to fortunate elements in the nation including the king, who was entitled to a fifth of the value of all gold mined. As a result he had no need to call the Cortes (or Estates) after 1698 and behaved as an absolute ruler. It was king John V, who reigned from 1706 to 1750, who benefited most from this bonanza.[28] His most conspicuous extravagance was the vast palace-monastery of Mafra, built by a German architect, J.F. Ludwig, between 1717 and 1730 in a relatively chaste Baroque style, and intended to outdo the Escorial, if not the Vatican (Ill. 19). But this was not the only monastery on which he lavished some of his wealth: he also rebuilt in the costliest manner the nunnery church of the Mother of God in Lisbon.[29]

Partly as a result of this expenditure, John V was considered by Enlightened persons to be exceptionally bigoted. 'When he wanted a festival,' wrote Voltaire, barely exaggerating, 'he ordered a religious parade. When he wanted a new building, he built a convent, when he wanted a mistress, he took a nun.'[30] During his reign the Inquisition was still persecuting heretics, mostly 'New Catholics', and having them burned at the stake – between 1734 and 1743 a total of fifty-one.[31] In the view of contemporary travellers the Church and the Orders were unusually powerful and the people exceptionally superstitious.[32]

AT THE BRIM OF PROSPERITY

ILL. 20 Painting of Cistercian monks harvesting in the fields under the protection of the Virgin and St Bernard, in the abbey of Santa Maria de Alcobaça, Portugal

Unfortunately, Portuguese historical statistics seem to be peculiarly sparse and unreliable, at least where the Church is concerned. Respected historians accept improbable and ill-supported estimates of the Church's share of the land as a third of the whole country and of the number of regulars in 1765 as 42,200 in 493 convents. The latter figure is impossibly high, assuming as it does that the average population of a monastery was almost a hundred, but not so high as would be required by the belief of some contemporaries that the average was 250![33] We have a series of more or less plausible estimates of the total number of houses at different dates from the mid-seventeenth century to 1826, which range from 450 to 577. It is true that one or two monasteries are reliably credited with remarkably large populations: Mafra itself is said to have housed over three hundred Franciscans in its early days; Alcobaça, an enormously rich Cistercian abbey, had 110 monks around 1700 (Ill. 20).[34] But, when at last we have apparently convincing overall figures, based on official enquiries, for the total number of houses *and* inmates, for the admittedly very late date 1822, they state that there were 402 for men and 132 for women, containing respectively 5,061 and 2,980 professed regulars, that is, an average of 13 monks and 22 nuns per house.[35] In 1826 Cardinal Saraiva reckoned that there were a few more male houses and 44 more nunneries, bringing the total up to 577, and that the number of male inmates was around 7,000 and of female 6,000. It seems that he arrived at his higher figures by including recently founded Orders with limited resources, in which the government had taken little interest.[36] There cannot have been a great many more monasteries in 1750 than in 1822, because suppressions other than of the Jesuits were minimal between those dates; and it would be astonishing if the average number of inmates per house in the mid-eighteenth century was in reality more than, say, thirty. Even on this basis the total monastic population would have numbered not more than 20,000 and the ratio of regulars to the whole population would have been roughly 1 in 125, lower than in Spain – though more than double what it was in France, which, it will be remembered, seemed to travellers to be swarming with monks and nuns. I conclude that for the mid-eighteenth century a figure approaching 20,000 is plausible.

In Spain and Portugal it was not until the 1830s that a general suppression of monasteries was decreed. In the period covered by this book the major contribution of these countries to the assault on monasticism was their prominent role in the destruction of the Jesuits. This I shall describe in Chapter 6.

CHAPTER 5

ITALY

Italy ranks as the head and fount of European monasticism. It was in Italy that St Benedict founded in the sixth century communities at Subiaco and Cassino from which the Benedictine Order directly, and many other Orders indirectly, derive. Italy, too, was the land where in the thirteenth century St Francis founded at Assisi what developed into a large family of mendicant Orders, the various brands of Franciscans, which, taken together, still in the eighteenth century constituted the majority of all monks and nuns in Italy and in Europe. In Rome were situated the headquarters of the Church and a vast range of institutions central to the life of Catholic monasteries everywhere. Montesquieu wrote during his visit to Italy in 1728–9:

> On the roads of Italy you cannot turn your head without seeing a monk, and in the streets of towns without seeing a priest. All carriages, all boats are full of monks... Italy is the paradise of the monks. There is no Order that is not lax. The business that all the world's monks have in Rome makes the roads crowded.[1]

Absolutely, and also relatively to its population, Italy had many more monks and nuns even than Spain.

Unfortunately, Italian monasticism in the eighteenth century is especially difficult to study both because it has attracted relatively little critical work – though Owen Chadwick's *The Popes and European Revolution* is a glorious exception – and because the peninsula was politically fragmented. What is now the territory of Italy contained in 1750, as well as several minor states, seven major political units: the papal state straddling the whole centre of the peninsula; the republic of Venice in the north-east; in the north-west the republic of Genoa and also the kingdom of Sardinia, which comprised the island of Sardinia and the duchies of Savoy and Piedmont on the mainland; in the south the kingdom of the Two Sicilies, that is Naples and Sicily, ruled by king Charles, heir to the throne of Spain; the duchy of Milan or Lombardy, part of the Austrian Monarchy; and the grand duchy of Tuscany, governed separately by the emperor. Politically, the republics of Venice and Genoa, with their maritime empires and oligarchical constitutions, were strikingly different from all the others. Even more peculiar was the papal state, ruled absolutely by the pope with the assistance of clergy but with no participation by laymen. Naples and Sicily were much more closely associated with Spain, which had ruled them for two centuries before 1700, than with the rest of the peninsula. The subalpine kingdom of Sardinia, whose kings were warriors and whose inhabitants on the mainland spoke French rather than Italian, had little in common with any of the other states of Italy. Although Innocent X had had considerable success in the mid-seventeenth century in imposing his reform of the male monasteries on the Italian states, and the pope's continuing ecclesiastical influence in the peninsula made him the nearest approximation to a pan-Italian ruler, his authority had diminished by 1750 and continued to dwindle thereafter. In the second half of the eighteenth century he faced not only the coalition of Catholic Powers that forced him to abolish the Jesuits but also revolts against his interference by almost every other state in Italy. Venice had never been ready to bow to his authority; Naples was jealous of his ancient claims to suzerainty; the Habsburgs challenged his influence over such matters as the appointment of bishops and the reform of monasteries; and even the tiny duchy of Parma, once under direct papal control, defied Clement XIII in 1768 by expelling its Jesuits. So it is impossible to treat Italy as a unit comparable with France, Spain, Portugal, the Austrian Monarchy – or even Germany, to which the Empire gave at least a measure of national identity. Even the recruitment areas of Italian monasteries seem in this period to have been determined by these political divisions.[2]

All the same, Italian monasticism had certain common characteristics – or at least emphases – that distinguished it from that of other countries. In the first place, the exceptional antiquity of a good many Italian monasteries helped to ensure that their property was particularly extensive. And, although the Church had been well supplied with lands, buildings and personnel in the Middle Ages, it acquired more and more of them in the sixteenth, seventeenth and early eighteenth centuries. The Counter-Reformation was largely Italian in inspiration, the Baroque style in architecture was an Italian invention, and Italians adopted with enthusiasm both the movement and the style. Both secular and regular clergy were remarkably numerous, but monks easily outnumbered seculars. The best figures we have for monasteries come from Innocent X's enquiry of 1649–50 – the sole example of a pan-Italian survey in this period. It found that the country possessed more than 6,000 male monasteries and nearly 70,000 monks of major Orders (including lay brothers), of whom 60 per cent were Franciscans of some kind. Although on the strength of this enquiry the pope abolished more than a thousand small monasteries, it did not take long for the total of 6,000 to be reached again, and monks increased in numbers until about the middle of the eighteenth century. Boaga, who wrote a fine study of Innocent's enquiry, concluded:

The evolution of the Orders in the second half of the seventeenth and the beginning of the following century is marked by two phenomena: first of all, [there is] stagnation so far as the geographical distribution of the monasteries is concerned; the enormous thrust and power of expansion characteristic of the previous period seems in many cases completely nullified – as for example the Dominicans, the Carmelites (332 houses in around 1686 and 353 in 1765), the Capuchins (806 houses in 1650 and 802 in 1761) and the Servants of Mary. The second phenomenon is the significant growth in numbers of monks in some Orders while others display the opposite tendency. Some examples: the Capuchins who in 1765 have almost 4000 more friars compared with 1650 [when they numbered nearly 11,000], and the Jesuits who in 1710 are 3395 as against 2677 in 1650. The same situation emerges from the statistics for the Observant and Reformed Franciscans. But the 4249 Carmelite monks of 1650 slip to 3780 around 1686, and the 6240 Dominicans of 1650 fall to 5873 in 1700.[3]

Overall, largely because of the Franciscan contribution, these figures imply a substantial increase in numbers of monks between 1650 and 1750, though perhaps not enough to match the rise of the population as a whole in the later decades of the period. But even if there were still only 70,000 monks in the latter year, that figure would still represent about 1 in 210 of all Italians. However, the enquiry of 1650 showed that in the north the density of monks was much lower than in the papal state and the kingdom of the Two Sicilies. More than 60 per cent of all monks were to be found in these two states, though they contained less than half the population of Italy. This discrepancy still existed in the late eighteenth century.[4]

In addition to the growth of old Orders, new Orders were founded and one, the Scolopi or Piarists, refounded. To take first the Scolopi, they had been originally created in 1597 by a Spanish priest living in Rome, José Calasanz, solely to educate children, particularly poor children, in *scuole pie*, that is religious schools. They were recognised as a religious Order with solemn vows in 1621. Their main work was in what we call primary education, but they soon became involved at the secondary level, where of course they competed with the Jesuits. Having shown a particular interest in natural sciences, they incurred the displeasure of pope and Inquisition by their admiration and sympathy for Galileo. For this and other reasons the Order was suppressed by Innocent X in 1646. But it was revived by Clement IX in 1669 and expanded notably during the eighteenth century.[5] Few new Orders for men were founded anywhere in the eighteenth century, but the two most important were Italian: the Passionists, associated especially with the cult of the Sacred Heart, provisionally approved by Benedict XIV in 1741, and the Redemptorists, rural missioners first and foremost, authorised in 1749.[6]

Innocent's survey did not deal with nuns, and there is no comparably full evidence for secular clergy either. But local figures confirm the conclusion that Italy, especially its cities, had a quite exceptional number of clergy of all types. In 1630 the town of Lecce in the kingdom of Naples had a population of 10,000, divided into only four parishes; but, according to good authority, its seventeen male monasteries housed 480 inmates and its eight nunneries 593, that is, more than 10 per cent of the inhabitants were regulars. On a larger scale Naples, the most populous Italian city by far, had rather more than 200,000 inhabitants around 1580, including 1,995 monks in 68 monasteries and 1,774 nuns in 22 nunneries. In 1781, when it had reached a population of 376,000, it contained more than 100 male monasteries, nearly 100 female communities, 4,617 monks and 5,871 nuns. Not only had the absolute numbers grown enormously, but the proportion of regulars to the whole population had also risen, from the already exceptional figure of 1 in 53 to almost 1 in 36.[7] In a number of cities more than 10 per cent of adult females were nuns; as already mentioned Florence in the mid-seventeenth century actually contained more nuns than married women.[8] Secular clergy increased too. In the Naples of around 1580 the 3,769 regulars were apparently matched by only 1,000 seculars. By 1706 there were 337,000 inhabitants and 3,849 secular priests, that is, the population had grown by nearly 70 per cent and the number of secular priests by almost 300 per cent, so that there was now a secular priest to every 88 inhabitants. But the figure of secular priests given for Naples in 1781, only 3,332, means that they were still heavily outnumbered by monks, not to mention nuns.

In the very special case of Rome the proportion of secular priests to population had risen from 1 to 81 in 1592 to 1 to 55 in 1760, while in the latter year the proportion of monks (in nearly 120 monasteries) had reached 1 in 40 and of nuns (in 53 houses) 1 in 80, adding up to an overall ratio of clergy to population of more than 1 in 20. According to another set of statistics, around 1700 7 per cent of the Roman population were clergy of some kind, and the figure remained above 6 per cent until after 1770, although the city's population was by then growing fairly fast.

Although these examples were naturally among the most spectacular, they reflect the general upward trend throughout the peninsula, with the seculars usually growing more rapidly than the regulars, especially in the previously less well-supplied north of the country, but not equalling them. Hanns Gross has suggested in his book *Rome in the Age of Enlightenment* that 6–7 per cent is a rather low proportion of clergy to find among the population of the capital of Catholicism. This looks a rather strange judgment when it is remembered, for example, that the cities of Rome and Naples, taken together, boasted far more clergy than the entire establishment of the eighteenth-century Church of England. Rome by itself contained approximately the same number of clergy in the eighteenth century as the Church of England possesses in total at the beginning of the twenty-first, and Naples had a third as many again.[9]

Looking now at whole states, in the mid-eighteenth century the Venetian empire is credited with more than 46,000 ecclesiastics for nearly 2.7 million inhabitants; Lombardy had more than 14,000, the small state of Modena nearly 7,000 and the still smaller republic of Lucca apparently 15,000, that is more than 1 in 10 of the population.[10] So Italy possessed both the densest monastic network and the highest proportion of regulars found in any large country; and, apart perhaps from France, with its unique wealth of female congregations, the greatest concentration of nuns. It seems probable that around 1750 approaching 1 in 100 of the peninsula's 15,000,000 inhabitants was a monk or nun. If secular clergy are taken into account, something like 1 in 75 of the population must have been an ecclesiastic of some sort. I know of no reliable figure for the total number of nunneries in all the Italian states, but it must at least have come near to the figure for male houses. Let us suppose, or guess, that there were 3,000 nunneries altogether, which seems certain to be an underestimate. On this basis Italy had altogether more than four times as many monasteries as the entire Austrian Monarchy and significantly more than France, though both these states had substantially larger populations. It seems almost incredible that the discrepancy should be so great, but the evidence proclaims that Italy contained *roughly fifteen* times as many houses as Catholic Germany. Statistically it cannot be doubted that Italy was by far the most priest- and monk-ridden of the countries of Europe (Ill. 27).

As always, to find reliable figures for the monasteries' ownership of property presents great difficulties. For the Italian Church as a whole, it is accepted that its wealth was 'much greater than that of the French clergy' and, as elsewhere, it seems that the monasteries accounted for at least half of it. Where detailed research has proved possible, the percentage of land owned by the Church has turned out to be less than tradition alleged. But in the kingdom of Naples it seems that about 10 per cent of land was monastic, in the papal state the proportion must surely have been as high, and only in the north was it significantly lower. In individual towns larger percentages are recorded: in Bologna, for instance, seventy-six monastic houses owned a quarter of the area of the city; and the four great abbeys of Ravenna, which included the gorgeous, uniquely ancient Byzantine house of S. Apollinare, had 34 per cent of the city's land in 1731. If historians have not found it easy to determine the global value of monastic lands, they are confident that, as a result of continuing benefactions, favourable economic circumstances and reasonably good management, the proportion of land owned by monasteries grew substantially between the sixteenth and the eighteenth centuries. The most striking piece of evidence produced for this conclusion is that in every Italian state between 1500 and 1700 church revenues increased by an annual average of between 5 per cent and 10 per cent, providing a huge sum from which both the papacy and efficient secular governments could exact ever growing taxes.[11]

In Owen Chadwick's words,

The life of an Italian country-town had an *ecclesiastical* atmosphere – cassocks everywhere, processions in streets, bells frequent, crowds at services, priests not highly respected for their priesthood (too numerous for that) . . . No child could escape the stamp of liturgical experience. It was part of the social order; at times it was the social order; at times it was too much of a social order.[12]

Monks often played a larger part in this scenario than ordinary secular clergy, first because only a small proportion of the latter were parish priests, most of them being private chaplains, priests supported by an endowment to say Masses for the souls of particular dead or what might be called free-lance priests, and secondly because male regulars of many Orders were customarily conceded pastoral and parochial roles. Despite the emphasis of the Catholic reformers of the sixteenth and seventeenth centuries on the centrality of parish worship and the need for good parish priests, religious institutions that cut across the parish – especially brotherhoods or confraternities in great variety – multiplied, and

the penetration of regulars into secular institutions was so widespread and their presence among the people so ubiquitous as to make it impossible to marginalize them and also to render projected reforms unattainable without relying on their collaboration. Centuries of neglect of the cure of souls by clergy and parish priests had finally transferred huge numbers of Christian people and entire areas of pastoral ministry – such as preaching and to a large extent also confession— to the religious Orders, especially the Franciscans and Dominicans.[13]

Significant proportions of parishes, in some places a third, were under the control of monks or nuns. Although many dioceses set up the seminaries required by the Council of Trent, others did not; and those that were established in small and poor bishoprics were ineffective in raising the level of the parochial clergy. In any case monks usually ran them. It was the monks and nuns who were active in education and, to a lesser extent, in charity. A fifth or more of bishops, and several popes, were drawn from their ranks.[14] On the other hand, rather paradoxically, the governments of the Italian states, other than the papal, were emphatically lay, and the clergy were not active in Estates because such bodies had virtually ceased to exist in the peninsula.

Despite much more or less good-natured and well-justified scoffing at their greed, idleness and laxity, monks and nuns seem 'to have enjoyed a broad and established popularity',[15] and to have retained social respect far later than their brethren and sisters in France. The ideal of the good parish priest as the true embodiment of the Church, so generally accepted in early eighteenth-century France, seems not to have won general favour in Italy until after the middle of the century and, when it did, owed much to the propaganda and example of S. Alfonso de' Liguori and his followers who, ironically, in order to spread their message, formed the new Redemptorist Order of missionary monks.[16]

Social structures and constraints had much to do with this state of affairs. As in France, the *commende* appears to have flourished to the mutual advantage of the ruler and his nobles, including the pope and his cardinals, while threatening the integrity of the monasteries subjected to it.[17] The further south one went in Italy, broadly speaking, the more 'feudal' society seemed. Everyone knew that, in order to keep their estates intact, wealthy Italians pursued more ruthlessly than was usual elsewhere the policy of committing their surplus male and female children to celibacy and the Church. The 'dowry' required by a nunnery for a nun, though substantial, was much lower than the likely dowry of a bride. This was the Liberal Carlo Cattaneo's explanation, written in 1844, with reference to Lombardy: 'Girls were condemned at birth to irrevocable vows, to minister to the pride of first-born males.'[18] An episcopal report blamed the grandeur of nunneries' buildings on the pride of the inmates' families. In some houses a cell was passed down from generation to generation of the same noble family.

Despite the imposition of stricter seclusion by the pope in 1566, contacts between nuns and outsiders were in many houses regular and frequent. Most

ILL. 21 Pietro Longhi, *The Convent Visit*, showing the parlour of a Venetian nunnery

nunneries were sufficiently lax to enable relatives to see the inmates often and to converse with them through grills or in their parlours (Ill. 21). Many nuns, like monks, were allowed annual holidays when they could go and stay with their families.[19] Although there were strictly observant houses, at the other end of the scale there were nunneries where flirting was easy and scandal not uncommon. In towns no nunnery was likely to be far away from a male monastery, and permitted relations between the nuns and monks could be astonishingly close. Mary Laven has described what went on at the nunnery of San Servolo in Venice in 1571:

The friars [of San Antonio and San Salvador] came to San Servolo in search of entertainment and sociability. The nuns provided them with meals – sufficiently grand to be described as 'banquets' – and, after dinner, male and female religious played cards and dice together. They played for money, and by all accounts the nuns tended to win. At any rate, it was rumoured that Don Fedrigo, the prior of San Antonio, had lost his community some 800 ducats in the course of these evenings of recreation. During carnival, as was customary in Venetian convents, the nuns put on theatrical shows; the friars sometimes stayed at San Servolo all night to watch the nuns perform. Such events were the highlights . . . but the relationships between female and male religious continued at a more prosaic level throughout the year. The nuns took in the washing of the friars, and they did their mending for them. Within the convent there were *converse*, lower-status nuns who were admitted to do the menial tasks for the rest of the community, and who were sometimes given greater freedom to leave the enclosure; these took food parcels of biscuits and fresh eggs to the friars at San Antonio and San Salvador. The friars sent back covered baskets with concealed reciprocal gifts.[20]

Intense relationships developed between friars and nuns, described as 'spiritual daughters'; a ring might be sent to signify 'betrothal', a sonnet written, a portrait commissioned and 'marriage' be spoken of – all, apparently, platonic. If this sort of thing could go on five years after the pope's notorious decree, which the Venetian state was anxious to enforce, how much more must have been tolerated two centuries later!

'Conservatories', a peculiarly Italian brand of community which imposed only limited discipline, became a fashionable milieu for educating the young, especially girls, who were destined for marriage if possible, or for the cloister if not: Naples in 1781 contained no fewer than forty-four 'conservatories and retreats for women'. Some of these institutions paid special attention to musical training, and in this country of opera and opera houses – and oratorio, which Oratorian monks had virtually invented – many an opera singer began his or her life in a conservatory or similar quasi-monastic 'hospital' or orphanage; and some of them made it their permanent base or returned to it when their theatrical careers were over. Vivaldi spent productive years teaching in such an 'ospedale' in Venice, and Pergolesi, the product of a Neapolitan conservatory, wrote his *Stabat mater*, the musical work most widely printed in eighteenth-century Europe, in the Franciscan house at Pozzuolo, where he was being looked after in his final illness.[21]

Like other Catholic countries, Italy possessed many splendid monasteries and nunneries that had been deliberately founded in remote places, of which some of the most famous are Montecassino on its hill in the kingdom of Naples; Subiaco, near Tivoli, in the papal state; and Vallombrosa, Camaldoli and Monte Oliveto Maggiore in Tuscany. Subiaco still in the eighteenth century had its two historic houses of S. Scolastico and the Sacro Speco, and only lost its virtual independence within the papal state in 1754.[22] Camaldoli deserves special mention as the chief house of an Order founded in the eleventh century which offers both facilities for hermits and the usual opportunities of the communal life. From the start it had a hospital open to all comers, and it retains a splendid pharmacy dating back to the fifteenth century, one of the best examples of a public service that was provided by many monasteries across Europe.

The Franciscans and Dominicans, however, had originally focussed their attentions on the towns and, although these Orders were diversifying in our period, they remained essentially urban; while older Orders like the Benedictines had by now established themselves in towns.²³ It seems that Pope Pius V, in imposing stricter enclosure on nunneries, propelled them into towns for supervision and security. So Italian monasteries, more than elsewhere except perhaps in Spain, had come by the eighteenth century to be heavily concentrated in or on the edge of towns, at a time when rural population was growing faster than urban. Complaints grew that the cities of Italy were becoming ever more crowded with ever more numerous and spacious monasteries.²⁴

Although by the eighteenth century many nuns had succeeded in escaping the constrictions that Pius V had imposed, and had set about extending their buildings in order to improve their amenities, this development only made matters worse for city governments. In Naples the nuns were so little in awe of the lay authorities that in a few cases they actually seized by force the property of neighbouring male houses which they alleged stood in the way of their work or comfort.²⁵ The aristocratic Clarissan nuns of Santa Chiara in the same city claimed to need their five cloisters, three of them strictly enclosed, the fourth for the Franciscan monks who ministered to them, and the fifth ravishingly rebuilt in 1739–42, furnished with pergolas and fountains and charmingly decorated with maiolica tiles illustrating daily life, carnivals, music and dance, ships and landscapes (Plate 8). This was a place not for prayer and meditation but for diversion and conversation with outsiders – king Charles III is supposed to have dubbed it 'the coffee-house of Europe'. Such a level of luxury was rare, but in many towns as well as Naples the ubiquitous presence of these privileged institutions with their extensive buildings made any kind of secular civic improvement almost impossible.²⁶

Monastic building took place on a huge scale in old as well as new institutions, but its chronology differs from that of France or Germany. Although there were conspicuous signs of monastic decay in the old Orders during the late fifteenth and early sixteenth centuries, they built much during the Renaissance, as did the still flourishing mendicants. Indeed, two well-known facts suggest that there is a tale to be told about the role of monasteries in the Renaissance itself. It was at Subiaco that books were first printed in Italy. And Fra Angelico, acknowledged as one of the major figures in the development of Italian painting of the Quattrocento, was abbot of the Dominican monastery of San Marco in Florence, where he saw to it that each cell was provided with a fine religious picture painted by himself or his underlings. Monasteries constantly appear in the standard literature as places for which artists painted their great masterpieces, but as though the impulse came entirely from outside. This can hardly be the whole truth.²⁷

ILL. 22 The great cloister of the Carthusian abbey of San Martino, Naples, 1623–56

Italy experienced no Reformation or religious wars such as emptied and destroyed monasteries elsewhere. But the Counter-Reformation led to new liturgical requirements and therefore to partial reconstructions of old houses; and new Baroque monasteries were built in hundreds, though mainly on restricted sites in towns and mainly in the seventeenth century. For all these reasons the eighteenth century ranks as a less notable period for monastic building in Italy than it was in the German lands. But churches and cloisters were rebuilt by many houses, including some of the greatest, Montecassino, Camaldoli and the charterhouse of San Martino in Naples (Ill. 22). Two major individual works deserve special mention. First, Superga, a spectacular almost neo-classical work by Filippo Juvara, overlooking Turin from the nearby hills, was built *de novo* for king Victor Amadeus II of Sardinia between 1717 and 1731 as a royal mausoleum to be guarded by a newly created body of monks. The king established it in fulfilment of a vow he had made when with prince Eugene he was planning to raise the French siege of the city during the War of the Spanish Succession (Ill. 23). Secondly, the unquestionably neo-classical cathedral of Subiaco was built for the

ILL. 23 The basilica of Superga, near Turin, built by Filippo Juvara, 1717–31: painting, school of Pannini

ILL. 24 Nave interior of the neo-classical cathedral of Subiaco, Italy, built by Giacomo Quarenghi, 1769–73

bigger of Subiaco's monasteries between 1769 and 1773 by Giacomo Quarenghi, soon to exploit even more splendid opportunities at the court of Catherine the Great (Ill. 24).[28] Additionally, earthquakes and eruptions led to a large-scale reconstruction of some towns in the far south, of which the most famous case was Lecce, especially its Celestine monastery, after the earthquake of 1693. The same earthquake affected much of Sicily, where the aristocratic Benedictine house of Catania, afflicted also by an eruption of Mount Etna, was rebuilt on a massive scale, with a large library, a museum and a grand organ whose capabilities were admired by Goethe.[29]

As in other Catholic countries, many monastic libraries grew, and many monks pursued learning, including some who made significant contributions to mathematics and natural sciences. Muratori, himself a secular priest, depended on monastic collaborators in his great enterprise of publishing the documents of medieval Italian history. The first modern alphabetic encyclopaedia, the *Biblioteca Universale Sacro-Profana*, was published in 1701 by a reforming general of the

Conventual Franciscans, Vincenzo Coronelli.[30] Among learned monks no one had greater fame than the Franciscan Padre Martini (1706–84), a pioneer musical historian, the Italian equivalent of Burney for England and Gerbert for Germany.[31] The Camaldolese Order was especially respected for its scholarly achievement and for its readiness to accept able novices from families too poor to provide the usual subvention. Isidoro Bianchi, one of its monks, belonged to the circle that published the progressive Milanese periodical, Il Caffè, in 1764–6, won a considerable reputation as a writer and educationist, defended Freemasonry, travelled abroad and hobnobbed with *philosophes*. It comes as no surprise that the Inquisition wished to arrest him, and that he eventually tried to leave his Order, but by keeping out of the papal state and under the patronage of the duke of Modena he preserved his liberty.[32]

In Italy, as in most of Catholic Europe, there were signs that both the fervour and the appeal of monasticism were diminishing already in the early eighteenth century. The proportion of boys and girls from noble families entering monasteries declined significantly: among the Milanese patriciate, for example, 30 per cent of children had gone into the Church between 1600 and 1650, whereas between 1700 and 1749 the proportion was only 12 per cent.[33] But it was not until the 1760s that the institution began to suffer seriously both from internal decay and external assault. This phase will be described in Part II of this book.

PART II

PATTERNS OF MONASTIC REFORM

CHAPTER 6

THE SUPPRESSION OF THE JESUITS

INTRODUCTION

The 1740s and 1750s felt the first shocks of the mental and political earthquake that was to rock the Catholic Church, and particularly monasticism, to its foundations. Quite suddenly, the Church found itself on the defensive in most of the lands that till then had seemed securely in the grip of the Counter-Reformation. The Enlightenment now began to gain wider support in Catholic countries, in most of which traditional monasticism entered upon a period of accelerating decline.[1]

Among the more conspicuous illustrations of the change of mood are architectural developments. As already mentioned, at her accession in 1740 Maria Theresa stopped work on the palace her father had begun to build, which was to incorporate the monastery of Klosterneuburg.[2] John V of Portugal had carried to completion the construction of a still vaster new palace-monastery at Mafra, but his successor, Joseph I, when he came to the throne in 1750, more or less abandoned it – to the monks.[3] More generally, the style of church architecture moved away from the grandiose, demonstrative, aspiring, colourful, figurative, populist, all-embracing Baroque, first to the lighter, more frivolous, less assertive Rococo and then, more dramatically, to the chaste, scholarly, introverted, whitewashed neo-classical of which the new Ste-Geneviève in Paris was the epitome.[4] This revolution in style was associated with a fundamental shift towards a more individualistic, private, quasi-Protestant theology and piety – though it would be absurd to suggest that the religious development was anything like as clear-cut or rapid as the architectural.[5]

143

During the 1740s the French government became more sympathetic to anticlerical views, partly because of political and personal accidents: France was allied with Voltaire's friend, the agnostic Frederick II of Prussia, in the War of the Austrian Succession; cardinal Fleury died in 1743; and the debts incurred during the war could only be met by increased taxation. In this mood the government lent support to the plan to publish a new, large-scale *Encyclopédie*; it made use of Voltaire as unofficial diplomat and appointed him historiographer royal; and in 1749–50 Louis XV launched his abortive campaign against the tax immunities of the clergy.[6]

By 1750 the number of vocations for monasteries of the old Orders was evidently declining in France and in some other countries. Newer Orders, even the Capuchins, were either scarcely growing or actually stagnating.[7] Soon afterwards, in the sixties or seventies, the pattern of bequests in Catholics' wills began to change. Fewer Masses were endowed, and among them fewer were founded in monastic churches than hitherto.[8] From around 1750 the rulers of Catholic states began to vie with each other in introducing reforms which were regarded as enlightened, most of them affecting religion, such as restricting donations of property to the Church, curbing its legal privileges, challenging the claims of the papacy to control their churches, expelling the Jesuits and imposing limitations on other Orders, reducing the Church's control of education and the press, establishing a measure of religious toleration and even interfering with the liturgy.[9]

If the impact of 'the crisis of the European consciousness' had been remarkably limited in Catholic countries down to the mid-century, it became palpable thereafter especially of course in France. The point is easily made by describing some of the landmark books published in these years which manifestly had a broad influence from the moment of their publication. In 1748 Montesquieu brought out *De l'esprit des lois*. The title is best translated *The Spirit of Laws*, to convey that it was the nature of law in general that he was concerned with. His approach was seen as revolutionary and subversive, since he treated law not as essentially a body of commands, either from God or ruler, but as a set of norms generated by society, and saw the variations in laws and constitutions between states as corresponding to variations of climate and geography across the globe. The work immediately established itself as one of those books that every educated man had to know about. Within a year it was being cited in the British parliament, and within three years was available to the Hungarian Diet. Its defence of limited monarchy, as distinct from despotism, became the starting-point of much political discussion in France.[10]

In 1750 appeared the prospectus of the French *Encyclopédie*, written by the radical mathematician, Jean d'Alembert, glorifying the advances of natural science and promising to provide a universal account of useful knowledge. In the following year the great compilation itself began to be published, with another radical, Denis Diderot, as its principal editor. Altogether, by the time the text was completed in 1765, nearly three hundred writers had contributed to it. About thirty of them were clergymen of some sort, mostly Catholics, though none of them was a monk.[11] But many of the 72,000 articles – and those that attracted most attention – were critical of authority, especially that of the Roman Catholic Church, with its pope claiming infallibility, its dubious saints and their implausible miracles and relics. The work trumpeted the achievements of science and technology and amounted to a vindication of lay expertise and secular attitudes against the pretensions of the learned clergy, which meant particularly the Jesuits. From the start more than four thousand persons took out subscriptions to the project, a huge number for such a costly enterprise at a time when even best-sellers were printed in editions of less than a thousand. Despite the fact that after the appearance of the second volume in 1752 the project was briefly banned, the first seven volumes had appeared by 1757, and the remaining ten volumes of text came out in 1765. The *Encyclopédie* was a repository of knowledge as comprehensive as its only competitor in scale, the German *Lexikon* of Zedler, and infinitely more lively: it remains the most opinionated and entertaining encyclopaedia ever produced. It was written in the language generally used by the European elite, and it was sumptuously illustrated by eleven additional volumes of magnificent prints. By 1789 25,000 copies had been sold of the successive editions, just over half outside France; and it can hardly be doubted that it had immense influence in an anticlerical direction.[12]

While it was appearing, several other notable French writings made a sensation across the Continent. In 1750 and 1754 Jean-Jacques Rousseau, a contributor to the *Encyclopédie*, published two *Discourses*, the first denouncing fashionable views of scientific and artistic progress, the second social inequality. Rousseau's views were rejected by most encyclopaedists, but they entered into the common currency of Enlightened debate. Since his premises were as secular and untheological as those of Diderot and D'Alembert, they proved equally objectionable to the Church. Voltaire's *Essay on Manners* of 1756 represented a new brand of history, trying to identify long-term secular causes and scoffing at religious interpretations. In his *Candide* of 1759 he attacked not only optimistic philosophers but also the desperate attempts of clergy to explain how an omniscient and beneficent God could permit a catastrophe such as the Lisbon earthquake of four years before. Helvétius's apparently atheistical *De l'esprit*, which appeared in 1758, 'brought together', according to the Sorbonne, 'all the brands of poison spread by modern writings'.[13] In two novels that achieved enormous sales, *La nouvelle Héloïse* of 1761 and *Emile* of 1762, and in the *Contrat social*, also of 1762, Rousseau celebrated love outside marriage, education uninfluenced by clergy and popular democracy. Although the French Church and the papacy condemned all these works with uncharacteristic alacrity, there was no stopping their publication or dissemination. Between 1762 and 1766 the anticlerical campaign intensified: the Jesuits were expelled from France, the bulk of the *Encyclopédie* was published and Voltaire's crusade against what he and Frederick the Great called the *infâme* – the malign influence of the Church – was successful in obtaining the posthumous rehabilitation of the Protestant Jean Calas, unjustly condemned to death at Toulouse in 1762 for murdering his son, a convert to Catholicism. All these incidents aroused passionate interest throughout Europe. In Catholic countries a wider intellectual rift was opening up than at any time since the Reformation between the official attitudes of the hierarchy and those of the more advanced lay elites.[14]

It is tempting to see the shift in the style of piety and the growing acceptance of Enlightenment ideas as coalescing into one profound and overwhelming movement which transformed society and inspired the measures taken by governments against the Church. This view has had many supporters at the time and since, chiefly among the more radical promoters of Enlightenment and the more extreme conservatives. But it requires only a little study and reflection to see that such a picture is false. In the first place, Catholicism was still making significant gains: we have seen that pilgrimages were attracting ever more participants, and that brotherhoods continued to multiply and expand after as well as before 1750. Secondly, though so many of the more affluent and better-educated lay men and women supported at least moderate reform, chronology and the detailed history of its enactment make it impossible to accept that its inspiration generally came from below. It was often rulers, government officials and even higher clergy who took the initiative. In fact governments in both Catholic and Protestant countries constantly complained down to the late eighties that their secular and religious reforms met with stubborn opposition from ordinary people.[15] Thirdly, even among the top people, especially outside France, a generalised Catholic Enlightenment was much more widespread than the full-blown anticlericalism and scepticism of the more radical French *philosophes*. As has been shown already in discussion of the Jansenists and of the ideas of Muratori, many proponents of reform advocated it as loyal Catholics – clergy as well as laymen – because they thought it in the best interests of the Church and in accordance with its true doctrine. Such reformers commonly abominated the religious attitudes of Voltaire, Diderot and their sympathisers.[16]

Perhaps the greatest stumbling-block of all in the way of arguing for a simple explanation for the decline of the Church and of monasticism is the story of the suppression of the Jesuits, finally decreed by pope Clement XIV in 1773. This was a truly momentous event, the dissolution of the very Order that alone took a special vow of obedience to the papacy and had notoriously supplied 'the shock-troops of the Counter-Reformation', the Order that imposed the strictest tests on entrants, required of its novices a longer and more rigorous training than any other and by common consent included among its members a high proportion of the ablest scholars, the best teachers, the most subtle confessors and the most persuasive missioners in the Church. In 1750 it was still riding high, with its more than 22,000 members (world-wide) dominating university and secondary education in almost every Catholic country and its royal confessors entrenched at almost every Catholic Court. No one could dispute that it numbered among its members some of the leading philosophers of the age. To mention just one of the most distinguished, Rudjer Boskovic, born in Dubrovnik, became internationally known as mathematician and astronomer as well as diplomat and administrator and, among many honours from several countries, was made a Fellow of the Royal Society.[17] The Jesuits' astonishingly rapid downfall, one of the most remarkable reversals in history, deserves a greater book than any that has yet been written about it.[18] Here it certainly cannot be treated fully, but such a portentous incident in the history of monasticism must be discussed. What will emerge is that the outcome was related only in complex and sometimes perverse ways to any European social movement, to the Enlightenment, to Jansenism, or even to the general decline of monasticism.

The Jesuits had always evoked extreme reactions, from unalloyed admiration to bitter hostility. The total number of their members in Europe was less than 20,000, less than that of the Capuchins and no more than a tenth of all monks. But unlike the old Orders the Society was activist in principle and, unlike the mendicant and other Orders which were socially activist but only at a local level, it was under strong central direction, had an agenda for the Church as a whole and paid particular attention to cultivating the political and social elites. Its success in seizing control of university and secondary education, in influencing Rome and other Courts, and in missionary activity within and outside Europe had been largely due to the calibre of its members, the thoroughness of their training and the effectiveness of its organisation, but it had inevitably aroused not only the hostility of critical laymen but also intense jealousy among monks of other Orders and the secular clergy. Its members' vow of obedience to the pope and their strict subordination to their general had always made lay rulers doubt their loyalty. There was a sinister air to its cult of secrecy, as for example in the mysterious elite brotherhood it had founded, the Aa.[19] Contrariwise, its royal confessors were suspected of breaching their trust in order to serve the interests of the Society or the papacy.[20] It was believed to exercise undue pressure on dying testators to bequeath property to the Society or the Church, and by this and other means was supposed to have become fabulously rich. In achieving its ends it was commonly supposed to practise poisoning.[21] Some of its real or alleged theological positions had aroused strong opposition. Parts of the work of one of its foremost theologians, Hermann Busenbaum, had been condemned by the papacy – and, to be fair, by some members of the Society itself – for putting forward, among other objectionable positions, the view that the assassination of tyrants might be justified. The Jansenists were only the most prominent of those who considered Jesuit confessors, with the authority of the Order, too ready to grant absolution on dubious grounds, especially to those who possessed power and wealth.[22] These charges against the Jesuits, which were lent credence by several well-known forged documents, help to explain why they had never been allowed into a devoutly Catholic state such as Salzburg and were excluded on and off from many others, especially Venice. In 1729 they were expelled from the universities and schools of the unprogressive kingdom of Sardinia.[23] In their successful missionary work in China the Jesuits had allowed ancient rites of ancestor-worship to be subsumed into Catholic ritual – a practice eventually condemned by the papacy in 1715, with the result that Christianity virtually died out there. It was they, together with Louis XIV, who had extracted the bull *Unigenitus* from pope Clement XI, thereby provoking anguished dissent within the Church, weakening its theological and moral position and justifying a disagreeable persecution of otherwise pious and blameless Catholics. Pope Benedict XIV was rather lukewarm in their support and there was a powerful anti-Jesuit minority among the cardinals.[24] Yet, despite all this, the extraordinary power and influence achieved by the Jesuits in the seventeenth century were still virtually intact in 1750 – in fact their position seemed stronger than ever in at least three respects, first because the number of their members and colleges was still growing, secondly through the enforcement of *Unigenitus* and thirdly, as we shall see, through the political and economic importance they had attained in the South American colonies of Spain and Portugal.

THE PORTUGUESE INITIATIVE

If the movement for the suppression of the Society had been straightforwardly due to the influence of new trends in theology and piety and to the impact of the Enlightenment and Jansenism, it would surely have begun in the country most influenced by these tendencies, France. But in the event the effective assault on the Society began in Portugal, a country which seemed to outsiders one of the most obscurantist in all Europe, overrun with priests, monks and nuns.[25] As in Catholic Europe generally, the Jesuits supplied confessors for most members of the royal family, though not, after 1712, the king himself; and they had a near-monopoly of higher and secondary education, tempered by the favour he showed to Oratorians towards the end of his reign.[26] When, in 1749–50, he became incapable and failed to replace principal ministers who had died or were dying, the conduct of public affairs was effectively left in the hands of two monks, his Recollect confessor and a Jesuit.[27]

At this point it becomes impossible to confine the story to the Continent of Europe. What went on in Portugal's vast, gold-rich colony of 'Brazil', which until 1750 covered an ill-defined area larger even than that of the modern state, was naturally of paramount importance to the Portuguese government, and here the Jesuits had a pre-eminent role. During the process of colonial expansion under the aegis of the Counter-Reformation Church, they had taken the major part in missionary activity in both the Spanish and Portuguese empires from the middle of the sixteenth century. In South America they had been very successful in converting the Indians, whose traditions and communities they protected from other settlers and from the slavery on which the sugar and tobacco crops depended. There being no effective lay authority, the Jesuits had created what were virtually independent states covering very large areas of the Continent and yielding immense profits. Of these 'states' the largest and most notorious was known as Paraguay. When disputes arose in the early eighteenth century between Spain and Portugal about the boundaries of their South American territories, the status of the Jesuits was inevitably called into question. By the treaty of Madrid of 1750 between the two Powers the borders of Brazil were defined and some of the Jesuit missions in Paraguay that had formerly owed allegiance to Spain were transferred to Portugal, requiring some Indians, despite protests from the monks, to migrate hundreds of miles in appalling conditions.[28]

When Joseph I became king in 1750 it was generally felt that the position of Portugal, both domestically and internationally, had deteriorated and that reforms were urgently needed. With this in mind, and in order to save himself the trouble of ruling, Joseph appointed as his chief minister the man who is known to history by a title he was given in 1770, the marquis of Pombal, previously his country's envoy in London and Vienna. In England he had been initiated as a Freemason and elected a Fellow of the Royal Society, an honour it did not accord even to the minister of a foreign Power unless he showed some intellectual capacity and openness. In Austria he had become a friend of Gerard van Swieten, Maria Theresa's progressive physician, and had watched with admiration her centralising reforms of 1748–9 which curbed the independence of the provincial Estates.[29]

Pombal was convinced that 'the power and wealth of all countries consists principally in the number and multiplication of the people that inhabit it'.[30] He believed that the population of Brazil was too low, and so he decreed that slaves must be shipped in from Portugal's African territories to augment the workforce. The Indians must be freed from Jesuit protection, which kept them in ignorance, idleness and superstition, and Portuguese and Indians must be encouraged to intermarry and breed. In June 1755 a monopolistic state company was created to take over the Jesuit estates. Exasperated by the pursuit of these policies, and by the terms of the Spanish–Portuguese agreement, some of the Jesuit Indian missions took up arms against the government.[31]

In the middle of the war against the Jesuits, on 1 November 1755, All Saints Day, while many of the faithful were at church, an earthquake followed by a tidal wave destroyed the old city of Lisbon, killing at least 10,000 people. The earthquake was the subject of intense debate. Traditionalists saw it as divine retribution – but for what? There were those who claimed that God was indicating his disapproval of Pombal. By contrast, the Methodist preacher, George Whitefield, had visited Lisbon in the previous year and published an appalled account of 'the Blasphemy and Idolatry of Popery' he had witnessed there during Passion Week and Holy Week. He regarded the earthquake as God's revenge on these works of Antichrist. A third approach was favoured by an English nun, Sister Catherine Witham of the Bridgettine house in Lisbon, who was thankful to God that the earthquake had not occurred at night or during the nunnery's High Mass.[32] Pombal, FRS, insisted that it was just a natural calamity and with consummate skill turned it to his advantage. He persuaded the king that the city should be rebuilt on the same site, with appropriate precautions, according to a rational plan and in an elegant style, and forced the work through against all difficulties. The earthquake and the war with the Jesuit missions had created an atmosphere of crisis in which desperate measures seemed necessary, and the king now accorded Pombal virtually despotic powers. Hitherto he had shown no particular interest in church reform, but after the earthquake many new churches had to be built, and the government, with papal approval, set up an enquiry into monastic wealth and behaviour. Rome and its representative in Portugal accepted that there were too many monks in the country and that their conduct was sometimes scandalous.³³ Soon this general enquiry was eclipsed by an assault on the Jesuits. A joint Spanish–Portuguese force smashed the resistance of their missions early in 1756, but by bearing arms against the king they had apparently substantiated some of the most damaging charges that had regularly been brought against the Society since its foundation. Pombal made sure that these enormities were known throughout Europe by writing, publishing and widely circulating a slanted *Brief Account of the Republic that the Jesuit Monks of the Portuguese and Spanish Provinces Established in the Overseas Dominions of the Two Kingdoms and of the War which they Provoked and Waged against the Spanish and Portuguese Armies.* It spoke of 'the usurpation of the liberties of the Indians', and of 300,000 families 'like so many slaves working for the Jesuits for a crust of bread' while the Society was busy constructing its magnificent and luxurious churches.³⁴

In September 1757 Pombal had all Jesuits removed from the Court, and early in the following year extracted from the dying pope, Benedict XIV, the public statement that the Society needed reform, together with the appointment of a Portuguese cardinal to carry it out. Later in 1758 an attempt was made to assassinate the king. It failed, though he was wounded, but after a secret investigation Pombal had twelve nobles executed for allegedly planning it, among them the duke of Aveiro, 'the most powerful noble in Portugal after the royal family itself, and president of the supreme court', who was first broken on the wheel but carefully kept alive in order to be burned to death, and the marquis of Távora, a general and former viceroy of India whose wife was well known to be the king's mistress. Eight Jesuits were arrested for complicity, including a half-mad old man called Malagrida who had attributed the earthquake to divine intervention. Pombal appointed his brother Inquisitor-General and, with the aid of compliant archbishops, had the whole body of Jesuits declared to be in rebellion. They were supposed to have tolerated heresy among their Indian subjects, to have encouraged them to rise against the Crown and to have amassed untold treasures of gold and silver in their inaccessible missions. In 1759 their lands and property were seized by the state, and they were all either imprisoned or exiled, with no compensation of any kind. Two years later, with savage irony, Malagrida became the last victim of the Portuguese Inquisition to be burned at the stake.

Secure now in his despotism, Pombal introduced a wide range of measures which were at once Enlightened, or apparently Enlightened, and unquestionably authoritarian: the Inquisition was turned into an arm of the state; the same happened to the censorship; the huge gap in education left by the Jesuits was

ILL. 25 Satirical depiction of the Jesuits' expulsion from Lisbon, from a print collection published in Amsterdam as *Receuil de figures historiques, symboliques, & tragiques*... (1762)

filled, or partly filled, by a new system of schools organised by the state but relying heavily on the participation of Oratorian monks; one small monastic Order, that of canons regular of St Anthony, a body long in decay and disrepute, was abolished – by the pope;[35] some monasteries were reformed; the curriculum of the University of Coimbra was modernised, mainly with a view to providing a better-trained bureaucracy; the distinction between Old and New Christians was abolished; and religious toleration was accorded to Protestants and Jews. But these measures were not enacted as swiftly as the expulsion of the Jesuits had been and, by the time they were brought in, other Catholic states had taken the lead in reform. Doctrinally, in fact, Pombal showed himself a rather conservative Catholic when, in prescribing the type of theological teaching to be established at Coimbra, he drew heavily on the writings of abbot Gerbert of St Blasien.[36] Had he been determined to assail monasticism, the Lisbon earthquake would have provided a golden opportunity: he could have greatly diminished the number of monasteries in the capital by not including their rebuilding in his plans. In fact he had virtually all of them rebuilt. At the Cistercian monastery of Alcobaça, where one of his numerous well-placed relatives was abbot, he sponsored the building of a factory to produce cloth and kerchiefs.[37] When Beckford visited Portugal in 1787 and 1794, there was no shortage of grand monasteries for him to visit, in which he heard splendid Masses and enthusiastic sermons, admired fine books and was offered a heavy dinner. At Mafra everything was extreme: 'a confounded jingle of all the bells' half stunned him; 'the service was chanted with the most imposing solemnity to the awful sound of organs, for there are no fewer than six in the church, all of an enormous size'; but, 'the vigil of St Augustine's day being observed as a fast with the utmost strictness,' supper consisted only of apples and salad with wine.[38]

In other words, it was only in their assault on the Society, their confiscation of its property and their expulsion of its members that Pombal and Portugal took a uniquely early and an especially ferocious initiative. Hence it is plain that religious and ecclesiastical reform in any broad sense was not the minister's chief concern. The destruction of the Society in Portugal was an act of state, facing down rebellion and ruthlessly asserting the absolute power of the Crown. Its implications for the Church and religion proved to be enormous – but not so much inside as outside Portugal.

FRANCE

While the Portuguese initiative has attracted the attention of few historians, a huge literature has grown up around the suppression of the Jesuits in France. Many of these writings treat the event as more or less hermetically sealed within the history of France and its colonies.[39] This is difficult to justify. That a particular change should occur in one country soon after a very similar change in another certainly does not prove that the earlier influenced the later, still less that the earlier alone made the later possible. But in this instance the causal chain is clear. Of course, attacks by French Jansenists on the Jesuits were more than a century old, and the Jansenists had long constituted a powerful, well-organised minority of the *parlement* of Paris, now led by Louis-Adrien le Paige. During the 1750s several local developments intensified feeling against the Society in France. The archbishop of Paris, Christophe de Beaumont, was making ever more enemies for the cause of the Jesuits by pursuing with callous zeal all avowed sympathisers with Jansenism, denying them the sacraments even on their deathbeds. The hostility of the *philosophes* to the Society became fiercer after the row over the *Encyclopédie* in 1752. In 1757 one Robert Damiens made a feeble attempt to assassinate Louis XV. He spoke against the archbishop of Paris and had had only the most tenuous connexion with the Jesuits, but this was enough to ensure that they were widely believed to have conspired with him. He was executed with maximum cruelty, and the anxieties aroused among Frenchmen were heightened by the heavy taxation and military disasters of the Seven Years War. Yet it was only after the Portuguese assault had succeeded that suppression of the Order, as opposed to merely limiting its influence, became a serious option in France. Not only had Pombal effectively publicised across Europe the iniquities, real and supposed, of the Jesuits and his achievement in suppressing them. In the process he had enlisted the bemused but none the less decisive support of the papacy, opening up the hitherto unimaginable possibility that Rome itself might abandon the Jesuits to the mercy of Catholic rulers. Dale Van Kley, author of *The Jansenists and the Expulsion of the Jesuits from France*, concludes that it was at the very end of 1759, precisely because of what had been achieved in Portugal, that the Jansenist leaders in the *parlement* of Paris decided to give up lesser campaigns and work for the total destruction of the Society.[40]

In some respects the scenario in France bore an uncanny resemblance to that in Portugal.[41] The duc de Choiseul, Louis XV's principal minister, was hostile to the Jesuits and appears to have plotted with the Jansenist leadership of the *parlement* to bring them down. In both countries an attempt on the king's life was, with little or no justification, blamed on the Society. As in Portugal, so in France, Jesuit misbehaviour in a colony proved disastrous. The Society had substantial estates on the Caribbean island of Martinique, some of which were managed by Father La Valette, who in 1753 became superior of missions in the West Indies. Early in 1756, before the Seven Years War officially broke out, English ships seized several vessels carrying cargo from La Valette to his creditors in France. As a result, they lost very large sums and went bankrupt, followed in turn by their creditors. Court cases naturally ensued. It was evident that La Valette had been engaging in practices from which as a monk he was debarred, including some complex money-laundering intended to counteract the weakness of Martinique's currency against the French. He had accumulated total debts of six million livres. His creditors at first sued him as an individual, but early in 1760 a court declared in the case of two of them, Lioncy and Gouffre of Marseilles, to whom he owed more than one and a half million livres, that it was the entire Jesuit Order that was responsible for the debts he had incurred because all its members were subject to the dictatorial control of its general. This decision threatened the Society, which was in fact far from wealthy, with financial ruin.

Lawyers now began to argue that the Jesuits had no legal right to operate in France, either for technical historical reasons or because of their inherent malignity and 'despotism'. Although the king and some ministers worked to frustrate the *parlement*'s campaign, their efforts only resulted in expanding the scope of the semi-public enquiries into the affairs of the Society. On 6 August 1761 the *parlement* of Paris – ostensibly on a provisional basis – forbade the Jesuits to recruit any more novices or accept any more vows, dissolved their confraternities and closed their colleges. The king required the *parlement* to suspend these decrees for six months while he tried to negotiate a compromise with the Society under which it would make a declaration against tyrannicide, accept the 'Gallican Articles' that declared the French Church autonomous and submit to the appointment of a general for France alone. Apart from the fact that the pope and the Order's general would not agree to this deal, the *parlements* of other provinces now joined that of Paris in rejecting it and defying the government by such measures as closing the Jesuits' colleges. After dithering for two years the king finally, in November 1764, bowed to the will of the *parlements* and dissolved the Order in the greater part of France by royal decree.[42] The best that he felt he could do for the Jesuits was to secure them pensions. His essential difficulty was that, because of the huge cost of the war, he needed the goodwill of the *parlements* in order to obtain approval for higher taxes necessary to stave off state bankruptcy. As one of the best placed of contemporaries, Bernardo Tanucci, chief minister of the king of Naples, commented earlier in 1764:

God allowed this whole storm over the Jesuits to originate with the pope, the learned and uncorrupt [Benedict XIV], who issued the bull instructing the Portuguese patriarch to visit and judge the Jesuits, from which sprang the condemnations of Jesuit commercial activity, and step by step the case of Lioncy and Father La Valette.[43]

From this compressed account of an extremely complicated story it will be apparent that the Portuguese and French cases, despite striking similarities, differed in crucial respects. A broader reading public than existed anywhere else in Catholic Europe was to be found in France, and all factions appealed to it. In addition massive popular hostility was turned on the Society. The headlong pace of events and the febrile atmosphere in which they took place anticipate the French Revolution itself. In France the king was not a tool in the hands of his principal minister, but nor was his theoretical absolutism effective. Louis XV plainly was at a loss to know how to handle the situation. He had twice previously challenged the *parlements* and then receded. This time too, overborne by his financial difficulties, he caved in. No parallel to the *parlements* existed in Portugal. Nor was a substantial body of *philosophes* to be found there. In France, after the Jansenists had made the early running, Louis-René de la Chalotais, of the *parlement* of Brittany, won fame with his *Compte rendu des constitutions des Jésuites* (1762) which defenders of the Society popularised by their attacks on it. La Chalotais argued on more general and rationalist grounds than the Jansenists and extended his assault to all monastic Orders. His work was the best evidence for the claims made after the event, by D'Alembert in his *Sur la destruction des Jésuites* (1765), that it was the *philosophes* rather than the Jansenists whose campaign had caused the suppression. In fact it is clear that the *philosophes* played only a subordinate role, and in any case La Chalotais was not a conspicuous figure among them.[44] But the relative strength of intellectual radicalism in France gave a special character to the debate there, helping to make it into a general critique of the Jesuits and of everything they stood for. All these factors ensured that, whereas in Portugal the suppression of the Society did not lead to a campaign against monasticism as a whole, in France it did.

SPAIN

In the 1760s, compared with the other major Catholic countries, even with Italy and southern Germany, Spain appeared remarkably uninfluenced by the Enlightenment as usually defined. The Inquisition, in which the Jesuits remained powerful, had banned both the *Encyclopédie* and *De l'esprit des lois* in 1759. In 1764 all of Rousseau's works were condemned, and in the following year what was supposed to be a copy of his *Emile* was solemnly burned in the Dominican church in Madrid. The Inquisition even succeeded in outlawing works by non-Jesuit theologians which the Vatican itself had positively recommended to the faithful. However, Spain is the perfect instance of *Catholic* Enlightenment, precisely because the country produced so few representatives of any other brand.[45] Within the Spanish Catholic Enlightenment monks played a large part. Benito Feijoo, Benedictine and professor at the University of Oviedo, published between 1726 and 1739 nine volumes under the title *Teatro critico universel*, the avowed aim of which was to introduce Spain to modern science: to Bacon, Descartes, Newton and the inductive method. These and other works of Feijoo received from king Ferdinand VI in 1750 the ludicrously unenlightened accolade of an order prohibiting the publication of any writings that criticised them. They became the books most frequently reprinted in eighteenth-century Spain. Although Feijoo introduced many ideas of French and Protestant origin into the country – or at least into the Spanish language – he wrote for the glory of God and in order to advance

Catholicism as he saw it. But in the process he criticised errors, superstitions and beliefs which many Spanish Catholics regarded as part of their faith. Similar comments can be made about *Fray Gerundio*, a satire on contemporary preaching, directed particularly at the friars, published by a Jesuit, José Francisco de Isla, in 1758. This book, however, was swiftly banned by the Inquisition because, unlike Feijoo's, its tone was combative and supercilious and it gave real offence to other clergy. This incident illustrates how skilled the Spanish Jesuits were at overplaying their hand.[46]

Despite the services of the Spanish Habsburg kings to the Counter-Reformation and despite the despotic power that the pope had granted them over the Church in their empire, they had never been accorded the same rights as the French king over the national church. Rome still made appointments to many church posts in Spain and drew substantial revenues from the country. After the failure of the Habsburg dynasty with the death of the cretinous Charles II in 1700, the Bourbons who eventually obtained possession of the throne set about trying to restore and, if possible, enhance the authority of the monarchy. One of their weapons was administrative centralisation; another was to build new palaces and refurbish old ones, trebling their total space;[47] the third was to reduce the influence of the pope over the church. To this end they obtained in 1737 a new concordat which, with a revision in 1753, placed them more or less in the position of the king of France, able to appoint whomever they chose to the major benefices of the kingdom and to draw substantially on ecclesiastical revenues.[48] They used these new powers, among other things, to reform the parochial system and to implement more fully the decrees of the Council of Trent which ordered the establishment of proper seminaries for the training of parish clergy.[49] In Spanish America king Ferdinand VI carried through between 1749 and his death in 1759 a reform of peculiar interest: he forced the monastic Orders to give up control of the parishes they governed, which in Mexico constituted a majority of all parishes. Monks were expelled from parsonages and from some of their lesser establishments, strict controls were placed on their recruitment and, as the measures took effect, their total numbers fell substantially. This is an example of 'secularization' of a peculiar kind not found elsewhere, the compulsory transfer of parishes from regular to secular clergy.[50]

In 1759 Charles III, who had previously been duke of Parma and then king of Naples, succeeded to the Spanish throne.[51] While in Italy, he had become associated with certain minor reforms, diminishing the rights of the clergy and enhancing those of the state, trying to restrict the numbers and property of priests and monks. But, disregarding the strong advice of his trusted Neapolitan minister, Tanucci, he had proved unwilling to take any drastic action against the Jesuits or other monastic Orders. It was just after the Jesuits' expulsion from Portugal that he assumed the government of Spain and, since the two countries had similar problems with the Order in South America, it was to be expected that he would follow Pombal's example. But he at first made no move against the Society in Spain, although Tanucci continued to urge him on from Naples, and despite a campaign mounted by officials in the colonies against the recent concession to Jesuit estates there that they need pay only one thirtieth, instead of one tenth, of their produce in tithe. It is striking that these anti-Jesuit arguments were strongly supported by the king's confessor, Fray Joaquin de Osma, who was a Franciscan.[52] But Charles seems to have been little affected by these representations, or by the expulsion of the Jesuits from France.

As well as having a Franciscan confessor, he was a devout member of the Franciscan Third Order, and on arriving in Spain offered to pay for the rebuilding of the main Franciscan church in Madrid (Ill. 26). He fulfilled his promise, making the new church, against much opposition, the prime Spanish exemplar of the neoclassical style recently adopted for Ste-Geneviève in Paris and soon to be employed at St Blasien in Germany.[53] He included the Escorial in his annual round of palaces,

ILL. 26 Façade of the Franciscan church of San Francisco el Grande, Madrid, 1760–84

though he created within it a sumptuous Rococo suite for his Court. Evidently he was no enemy to monasticism as such, even though he was thought to be unfriendly to the Jesuits. In 1765, however, he allowed the publication of a tract by Pedro de Campomanes, a junior lay official, which asserted the power of the king to curb the alienation of landed property to the church in mortmain. The censors who approved the book were an Augustinian, a Benedictine and a Dominican. The pamphlet made a considerable stir abroad and seemed likely to lead to legislation in Spain.[54]

But on Palm Sunday 1766 serious rioting broke out in Madrid. The disturbances, which took place during a period of severe food shortage, were sparked off by the attempt of the king's chief minister, Squillace, an Italian whom he had brought with him from Naples, to enforce an old edict that forbade the wearing of traditional Spanish cloaks and hats, on the ground that they made it easy for criminals to conceal their identities. So alarming were the riots that the king finally came to the balcony of the royal palace and, with a Franciscan standing by, swore to abandon the edict, dismiss Squillace and lower food prices. This direct confrontation between king and people – quite exceptional in pre-revolutionary Europe – terrified Charles, who left the city overnight for his palace at Aranjuez, appointed the count of Aranda his chief minister and began elaborate consultations with his advisers about the causes of the unrest and the measures to be taken to restore the situation.

After secret investigations and deliberations, and 'for urgent, just and necessary reasons which I reserve in my royal breast', he ordered and arranged for the expulsion of the Jesuits from all his dominions, without warning and by military force. In Spain itself the deed was done in April 1767, when 2,746 Jesuits were driven out. This was easily the most decisive action of his reign.

Although those who knew the nature of the secret reasons were sworn to keep them secret and the documentation was thought for two centuries to have been destroyed, much of it was found in the 1970s in the papers of Campomanes, who was the official in charge of the enquiry and who drafted much of the advice to the king which led to the expulsion. The small Extraordinary Royal Council and the enquiry it instigated, both working in secret, had come up with the conclusion that, wherever disturbances had occurred, Jesuits had planned or fomented them. Improbable though this seems, the evidence adduced was accepted by the king and his ministers; and the same argument that had been used against the Society so effectively in France now proved equally fatal to it in Spain. Since all Jesuits owed unquestioning obedience to their general, it was maintained that any and every act of each single Jesuit must have been willed by, and be the responsibility of, the whole Society. Campomanes's crucial memorandum declared that the Order had seven major vices. First, it was 'united under a foreign government contrary to the spirit of its foundation'. Secondly, its greed for wealth had led it into taking up arms against the government in South America. Thirdly, it peddled the doctrine of probabilism, which could encourage rebellion. Fourthly, its whole spirit was seditious, treasonable and irreligious; it was 'a cancer seeking to take over the state under the guise of religion'. Fifthly, it showed animus against all rulers and established institutions – chiefly in its attempts to rebut the charges levelled against it in Portugal and France. Sixthly, it pursued vengeance against its detractors, which helped to account for its trouble-making and its alleged attacks on the sacred person of the king. Finally, it possessed external allies. This indictment, for all its tendentious repetitions, was enough to persuade Charles – or perhaps to confirm his instinctive feeling – that the Society's continued existence in Spain was incompatible not merely with royal authority but with his personal safety. Because the popular mood was thought to be so dangerous, he was also advised to act secretly, suddenly and with overwhelming force.

At the same time the Society's lands were to be seized. The Jesuits themselves would be granted a pension if they went into exile, so long as they did not publicly criticise the expulsion. Although the terms of the suppression were kinder to individual monks than Pombal's had been, the understandable refusal of the pope to offer asylum in his states to a sudden influx of more than 5,000 Jesuits from the Spanish dominions led to many of them suffering great hardship in the search for a new domicile.[55]

Between the riots and the expulsion, Campomanes's anti-mortmain legislation was quietly abandoned, presumably for fear of opposition and in order to reassure the Church and, in particular, other Orders. When, after the event, the Spanish bishops were asked their opinion of the expulsion, a large majority applauded. In material terms they were its chief beneficiaries: many of the Jesuits' buildings and much of their land were used to found or assist diocesan seminaries. As for other monks, they too, long jealous of the Jesuits' privileges and pretensions, welcomed the expulsion and the opportunity to take over some of the Jesuits' colleges and university posts. On the other hand, half the Order's land had been sold off to laymen.[56]

Charles's motives in suppressing the Society had had little to do with religion, nothing to do with monasticism and almost everything to do with securing and strengthening his personal position and his absolute power. After taking this great step, he reverted to his policy of moderate and cautious reform. He only began to limit the independence of the Inquisition in 1768 and, though he eventually turned it into a governmental tool, he never abolished it for fear of the public's reaction. He allowed the burning of witches to continue until 1781. He showed no interest either in freedom of expression or religious toleration. As far as monasteries were concerned, a few houses were suppressed, but only one Order, and that by the pope: the Order of St Anthony, as in Portugal. Otherwise, Charles insisted on various Orders observing their rules more strictly and in 1770 imposed certain restrictions on the number of inmates each house might admit. But he abandoned proposals to restrict gifts to the Church and to raise the age of profession. It seems that by the end of his reign in 1788 the number of regulars had not been reduced and the growth of their property had hardly been stemmed. Apparently, no attempt was made to take away parishes from monasteries, as had been done in the Spanish Empire. The truth of Hermann's trenchant comment can hardly be denied: 'the expulsion of the Jesuits masks the fact that Spanish regalism backed away from confronting the regular clergy'.[57]

THE AUSTRIAN MONARCHY

Having made up his mind to expel the Jesuits from Spain, Charles III now became obsessively determined to destroy the Order completely. He worked indefatigably to persuade other Catholic Powers to follow his example and then to join him in putting pressure on the pope to abolish the Society.[58] Naples and other Italian states swiftly followed his lead by expelling it. It was worse than useless that pope Clement XIII reacted vigorously and reasserted the papacy's ancient claims to punish and ultimately to depose contumacious secular rulers. In the spring of 1768 the emperor Joseph II, who was also co-regent of the Austrian Monarchy, wrote to his brother Leopold, grand-duke of Tuscany:

Now that the times are more enlightened, the Court of Rome no longer has so much weight in European politics. Some wise and prudent popes, however, have contrived to preserve some influence by not committing themselves to unreasonable positions. But the present pope . . . seems determined to ruin everything . . . To preserve a religious Order proscribed by four Great Powers, which is now impossible, Rome, instead of secularising it as they desire, has been behaving in such a way as to challenge them to break away completely and so deprive herself of the little influence she still has . . .

In these circumstances all the Powers, to avoid a crisis, are virtually agreed that they should wait until this pope dies . . . The abolition of the Jesuit Order . . . will assuredly be a *sine qua non* at the election of a new pope.

So far as we are concerned, we have not been ready to involve ourselves either for or against, having insufficient reason to desire their destruction, but not regarding their existence as so necessary that we must protect them.[59]

Paradoxically, the fate of the Jesuits was sealed by the fact that, for the first time in history, all the major Catholic states were allies in international politics, France and Austria since 1756, Spain and France since 1762, Naples and Spain of course, even Portugal for a time. As the temporal sovereign of a minor but sizable state, the pope was at the mercy of this combination, especially since some of his outlying territories could easily be seized by anti-Jesuit Powers: in 1768 France occupied the enclave of Avignon and Naples that of Benevento. Early in 1769 Spain, France and Naples formally requested the pope to dissolve the Society. Clement XIII would not hear of it, but within a few weeks he was dead. As Joseph had predicted, the anti-Jesuit Powers procured the election of the pliant Clement XIV, a Franciscan believed to be ready to suppress the Society.[60]

The new pope, however, was able to procrastinate since no German state was ready to expel the Jesuits. Bavaria, the most important after the Austrian Monarchy, was ruled by an elector who was committed to their support; and even Austria refused to join the other Catholic Powers in putting pressure on Rome. Maria Theresa repeatedly declared to diplomats and others that she was unimpressed by the actions of the other Powers, that the Jesuits in her lands were certainly not guilty of the alleged crimes which had been held to justify their expulsion from other countries, and that she regarded them as a thoroughly useful and respectable Order. She announced herself neutral, though at the end of 1769 added a rider to this policy: if the pope decided that it was for the good of the Church that the Society should be suppressed, she would acquiesce. This shift of position represented a concession to Choiseul, the minister of her ally, France, during the negotiations for the marriage of her daughter, Marie Antoinette, to the future king Louis XVI. In secret instructions given to Marie Antoinette when she left for France early in 1770, the empress wrote:

I have one more point to make, concerning the Jesuits. Do not talk about them at all, either for or against them. You may cite me and say that I have asked you to speak neither good nor evil of them: that you know that I esteem them, that in my lands they have done much good, that I should be sorry to lose them, but that if the court of Rome believes it must abolish this Order, I shall put no obstacle in the way; moreover, that I always used to speak of them with respect, but that even in private I did not like people to talk about these unhappy affairs.[61]

Maria Theresa's attitude remains somewhat surprising given, as she herself admitted in 1774, that she had 'not been well disposed towards the Society for many years'.[62] Its power within the Monarchy had been immense, probably greater than anywhere else in Europe. Before 1759 it monopolised the direction of most of the universities of her dominions, its members occupied most of the Chairs of philosophy and theology, they were in charge of most aspects of censorship and they supplied all the confessors of members of the royal family. With a view to making their ministry and missions more effective, they had become notable as promoters of the use and study of the numerous vernacular languages that flourished in greater Hungary: Hungarian itself, Illyrian, Croatian, Serbian, Romanian, Ruthene, Slovak and Czech. By establishing in 1746 the college in Vienna that became known as the *Theresianum*, where the training of young nobles and government servants was entrusted to the Society, she had actually enhanced its standing. It was also given charge of the Oriental Academy, founded in 1753 to train future diplomats. But from this time onwards the Society's power in Austria was gradually weakened until, just before the suppression, they had few Chairs and royal confessorships left to them, and no representatives on the censorship commission.[63] In initiating or permitting these changes, Maria Theresa had been influenced by the hostility to the Jesuits of the secular clergy, headed by archbishop Migazzi of Vienna, and of the Augustinian, Benedictine and Dominican Orders whose theologians sought at least equal rights with the Society to teach their particular brand of theology in universities. Her personal religious attitudes have been described as Jansenist: she recommended her children to read certain Jansenist texts, she strongly disapproved of the Jesuits' advocacy of probabilism and disliked their partisanship in support of the bull *Unigenitus*. She gave authority to her physician, the learned Gerard van Swieten, to carry out what he called in November 1758 'the intention of Your Majesty . . . to limit the exorbitant power that the Society has everywhere appropriated to itself'. His belief was 'that the true aim of the Society was to make money, and that the religious motive was only a pretext to take advantage of the piety of Your majesty and her ancestors'. So arrogant had they become, he alleged, that they claimed copyright in publishing the Holy Scriptures. In 1759 – it can hardly be accidental that this was the year after the pope had acknowledged that the Jesuits of Portugal needed reform and the year in which they were expelled by Pombal – Maria Theresa took away their monopoly of university Chairs and of places on the censorship commission. Despite considerable opposition to this policy, in the face of which her determination fluctuated, she continued to whittle away their power so that by 1770 most of it had gone. In

1767 she had ceased to confess to Father Kampmiller, SJ, turning instead to the provost of the Augustinian monastery of St Dorothea in Vienna, Ignaz Müller.[64]

Many writers in the eighteenth century and since have maintained that, in contrast to his mother, Joseph II was an enemy to the Jesuits. In 1790, the year of his death, apparently powerful evidence to this effect was published by the unknown compiler of a collection called *Letters of Joseph II*. The evidence consists of two letters, the first supposedly written to Choiseul, dated January 1770:

If I were sovereign, you could count on my support, and you have my approval as regards the Jesuits and the plan to suppress them.

On my mother do not rely too much... But Kaunitz is your friend...

Choiseul! I know [the Jesuits] as well as anyone does:... their efforts to spread darkness over the earth, and to rule and embroil Europe from Cape Finisterre to the North Sea.

The second letter, dated July 1773, is allegedly addressed to the count of Aranda, the Spanish minister who was in power when the Jesuits were expelled from his country:

Clement XIV has acquired eternal glory by suppressing the Jesuits... Before they were known in Germany, religion was a doctrine that brought happiness to peoples; but they have made it inspire fear... [Their] principal objects were to acquire glory, to extend their power and to spread darkness over the rest of the world. Their intolerance caused Germany to suffer the horrors of a thirty years war. Their principles cost the Henries of France their lives and thrones; they were the originators of the loathsome [revocation of the] Edict of Nantes. The powerful influence which they had over the princes of the house of Habsburg is only too well known... To their wise direction were entrusted the education of youth, literature, patronage, the distribution of the principal offices of state, the ear of kings and the heart of queens. We know too well what use they made of their power, what plans were carried out and what fetters they imposed upon the nations... If I was inclined to hate anyone, [it would be the Jesuits].

Each of these incendiary letters has been quoted, often at even greater length than here, by many historians, including some of the greatest authorities.[65]

That such views were held, and were ascribed to Joseph II, in 1790 is significant. But the documents in which they occur are pure invention, giving a quite false impression of the attitudes not only of the emperor but also of the supposed addressees; and acceptance of these letters as genuine by so many scholars has led to a serious distortion of history.[66] In the letter to his brother Leopold that I quoted earlier, Joseph treats the whole issue of suppression as almost a joke, and he did the same on other occasions. For example, in 1769 he cruelly teased the general of the Jesuits about their imminent suppression; in 1771 he scoffed at the methodical way in which they required penitents to list their sins; and, when writing from his annual military camp to the elector of Trier in 1781 in defence of his early church reforms, he expressed regret at having left his copy of Busenbaum at home. But he had been largely educated by Jesuits and he did not criticise the teaching he had received. In 1776 he paid for an expensive funeral for one of his old Jesuit tutors, Father Franz. He retained his Jesuit confessor, Höller, until he died in 1770. Many of the tutors he appointed in the 1780s for his nephew, the future Francis II, were ex-Jesuits. The most revealing of his remarks about the Society is what he said, travelling incognito in Italy early in 1769, to count Papini, whom he met casually as they waited to change horses:

The [count] asked him about the Jesuits of Germany. The emperor replied that they behave very well there; they are learned and zealous – adding other praises – and concluding that what has happened to them elsewhere wouldn't happen in Germany. Hearing these praises, the count supposed that this was a young man educated at the *Theresianum*, who spoke out of loyalty. 'No,' the emperor replied, 'I was educated at home and I said that out of simple regard for the truth.'

In 1780 Catherine II of Russia was equally surprised by the warmth of his praise for the Society.[67]

Other aspects of Joseph's views come out in a memorandum that he wrote in 1773, when he was about to go on his travels for several months, giving his opinion on what action ought to be taken when the expected papal bull of suppression reached Vienna. He began by saying:

The education of youth, at least of the most important part of it, in religion as well as in other subjects, has been until now almost entirely entrusted in these lands to the Fathers of the Society. Neither among the secular clergy nor in the other regular Orders will it be possible to find immediately, especially in the bigger towns, a sufficient number of qualified persons to fill the places of the Jesuits, with comparable success, in *Gymnasien*, academies and universities, and to occupy the many endowed teaching posts.

So it must be considered what provision should be made in education, especially in the noble academies and foundations, in the *Theresianum*, in the colleges at Olmütz, Prague, Tyrnau and all other academies and *Gymnasien*, and whether it would not be desirable – indeed, for the good of religion and the state, necessary – that even after the suppression of the Society the teachers of this Order should remain in their existing posts, and on what basis one could keep them on at least until [other] able persons can be trained to fill the teaching posts in future and match the existing provision.

It will take long application and preparation to educate teachers for this [sort of] instruction, to which the whole institution of the Society was especially devoted.[68]

The emperor evidently admired the intellectual and pedagogic achievements of the Order. He clearly minded less about their alleged theological errors than his mother did. But he had supported her loosening of the censorship, and indeed wished to carry it further. After the death of Father Höller, he made his parish priest his confessor.[69] He desired to reform education, which the suppression of the Society rendered necessary and the windfall of its lands and revenues made more feasible. He wanted a drastic reform of monasticism. But the Jesuits would not have been his first target. In this his views resemble, and were doubtless influenced by, Kaunitz's.[70]

When, however, the pope concluded that he had no choice but to suppress the Society, Maria Theresa made no effort to save it. What she stipulated was that the property of the Jesuits should pass to the state rather than, as he had envisaged, to the church. After the promulgation of the bull, she asked the pope whether he would permit her, contrary to its terms, to appoint ex-Jesuits to serve in parishes that lacked priests. The pope replied that it was her affair, and a large number of ex-Jesuits found employment in this and other spheres, both before and after she was succeeded as ruler of the Monarchy by her son.[71]

CONCLUSION

It is plain that the principal motive of the rulers who expelled the Jesuits and urged the pope to suppress the Society was to enhance their absolute authority as against what they saw as an arrogant and overmighty body that owed allegiance to a foreign ruler and apparently did not scruple to foster rebellion when its interests were threatened. Those Catholic Powers that possessed a colonial empire had in earlier centuries cheerfully accorded great independence to Jesuit missions. When that independence was abused, resurgent absolutism victimised them. But, where these considerations did not apply, as in the German states, the suppression was the work not of the local rulers but of the pope, under pressure from the sovereigns of France, Spain, Portugal and Naples.

Dissolution of the Jesuits established a precedent for rulers seeking to limit the numbers and wealth of monks and nuns. When it later came to the suppression of other Orders in France and the Austrian Monarchy, the pattern devised for the case of the Jesuits was applied with only slight alteration: seizure of property by the state accompanied by opportunities for the monks to become parish priests or obtain other suitable employment, together with some provision of pensions. But, at the time when the suppression of the Jesuits took place, this seemed an unlikely prospect. Other Orders had assisted and applauded the suppression. At the Bavarian monastery of Polling, which had set itself up as a rival to the Jesuit University of Dillingen, the monks had hoped that, 'with God's help, the [Jesuits] will suffer the fate of the Templars. They harm our religion, the pious as much as the scholars.'[72] In general the suppression was seen by rulers, governments and most observers as a unique measure not affecting other monks and nuns. Neither the attacks of the *philosophes* nor popular feeling had played a crucial role. Some of the ministers involved can be found expressing hostility to all regulars: Campomanes, Aranda and Kaunitz for example. But, at least in the last two cases, their more extreme remarks are balanced by many more judicious statements and, in the case of all three, by the pursuit of relatively moderate policies.[73] So far as most of those who masterminded the suppressions are concerned, they saw themselves as reasonable or enlightened Catholics, critical of the intolerance, empire-building, ruthlessness, greed and forms of piety especially associated with the Jesuits, and jealous of their power, but not hostile to monasticism in general any more than to the Church as an institution or to the central doctrines of Catholicism.

Yet some observers, such as Sonnenfels in Austria and D'Alembert in France, welcomed the suppression as sounding the death-knell of all monastic Orders,[74] and they proved in a sense to have been right. It is hard to overstate the general impact of the measure, however limited the aims of many of its promoters. Intellectually the ablest, educationally the most effective and politically the most powerful of all the Orders, the Society of Jesus had been destroyed by a concert of the Catholic Powers. The papacy, in doing the deed, had asserted its absolute authority in a way that would strengthen its power in the distant future. But for the next generation the suppression was seen as a tremendous defeat for the pope, and that was also how it was viewed in Rome. It surely goes far to explain why Pius VI, who reigned from 1775 to 1799, acquiesced in nearly all of the church reforms imposed by secular rulers until he brought himself to condemn in 1791 the French National Assembly's Civil Constitution of the Clergy, and why he never made a strong stand in support of any type of monasticism. The fact that the papacy had been compelled to abandon the very Order that had been founded to uphold it shattered morale in the Vatican and shifted the balance of power away from Rome in favour of lay Catholic rulers.

Yet the main theme – the destruction by the pope and the Catholic Powers of the most effective and powerful of all the Orders – was accompanied by a maverick counterpoint. The officially Protestant and actually agnostic Frederick the Great of Prussia, and Catherine the Great, a convert to the Russian Orthodox Church – both of whom had prided themselves on extending toleration to their Catholic subjects – now demanded that the pope should allow them to maintain the suppressed Order in their dominions. They recognised it as a uniquely successful educational machine for their Catholic subjects which it would be impossible, at least in the short run, to replace. The pope, in some embarrassment, told Frederick that, having solemnly abolished it, he could not allow the Order to survive as such, but agreed that ex-Jesuits could continue their work in Silesia under a new name and under the king's direction. Catherine refused to publish the papal bull suppressing the Society and ordered the Jesuits to carry on. The pope, when challenged by Catholic rulers about the position in Russia, declared that these were ex-Jesuits, but he privately told the Russian monks that he approved their activity, which included taking in novices and electing a general. So, while the government of independent Poland and Maria Theresa in Galicia suppressed the Jesuits and reduced the number of monasteries of other Orders, these non-Catholic rulers sustained them, Catherine actually maintaining them as a community. That Frederick and Catherine took this line appears all the more remarkable given that no such toleration was yet shown by the London government towards any monks or nuns in Britain and Ireland.

In 1801 Catherine's successor, Paul I, obtained a formal statement from the pope that the Russian ex-Jesuits had been real Jesuits all along. But, soon after the Order had been re-established elsewhere, they were expelled from Russia in 1820. Despite these vicissitudes, the protection of the Jesuits by Prussia and Russia after 1773 is a striking example of toleration towards Catholic regulars on the part of non-Catholic rulers, a phenomenon which in the nineteenth century made possible a vast growth of monasticism in lands, such as Ireland, from which it had been banished at the Reformation.[75]

CHAPTER 7

FRANCE: THE *COMMISSION DES RÉGULIERS*

Some reform of monasteries was imposed or attempted between 1765 and 1790 in almost every Catholic country. But the two most notable and influential examples were, first, the changes brought about by the *commission des réguliers* established in France in 1766 and, secondly, the developing programme of reform in the Austrian Monarchy under Maria Theresa and Joseph II. To compare them yields unexpected results. Although an essential aim of both was to reduce the number of houses of monks, they embodied revealingly different approaches to the religious and social functions of monasticism.

The suppression of the Society of Jesus in France rendered changes in some areas more likely, and in others inescapable. Since the Jesuits had been driven out of the educational system which they had dominated for so long, it was necessary to take measures, so far as possible, to fill the vacuum they left behind. The government took the matter out of the hands of the Church and placed the hundred-odd former Jesuit colleges under the control of local committees composed mainly of laymen, chaired by a bishop. Although the conduct of about a third of the colleges was entrusted to other Orders, especially the Oratorians and the Doctrinaires, this was done at the behest of the state operating through these local committees, not of the church authorities. In some places the bishop was refused control over any aspect of the teaching except the strictly theological. Soon those colleges run by Orders were removed from secular control, but the majority remained under local authorities. In principle this transfer of authority represented an epoch-making triumph for the laity over the clergy and an important stage on the way to secularised education.[1]

In practice its effects were more limited. At first nearly all the teachers appointed by the local committees were clergy, largely because there were few trained laymen, though a counter-trend showed itself in the growing preponderance within the Oratorians of *confrères* who had not taken orders; the colleges remained emphatically Catholic; and money to fund new initiatives was always in short supply. No doubt the reformed system strengthened and accelerated modernising tendencies in education, but these trends had been operating for decades, even in the Jesuits' schools: a reduction in the importance of theology, Cartesianism and Latin in the curriculum and a corresponding increase in the time given to 'modern' subjects like natural sciences and living languages. Each college had its own particular history. To give just one example, the citizens of Vienne had to fight a long battle to retain for the town its former Jesuit college, and succeeded only at the cost of losing some of its considerable revenues to the college in Grenoble. In 1774 the Vienne curriculum was widened by the inclusion of a design class, part of a national movement to provide training in practical subjects. But the school remained the preserve of the children of the local professional elite, and many of the pupils continued to receive the tonsure at an early age, in order to be qualified for a possible ecclesiastical career.[2]

Although the fall of the Jesuits had come about for reasons peculiar to the Order, it none the less opened up debate about monasticism as a whole. In 1765 the General Assembly of the Clergy held its quinquennial meeting, conscious that since its last gathering the situation of the Church had dramatically deteriorated. The king had failed to give it his accustomed support over the suppression of the Jesuits and over the disposal of their colleges. Hence the identification of Church and state exemplified by the incorporation of *Unigenitus* into the law of the land had effectively been destroyed. The *parlements* and the *philosophes* were in full cry against the clergy. It was clearly prudent for the Church to show itself ready for further reform and, so far as possible, to keep control of the process. Among the issues the Assembly addressed was the condition of the monasteries.

It will be remembered that the Assembly did not include representatives of the regular clergy and so offered a free field for the anti-monastic resentments of some secular clergy. In particular, the bishops had always objected to the fact that in each diocese there were 'as many little individual dioceses as there are monasteries, where the bishop has no right of access for inspection'.[3] The Assembly's effective leader, Loménie de Brienne, archbishop of Toulouse, proposed that, in view of the lamentable state of the monastic Orders in France and in order to save them from ruin, it should ask the king to request the pope to establish a *commission*

FRANCE: THE *COMMISSION DES RÉGULIERS*

made up of higher clergy to reform them. Brienne wrote in 1769: 'In 1765 the monastic estate in Europe was threatened with a revolution. In France its coming was signalled by moral decline, the decay of scholarship and above all by the spirit of faction within the monasteries, which led to many cases in the secular courts.'[4] His last point weighed heavily. The fall of the Jesuits had been precipitated by the court cases arising from La Valette's misbehaviour. Other legal battles arose from disputes within monasteries, usually between superiors and ordinary monks and nuns about the conduct of the house's affairs, since a procedure existed, *l'appel comme d'abus*, under which such quarrels could be taken to the secular courts, where the proceedings provided material for the enemies of monasticism and where the decisions were likely to be unwelcome to the church authorities. In addition, it was believed that the mere threat of such cases discouraged some superiors from exercising proper discipline.

Choiseul, the king's chief minister, welcomed the idea of an enquiry but gladly acceded to the demand of the *parlements* that the king should set it up himself. So Louis established in 1766 by his own authority, without even informing the pope, a *commission des réguliers* consisting of five archbishops and four lay councillors of state, to be assisted by sundry lawyers and theologians. Many churchmen objected to the exclusion of Rome. But, as with the new arrangements for the running of colleges, the clergy did not in general refuse to join a committee containing lay members which was presuming to deal with an ecclesiastical issue. Nor did they co-opt, as they were expressly allowed to do, monastic representatives. Brienne himself acted as secretary to the commission.

Nunneries were excluded from the *commission*'s terms of reference, as were all new, post-Reformation Orders. As already stated, the total number of monks affected was over 26,000 in nearly 3,000 houses. Among them, Cluny and its daughter-houses, though partially investigated, were left to the very tender mercies of the commendatory abbot of Cluny and head of the congregation, cardinal de la Rochefoucauld, archbishop of Rouen.

When the edict establishing the *commission* was published in May 1766, a pamphlet debate was unleashed. Some radicals declared that monasticism was in all respects pernicious. It removed subjects from society; it took much property out of circulation, thus damaging the economy; its insistence on celibacy limited the growth of population.

What honour can be done to religion by these swarms of monks, who, required by their vows to lead a life of poverty and mortification, differ from the most voluptuous and perverted laymen only in their distinctive and bizarre dress – monks who, induced to enter the monastery out of laziness, live there in idleness? How many abbeys are there in

France where strangers are attracted only by the magnificence of the accommodation and the pleasures of a good table? You go there and come upon the most frightful scandals; you leave, filled with indignation at the folly of the people who founded and maintain rich menageries for such animals.

Mendicant Orders came in for especially violent denunciation: their 'poverty forces them into all kinds of low behaviour, ... to conjuring, imposture, charlatanry, thieving ... Would it not be a benefit to religion to destroy all these nurseries of loutish monks?'

If abolition was not practicable, it was demanded that the age of profession should be raised, say, to twenty-five, which it was assumed would gradually but infallibly reduce the number of monks and monasteries.

By contrast, the defenders of the monasteries declared them to be the bulwark and ornament of the Church, and branded their attackers as secret or implicit enemies of Catholicism, if not of Christianity. Where abuses existed, they should be reformed, not made the excuse for suppressions. The Church's property was necessary to assist the poor, to maintain the monks and to provide decent worship.[5]

The *commission* sent questionnaires to all bishops and to the monasteries of the relevant Orders, and some *curés* and laymen also submitted their views. To summarise this welter of often detailed statements is naturally difficult. It was the bishops who gave the fullest answers and to whom the greatest attention was paid. In general they simply accepted that French monasticism was in decay. In particular, they condemned the prevailing 'spirit of property', as shown in the practices widespread in the richer Orders of paying monks what amounted to an income and of allowing them an agreeable set of rooms in often new, proud and opulent buildings. They deplored the fact that monks in many houses were permitted to consort freely with lay men and women; the abandonment by some monks of their sober habit in favour of more elegant costumes; their lax observance of the offices and of fasts; and their readiness to flirt with *philosophie*. It was pretty well agreed that there were too many regulars – the aim of the founders, it was stressed, was quality, not quantity. Further, it was considered absurd that in many towns more than one house of the same Order was to be found. As the pope had long ago decreed, monasteries with fewer than ten or perhaps twelve monks could not be regarded as viable. That monks should be appointed parish priests was generally condemned, and the bishops insisted that the remaining exempt houses ought to be placed under their control.

As for the mendicants, while many bishops and secular clergy made hostile comments about them, others declared that, in order to provide adequate pastoral care, they needed the devoted aid of these monks as parish priests, preachers, confessors and missioners. The division of opinion roughly reflected the differences between regions in which the Church was well endowed, especially in the north and northeast, and regions where the Church had little land. In the former areas the mendicants were likely to be seen as interfering with the work of the secular clergy and, by taking fees for preaching, celebrating marriages and conducting funerals, reducing their income. In the latter areas the mendicants' help was considered indispensable and useful.[6] But, in general, the work of the mendicants was valued much more highly than that of the propertied Orders.

A few secular clergy and laymen condemned monasticism root and branch, but the majority of such respondents accepted the validity of the institution, although they almost all acknowledged that it was in decline. Laymen, in their replies, tended to concentrate on the disorderly conduct of local monks and to criticise the wealth of the monasteries. It was an important factor that the inalienable property of a monastic house often stood in the way of both private building and municipal improvement. Strongly critical attitudes were more common south than north of the Loire.[7]

Though no regular was a member of the *commission*, it made a point of collecting views from numerous monks, both superiors and their inferiors, the latter often anonymous. No other body of documents reveals so much about the thoughts and feelings of eighteenth-century monks, about the life they led and the work they did. In the more decayed Orders the members often appear content with manifest abuses, but in almost every Order there were monks ready to admit that the rule had been damagingly relaxed. The prior of the Celestine house of Verdelais wrote to Brienne's representative:

I feel as strongly as anyone the unhappy state of the Congregation and the moral impossibility of maintaining us in the type of life we have embraced without a total reform which will be accepted by no one, least of all myself, because I do not feel myself strong enough or virtuous enough to support such a change as would be absolutely necessary. [He would welcome secularisation, but fears that to say so publicly would damage him, because the archbishop of Paris will oppose it and might do so successfully.] Act as though you have our agreement and burn my letter, as I shall burn yours.

Another monk declared: 'I hope you will do all you can to secure us a decent pension. We're all interested in the prospect. I would give everything to finish the business and for us all to be secularised, having been provided with a pension of 1200 to 1500 livres.'[8] Many respondents remarked that monks, except the strictest, were by no means insulated from society and were well aware that monasticism was not valued as it had once been, as falling recruitment figures confirmed. This climate of hostility or indifference had naturally unsettled them, and the assault on the Jesuits had inevitably worried them further. Deep divisions were revealed within many monasteries, ordinary monks often complaining of the 'despotism' of superiors and their indulgent way of life. These complaints were directed not so much against commendatory abbots as against regular priors and office-holders. Many mendicants found begging disagreeable and even dangerous now that opinion in society was turning against the practice.[9]

Respondents to the *commission*'s questionnaire often considered whether particular Orders and houses of which they knew something lived up to their professions. They ask: does an Order obey its rules, and is its rule consonant with the intentions of its foundation and of the monastic vocation; are the Orders run properly and consensually; do individual houses function as they should; do monks in particular houses behave properly; are the Orders and their houses useful to the Church and society? In the case of a small number of little Orders nearly everybody answers 'No' to most or all of these questions. An extreme example was the Exempt Benedictines, who had abandoned living in communities centuries ago and now resided in their own houses, sometimes supporting their families, perhaps with male and female servants whom they paid out of the Order's endowments. Though this state of affairs had existed for so long, it was plainly scandalous in relation to the proper objects of the foundation. The canons of St-Ruf had already asked to be secularised. Even in the great reformed congregation of St-Maur scholarship was said to be declining because the monks were not compelled to be on their own for so long as previously; the inmates of many houses were at odds with each other, partly because of the residue of the Jansenist controversy; and the great wealth of some houses had not prevented them from incurring huge debts.[10]

Despite all this self-criticism and defeatism, a strong body of opinion within the monasteries vigorously defended the institution, usually arguing for a return to stricter observance of the rule as the means of saving it. The bishops' line was similar. The archbishop of Cambrai, Mgr Choiseul, stated the case especially intelligently:

In general, the religious are less necessary today to pastoral government... because the education of the clergy has improved and the ignorance that was once the lot of secular clergy has now, on the contrary, retreated into the cloister... [But] let us take care not to destroy a still useful refuge and a resource which may in the future become necessary to us.[11]

PLATE 1

P.A. de Machy, *Louis XV laying the foundation stone of the church of the abbey of Ste-Geneviève* (detail), Paris, 6 September 1764. The church was designated under the Revolution as the Panthéon.

PLATES 2 AND 3

The so-called 'Turkish bed' by L. Sattler in the Prince Eugene Chamber, Augustinian Abbey of St Florian, Upper Austria, c. 1707.

The 'Marmorsaal', Melk Abbey, by Jacob Prandtaure, completed 1726; ceiling fresco by Paul Troger.

PLATE 4

Monastic staircase (*Kaiserstieger*) Göttweig, by F. A Pilgram, 1738 with frescoes by Paul Troger, 1739.

PLATE 5

The pilgrimage church in Viezehnheiligen by Johann Balthasar Neumann, begun 1744.

PLATE 6

The church of the Cistercian abbey of Stams, Tyrol, Austria, showing the medieval nave, the high altar (1613) and baroque decorations of c. 1734.

PLATE 7

Interior of the library at St Gall, Switzerland, 1757–63, by Peter Thumb, with stucco work by the brothers Gigl, and bookcases and other wood carving by Gabriel Loser, a monk.

PLATE 8

The pergola gallery of the cloister of Santa Chiara, Naples, Italy, 1739–42, by Domenico Vaccaro.

PLATE 9

Detail of the *sagrario* of the charterhouse of Granada, Spain,
by L. de Arévalo and F. Manuel Vasquez, 1727–64.

The remedy, very generally favoured, was to revitalise and enforce the old rules, to 're-establish conventuality'.

After the relatively short period of two years the king issued in March 1768 an edict based on the recommendations of the *commission*, which in turn were firmly grounded on the submissions made to it. He began by applauding those monks 'who gave an edifying example of a regular and laborious life' while regretting the counter-examples of corrupted rules that had brought relaxation and consequent evils. What mattered, he went on, was to strengthen the vocation of those who become monks by ensuring obedience, discipline and strict observance of the rule. To this end the age of profession for men would now be fixed at twenty-one and for women at eighteen (as against the previous sixteen in both cases). The edict incidentally claimed that this would increase the number of secular clergy, including parish priests, at the expense of monks. The bishops did not immediately get their way about abolishing monastic exemptions, but the edict required them to carry out a visitation of the monasteries already subject to them in order to scrutinise their rules, clarify them and thus, it was hoped, ward off litigation and restore the fervour of their primitive institution. The same requirement was imposed on general superiors to visit the monasteries remaining under their jurisdiction. Finally, the edict gave power to the *commission* to propose the suppression of particularly corrupt Orders and of unsatisfactory individual houses. In principle, all houses were to go that had fewer than sixteen inmates, or fewer than nine if the house was part of a congregation. There was to be no duplication of houses of the same Order in any town except Paris, where only two establishments of any one Order were to be permitted.[12] By a further edict of 1773 the powers of the bishops over the monasteries subject to them were enhanced.[13]

In detail, the *commission*'s laborious programme of recommendation, consultation, legal argument and execution involved long delays and led to many inconsistencies. So far as suppressions were concerned, the case of the Dominican house of Grasse offers one of the more striking examples. It had had ten inmates in 1729 but the number had fallen to four by 1768. Their revenues were far too small to enable them to repair their increasingly dilapidated buildings, and evidence was given that they neither preached nor took confessions. In 1771 the bishop successfully proposed to the *commission* that this manifestly degenerate house should be suppressed at the end of June. The rest of the story should be told in the words of Bernard Plongeron:

Bizarrely, the storm broke. The general council of the city held an emergency meeting on 30 June and criticised Mgr de Prunières... What was he up to? How could he not have realised what harm he would be doing to the worship of God? Do not the inhabitants regard the (?ruined) church of the Dominicans as a 'second parish church', easy for the rural population to get to and useful 'on account of the number of Masses celebrated there on feast-days and Sundays at the most convenient times'?

The saintly bishop was at a loss... but began to understand when he learned that the conventuals, magically increased to six, had stirred up their relatives among the bourgeoisie of Grasse. A procession of new sympathisers hastened, with southern volubility, to praise 'the enlightenment, the edifying example and the regular observance' of their *protégés*. On 3 July the royal commissioners, fearing disorder, had to give up the attempt to carry out their instructions.[14]

This was a highly unusual case. Often neither the monks nor their neighbours much regretted a house's suppression. But Chateaubriand remembered stopping

for dinner at a Benedictine abbey which, for want of a sufficient number of monks, had just been incorporated in a more important community of the Order. We found nobody there but the bursar, who had been given the task of disposing of the furniture and selling the timber. He provided us with an excellent meatless dinner in what had been the Prior's library: we ate a considerable number of new-laid eggs with some huge carp and pike. Through the arcade of a cloister I could see some great sycamores bordering a pond. The axe struck at the foot of each tree, its crown trembled in the air, and it fell to make a show for us... My heart bled at the sight of these decimated woods and that deserted monastery.[15]

It is thought that ultimately 458 out of the 2,966 examined houses were suppressed, that is about a sixth of them, with probably fewer than 3,000 inmates, amounting to perhaps a ninth of all the monks of the Orders concerned.[16] Some of their inmates ceased to be monks and were pensioned, others were taken into surviving houses.

More important than the suppressions was the revision of the rules of the Orders. It was a slow process. Twelve years passed before the *commission* was dissolved, and even then it was replaced by a modified *commission* under another name. So the old Orders were subjected to a long period of uncertainty after the initial edict had been published. This ordeal, together with the raising of the age of profession, they and the General Assembly of the Clergy blamed for the steep decline of overall monastic numbers during these years: the Assembly claimed in 1780 that, if the present trends continued, the religious Orders would disappear altogether within three generations.[17] It is true that the 24,000-odd monks who in 1768 had belonged to the monasteries examined by the *commission* had been reduced by 1790 to 18,845, a fall of almost a quarter.[18] But, as usual, the story is not so simple. The 1780s saw a recovery of vocations to the old Orders: recruitment to the Maurists, for example, rose to a level higher than the peak of the 1740s – not enough to repair the great losses they had suffered in the previous two generations, but a striking phenomenon none the less.[19]

Bitter controversy has surrounded the *commission*'s work. Loménie de Brienne, who was effectively its manager, was the friend and admirer of *philosophes* such as d'Alembert and was to be excluded from the see of Paris by Louis XVI on the ground that he did not believe in God. Hence he has been accused of scheming to destroy monasticism under cover of reforming it.[20] The other commissioners, if less radical intellectually, were scarcely friends of the monks. They and the government freely avowed that they wanted the numbers of monks, at least of the traditional type that fell within their remit, much reduced; and the raising of the age of profession was avowedly intended to have this effect. But they also said that they wanted better if fewer monks, and the measures they took seem well adapted to produce this result. In 1773 their efforts were backed up by a royal edict laying down remarkably detailed regulations for the conduct of monasteries and their monks: the revised rules must be strictly observed; there must be provision for the education and separate housing of novices; with only rare exceptions, monks must reside in their house; they must not transfer to another; they must not go out of it except with permission; they must not own property, and the amount they could be given as pocket money was strictly limited.[21] The outlook of the commissioners was best shown in their treatment of the Carthusians, the strictest of the contemplative Orders, devoted entirely to prayer, meditation, worship and manual work within the monastery. So few complaints had been received about the Order that the *commission* made only minor recommendations about it, accepting that it had retained its purity and austerity and therefore could not be said to need reform. Brienne spoke of its houses as prisons – but voluntary prisons. 'It is impossible', he said, 'to desire that a Carthusian should be an enlightened man.'[22] In other words, the *commission* was not concerned to draw monks into the world, to make them more useful in a modern or Enlightened sense. Its avowed aim was to reinvigorate the institution by restoring the ancient monastic observance and enclosure.

The form of the *commission* has also been much criticised. By ultramontane criteria and by the standards of nineteenth- and twentieth-century Catholicism it was appalling to establish a body to deal with such matters without first seeking papal approval – but, after a little negotiation about the detail and the fate of the property of the suppressed houses, the pope gave his blessing to its proposals retrospectively and backed them with his influence.[23] The general acquiescence of Frenchmen in the state's interference in these matters, which plainly involved morality, church law and discipline, showed how strongly rooted Gallicanism was and, like the expulsion of the Jesuits by the state, appears to anticipate the claims of the revolutionary regimes in and after 1789 to regulate the French Church without paying much attention either to the pope or the clergy.

From a quite different standpoint the *commission* – and the government – have been criticised for their unquestioning acceptance of the Church's position as a great property-owner and as providing a system of outdoor relief for the aristocracy. The lands of the few relatively small monasteries that were dissolved were retained by the Church for charitable purposes, and among the bishops and the commissioners there was no challenge to the Church's wealth and taxation privileges, or even to the grotesque system of commendatory abbots – surely one of the main causes of monastic decadence. The subject seems to have been virtually tabooed. No doubt the failure to address the question of the *commende* was due to the fact that it was so advantageous to the government and to the bishops. All the archbishops on the *commission* held at least one abbacy in *commendam*, and to attack the practice would have threatened the incomes not only of many nobles but also of most of the great dignitaries of the church. But to attempt a reform of the monasteries without addressing this major cause of their debility was a classic case of failing to grasp the nettle.

CHAPTER 8

THE AUSTRIAN MONARCHY: THE JOSEPHIST SOLUTION

INTRODUCTION

The second and more radical of the major schemes of monastic reform undertaken during the last years of the *ancien régime* was carried through in the Austrian Monarchy.[1] Here suppression of monasteries formed part of a much broader programme of church reform which included the limitation of papal authority over the Church, the curbing of its wealth, the creation of new dioceses and parishes, the imposition of a state-run system of education for intending clergy, liturgical change, the abolition of brotherhoods, a remodelling of poor relief and other charitable activities, relaxation of censorship, and the toleration of Protestants and Jews. Since it was Joseph II who enacted most of the relevant legislation during his years as sole ruler from 1780 to 1790, the programme has become known as *Josephinismus* in German and 'Josephism' (or 'Josephinism') in English.[2] But its origins have been traced back at least to the early years of his mother, Maria Theresa's, reign, to a period well before he began to take a part in policy-making; and it was certainly well under way when she died.

The Monarchy comprised a huge collection of territories, including all of modern Hungary, Slovakia, Croatia, Slovenia, Luxembourg and the Czech republic, most of modern Austria and Belgium, substantial parts of Italy, Germany, Romania, Serbia and (after 1772) portions of Poland and Ukraine. The total area of this great agglomeration easily surpassed France's, but it lacked unity partly because certain of its component parts – Lombardy, some of the German possessions, Belgium and Luxembourg – were widely separated from its central lands.

Its population, on the other hand, was rather smaller than that of France, though it grew rapidly after 1750 and is estimated by Professor Peter Dickson, who alone has mastered the relevant sources, to have exceeded 20,000,000 by 1780.[3]

Largely owing to Joseph II's zeal for accurate statistics, we have unusually convincing figures for the number of monastic houses and their inmates in the Monarchy in the early 1780s, before he introduced his main reforms.[4] Then, it appears, there were barely 2,000 houses in his entire territories, containing about 40,000 regulars of both sexes. Thirty years earlier, before the 343 houses of the Jesuits and a batch of Italian monasteries had been suppressed in his dominions, the total must have been rather higher, but the annexation of Galicia in 1772 had made up part of the loss. These, however, are paltry figures compared with the tally in France, Italy as a whole, Spain and (having regard to population) Portugal. The overall calculation hides a further major difference between the central provinces of the Monarchy on the one hand and most Catholic countries, including Lombardy and Belgium, on the other: the regulars of the Austrian and Hungarian lands included only a tiny proportion of nuns – roughly one eighth – whereas in Lombardy nuns outnumbered monks and in Belgium nearly equalled them. In fact Lombardy and Belgium each had more nunneries than the central lands of the Monarchy put together. There were even greater variations between the regions of the Monarchy than within, say, France. Lombardy had more than one regular to a hundred people. In the Belgian lands and the Austrian duchies the ratio of regulars to the population as a whole was comparable with that in France: very approximately, about 1 to 220 in the Belgian lands and around 1 to 400 in the Austrian provinces (notably denser in Lower Austria than in the other duchies). In the Bohemian lands it was more like 1 to 800 and in the Hungarian lands 1 to 1,600. These last two proportions are far lower than any we have previously encountered. In the case of the Hungarian lands it needs to be remembered that in some areas Greek Orthodox monasteries were also to be found. But the low density of regulars appears even more striking when it is realised that in every province they outnumbered the secular clergy, often by a large margin, or, to put it another way, in most provinces the relatively meagre corps of regulars made an exceptionally large contribution to the relatively still more meagre overall provision of clergy – and yet it seems clear that the mid-eighteenth century was the time when the total number of clergy in the Monarchy, as in many Catholic countries, reached its highest ever proportion of the population.[5]

That serious monastic reform should have been promoted in France, the land of the *philosophes*, immediately after the suppression of the Jesuits, appears only natural. The Austrian Monarchy, by contrast, seemed literally to owe to the missionary zeal of the Counter-Reformation its recovery in the seventeenth century and its rapid expansion eastwards in the early eighteenth century – if not its very identity.[6] The emperor Charles VI, ruler of the Monarchy from 1711 to 1740, was a bigoted and intolerant Catholic. Although the character and religion of his daughter, Maria Theresa, were markedly less gloomy, to the end of her life she considered it her sacred duty to promote the conversion of Protestants, Orthodox, Muslims and Jews to Roman Catholicism and to refuse them the right of public worship except in some cases where treaties guaranteed it.[7] As we have seen, neither she nor her son Joseph was prepared to work for the suppression of the Jesuits, though she had curbed their power.[8] Most of her lands scarcely felt the influence of the French Enlightenment until the 1760s, and its mockery of the Catholic Church never attracted much sympathy among her subjects.[9] In admittedly backward Hungary, Jesuit and Mendicant missionaries were still making converts, and it required a direct order from Maria Theresa to stop a wave of prosecutions for witchcraft there in 1766.[10] Austrian historians, searching for a parallel in their country to the independent and iconoclastic public opinion that flourished in France, can point only to a 'flood of pamphlets' in the 1780s, most of them brief and crude productions; while the Austrian 'public sphere' hardly extended beyond the nobility and the bureaucracy.[11]

It is true that cracks existed in the Monarchy's façade of Catholic loyalism. In Hungary a substantial minority of the population was Protestant, in Transylvania Lutherans, Calvinists and Unitarians (though not the Greek Orthodox majority of the population) all had official standing, and treaties purported to bind their Habsburg rulers to accord these groups religious toleration.[12] Prince Eugene, the Monarchy's greatest general, had delighted in anti-papal and deistic literature.[13] In the Austrian Netherlands Jansenism was thought still to linger;[14] little societies of religiously dissident nobles were to be found in Bohemia; Muratori's Catholic reformism made a substantial impact on the Church, especially in the southern parts of her dominions; and Freemasonry, condemned by the pope, attracted her husband, the emperor Francis Stephen, and his coterie.[15] But none of these factors stemmed the great wave of monastic rebuilding and Baroquisation until the 1740s.

From about 1750, however, signs began to appear of a retreat from the extremes of Counter-Reformation piety. Maria Theresa and her husband certainly had some sympathy with Jansenism and favoured a rather less elaborate style of ceremonial and worship than had been customary.[16] Partly at least because of the cost and depredations of the War of the Austrian Succession in the 1740s, the boom in church architecture came to an end, and such ecclesiastical buildings as were erected were decidedly plainer than they would have been earlier in the century.

Not only the monarchs, the bishops and some progressive clergy, but also the Court and the higher nobility were losing sympathy with the militant Counter-Reformation and the high Baroque.[17]

As part of this change, attitudes to monasticism, inside as well as outside the cloister, were changing in the Monarchy as in Germany, though the state played a much larger role in the process in the Habsburg lands. At Melk the journals kept by successive priors reveal a decline in obedience, austerity, contentment and conviction:

[In 1750] the monks suddenly begin to attach importance to showy clothing. The prior is embarrassed by the lack of concentration shown by his monks at prayer. A pamphlet appears in Vienna in 1752 advocating commendatory abbots. The chapter of the monastery begins to make difficulties about the abbot's economic activities, against abbot Thomas Pauer they even held a counter-chapter. The monks go into the town at night, speak to women, allow keys to the enclosure to disappear. When the prior remonstrates with them, they threaten to leave ... What the world finds exciting the monks immediately want to do as well ... There is no longer any love for the rule, monks interpret it as it suits them. The prior complains even about the abbot, who does not think it expedient to use the assigned prayers for the cessation of heavy rains because, if they are not answered, the faith of simple people is weakened rather than strengthened. Indiscriminate reading of Rousseau and Voltaire disturbs young monks and causes them to leave. The prior complains he doesn't know which way to turn, one way seems too tough, the other too mild. Suddenly the monks want to discuss when and to what extent music should be heard or wine be provided ... In carnival time the monks want to chat to each other in the refectory after Vespers. After much reluctance he has permitted this, because he doesn't want to give the impression that he wishes to forbid absolutely everything. They want to go into the garden more, become more and more insolent and constantly demand new freedoms.... Hontheim has recanted the extremely dangerous teaching of his book 'Febronius', but Eybel, the Professor of Jurisprudence at Vienna, has declared that he will none the less continue to teach it. May God grant, sighs the prior, that his eyes too may be opened. Recruitment encounters great difficulties because the interference of the state makes it hard for candidates to stay on. Father Ambrosius is punished because he has listened to Father Maximilian Stadler playing the *Klavier* late into the night.[18]

In the sixties, for the first time, the number of publications in German by monks of Melk exceeded the number in Latin. During the eighties one monk brought out an *Apology for Womankind* with an epigraph from the *Spectator*, and others published lyrics in radical journals. Some were avowedly writing on secular matters for the public at large.[19] It can hardly have helped the prior that two successive abbots became Freemasons and were, it is said, 'buried in their aprons according to the custom of the house'.[20] Melk was a particularly large and rich abbey, with unusual connexions to the Court, the Capital and the aristocracy. But in many other less favoured and well-documented monasteries signs of similar developments can be discerned.[21]

One historian, Michael Pammer, has claimed on the basis of a study of Upper Austria that Joseph II's reforms of the 1780s were 'only the administrative realisation of a long since completed change of mental attitudes', as shown by a decline in the number of Masses stipulated in testators' wills and in their bequests to monasteries, brotherhoods and pilgrimage sites. But his evidence scarcely proves his point. Still in the seventies 80 per cent of wills included bequests for Masses; and legacies to monasteries, in 10 per cent of wills, represented an increase on several previous decades. It was not until the eighties, when the government was already cutting down the number of Masses that could be endowed, abolishing all brotherhoods and suppressing many monasteries and pilgrimages, that the pattern of bequests changed significantly. That there was a shift of religious opinions from about 1750 among elements of the upper classes and of the clergy themselves cannot be doubted, but Pammer's material strongly suggests that no more general change of attitudes occurred before the legislation of the 1770s and 1780s began.[22]

It was probably in 1750 that Maria Theresa dictated the first version of her 'political testament'. This was just after she had forced through a reform of the constitution of her central lands, curbing the power of the Estates – and therefore of the great abbeys of Austria – in order to increase her revenue and army.[23] In this document she declared that the clergy of the German lands were in a good and flourishing condition and needed no more of the lavish assistance that they had been receiving from the state, or from her predecessors. In fact, she went on,

they do not, alas! apply what they have as they should, and moreover, they constitute a heavy burden on the public. For no monastic house observes the limitations of its statutes, and many idlers are admitted; all this will call for a great remedy, which I propose to effect in good time and after due consideration.

But, she continued,

I except from such measures the kingdom of Hungary, where much still remains to be done for religion, in which task I shall require the clergy there to co-operate, but not work with them alone, but concert chiefly with laymen on the principles to be followed, the chief aim of which must be to introduce seminaries, colleges, academies, hospitals for the sick and injured, conservatories (as in Italy) for unmarried women, for the better instruction of the young etc., taking careful pains to support and develop what is useful to the public, and not what profits the private advantage of the clergy, monks and nuns in any Province.[24]

This is deservedly a famous passage, and some historians have claimed that from it stems the whole gamut of church legislation associated with her and with Joseph II, that what is known as Josephism actually derives from Maria Theresa's 'great remedy'.[25]

Her remarks are certainly astonishing, coming from a young and devout monarch, heiress to Charles VI, with a Jesuit for a confessor; and they show a genuine awareness of the variations in the state of monasticism within her dominions. But there are many difficulties in the way of treating this statement as seminal. The first is that, under examination, the programme, like the syntax, appears both incoherent and elusive. On the one hand, she says it is desirable that the Catholic religion should flourish and that the condition of the clergy should be good; on the other hand, *what is useful to the public* is a touchstone. She declares that monasteries should observe the limitations of their statutes and not admit idlers, but she does not condemn them – or any particular Order – in principle. She envisages different remedies for the central lands and for Hungary. It is with specific reference to Hungary – not to the Monarchy as a whole – that she makes one of her most radical statements, that she will require the clergy to co-operate with laymen in reform. But she evidently thinks that the Church in Hungary, unlike that in the central lands, needs *more* priests and *more* endowments. One cannot tell from her words what her concept of 'utility to the public' amounts to, or what her attitude is to monasteries of contemplative orders. The meaning of 'useful' can be almost infinitely variable. Even in Joseph II's reign, in 1781, one of his most trusted ministers, count Hatzfeld, president of the *Staatsrat* (Council of State), argued that contemplative Orders ought to be regarded as contributing to *das allgemeine Beste* – the general advantage – through their prayers and worship.[26] It is virtually certain that Maria Theresa would have agreed with him and it is therefore most unlikely that she would have suppressed such Orders, as her son did.

Among other reasons for doubting the significance of this passage in the actual shaping of policy are the facts that in the second version of her testament, written in 1756, there is no discussion of monasteries at all and that she did nothing concrete about monastic reform (except for curbing the power of the Jesuits) until after 1765. Further, the document was composed to be read by her heir on his accession, was kept strictly secret and may never have been seen by Joseph II at all.[27]

In 1765 he succeeded his father as Holy Roman Emperor and co-regent of the Austrian Monarchy. As emperor he had some rather ill-defined powers over the Church in the *Reich*, that is, Germany. As co-regent he had no power within the Monarchy in his own right, but much opportunity to put his views and influence his mother's policy. In a memorandum of 1765 'on the defects of the present system and the most effectual means of remedying them' – a document which is perhaps even more famous and was certainly more instrumental than Maria Theresa's political testament – he set out his plans for the reform of the Monarchy. He devoted a section to the monasteries. He declares that they are too thriving for the good of the state. They ensnare people into taking vows who are too young to know what they are doing, thus depriving the state of the services of men of genius. He would raise the age of profession to twenty-five – that is a very big rise from the sixteen laid down by the Council of Trent. He would appoint a commission to investigate all monasteries, to reform them and use them 'for pious purposes which would be at the same time useful to the state, such as the education of children who, while becoming Christians, would become good subjects'. Perhaps one in twenty monasteries should be reformed, in order to distribute ecclesiastics more evenly over the country.

This pronouncement shows that Joseph had no thought of abolishing all or even many monasteries, at least in 1765. To reform one in twenty is a very modest proposal. On the other hand, he spoke very ill of Catholic education, much of which was in monastic hands, and urged that it should be drastically reformed.[28] His remarks bear little relation to what his mother had said in her testament fifteen years earlier. Still less do they derive from the inchoate French proposals of 1765.

At Maria Theresa's request, prince Kaunitz, her chief minister, wrote a lengthy response, dated 18 February 1766, to the vast range of suggestions in Joseph's memorandum.[29] What he had to say on monasteries is unexpected – indeed, given his reputation as an Enlightened reformer of the Church, positively embarrassing. In his five indispensable volumes of documents on Josephism, Ferdinand Maaß, whose thesis is that Kaunitz was the mastermind behind the movement, does not bring himself even to mention it; and Dickson gives it only a reluctant footnote as evidence of Kaunitz's inconsistency.[30] The chancellor refutes the emperor's statements point by point. He questions whether there are too many monks in the German hereditary lands. There are only 23,000, he says – in fact, as we have seen, this was too high a figure. He scoffs at the idea that they include thwarted geniuses. Most monks are virtually unemployable outside their houses, and there are too few benefices to go round in any case. The convents are performing a service by maintaining such people. Then he defends the usefulness of monasteries. Unless religious worship is to be curtailed, the monks' contribution to it is indispensable:

> It is true that there could be fewer monks if there were more secular priests. But it is not less true that the cost of priests is much higher than that of monks, for it is clear that three monks can live in a community on what it would be necessary to pay one priest living on his own.

Among the assumptions behind this defence are, first, that the provision of parish priests is of prime concern to the state; secondly, that such provision is or ought to be the most important function of the Church, overriding all others; and thirdly, that monasteries have a vital role in this provision. In other words, Kaunitz knew and approved of the contribution made by the Austrian monasteries to parochial work. Although he was arguing against the dissolution of monasteries, he was already approaching the question from a standpoint which was crucial to Joseph's policy of suppressions.

EARLY REFORMS IN LOMBARDY AND GALICIA

Despite his arguments in this document, in the following year Kaunitz began promoting monastic reform in the duchy of Milan, of which he was effectively the ruling minister. Why he should have done so is an intriguing question. A large part of the answer must lie in the fact that Catholic opinion, and all the Catholic Powers, were moving in a similar direction. Restrictions on the Church's right to perpetual ownership of all the land that it acquired had been enacted by most Catholic states since France had shown the way in 1749. This spate of legislation marked an important shift of attitude, though the new laws were not particularly effective, partly because rulers went on granting exemptions as favours or in return for services: even Joseph II was regularly doing this in Belgium in the early 1780s.[31] Governments were also trying to control the Church better in other, not yet very drastic ways, for example by claiming the right to ban the entry of papal bulls and by increasing taxation of the clergy. Even the suppression by the new Russian empress, Catherine II, of nearly five hundred Orthodox monasteries – two-thirds of the total number – and her seizure of their lands and serfs for the state were noticed and applauded by anticlericals in Catholic states.[32] The edicts arising from the French *commission des réguliers* can hardly have made an impact by the time Kaunitz decided to act. But it is hard to separate the measures of government from the movement of opinion. Pombal's campaign against the Jesuits and the movement for their expulsion in France had evoked a large literature and excited everyone in Catholic Europe who took any interest in public affairs. The fate of the Jesuits naturally led to discussion of the merits of other Orders. As we saw in the last chapter, the establishment of the *commission des réguliers* provoked a lively public debate in France about the monasteries.[33]

For a short period in the mid-sixties Italy became the leading centre of reformist writing and activity, especially in Lombardy and Venice.[34] In Milan a brilliant group of young nobles got together to produce the first critical journal to be published there, *Il Caffè* (1764–6). One of the coterie, marquis Beccaria, published in 1764 *Crimes and Punishments*, an outright attack on torture, on the death penalty and on the inclusion in secular law codes of offences which did not harm society but were branded by the Church as sins. The only justification for laws and punishments, he maintained, should be their 'utility', measured against the yardstick of 'the greatest happiness of the greatest number'. Not only was Beccaria's book swiftly translated into French, but within three years some of its recommendations had been published by Catherine the Great to the Russian people. Beccaria and others in the circle of *Il Caffè* were soon given employment by the Austrian regime.[35] The resident governor of Lombardy, count Firmian, a collector and student of Enlightened literature in French and English, sympathised with some of their views. In 1765 a *Giunta economale* was appointed in Lombardy to examine the position of the Church, and its powers were notably expanded in 1767–8.[36] In 1767 was published the first volume of *Di una riforma d'Italia* (On a reform for Italy) by Carlantonio Pilati, a professor in the prince-bishopric of Trent, which assailed the dominance of religious and intellectual life by the Church. Voltaire declared: 'There is scarcely a stronger and bolder work: it makes all the priests tremble and gives courage to the laity... By comparison, French books are all circumspect and gentlemanly. When the author speaks of monks, he never calls them anything but scoundrels.' Pilati was one of the first to recommend abolishing all monasteries of every Order as useless or pernicious.[37]

In Venice, too, a spate of anticlerical works was published, some of which had been banned or burned in France. Their special significance, so far as the monasteries were concerned, lay in their attacks on forced religious professions, and on lifelong vows. Plays and operas like *Idomeneo* and *Jephtha* were drawn upon to show the 'fateful consequences of ill-considered vows'. It was now permitted in Venice to express revulsion at the neglect of their rules by all monasteries and to assert that all of them had become too comfortable: even Capuchin poverty, it was pointed out, was not the true poverty experienced by such people as unpublished writers and students without scholarships (Ill. 27).[38]

ILL. 27 Pietro Longhi, *La frateria di Venezia*, depicting various types of Venetian monks. An autograph note on the back of the picture divides the personnel up between 'those who have a good time', 'those who study' and 'the devout'

The Jesuits of course attracted the bitterest enmity, and several Italian states followed the example of Portugal, France and Spain in expelling them before the pope suppressed them: Naples in 1767, Parma, Modena and Malta in 1768. So far as monasticism in general was concerned, all Italian states – except the papal – took some action to curb it in the 1760s and 1770s, but most of them enacted only very limited measures such as laws against the extension of mortmain, or the abolition of a tiny Order here and a few nearly empty monasteries there, usually with the prior approval of the pope.[39]

Three Italian states, however, embarked on a more serious programme. Of these Venice was the first. While the relatively free press of the republic had been publishing ever more and more radical critiques of monasticism, the government had begun chipping away at the powers of the Inquisition and other obvious ecclesiastical targets. More important, it had set up in 1766 a commission to investigate church property and its uses. The commission made its thorough and powerful report in the following year, and in 1768 the republic, urged on by its most prominent statesman, Andrea Tron, enacted a sweeping reform of the monasteries under the following heads:

Abolition of exemptions, placing all regulars under the ecclesiastical control of the bishops – limitation of the disciplinary powers of monastic superiors – clear rights to arraign and punish regulars assigned to the secular authorities – prohibition on recourse to foreign courts – destruction of monastic prisons – prohibition on professions in the mendicant Orders, in the other Orders prohibition on professions before the age of twenty-one, total ban on children from entering monasteries – no [preparation for the monastic state] to be undertaken outside the country, and no foreigners to be accepted – no begging to be permitted except for those with no fixed abode – all houses to be abolished that have fewer than twelve inmates – prohibition on undertaking a pastoral cure beyond the vicinity of the monastery (except for certain Franciscan Orders in Dalmatia and Albania).[40]

This sweeping programme, implemented progressively during the next five years, led to the suppression of more than half of all Venice's monasteries, 306 out of 441. Most of them were small, but the effect was to reduce by 45 per cent its population of monks. No attention was paid to the protests of the pope. This proved to be, proportionally, the largest purge of Catholic regulars imposed by any government before the French Revolution. It greatly influenced the actions of the two other Italian states which took serious measures to curb monasticism, Austrian-ruled Lombardy and the grand duchy of Tuscany. Just as Portugal, small and apparently somnolent, began the process that led to the suppression of the Jesuits, so the allegedly decadent republic of Venice gave an example to other countries in dealing with the remaining Orders.[41]

Firmian recommended to Kaunitz that he should follow the radical example of Venice. But Kaunitz replied that they must proceed cautiously, because, first, it was necessary not to offend the religious sentiments of Maria Theresa, and, secondly, 'the number of monastic professions in Italy, though prodigious, is to some degree the result of the constitution of the country and of families'.[42] Kaunitz was of course referring to the practice, notoriously widespread and generally accepted among the Italian landed classes, of placing surplus sons and (especially) daughters in monasteries. While Maria Theresa had to be humoured, pressure in the opposite direction from the new co-regent, Joseph II, must have been a factor in Kaunitz's espousing monastic reform. An enquiry was set up, and in 1769 the process began of abolishing small convents. The same justification was put forward as pope Innocent X had given in the mid-seventeenth century, that a house with fewer than twelve religious was not viable. A deal was then done by Maria Theresa's government with pope Clement XIV under which small monasteries, rather than being straightforwardly dissolved, were united with others. The resulting rather limited profits were applied to parishes, hospitals and orphanages. By the death of Maria Theresa 65 out of 291 male monasteries had been suppressed in Lombardy, and the number of monks had fallen from 5,500 to 4,330. Only 6 out of 176 nunneries had gone, because the bishops fought for their retention. Monasteries had been suppressed mainly on the ground that they were small, but with some regard to their 'uselessness' and to the possible utility of their buildings. These Italian measures are often treated as a trial run for monastic reform throughout the Monarchy, and certainly any dissolutions constituted a precedent for other dissolutions. It is also true that much the same criteria were adopted in dissolving a rather similar proportion of the monasteries of Galicia soon after Austria acquired that province by the first partition of Poland in 1772. There 214 houses were reduced to 187, and 3,212 regulars to 2,895 by 1777.[43] But the situation in wealthy Lombardy was very different from that in Galicia, and both were quite unlike the German lands. Hardly any of the numerous Milanese monasteries were involved in parish provision; in Galicia monks and nuns constituted a relatively small proportion of a not very numerous total of clergy; and in neither province did they have a role in any form of Estates.

In the late sixties and early seventies a serious discussion took place at the highest level in the Austrian government about improving public education. Famously, Maria Theresa in 1770 declared education to be *ein Publicum* – that is, a matter for the state rather than, as hitherto, the clergy. But this pronouncement has to be seen in conjunction with a much less progressive-sounding decision that accompanied it. The current ministerial expert on education was count Pergen, who took the almost revolutionary position that the regular clergy were so self-seeking and obscurantist that they ought not to be allowed to have anything at all to do with lay education in future. No doubt he had the Jesuits in mind more than any other Order, but there were other teaching Orders operating in the Monarchy, most notably the Piarists and small communities of nuns, which were not tarred with the same ultramontane brush. If this proposal had been accepted, it would have made necessary the training of a completely new cadre of teachers. Not only Maria Theresa but also Joseph II and Kaunitz were quite clear that this was an impossible policy. On the contrary, they considered the best guide in these matters to be the provost (or abbot) of the Premonstratensian house of Sagan in Prussian Silesia, Ignaz Felbiger, whose published catechism they much admired and whom they were to 'borrow' from Frederick the Great to oversee the establishment of a new primary school system in their lands.[44]

Meanwhile, in 1770 Kaunitz emerged as a monastic reformer for the whole Monarchy. In this case he himself stated that he was partly influenced by the wishes of Joseph II. Kaunitz is now to be found vigorously arguing that the number of monks and nuns was 'far too high' and should be reduced by the state raising the age of profession to twenty-four. This should be done without papal authority or concurrence. It was clear, he said, that Protestant countries benefited from having fewer monks, and fewer celibates generally. Monasteries, because their property was inalienable, distorted the market in land. Monks are not necessary to Christianity – they are not to be found in the Church before the fourth century. Then he produced another telling calculation: 'A parish priest in the countryside with three chaplains or "co-operators" can provide worship and cure of souls for 4,000 persons.' If that is so, he continued, the same four clergymen can do as much in a town. Yet the density of clergy in Vienna is far higher than that. The position will be better in every way if there are fewer monks and priests but all have a genuine vocation.[45] He has certainly changed his tune since 1766, but he still assumes that many parish priests will be regulars. However, he insists that they must be educated not as they have been hitherto, in their monasteries, but on the same basis as in the universities, according to a curriculum approved by the government. He does not yet propose that the training of priests be taken out of the hands of their monasteries altogether.

Maria Theresa agreed in 1770 to raising the age of profession to twenty-four, and later (not necessarily in every province) to abolishing monastic prisons and imposing all kinds of often petty restrictions on monasteries, as to number of monks, reception of novices, the permitted size of their 'dowry', the education of priests, relations with superiors and foreign houses and so forth.[46] To raise the age of profession was to adopt a policy already enacted in France and Venice (though less drastically) and designed to reduce the number of monks and nuns. But she never appointed a commission of enquiry into monasteries and she dissolved none in the German lands or in Hungary – with the enormous exception of the

Jesuits', abolished, as we have seen, only under pressure from other Powers by the pope himself.

So the only suppressions of monasteries in Maria Theresa's reign were the limited measures carried through in Lombardy and Galicia. On this basis it is impossible to accept her actual legislation as amounting to the 'great remedy' which she spoke of in 1750 but never defined, and neither that passage in her testament nor her enactments can be regarded as the blueprint for Joseph's programme.

JOSEPH II'S ACTIVITY AFTER 1780: THE CENTRAL LANDS

Within a few months of her death, however, Joseph turned his attention to the monasteries of the Monarchy as part of his all-embracing scheme to reform the Church. He was convinced – and no doubt strengthened in his conviction by knowledge of Febronius[47] – that it was the right and duty of the secular ruler to carry out such reform, at least when the pope and the church authorities were failing to do it themselves. More than that, as he wrote to the pope in 1782,

Without going and searching the texts of Holy Scripture and the holy Fathers, I have a voice within me which tells me what it is proper for me as legislator and protector of religion to do or to leave undone; and this voice, with the aid of divine grace and of the just and honest character that I recognise in myself, can never lead me into error.[48]

Very early in his reign a case of abuse came to light in Mauerbach, one of Austria's few Carthusian monasteries, and it has been maintained by some, both at the time and since, that it was this incident that provoked his policy of suppression.[49] But, if that special case strengthened the arguments for the abolition of contemplative Orders, Joseph seldom offered as a justification for his policies the existence of abuses such as laxity, frivolity and cruelty in particular houses. He operated instead on general principles. First, monasteries must be stripped of their extra-territorial character: he abolished all the connexions that existed between houses in his lands and superiors or monasteries in other states. Secondly, monasteries must be 'useful' – and Joseph understood by that adjective 'contributing to a tangible secular purpose'. So, late in 1781, he decreed the suppression in all his lands of all purely contemplative monasteries which, being 'utterly and completely useless to their neighbours', 'could not be pleasing to God'. These were the houses of Orders like the Carthusians whose rule and vows prohibited them from doing what Joseph saw as useful work. In taking this step he was, consciously or not, adopting a policy opposite to that of the *commission des réguliers*. Far from wishing to restore the observance of the ancient monastic rules, he abolished the very Order which Brienne considered irreproachable. It is ironic that the *philosophe* presided over a reform that rehabilitated the contemplative Orders while Joseph, a devout Catholic who scarcely understood the French Enlightenment, abolished them.[50]

Thirdly, he turned to other Orders, intending that no monastery of any kind would be allowed to survive unless it performed a useful function. That meant, in Joseph's own first draft for the *Staatsrat*, either educating youth or looking after sick persons. To these qualifying functions were added, after discussion, 'preaching, hearing confessions and attending deathbeds' and, later still, the cure of souls.[51] This last addition, which enters the documents almost as an afterthought, became the essence of the whole programme. It is striking how long it took for Joseph's policy of monastic reform to develop from its tentative beginnings in the memorandum of 1765 into the drastic and idiosyncratic scheme of the 1780s.

In the summer of 1782 an Ecclesiastical Commission was established to implement this policy in the central lands and in Hungary. The emperor appointed as its chairman Freiherr von Kressel, declaring that under his direction he was confident that the commission would produce 'in this business so near to my heart... the best results for religion and the state'.[52] Thirty-two years after Maria Theresa had spoken in her political testament of applying a 'great remedy' to the Church, Joseph at last ordered a full survey of monasteries as part of an elaborate and detailed census of all church land. Pending its report, he forbade monasteries to take any new novices. On 24 October 1783 a decree was issued that envisaged the establishment of new parishes wherever too many people (usually, over 700) were included within an existing parish or where parishioners were too far away (an hour's journey) from an existing church or had to brave flood or snow, mountain or bad roads to reach it. It was now within this context of improving the provision for the cure of souls that the fate of every single monastery was to be decided:

Among monasteries, those will be retained which are necessary either to staff their own parishes or to assist the cure of souls, and for these houses an appropriate number of clergy will be laid down, enough to meet all contingencies. The other monasteries that are entirely unnecessary for the cure of souls will wither away (*gehen nach und nach ein*).

Monks were encouraged to leave their Order and become parish clergy or be pensioned. If they stayed in their Order, they might still become parish priests but otherwise would find themselves in the course of time moved, and brought together with members of other suppressed monasteries of their Order into one house until they died out. It must be emphasised that, unlike the initial dissolution of contemplative Orders, these measures were not, at least in principle, directed at entire Orders. There was at least one exception: it was decided to suppress the Trinitarians, who for some time had scarcely used their substantial resources for their designated purpose, which was in any case held to be obsolete, namely, the rescue of Christian captives from the Turks.[53] In general, though, every single monastery was to be considered on its merits – a recipe, of course, for delay, uncertainty, ill feeling and inconsistency.[54]

The financial mechanics of the process were that the property of the suppressed houses, or the proceeds of its sale, were transferred to a Religious Fund, established early in 1782. Maria Theresa had set up a fund of the same name, but that had been entirely devoted to converting Protestants to Catholicism.[55] The first charge on the new fund was the payment of pensions to the ejected monks and nuns who could not find employment. The emperor was especially hostile to the old Orders of nuns as almost wholly useless: their members could not become priests, confessors or preachers. He approved of what his mother had called 'conservatories (as in Italy) for unmarried women' and also of communities of nuns who taught children or cared for the sick, but such houses were not numerous in the central and eastern lands of the Monarchy. Most nunneries were therefore suppressed but, since their inmates were unlikely to find jobs, to pension them proved particularly costly.[56] The second charge on the Religious Fund was the creation and endowment of the new parishes, parish clergy and parish churches.

In Joseph's mind no element of his church reform mattered more than the establishment of 'general seminaries', only twelve in the whole Monarchy, where all future clergy were to be trained. The aim of this scheme, which he carried through despite strong opposition from his ministers and from the clergy, was to remove from dioceses, and especially from monasteries, any role in educating the clergy. Further, the curriculum of the general seminaries was to be established by the government and to inculcate the officially approved theology and the government's view of the role and functions of clergy and the Church. Some of the costs of these institutions were met by the Religious Fund, and many of them operated in former monastic buildings.[57]

It soon became clear that the Religious Fund would be very heavily burdened for decades with the cost of the pensions to former monks and nuns, leaving too little for the vast programme of parish creation which the emperor's plans envisaged. On the other hand, what was achieved was remarkable – far beyond anything attempted in any other Catholic state before the Revolution. In the whole Monarchy, according to official tables, over 700 monasteries were dissolved and more than 5,000 were added to the previous total of secular clergy, while the number of regulars fell by 14,000. Recent work has shown that, at least in some parts of the Monarchy, these figures exaggerate the degree of change. Two classes of regulars give particular difficulty. There were, first, those whose houses were dissolved but who remained regulars and moved into other houses or Orders. It is not clear that they always showed up in the official statistics of regulars. Secondly, a considerable number of monks became parish clergy while remaining monks, and it looks as though they may, at least in some cases, have been counted as 'new secular clergy'. Allowing for these statistical problems, 5,000 might be the number of new *parish* clergy but the fall in the number of regulars would be significantly lower than 14,000. Among the listed new seculars, moreover, the huge proportion of more than two-fifths are described as students in one of the new general seminaries, and it is quite unclear how far they were able to contribute to parochial work.[58] The number of new parishes created is also a matter of dispute. Professor Dickson gives a figure of only 628 for the whole Monarchy, but in addition 1,161 new 'local chaplaincies' were established.[59] Whatever the precise figures, by the end of the reign the bishops and the *Staatsrat* were gravely concerned at the decline in the total number of clergy and also at a serious fall in the level of vocations. This was partly attributed to the lower esteem in which the government and society now appeared to hold the clergy, especially the regulars.[60]

Although the government pursued virtually the same policy in every province, the manner and effects of its implementation varied in important ways. We know more about the case of the Austrian duchies than any other part of the Monarchy. We learn from Dickson's tables that in these provinces 1,178 additional secular clergy, over and above the 6,500 recorded in 1780, were in post or in training in 1790 as a result of the suppressions.[61] So far as the creation of new parishes was concerned, although rural areas benefited to some extent, the impact of the programme was greatest in Vienna, where, counting the suburbs, the astonishing tally of forty-seven parishes was created. Half of these were erected with assistance of some kind from monasteries. Some of them were actually endowed by surviving monasteries, others were aided by the Religious Fund; some of them were staffed by monks, others by secular clergy, of whom some resided in monasteries.[62]

As well as the already mentioned difficulties of interpreting the official figures, an important study by Dr Ludwig Raber of the impact of Joseph's legislation on the (Observant) Franciscan houses of Austria, with special reference to Lower Austria, has engendered yet further doubts.[63] The Franciscan Order, of course, is a mendicant Order, which raises an important question not yet addressed, the emperor's and the government's attitude to begging. He would have liked to stop it altogether and issued an order prohibiting it. He disapproved of it on principle, as obstructing market forces, discouraging people from working hard, denying personal responsibility and provoking disorder. He believed that the regularised mendicancy of the Orders imposed a special and unjustifiable burden on the poor. Further, he and his sympathisers thought that mendicant monks used improper spiritual inducements to extract alms, and that during their begging tours they preached superstition and bigotry. However, he was forced to admit that the monasteries of these Orders were useful, indeed indispensable, and that they could not survive financially without some revenue additional to that supplied by their endowments. He was therefore compelled in the short run to make numerous exceptions to the prohibition on begging, and in the longer run to provide alternative revenue for the monks, confusingly known as 'pensions', further reducing the financial returns from the suppressions.

There were sixteen Observant Franciscan monasteries in Austria at the beginning of Joseph's reign, making them the largest single Order in the area. On the basis of the returns they made to the enquiry on ecclesiastical revenues and provision, the commission decided that thirteen of the sixteen should be suppressed, leaving only the three located in Vienna and its suburbs. These three were to supply parish priests from their own number, to house secular priests to whom some of the Franciscan monks would act as assistants in parish work, and to maintain a kind of reserve of clergy to stand in when incumbents were ill or absent or died. Perhaps the most striking detail to emerge from Raber's account is that the thirteen monasteries were not all suppressed at once. The bureaucracy pointed out that, under the terms of the emperor's edicts, this was impossible. In Raber's words,

The priority was to make room in the monasteries by transferring the younger Fathers, and later the lay brothers, to the cure of souls or to other available posts. Thus... monasteries were suppressed in order to provide personnel for the cure of souls, and monks were sent to parish work in order that monasteries could be dissolved.

The most that could be hoped for was to suppress one house a year, and that target was not always achieved. By the time Joseph died in February 1790, four of the thirteen houses had still not been dissolved, one saved by the intercession of the bishop of St Pölten, the others waiting their turn to be suppressed. The death of Joseph and the accession of Leopold II procured them a stay of execution. If this pattern was applicable to all Orders, it becomes easier to understand how Joseph's policy turned out to be less drastic in result than in intention.

However, the policy of converting monks into parish clergy certainly achieved notable success with the Franciscans of Austria. Raber reports that

Between 1783 and 1790 were transferred to the cure of souls:

in the diocese of Linz	15 Fathers
in the diocese of St Pölten	55 Fathers
in the archdiocese of Vienna	107 Fathers
as army chaplains	4 Fathers
Total	181 Fathers

In Lower Austria there had been 325 Fathers in 1783. Clearly that figure is not calculated for the same area as those in the table, but it would appear that a very considerable proportion of all Franciscan priests – perhaps a half – became parish clergy.

Many aspects of Joseph's programme are summed up in a well-known print (Ill. 28). I was lucky enough to find in the Vatican Archives a spirited contemporary description of it by cardinal Garampi, the papal nuncio in Vienna, which makes its allusions perfectly clear. He reports in March 1783 that since the last week of January two shops have been selling, as though they are of foreign origin, with the approval of the censorship, this and another 'scandalous and heretical' print.

Curiosity, the mother of temptation and heresy, caused sales to be so rapid and numerous that buyers could hardly get in and out of the shops. What astonished me still more is the exorbitant price, . . . two and a half florins, and despite such a price many many thousands have been sold.

. . . St Peter and the emperor are shown standing on the top of a great hill. In front of them is a net with naked souls climbing one after another to heaven. The emperor holds it with his right hand, St Peter with his left. The latter looks modestly down, holding his keys in his right hand. The emperor has his left hand raised, pointing to the symbol of God or the Trinity shining on high.

On one side of the hill is a Freemason, or someone dressed as a builder with a lantern in his hand, from which a ray of bright light illuminates a group of weary poor men – as though Christian charity to the poor was unknown before the introduction of Freemasons.

On the other side is seen the façade of the Schottenkirche [a great Benedictine house in Vienna] with an inn sign; and the sacristan . . . begging for alms and calling people to worship . . .

At the foot of the hill are regulars of both sexes crowded and enclosed in a net, and holding sacks full of money. Under the net is a box into which have been thrown rosaries, votive offerings, instruments of penitence, religious habits and banners of confraternities.

ILL. 28 Engraving illustrating the impact of Joseph II's reforms, 1783

Between the hill and the net stand spectators...and, as well as a bishop with pastoral staff and mitre, are seen two persons with rochets, by whom it is perhaps intended to represent the Cardinal Archbishop and the Nuncio, the former with a French-style stock, the latter with a Roman one; two Greek priests and a Protestant minister with wife and children.

Finally they have irreligiously placed at the bottom in Latin, French and German the text of St Luke [ch. 5, vv. 6,10]: 'They inclosed a great multitude of fishes: and their net brake...and He said, "Fear not; from henceforth thou shalt catch men."'

The moral of this print seems to be that the best use will be made of the property of the church for the benefit of the poor, and that, now that external devotions have been abolished, there will be purer worship rendered to God.

The only point Garampi refrained from making is this: the artist appears to be insinuating that the pope, on his recent visit to Vienna, has approved Joseph's measures, a claim that it was possible to make since, contrary to the nuncio's advice, Rome had issued no condemnation of them.

In the other print described by Garampi are to be seen the Greek Patriarch, pope Leo X, Luther and Calvin, all congratulating Maria Theresa and her husband on having given Joseph II to the world. Among the admiring spectators is a rabbi. It is remarkable to find such good evidence as this despatch supplies of the popularity of these images, though the nuncio also reports that they evoked protests from the faithful.[64]

Among all these changes it is the suppression of more than a third of the monasteries that has made the greatest impression. But it is important to understand that Joseph did not leave the remaining two-thirds untouched. It was not only the dissolved monasteries whose funds were tapped. If a house had surplus revenue, the Religious Fund might take it without the house being dissolved. When the abbot of a major house died, Joseph generally forbade the monks to elect a successor. Instead, they were allowed to choose a prior to be the spiritual head of the institution on a three-year tenure, while a commendatory abbot or other outsider, perhaps a layman, was appointed to administer the temporalities to the benefit of the Religious Fund. This arrangement incidentally deprived the abbey of representation in the Estates. A house might be peremptorily ordered to create a new parish out of its existing benefices and to build a parish church out of its own revenues – as the Schottenstift was compelled to do with the church of St Laurenz in the eighth district of Vienna. According to a modern abbot of the house, his predecessor in Joseph's reign, Benno Pointner, had

> made a courageous stand against the Josephist pamphlets and also fought for the rights of the parishes, to which he sent at least half his priests for the cure of souls...There was no avoiding the incorporation of more parishes into the foundation, so that the number of Schotten parishes reached eighteen – a much too high number considering the heavy obligations associated with the foundation in Vienna. But perhaps that excessive burden was necessary in order to stave off the danger of

Table 4 *The monastic day as reformed by Joseph II (cf. p. 50)*

5.00 a.m.	Wake up
5.30	Call to meditation
6.00	Prime, then Mass and academic studies
9.00	Terce, Sext, None and corporate Mass, followed by Studies, which could be carried on individually in the garden
10.45	Examen particulare (searching of conscience about the previous twenty-four hours)
11.00	Midday meal with readings from the Fathers, opportunity to walk in the garden
13.30 to 15.30 p.m.	Study Silence
15.30	Vespers and Compline
16.00	Study, from 17.00 allowed to be carried on individually in the garden
17.45–18.00	Opportunity for private prayer
18.00	Evening meal, then *amica confabulatio* (friendly conversation) until 20.00
21.00	Night silence

the monastery's suppression by Joseph's administration or of the appointment of a so-called 'commendatory abbot' who would not have to belong to the Order.

Melk too now sent the majority of its monks into parishes. The Premonstratensian monastery of Geras raised the number of parishes it owned and serviced from ten to seventeen. Between 1782 and 1791 it spent 14,000 florins on four new priest-houses, eight schools and a new church.[65] This must have been the pattern in all the surviving houses, except for the few which had been allowed to exist because of their contribution to education and the care of the sick rather than because they provided parishes and clergy.

With their young monks away at the general seminaries and their able-bodied priests working in parishes, monasteries found it difficult, if not impossible, to maintain a proper community life. Choral services were drastically cut down on the ground that, now that monks were required to be useful, all this singing, especially in the middle of the night, would be injurious to their health and therefore to the spiritual well-being of their flocks.

More than half the monasteries survived, it is true, but only as half-monasteries. In cases where it seemed to the government more convenient or economical, they were allowed to continue in existence, but as depleted, cowed communities to be bullied, mulcted, scattered and stripped of their traditions, of their independence and of their role in the Estates.[66]

Why did Joseph adopt this particular policy, drastic by any standards other than those of the Reformation and the great revolutions, but with so heavy an emphasis on the provision of parishes and parish clergy, and permitting such a large number of houses to live on to fight another day?

One part of the explanation lies in the relations between the emperor and his civil servants. On this point the despatches sent to Rome by the papal nuncios, Garampi down to 1785 and Giovanni Battista Caprara thereafter, contain invaluable and neglected evidence.[67] Among their most interesting features are the strikingly different impressions that the two nuncios give of Joseph II's relationship with his officials. Garampi, who had been in Vienna during the last five years of Maria Theresa's reign, was emphatic that tremendous changes were occurring. Even before a single monastery had been suppressed, he talked of 'a crisis similar to that which the Church suffered in the sixteenth century'.

All the regulars [he wrote] are so shaken that they not only carry out punctiliously the orders they receive but they actually go beyond the royal instructions ... I am reminded at this juncture of the fatalism of the Turks who, unnerved by the fear that their monarchy is in decay, calmly await its end, making no effort to prevent it, and excusing their supine inaction as what they call resignation to the divine will and to the inevitability of Fate.

He had no doubt at all that the emperor himself was the prime mover and that he was having to dragoon his officials into implementing his policy. Garampi informed Rome in July 1781, and again in November, that he could not square it with his conscience to administer the Easter sacrament to Joseph, the nuncio's traditional privilege, because his measures revealed him to be a Jansenist heretic. This suggestion clearly alarmed the pope and must have helped to induce him to make his famous journey to Vienna, where he arrived in time to administer Communion personally to the emperor on Maundy Thursday.[68]

One of the commonplaces of historians, without a single exception, is that the president of the Ecclesiastical Commission, baron Kressel, often said (without proof) to have been a Freemason, was a zealous promoter of church reform.[69] As we have seen, Joseph thought so too. But on 5 May 1783 Garampi, in one of his huge, especially confidential despatches sent by safe courier, reported a secret conversation with Kressel. The baron in no way concealed the torment he suffered [in carrying through these reforms]; but he added that... despite his feelings he remains in his post, no longer with the hope of doing good, but merely of diminishing evil. He foresees that, if he gives it up, there are now too many capital enemies of the Church and blind flatterers of the sovereign who would weakly follow instantly every hasty idea or command he gives.

Kressel, while bitterly regretting the harm done to the Church, thinks he has succeeded in minimising its effects. 'He assured me that, once the emperor has adopted a principle, it is a waste of time to try to oppose it. The only thing to do is to bring up one by one the difficulties that make it awkward to carry out.' By this means, he said, he had succeeded in preventing Joseph carrying out his plan to put all clergy on fixed salaries, and had persuaded him that the best course was to leave them with their possessions and in control of them. He believes that anyone else would have acquiesced in Joseph's initial scheme of destroying all ecclesiastical foundations. Some of his colleagues, he said, 'professed a hatred of everything that is piety, church, order, hierarchy and monks'. He reckoned, as did Joseph's brother, Leopold, that 'the multiplication of parishes was a bottomless pit for which the funds would never suffice'.[70]

The nuncio can hardly have invented this conversation, astonishing though it is, and Kressel would hardly have spoken in this foolhardy way if he had not felt passionately about these issues. But, as the nuncios reported with horror, there were also genuine radicals near the centre of power. I have already quoted the excited remark made in 1782 by Joseph von Sonnenfels, famous as professor of political economy, dramatic critic, official censor and Freemason, that all other Orders would shortly experience the fate of the Jesuits.[71] Ignaz von Born, a noted metallurgist and an even more prominent Freemason than Sonnenfels, published in 1783 *Monachologia*, a satirical classification of monks on the Linnaean system, anticipating the extinction of all their species.[72] The progressive canonist, Johann Valentin Eybel, wrote not only *Was ist der Pabst?* (What Is the Pope?), *Sieben Kapitel von Klosterleuten* (Seven Chapters of Monks and Nuns) and sundry other pamphlets highly critical of the traditional Church, but was also employed by Joseph II as ecclesiastical commissioner in Upper Austria, where he derived obvious pleasure from ordering great abbots about and taking part in the formalities attending the suppression of monastic houses.[73]

Caprara was as certain as Garampi had been that it was Joseph who genuinely took the decisions. But he saw the emperor, for all that he abominated his measures, as the only bulwark against still worse changes. Joseph alone, he thought, stood in the way of the total abolition of clerical celibacy, which Eybel and others advocated. If Caprara both exaggerated the influence of the extremists and sometimes proved too optimistic about Joseph's attitudes, he was certainly right that the emperor's radicalism had its limits, and that a married clergy was beyond them.[74] Joseph also stood out against allowing monks and nuns in general to abandon their vows. Although in the last months of his reign he permitted the sale of some former monastic lands, he always insisted that the proceeds should go to further religious or charitable activities through the Religious Fund, not to fill the state's coffers for general purposes.

He undoubtedly saved some individual monasteries from suppression. Eybel kept on recommending that the great house of St Florian should be dissolved to endow the new bishopric of Linz. In the end the bishop was assigned some of the monastery's revenues and the provost's house in Linz for his palace. But Joseph angrily ordered Eybel never again to raise the question of suppressing the abbey: it was too useful as a provider of parish priests.[75] In Bohemia, the emperor was asked to suppress the rich Premonstratensian house of Strahov on the castle hill in Prague. It had just built itself a second 'philosophical' library to match its 'theological' library of the seventeenth century. In so doing it used bookcases and accommodated books from dissolved monasteries, and placed a bust of Joseph in the pediment of the new building (Ill. 29). He declared the monastery too useful to destroy.[76] On the other hand, as late as 1789, he agreed to suppress the major Cistercian monastery of Lilienfeld on the special ground that its spendthrift abbot had run it into debt. Since the Religious Fund was overstretched, Joseph's officials were always looking for excuses for dissolving juicy foundations.[77]

The emperor had travelled a long way since he had proposed to his mother in 1765 that one in twenty monasteries should be abolished. He had suppressed over a third of them. Anticipating the French revolutionaries, he had ordered that the streets created on the former property of monasteries should be given names that would efface their previous ownership from memory.[78] He had been prepared to take over the property of all monasteries; he had removed from them the right to train clergy; he had abolished purely contemplative Orders; and he had substantially reduced the place of prayer and worship in the life of the surviving houses. I do not know whether by the end of his life he would have had any religious qualms about suppressing all monasteries. But, despite his radicalism, he certainly still held the view that there were practical advantages in preserving – on his terms – a large number of them.

ILL. 29 Façade of the philosophical library of the Premonstratensian monastery of Strahov, Prague, 1784

So far my account of his monastic policy has been illustrated entirely by examples from 'the German hereditary lands' or 'the central lands' of the Monarchy, that is, the Austrian duchies and Bohemia. Two other parts of his dominions, Hungary and the Netherlands, merit special attention because their story was so different. They were the least docile of his lands, boasting constitutions of medieval origin which restricted the ruler's power. While Maria Theresa lived, Joseph had been largely excluded from meddling in their affairs: she knew both how impatient he was with such restrictions and how damaging his plans to abolish them might be, since his frequently stated aim was to achieve *Gleichförmigkeit* (uniformity) of law and administration throughout the Monarchy.[79] The upshot showed how an attempt at imposing uniformity on disparate territories can produce widely varying effects, either as a result of the direct application of the laws in differing situations – as happened in Hungary by comparison with the central lands – or through the violent reaction they may provoke, as in the case of the Netherlands.

HUNGARY

Under Maria Theresa Hungary or 'the Hungarian lands' included, as well as modern Hungary, modern Slovakia and Croatia and small portions of Romania, Serbia, Ukraine and Italy. Under Joseph II Transylvania, roughly a third of modern Romania, was united with Hungary. So this was a vast country of many races, languages and religions. In her testament of 1750 Maria Theresa had promised to give special treatment to Hungary, 'where much remains to be done for religion'. It is likely that she had in mind, first, that there remained many Protestants in Hungary – perhaps a quarter of the population – and that the campaign waged by the Catholic Church, with the support of the Habsburg dynasty, to convert them to Rome had so far achieved only partial success. Secondly, she must have known that the overall provision of Catholic parishes was woefully thin. To try to remedy this lack, her father Charles VI had established in 1733 a fund to create new parishes. But after her death, while the population of Hungary was twice as large as that of the Austrian lands, there were still one and a half times as many Austrian as Hungarian Catholic clergy, and the total revenues of the Hungarian Church fell much below those of the Austrian. The provision was also very uneven. In the western and north-western counties the Church was strong and comparatively rich, in the rest of the country much less so. In two of the ten districts into which Joseph divided Hungary, his inspectors in 1786–7 credited the Church with a million florins of income, and four districts had over a thousand clergy. But in the other four there were under five hundred clergy and church income was under 300,000 florins. This variation arose partly because most of the Greek Orthodox population and some of the strongholds of Protestantism lay in the east. But that itself had much to do with the historical experience of the different regions of the country. The extreme west and north had experienced only rare Turkish incursions and was closely tied to Austria. An intervening area had been won back from the Turks immediately after the siege of Vienna of 1683. But the more easterly regions had come under the effective control of the Habsburgs only after the great Rákóczi revolt had been defeated in 1711. Here the Catholic Church was truly a missionary church. Whereas the central and western lands of the Monarchy had seen a massive rebuilding and refurbishing of churches and monasteries in the late seventeenth and early eighteenth centuries – already by Italian standards a much delayed flowering of the Counter-Reformation – in Hungary it came even later. Hungarian churches were mostly rebuilt from ruins or from scratch in the eighteenth century, and in a distinctly less opulent manner than to the west. Whereas the Austrian Church seems virtually to have stopped building and to have lost its missionary

ILL. 30 The refectory of the Benedictine archabbey of Pannonhalma, Hungary, showing frescoes of 1728–30

Table 5 *Monasticism in Lower Austria and Hungary compared*

Region	Population (approx.)	Mendicants	Endowed monks	Monastic revenue (approx.)
Lower Austria	1 million	1,805	1,047	1.4 million florins
Hungary	8 million	3,736	9,88	1.2 million florins

élan around 1750, the Hungarian Church was advancing and expanding right up to Joseph's accession.[80]

In Henrik Marczali's words,

In the counties formerly occupied by the Turks, where there was scarcely any other foe to contend with except the havoc and destruction that had been wrought, and where the life not merely of the Catholic Church but of Western Christianity had become entirely extinct, the chief rôle among the champions of the Church was still played by the Franciscans . . . their numbers continually grew.[81]

In Hungary there were four times as many mendicants, mainly Franciscans, as there were endowed monks, whereas in Austria the mendicants outnumbered the non-mendicants by less than two to one. The ancient Orders that dominated Austria had only a few houses in Hungary, and their role in the Church was relatively insignificant. The grandest of them, Benedictine Pannonhalma, has lately celebrated its nine-hundredth anniversary, but in fact, like its brother-houses, it had ceased to exist during the Turkish occupation and had to be refounded after the Turks had been driven out (Ill. 30). The relative poverty and weakness of Hungarian monasteries overall is shown in Table 5, based on Dickson's figures.[82]

So Maria Theresa was absolutely right to say in her testament of 1750 that the religious situation in Hungary was quite different from that in the central and western lands of the Monarchy. However, despite her remarks, her legislation did not take much account of the difference, at least so far as the monasteries were concerned. The most distinctive of her Hungarian church measures was the establishment of five new bishoprics in 1776–7, though even that was paralleled in Bohemia.[83] Since the Jesuits had played a directing role in the recovery of Hungary for Catholicism and possessed large estates there, their dissolution by the pope had a greater impact even than usual. One of its particular results was a notable increase in the activities of the Piarists, who had already established themselves as promoters of a rather more up-to-date education than the Society favoured and who now took over much of its educational work.[84]

Joseph's approach was in some respects the opposite of his mother's. His grant of a measure of toleration to Protestants, Greek Orthodox and Jews had particular significance for Hungary, which contained substantial minorities of all three groups. His travels had given him unique first-hand knowledge of the varied character of his dominions and might have been expected to persuade him of the need for different policies in different provinces. But his determination to achieve *Gleichförmigkeit* caused him to give virtually the same instructions about monastic reform for Hungary as for the central lands, and Kressel's Ecclesiastical Commission, despite considerable Hungarian opposition, was placed in charge of both areas.[85]

The small group of purely contemplative monasteries was dissolved at the beginning of the reign together with a wealthy Order almost confined to Hungary, the Paulines, which had become discredited as decadent and aristocratic; but the main group of suppressions, which in Austria began in 1783, did not start in Hungary until 1786–7. This was nearly two years after the enquiry into the Church's revenues reported. But, once the process had started, it seems to have proceeded rapidly. As always, it is difficult to establish precise figures for monastic suppressions. A major problem is that the compilers of statistics for the emperor used varying definitions of Hungary. Moreover, the same uncertainty arises as in the Austrian lands, whether houses designated for suppression were actually dissolved. The most thorough study, a recently published article by Dr Márta Velladics, concludes that, in Hungary widely defined, there were in 1782 315 monasteries. Out of these, 140 were dissolved and 175 survived.[86] An additional and surprising peculiarity of the Hungarian story is that Joseph turned one of the dissolved Franciscan houses in Buda into a house and hospital for Elizabethan nuns.[87] To make a comparison with Lower Austria again, Dickson's calculations show that in 1790 the revenue of that province's monasteries was still almost a million florins, having been reduced by only a third since 1780. In Hungary total monastic revenue was in 1790 less than 600,000 florins, under half the total in 1780. However, the number of regulars had fallen by less than a third during the decade.

In total contrast to what happened in the German lands (and in Belgium), Joseph spared only two of the eight Benedictine houses in Hungary, and those not the richest; and all seven Premonstratensian houses were suppressed. Despite the prejudice of the emperor and his supporters against mendicant Orders, 80 out of 118 Franciscan houses and 12 out of 20 Capuchin houses survived.[88] This difference between Hungary and other parts of the Monarchy has scarcely been noticed, let alone studied. More research is needed before a full analysis can be provided. But the essential point is surely that over many centuries monasticism in Hungary had developed in a quite different way from monasticism further west. At no point in the eighteenth century did the old Orders possess many Hungarian houses, and they did not come near to rivalling the ancient Austrian monasteries in political, social and religious significance. The abbots of a mere three great Hungarian monasteries had places in the Diet, where they were completely overshadowed by the bishops, who dominated the First Estate.[89] However, this difference was of limited political importance because Joseph had no intention of calling a Diet, whereas he continued to work with the Austrian Estates since they had lost most of their power to act independently. He deliberately flouted Hungarian susceptibilities, imposing his preferred policies regardless of opposition. But on the other hand the primate of Hungary, count Joseph Batthyány, retained a more than merely formal position in the administration until 1787. Although he spoke out strongly against the emperor's early reforms, he presumably welcomed the increase of pastoral provision even at the expense of monasteries. So far as their 'utility' was concerned, the Benedictines, and even the Premonstratensians, seem to have had relatively few of their monks working in parishes, as compared with their brothers in the German lands. When it was proposed to suppress the abbey of Pannonhalma, there was an inconclusive negotiation between the monastery and the government as to whether the monks would run a school in order to make their institution qualify as useful. But the idea that it could extend its parochial activities seems not to have been seriously considered. After its suppression even the use of its church by a parish was ruled out because it was on the top of a hill accessible only by a damaged road which the faithful could not be expected to climb.[90]

So, unlike in Austria, the monasteries Joseph suppressed in Hungary were the richest ones. The Benedictine and Premonstratensian houses might be few, but they were on average *forty* times wealthier than Franciscan houses.[91] Presumably, given the especially poor provision of clergy and the relatively low income of the Church in Hungary, the government simply could not have financed the creation and maintenance of a significant number of new parish clergy without taking over the revenues of the particularly wealthy monasteries. As a result the pursuit of the same policy in Hungary as had been pursued in Austria only intensified the differences between the two countries. In Hungary the old Orders became even less important. It was the Franciscans who had been conspicuous in parochial work before 1780, and they evidently played an even greater role in it after Joseph II's reforms. The overall provision of parishes in Hungary, and the wealth of the Church there, remained scanty compared with that in Austria, though the Hungarian suppressions seem to have made it possible to supply 2,212 additional parish clergy, including ordinands, a percentage increase much greater than elsewhere in the Monarchy.[92]

It is tempting to say that the trouble was that Joseph would not take *Gleichförmigkeit* far enough. What was needed to put the provision of parishes in Hungary on a par with that in Austria was to raise the income of Hungary's Church, and hence of its Religious Fund, to the Austrian level. The emperor maintained in his celebrated 'pastoral letter' to his officials, published in 1783, that the provinces, since all belonged to one state, should be ready to help each other; and certain financial transfers did occur from province to province by way of Vienna. But it appears that the net beneficiary was Austria, especially Lower Austria.[93] So far as I know, Joseph never contemplated any serious redistribution of ecclesiastical funding between the provinces.

THE AUSTRIAN NETHERLANDS ('BELGIUM')

Long before he succeeded as king of Hungary in 1780, Joseph had decided to set aside its medieval constitution so that he could govern the country despotically in what he saw as its own best interests and those of the Monarchy as a whole.[94] Hence he refused to be crowned, because that would involve his taking oaths to observe the constitution; and he soon had the Hungarian Crown removed unceremoniously to Vienna. At least in Hungary there was only one constitution. In the Netherlands,[95] small though they were by comparison, and despite the fact that the independent prince-bishopric of Liège divided his territories in two, he was ruler of ten distinct provinces under ten different titles according to ten different constitutions which, at several separate inaugurations, he would be expected to promise to uphold (see Map 3). The country was a veritable museum of medieval institutions. As duke of Brabant, the most important province, Joseph would have to subscribe to a fundamentally fourteenth-century document called the *Joyeuse Entrée*, which bound him, for example, to respect the privileges of its Church, to appoint only natives to official positions and to seek approval of all his edicts from both the Council of Brabant, a body resembling a French *parlement*, and the Estates. If a ruler failed to observe this constitution, it provided that his subjects were entitled to withdraw their allegiance. There were three Estates in Brabant of which the First, the clergy, consisted entirely of thirteen abbots of ancient monasteries of the old Orders. As count of Flanders, the major province apart from Brabant, Joseph's position was less circumscribed because Maria Theresa and Kaunitz had made a deal with the Estates under which their composition was

THE AUSTRIAN MONARCHY: THE JOSEPHIST SOLUTION

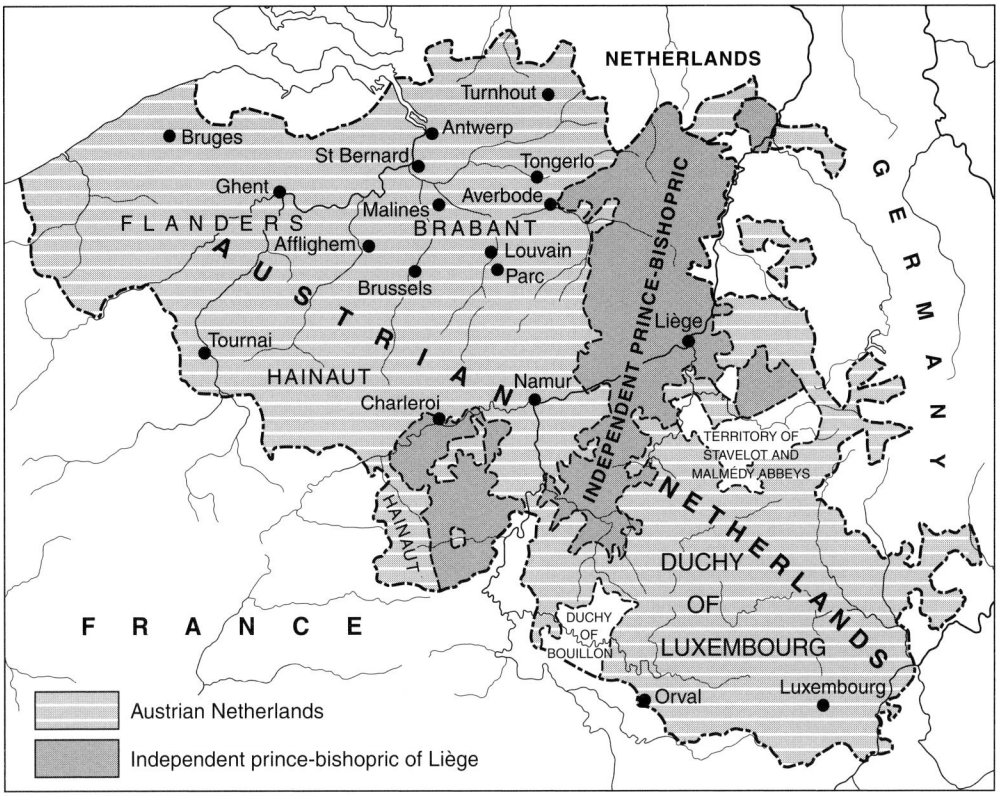

MAP 3 Belgian monasteries

updated and they gave up the right to withhold taxation that had been requested by the ruler. But in most of the other provinces the Estates, although they had no written constitution like the *Joyeuse Entrée*, claimed the same rights as those of Brabant to reject laws and to refuse taxes proposed by the government. These Estates varied in their composition but most of them included a First Estate of clergy consisting wholly or largely of abbots.[96]

As with Hungary, the constitutions of the provinces and the rights of the Estates as against the ruler were guaranteed by international treaties. But the force of these provisions was naturally much greater in the case of the Netherlands because Belgium was many hundreds of miles from the capital and the central lands of the Monarchy, and hence the Vienna government was much less well placed to send an army to quell a Belgian than a Hungarian uprising. In fact the government of the Netherlands had been entrusted to the Austrian Habsburgs after the War of the Spanish Succession only on condition that the river Scheldt would be closed to foreign commerce, thus preventing the exploitation of Belgium's economic potential and protecting the trade of Britain and the Dutch Republic from competition. Further, to give the dynasty these provinces to rule was inevitably to hamper any plans it might cherish to consolidate its territories into a bloc and to pursue a coherent and aggressive foreign policy. Because, like Lombardy, the Belgian lands were detached from the rest of the Monarchy, their domestic affairs were overseen from Vienna by the State Chancellery, whose head was prince Kaunitz.[97]

Most of the provinces of the Austrian Netherlands had in the late Middle Ages enjoyed exceptional prosperity and, despite being frequently fought over in the meantime, were still in the eighteenth century, by comparison with all other parts of the Monarchy except Lombardy, relatively wealthy and urbanised.[98] Their tax yield was substantial enough to produce a surplus, some of which was secretly transferred to subsidise the operations of the Vienna government.[99] For a period in the sixteenth century it had seemed that the provinces had been won for the Reformation but since, unlike the northern Netherlands, they had remained under Spanish rule they had been recovered for Catholicism by the Counter-Reformation. Subsequently they had developed in self-conscious contrast with the Protestant north and had become notorious for clericalism and obscurantism. Although in the late seventeenth and early eighteenth centuries Jansenism took a strong hold, it seemed to have virtually disappeared by the time Maria Theresa came to the throne.[100] Certainly the rule as viceroy of her brother-in-law, prince Charles of Lorraine, from 1745 to 1780 was relatively generous and enlightened, but French *philosophes* as well as Dutch and British Protestants who visited the country considered it benighted.[101]

The figures for Belgian clergy numbers in the eighteenth century are unsatisfactory, especially before the reign of Joseph II. It seems, however, that at mid-century, as in most Catholic countries, the clergy as a whole reached their highest proportion of the population, in Belgium about 1 in 100. Brussels, with only seven parishes for over 70,000 people, contained none the less in 1784 1,597 clergy; Antwerp with 50,000 inhabitants had 1,054. This proportion of rather more than one clergyman to fifty persons in both cities might seem exceptional, but in the university town of Louvain the ratio was more like one in thirty. Among the clergy there were substantially more regulars than seculars.[102] The provinces abounded both in rich monasteries of the old Orders and in houses of the newer Orders. In 1750 there must have been altogether about 450 since, after the dissolution of the 46 Jesuit houses, there remained almost 400. So the Austrian Netherlands, with a population of two and a quarter million, possessed in the early 1780s roughly 10,000 monks and nuns, about 1 in 220 of the population, *per capita* eight times as many as Hungary and nearly twice as many as the Austrian lands. Nearly half of all regulars were nuns.[103] Figures for the landholdings of the regular clergy are even more uncertain and include staggeringly high estimates, but it is probable that monastic property represented between 15 per cent and 20 per cent of the total area.[104] Certain houses had remarkably high incomes: the Benedictine abbey of Afflighem, whose titular abbot was the archbishop of Malines, received almost 300,000 francs a year, and the Cistercian nunnery of La Cambre – notorious for having staged in 1759 Molière's *Le médecin malgré lui* – over 100,000.[105]

It is possible to find in Belgium in the early eighties severe criticisms of the monasteries. For example, among the many thousands of petitions submitted to the emperor during his visit of 1781, one of the few which raised a general issue consisted of a denunciation of the excessive number and the mutually conflicting privileges of the clergy of Louvain.[106] But the general Belgian attitude to the regular clergy was remarkably benign. The bishops made this defence of them to Maria Theresa in 1773: 'It is the monasteries that supply the secular clergy with auxiliary troops always ready to help them in the burdensome discharge of parochial duties; in the towns the religious provide learned and zealous preachers; in the country they substitute for clergy who are sick.'[107] The Estates of Hainaut later told Joseph II:

The ecclesiastical communities which are the great landowners in this county have rescued the country from the ruin brought by 150 years of war: it is they who, by helping the labourer, repairing his cottage and his buildings, giving him cattle and seed, have provided work for the inhabitants ... They care about the prosperity of the farmer. He for his part feels honoured in a profession that enables him to live comfortably, knowing that his enterprise will not become a pretext to extort from him a greater quantity of produce.

It was often asserted too that the monasteries were generous in charity to the poor, though it was notorious that they spent much of their income on building. Many were noted for the excellent beer they brewed. But while it was generally acknowledged that the monks and nuns behaved respectably, they were not thought to display the fervour of previous generations.[108]

We luckily possess for the period 1779 to 1791 an exceptionally full and well-observed journal kept by a monk of the seventh-century Benedictine abbey of St Peter in Ghent, Emilien Malingié, recording 'everything remarkable that happened in the abbey ... and ... the principal events that occurred in the Austrian Netherlands'. To follow aspects of the story through his eyes and experience, controlled of course by other sources, reveals much about monasteries in general as well as about Belgian houses and his own in particular; and his journal is unique as an account from below of the measures of Joseph II and their impact.[109]

Malingié entered the house as a novice in 1779 at the age of twenty-three and took his solemn vows three years later, thus observing the new law on the age of profession. He prefaces his journal with a full account of his abbey and its buildings. As he proudly records, its privileges were almost uniquely extensive. Its abbot claimed the rank of prince, and this claim, though regularly challenged by the government, was never disproved. A more extended version of his title ran 'Prelate of the exempt abbey of Saint-Pierre-lez-Gand, primate of Flanders, prince of Camphin, count of Harnes, lord of the town of St Pierre etc. etc.'[110] The abbey, on the banks of the Scheldt, had nearly complete authority over its little town or suburb on a hill that dominated Ghent, once one of the richest cities of Europe. Though much of the monastery's large income during the eighteenth century – 15,000 livres per annum excluding significant revenue from lands in France – had been spent on rebuilding, Malingié held the well-justified opinion that it lacked elegance, unity, administrative convenience and a sufficient level of comfort. For example, the library was too near the admittedly impressive domed church and so readers were disturbed by the sound of the organ and the chant, and they could also hear what was being taught in the theology class below. The bookshelves were too high for all the volumes to be reached with the ladders provided but, despite an accident to the librarian, the abbot refused to have longer ladders made. An impressive infirmary had been built to an architect's design, but at the price of taking away some of the monks' individual gardens, a measure which had aroused bitter opposition – indeed, one monk was never the same again after these gardens had been built over and died soon afterwards. The abbot had duly offered rooms in the new infirmary to the older monks, but all had refused: they preferred their existing spacious rooms on an upper floor, affording magnificent views. So the infirmary had never been used for its intended purpose. No account of a monastery illustrates better than this the uncanny affinity between these functioning Catholic houses and old-style Oxbridge colleges. As I read Malingié's comments, I can almost hear the voice of a long-serving bachelor Fellow complaining about his head of house and the management of his college.

When Malingié joined the community, there were forty-eight monks, all of them apparently of local origin and ten of them of noble stock, including abbot Seiger – 'at least, so he claims'. Fourteen of them worked in parishes. While still a novice Malingié was not privy to all the affairs of the house but he records with relish the celebration in November 1780 of the golden jubilee of a monk aged seventy-one called T'Servrancx, who was pastor in Destelberghen. Of course a special service was held. The monk was crowned, and the presbytery was adorned with flowers by four decently dressed little girls. 'During this ceremony and the Mass two little cannons were fired several times, but as the noise prevented all the solemn liturgy being heard, the abbot ordered the firing to stop.' The jubilarian's relatives came, twenty-three men and twenty women. At noon a magnificent meal of seventy-nine covers was served. The jubilarian sat on the abbot's right, the mayor on his left. The cannons sounded again, as at Elsinore, when each toast was given. After supper eight monks performed a comedy 'representing all the dramatic actions done by the jubilarian during his life'.[111] There followed a concert and 'a sort of ball'. The ladies had not been allowed to dine but had been permitted by the abbot to attend the play and the dance, to the indignation of the prior. As Malingié wrote, though the occasion was in fact decorous, it did not edify the world that monks put on mixed dances. The next day the abbot entertained the twenty ladies and the jubilarian to a meal in his lodgings. Such a celebration, which doubtless had parallels in many monasteries, helps to account for the widespread perception of monks as gluttonous and abbots as fat. This impression would have been enhanced by the sumptuous meal served after the funeral of abbot Seiger in September 1789. Following two vast *services* of meat and fish of almost every kind, including sturgeon, came the dessert of 107 plates of pineapples, melons, grapes, pears, apples etc.; coffee and liqueurs; and at eight o'clock a second offering of oysters. At ten o'clock the monastery's carriages ferried the guests home.

The abbey's status as a royal foundation and the premier abbey of Flanders was understood to involve giving regular hospitality to the viceroy, his family and his guests – and to high society generally. Both Catherine the Great's son, the future tsar Paul, and George III's brother, the duke of Gloucester, came in 1782; and a throng of notabilities descended on the monastery to see Blanchard take to his balloon – and nearly come to grief – in 1785.

St Peter's exceptional privileges, as Malingié's account underlines, depended on its association with the counts of Flanders and its unique role at their inauguration. Custom dictated that after the death of Maria Theresa a catafalque should be erected in the church, a solemn requiem be sung without instrumental accompaniment and the great bell be tolled for half an hour three times a day for six weeks. A few months later, to the general astonishment, Joseph II came to visit his Belgian provinces, the only part of his dominions that he had never previously seen. As was his custom he travelled incognito so that he could be spared the normal ceremonies and formalities; and he gave offence by staying in hotels rather than in official residences such as St Peter's. But at times he played the ruler's part. On 16 June 1781, after having watched the soldiers exercising at the barracks behind the abbey, he gave an audience in the city centre. First to be received, according to precedent, were the bishop of Ghent, a prince Lobkowitz from Bohemia, and the abbot of St Peter's. Both were aware of the emperor's intention to carry out reform in Church and state, though no one knew what his detailed proposals would be. The bishop asked him to swear at his coming inauguration the customary oath in the cathedral to maintain the rights and privileges of the Church. Joseph replied that he would not do so because the general promises that he would make in the town square to observe the constitution rendered such special undertakings unnecessary. After this the abbot naturally expected that the emperor would decline to swear another customary oath, which generations of counts had taken in St Peter's before proceeding to the square, to uphold the rights and privileges of the abbey. But he forestalled the abbot's request, saying: 'I am aware of the custom to take the oath at your abbey. Be confident... that it will be done in the usual form.' Less gratifying was his curt refusal of the petition of a young aristocratic lady to be allowed to take monastic vows before the statutory age of profession.

In the event Joseph did not himself swear the oath in St Peter's. But his deputy, prince Albert of Saxe-Teschen, did so on behalf of himself and his wife, the emperor's sister, Marie Christine, joint governors-general, on 31 July, promising 'to maintain against and in the face of everyone the privileges, franchises, usages, customs, goods, possessions... of this church'. He then swore the oath to uphold the constitution of the province. 'What stronger bond can there be', wrote Malingié, 'than that of an oath?'[112]

Only two months later the monk was lamenting what he saw as two breaches of these oaths, Joseph's edict of toleration and his abolition of monasteries' dependence on foreign superiors. Then in 1783 he wrote: '**alas!** the sacrilegious arm of Joseph II, our unworthy sovereign,... has suppressed the Carthusian monastery at Ghent'. This house was one of the victims of his edict, applied to all his provinces, abolishing the 'useless', purely contemplative Orders. By the time the full effects of the measure had been felt in Belgium, over 150 monasteries had been closed, most of them nunneries.[113]

And you, [wrote Malingié,] impious emperor, sacrilegious sovereign, limb of Satan, you dare to tear these holy souls from their retreat to plunge them into this stormy sea, to make them sustain themselves in this den of vice that you continually poison more and more by your edicts drawn from the founts of irreligion and impiety. But be assured, villain that you are, that you will soon feel the weight of the avenger's arm on your head and on your realm. It already seems to me that he has commanded the infernal furies to preside at your death. Tremble then, unnatural monster, and quake!

But at this stage the monk can only lament the passivity with which the Council and Estates of Flanders have received Joseph's decrees. They have even suggested how he might best spend the money accruing from the suppressions.[114]

However virulent Malingié's account, it remains factually accurate. His emphasis on Joseph's readiness to take the oath to maintain the privileges of St Peter's and the general oath to uphold the constitution of Flanders is well justified. The emperor had also allowed prince Albert and other deputies to swear on his behalf to abide by the constitutions of the other provinces. One is bound to wonder why Joseph, so scrupulous in Hungary, proved so complaisant in Belgium. There was of course no occasion for him to justify his action in 1781. When, in and after 1787, he openly flouted the *Joyeuse Entrée*, he declared that many of the provisions of the document were so manifestly absurd and out-of-date that it was impossible to observe it fully. He also maintained that, if the measures he put forward were clearly beneficial, it did not matter that they contravened the constitution. 'I do not need your consent', he told the Estates of Brabant, 'to do good.'[115] But, in view of his attitude in Hungary, it seems improbable that in 1781 he already intended to break his oath and abolish the *Joyeuse Entrée*, as he eventually did – or tried to do – in 1789. As regards his almost more surprising readiness to take the oath in St Peter's to maintain the abbey's privileges, he could reasonably have replied to Malingié that his early measures did not in fact infringe them.

A complicating factor was his long-held desire to exchange Belgium for Bavaria in order to concentrate his territories. Although one attempt to achieve this *arrondissement* had just failed in the War of the Bavarian Succession of 1778–9, he never ceased to plan others, and he tried to obtain the exchange by negotiation in 1784–5. Maybe, when he allowed all these Belgian oaths to be taken on his behalf, he said to himself that he would not be ruler of the country for much longer. But in the special case of the monasteries there is a further possible explanation. As we have seen, the great scheme to apply the manpower and revenues of monasteries of all Orders to the creation of parishes did not surface until 1782, when it was promulgated for the central lands and Hungary. It was not applied to the Austrian Netherlands until 1786. No doubt the delay between 1782 and 1786 is largely explained by the Bavarian exchange negotiation and also by the war Joseph fought against the Dutch in 1784–5 in an attempt to force the opening of the Scheldt. But back in 1781 his characteristic scheme for the reform of the monasteries had not been invented. A final justification of Joseph's taking the oath to preserve St Peter's can be found in the fact that, until very late in his reign, he refrained from dissolving any Belgian houses that were represented by their abbots in the provincial Estates. To this degree he respected their constitutional position.[116]

Malingié records with mounting indignation the hail of edicts that rained on the Belgian Church during the year 1786, most of which had been imposed earlier on the central lands and Hungary and were directly copied from those just introduced in Lombardy. Now acting as the abbot's and the chapter's secretary, Malingié knew how cunningly the abbot sought to frustrate the government's measures. He would feign illness in order to avoid meeting official guests; he would blandly inform a visiting general that the abbey had no stables. He adopted various ruses to preserve the house's property. For example, he wrote to the emperor saying that, in order to comply with an edict of Maria Theresa's, it needed to spend a very large sum on the parish churches and vicarages for which it was responsible. His object was to show that all the abbey's income was committed to useful purposes and there was nothing to spare. To his surprise Joseph approved the expenditure, but nothing was ever spent. One of the edicts of 1786 established an Ecclesiastical Commission like that of the central and Hungarian lands, announced the new plans to determine the fate of all monasteries according to their capacity to provide parish priests and required all houses to make a return of their condition, lands and revenues.[117] The abbot of St Peter's delayed sending in his return, which it must be admitted, especially since the house had considerable property over the border in France, was no easy task to complete. He gave all the monks money ostensibly to pray for his health, saying that he wished to provide for them in case the monastery was suppressed. To this end also he passed a sealed box of confidential papers to his sister for safe keeping, which included bank drafts and lottery tickets.[118]

Of all the emperor's ecclesiastical measures it was the establishment of the general seminary at Louvain that caused the greatest indignation. An English contemporary wrote: 'With a view of enlightening the Flemish clergy, who have not been thought to possess the most liberal sentiments in matters of religion, a rector and professors were sent from Germany' to run the courses.[119] All Belgian abbeys were ordered to send their novices to be trained there, and most, after making many excuses, eventually complied. But in December 1786 the seminarists rioted against their teaching and conditions, most particularly the weakness of their beer, the first sign of violent opposition to the government's policies. As no concessions followed, but instead further edicts drastically altered the constitutional and administrative arrangements of the provinces, unrest mounted. Whereas the nobility and other laymen had not felt inclined to fight for the preservation of contemplative monasteries, they now backed churchmen, secular and regular, in opposition to the emperor's programme of further church reform.

The Council of Brabant and the Estates, led by Henri Van der Noot, demanded a return to the constitutional and legal position of two hundred years ago. This astonishingly conservative stance was supported by a flood of pamphlets and by the propaganda of an ex-Jesuit, F.-X. Feller, who in his *Journal historique et littéraire* and other writings denounced rationalist reform in ways that anticipated Burke's attack on the French Revolution in 1790. In May 1787 a popular rising, 'the Little Revolution', took place in Brussels which the governors-general had not the forces to suppress, and in June they ventured, without Joseph's prior authority, to withdraw all his recent legislation and to suppress the general seminary. Countrywide celebrations greeted this victory of reaction.

Joseph, infuriated, played for time, reinforced his troops in Belgium and then reimposed his measures. The new criteria for monastic suppressions had come as a shock to the Belgians: in the Netherlands the application of monastic revenues and personnel to parochial work, which appeared generally acceptable in other parts of the Monarchy, was heavily criticised, mainly because it was deemed unnecessary and unconstitutional but sometimes on the ground that it ignored the fundamental distinction between the secular and the regular clergy.[120] But so long as the government was busy obtaining and collating the answers to their questionnaire from the monasteries the process of suppression was held in abeyance. Needless to say, the abbots dragged their feet about it, as about sending their novices back to Louvain. But early in 1789 Joseph wrote to the abbot of St Peter's and others, 'demanding to be obeyed without delay and without argument'.[121] It had been true for some years that, when an abbot died, the house was denied the right to elect a successor. Now the government began appointing commendatory abbots, another infringement of the *Joyeuse Entrée*. As disobedience continued, troops were sent in to recalcitrant abbeys to occupy them and seize their property, and the government sought to arrest the leading dissident abbots, who fled to the Dutch Republic.[122]

One naturally asks how many monasteries were suppressed under the new criteria during this disturbed period, and how many parishes were established. It is very hard to give an answer. The government had found itself frustrated at every turn. They decided, after bitter early experience, that houses with poor resources could not be suppressed because that would cost the Religious Fund more in pensions than would be gained from the seizure of their property. This consideration saved most of the mendicants' establishments. Then the numerous houses that had property outside the emperor's dominions were to be left alone unless – a most improbable condition – the other state concerned would surrender it. This difficulty caused the wealthy monastery of Orval in Luxembourg, just lavishly rebuilt, to

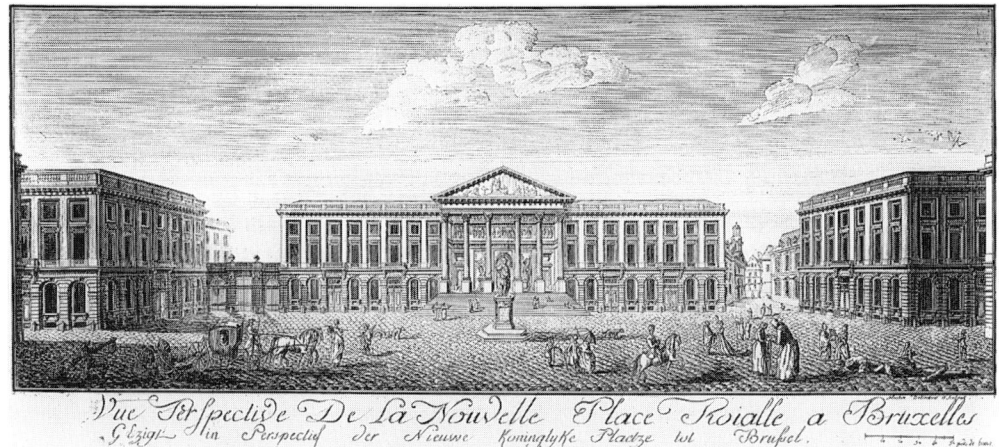

ILL. 31 Late eighteenth-century print of the 'Nouvelle Place Royale', Brussels, showing the buildings intended for the abbey of Coudenberg

be spared. On the other hand, the Augustinian monks of Coudenberg in Brussels made things easy by asking for their house to be dissolved. Their fate constituted an awful warning. Their abbot having obtained a seat in the First Estate of Brabant as late as 1775, the house was induced to collaborate with Charles of Lorraine in rebuilding their monastery as part of the grand remodelling of the quarter around his palace. The cost of their splendid new church and buildings, which still dominate the district, had plunged them into irretrievable indebtedness (Ill. 31).[123] Otherwise an unknown number of houses was earmarked for suppression, but very few indeed of them appear to have been actually suppressed.

So far as the erection of new parishes was concerned, within the Monarchy the Belgian situation was peculiar. Although monks were numerous, the seculars, most unusually, far outnumbered them. In most districts the provision of parishes already fell not far short of what Joseph considered appropriate, and most bishops thought that there was no great problem to be addressed. A few new parishes, however, were created. In Luxembourg, on the other hand, not only was there a real shortage of parishes but there was no bishop. The government had ideas of applying the revenues of Orval to a new bishopric but, as we have just seen, that plan was frustrated. If so rich a monastery could not be suppressed in Luxembourg – and if no assistance could be obtained from outside the duchy – then there was no hope of finding the money to create the required parishes. Joseph resorted to accepting financial assistance from rich clergy, including Hontheim, in the diocese of Trier, of which Luxembourg formed a part. But even that had not materialised by the time rebellion triumphed. All in all, it appears that the programme of monastic suppressions and parish creation planned in 1786 hardly got off the ground.[124]

As the Council and Estates of Brabant continued to obstruct his measures, in June 1789 Joseph formally quashed the *Joyeuse Entrée*.[125] Van der Noot had already fled to the Dutch Republic where at Breda he was collecting troops and negotiating for the support of foreign rulers. A rival opposition party arose, led by Jean-François Vonck and called the Democrats, which looked with some sympathy to revolutionary France and accepted the desirability of some reforms while objecting to Joseph's despotic methods. Vonck tried to persuade Van der Noot not to rely on foreign assistance but instead to raise a force of Belgian patriots to fight the Austrians. Since Van der Noot refused, Vonck took action himself and set about trying to recruit an army. A group of Democrats around Vonck also began to plot a revolutionary outbreak. In 1788 one of them, perhaps the prime mover, J.B. Verlooy,[126] published the first defence ever made of Flemish as a national language; and resentment at the dominance of French in government and aristocratic circles clearly played some part in the opposition to Austrian rule. It was crucial to all these efforts that the British, the Dutch and their Prussian allies were hostile to Joseph II and his plans, that France was disabled by her own revolution from assisting her ally, the emperor, that a radical revolution broke out in Liège in August, that it was so easy for Belgian opponents of the Austrian regime to take themselves off to the Dutch Republic or to Liège to write and publish pamphlets or raise and train troops – and, most important of all, that Joseph had become involved in a costly and difficult war against the Turks, which prevented him from sending as many troops as he would have liked to the Netherlands.

It is time to bring on to the stage Godfrid Hermans, abbot of the Premonstratensian monastery of Tongerlo near the Dutch border and a prominent member of the First Estate of Brabant.[127] A man of peasant origin, genial, energetic and able, he had hitherto been known as an effective abbot in three spheres. First, he had proved an excellent agriculturist, bringing marshes and heaths under cultivation and greatly increasing the yield of the monasteries' estates, especially those lying in the Dutch Republic. Secondly, he had worked hard and successfully to expand the holdings of his abbey's library. Thirdly, he had very recently done a deal with the government under which, at considerable expense to his house, Tongerlo would accommodate and foster the work of the Bollandists – ex-Jesuits and refugees from the abbey of Coudenberg – on their series of *Acta sanctorum*, lives of the saints. The government officials who endorsed his proposal doubted the project's scholarly value but thought it a harmless encouragement to piety and patriotism, and of possible economic benefit.[128] Hermans now decided that his duty required him to go beyond peaceable opposition to the emperor and to promote armed intervention. Though his own opinions inclined him to Van der Noot's conservative programme, Hermans, with the abbot of the nearby Cistercian house of St Bernard, arranged to guarantee 100,000 florins to the Vonckists' choice as commander, the retired general Jean Van Der Mersch, if he would leave the Austrian service and head a rebel army, which he agreed to do. Although the Estates party and the Democrats differed over both long-term aims and short-term tactics, at this stage they were united enough in their determination to defeat Joseph II's plans for such leaders as the abbot of Tongerlo to be able to make use of both approaches. It is striking how close the interrelationships were between monks and politicans of both parties. If Van der Noot's conservatism and his association with the Estates of Brabant seem to make him the natural ally of Hermans, Vonck had worked as the abbey's legal representative and received in September 1789 a payment of 10,000 florins from the abbot to further his brand of opposition activities. In Vonck's own words:

Of all those to whom I talked of the revolution, I never encountered anyone who had it so much at heart and who was so enthused about it as [the abbot of Tongerlo] who one day frankly told me that he would stop at nothing to bring about so salutary a result and that he would try by all possible means to persuade several other members of the First Estate to enter into his views.[129]

Brussels had necessarily been the centre of the Estates' campaign, but Flanders was believed to have Vonckist sympathies and was certainly more vulnerable to attack than well-garrisoned Brabant. So when Van Der Mersch took his troops from the Republic into Belgium, he led them into Flanders. At Turnhout his force defeated a contingent of Austrians, who retreated and made a stand in Ghent. Malingié records watching from his abbey church tower the street-fighting that went on there for several days in mid-November.[130] The abbey was in the hands of the sequestrators and was the head quarters of the Austrian general, and a few monks were on the emperor's side. But the majority of monks took the side of the insurgents. All felt, however, that they had to preserve a degree of impartiality and they obtained the half-permission of the authorities to offer hospitality to the rebels as well as to the government forces. After the defeat of the Austrians, monks of this and other Ghent monasteries tried with success to prevent reprisals against the government's men. Despite its prudent display of moderation, however, the abbey of St Peter's had given more than any other in Flanders to support the patriotic cause: 43,000 florins of Brabant.[131]

Faced with this scarcely credible disaster the Austrian resident minister, count Trauttmansdorff, took it upon himself to close the general seminary, but it was too late to stop the momentum of the patriotic movement. By the end of the month a popular revolt in Brussels had driven out the minister and his officials – so precipitately that they had to leave their files behind, with the result that the rebels could publish some of the most damaging as evidence of Joseph's despotic and ruthless approach to Belgian affairs. In mid-December the abbot of Tongerlo was one of the group of rebel leaders who rode into Brussels in triumph with Van der Noot. They set Austria and Joseph II at defiance, called a States-General of all the provinces and formed a United Belgian Republic. Abbot Hermans, under the religious-sounding title of 'grand almoner', was effectively their war minister or 'the soul of the Brabant Revolution'. He raised troops, preached at them, fed them, clothed them, provided them with weapons and even gave them their orders. All in all he and his monastery spent more than 400,000 florins to support the patriotic cause in 1789 and 1790, and more than 3,000,000 was raised from the abbeys as a whole.[132] Of course others than abbots and their monasteries played essential parts: certain nobles were prominent, like prince Louis de Ligne, brother-in-law of Helen Massalska and son of Joseph's loyal general, who led some of the patriotic troops in the battle for Ghent; prominent bankers like viscount Walckiers made a notable contribution; and there was widespread popular support from both men and, unusually, women in the revolts in Brussels. But the abbots and their houses had special advantages and opportunities which they used with notable skill. In so far as the use of Flemish was an issue, they were in a very strong position to exploit it because many of the abbeys had for centuries conducted their affairs in that language. More important, they had lands and resources outside the Austrian Netherlands, wealth sufficient to fund an army, an assured political position as leaders of the First Estates of the provinces and a fund of goodwill among the population. Indeed the monks were accused by the Austrians and the Belgian radicals of using every inducement to whip up a bigoted and fanatical crusade against a basically well-meaning government (Ill. 32).[133]

By the end of November 1789 Joseph, desperate and dying, had abandoned virtually all his legislation. So, in the very month when the French National Assembly abolished monastic vows in principle and declared all church lands to be at the disposal of the state, the abbeys of Belgium had the major role in raising and funding an army and a rebellion that drove out the armies of the emperor and smashed his reforming programme. It was in Belgium that he was first forced to make the humiliating concessions that he then extended to Hungary and, less

PATTERNS OF MONASTIC REFORM

ILL. 32 Engraving showing monks chasing out Joseph II's troops ('Outbreak of the fanatical rebellion in Brussels'), 1789

comprehensively, to the Austrian lands. If this was almost the last political triumph of the old Orders, it was surely also the greatest – the crushing defeat of the most radical and authoritarian of the enlightened despots.

EPILOGUE AND CONCLUSION

Within three months of the Belgian *débâcle*, Joseph was dead. The furies may well, as Malingié predicted, have presided at the emperor's desolate deathbed, but it was still possible to muster the eight abbots whom custom required to accompany his corpse to the crypt of the Capuchins.[134] Throughout the Monarchy it appears that the programme of monastic suppressions ground to a halt.

His successor, his brother Leopold II, grand duke of Tuscany since 1765, had been pursuing church policies similar to Joseph's, including various measures aimed at reducing the numbers and reforming the activities of monasteries. Leopold seems to have had much the same view of monks and nuns as his brother, but he disapproved of Joseph's despotic methods and his approach was always more cautious, consensual and subtle. He recognised that monasteries, especially nunneries, had far greater significance for his Tuscan subjects than for most of Joseph's. When he became grand duke, more than 1 in 40 of the population of Tuscany were clergy, with the regulars in the majority and nearly twice as many nuns as monks among them. These proportions were among the highest in Europe. There were 345 male and 315 female establishments. Nineteen years later the numbers in all categories had fallen, but only by less than a fifth. This reduction was scarcely more than would have been expected from previous trends. In 1785, however, Leopold gave all nuns the opportunity to choose between the full contemplative life and living in a less strict 'conservatory' where the education of girls was a principal activity. The category of conservatories had long existed and, as we have seen, had been approved by Maria Theresa and Joseph, but Leopold turned them into lay institutions and greatly increased their number at the expense of the closed monasteries. About a third of all nuns chose to enter these new-style conservatories. By the time he succeeded Joseph, however, a reaction against some of Leopold's ecclesiastical reforms, such as the abolition of certain devotions and pilgrimages, had emerged, and he was beginning to make small concessions to it.[135]

Much more important to him than the fate of monasteries, of course, was the preservation of his heritage as ruler of the Austrian Monarchy and hence the recovery of Belgium. He had for some years been corresponding treasonably in invisible ink with his sister, Marie Christine, in Brussels, in preparation for his accession. Shortly before Joseph's death, he entrusted to her an extraordinary manifesto in which he declared his belief that all states should possess a constitution which their rulers should observe.[136] Unfortunately, by the time it was published in March 1790, Marie Christine had fled to Cologne, the whole of Belgium was in the hands of the rebels and they saw no need to take his protestations seriously. Undeterred, Leopold set about securing what he saw as the essential preconditions for saving the Monarchy, namely, staving off the threat of active Prussian intervention in Belgium and Hungary, and ending the Turkish war. He achieved the essential point amazingly quickly, in July 1790, by the Convention of Reichenbach with Prussia, which removed the threat of Prussian intervention and provided for the restoration of Austrian rule in Belgium. No doubt Leopold would now have been able to recover the Netherlands anyway, but his task was rendered easy by the bitter divisions which had arisen within the republican government in Brussels and among its subjects. When Austrian troops invaded Belgium in November 1790, the leaders of the Estates simply fled, and the country was reconquered with scarcely a shot fired.[137] During the following year Albert and Marie Christine stood in for Leopold at the inaugurations of his reign in most of the provinces.

In Belgium, under the rule of the Estates, the numerous demands that some at least of the dissolved monasteries should be revived had been favourably received. In Hungary Joseph had been induced at last to call a Diet which met after his death, and there too requests were made that some monasteries be re-established. Leopold, characteristically, expressed interest in the possibility in both countries, but took no action. In Austria he allowed the re-establishment of the Cistercian house of Lilienfeld. As for the surviving monasteries, the return of their novices from the abolished general seminaries and the withdrawal of some of Joseph's liturgical innovations enabled them to resume much of their traditional common life and pattern of worship.

Leopold's unexpected death in March 1792 was followed by another round of Belgian inaugurations on behalf of his son and successor, Francis II. In Hainaut, for example, prince Charles de Ligne, now estranged from Helen Massalska, took the oath on behalf of the new ruler, at Mons in June. The panoply of the *ancien régime* was on display for the last time. The immense procession was headed by the parish clergy, the dean and canons of Ste-Waudru, the five mendicant Orders and the canonesses of the chapter of Ste-Waudru, followed by the saint's major relic.[138]

A month later the French invaded and expelled the Austrians. In the following year the Austrian government was restored again, this time in a more reactionary mood. The restoration of suppressed monasteries was formally approved, and altogether thirty-eight were reopened.[139] Then of course the French armies returned in 1794, this time putting an end for a generation to the Belgians' aspirations for independence. The new dictatorial regime had no difficulty in dissolving and expropriating all the monasteries in 1796. None the less, the example of the Austrian Netherlands proves conclusively that the people of a Catholic country could still be fervent supporters and defenders of their monasteries well into the 1790s, and would not surrender them until forced to do so by a genuinely ruthless armed occupation.

In the central lands of the Monarchy the surviving monasteries were now pretty secure,[140] but Francis remained a convinced Josephist and was most reluctant to allow a monastic revival. Eventually, in 1801, he sanctioned the reopening of Pannonhalma and other suppressed houses, mainly in Hungary. Finally, in 1827 he permitted new foundations of contemplative Orders in his Empire. By 1847 there were as many houses altogether in Hungary as there had been in 1780.[141] In Austria some of the greater houses were given an important role in higher education, and there too new as well as old Orders founded a substantial number of new monasteries.

A book published in 1951 to celebrate the five-hundredth anniversary of the Franciscan Order in Austria contains this passage:

Certainly parishes were imposed on us by necessity, for both under Joseph II and also under the Nazi persecution the acceptance of a parish was the last expedient to preserve the monastery from suppression... [But] what originally happened under duress is also in the line of modern development, and it is possible to see here the hand of Providence.[142]

Austrian monasteries play a larger role in parochial work than those of any other European country. This peculiarity, and the fact that Austria is the one state in Europe where a large number of ancient and splendid Catholic houses can boast an almost continuous existence from the Middle Ages into the twenty-first century, are largely explained, first, by the fact that the country was never ruled by French armies of occupation after the Revolution, secondly by the fact that it never became part of the eastern bloc after the Second World War and, thirdly, by the complex story of Joseph II's dealings with the monasteries. Outside Belgium, Joseph's monastic policies must be accounted a success. Alone among the Catholic regimes of Europe, his succeeded in significantly increasing the number of parishes and parish clergy.

Finally, two aspects of Josephism should be emphasised here. First, unlike Henry VIII or the French revolutionaries, he did not seize monastic lands and property for state or purely secular purposes. In principle at least, and with very few exceptions in practice, all the revenue from the monastic lands that were not sold went into the Religious Fund. So did all the proceeds of the lands that were sold off – though it is true that too many were sold over a short period and therefore their full value was not obtained. If a monastery was handed over to the army for a barracks or to the state for an office, as often happened, a rent was paid to the Fund. Many of the works of art owned by the monasteries were taken for the imperial collections, or sold off and scattered over Europe, like the Rubens altarpiece of the convent of Whiteladies in Louvain, now in King's College Chapel, Cambridge; but in principle the money raised went to the Religious Fund.[143] The Fund still exists and helps to keep the Austrian Church afloat. As for the books and manuscripts in the libraries of the suppressed houses, they were put at the disposal of the university libraries or the Imperial Library. In Hungary Dr Velladics has been able to trace only 10 per cent of the carefully catalogued books of the dissolved monasteries. Records are incomplete, and there must have been many duplicates which it was reasonable to throw away or sell. But though care was taken to preserve what were then seen as worthwhile volumes, some works that would now be thought valuable were evidently destroyed, especially perhaps theological writings of which Josephists disapproved.[144]

Secondly, this strict policy of the emperor's goes far to account for the at first sight surprising fact that pope Pius VI did not publicly condemn his measures. Certainly, the papacy had become very reluctant to risk creating a schism and had learned from the campaign against the Jesuits that the demands of Catholic governments, if they were united, were almost impossible to resist. It would seem that Rome itself no longer regarded contemplative Orders as of the essence of the Church. If Joseph had followed his first inclination and had all clergy paid direct by the state, he would have presented the pope with a much more difficult problem. But he left the Church in control of such property as was not passed to the Religious Fund. The French revolutionaries took comfort from the pope's acquiescence in Joseph's reforms and did not expect their Civil Constitution of the Clergy to be condemned by the Vatican, not seeing that the emperor's policies and theirs were entirely different. This, as we shall see in the next chapter, was to prove a disastrous misconception.

PART III

THE TIME OF REVOLUTION

CHAPTER 9

THE REVOLUTION IN FRANCE

INTRODUCTION

In France, of course, what happened to monasticism in the last two decades of the eighteenth century was utterly and completely different from what happened to it in the Austrian Monarchy. For most of the 1780s, while Joseph II was grasping the nettle of monastic reform, virtually nothing was being done about it in France. Then – very early in the course of the French Revolution – came action far more drastic than any country had ever taken against monasteries, except in the name of Reformation. At the beginning of August 1789 the Church as a whole lost its privileges and its tithes; at the end of October the taking of perpetual religious vows was suspended; and in November all the property of the French Church was declared to be at the disposal of the nation – just when the reaction against Josephism was taking hold in the Monarchy, most strikingly in Belgium. In February 1790 all the Orders that required lifelong vows were dissolved. This was still not enough to satisfy revolutionary fanaticism: by the end of 1792 even the congregations with simple vows had been disbanded. Barely a year later, Catholicism itself was outlawed. In its place the state installed a brand-new cult of Reason and the Supreme Being.[1]

Why did things develop so differently in France compared with all other Catholic countries – at least down to the period between 1795 and 1810, when French occupation or influence helped to impose versions of the revolutionary solution on Belgium itself, on Germany, on mainland Italy and on parts of Switzerland and Spain? The comparison between France and Belgium in the 1780s is especially telling, since the conquests of Louis XIV had incorporated into France much of the southern part of the old Low Countries without changing its basic social and ecclesiastical structure. Artois and the parts of old Flanders now possessed by France, just like those under Austrian rule, had exceptionally rich abbeys and powerful provincial Estates. In fact the regular meeting place of the Estates of Artois was the abbey of St-Vaast in Arras, a house so rich and so conscious of its position that it had just completed one of the grandest neo-classical rebuilding programmes seen in France. It was known too, like most of its near neighbours, as an Observant house, untainted even by the fact that its commendatory abbot was the profligate cardinal de Rohan. Among the special privileges of its regular abbot were his role as patron of the English houses at nearby Douai and his right to nominate four scholars from Arras to bursaries at the fashionable former Jesuit College of Louis-le-Grand, Voltaire's old school. It is a tribute to the abbot's fairness if not to his prescience that one of those he nominated in 1769 was Maximilien Robespierre, who after graduation did legal work for the abbey but in 1788 began his revolutionary career by publishing a pamphlet that identified the Estates of Artois as the principal cause of all the province's ills.[2] Such an abbey as St-Vaast, if located across the frontier in Belgium, would surely have played a significant role in the rout of Joseph II's troops and the rejection of his church reforms.

Until after June 1789, in fact, French monasticism seemed to be much less seriously threatened than Belgian. The difference was chiefly due to the vigour of the Austrian government and the feebleness of the French. But in certain respects French monasticism was showing signs of new life such as were not evident across the border. First, as we saw in Chapter 7, the *commission des réguliers* had promoted some reforms. While in the short run it had provoked a crisis of confidence within the propertied Orders by reducing the number of their houses and their inmates, by its reinvigoration of the monastic rules it had paved the way for the rise in their vocations in the 1780s.[3] Such a revival in the Austrian Monarchy was rendered impossible until well into the nineteenth century by Joseph II's abolition of the contemplative Orders and the restrictions that he imposed, many of which his successors maintained, on the activities of the ancient monasteries that were allowed to survive.

Secondly, there can be found in France of the *ancien régime* a movement among the clergy, including the regulars, parallel to the Catholic Enlightenment which in central Europe was helping to promote many of the reforms of Josephism. Among a progressive minority of French monks of the old Orders were some, for example, who talked of having two great duties, the first, which they owed as citizens like everyone else, being to the state or to society, the second – but only the second – to God. Others stressed that monasteries ought to be *useful*, and some monks even declared that their very purpose in entering their communities was precisely to be useful to society: 'Our status cannot require us to refuse to society what it has a right to expect of all its subjects. Surely a monk occupied in forming citizens and inculcating religion and morality cannot be less pleasing to God than a monk who copies manuscripts?' Some opposed the absolute obedience due to abbots as contrary to the rights of Man, postulating a contractual relationship between superiors and ordinary monks. They acknowledged that they owed under their vows absolute obedience to God and to the rule of their Order, but they condemned the 'despotism' of the mere men who were their earthly superiors. Gérard Michaux, in bringing forward these examples, points to the apparent contradiction in their position:

They intend to fashion a 'new monk' more at grips with the preoccupations of state and society. They envisage a monastic life resolutely engaged in, and not cut off from, the world. Were they to blame or misguided? Does not this rather prove the internal dynamism of the regular clergy and its great readiness to respond to the needs of the time? But is such a monk still a true monk?[4]

This was the dilemma of monastic promoters of the Catholic Enlightenment in every country, though it was especially acute in the France of the *philosophes*. But the dilemma looks much clearer in retrospect than it looked to the participants. A new abbot of Prémontré began his reign in 1784 by publishing an intelligent defence of monasticism. He acknowledged the duty of monks to be useful to the state as well as to the Church and went on to declare that 'the monastic order is certainly not of the essence of the Church, but is none the less necessary to its glory'. It evidently did not seem paradoxical to the Augustinian Hervier that he should be an enthusiastic admirer of Mesmer and mesmerism, or to the Premonstratensians Lissoir and Hédouin that they should publish, respectively, a translation of Febronius and a selection from the writings of the radical anti-colonialist Raynal.[5] No wonder some of these reformers gladly welcomed and assisted the early ecclesiastical measures of the French Revolution.

Thirdly, as already described in Chapter 3,[6] alone among the Catholic countries of Europe, France saw during the eighteenth century a huge expansion of new, mainly female, Orders (or, strictly, congregations) which did not demand full vows and were dedicated to charitable activities. This truly remarkable development was generally acknowledged even by many of the enemies of traditional monasticism to be of great advantage to society, it was to be a major inspiration of the nineteenth-century monastic revival and it provided new opportunities for women to conduct major enterprises independently of men. But for the hiatus of the French Revolution, this movement would surely have advanced uninterruptedly through the 1790s.

Unfortunately for the monks and nuns of France, negative factors were at work which proved far more powerful. Some affected the Church as a whole. Madame de la Tour du Pin, who had been nineteen in 1789, described in her *Memoirs* the last years of the *ancien régime* and the early years of the Revolution, drawing on her recollections of the Court of Versailles and of her family. Her great-great-uncle, whom she knew well, was archbishop Dillon of Narbonne, though he seldom visited his diocese. He was both commendatory abbot of the great Benedictine house of St-Etienne at Caen and president of the Estates of Languedoc. Her father-in-law became minister for war in July 1789, but her mother-in-law had been confined for some misdemeanour to a convent. She herself was regularly threatened by her grandmother with the same fate. With hindsight she wrote:

The hierarchy of the Church . . . had been corrupted by contact with the dissolute habits of the Court. Almost all the bishops were of noble birth . . . When they were raised to a see, they looked on the appointment as honourable exile which separated them from their friends, their families and all the worldly pleasures of society . . . The rot started at the top and spread downwards. Virtue in men and good conduct in women became the object of ridicule and were considered provincial . . . The older I grow, the more sure I become that the Revolution of 1789 was only the inevitable consequence and, I might almost say, the just punishment of the vices of the upper classes, vices carried to such excess that if people had not been stricken with a mortal blindness, they must have seen that they would inevitably be consumed by the very fire they themselves were lighting.[7]

If no historian would accept that the relation of cause and effect could be so simple and straightforward as this, the conclusions of such an intelligent and knowledgeable witness have to be taken seriously. Intellectually, too, belief in the elaborate structure of Catholic dogma appeared to have given way, at least for many, to the identification of Christianity with a general and unspecific benevolence towards others. The Catholic ideal of the good parish priest seemed assimilable to Rousseau's portrait of a simple Savoyard vicar, a well-meaning pastor virtually innocent of theology. After the 1760s educated opinion ensured that the laws against Protestants were scarcely enforced, and a measure of toleration was granted to them by the government in 1787 – opposed in general by the leaders of the Church but accepted by many Catholics. Jansenists were now rarely persecuted, and even toleration of the Jews was seriously canvassed.[8]

Monks were inevitably affected by such changes of attitude. In 1771 Horace Walpole, a frequent visitor to France, wrote:

It is very singular that I have not half the satisfaction in going into churches and convents that I used to have. The consciousness that the vision is dispelled, the want of fervour so obvious in the religious, the solitude that one knows proceeds from contempt, not from contemplation, make these places appear like abandoned theatres destined to destruction. The monks trot about as if they had not long to stay there; and what used to be holy gloom is now but dirt and darkness.[9]

This was written very soon after the initial shock of the measures arising from the *commission des réguliers*. But, despite the partially successful attempt of the *commission* to rehabilitate the old Orders, including the purely contemplative ones, it seems that in 1789 few clergy, and not many laymen, could see the point or merit of a life devoted solely to prayer and worship.

Whereas piety and discipline were still generally found among the monks of Artois, and still earned respect, in other provinces they were rarer. We have already seen that in a great many male houses the grand state kept by the abbot, the wealth and amenity of the house, the comfort and laxity of the monks contrasted sharply with the original aims of the Order; that the same applied to the major nunneries; and that the royal use of the *commende* was indefensible and immensely damaging to the monasteries concerned. The head of the Trappists declared: 'the monastic order swarms with scholars but has few saints'.[10] But even the scholarship of the Maurists was thought to be in decay. The government had recently decided that for its own ends it was worthwhile to support their efforts to establish the truth about ancient usages, and had also entrusted to them five of its new military colleges, which meant that the abbatial buildings resounded with 'drums and bugles, drill and dancing'. But their Order was riven with disputes and some of its houses were crippled by debt.[11] In any case its publications, however impressive, had a diminishing place in French intellectual life as the total number of books, pamphlets and journals published grew by leaps and bounds and the percentage of religious works among them fell.[12]

Because the rise in vocations to some of the old Orders during the 1780s affected relatively few houses, and perhaps because it ran counter to the main tendencies of monasticism and of French society, it was scarcely noticed at the time. What struck contemporaries was the admittedly much greater scale of their previous decline, which it would have taken decades of improved recruitment to reverse.

When the commissioners of the revolutionary government entered the great male monasteries in order to take the prescribed inventories after the decisions of November 1789, they commonly – though by no means invariably – found few monks remaining, and many of those quite ready to give up their vows and leave the life of the cloister:

From 1766–70 to 1790 the [membership of the] Cluniac Order had gone from 671 religious to 301; the Cistercian Order from 1,873 to 1,624; the Congregation of St-Maur from 1,917 to 1,652; the Cordeliers from 2,395 to 1,544; the Capuchins from 4,397 to 2,674; the Recollects from 2,534 to 1,558; the Dominicans from 1,441 to 1,001; the Order of Ste-Geneviève from 662 to 567; the Carthusians from 1,004 to 821.[13]

If contemplative Orders were commonly thought pointless, the wealth of the propertied Orders in general was condemned ever more stridently as contrary to their original spirit and damaging to France. The article on 'Foundations' in the *Encyclopédie*, written by the economist and future minister, baron Turgot, declared that all foundations tend to lose sight of their original purpose and that those which distributed charity indiscriminately and on outmoded principles did much more harm than good. The article 'Monasteries' held up the example of Henry VIII's dissolution of all religious houses:

Since this change the spirit of commerce and industry has established itself in Great Britain, and the public revenues have notably benefited from it. In general, every nation which has converted monasteries to public use has gained, humanly speaking, without anyone having lost. In fact it did harm only to the passing generation that was despoiled, but they left no children to lament it. It is the injustice of a day which yields benefits for centuries.[14]

The first article in Voltaire's *Dictionnaire philosophique* of 1765, entitled 'Abbé', contrasted the poor and humble abbot elected by primitive monks with the rich and powerful abbots of the eighteenth century:

'A poor man who has taken a vow of poverty and in consequence is a sovereign!' ... it must be repeated a thousand times, this is intolerable. The laws protest against this abuse, religion is ashamed of it, and the genuine poor, without food and clothing, cry out to heaven at M. the abbé's gate ...

You have profited from the times of ignorance, superstition and folly to despoil us of our birthright and to trample us under your feet, to fatten yourselves on the substance of the unfortunate. Tremble lest the day of reason come.

These are condemnations by *philosophes*, especially influential at this juncture when the concept and force of public opinion were for the first time being recognised in France.¹⁵ But in fact such radical views did not command general support, and the relaxation of censorship and the rise of the press ensured that other standpoints too were receiving wider publicity than before. Much was still being published in criticism of the *philosophes* and in support of traditional Catholicism. Writings influenced by Jansenism combined hostility to Jesuits and doubts about other branches of monasticism with rigorous morality and theology. And, as the 'new religious historiography' of the period stresses, attitudes that have been seen as Enlightened and anti-religious were often espoused by sincere believers as tending to renew the Church and to purify its theology.

Mendicants of course attracted particular condemnation. The economists disapproved of their refusal to participate in buying and selling, working and earning, of their encouragement of idleness and of their exactions from the poor. In a striking tract of 1775 the notorious maverick journalist Linguet made the astonishing claim that the mendicant Orders amounted to a conspiracy devised by the pope to enable him to control the world.¹⁶ This was a topic on which some people would believe anything, but the work of the mendicants was much more visible and acceptable to ordinary people and to secular clergy than that of the propertied Orders.

The anonymous author of a more reasonable and better informed *Philosophic History of Monasticism*, published in 1788, acknowledged the observance, scholarship, urbanity and hospitality of modern monks, while highlighting the paradoxes of their way of life. An abbot, perhaps the son of a hairdresser, lives surrounded by brilliant and sumptuous luxury. How little the dirty monks of old have in common with modern monks of the old Orders, 'white-powdered, well scented, [their habits] most elegantly hitched up, in silk stockings, with jewelled buckles and a gleaming skull cap'! When they entertain you, they go off punctiliously to the choir, leaving you to play tric-trac or cards, read newspapers or view the park. How pernicious the institution is has been demonstrated by Montesquieu, Helvetius, Rousseau and Raynal. Monastic vows are against Nature. To vow to be celibate is to hold back population growth; to vow to be poor is to identify oneself with the inept and lazy; to vow obedience is to be subjected to the 'pure despotism' of St Benedict or the 'unlimited monarchy' of the Jesuits. Regrettably, the *commission des réguliers*, instead of reforming the Orders, sought to enforce their ancient rules. England has gained enormously by having married clergy who serve the state and, unlike the French clergy, are not educated in a spirit hostile to the state.

Compare the buildings of London with those of Paris. Instead of founding useless monasteries private Englishmen endow hospitals for the old, bridges, botanical gardens, medical schools, orphanages, museums, stock exchanges. In France the state has to take on that work. Maybe the monasteries could be preserved if they were pruned and 'an active and social life' could be introduced into them. Certainly the nuns who staff the hospitals of France, unlike nuns in general, are to be admired. But to seize the monks' lands would get rid of mendicity and, rather than attempt to reform them, 'there would be infinitely fewer difficulties and dangers in cutting them off at the roots'.[17]

A conspicuous characteristic of the late Enlightenment in France was its exploitation of pornography and scatology to besmirch all branches of the Establishment. Here the monks were easy game, especially the substantial number of them whose duties included ministering to nuns. Libidinous clergymen were not invented by the eighteenth century but they were relished by a wider public in that period than ever before: *Thérèse philosophe*, describing the seduction of a young girl by her confessor, and the *Histoire de Dom B*, recording the conquests of a Carthusian gate porter, maintained their position as bestsellers from their publication in 1741 down to the Revolution.[18] At a more elevated level, one of Baculard d'Arnaud's plays, *Euphémie*, of 1768, portrayed the inner struggle of a nun between her religious obligations and her love for a man, though in this case the battle was ultimately won by the Church.[19] Such salacious tales assisted the growth among the educated classes of the interlinked convictions, fostered by the *philosophes* though by no means confined to them, that societies needed population growth; that it was against Nature, and probably unhealthy, to make a vow of eternal chastity; and that it was illogical and preposterous for men and women to use their freedom to surrender their freedom.

Before the beginning of the Revolution, then, general educated opinion in France, a force much more conspicuous and influential than in other Catholic countries, had become at best lukewarm in support of monasticism. It seems that many French churchmen had come to doubt that the institution was of the essence of Catholicism. Whereas in the seventeenth century monks and nuns were reckoned necessary instruments in the work of the Counter-Reformation and were regarded as generally superior to secular clergy in piety and effectiveness, by the late eighteenth century secular priests were valued more highly, and considered to be of better quality, than regulars. But even so, as we shall see, only a few extremists contemplated abolishing monasticism. Its *débâcle* in late 1789 and early 1790 – like other upheavals of these years – cannot be explained except in the context of the sequence of events, or chapter of accidents, that led to the

Revolution and propelled it forward, making radical solutions appear unavoidable and creating a political situation which favoured them. To attempt here to give a full account of these events and accidents would be absurd, but a sketch including the most relevant is indispensable, especially since even those accounts of the Revolution which give due weight to religion and the Church rarely devote much space to monks and nuns.

THE APPROACH TO REVOLUTION

From the 1760s onwards the king and his government, burdened with the debts they had incurred during the Seven Years War, lurched from one crisis to another, while demands grew for an end to the so-called 'despotism' of the monarchy and for the summoning of France's ancient representative assembly, the Estates-General, which had last met in 1614. At the very end of 1786 Louis XVI accepted the advice of his minister, Calonne, to call an Assembly of Notables, rather than the Estates-General, and put to them a plan of financial reform. The 144 members of the Assembly contained eighteen clerics, none of them monks. Among the many proposals before them was one to repudiate the Crown's debt to the Church, a debt which from the point of view of the clergy had been incurred as a favour to the monarchy and ought to be repaid but according to anticlericals should be regarded as the grudging contribution of a bloated Church to the well-being of the state. Like all the other privileged groups represented among the Notables, the clergy eventually announced that they could not give an opinion without first consulting their constituency, in their case the General Assembly of the Clergy. Since the calling of the Notables was not achieving what had been hoped of it by the king, he sacked Calonne and appointed a new minister, none other than archbishop Loménie de Brienne, who had naturally been a Notable. But he could not control the Assembly either and it was dissolved in May 1787. The General Assembly of the Clergy, summoned prematurely in 1788, followed the Notables in demanding that the Estates-General be called. Almost all elements in France had persuaded themselves that this step would benefit them, not only by ending royal and ministerial 'despotism' and creating a new constitution but even, it was supposed, by reducing taxation. The government gave in, though at first it prevaricated about the date of the meeting. Meanwhile, on 16 August 1788, it declared itself bankrupt. Brienne resigned, to be replaced by Necker, who claimed and was believed to have righted the state's finances during an earlier spell as minister. So a great French Catholic prelate – the last such first minister in France – was replaced by a Protestant Swiss banker, and all the constituted authorities had effectively abdicated their roles to the Estates-General, which the king had by now agreed to call together in 1789. Necker saw his role as 'little more than a caretaker until the Estates-General met. The bankruptcy of the monarchy was therefore not only financial, but political and intellectual, too. It had collapsed in every sense, leaving an enormous vacuum of power.'[20]

It was a traditional preliminary to meetings of the Estates-General that most of the established organisations of the kingdom should be asked to send in statements of their grievances, known as *cahiers de doléances*, as well as to elect representatives to one or other of the three Estates. For these purposes delegates of the clergy, the First Estate, met in their localities; representatives of the nobles, the Second Estate, did the same; while members of the Third Estate, the remainder of the population, met in every village or town in order to prepare statements that in most cases would be collated at a higher level. The resulting documents constitute an extraordinarily wide expression of opinion, far broader than anything to be found anywhere else in Europe at this period. They reveal a great deal both about the views of the clergy and about others' attitudes to the Church.

Like all documents, and especially all collections of documents on this scale, they present difficulties of interpretation and have serious limitations.[21] Some have been lost, which may distort the overall picture. In many cases the *cahiers* of the Third Estate can be observed undergoing a process of refinement, or laundering, from the original village documents through intermediate collations to final regional submissions. Some of them clearly followed a circulated model. Lawyers often presided over the preliminary meetings and naturally left their mark on the resulting documents, while in other cases parish clergy played this role. Wide though participation was in the process of compiling them, poorer people were excluded because they did not pay taxes.

As for the separate *cahiers* of the clergy, for our purposes they have a major weakness: they do not, as the reports gathered by the *commission des réguliers* did, report or represent the opinions of regulars. Female regulars, like all women, were excluded from any participation in the process, though abbesses could send male deputies to the meetings of the clergy. More surprisingly, male regulars were grossly under-represented at the meetings that prepared the *cahiers* of the clergy: the government had decided that every clergyman in charge of a parish would be entitled to attend, but only one representative of each monastic house. Hence the monks of France played a very limited part in the proceedings leading up to the Estates-General, as in the assembly itself.

If the regulars could not express their own opinions effectively through the *cahiers*, both the secular clergy and the other Estates were able to give their views about the regulars. The *cahiers* of the clergy show no awareness that the Church's very existence would soon be threatened. They were confident of the faith of the mass of the population, often critical of the relaxation of censorship and of the recent modest measure of toleration for Protestants. Concerned though they were to protect church land and revenue, many accepted that their exemption from ordinary taxation must be abandoned or limited. Objection was made in more than half the *cahiers* of the clergy to some aspects of the modest reforms of the *commission des réguliers*. Some wanted certain dissolved monasteries restored. A few even regretted the loss of the Jesuits. Over half also advocated partial reforms of the Orders, including some suppressions, transfer of some monastic property to other religious purposes and the abolition of the *commende*. But in general the clergy defended most monastic houses as fundamentally useful, and not one of their *cahiers* envisaged the total disappearance of monasticism.

Despite the conservatism of these collective views, the district meetings of the First Estate produced one crucial radical result. They provided for the first time a forum in which the lower clergy could express their bitter feelings at the meanness of their salaries, especially as seen in relation to episcopal, canonical and monastic wealth, and at their exclusion by government policy from virtually any possibility of promotion to bishoprics. As a result the majority of the bishops, to their astonishment and chagrin, were not elected by their clergy as deputies to the Estates-General, and the 51 bishops who were chosen were outnumbered by more than 200 relatively humble parish priests.[22]

Of the *cahiers* of the Third Estate, a good percentage of those from rural areas confined themselves to local affairs. Religious matters of all kinds were mentioned less frequently than questions concerning the government and constitution, the rights of the individual, privileges and feudal obligations, taxation and the economy. Only about a quarter to a third brought up any religious or ecclesiastical issues at all: in one calculation such topics come forty-fourth in the list of fifty topics most frequently occurring.[23] The comments themselves were not in general particularly anticlerical or anti-monastic. Only about 7 per cent of all the *cahiers* mentioned the regulars at all, and only 2 per cent asked for partial or total suppression of monasticism.[24] A few, admittedly, were radical. Brest, 'the most anticlerical town in the kingdom', demanded that the clergy should cease to constitute the First Estate, a pretension 'as incompatible with the vows of humility and disinterest that they profess as with the constitution of the kingdom'. A neighbouring small town asked for 'the suppression of several monasteries and abbeys that serve only to foster indolence', the conversion of mendicant houses to barracks and even the abolition of the Sisters of Wisdom because their discriminatory treatment of the sick 'has resulted in mistakes damaging to Humanity'.[25] One *cahier* from the Nîmes area, where Protestantism was strong, declared monks to be 'useless to the state and to religion'. Cahors thought that celibacy made men wild and that marriage would 'phlegmatise them in every way'. But, by contrast, there were many places whose grievances in this field seem reactionary: a parish near Sens was not alone in declaring that 'it is important and to the advantage of the Third Estate to allow monastic houses of both sexes, propertied or not, to subsist. They are the only quiet places to which the Third Estate can aspire.' Their alms, it went on, are useful and they create employment.[26] The educational work of the monks was often applauded and never criticised. The most frequently mentioned ecclesiastical issue was the tithe but, of the comparatively small proportion of parishes which referred to it, only 29 per cent asked for its abolition and 39 per cent for its reform. In general they wanted it made more equitable, and particular problems in its allocation and collection ironed out. They commonly asked that it should no longer be owed to the many abbeys and other corporations that were entitled to it, but instead be returned to the parish priests for whose support it was believed to have been intended. Regional variations were marked: Paris, certain towns and an area west of Paris were relatively more radical than the rest of the country and than rural areas in general, but they still produced only a small minority of full-blooded attacks on monasticism.

Among the *cahiers* of the nobles, too, a few demanded complete suppression of the monasteries, but the majority sought only to restrict their numbers and property.[27] The message from the people and the provinces about the monasteries, their properties and their revenues, as about most things, was mildly reformist, betraying little sign of the influence of the *philosophes* or of any rational blueprint for radical change. It was common to ask, as the Belgian opponents of Joseph II had, for the revival of what was seen as the old constitution. If that certainly included calling the Estates-General, it was also understood to embrace the right of the monarchy to reform and control the Church without reference to the pope. Gallicanism was axiomatic, as, for the vast majority, was loyalty to Catholicism. Though these views overall were rather less conservative than what a similar exercise would have been likely to produce in Belgium, they resembled the views of the opponents of Joseph II in that country much more closely than they prefigured the work of the French Revolution.

It was the Estates-General, transformed into a National Assembly, that, in defiance of the opinions of the people as expressed in the *cahiers*, destroyed French monasticism, and much else. The Estates-General of 1789 was bound to be different from any of its predecessors. An assembly that had not met for 175 years could not be restored unchanged; it had to be reinvented. There was no living tradition, let alone continuity, of membership and procedure. Few parts of France had long-standing provincial Estates to provide delegates with appropriate experience. In addition, the government had ensured that the new assembly would be seriously different from the old by making changes in the method of election. No individual was guaranteed a seat in any of the Estates: all delegates were elected. This was true of no other representative assembly in the Old World. The decision to give the vote to every parish priest enabled the lower clergy to take control of the First Estate. Further, the government gave double representation to the Third Estate, which now obviously stood for much more powerful sections of the population – including a *bourgeoisie* – than it had in 1614. However, its membership by no means reflected its constituency: two-thirds of its deputies had some legal training.

Having made these arrangements, the king and his ministers then vacillated about the all-important question whether, as in most such assemblies and in the historic Estates-General, the Estates should deliberate and vote separately, thus preserving the 'society of orders' or Estates and the privileges of the clergy and nobility, or whether they should unite to form one body. The point had not been decided by the time the formal opening of the assembly took place at Versailles in early May. This uncertainty gave the leaders of the Third Estate time and opportunity to campaign for the view that the three Estates should be merged and that in the resulting assembly each individual member should have one vote. On 17 June the Third Estate adopted the title 'National Assembly' for the single chamber of all deputies which it hoped to create, and effectively claimed to exercise the sovereignty previously inherent in the king. Since the First Estate showed reluctance to join the Third, 'the clergy were publicly insulted in Paris. The people could not see an ecclesiastic, especially a secular, without stopping him and demanding that he take the side of the Third Estate. But it must be said that the monks have been privileged not to receive any insults.' Under this pressure and after much heart-searching, the First Estate, most of whom felt much closer to the members of the Third Estate than to nobles and noble bishops, agreed by a narrow majority to join them. Having at first objected, the king acquiesced and reluctantly ordered the nobles to follow suit. The resulting assembly had the huge membership of nearly 1,200. During the next month Louis tried on and off to reassert his authority, invariably mishandling the situation and making matters worse. On 11 July he dismissed and banished Necker, a necessary preliminary to a military coup intended to discipline or dismiss the Assembly.

THE TIME OF REVOLUTION

ILL. 33 Depiction of the sacking of the convent of St-Lazare, 1789

THE REVOLUTION, TO FEBRUARY 1790

What saved it at this point was a popular rising in Paris. Between 12 and 15 July the city was out of control and the king was told that he could not rely on his army. St-Lazare – part monastery, part hospital, part prison – was among the buildings sacked because it was believed to contain an arsenal for the royal troops (Ill. 33), and the dreaded prison fortress of the Bastille was stormed. The king surrendered, recalled Necker and gave his blessing to the citizen National Guard that had restored a kind of order. It is from these incidents that the Revolution is usually dated.

In the provinces a bad harvest had created a food shortage and severe hardship, for which the privileged classes were widely blamed. Now rumours of a plot to dismiss the Assembly and – ironically, in view of Joseph II's difficulties – fear of an invasion from Belgium helped to cause an extraordinary wave of violence and panic. In late July and early August peasants in many rural areas attacked the symbols of oppression and privilege, châteaux and abbey buildings, especially granaries, often burning the records that authenticated feudal obligations. It seemed as though rents, tithes and all traditional rights, dues and privileges were at risk. A study has been made of the attacks on abbeys in the far north-east of France, the future *département du Nord*, an area rich in monasteries that had been won from the then Spanish Netherlands by Louis XIV. Between 23 and 30 July 1789 seven abbeys were assailed by peasant crowds. Two of them, the nunnery of Prémy and the Benedictine abbey of Maroilles, were sacked. No peasants came to their rescue. But there was no sign of hostility to religion or monasticism as such. Just before sacking the abbey of Maroilles the inhabitants of Taisnières had attended Mass. It is clear that what was resented by the rioters were the abbeys' feudal and fiscal exactions, especially tithe, and their readiness to resort to the courts to enforce them.[28]

The Assembly could do nothing but endorse the popular Parisian revolution that had preserved it. Although the deputies were still meeting at Versailles, they could not escape the influence of the Capital, where

the bishops are humiliated, the priests are insulted, openly persecuted; the monks, though less badly treated, are not favourably viewed. The warehouses of St-Lazare encouraged a low opinion of populous and rich communities. An attack was made on St-Martin-des-Champs, Order of Cluny; they went on to the Carthusians, then to the Dominican novitiate and several others. But there was no repeat of the unhappy story of St-Lazare because nowhere were similar stores of provisions and arms discovered.[29]

The atmosphere in and around the Assembly was unique: despite the massive evidence for it in the sources, its febrility remains hard to credit. A minority of nobles, clergy and others already feared for their privileges and property, and the emigration was beginning. Those who remained suffered physical intimidation, oral and printed abuse: the threat of disorder was ever present. But none the less there reigned among the majority an extraordinary spirit of elation and hope, together with a readiness for radical change and sacrifice which infected some noble deputies and nearly all the representatives of the clergy, including even archbishops who had initially been known as conservatives. The country clergy were required, but also were often delighted, to read to their congregations the voluminous and amazing decrees of the National Assembly. Never had so many *Te Deums* been sung to celebrate public achievements. During this phase of the Revolution, while the leaders of the Third Estate harped on the importance they attached to the Church and religion, the Church in turn endorsed the revolutionary programme.[30]

THE TIME OF REVOLUTION

ILL. 34 Pen and wash drawing by Jacques-Louis David, *The Tennis Court Oath*, 1789

Though monks were represented in the National Assembly by only ten deputies,[31] one of them became well known, Dom Gerle, a Carthusian, Visitor of his Order, who saw in many of the aspirations of the revolutionaries laudable aims that a Christian ought to welcome and assist. Belying Brienne's *mot*, Gerle was a Carthusian who was an enlightened man. He was given a starring role by David in his famous picture of the *Tennis Court Oath* which led to the formation of the National Assembly in June 1789 (Ill. 34). The painter depicted a secular priest, a Protestant and Dom Gerle prominently administering the oath. The force of the painting's propaganda might seem to be weakened by the facts (i) that Dom Gerle was actually not present on the day in question, indeed had not yet been elected to the Assembly, (ii) that the whole picture is a highly imaginative reconstruction and (iii) that it was not even completed during the revolutionary period because the featured participants fell out so quickly and violently that a depiction of their fraternal unanimity became entirely unacceptable.[32] But Dom Gerle was a prominent leader of the Assembly for most of 1790. The comments quoted earlier suggest that monks were seen as more favourable to the Revolution than seculars, and it is clear that the early actions of the Assembly commanded broad support within the male monasteries, though not in the nunneries. There was much that ordinary monks might rejoice in: the attack on the aristocracy and the upper clergy, who were the principal beneficiaries of the *commende*; the advance of liberty and enlightenment, if properly defined; the hope that France would be better governed at home and more highly respected abroad; and, for some, the prospect of freedom and a pension. Many monastic houses enthusiastically celebrated the fall of the Bastille. It was by invitation that the Jacobins met in the library of the Dominican monastery that gave them their nickname; and the Carmelites provided the National Guard with buildings for a barracks.[33]

On the other hand, much that was published during this heady period criticised the Church, including the monasteries, often violently. Among the many strident caricatures published in France at this time, anti-monastic cartoons were not in fact especially numerous. But two are illustrated here. The first belongs to a tradition of pictures showing France borne down by various oppressors, usually the king, the Court, the ministers, the farmers-general, the nobles and the Church as a whole – here it is society ladies and nuns who are singled out (Ill. 35). The second gleefully depicts clergy, including monks, having to surrender their money and property (Ill. 36). There appear to be no cartoons at all that show sympathy with monks, nuns and monasteries.[34]

It is only against this background of riots, panic, distrust, vituperation, social animosity and optimism that the events of the astonishing 'night of August 4' can be comprehended. Certain noble deputies had agreed beforehand to go to the Assembly and make an ostentatious sacrifice of their privileges to the nation and the Revolution. The debate got completely out of hand, as one by one nobles and bishops joined in an auction of promises. It was an intoxicating occasion which seemed to the participants and to observers more like a dream than reality. When the bishop of Chartres proposed the end of hunting privileges, the duc du Châtelet exclaimed: 'the bishop takes away our hunting, I'll take something away from him'.[35] The duke proceeded to suggest the commutation of tithes. By the end of the night privilege, social divisions and 'feudalism' had all been abandoned – at least in principle. When the issues were raised again on the 11th, though the Assembly was in soberer mood, there was no question of undoing the work of the 4th: the members now put into decrees the declarations of that extraordinary night. The bishops decided that the only thing to do in the circumstances was to go even further than they had before, to surrender tithes altogether, voluntarily. This did not take immediate effect, at least not in theory, though in practice tithes became very difficult to collect. But the clergy were given to understand that, in compensation, their salaries and a range of ecclesiastical activities would be financed directly by the state:

THE TIME OF REVOLUTION

ILL. 35 Caricature showing a peasant woman supporting a noblewoman and a nun, 1789

ILL. 36 Caricature of the French clergy being forced to surrender their property (*Le déménagement du clergé*), 1789–90

Tithes of every kind are abolished [the new law stated], subject to a decision on other ways of meeting the cost of divine worship, paying the ministers of the altar, relieving the poor, repairing and building churches and presbyteries, and [maintaining] all the establishments, seminaries, schools, colleges, hospitals, communities etc. to which tithes are at present due.

As yet, only the more suspicious and alarmist clergy doubted the good intentions of the Assembly. The archbishop of Paris ordered the singing of a *Te Deum* to celebrate this 'epoch-making moment, ever memorable in the nation's history'.[36] It was evident that the monasteries would suffer greatly by these decisions, but their position was barely mentioned.

On 24 September Necker made one of his long speeches to the deputies declaring even more forcibly than before that the financial situation was so desperate that it required immediate drastic action to save the country from internal disorder and to restore its standing abroad. The position had materially worsened since the Estates-General had met, largely because it had rashly decided not to go on collecting the existing taxes.[37] Necker particularly asked for a patriotic contribution from every citizen in comfortable circumstances. Following him,

Dupont de Nemours, respected as an economist, spoke at equal length, accepting that it was 'the state that you have to save'. A patriotic contribution would not be enough. He concentrated on the possibilities of mulcting the Church. 'The clergy', he said, 'have done their duty... The tithes are at your disposal.' He went on to calculate what sum would be needed to support adequately parish worship, bishops and cathedrals. Next he praised the work of hospitals and colleges, which he maintained ought to be better funded than hitherto. Only then did he mention monasteries, and only in the context of the pious foundations of Masses. Pointing out that the clergy had long ago ceased to be numerous enough to say all the Masses required of them by testators, and that the Church had found a way round this difficulty by lumping benefactions together, he went on: 'It is up to the bishops to combine with parish Masses the observance of the foundations made in favour of abbeys and priories; and that becomes indispensable when the suppression of tithes, or their transfer to the domain of society, destroys half the monastic houses.' A few sentences later, he was envisaging the total disappearance of non-parochial clergy. He assumed that monks and nuns would be given pensions. But even so he maintained that the seizure of their lands, together with the tithes and other dues, would so enhance the credit of the state that it would be able to borrow enough to solve the financial problems described by Necker. Nowhere in his speech does he give the slightest recognition to the prayer and contemplation, the worship, the scholarship, the artistic achievement and the economic contribution of the monasteries.[38] It was already plain that the Assembly contained much more than its fair share of *philosophes*, as of Protestants and of persons influenced by Jansenism.

Debate on the finances continued on and off for the next few weeks. What Dupont had proposed in detail was not universally approved, but the notion of seizing church property was found highly attractive by many deputies, and soon came to seem inevitable to many of them. Most of its proponents favoured selling off the lands, once acquired, so that the state would receive an immediate financial boost. On 28 September a letter from the Cluniac monks of St-Martin-des-Champs was read to the Assembly:

They beg [you] to accept the voluntary offer which they make of all their property to the nation. They can make this renunciation, in the name of their whole Order, confident that all its members (except a very small number) enthusiastically subscribe to it... The Cluniac Order... has a total estimated revenue of 1,800,000 livres, half of which belongs to commendatory abbots and priors. The sites of its three houses in Paris are valued at 4 millions at least, which with the sites of its other houses in different provinces can provide a pension for each individual of 1,500 livres. This arrangement would give to the state a revenue of 900,000 livres, and to the monks *liberty*, which they will have the happiness of sharing with all Frenchmen.[39]

The superior of the Order had known nothing of this approach and soon disavowed it, as did many of the monks, but it had made a considerable impression. St-Martin-des-Champs was extremely well endowed and had rights of presentation to two-thirds of the parishes of the Capital.[40] A few days later, on 1 October, other similar addresses were read. For example, the monks of the great abbey of Bec in Normandy applauded the abolition of tithes and seigneurial rights and begged to be allowed 'the inestimable benefit of liberty' accompanied by a suitable pension, while the monks of Bonneval said that, though they would prefer to remain as they were, they would submit to being suppressed, subject again to receiving a pension.[41]

Decisions about church property were delayed by other discussions, especially the debates on the Declaration of the Rights of Man and the Citizen and on the Constitution. When the king refused to surrender his executive power, the march of the women on 5 October forced him to move to Paris, calling upon the Assembly to follow him. On Saturday 10 October, the deputies, still at Versailles, returned to the issue of church lands. They heard Talleyrand, bishop of Autun, once known as the financial genius of the General Assembly of the Clergy, explain, in a lucid and cunning speech, how they could get round the difficulty that the Revolution, and especially the new Declaration of the Rights of Man, had enshrined the right of individual property. The Church's property, he declared, had been given not for the benefit of individuals but to enable them to fulfil certain functions. While the nation cannot 'destroy the entire body of clergy, because this body is essentially necessary to the practice of religion, it can certainly destroy particular groupings within this body, if it judges them harmful, or simply useless' and has therefore 'a very extensive right to dispose of their property'. On this basis he produced a scheme under which all church property would become the property of the nation. He estimated that its total value was 150,000,000 livres per annum. In return the state would guarantee to pay the Church 100,000,000 to maintain the clergy and their work. This sum would diminish as old incumbents died off since they would be replaced, if at all, at a lower salary. As part of this reorganisation, he remarked in passing, 'from now on every community will be forbidden to let anyone take vows, until it has been decided which of the former communities will continue'.[42]

The issues were further debated over the next few weeks. Some powerful speeches were made against Talleyrand's and similar proposals. Of these the most effective was that of the abbé Maury. He pointed out that neither the king nor the nation had given the land and money now possessed by the Church, and that the individuals who had actually made the donations had made them to individual churches and communities, not to the Church as a whole. He maintained that it was positively desirable that the clergy should be propertied, that all property was equally sacred and that in any case, before assailing the Church, the Assembly should consider its attitude to religion in general and Catholicism in particular. The group who really wanted the state to take over the property of the clergy, he claimed, were the speculators, who, unlike other sections of the population including the Church, had shown no readiness to make sacrifices themselves to save the state.[43] Certainly, declared the abbé Gouttes, the monasteries should be reformed and reduced in number. But the Assembly has no power to break the vows of regulars; and

it would not be in your interest, nor in that of religion and morals, to release into society men like the monks of the Order of Cluny, who have been so rash as to give you what does not belong to them on condition that they receive a pension much higher than is due to persons useless and even harmful to society, who can be compared to the greedy and lazy hornets that devour the substance of the wise and laborious bee.[44]

But keep the useful monks: some do exist, like the Maurists, . . . [and] the mendicant Orders which have rendered such great services to the Church.[45]

No discussion specifically devoted to monasteries took place until 28 October. Then letters were read from two monks and a nun asking for a decision to be taken whether the temporary suspension of monastic vows should be made permanent. It was pointed out that, by the rules of the Assembly, so important a step, which appeared to prejudge a major question, should not be taken the first time it was proposed; but the cause of the regulars attracted so little sympathy that after the briefest of discussions a decree was duly enacted suspending the taking of perpetual vows.[46]

As the debate on church property continued, powerful warnings were issued that Talleyrand's proposals were unwise: that the wealth of the Church would be dissipated by the state and would in any case prove inadequate to stave off bankruptcy; that those who were at present enjoying more church property than ideally they ought to have should not be forced to give it up, for 'no Frenchman should have reason to groan at being free'; and that 'the innumerable quantity of monks and nuns who implore divine mercy to remain in their estate' should be indulged.[47] Archbishop Boisgelin of Aix made a telling late appeal for moderation, for judicious reform rather than confiscation. But, like most speakers, he said remarkably little about monasteries – only that 'houses and communities will be reduced in such a way that the number of their members will suffice to fulfil their aims and the useful purposes to which their labours should be directed'.[48]

It was left to the comte de la Marck to venture a strong defence of monasteries. He described himself as a representative of 'the Belgian provinces', that is, of the former parts of the Netherlands now annexed to France. He argued that the confiscation of church lands would have the result that, as compared with other provinces, his region would be contributing an unfairly large part of its wealth to the French state.

> Why? A very great part of the land of these provinces belongs to the clergy, the hospitals and the colleges. The farmers of these lands, secure in the length of their leases, ... are used to regarding this rented land as a property; they spare no effort in cultivating ... the land they occupy ...
>
> The majority of the owners, the monks, the chapters, consume their wealth on the same land that produces it; they have no idea of those objects of luxury and curiosity that are sought in distant parts and cause the money of one country to be transported to another. Their revenues, far superior to their needs, are partly used to construct and maintain immense buildings, partly to meet the cost of public education, and always for enlightened assistance to the poor.
>
> This source of wealth and happiness, attested for centuries, ... will dry up if the National Assembly ... disposes of this property ...
>
> It is not the cause of the clergy that I am upholding, it is that of the people.

During the course of his speech he stressed more than once how important it was that his region had always resisted the appointment of commendatory abbots. He also cast doubt, as had some other speakers, on the optimistic assumptions commonly made about the likely yield of massive sales of church land.

Having put his detailed case, he ranged far beyond his brief to challenge one of the fundamental axioms of the Revolution. Why, he asked, should all the provinces of France be treated the same, as though part of a machine? Why should there not be 'several little states, each administered separately and differently according to the genius of its inhabitants but united under a general government for mutual support?'[49]

It is no wonder that this arresting speech was unwelcome to the Assembly. But it beautifully illustrates, at the decisive moment, the parallels and the differences between the Belgian and French Revolutions. The comte de la Marck, one of the great nobles of the Austrian Netherlands, was already active in helping to prepare their uprising against Joseph II, whose church policies he opposed on the same grounds as he now opposed the secularisation of church lands in France. But he clearly recognised that French opinion about monasteries – particularly in the National Assembly – differed from Belgian and also that, outside the former Belgian provinces of France and a few other areas, recent French experience of monasteries was less encouraging than Belgian. The determination of Joseph II to unify and homogenise his territories closely paralleled the aims of the French Revolution, but the historical traditions of the two countries made centralisation much more palatable in France than in Belgium.

Finally, on 2 November, at the end of the day's debate in which the count had spoken, the following decree was enacted by 568 votes to 346: 'That all ecclesiastical property is at the disposal of the nation, subject to provision, in a convenient manner, for the expenses of worship, for the payment of ministers and for the relief of the poor, under the supervision and according to the instructions of the provinces.'[50] A deputy more sanguine than the comte de la Marck wrote to his constituents in Flanders telling them what had been done, adding: 'After that you will not say that your abbey is suppressed nor that your good monks will die of hunger. Provision will be made. You can rest assured about that. People are not so inhuman in France.'[51]

Within a week it was further agreed that church property should be placed in the charge of the king and the state officials, ostensibly to protect it against theft but also so that it could be inventoried. A regular abbot who was a deputy, M. de Coulmiers, abbot of Abbecourt, had attempted unsuccessfully to resist this measure, saying that heads of houses were in the best position to supply the necessary information. The Assembly preferred to entrust the task to the local authorities.[52] Before the end of 1789 the collection of this information had begun and the first sales of church land had been authorised, to the tune of 400 million livres.[53] But many still believed at this stage that localities would have the power to decide on the details of the programme, that only some monasteries would be suppressed and only some lands would be seized.[54]

In December also, however, the Assembly's ecclesiastical committee produced its major report on the fate of the Orders, the regulars and their houses. M. Treilhard, its radical chairman,[55] introducing it, spoke of the almost universal decadence of monasteries and the public's conviction that they should be suppressed. The report of course rejected lifelong vows. It proposed to offer every monk and nun the opportunity to choose within three months whether to remain in the cloister or to enter the world. Those who elected to stay would be gathered together in certain houses, mostly in small towns and the countryside, and the state would pay the house 500 livres annually per inmate to maintain them and keep up the buildings. Those who elected to leave would receive a somewhat larger pension, increasing with age, with an especially generous provision of 2,000 livres for former abbots. All this would increase liberty and gloriously destroy 'this revolting contrast which allows certain Orders to be surrounded by all the luxury of opulence but condemns the others to the shame of begging'. The houses that would survive in the major towns would be those devoted to education, to care of the sick or poor or to the advance of knowledge. This arrangement, M. Treilhard claimed, would have a double utility: 'the presence of the religious would revivify the countryside where they lived, and you would obtain free disposal of the lands they possess in the major cities, an immense resource very precious in our critical situation'. Up to this point, what was being proposed was not total, but only partial, suppression.

The report was debated on 11, 12 and 13 February 1790. The bishop of Clermont powerfully defended monasticism, reminding the Assembly that his constituents had required him to do so. More acceptable to the Assembly were opinions like those of Roederer or Pétion. Roederer claimed that ordinary cultivators would do as much for agriculture as monks would; that the poor could be looked after by the state as well as they would be by the monks; and that, 'if it is right to allow pious men the freedom to lead a sedentary, solitary, contemplative life, I shall reply that everyone can be sedentary, solitary and contemplative in his study'. Pétion declared:

Nowadays monks do not work any more; they are workers lost to society, wealth taken from it. So monks are individually harmful, dangerous as a body. If Spain, once so populous, is now deserted and impoverished, this is entirely due to the establishment of monasteries. If England is flourishing, she owes the fact partly to the abolition of monks . . . You must destroy these orders entirely. If you keep some, you will prepare the way for the revival of all.

The superior-general of St-Lazare argued that Paris would be vastly poorer without its monks, provoking Barnave, a Protestant member of the Ecclesiastical Committee, to denounce the Orders as 'incompatible with the Rights of Man' because their members deliberately surrendered their liberty. They are 'outside society', he declared, 'against society'. The Assembly was carried away by these radical ideas.

It was decided that solemn vows should no longer be recognised, and that all Orders that required them should be suppressed 'without the possibility of any such being established in the future'. Regulars should be free to leave the cloister, in which case they would be pensioned. Those monks who did not wish to leave would be moved to a house selected by the local authorities; but nuns who so desired could stay on in their present houses. Teaching and charitable institutions should survive – but only for the time being, until better provision could be made.[56]

By now, a week before Joseph II died, the Revolution had already enacted far more radical legislation on monasticism than his. He had abolished only certain Orders, mostly contemplative, and overall suppressed less than half the monasteries in his dominions, whereas France had now abolished all the traditional Orders, leaving only a remnant of them to die out on sufferance. He had maintained state recognition of perpetual vows, which the Assembly had rejected. The lands and revenue he had seized were exploited for religious ends, not, as in France, for the state's general purposes. No country that had remained Catholic had ever previously abolished all the Orders that required solemn vows. In no Christian country had all church property been confiscated. The Assembly had gone far beyond what the people had contemplated in their *cahiers*. In fact it is difficult to find anyone who, before the event, recommended so ruthless a confiscation.

In November 1790 there appeared in London Edmund Burke's *Reflections on the Revolution in France*, the classic statement of the case against its rationalism, despotism, irreligion and spoliation. The book was to become enormously influential, in the long run as the most powerful of all defences of conservatism, in the short run as the most compelling critique of the new French regime. But it was regarded by most politicians and observers for at least two years after its publication as wildly exaggerated in its indictment; indeed some thought it proved that Burke was mad. When later he appeared to be vindicated by the expansionism that led to war in April 1792, by the September massacres of 1792 and by the execution of Louis XVI in January 1793, it was admitted that he had turned out a wonderful prophet. But even so he had been 'right too soon'. One of his recent editors tells us that Burke had formed his views by September 1789 on the basis of inadequate information supplied to him by a group of reactionaries he happened to have met and corresponded with, and that neither the material he possessed nor the actual developments in Paris justified the account he gave. This is proved, we are told, by the fact that, when he had virtually completed his text, even the Civil Constitution of the Clergy of July 1790 had not yet been passed.[57]

His contemporaries noticed, with a mixture of mirth and alarm, that he concentrated to a remarkable extent on the fate of the French Church and, in particular, of French monasticism. Windham, an originally sceptical friend who was later to become one of his most fervent allies, declared: 'What shall we say of a book of which the best argued & most forcibly written part is a vindication of convents?'[58] It is certainly extraordinary that Burke should have ventured to write so much on this theme. Protestant Britain was as yet quite unprepared to show the slightest sympathy with monasticism. As an Irishman of Catholic origin who fought for greater toleration of Catholics, Burke frequently had to rebut the potentially ruinous charge that he was not a member of the Church of England at all but himself a Catholic who had been educated by Jesuits at St-Omer. Had these accusations been true, he would have been ineligible to sit in parliament and hold the offices he had held and would have laid himself open to heavy legal penalties. But of course the reason why he stressed the fate of the monasteries was that it was in their case that the Revolution had already shown itself contemptuous of prescription, the rights of property and established institutions on a grand scale. He had made a point of reading the voluminous proceedings of the National Assembly. They told him that by November 1789 the fate of the monasteries had been virtually sealed and that in February 1790 the decision was ratified. By the same date the principle of seizing all church property had also been agreed, together with the mechanisms for so doing and for selling it off. The Civil Constitution of the Clergy, which Burke in fact discussed, certainly carried further the process of reforming the Church but added little to the decisions already taken about its lands. He undoubtedly drew out the implications of some of the early measures of the Revolution, in secular as well as ecclesiastical matters, before they were applied in practice. In this sense he certainly ranks as a prophet, though one who was prompted by documentary evidence rather than by divine inspiration. But on the fate of the monasteries he was talking of what had already been settled and was already being acted upon. He was not only exceptionally well informed about the state of affairs at the end of 1789. Unlike most of his contemporaries and many subsequent historians, he was equipped to see the significance of what had been done to the monasteries of France.

THE REVOLUTION AND THE MONASTERIES FROM MARCH 1790

Faced with the choice of leaving the cloister or staying on but in much less favourable conditions, many French monks seized the opportunity to leave. As usual, the available figures are hard to interpret. A monk who at first declared he wished to leave might well change his mind. If, as in the majority of cases, a monk's house was being dissolved, he might well feel and could certainly argue that his commitment was thereby terminated. 'It is not we who are leaving our Order, it is our Order that is leaving us.' It was not a case of Observant houses being retained and slack ones dissolved. A good many houses contained only tiny numbers, in spite or because of the efforts of the *commission des réguliers*. Whereas a high proportion of the monks of the old propertied Orders left the cloister, certain other Orders, especially the Capuchins, showed much greater attachment to their common life and vows. In Paris, where the evidence has been studied in depth by Plongeron, it seems that roughly a half of all monks decided to go into the world, and roughly half to accept the offer of a place in one of the houses where such persons were to be allowed to live a communal life.[59] Some gladly became parish priests, some sought to be fully secularised and married. In general, wrote La Gorce, the monks showed themselves neither heroes nor renegades: it was as though they were 'suddenly woken up from their tepid tranquillity, their soporific psalmody'. Their pacific habits and the lack of collaboration between houses and Orders made their suppression easy to accomplish.[60]

The great majority of nuns, on the other hand, declared their intention of remaining in their commuities, often making powerful protests to the officials who came to offer them their freedom: they did not desire, they said, that kind of liberty; they already possessed the one freedom they sought, the freedom to worship and pray in their community. The idea prevalent among caricaturists and deputies to the Assembly that the nuns were only waiting their opportunity to leave their prisons and find husbands, perhaps among former monks, was shown to be a fantasy. Only a small percentage of former nuns married, and of them only just over a fifth married a priest or regular, while only 4.5 per cent of the male clergy who took the opportunity to marry chose nuns for their wives.[61]

Some abbots and abbesses proved obstructive, at least to a point, and a considerable number of towns and villages petitioned to keep their monasteries, but there was scarcely any violent opposition. That the regulars themselves should submit peaceably was only to be expected. It is more surprising that their lay sympathisers mostly remained passive. At Montauban, however, riots occurred in May 1790 when the making of inventories of monastic property began: five people were killed. In much more serious disturbances at Nîmes in the following month, during which perhaps 300 died, hostility to the measures of the Assembly was obviously intensified by Catholic resentment at the control newly established by a Protestant elite over the local administration.[62] Pious Catholics were mortified that the majority in the Assembly refused in the spring of 1790 to accept a motion proposed by Dom Gerle, and promoted by traditionalists especially in the south, declaring that the Catholic religion was the religion of France.[63] At Toulouse, where only 5 per cent of monks had seized the chance to leave the cloister, 313 citizens met in April 1790 to call for the maintenance of Catholicism, and in particular of the local chapters and religious houses. What followed is highly instructive. The meeting was forbidden by the mayor on the grounds, first, that no one could possibly intend to threaten 'this holy religion' and, secondly, that such 'secret machinations' were designed to 'form a party in the heart of Toulouse opposed to the regeneration of the French empire'. Local newspapers attacked lazy priests and opulent congregations, and in July the mayor attended a patriotic, revolutionary festival where he and the local National Guard swore 'in the presence of the Supreme Being to live and die as citizen soldiers, comrades and brothers, to be faithful to the nation, to the law and to the king'.[64] One can already detect in the official reaction the shrill intolerance of the propaganda that in a more virulent form was to justify the savage repression of the Terror. Dom Gerle's motion had evoked not only loyalty to the Church but also, in response, strident anticlericalism. But the mildness of the opposition to the Assembly's monastic policies, although they had become so much more radical than what had been envisaged in the *cahiers*, suggests that they commanded a substantial measure of support, at least among the politically aware.

Of course it mattered that the legislation did not take immediate effect. Sales of land and property began in earnest only in the last months of 1790. The government, in ever deeper deficit, decided to issue *assignats*, effectively paper money, to the value of the confiscated lands. At first the property fetched good prices. It took time for the market to be glutted, for more *assignats* to be issued and for inflation to render them almost worthless.[65] The process aroused very little opposition, except in Alsace, where it was feared that the land would be bought by Jews.[66] In general, monks did not leave their monasteries until the end of 1790, since their pensions were not payable until 1 January 1791; and Paris cannot have been unique in having half of its male monasteries still open, for those who had chosen to continue as monks, until after the end of 1791.[67]

Meanwhile, the Assembly had enacted further revolutionary legislation on the Church, making the prospects of the monks and nuns seem ever bleaker. A sweeping reform of the Church, the Civil Constitution of the Clergy, was enacted in July 1790. This law completely redrew the map of dioceses, depriving many bishops of their sees; it abolished all offices in chapters, colleges and monasteries of both sexes, leaving no benefices except those with cure of souls; it fixed the stipends of all clergy; and it set up electoral bodies, dominated by laymen, to choose parish priests and bishops – all without prior reference to the French Church itself or to the pope, and explicitly excluding the pope from any future involvement.[68] This measure went far beyond what any Catholic country had ever enacted, and further than most Protestant states had gone, in rationalising church geography and prescribing the election of clergy. Almost all the bishops opposed it, most of them having refused even to take part in the debates on it. Most of the lower clergy in the Assembly voted against it. At first the king would not approve it, partly on the ground that the role of the pope in the Church had not been taken into account; and the Assembly eventually asked the king to seek papal approval for it. This approach was generally believed by the revolutionaries to be a mere formality. After all, the papacy had been forced to suppress the Jesuits, and Pius VI had not officially condemned the measures of Joseph II. The Vatican, like the French bishops, was most reluctant to precipitate a schism in the Church and hoped that some compromise could be negotiated. Knowing how serious a step it would be to condemn the Civil Constitution, Rome naturally took a long time to produce its answer.

Although so many clergy were hostile to the measure, others welcomed its downgrading of hierarchy and its emphasis on pastoral care. The opinion of the pope on the affairs of the French Church was considered by many to be unimportant. Dom Gerle not only supported the Civil Constitution; he persuaded himself that it had acquired divine sanction through having been prophesied two years earlier by a poor girl called Suzanne Labrousse.[69] Before long, however, while the pope's answer was awaited, serious resistance appeared in the provinces to the new arrangements. So the Assembly decided in December 1790 to require all clergy holding church offices to take an oath to the state and to the Civil Constitution, and at the end of the month the king was induced under strong pressure to accept this decree, even though Rome had not yet pronounced on the Constitution itself. Just at this time, ironically, Austria re-established its rule in Belgium.

Faced with the necessity to commit themselves one way or the other, nearly all the bishops and many ordinary priests refused to take the oath, unable to accept either the total exclusion of the pope or the popular election of clergy. Precise figures are as always difficult to give. A surprising number managed to avoid ever being confronted with the oath. Some were allowed to take it with reservations. Some who would not take it at first took it later. Others who took it initially later retracted. Very roughly, half of the clergy refused the oath, many fewer than half in Paris and the south, far more than half in the north and west. As for the regulars, nuns did not qualify to take the oath but many monks did. Dom Gerle had made a point of taking it, unnecessarily, in the Assembly; and, in Paris at least, about half of the monks took it; among them, roughly as many of those who had left the cloister took it as of those who had stayed.[70] Although in the nineteenth century it was assumed by the Church that the refractory priests took the obviously right decision and the constitutionals the obviously wrong one, the situation was anything but clear-cut in 1790–1. The French Church had long been accustomed to obeying the secular power and virtually ignoring the pope. It was a serious question for a priest whether it was more important to cling to traditional notions of the Church's independence from the state than to do one's duty to one's flock; and, if he refused the oath, he risked losing his livelihood. On the other hand, the deepest feelings of many were offended and aroused by the radical changes made by the Civil Constitution. In every region the attitudes of lay Catholics, especially of women, made an immense difference: in some areas the large majority of the faithful pressed the clergy to refuse the oath; in others the pressure to take it was equally strong. Ex-monks perhaps had special reason to adhere to the Civil Constitution, having just decided to abandon their regular life precisely in order to become good citizens and do useful work.

Pius VI eventually produced his condemnation of the Civil Constitution on 10 March 1791: 'from beginning to end', he proclaimed, 'it contains nothing that ought not to be censured, and all its regulations are so intertwined that hardly any part of it is free from suspicion of error'.[71] He seized the opportunity to denounce almost all the work and ideas of the Revolution. A fortnight earlier, Talleyrand, the only one of the old bishops who would agree to do so, had consecrated the first 'constitutional' bishops. The French Church was now to be split from top to bottom. The old aristocratic bishops, appointed by the Crown to ancient dioceses – many of whom had already emigrated – were set over against an almost completely new bench of elected bishops, mostly of much humbler origin, whose dioceses coincided with the new *départements*. The lesser clergy, including the monks, were divided into those who, having taken the oath, could hold a post in the Church and those who, having refused the oath, were excluded. This issue overshadowed the emptying and spoliation of the monasteries, and the sale of church lands bound the numerous purchasers, most of them already persons of substance, to the revolutionary regime. At the same time as passing the Civil Constitution the Assembly had abolished nobility, so that large numbers from both the old First and Second Estates were alienated.

The leaders and beneficiaries of the Revolution became ever more convinced that its entire achievement was being put at risk by the evident disloyalty of the king, the scale of the emigration, the threats of foreign Powers and mounting opposition at home. From the revolutionaries' standpoint refractory clergy ranked as traitors, ready to assist the king, the *émigrés* and the enemies of France to overturn the new order. On the other side, in many parts of the country the dissidents commanded wide sympathy. This religious division was the major factor in reducing much of France to a state of virtual civil war, with rival gangs using violence against whichever kind of clergy they disliked. In November 1791 the new Legislative Assembly required priests who had so far refused to swear the oath, or had recanted, to take it forthwith or else lose their pensions and be debarred from officiating in parish churches. Further, if the mere presence of non-jurors was reported to have encouraged any kind of opposition to the regime, they became liable to imprisonment. Although the king refused to sign the new measure, many localities acted on it. Soon the persecution was intensified. If a refractory priest was denounced, he could be banished. If he then returned to France, he would be imprisoned for ten years. Former monks suffered under these measures together with clergy who had always been seculars.

By the beginning of 1792 the revolutionary leaders appeared paranoid in the face of foreign threats and internal dissension, and a declaration of war against the princes who were assisting the *émigrés* was demanded. It came in March. In this still more febrile atmosphere the reports and decrees of the Legislative Assembly abounded with wild statements by progressive deputies which were not only dogmatic and despotic but often manifestly untrue. A few quotations from one document will suffice to illustrate what was said of monks and nuns: the report of the Committee of Public Instruction on the secular congregations, dated 10 February 1792, as given to the Assembly by Gaudin, a deputy from the already rebellious Vendée:

Philosophy had taught us long ago the need to suppress the monasteries, and experience has now convinced us of the advantages that this suppression has brought to society. There is almost no one who does not applaud it. I do not except even the great majority of those who lived in these houses who, seeing their chains broken by the Constituent Assembly, have offered their thanks to their liberators.

Those indissoluble bonds, equally objectionable to Nature and the fatherland, no longer exist: the first breath of liberty caused them to disappear...

However, the Oratorians and Doctrinaires were allowed to continue in their work of public education. It was naturally expected of them that their efforts would match their former reputation; but this hope has been utterly disappointed. It seems that these bodies have been preserved merely to demonstrate to the nation the impossibility of associating any ecclesiastical corporation with our constitution... The aim of the legislator has been to unite more closely all citizens with the public interest, and every corporation is inevitably an intermediary interposed between the individual and the nation.

We must not then be surprised if these congregations have visibly and rapidly decayed...

Disputes have occurred about everything, but principally on the question of the civic oath...

Your committee... proposes to suppress them from this very moment...

The possessions of these congregations will then pass to the national administration and will add to the funds for public education...

The consolidation of all this property being necessary to the execution of your plan, you cannot delay destroying all the congregations hitherto charged with seminaries and theological teaching, Lazarists, Sulpicians, Eudists and so many others; and finally the Sorbonne,... which so well deserves to be condemned in its turn by the Reason which it has so often proscribed.

All these associations, intimately tied to the old episcopal regime,... were born under the auspices of superstition and steadily became more and more perverted by the nature and form of the teaching entrusted to them...

Their houses have remained asylums and breeding-grounds of fanaticism... These societies draw their strength from their union... You have seen it in the case of the monks. Their dispersion has furnished the nation with a certain number... changed into useful citizens. The ancient tree of monasticism has been entirely uprooted by the good work of the Constituent Assembly. It will be your glory to extirpate these last remnants...

The Filles de la Sagesse,... uncloistered nuns,... under the direction of their spiritual fathers, have continually circulated the poison of fanaticism into the furthest corners of society... Their manner of life, divided between retreat and dissipation, serves both to concentrate fanaticism and to spread it.

So all these congregations were duly dissolved, though it took until 18 August to carry the whole programme of the committee into law. Those who had belonged to congregations concerned with care of the sick and the poor were ordered to go on working, but as individuals in ordinary clothes, not as members of banned communities in religious habits. In future only those who had taken the civic oath would be allowed to teach. Small pensions were paid to those members of the suppressed organisations who had taken the oath. On the previous day all monks and nuns remaining in communities were ordered to vacate their premises before 1 October. These laws marked the official end of all monasticism in France.

At the beginning of August a 'second revolution', spearheaded by the Paris mob, had forced the Assembly towards more radical positions. On 26 August it was decreed that all refractory clergy must leave France within a fortnight. Those who did not would be taken to the penal colony of Guiana. Parisian radicals – and thugs – now took the law into their own hands and between 2 and 7 September rampaged through the prisons and monasteries, massacring or summarily executing well over a thousand presumed refractories or traitors, including at least 200 priests and many monks and nuns.[72] Such episodes of lynch law recurred over the next two years in many parts of the country, often more or less encouraged by the authorities.

Late in 1792 the monarchy was abolished, and in January 1793 the king was executed. Eleven days later the Republic declared war on Britain. The destabilising effects of external and civil war were enhanced by bad harvests and rampant inflation, largely caused by the method and speed of disposal of church lands. Under the regime of the Committee of Public Safety in 1793–4, despite the guarantee of religious freedom in the new constitution, 'the Terror' assailed a vast range of supposed 'enemies of the Revolution', including Catholicism of every type and Catholic clergy of all persuasions. In July 1793 it was decreed that all church bells must be removed and melted down for the war effort. In practice, however, it was often found that taking down bells would endanger the whole structure of a church, and so many bells survived, though condemned to silence. In October the Christian calendar was replaced by a rationalistic calendar with a ten-day week and absurd new-minted names for the days and months – a scheme of course wholly unimagined in the *cahiers*, many of which had demanded better observance of Sunday.[73] The revolutionary government tried to efface the memory of the old religion. The names of saints, churchmen and monasteries were expunged from the map. Pont-l'Evèque became Pont-Libre; Pont-l'Abbé Pont-Marat; Port-Royal Port-Libre; the town of St-Denis was renamed Franciade and St-Quentin Egalité-sur-Somme.[74] The buildings themselves and commemorative statues were threatened by declarations such as this: it is 'a manifest wish of the nation' that 'no public monument should continue to exist which recalls the reign of despotism'.[75] The current National Assembly, the Convention, legalised divorce and favoured the marriage of priests, including bishops. Since some clergy could not accept this position, it was decreed in July 1793 that any bishop who opposed clerical marriage was to be deposed or deported. In September the unfortunate sisters who had been ordered to go on tending the sick and succouring the poor as individuals received a further blow: only if they took oaths to the constitution could they continue their work. Their presence and assistance at births, illnesses and deaths was held to have given the traditionalists among them too much power over the minds of those they served.[76] By the end of 1793 the constitutional Church had been virtually abandoned by the government that had established it; clergy were being forced to abjure their vocation, churches were being desecrated and vandalised. Cults of Reason and of the Supreme Being were introduced and celebrated in a 'purified' Notre-Dame and many other churches across France, while Catholic Masses were banned. By the summer of 1794 not merely the Roman Catholic Church but Christianity itself seemed to have been outlawed.

In this welter of change not only the wealth and standing but also the sheer number of the clergy had been drastically reduced. A significant body of monks, and a small number of nuns, had been secularised. From the beginning of the Revolution 30,000 to 40,000 priests emigrated, at least a third of the total. Among them were numerous monks but, if the case of Paris is at all representative, a much lower proportion of regulars than of seculars went into exile. On the other hand, many Parisian clergy prudently withdrew to the provinces.[77] Those refractories who stayed in France after 1790 officiated only illegally and at great risk to themselves and their flocks. Then, in the period of persecution from 1793, a high proportion of the constitutional clergy, perhaps 20,000, abdicated their functions, either formally or by simply ceasing to act, and more than two thousand priests and other clergy were killed, with or without trial.[78] Many of them died with extraordinary courage, most particularly the many nuns who refused to compromise with the regime. Their sacrifice, and the reaction of others to it, made possible the ultimate revival of the Church, but in the short run further reduced the strength of the clergy.

During this period, too, the religious buildings of France were remorselessly targeted by both mobs and officials. Taking just monastic structures, an early example of desecration was the secularisation of the new church of Ste-Geneviève, the destruction of its relic of the city's patron saint, and its conversion into the Panthéon, where the remains of Voltaire and Rousseau were reburied in 1791. However, in this case the main features of the building itself survived the change. Some monasteries were attacked before their inmates left, such as St-Lazare. Once buildings were empty, they were more easily vandalised, whether criminally or by those to whom they were assigned by the government after its seizure of the property. The vast complex of the abbey of Cluny was devastated by a force of 200 men in 1793, though it took many more assaults to reduce it to its present-day condition (Ill. 37). The tombs of the Bourbons in the abbey of St Denis inevitably attracted the attention of revolutionaries, and the government solemnly decided to destroy them. Monastic buildings, if they survived at all, most often became government offices or institutions of some kind, but a minority were employed in unlikely ways: a famously

(a)

(b)

ILL. 37 The French abbey of Cluny (a) before its destruction during the French revolution and (b) in the process of being destroyed c. 1810

shocking case was the installation of a gunpowder factory in St-Germain-des-Prés, with predictable results. Clairvaux became a glass factory. Ornaments, paintings, sculptures, stained glass, manuscripts and books fell victim to various perils: the government's call for patriotic contributions; the widespread contempt for Gothic art and architecture; the needs of the new occupiers; and the demands of museums.[79]

By mid-1794 the Catholic Church had been virtually wiped out in France. But within a few weeks the extremist government was toppled, to be replaced by a somewhat less fanatical, but still officially irreligious, regime. It became less dangerous and less rare for priests, both refractory and constitutional, to celebrate Mass, which was soon legally permitted again. Much more important, the fervour of devoted lay men, and especially lay women, kept Catholicism alive with or without the presence of priests. But until 1801 the government of France formally associated itself with no religion, a state of affairs not seen in Europe since the Dark Ages; many of its supporters continued to regard Catholicism, if not Christianity, as incompatible with the Revolution; and from time to time the persecution of Catholics recurred.[80]

When Napoleon became Consul and the effective ruler of France in 1799, he set about trying to reconcile his regime with the Catholic Church. One of his generals had reported to him: 'Our religious revolution is a failure. People have become Roman Catholic again.'[81] Napoleon calculated that only a resolution of the religious question would lay to rest the bitter internal divisions created by the Revolution in France. The election of the moderate pope Pius VII in 1800 assisted him. Napoleon cynically reckoned the value of his support at 'a corps of 200,000 men'. In 1801 he succeeded in making a concordat with the pope. With the blessing of Rome the church hierarchy was re-established and the state agreed to pay its salaries. The clergy who had staffed the constitutional Church were virtually abandoned in favour of returning exiles loyal to the papacy. But no attempt was made to recover the lost church lands and no mention was made of monasticism. The Benedictine pope had silently acquiesced in the re-establishment of the French Catholic Church without a monastic element.[82] The precedent was very soon to be copied in Germany.

Napoleon had been prepared to allow, even to welcome, the publication in 1802 of Chateaubriand's *Le génie du Christianisme* (The genius of Christianity), as likely to influence his hitherto anti-religious followers to support the concordat. The book certainly had a huge impact, appealing to sentiments long driven underground in France, and virtually inventing both French romanticism and romantic Catholicism. Chateaubriand's main emphasis was on the contribution of the Church to beauty and on its appeal to the emotions through its liturgy, its art, its architecture and its music.

He said little about monasteries, but what he did say was striking. Monasticism is beautiful because it is very old. 'History, the passions of the heart, charity, vie with each other at the origin of our monasteries.' He even praised monasteries for having beautiful names, like Vallombrosa.

Perhaps it will be said that, since the causes that gave rise to the birth of the monastic life no longer existed among us, the monasteries had become useless refuges... Are there no longer orphans, sick travellers, poor, unfortunates?... It is a barbarous philosophy and a cruel policy that force the unfortunate to live amid the world... It has been claimed that a great service has been done to the monks and the nuns in forcing them to leave their retreats. What is the result? The women who have been able to find refuge in foreign monasteries have fled there; others have banded together to form monasteries for themselves in the midst of the world; several have died of grief; and these Trappists, so much *to be pitied*, instead of taking advantage of the charms of liberty and life have gone to continue their austerities in the heaths of England and the deserts of Russia.[83]

Napoleon was reluctant to restore any monastic communities. But, with or without his sanction, they began to revive. In 1804 he was persuaded to give legal status to some male missionary congregations (Lazarists, Fathers of the Holy Spirit) and many female ones devoted to charity, and even to recognise perpetual, though not solemn, vows – a major departure from the principles of the Revolution. Already a number of groups of Christian Brothers had returned from exile to assist in rescuing primary education from the parlous state to which the Revolution had reduced it. They were refused legal recognition, but between 1805 and 1808 they established themselves in more towns than they had served before 1789.[84] The female group of congregations was placed under the protection of Napoleon's mother, and by 1808 could muster 10,000 sisters, divided roughly evenly between those who cared for the sick and those who educated children. One male Benedictine and one male Trappist monastery also obtained recognition on tortuous grounds. The position of all these houses remained precarious because their recognition could be withdrawn at any time.[85]

Following the restoration of the Bourbon monarchy in 1815, monasticism experienced a remarkable revival in France, and the numbers of regulars reached pre-revolutionary levels by the 1860s. But the developments of the later years of the *ancien régime* and the Revolution left their mark. The great majority of the new regulars were female, and none of them could hope to enjoy grandeur and opulence such as the old Orders had known in the eighteenth century.[86] Only in rare instances, as at Solesmes, have old monastic buildings been recovered and reoccupied by monks. Moreover, it was an inescapable legacy of the revolutionary period that monasticism remained always bitterly controversial in France, seen by many Frenchmen as anti-republican and unpatriotic. Under the Third Republic monks and nuns were to suffer fitful persecution.

CHAPTER 10

THE IMPACT OF THE REVOLUTION OUTSIDE FRANCE

This, broadly, was the story of monasticism outside France between 1792 and 1813: the victories of French armies made it possible to transport the anti-monastic policies of the Revolution to most of western and much of southern Catholic Europe, excepting only Sicily and parts of Switzerland and of the Iberian peninsula. But when and how the policies were carried out varied from country to country; and the process in Germany was entirely different from what occurred anywhere else. Everywhere the precise nature and timing of the measures imposed or promoted by the French was to some extent influenced by the local situation and by the nature of the regime in Paris at the moment when they were devised. Ultimately, though, the monasteries received almost the same treatment in all the territories which France conquered or dominated for any length of time. The crucial decisions were those that had been taken by the National Assembly and its successor, the Legislative Assembly, in the first three years of the Revolution.

One province was actually annexed – or 'reunited' – to France before the wars got under way: the enclave of Avignon, belonging to the pope, in September 1791. What the revolutionaries did to this city, which had requested annexation, gave little encouragement to other populations to follow suit.

From 1792 to 1794 [wrote the historian of revolutionary vandalism] a violent campaign was carried on to obtain from the Convention permission to demolish the Bastille of the Midi, the *papal Bastille*, as in Jacobin style they called the Palace of the Popes. The fortress owed its survival only to the immensity of its structure which defied the picks of the demolition squads. Having failed to destroy it, they allowed it to be pillaged... Each citizen was allowed to take away whatever he wanted: tapestries, woodwork, furniture. It was a legalised sack, done in cold blood... The devastation extended to all civil and religious monuments... The lapidary museum of Avignon... [is a] veritable charnel-house of stones and marbles where the pity of archaeologists has collected and ordered a few rare fragments spared from the savagery of the vandals. This is all that remains of the masterpieces which once made Avignon one of the most beautiful towns in the world: broken columns, shattered capitals, dreadfully defaced statues. Here is the debris of the Benedictines, there that of the Celestines, further on that of the cathedral cloister.[1]

Soon after the first victory of the revolutionary army against Austria and Prussia at Valmy in September 1792, the Convention decreed that all territories located within the 'natural frontiers' of France should be 'reunited'. It also offered 'fraternity and assistance to all people who wish to recover their liberty'. The first case to which these principles were claimed to apply was the duchy of Savoy, annexed in November 1792, part of the kingdom of Sardinia, like the county of Nice, which was seized in January 1793. They were taken over with little difficulty and, like Avignon, became subject to French law, including by then the suppression of all monasteries and the confiscation of all their lands.

EARLY CONQUESTS, ESPECIALLY BELGIUM

After general Dumouriez's victory over the Austrians at Jemappes in November 1792, Belgium was occupied and it was proposed in Paris to 'reunite' it, since France's 'natural frontiers' extended to the Rhine. The long-standing treaties which closed the Scheldt in the interests of British trade were denounced, and it seemed clear that the Dutch Republic would soon be invaded. Since Britain insisted that the Low Countries must remain independent of France, on 1 February 1793 the Convention unanimously agreed to declare war on her. A fortnight later Dumouriez invaded the Dutch Republic, but the Austrians defeated him at the battle of Neerwinden in March. Dumouriez then defected, the emperor Francis II regained control of his Belgian provinces in May and his armies crossed into France. The Belgians, who had seen off Joseph II, had now, it seemed, humiliated the revolutionary regime too.[2] The retreating French 'had time only to devastate a certain number of churches and convents'. During this second Austrian restoration, as we saw in Chapter 8, while France was outlawing Catholicism, Francis II permitted the re-establishment of thirty-eight monasteries suppressed by Joseph II, mostly nunneries.[3]

In the aftermath of Jemappes the elector-archbishop of Mainz and neighbouring German princes were also driven from their lands, which were annexed by

France with the aid of puppet revolutionary governments and rigged plebiscites. But, as in Belgium, this phase of French rule lasted only a few months, until in July 1793 the French garrison of Mainz surrendered to the Austrians. In the first few years of the French Revolution radicalism had had its supporters in the Rhineland. Beethoven, for example, based at the elector's Court in Cologne, had written music for an Ode on the Death of Joseph II in 1790, which included the words: 'A monster, whose name was Fanaticism, rose from the caverns of Hell, got between the Earth and the Sun, and it was Night. Then came Joseph, . . . dragged the frenzied monster down . . . and crushed it. Then Mankind rose up into Light.'[4] Experience of French government, however, had rendered it very unpopular, especially because it threatened the clergy, secular and regular, who provided much of the economic basis of the area's relative prosperity and whose religion commanded the fervent support of the people at large. In the period of French occupation monks were conspicuous among those who were exiled across the Rhine, and with the restoration of the sovereigns they returned in triumph.[5]

So, in these early instances where French armed might proved inadequate and the views of the populace could make themselves felt, the Revolution's ecclesiastical policy was rejected. But the Austrians' victories and invasion galvanised the regime in Paris to carry out the unprecedented mobilisation of the French people that, with the aid of universal conscription and savage punishment of disloyalty and failure, created an army inherently superior to any other, especially in its size. It was to win most of its numerous battles and, because it had been given the power to punish and expropriate the property of all 'enemies of the people', it enabled the occupying governments that it sustained to treat the opposition of the inhabitants with a degree of contempt that no ordinary civil regime based on well-established laws, respectful of property rights and anxious to rule by consent could begin to match.[6]

Again it was Belgium and the Rhineland that were the first to be conquered and governed by the new order, from the summer of 1794. Of the two, Belgium was subjected more speedily to more of the Revolution's legislation because it was officially incorporated into France in July 1795. With the end of the Terror in France, Catholicism was no longer actually proscribed, but monasteries remained beyond the pale. Bouteville, the administrator sent by the French Directory to rule in Brussels, had no doubt that the taking of lifelong vows was incompatible with the liberty gloriously established by the Revolution. At first, though, he hesitated to act against the monasteries because he knew that they enjoyed the sympathy of the population. But, encouraged by orders from Paris, he embarked in June 1796 on inventorying all monasteries with a view to dissolving them and seizing their property. Then in September 1797 the Directory enacted a special law suppressing all houses of men and women in Belgium except for those concerned with education and caring for the sick. This, of course, was to revert to the position reached in France in 1792. All the monastic lands were sold off. The monks and nuns were not given pensions but vouchers, which, by 'a refinement of persecution', were usable only for the purchase of confiscated church lands. Many refused to accept this tainted compensation. Some who did found themselves prevented from buying monastic lands, but others were allowed to do so and even to purchase, directly or indirectly, conventual buildings and re-establish some form of religious community within them. Within a year, after the relatively moderate Bouteville had been recalled, the regime became more anti-religious. The previously exempted congregations were suppressed and the laws against monasteries of all kinds were enforced with fresh zeal. The rebuke received by one lowly official who had shown sympathy with some dispossessed nuns illustrates the new attitude of the government:

Your too great indulgence for your ex-nuns, citizen, has got me into hot water with the Minister of Police. I honestly don't know how an enlightened republican such as you appear to be can seriously ask me whether it is possible to leave a community of stupid old women undisturbed when it is notorious that they stay together only to pass on their prejudices and their fanaticism to the girls whom the aristocracy entrust to their care. I declare that if you do not certify to me within ten days that they have left their old convent, I shall not be able to refrain from reporting that you are responsible for a scandal unexampled in the Republic, namely, a religious institution still in being after three years of suppression.

No one is more of a friend to humanity than I, but this feeling cannot justify the propagation of the fanaticism and prejudices which the government is determined to destroy completely. Piety of course consists in succouring the unfortunate by providing them with the necessities of life, not in banding together to defy the law and the institutions of the Republic.

During this period the ringing of church bells was banned, the clergy were forbidden to wear their distinctive costumes, and they were required to take an oath of submission and obedience to the laws of the Republic. Among the government's commissars was Johann Matthias Konz, a former Premonstratensian from Luxembourg who had came to hate the monks and had rallied enthusiastically to the French cause. But he was a rare and unpopular bird. Only a small fraction of the clergy would take the stipulated oath, with the result that thousands of them were condemned as traitors and more than eight hundred were deported. When in addition conscription was imposed, a widespread rebellion occurred in late 1798, which was savagely repressed. The ferocity of the government's intentions is shown by the fact that nearly eight thousand clergy were listed for deportation. That fewer than nine hundred were actually deported demonstrates the scale and determination of the Belgian population's resistance, helped a little by the British naval blockade. The position of the Church remained miserable until the Concordat came into effect in 1802.

During the long years of French occupation down to 1814 the Church, including former monks and nuns, had a major role in the national opposition to the French, as earlier to Joseph II. This heritage, together with resentment against the union with the Dutch Republic imposed by the congress of Vienna, made Belgium a natural centre for Liberal Catholicism after 1815 when the Church in most countries was identified with reaction and opposed to nationalism. But the long period of French rule also ensured that the country became bitterly divided between friends of the Church and strong anticlericals drawing their inspiration from revolutionary and republican France.[7]

What happened in the Rhineland under its second occupation is best considered later, in relation to the peculiar history of secularisation in Germany as a whole. Chronologically and logically, it is more satisfactory to deal first with Italy and the other countries in which French occupation was decisive.

ITALY

All the Italian states active in monastic reform in the last decades of the *ancien régime* had experienced a reaction against it by the time the French arrived in 1796: Parma in the 1770s, Venice in the 1780s, Lombardy and Tuscany in the last days of Joseph II and the early 1790s, and Naples in the 1790s.[8] The papal state, by contrast, had done almost nothing to take its monasteries in hand, partly because from the 1760s it was swamped by Jesuit and other refugees, though Pius VI was credited with reforming Subiaco. In 1791, by condemning the Civil Constitution of the Clergy and denouncing the French Revolution and all its works, he abandoned his earlier policy of appeasing rulers who had presumed to reform the Church.[9] So, when French armies occupied the mainland of Italy, between 1796 and 1799, they found a country in the grip of reaction. Their ruthless dynamism completely transformed the situation.

In 1796 the army of general Napoleon Bonaparte conquered Lombardy, established a puppet republican government and began introducing revolutionary measures. By this time the suppression of almost all monasteries, considered irreconcilable with individual freedom, was the settled policy of French and French-inspired rulers. Bonaparte himself liked to call monks 'worms' and 'madmen' and to point out that they had not been found necessary by the early Church, Muslims, the English or Protestants.[10] But Bonaparte knew that he needed Catholics and their priests as allies, especially at certain times, and he would sometimes make statements and issue orders apparently sympathetic to monks: he told general Joubert to 'try to get support from among monks' in the Tyrol.[11] However, any monastery that offended him was swiftly suppressed, and the same financial desperation that had promoted the seizure of church property in France soon came into play in Italy. So in 1798 the Milanese republic abolished most monasteries and set about selling off their lands. At least it revived the exception that in France had been abandoned late in 1792, namely that institutions concerned with education and care of the sick should survive.

Next the French invaded and subdued the papal state. In 1798 they exiled the pope and erected a republican government in Rome which dechristianised street names and abolished monastic vows. As in Milan, a minority of priests and monks, especially Capuchins, supported the new Republic, but it was soon threatened by rebellion, partly at least of religious inspiration. In January 1799 a Parthenopean Republic was declared under French auspices at Naples which started the process of suppressing monasteries. It won the support of some bishops and monks, especially, it seems, of Dominicans, but it was not long before a scratch army under cardinal Ruffo drove out the French and brought down the Republic. The fanaticism and brutality displayed by the defenders of religion in this as in other such revolts appalled the civilised at least as much as the barbarities of the French Revolution.[12] Meanwhile, early in 1800, the cardinals, unable to meet in Rome, elected a successor to Pius VI in the monastic church of S. Giorgio Maggiore at Venice, choosing a Benedictine monk, Pius VII, one of whose claims to the office was that as bishop of Imola he had preached a sermon suggesting that Catholics might justifiably co-operate with a revolutionary government.

For a few months in 1799 the military tide turned and the French were in retreat all over Italy, with the result that many monasteries that had been suppressed were restored. But France recovered quickly and over the next few years regained control of the mainland, establishing a new set of regimes to govern it. Meanwhile the pope had made concordats with Napoleon for both France and Italy, in neither of which were there any clauses concerned with monasteries – except for the pope's assurance that he would in no way challenge the right of the purchasers of confiscated church lands to their new possessions. In Piedmont partial suppressions occurred; in Lombardy, Tuscany and the former papal state nearly all monasteries, with the now customary exception of those concerned with teaching and care of the sick, were abolished. When the policy was extended to Rome, the pope protested, declaring that monasteries were necessary to the Church. In the short run this stand led to his deportation, in the long run it encouraged the monastic revival of the nineteenth century. The prefect of Rome from 1809 to 1814, Camille de Tournon, regretted the suppression of the city's monasteries as politically foolish and managed to preserve 'the four largest nunneries', while devoting immense effort to the cleaning and repair of the great monuments of ancient Rome. In Naples one of the officials most involved, Pierre Roederer, whom we encountered earlier as a member of the National Assembly, took the view that laziness characterised the population, accounting for the country's backwardness, and that the principal cause of idleness was the monasteries, especially 'the 100,000 monks who daily boil up soup for 500,000 layabouts'. But, in the face of popular disturbances directed against the French regimes, the policy initially adopted in Naples resembled the tinkering of pre-revolutionary governments: suppressing small monasteries, selling off some lands but allowing viable houses to survive. Later a more radical variant was enacted under orders from Napoleon, who in 1810 decreed the general suppression of monasteries throughout mainland Italy: wealthy and solvent houses were dissolved and their property seized, while propertyless mendicant houses and useful or poor female congregations were spared. Between 1806 and 1814 a total of 1,322 monasteries were suppressed in Naples, but 401 mendicant houses and a few nunneries remained.

French rule, or regimes maintained by France, generally left alone female (and a very few male) communities that did not demand full vows and devoted themselves to teaching and caring for the sick. Other exceptions to revolutionary principles were sometimes allowed. For example, a special decree revoked the suppression of the ancient monastery of Camaldoli in the hills of Tuscany since its services were deemed necessary for the comfort and safety of travellers. But, except in Sicily, which the French never conquered, 'the paradise of the monks' saw nearly every monastery abolished, or in the process of being abolished, by the time the Napoleonic empire collapsed in 1814. So far as their lands were concerned, the policy adopted was that of the Revolution and not that of Joseph II and Leopold II: that is, all their lands were seized for general secular purposes without recompense to the Church or consideration of the wishes of the original donors, although pensions were paid to the expelled monks and nuns so long as they remained docile. The considerable numbers who resisted were deported, probably 350 of them to Corsica.[13] Most of the lands were in fact sold off, though the regimes

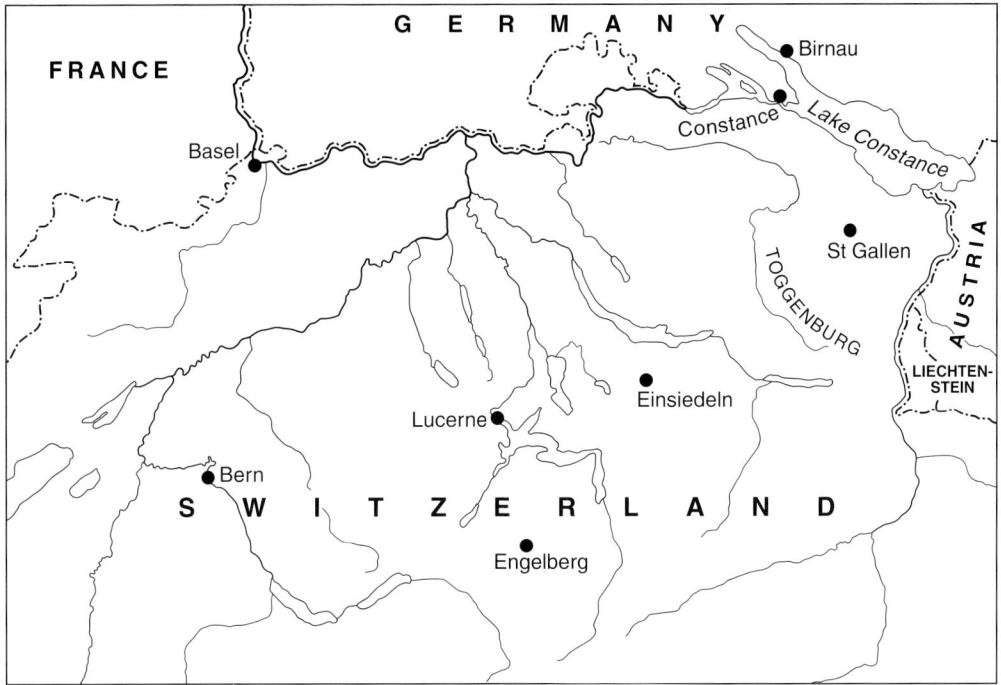

MAP 4 Swiss monasteries

did not last long enough to bring the process to completion. Most monastic buildings were commandeered or destroyed, while museums and picture galleries, especially those of Napoleon himself and of Paris, were greatly enriched from their treasures.[14]

SWITZERLAND

Switzerland was an even more varied museum of medieval institutions and practices than Belgium. By the eighteenth century it had become a republican confederation made up of thirteen semi-independent cantons, sundry cities and other units, and its population was divided between Catholics and Protestants, with religious divisions often cutting across political. In its areas of dominance Swiss Catholicism flourished, notoriously truculent towards its bishops and the pope. In the town of Lucerne the proportion of clergy to adult males reached the extraordinary figure of one in five, as high as anywhere in Europe.[15] Of Switzerland's roughly 120 monasteries the two grandest were the learned St Gall and Einsiedeln, with its miraculous image of the Virgin that attracted pilgrims in vast numbers, including Gibbon in 1755:

From Zurich we proceeded on a pilgrimage not of devotion, but of curiosity to the Benedictine Abbey of Einsidlen [sic], more commonly styled our Lady of the Hermits. I was astonished by the profuse ostentation of riches in the poorest corner of Europe: amidst a savage scene of woods and mountains, a palace appears to have been erected by Magic, and it *was* erected by the potent magic of Religion. A crowd of palmers and votaries were prostrate before the Altar; the title and worship of the Mother of God provoked my indignation; and the lively naked image of superstition suggested to me, as in the same place it had done to Zuinglius, the most pressing argument for the reformation of the Church.[16]

Archdeacon Coxe, another English historian, condemned it more comprehensively a generation later:

As I walked to this celebrated convent, I found the whole way furnished with stalls, provided with cakes, whey, and other refreshment for the numerous pilgrims then on their road. I saw several hundreds, in groups... I also saw several bevies of merry damsels, who seemed to enjoy the pilgrimage as much as Welsh lasses relish a wake...

The ridiculous tales... of the origin and aggrandizement of this abbey, are so many melancholy instances of the credulity of the darker ages: that they are still believed in the present enlightened century, must be attributed to the force of habitual prejudice; and at the same time proves, how difficult it is for the human mind to shake off those superstitious errors, which it has early imbibed under the name of religion...

Whatever was its origin, and whoever was its founder; crouds of pilgrims resort hither from all quarters to adore the Virgin, and to present their offerings: and it is computed, that upon the most moderate calculation, their number amounts yearly to 100,000.

He thought the Baroque church 'in false taste' and the relics and 'skeletons of saints in masquerade' 'a wretched insult upon poor human nature' (Ill. 38).[17]

From the first, Switzerland felt the influence of the French Revolution, and in 1792 France annexed a part of the bishopric of Basel. The numerous monasteries became concerned for their survival as some of their subjects and tenants were inspired by French example to challenge their authority and their very existence. The power and wealth of the abbey and principality of St Gall had long been resented, especially by the adjacent Protestant city and by its Protestant subjects in the Toggenburg. Like St Blasien, its complement and standing reached a high point in the 1790s. But the abbot and the chapter found themselves forced to consider whether, in order to save the abbey as a spiritual institution, they should surrender its secular power. In 1795 the abbot made what he considered

ILL. 38 Early nineteenth-century lithograph of the Benedictine abbey of Einsiedeln, Switzerland

the necessary decision to yield up the abbey's feudal rights, his monks concurring most reluctantly. When in the following year a new abbot was elected, Pankraz Vorster, his first task was seen as retrieving the house's financial position. His attempts to secure the monastery its due payments naturally reduced his popularity. Then in 1797 the French invaded, the Helvetic Republic was set up in place of the Swiss Confederation and the abbot made further minor concessions. In the following year the chapter of St Gall renounced all its political rights to the people and Vorster departed in protest. 'What sort of an absurdity', he asked, 'is a monastery in the power of modern *Aufklärer* without spiritual and worldly support?' He was able to return in 1799 for a few months, then left for good. From this time he fought to have his abbacy restored by any means, appealing more than once for help to George III, even suggesting in 1803, when he lost the emperor as suzerain, that the king of England might like to take over. In the same year the French reshaped the political geography of Switzerland while allowing it a measure of independence. They created a canton of St Gall, whose leading minister, Karl Müller von Friedberg, had previously served the prince-abbot as first minister. The abbey had meanwhile known a fitful existence, but in 1805 the new cantonal council agreed to dissolve it. This decision is hardly surprising: as well as the force of revolutionary ideology, the abbey had to contend with centuries-old local resentments, differences between the abbot and his monks, and the fact that all the great abbeys of Germany had been or were in process of being dissolved. What is remarkable is that the decision to suppress St Gall was taken by just 36 votes to 33. This was almost the only such decision ever taken by a reasonably free vote, and the narrowness of the majority demonstrates not only that monks and monasticism could still attract significant popular support but also that opinion was deeply divided. In 1814 the abbot lobbied the plenipotentiaries at the congress of Vienna for the abbey's restoration, but without success, and it eventually became the cathedral of St Gall, the bishop's palace and part of the town administration.[18]

It was a different story with many other Swiss abbeys, especially after the French relaxed their control over the country. Einsiedeln, having been abandoned by the abbot and his monks in 1797, resumed its common life in 1802 and survived thereafter. The other grand Benedictine house, Engelberg, whose abbot, said Coxe, had 'very considerable power, which renders him nearly absolute',[19] lost its secular privileges but remained in being. Nearly all the numerous monasteries of the city of Lucerne survived, including three Capuchin houses, even though they were not allowed to take novices for fourteen years from 1798 to 1812.

The case of Switzerland, like that of Belgium, shows that, where the state had not the power, or chose not to exercise the power, to suppress monasteries from above *en bloc*, many of them could command the support to survive, especially if they were prepared to give up some of their political, social and economic power and privileges. But, as usual, the Swiss story was unique.

SPAIN AND PORTUGAL

Spain had gone to war with revolutionary France in 1793. The propaganda of the Committee of Public Safety attracted some Spaniards, including a few monks, but many more were fired by the Church to join a crusade against the regicide, anti-Catholic French. Improvised forces of Catalan peasants were remarkably successful, in combination with Spanish regular troops, in driving out the invading French troops. In 1795 peace was made between Spain and France at Basel without any territorial changes. No opportunity had arisen to apply the monastic policies of the revolutionary assemblies in Spain. In the next year Spain allied with France and engaged with limited success in the naval war against Britain. These conflicts brought the government so near to bankruptcy that in 1798 a peculiar variant of monastic reform was devised to raise money, namely cajoling all monasteries to make over to the government a proportion of their land. The pope was induced to support this policy, at least to a certain point. 'One can be reasonably sure', writes Richard Herr, 'that a sixth of all ecclesiastical property was disentailed' (as the process was called) in Castile by 1808. But this scheme did not save the state from defaulting on its debt repayments.[20]

In 1807, however, Spain enabled France to invade and conquer Portugal, which had refused to accept the emperor's 'Continental System', a plan designed to cut off trade with Britain and turn the whole Continent into an economic unit working for the advantage of France. The Portuguese royal family fled to Brazil, and a guerrilla war ensued in Portugal between supporters and opponents of France, in which clergy including monks played a major role. Despite the involvement of France in its affairs, Portugal saw little in the way of church reform during the Napoleonic period, though monasteries suffered like the whole country from war and civil war and lost many of their treasures, destroyed, confiscated or looted. Expeditions were sent from Britain to assist the anti-French movement, and the country was fought over by British and French forces for four years until Wellington's army drove the French out in 1811.[21]

Meanwhile, in 1808, Napoleon intervened in a disputed royal succession in Spain and tried to resolve the issue by putting his brother Joseph on the throne. At the same time he issued decrees that suppressed the Inquisition and reduced the number of male monasteries by two-thirds. His intervention naturally provoked a revolt, in which monks were much involved. In Galicia the guerrilla leaders included the abbots of Valdeorras, Casoyo, Cela, San Manuel and Trives; in Castille a Capuchin, Délica; in Andalucia Fra Rienda. Battalions were raised entirely of monks: of Dominicans in Málaga, Carmelites in Logroño, Franciscans in Burgos and mounted friars in Murcia. The conflict was glorified as a holy war, another crusade against the infidel.[22]

Within a year of becoming king Joseph took still more drastic measures against the monasteries. He abolished all male Orders, giving the monks fifteen days to leave their cloisters and abandon their habits. All their lands were seized by the state, to be sold off. In the areas of Spain that the French controlled, chiefly the north and west, these policies were enforced. Monks who left or were expelled received pensions but were encouraged to work as secular clergy. Sales of monastic lands got under way, some of the proceeds going to enhance the pay of parish clergy, but most to supplement the revenues of the state. Monastery buildings were either adapted for other uses or left to decay or be sacked. Nuns, though not subject to a general suppression, were encouraged to leave their cloisters. Given the failure of Charles III and his successors to take bold measures at all against the monasteries after the suppression of the Jesuits, this programme amounted to a social and religious revolution.[23]

Following their withdrawal from Portugal, the French were slowly driven out of Spain by the British expeditionary force. In 1812 the official patriotic government in Spain framed a liberal constitution, adopting a middle course between restoration of the monasteries and the Napoleonic scheme. The number of houses to be restored was severely restricted: there were to be only 60 for men and 350 for women. The age of profession was raised to twenty-three, and all Orders' monastic rules were to be strictly enforced. However, at the Restoration in 1814 these plans were abandoned in favour of returning all monasteries to the monks and nuns. By 1820 there were 33,000 monks, still an impressive number though reduced by a third from the cohort of pre-Napoleonic days. Despite the sales of monastic lands, the number of houses was almost as great as before.[24] In the eccentric chronology of Spanish history it was left to the 1830s to seize all church lands, but it was clearly the experience of French rule that had put the whole issue on the practical agenda, while creating bitter divisions within Spanish society that persisted until far into the twentieth century. Similar shifts in attitudes to those seen in Spain prepared the way for the general dissolution of monasteries in Portugal, also in the 1830s.[25]

GERMANY

In 1794–5 the French again occupied the area on the left bank of the Rhine and began to extend French laws to it, including laws on religion. But the process advanced more slowly here than in any other part of Europe that the revolutionary armies conquered. Not until 1798, for example, were feudal rights and tithes abolished. Other characteristic measures were also introduced gradually, such as the revolutionary calendar, a ban on pilgrimages, religious toleration and so forth. All of them, though welcomed by a few radicals, were generally resented and passively resisted. Naturally monks were prominent in the opposition and some of them were punished for their behaviour:

seven months for the Capuchin Pacificus Höcker of Aachen, for preaching about the miraculous cross at Birgden in a provocative manner, four months for the Franciscan Lubentius Ophoven, for poking fun at republican costumes; and so on. They deported to the right bank: six Augustinians from Trier, a Capuchin from Bingen, thirty Dominicans from Jülich, a Capuchin from Bacharach, a Franciscan from Aachen; and so on.[26]

Occasionally penalties were more severe, but there was no parallel to the ferocious repression that occurred in Belgium after the full range of revolutionary measures against the Church had been imposed. The abolition of tithes and feudal dues in 1798 of course greatly reduced the income of the wealthier ecclesiastical institutions, but even then the enactment of the French laws seizing all church lands and abolishing nearly all monasteries was delayed in this occupied part of Germany until after its formal annexation to France in 1801.

Why? It is natural to ask whether the explanation for this anomaly might lie in the special role of the great German monasteries and the unusual degree of popular sympathy they seem to have enjoyed.[27] Certainly, there existed French officials who urged the authorities in Paris to proceed cautiously on religious matters in 1799.[28] But this suggested explanation cannot survive consideration of what the French did in Belgium, where it appears that the Orders were even more uncritically admired by the population than in Germany and yet were ruthlessly suppressed by the French regime.

The government's hesitations in the Rhineland rested on entirely different grounds. In occupying and annexing Belgium and Italian states France was dealing with isolatable political units: most of Belgium had been ruled by the Austrians, like Lombardy; Piedmont, Tuscany, the papal state and Naples were distinct sovereignties. Each of them could easily be conquered by French armies. But the left bank of the Rhine was part of the Holy Roman Empire, which covered an area so vast that at this stage no one could dream that it could all be conquered. In the very early days of the Revolution the French claimed to have abandoned power-politics and to have substituted for it such principles as fraternity and nationality. By 1795 at the latest, however, they had reverted to pursuing the interests of France through traditional means, diplomacy and war. Formal annexation of the left bank of the Rhine would completely disrupt the settlement made by the Peace of Westphalia, a settlement guaranteed and hitherto sustained by France since it ensured that Germany would be politically divided. Under the treaty the intricate political map of the Empire and its complex constitution were alike unalterable, except by agreement with other Powers. Hence the French government accepted that the Rhineland could not be formally annexed without the sanction of a new treaty.

Further, the existence of the ecclesiastical states within the *Reich* put a special complexion on the normal policy pursued by the French of seizing all church land, particularly since much of the German territory that they occupied had formed part of the archbishopric-electorates of Mainz, Trier and Cologne. In the circumstances it is not surprising that, when suppression of the monasteries was discussed in Germany, whether in the press or by statesmen, it was subsumed in, or more usually occluded by, what seemed the much larger and more pressing question: should some or all of the ecclesiastical states be secularised? Among these states the independent prince-abbeys were of trivial importance compared with the bishoprics, especially the three archbishopric-electorates. Plans to secularise them had been seriously mooted in the 1740s, when Frederick the Great and Bavaria cast greedy eyes on them; and the issue was revived in the late 1770s and early 1780s, when Joseph II's plans to exchange Bavaria for Belgium seemed likely to redraw the map of Germany. In the considerable pamphlet literature that the question attracted, Protestant writers almost all condemned the ecclesiastical states, though one of the most prominent, C.F. von Moser, thought it admirable that, unlike the majority of German rulers, the bishops were elected and were to some extent controlled by the cathedral chapters. Catholic authors of course showed more sympathy, but this was generally because they saw the ecclesiastical states as essential props of the Empire and of the Catholic position within it rather than for their intrinsic merit.[29] A new wave of pamphlets appeared in the second half of the 1790s, when the French occupation made the issue topical again, but with a new twist. Prussia and other Powers now began to argue that, if they were to acquiesce in the French demand to annexation of the whole left bank of the Rhine, they would need to be compensated elsewhere for their not very considerable loss of territories there – and where more conveniently than from the lands of the anachronistic ecclesiastical states? The theme was taken up in the negotiations leading to the Treaty of Basel in 1795, the Treaty of Campoformio in 1797, the Treaty of Rastatt in 1798 and the Peace of Lunéville in 1801. Already at Campoformio, despite having promised to maintain the integrity of the Empire, the emperor, Francis II, had secretly accepted a deal involving French annexation of the left bank and compensation for Austria in the form of the archbishopric of Salzburg. At Rastatt the principle of 'compensation through secularisation' was agreed. Whatever was pleaded in mitigation, the secular rulers were motivated by greed for land and sovereignty, and they found the policy of partition, recently pursued in Poland, far more attractive than preservation of the integrity of the Empire. In their efforts to salvage what they could from the impending wreck, the ecclesiastical princes showed no more compunction:

the bishops found themselves inclined to offer up the property of the monasteries; the archbishops believed it would be amply sufficient to seize only the bishoprics and out of their land, by way of consolation, allow the three ecclesiastical electors to gain a small increase of territory from Salzburg, Münster and Fulda; among the electors, finally, Mainz wished in God's name to say Yes to everything so long as it was arranged that Mainz would remain German patriarch and primate.[30]

The Machiavellian figure of Talleyrand, now French foreign minister, presided at Rastatt over what amounted to a decision to liquidate the Church's property in Germany, just as he had set going the process of French secularisation in the National Assembly.[31]

Before the decisions taken at Rastatt could be carried out, the War of the Second Coalition delayed matters for three years, and it was only at Lunéville in 1801, where a serious attempt at a general pacification of central Europe was made, that French annexation of the left bank was formally accepted and the emperor was charged with working out a detailed scheme of compensation to other Powers. A few months later Napoleon obtained the agreement of the pope to the concordat that re-established Catholicism in France but also ratified the sales of church lands. With the pope and the Holy Roman Emperor squared and the German princes in favour, all the obstacles had been removed which had hitherto prevented the French regime in the Rhineland from enacting the measures carried in France in the early years of the Revolution. They were duly brought in during the summer of 1802, with the now usual exception in favour of communities that cared for the sick and educated children.[32]

So on the left bank of the Rhine the French had always intended to introduce their revolutionary policies towards monasticism but waited before implementing them fully until they had obtained by treaty the right to annex the region. The position was quite different in the rest of Germany. Virtually all the lay rulers favoured a measure of secularisation involving the ecclesiastical states, though at first it seemed likely to be partial rather than general. Their motive was not religious or even particularly anti-religious, they simply desired to enlarge and consolidate their states and their control of them. Monasteries had hardly figured at all in the discussions that preceded the four treaties.

In Bavaria, however, proposals to dissolve monasteries suddenly became serious in and after 1798. The costs of the war were threatening to bankrupt the state and, as so often, the government saw hope in mulcting the monasteries. It knew that it could not legally suppress the large number of houses that had representation in the Estates, which included all the wealthiest, and so it imposed on these monasteries with papal sanction, a swingeing levy of 15 million gulden. But in the next year a new elector succeeded, Max Joseph IV. He was that rare phenomenon, the ruler of an *ancien régime* state who sympathised with much of the legislation of the Revolution, and the ruler of a Catholic electorate who had had a Protestant education. He was encouraged in his reforming views by an able and ruthless minister of French origin and education, count Montgelas, who had already advised that, so far as possible, the monasteries should be suppressed and their lands confiscated. But when Max Joseph succeeded, he thought tactically necessary to withdraw his predecessor's heavy taxation and to promise to maintain all monasteries. This undertaking proved worthless. In 1802 the elector suppressed all the monasteries in Bavaria which were not protected by the constitution of the Empire, that is, the mendicant houses and the lesser houses of the old Orders, a total of seventy-seven male and fourteen female houses. Though many petitions were received asking that particular monasteries should be spared, no attention was paid to them.[33]

More important, at the last moment Montgelas injected a new idea into the discussions of the committee of the *Reichstag* that had been set up to arrange the details of the general German secularisation: that, as well as transferring the prince-bishoprics and prince-abbeys to lay rulers, it should accord to all princes the right to dispose of all the monasteries within their territories. It seems that this massive extension of the scope of the discussion had never previously been contemplated, but the committee, largely composed of princes, agreed with alacrity. In the ultimate document of 25 February 1803, the *Reichsdeputationshauptschluss* (i.e. the decision of the imperial committee), the fateful clause was included. It comes in the modern printed version only after thirty pages providing for detailed redistribution of territory between states, large and small. The clause reads:

All the property of endowed foundations, abbeys and monasteries, in old as well as new possessions, Catholic as well as Protestant, mittelbar as well as unmittelbar, which have not been specifically assigned in the preceding sections, shall be left at the free and full disposition of the respective sovereigns, whether for the support of worship, education or other social purposes, or to ease their financial position.

The only qualifications were that cathedrals must be maintained and that pensions must be paid to clergy whose institutions have been suppressed. What had begun as a proposal to compensate a few rulers for relatively small losses to France on the left bank had developed into a total reorganisation of the map of Germany; and the suggestion that the compensation should come from the ecclesiastical states had turned into a general secularisation and sale of all church land (Ill. 39).[34]

All rulers did not act at once, but by 1812 all but a handful of monasteries had been suppressed in south Germany, rather over four hundred in all (Ill. 40). Almost the only survivors were a few houses set aside to receive monks and nuns

THE IMPACT OF THE REVOLUTION OUTSIDE FRANCE

ILL. 39 *Der Entschädigungs-Baum* ('The Compensation Tree') by F.L. Neubauer, 1803. The decaying tree, on which are displayed heads of the clergy, is being cut down with the encouragement of citizens

who declined to leave the cloister, with the intention that the inmates would die out and not be succeeded by others. Among the Benedictines, for example, the only house left in Germany was St Jakob in Regensburg.[35]

It will be clear that these decisions cannot be ascribed to the direct influence of the French Revolution or of the Enlightenment. It was German lay rulers who devised and implemented the measure, and most of them disapproved of the Revolution and by 1802 had become wary of the Enlightenment. The theoretical inspiration came not from Voltaire or even Muratori but from the advocates of state sovereignty and the opponents of priestly rule. Scheglmann, the reactionary historian of the Bavarian suppression, declared that the prime influence came from Pufendorf and the natural law school.[36] This is not so fanciful as it may seem. It was Pufendorf who had called the Empire a monstrosity because he could discern no absolute sovereign ruling over it. He and his school also argued that the contract which men naturally and necessarily made with the ruler whom they needed for their security accorded him absolute power.[37] The *Reich* and the old monasteries both belonged to an age when there were no absolute rulers, no

ILL. 40 I.S. Dürr, The secularisation of the Cistercian monastery of Salem, Germany, 1804

compact states, no strictly guarded frontiers, when the papacy was admitted to have sway in certain matters over the whole of Christendom, when Orders and universities looked to an international or supranational rather than a national community. The German secularisation marked the triumph of the territorial state, though not yet of the nation-state. From the *Reichsdeputationshauptschluss* was bound to follow the end of the Empire itself, which came in 1806.

Such a vast change in the German and European state system could not have occurred, or even been envisaged, without either a prior revolution in Germany, of which there was never the slightest prospect, or an upheaval caused by war. The victories of French armies had led to the French demand to annex the left bank. Either Napoleon himself or his acolytes exercised the major influence over the decisions taken at Campoformio, Rastatt and Lunéville. Without the French

Revolution there would have been no such victories, and without the French Revolution it is inconceivable that a ruler of France would have come forward, able and ready, like Napoleon, to redraw the map of Germany and smash the structure and constitution of the *Reich*. But for the Revolution, no Catholic country would have given to other Catholic states an example, such as revolutionary France did, showing that monasticism could be dispensed with altogether, and but for the Revolution the papacy would not have been reduced to acquiescing meekly in the disappearance of monks and nuns. To secularize all German monasteries was almost unthinkable in 1789. But by 1798 the policy had been imposed on France, Belgium and much of Italy. It was what governments did to get themselves out of debt; it no longer shocked. It had become thinkable in Germany.[38]

The dissolution of the south German monasteries, then, was part of a general secularisation of all Church property, including many ecclesiastical states and excluding only the lands of parishes. It was also part of a final *putsch* by the lay rulers of Germany to establish their sovereignty and destroy the *Reich*. In these respects it was unique. In several other ways it was unusual. It contributed to no serious civil disturbances, such as occurred in this context in France, Belgium, Spain and Naples. Unlike in most other countries, it was carried out at a time when most of the monasteries were well disciplined, had good membership figures and were held in high standing for their religious, social and cultural activities. The number of monasteries involved was relatively small, while the property involved was exceptionally large. But, once they had been agreed, the story of the German suppressions had many features in common with that of other examples.

For the Bavarian state, where the process has been well studied, it meant a huge injection of wealth. As a result of the dissolution of the greater monasteries that had standing in the Estates, it become lord of 28 per cent of all peasant holdings. A further 25 per cent accrued from lesser landowners, nearly all of them ecclesiastical, and some of them monastic. Particularly valuable was the vast area of woodland owned by the Orders. Against this bonanza had to be set the huge debts recently incurred by the state; the debts of the monasteries themselves; the cost of paying pensions to the ejected monks and nuns; and the liabilities incurred by the state to look after 1,330 churches, to ensure that worship was maintained in previously monastic parishes and that education continued in formerly monastic schools. It was often difficult to find uses for the vast and isolated buildings of the abbeys. Quite a number became factories, but the return from the sales did not match expectations. Overall the total net annual income obtained by the Bavarian state seems to have been less than 5,000,000 gulden (Ill. 41).[39]

THE TIME OF REVOLUTION

ILL. 41 Watercolour cartoon satirising secularisation in Bavaria, 1803, showing monks and nuns surrendering their property

An immense quantity of paintings, sculptures, gold and silver church plate and ornaments, fine furniture, music and musical instruments, books and manuscripts also fell to the state. What was not disposed of forms a major part of the holdings of the modern state libraries and museums of Bavaria. On the other hand, the value of much that was found in monasteries was not appreciated and the amount was so great that it could not all be retained.

Not only Bavaria and other south German states like Württemberg benefited greatly from the *Reichsdeputationshauptschluss*. So did northern, Protestant Prussia, which gained large amounts of Catholic territory including over a hundred monastic houses. Hitherto the Prussian government had tolerated some monasteries. Especially after 1810, it set about dissolving both long possessed and newly acquired houses, including large numbers that had previously belonged to Poland. These vast changes obviously had implications far wider even than the effects of a huge transfer of property – implications which will be discussed in the Conclusion.

CONCLUSION

THE MONASTERIES OF THE ANCIEN RÉGIME

I hope I have succeeded in making the case that the neglect of European Catholic monasteries by most historians of the early modern period, even by many church historians, amounts to a serious distortion of history. The number of monastic houses, their vast total wealth, the continuing growth of many Orders into the second half of the eighteenth century, their political, economic, social, charitable, educational and scholarly activities, their architectural, artistic and musical achievements – all these should have rendered them too important to be ignored. This applies whether one is inclined to sympathise with their rationale or is repelled by it. Only with an awareness of the scale and scope of their operations, of their heterogeneity, of their visibility both to friends and enemies, of their integration into the *ancien régime*, and of the admiration, hatred and controversy they aroused, can the significance as well as the ruthlessness of their suppression be understood and appraised.

To summarise some of my earlier discussion, in Catholic Europe in 1750 there were at least 15,000 monasteries for men and 10,000 for women, containing in total roughly 200,000 monks and at least 150,000 nuns, making the regular clergy as a whole more numerous than the secular, and the monks by themselves comparable in number to the seculars. These figures may well have represented the peak of monastic growth since the crisis of the Reformation, because in some, perhaps most, countries and Orders the total of regulars fell in the decades between the mid-century and the revolutionary period, decades which included the complete extinction of the Jesuits in Catholic countries, the reforms instigated by the *commission des réguliers* in France and the partial suppressions carried through by the Venetian Republic and by Joseph II. But some increases also occurred, most spectacularly the growth in the number of French nuns who had taken simple vows and were engaged in teaching and caring for the sick, children, the old and the disabled. Taking these nuns into account, the total of regulars in 1789 can have been scarcely, if at all, lower than that of 1750. The number of *monks*, however, had certainly declined.

Before 1789 the monasteries' landholdings varied greatly from region to region but, since their estimated portion of about 5 per cent of the total land in France is compensated by much higher figures elsewhere, they must on average have owned 10 per cent or more of the total surface area. The houses of the old Orders were great lords, in many areas major feudal lords, who controlled and employed many labourers and servants and ran not only farms and forests, vineyards and breweries but also town estates, spas, mines and factories. Many had built-in political power through representation in the Estates of their province. Indeed they often had more entrenched political power than the bishops, from whose authority they were commonly exempt.

They fulfilled a great variety of social functions. The original purpose of the old Orders, namely prayer, meditation and worship of God, was still central, still commanded widespread support in Catholic countries and was seen by many as 'useful' to society; and monasteries in general attracted a significant proportion of the large sums of money left by the faithful in their wills to be expended on prayer and Masses for their souls – though in many areas they were beginning to lose the patronage of the elite in the later eighteenth century. Monasteries fulfilled their duty of hospitality, some of them at a level grand enough to please sovereigns, others at lower levels. They ran semi-public hospitals and dispensaries. They distributed doles of food and drink to their neighbourhood and to visitors, usually in a manner considered by enlightened statesmen and economists to be random and irresponsible; but this practice was crucial to the well-being of many individuals and communities that lacked other means of support. When in 1829 William Cobbett published his *History of the Protestant Reformation in England and Ireland*, he claimed that it was the dissolution of the monasteries that had made the Poor Law necessary, and backed up his claim by recalling the complaints that he had heard in France in 1792 about the suppression of a Carthusian house.[1] This is a branch of monastic activity which historians have largely neglected. An enormous proportion of education was in the hands of regulars, including almost all the universities in Catholic lands; the best of what we would call secondary education, especially in the Jesuit Colleges; much of what we would call primary education and most of the education available to girls; and much of the training of secular priests as well as of the regulars themselves.

If you wanted to become a scholar, unless you had a substantial private income, by far your best chance lay in entering a monastery. Many houses possessed splendid libraries, commonly much enlarged in the eighteenth century, which rivalled those of universities. The wealthy Orders offered, usually in return for a sizable initial donation, a life such as the ex-Jesuit Feller found in 1788 at Averbode, a Premonstratensian abbey near Liège, 'one of those precious solitudes where religion, study, the arts, agriculture etc. are vigorous in the bosom of peace and contentment'.[2] It was an attraction to some – and a cause of criticism by outsiders – that to become a monk released one from the burden of looking after an indebted estate or a troublesome family, and from taking part in local government or being conscripted for military service. The less wealthy and scholarly Orders would at least give a certain status, a home, some peace and a measure of security, though mendicancy, which some branches of the Franciscans still practised, involved both discomfort and risk. All Orders gave opportunities to develop and use some or all of the following talents: preaching, teaching, learning, writing; ministering to a parish or brotherhood; singing, playing instruments and composing music; acting; designing buildings; painting; craftsmanship and labour of various kinds. The internal hierarchies of monasteries offered the inmates the chance to shoulder administrative, financial, pastoral and political responsibility. For women, such opportunities were especially rare outside nunneries. While many of the grander monasteries catered only for members of the aristocracy, in a good proportion of the greater houses, especially in the German lands, a man of humble origin could rise to become an abbot equal in status to a count or even a prince.

Some of the functions fulfilled by monasteries now seem quite incongruous. They ranked as important sources of loans to governments and others, since the security of their large inalienable estates, so long as they were being well managed, was unrivalled. Some, especially those sited in remote areas, acted as hotels for travellers. They trained a large proportion of musicians, including opera singers, male (including *castrati*) and female.[3] A few boasted picture galleries. Some had observatories, cabinets of curiosities and museums which made it possible for their inmates to carry out important scientific work.

On the negative side, many houses were slack, some downright disgraceful, offending against both their Order's rule and the Church's laws. This is hardly surprising since monks and nuns had often been induced to join communities and take vows by being 'ensnared' too early, by more or less brutal pressure, by brain-washing and by the absence of any alternative hope of security and a degree of comfort. In all regions of Catholic Europe it was an understood strategy of propertied families to put into monasteries their surplus younger sons and the daughters whom they could not afford to supply with dowries. In some areas, especially Italy, this was done on a prodigious scale, though the practice declined somewhat during the eighteenth century.

If the head of a monastic house cared to use his or her almost absolute authority ruthlessly, it was difficult for a monk or nun to do anything about it. Disobedience might incur significant penalties: enforced fasting, public humiliation, corporal punishment and committal to the monastery's prison; and the state upheld monastic vows and pursued monks and nuns who tried to escape. Since, however, very few nuns and only a minority of monks welcomed the suppression of their monasteries in the revolutionary period, it must be presumed that on the whole they were content with the life they had chosen or acquiesced in; and many clearly found it fulfilling.

Certain monastic achievements command our admiration. It may seem to the tourist that almost too many Baroque, Rococo and neo-classical monastic churches and ensembles survive, and some of them, as with the lesser examples of all styles, are certainly uninspired. But few travellers nowadays would accept the view found in such guidebooks as the first Baedeker for Sicily: 'In the seventeenth century numerous edifices in the 'baroque' style were erected on a very extensive scale, but characterised by an only too florid richness of decorative detail'.[4] Melk, Vierzehnheiligen, St Gall, the two great abbeys at Caen, the charterhouse at Granada, the cloister of Santa Chiara in Naples, S. Nicola in Catania, Superga, St Blasien and what is now the Panthéon in Paris are just a few of the buildings that dazzle the observer with their grandeur, their beauty and their audacity. Even people who are allergic to the Baroque and subsequent styles would have to acknowledge that the monasteries of this period preserved for posterity many great Romanesque, Gothic and even earlier edifices, some like Cluny and St-Denis ruined by the Revolution, but others, such as S. Apollinare at Ravenna, Maulbronn, Heiligenkreuz and Assisi, still substantially intact. A few monks were themselves notable architects like Dom Guillaume de la Tremblaye, painters like Fra Angelico or Bernardo Strozzi, or musicians like abbot Gerbert and Padre Martini; and of course the monasteries gave employment and opportunities to almost all the great lay practitioners of these arts as well as to thousands of lesser men: Tintoretto, Rubens and Tiepolo supplied a large number of them with altarpieces; architects such as Hildebrandt, the Asam brothers, Soufflot and Quarenghi built for them; and Michael Haydn devoted his life to providing music for St Peter's in Salzburg.[5]

For a historian one of the greatest claims to fame of the monks of this period rests on the work of the Maurists who, led by Mabillon, developed many of the techniques of the modern scholar, laying down strict criteria for the use of evidence, establishing the texts of many of the essential sources of medieval history and denouncing the credulity of their pious predecessors and rivals who had cheerfully accepted the authenticity of every anecdote, relic or miracle that might enhance the appeal of their institution. This was a major monkish contribution to Enlightenment. If it was not *because* or even while Prévost was a monk that he wrote a classic novel, and not *because* Baudeau was a monk that he became known as a physiocratic writer, both owed many of their opportunities to their Orders. And the Jesuits included among their number the scientist Boskovic, the architectural theorist Laugier and the teachers at Louis-le-Grand whom their pupil Voltaire praised to the skies.

Within the Church as well as outside, the role of the regulars has been consistently underestimated. McManners described the wealthy monasteries of the old Orders as 'a great hulk, laden with treasures, which the receding tide of the Middle Ages had left stranded on the shores of the modern world'.[6] But this vivid image takes no account of the post-Reformation development of the old Orders. It is true that the thrust of the Counter-Reformation, of the Council of Trent and of most religious reformers, lay or clerical, was in favour of increasing the number of secular clergy, especially secular parish priests, and reducing the number of monks. The Orders, both the old and the new, by maintaining their independence from the bishops, in some cases by tempting worshippers away from their parish churches, and by making it more pleasant and fulfilling for young men to enter a community than to become secular priests, were frustrating these aims. If the manpower and resources of the Church were considered globally and on first principles, it was difficult in the climate of Counter-Reformation Catholic Europe to deny that too much of them was devoted to supporting monks and nuns in lives of contemplation and worship, to encouraging lavish expenditure by monasteries on churches and buildings many of which were open only to a few, and to sustaining the political and social position of abbots, abbesses and their communities. But monasteries were for most people in Catholic Europe part of the social milieu which it was impossible to think away. For Catholic rulers they had proved very useful as a counterpoise to the nobility, in offering opportunities for royal patronage, as a source of loans and revenue, and in providing education, pastoral care and other social services. Further, to augment the number of parishes raised serious legal and financial problems, and many bishops had still found it impossible to establish worthwhile seminaries to train their clergy. To found a new Order, on the other hand, was not too difficult, to found a new monastery of an established Order relatively easy and to reform an existing house perhaps easier still. The 'shock-troops of the Counter-Reformation' – monks who could be sent anywhere to bring the faith to heathen or Protestants – were not just the Jesuits, but also the Capuchins and other new Orders; and in the seventeenth and eighteenth centuries the old Orders too became associated with many aspects of church reform, building great hall-churches, supplying preachers, confessors and parish priests, running missions, promoting pilgrimages, founding or assisting brotherhoods, and educating students at all levels. In a sense they became victims of their success in this regard. It is accepted that the secular clergy of France had by the mid-eighteenth century become a well-trained and dedicated body. This was largely the work of the monks who ran the new seminaries, but the achievement had the effect of making regulars more dispensable than hitherto.

In the eighteenth century almost all Orders had members who attempted to reconcile the monasteries with social changes and with the rise of Enlightenment, at least in its Catholic variety. Some came to doubt the merit of celibacy and to question the value of the traditional monastic timetable. Some even became publicists, either arguing for change like the Benedictine Werkmeister or defending the *status quo* like the Jesuit Feller. But, as is shown by the cases of Werkmeister's Neresheim and of some French monasteries, if monks went beyond a certain point in proposing reforms they found it difficult to remain monks.[7]

If a country was Catholic before 1790 and therefore contained many monasteries, it was inevitably different in many important ways from Protestant countries, and the fact needs to be recognised more often than it is when the history of Europe is being written. The total numbers of clergy in Protestant countries were inevitably lower than in Catholic lands. In England, for example, there were far fewer opportunities than in Catholic countries for a man to make a career in the Church, and of course none at all for a woman. Education, except in Oxford and Cambridge, was not in the hands of persons bound to celibacy, though for boys it remained largely the affair of clergy. Charity was not dispensed, randomly or otherwise, at abbey gates – except in the extraordinary case of St Cross at Winchester. There were no abbots now to outrank bishops, as once they had, in the House of Lords. There was no network of institutions providing sanctuary for unmarried women. It would be highly desirable to have more comparative studies of the social structure of Protestant and Catholic communities, taking account of monasteries, especially in relation to Germany and Switzerland where Protestant and Catholic villages and towns were often contiguous.

In this book, however, I have confined myself to a comparative study of Catholic countries – a sufficiently rash undertaking – from which it has emerged that the place of monasteries in society varied substantially within Catholic Europe from region to region, and especially from state to state. The monastic population was far denser in Italy than anywhere else, denser in Spain than in France or Portugal, and denser in France than in Germany or the Austrian Monarchy. The ratio of regulars to population ranged from more than 1 to 100 in favoured areas like Rome and Cologne – in Naples it reached 1 in 36 – to less than 1 to 1,000 in parts of Hungary and Poland. No area was without houses of the old Orders and of the numerous branches and offshoots of the Franciscan Order. But the former were relatively weak in Italy and the latter strong there, while the Dominicans and military Orders were especially powerful in Spain, the Piarists particularly important in Italy, the Austrian Monarchy and Poland, and the mendicants less numerous in the central lands of the Monarchy than in most other countries. In small regions particular Orders might seem dominant, like the Recollects, as Joseph II noticed, in Slavonia.[8] Nunneries were relatively few in the central lands of the Austrian Monarchy but very numerous in Spain and still more in Italy; and the burgeoning new female Orders of eighteenth-century France had no real parallel elsewhere. The true monastery-state was to be found only in Germany; the abbot as a virtual government minister only in Austria; the monastery as a provider of parish clergy more generally in the German lands than elsewhere; abbots as leaders of a national uprising only in Belgium and, to a lesser extent, in Spain; and the use of nunneries in family strategies most conspicuously in Italy and Spain, and much less commonly in the German lands. These variations between Catholic countries and regions in the number, density, mix, independence and social involvement of houses of monks and nuns were sufficiently wide to give a distinctive character to their societies.

Before the revolutionary period, old-style monasteries were at their most powerful politically in the German Catholic lands, because of the presence in the Empire of independent monastery-states and because their dominance of intellectual life was exceptionally complete. Among the major countries, such monasteries were probably least powerful in France, despite their wealth, even before the reforms of the *commission des réguliers* made them less rather than better able to justify themselves in the climate of the Enlightenment; and their lack of representation in the General Assembly of the Clergy and the Estates-General helped to account for their rapid suppression in the early days of the French Revolution.

CONCLUSION

THE SUPPRESSIONS

Special power of another kind was exercised by the Jesuits, whose organisation was centralised, and who at the height of their influence controlled most university and secondary education and provided confessors for the majority of Catholic rulers. It was partly for these reasons that the campaign against them, beginning in Portugal in the mid-1750s and leading to the papal suppression of the Society in 1773, had such huge significance and impact. Although it owed something to the widespread criticism of their theology and of their persecution of Jansenist sympathisers, its essential motive was the determination of secular rulers to put an end to the Order's defiance of their power, as blatantly shown in Latin America, and to destroy a body whose members obeyed a general based in Rome and took an oath of obedience to a foreign ruler, the pope. It was seen by some as the first step towards the destruction of all monasteries, and it was certainly later treated as a precedent. But other Orders had gleefully joined in discomfiting their proud rivals; and Portuguese and Spanish governments that had been so determined to crush the Jesuits seemingly did not wish, or did not dare, to move against other Orders. Moreover, neither Maria Theresa nor Joseph, though both were anxious to reduce the number of regulars, wished to see the Jesuits dissolved, since they were an elite corps who appeared indispensable to the educational system. The point was nicely made by Maria Theresa when refusing to establish an Academy in Vienna after their suppression, in 1775: 'I could not possibly decide to start an academy with three ex-Jesuits and a worthy professor of chemistry. We would be the laughing-stock of the world.'[9] In every Catholic country their fall led to a crisis in education, which it took many years and the assistance of other monastic Orders to overcome. Although Clement XIV himself decreed the suppression, he did so only under the strongest pressure from the Catholic Powers, and Rome recognised the outcome as a crushing defeat. As a result, the papacy became very reluctant to condemn formally the church reforms proposed by secular rulers such as Andrea Tron in Venice and Joseph II in the Austrian Monarchy, leading the French revolutionaries to assume that the Civil Constitution of the Clergy would be accepted in Rome.

Why did rulers and other Catholics come to favour suppressing other Orders? It had long been very generally agreed by the governments of Catholic Europe that monasteries, however admirable in principle, were far too numerous; that many of them were useless or of little use to society, pernicious in their outlook and perhaps in their educational activities; that their international networks made them fundamentally disloyal to the states in which they operated; that they possessed far too much land, which, since it was protected against the forces of the market by the laws of mortmain, could only increase further; and that they were in general sustainers of an economic system that discouraged population growth and free economic development. Most rulers cared that the Church in their dominions should be an effective proponent of morality and patriotism. In this light the monasteries were seen to remove from society men who might have become good and useful secular clergy; and the exemption of most houses from the control of bishops was held to diminish respect for pastoral work. The success of Protestant countries in eighteenth-century wars and in economic development had a profound effect: the victories of Prussia galvanised the rulers and ministers of the Austrian Monarchy, the triumphs of Britain led to demands for reform in France.

In the background lurked a fundamental change of attitudes, away from the belief that men ought to give pre-eminence in their lives to preparation for death and the afterlife to the conviction that they ought first and foremost to try to improve their and others' lot on earth. The apostles of individual liberty and the rights of Man mostly considered these principles incompatible with the taking of lifelong vows of poverty, chastity and obedience. Further, in the seventeenth and early eighteenth centuries most Catholic rulers had believed that their authority, and even their salvation, depended on all their subjects being Catholic. In this context monks and nuns were seen as an essential part of the missionary force not only of the Counter-Reformation but also of Catholic princely absolutism. By the late eighteenth century most rulers had ceased to think in these terms, had come to believe that they could maintain their government without imposing uniformity of faith among their subjects, and were no longer horrified by proposals for religious toleration. Some were now ready to treat a subject's religion as of no consequence if he gave the state good service. This change of course owed much to the Enlightenment, but most Catholics and rulers of Catholic countries accepted only certain aspects of the teachings associated with that movement, aspects which they regarded as compatible with being faithful members of the Church.[10] Once these shifts had occurred and monasteries came to seem expendable, their property stood out as an obvious resource which could be exploited to render the work of the secular clergy more effective. Hence it could be asserted that 'Every Catholic who wished to follow the developed principles of his religion has for a long time wanted the suppression of the monasteries . . . [and] their revenues, in accordance with the needs of the time, applied in a beneficent fashion.'[11] But in fact this was a minority view among Catholics, the great majority of whom supported only partial suppressions.

It is important to distinguish between the various policies adopted by governments towards the monasteries in the eighteenth century. Some states, at least until the Revolution, confined themselves to assailing the Jesuits and to enacting such measures as putting restrictions on the extension of mortmain, raising the age of profession and limiting the number of novices. The *commission des réguliers* in France followed a long tradition in suppressing houses with very small membership but placed unusual emphasis on regenerating the contemplative Orders. Joseph II, by contrast, abolished the contemplative Orders in his dominions and devoted the proceeds from these and other piecemeal suppressions chiefly to the creation of new parishes. None of these reforming initiatives involved removing property from the Church and putting it to wholly secular uses. The French Revolution, in abolishing vows, suppressing all monasteries and justifying the seizure of all their lands to bail out a bankrupt government, was in all three respects going far beyond anything hitherto enacted by the government of a Catholic country since the Reformation.

Why, when it came to it, was it physically so easy to suppress the monasteries? In general, monks and nuns obeyed the precepts of their calling and did not resist their suppression by force, encouraged in most cases by the promise of a pension or other employment if they left the cloister and, if they declined to leave, of an opportunity to live out their lives in houses set aside for the purpose. For most of them, hardship came only later, as pensions lost their value or were withdrawn, as the rump of houses was suppressed and as revolutionary regimes branded all ex-regulars as incorrigible traitors. The Jesuits, however, had been exiled from several countries and did not in all cases receive pensions. The militant abbeys of Belgium constitute a striking exception to the docility of most monks: they and their supporters saw off both Joseph II and the early efforts of the French Revolution's armies. In Spain, too, the monasteries mustered enough defenders to resist two French invasions with considerable success. But otherwise it was only in some parts of Switzerland and Italy that popular sympathy encouraged monks to resist suppressions. The monasteries of Germany, whose lands and status had been preserved in aspic for a century and a half by the settlement of Westphalia, found themselves in 1803 at the mercy of the transformation in power-politics brought about by the French Revolution. To resist not only the armies of France, but those of all German rulers including Prussia and Austria, united in their desire to seize monastic lands, was out of the question.

Over most of Catholic Europe popular sympathy for the regulars' cause was muted, largely due to the very general feeling, found at all levels of society, that it was no longer appropriate for monks and nuns to play the parts of sovereigns and feudal lords and that the ostentation, ease, gluttony, wealth, political power and taxation privileges of the greater houses were irreconcilable with the vow of poverty. The Orders had not helped themselves, either with the people or with governments, by their public rivalries and squabbles. Popular opposition to monastic suppressions was less conspicuous than hostility to other Enlightened reforms such as legislation against religious holidays, processions, the veneration of relics and so forth. However, there was little demand, even in France, for total suppression.

It is tempting to suggest that the numerical or the political strength of monasticism – or the extent to which it had already been reformed – explains why it survived the revolutionary period in some areas and not in others. But this cannot be true. It is just possible to imagine that, if the regulars had been fairly represented in the French assemblies, the First Estate would not have joined the Third in forming a National Assembly and that then the course of the Revolution might have been utterly different and some French monasteries might have survived. But, once the actual National Assembly had been created, the Paris mob had been aroused and the true state of the finances had been revealed, the monasteries of France were doomed, whatever anyone could say on their behalf. Soon other Catholic countries fell under French control and were forced to take the same road. It was the *élan* and ruthlessness which the Revolution generated in the French army and administration that explains the almost total suppressions that occurred in Belgium, mainland Italy, Germany, Switzerland and parts of Spain. Belgium's monasteries were pitilessly cut down by the French despite their wealth, power and discipline, despite Joseph II's reforms, and in the face of popular opposition. Mainland Italy's monasteries were suppressed during periods of French occupation. The fact that Venice and Tuscany had carried through a reform of monasteries did not save them from Napoleonic suppression. Germany's houses succumbed to the combination of French power and the greed of German princes. In the central and eastern lands of the Austrian Monarchy Joseph II's reforms had made them more 'useful' and acceptable to the elite, but their survival in these lands was ultimately due to the fact that Austria was not annexed or restructured by Napoleon. Nor was Poland, but there the monasteries found themselves instead at the mercy of the three partitioning Powers, which meant that a good proportion survived into the nineteenth century under Austrian and Russian rule; but after 1810 those under Prussian rule were soon suppressed, and from 1820 onwards Russia too reverted to a policy of suppression.[12]

CONCLUSION

THE EFFECTS OF THE SUPPRESSIONS

How much did it matter that all these monasteries were suppressed? The most conspicuous losses were, in the broad sense, artistic: of buildings, statues, stained glass, manuscripts and books. Henry James wrote in his diary of a visit to France, having just seen the abbey of Montmajour: 'Everywhere one goes, one meets, looking backward a little, the spectre of the great Revolution and one meets it always in the shape of the destruction of something beautiful and precious. To make us forgive it at all, how much it must also have destroyed that was more hateful than itself!'[13] Although the depredations were at their worst in France, examples ranging from neglect through tasteless adaptation to wanton vandalism were to be found everywhere in Catholic Europe. Of course, even if all the monasteries had survived as communities, their buildings and treasures would not all have remained intact; and the monasteries themselves had destroyed much of value in their building campaigns during the seventeenth and eighteenth centuries. Some French historians palliate the excesses of the revolutionaries, for example Christian Péligry, writing about Toulouse:

We must consider acts of spoliation and vandalism as a constant phenomenon which alas! appears throughout the length of human history. The balance sheet of the Revolution, tarnished by excesses committed under the influence of anger or folly, seems to us, despite everything, positive if one acknowledges that it gave libraries an institutional framework which enabled them to survive through all the troubles of the nineteenth and most of the twentieth century.[14]

But the extent of the damage to France's heritage inflicted by Frenchmen themselves during the revolutionary years was surely unparalleled for such a short period.

It is far from easy to appraise the more general effects of the secularisation of the monasteries. In the first place, there is no pure example. Except in the central and eastern provinces of the Austrian Monarchy, other church lands were confiscated at the same time as monastic property; and there only a third of monasteries were suppressed, while the contemporaneous abolition of brotherhoods complicated the issue, as is graphically brought out by the engraving reproduced on p. 198. Whereas in France and in some of its satellite states much aristocratic property was confiscated as well as the Church's, and the surviving relics of feudalism were also abolished, in Germany and the Austrian Monarchy the aristocracy lost little and serfdom persisted until at least 1848. In France, uniquely, the Church suffered a schism between those who would accept the Civil Constitution and those who would not, and Christianity itself was for a short time proscribed. In many areas, perhaps especially in western and southern Germany, the effects of the secularization are difficult to disentangle from the damage inflicted by the armies and battles of the Napoleonic Wars. All these factors make it very difficult to isolate the suppression of the monasteries for examination.

With a view to evaluating the social and economic changes caused by the secularisations, scholars have devoted much labour to working out what sort of people bought monastic lands. The result for south Germany is that 'through the purchase of monastic lands the social structure was only altered to a quite unimportant extent'.

Where, as in Bavaria, in the context of monastic landowning, independent working peasants resided on their holdings, they were still there after the suppression of the monasteries. The property managed by the monasteries themselves was usually bought by wealthy citizens, nobles or peasants. In the Rhineland...the prosperous bourgeois and peasants were the real gainers.[15]

One of the most thorough of such enquiries concerned Piedmont, where again no revolutionary change can be identified. Only 2.7 per cent of the entire land surface was actually sold off, three-quarters of which came from the property of 411 monasteries. The total number of purchasers was small, 3,555, constituting 0.2 per cent of the population. The already rich were naturally in a position to buy the most land, the poor could buy none. However, nobles bought 16.6 per cent, a fairly low proportion, and other 'proprietors' and 'merchants' bought 15.2 per cent each. Churchmen themselves managed to buy 4.2 per cent.[16]

Such calculations, though the research and effort involved in them arouse admiration, seem less worthwhile now than they did in the decades after the Second World War when, in the West as well as the East, class relationships were thought to be the key to explaining historical change. In the first place, the conclusions are invariably less than dramatic, while always seeming to show a modest improvement in the position of people who can reasonably be called *bourgeois* or middle class as against the aristocracy, and very limited gains for the poorer classes. But, secondly, classes are very hard to define even in more modern societies. Rather than talking of classes, it is far more instructive to see the process as a crucial stage in the supersession of a 'society of orders', i.e. legally privileged estates, by a society in which individuals are legally equal. No one would call the clergy a class but, if they owned, as in the extreme case of Bavaria, over half of all the land, they had an economic and social significance as great as any class could have, and much more precisely definable. On the other hand, they were certainly an order. It can hardly be doubted that clergy have a certain *esprit de corps* and that they differ in outlook and behaviour from the laity; and this is particularly true of monks and nuns. As contemporaries thought, the main point at issue was whether to remove from the clergy their status as a privileged order, or from the regulars their part in this status, or at least some of their land and their political and social power. The dissolutions represented a vast transfer of land from the clergy to various types of laymen. These elaborate statistical enquiries tend to miss the point that, even if the monastic and other church lands were redistributed in such a way as to leave the relative positions of aristocracy, bourgeois and peasants little altered, all three had gained in absolute terms – in a state like Bavaria, hugely – by purchasing the land that had previously belonged to the Church.

The state, too, benefited substantially, though more in some countries than others. Of course the results of confiscation and sales disappointed initially inflated hopes. In Bavaria, for example, it is doubtful whether the revenue accruing from the vast accession of land to the state actually outweighed the costs of paying pensions and maintaining parishes and schools. Many of the remote and rambling monastic complexes could not be let or sold, or only for tiny returns. Five million florins was all that the state obtained in income annually from the properties it had seized.[17]

It is the case of France that matters most, because the suppressions there were part of the Revolution, because they helped to make possible the victories of her armies and because their example was exported to more than half of Catholic Europe. Here the story is immensely complicated by the issue of paper money, *assignats*, with which it was possible to buy church land. This is Florin Aftalion's summary:

Whatever the cause may have been, whether it was the depreciation of paper money or fraudulent bidding, the revolutionary governments squandered the immense wealth which they had confiscated. A necessarily crude estimate suggests that the greater part of the *biens nationaux*, worth around four billion *livres* in 1790 (two billions in church property, to which were added two further billions' worth of properties belonging to suspects, émigrés and those condemned to death), had been surrendered before 1797, whereas the sum total of payments received by the Treasury by this date amounted to no more than one billion... In a relatively short period of seven years the state carried out, involuntarily and on an arbitrary basis, an extraordinary redistribution of wealth involving three billion *livres*, which comes to around double the national product of the pre-revolutionary period. Contrary to the purposes of Jacobin ideology, the beneficiaries of this massive wealth were not the poor, but rather, in varying proportions depending upon the region, well-to-do peasants, bourgeois and even, through their use of catspaws, nobles and émigrés.

But the greatest beneficiary, of course, was the state itself, though it is impossible to calculate how much it retained of the forty-five billions it originally made by the issue of *assignats*.[18] As everywhere, the sale of the lands bound the purchasers to the support of the anticlerical regime.

What difference the secularisations made to general economic development is a question no less difficult to answer. In the twenty-first century it seems self-evident to almost everyone that the dedication of so many people and so much property to monasteries must have stood in the way of economic and social progress. But historically the case is not straightforward. At the time of the French Revolution the economic advance of Protestant Britain already stood out and was ascribed by many commentators partly to the expropriation of the monasteries under Henry VIII. But one of the most industrialised areas in Europe lay on the borders of Belgium and France, located in a strongly Catholic region dominated by monasteries.[19] Having carried through the most drastic of all the secularisations, France suffered economically during the revolutionary and Napoleonic Wars, fell further behind Britain and proved notoriously slow to develop industrially in the nineteenth century.[20]

Education ranks as the most important social activity of monks and nuns. It was and is often suggested that, if a society is to 'modernise', it must prevent the clergy from purveying their pernicious or at least obscurantist notions to generations of school-children. The suppressions carried out under the aegis of revolutionary governments involved the deliberate removal of secondary and higher education from the monks and nuns and from the clergy generally. But in this field too the story is paradoxical. As with the suppression of the Jesuits, the revolutionary suppressions initially reduced the sheer amount of education available. The rich university provision in south Germany all but disappeared with the monks. In monk- and nun-ridden Paris in 1789 66 per cent of widowers and 62 per cent of widows had signed the inventory of their inheritance, and in northern France generally the literacy rate, so far as it can be calculated, exceeded 50 per cent.[21] It can hardly be coincidental that French literacy rates diminished during the revolutionary period.[22] All three of the great enlightened despots, Frederick, Catherine and Joseph, had employed abbot Felbiger as their education czar to improve primary education in their dominions, with some success; and the percentages of literates in the three Catholic electorates on the Rhine were among the highest in Europe. On the other hand Italy, with by far the highest density of monks and nuns, had shockingly low literacy rates even by eighteenth-century standards; and it would seem that, the more monks an Italian province had, the worse its rate was likely to be: in Naples and Sicily it fell well below 20 per cent.[23] But at least the better teachers among the monks and nuns must have opened up intellectual possibilities to their students that went beyond the catechism and represented a significant improvement on no education at all.

Musical education was naturally much affected. In the special case of France the admittedly limited and biased musical education that had previously been available in numerous monasteries and churches up and down the country was replaced by a more professional course confined to one state-run conservatoire in Paris.

The Austrian Monarchy, Portugal, Poland, Sicily and parts of Spain escaped direct rule by France. Of these areas, only the Austrian Monarchy had carried out serious monastic reform, suppressing a third or more of all monasteries and reducing rather more drastically the number of monks and nuns. The process can be said to have caused some damage. Some of the suppressed monasteries' buildings were destroyed or spoiled, their libraries and treasures were dispersed and some losses were incurred. As in every country, some villages had depended economically on monasteries and had reason to regret their demise. Research has been published on the effect of Joseph II's global policies on the scale of the musical establishments of Vienna's churches. The total number of musicians employed in them before the reforms had been over 300, and those who sang or played in the more than fifty old parish churches had been paid altogether 28,000 florins per annum. With the suppression of the brotherhoods and of some old churches, and the simplification of the liturgy, the cost was halved. A further fifty-five churches, many of them monastic, employed relatively few musicians since the monks or nuns themselves performed much of the music, but the overall expenditure on music was further reduced by the suppression of a few of these institutions and the conversion of many others to parish churches. The affected musicians naturally felt aggrieved, and presumably Vienna's musical life was somewhat impoverished.[24] Similar changes must have occurred throughout the Monarchy.

However, what is most striking about the Monarchy for us is that so many of the monasteries, including nearly all the greatest, survived Joseph II's reign and returned to operating much as they had before the 1780s, though with more of their monks working as parish priests. After his death they recovered their role in the Estates and much of their previous independence. Some of them were designated

CONCLUSION

by the government to contribute to higher education, for example St Florian in historical studies. In the Revolution of 1848 they lost their feudal rights, but the Estates' committee that worked out the details of this change in Lower Austria was still presided over by the abbot of Melk.[25] Even after this they still retained much of their income from land, and in the second half of the nineteenth century they can be seen playing roles as varied as ever. The abbot of an Augustinian monastery in Brno, Gregor Mendel (1822–84), seized the opportunities offered him to experiment on plants in the monastic garden to such good effect that he is revered as one of the founders of modern biology.[26] It was at St Florian that Anton Bruckner (1824–96) was choirboy and later organist, and received much of the encouragement and support he needed in his career as a composer.[27] In the last decade of the nineteenth century and the first of the twentieth, the Premonstratensian house at Tepla in Bohemia, rich by virtue of its development of the spa at Marienbad, behaved in a manner more characteristic of the eighteenth. When the future Edward VII visited the spa as prince of Wales, he got to know the abbot. On 7 September 1905, now king, he wrote to the future George V:

the Abbot & Monks of Tepl entertained me at luncheon last Monday at the Monastery & afterwards gave me a day's partridge driving! There were more beaters than birds as there were quite 200 of the former & we killed between 20 and 30 of the latter & a few hares... as the day was lovely it was very enjoyable.

The next day the abbot was made an honorary CVO, and in the following year he was shown round Buckingham Palace by the king.[28] When monasteries have such importance in society, they inevitably have dealings with some black sheep. Just as the abbot of St-Vaast had awarded a scholarship to Robespierre, so the Upper Austrian abbey of Lambach provided singing lessons for the future Adolf Hilter.[29] They turned into two of the most dangerous enemies that the Church and the monasteries have ever known.

In common with other landlords the monasteries suffered a huge loss in income during the hyperinflation of the 1920s,[30] but few of them actually went under, and they continued to function not only in the Republic of Austria, but also in Czechoslovakia and in Hungary. It was only during the Nazi period that they were all closed. One of the most notable of twentieth-century Austrian historians, Hugo Hantsch, a Benedictine of Melk, was one of those who suffered a spell, fortunately brief, in a concentration camp.[31] In the areas included in the eastern bloc the lands of the monasteries were confiscated by communist governments after 1945, but in Austria the main houses were restored and still flourish. To outsiders their place in modern Austrian society is astonishing. It was the abbey of Stams that trained the triumphant Austrian skiing teams of recent years; Melk, among other educational activities, teaches cookery. I mention all this to make the point that these monasteries, at least after having been reformed and made more 'useful' by Joseph II, have found no great difficulty in fitting into, and contributing to, a modern society. While it was clearly not Joseph II's monastic reforms – though it may have been his army reforms – that saved Austrian monasteries from the direct impact of the French Revolution, it seems highly likely that his work rendered the surviving houses so acceptable and useful that there was little danger of their undergoing the periodic persecution that afflicted the monasteries of France, Spain and Portugal during the nineteenth century.

No part of Catholic Europe can be said to have had a typical experience of monastic secularisation, since both the previous situation and the process of suppression varied so much from region to region. But the case of Bavaria was at least more or less typical of Germany and, since it happens to have been particularly well studied, I shall use the views of five commentators on the effects of the suppressions there to illustrate how fundamental the issue could seem at the time and can still seem today, and how differently it could and can be regarded.

First, here are the views of an intelligent young noble, Freiherr J.C. von Aretin, who, at the time of the suppressions, was given the task of combing the libraries of the dissolved monasteries for books and manuscripts worthy to be taken into the Royal Library at Munich. He wrote, in 1803:

Between yesterday and today lay a gulf of a thousand years. Today we have dared to take the giant stride across this immeasurable gulf. From today is to be dated an epoch in Bavarian history as important as any there has ever been. From today the moral, spiritual and physical culture of the country will take on a totally changed aspect. In a thousand years' time people will still feel the effects of this step. Philosophical historians will date a new era from the suppression of the monasteries, just as they did from the abolition of private warfare (*Faustrecht*), and people will approach the ruins of the abbeys with the same mixed feelings with which they now regard the crumbling old castles of the robber barons. Don't suppose, dear friend, that I am being carried away by enthusiasm. If you find out more about the influence hitherto exerted by our monasteries, which owned a third of the country, I am convinced that you will grasp the importance of the change that contemporaries can never or seldom see in its true light.[32]

By contrast a Catholic historian, A.M. Scheglmann, writing in the 1900s, considered that all the monasteries of Bavaria had passed the one test that mattered, that they followed their rule; and he therefore maintained that all should have been allowed to survive. The *Reichsdeputationshauptschluss* had to be regarded as 'morally, theft from God; juridically, an illegitimate usurpation; politically, high treason; and, at the bar of reason, folly and madness'.³³

Eberhard Weis, who has made a profound study of the Bavarian secularisation, concluded that, while it had led to terrible losses of priceless buildings, artefacts and manuscripts, if it had not happened in 1803, the monasteries would have slowly decayed anyway and would have lost their rights of lordship over land, at latest in 1848–9.

Dietmar Stutzer has written the most accessible general account of the Bavarian suppressions, emphasising the huge range of their impact. Symbolically, the monastery bells, hitherto audible over much of the countryside many times a day, were silenced and melted down. The elaborate infrastructure of the great houses had to be taken over or replaced: the mills, the bakeries, the breweries, the infirmaries, the dispensaries, the schools. The monks and nuns and the few remaining lay brothers and sisters had to be shepherded out of their monasteries, some to go to certain specially preserved houses, many to go into the world. The library's books, the gold and silver, the pictures and other artefacts had to be processed, either sold or taken into the state libraries, museums and galleries. The state cavalierly undertook not only to pay pensions to the monks and nuns but also to look after those lay people whose livelihood had absolutely depended on the monasteries, a commitment that has been seen as anticipating later systems of social security. It was reckoned that over 4,000 full-time workers had been employed to work solely for the sixty-five monasteries, together with more than twice as many part-time employees, directly affecting a total of more than 30,000 people altogether, including family members. The management of the very considerable lands and revenues of the major houses proved to have been conducted not with the aim of obtaining maximum profit but to promote the mutual interests of the entire community of the monastery. After the suppressions, alternative sources of credit had to be found, since the monasteries had been largely responsible for necessary agricultural loans. The whole enterprise of secularisation amounted to a revolution from above, which could only have been accomplished in a state where public opinion was of no consequence and vested interests could be ignored.³⁴

Most striking of all are the opinions of a descendant of the optimistic nobleman of 1803, the noted historian of the *Reich*, Karl Otmar Freiherr von Aretin. He wrote in 1990 that, while the secularisation was a necessary prelude to modernisation, in the way it was carried out it had had effects 'from which Catholic Germany did not recover until the twentieth century'. It had not been necessary to take all church land or to destroy eighteen south German universities. The provision made by the Bavarian state for those economically disadvantaged by the process had been quite inadequate. It was unfortunate enough that armies fought over the region during the revolutionary and Napoleonic Wars and that the remodelling of the political map of Germany in 1803 replaced a Catholic political predominance in the *Reich* by a Protestant majority in the German Confederation. But 'in areas where the monasteries were suppressed, south Germany suffered a further wave of poverty and cultural retardation'.[35]

The French revolutionaries had not dreamed that monasteries would ever be revived; and Aretin senior clearly thought in 1803 that in Bavaria they had been eradicated for ever. But the pope re-established the Jesuits on a general basis in 1814 and they were soon permitted back into one country after another, though always controversially and often only temporarily. After the Restoration some Catholic regimes, as in Bavaria and most of the Italian states, gave back or succeeded in recovering parts of the old monastic lands for the Church, and everywhere in Catholic Europe the foundation or refoundation of some monasteries was permitted. It made a considerable difference how long the blanket suppressions had lasted. In France the drastic church reforms of 1789–92 remained in place until at least 1801, and until after the Restoration male monasticism was greatly restricted and female Orders were strictly controlled. The new owners of church lands therefore had possession of them for a generation before there was any question of re-establishing monasteries of the traditional type. Most of the old monastic buildings of France had been destroyed, were in ruins or had been seized for other purposes. In Belgium the new order lasted almost twenty years, in Germany a dozen years or less, but in mainland Italy the French ruled only for two comparatively short spells, especially short in the cases of the papal state and Naples. The parts of Spain controlled by the French experienced an even shorter period of partial suppression. So, whereas at one extreme there were hardly any French Benedictines still alive when it came to restoring their Order in France in the 1830s and all their old lands and buildings had been sold off long ago, in parts of Spain and Italy the buildings of many houses had been vacated for only short spells by the time the Restoration permitted the return of monastic communities, and some of the lands had yet to find a buyer.

As might have been expected, the clearest effects of the suppressions were felt by the Church itself. They overturned, as of course was intended, the previously normal superiority in numbers of the regular over the secular clergy, at least so far as monks were concerned. But the intention of nearly all the reformers to improve the number and lot of secular, especially parish, clergy through the dissolution of monasteries was not generally realised. In many cases the effect of the whole process was to reduce the total number of clergy serving parishes, partly because regulars had contributed notably to that task, but more because of the damaging effect of the legislation and the events of the reforming and revolutionary years on the recruitment and morale of both regular and secular clergy. Even in the Austrian Monarchy, despite all Joseph II's efforts, a shortage of parish clergy was causing alarm by the end of his reign. Napoleon enabled the Catholic Church to re-emerge, through the Concordat, as the Church of the majority of the French nation. But in 1815 the number of parish clergy in France was little more than half what it had been in 1789, and there were as yet virtually no monks to assist them. There were parts of France where parish priests were scarcely to be found.[36]

So great was the change in attitudes in Napoleon's later years and after 1815 that Stendhal could depict in *Le rouge et le noir*, published in 1830, a young man who saw joining the Jesuits as the career to take up if one wanted to emulate in the post-Restoration era the meteoric rise achieved by Napoleon as a soldier in the previous generation. It turns out that 1830 was the peak year of the nineteenth century for ordinations to the priesthood.[37] The hero listens to some clergy discussing with a minister whether the state will return to the Church its woodlands, said to have constituted the bulk of its wealth.[38] Male monastic Orders had resumed their role in education, though now in competition with lay teachers; and in the hospitals, and particularly those that served the mentally and physically incurable, and in the lower schools, particularly girls' schools, the nuns found roles which no one else was ready to fulfil. Although in fact no property was returned to the Church by the French state, by 1880 there were almost twice as many French regulars in total as there had been before the Revolution, though a much higher proportion of them were now nuns.[39] The experience of the Revolution made sure that the revival of monasteries would always be controversial in France, with the result that monks and nuns endured two periods of exile under the Third Republic.

Of course the revived communities, especially those of Orders that had previously been propertied, were unlike their predecessors in important ways. If some of them managed by benefaction and sacrifice to acquire or build substantial edifices, they remained genuinely poor, without political influence, and subordinate to their congregations, the bishops and the pope. Most of the new monasteries and Orders that were founded did not even aspire to grand buildings or to emulate monks or nuns of the old regime. They were all part of a newly fashioned Church, still staffed by celibates but no longer integrated into the state and the nobility, no longer existing on ancient endowments, concentrating on its basic purposes rather than active, as it had been, across almost the whole range of secular affairs. After 1830 the great majority of recruits to the clergy in France were from poor rural families, and this was the tendency everywhere. The line between lay and clerical had been accentuated, and had shifted an immense distance. The clergy were no longer an order, but a profession. There would be no more bishops who were also government ministers. The Catholic Church, even in a country where it had the majority on its side, would in principle be only the major sect in a secular society where many sects were tolerated. Paradoxically, as a result of the changes brought by the Revolution, the authority of the papacy over the Church was greatly enhanced, as the new profession closed ranks against unsympathetic governments.

A perhaps surprising corollary of these developments was the extension of monasticism to countries where it had previously been banned. Protestant as well as Catholic states ceased to identify themselves with a particular brand of Christianity. In the wave of sympathy for the victims of the French Revolution, exiled monks and nuns received a remarkably warm welcome in Britain, and a few monasteries established themselves in England, including the community that later moved to Downside. By the second half of the nineteenth century Catholic Ireland, where monasticism had earlier been outlawed, pullulated with monasteries; and Anglican England, Presbyterian Scotland and Lutheran Prussia had become places where Catholic monasteries could flourish and to which monks and nuns persecuted in Catholic countries could flee. It was not long before the Church of England, to the horror of its Protestant wing, had monasteries of its own.

Almost no one in a modernised, westernised society can feel that it would be sensible or desirable to return to a society in which monasteries had the place that they occupied in Catholic countries of the *ancien régime*. The pundits of the age were surely right to believe that there were too many monasteries, especially in a country so full of them as Italy was. They engaged in unseemly competition, and their original purposes had become overlaid by other, in some cases barely compatible, aims, like locking away surplus sons and daughters of the upper classes. Since monks and nuns were so numerous and since many of them entered monasteries without fervour or under duress, they were bound to fall below the standards expected of them. On the other hand, even now, when numbers of monks and nuns are falling so rapidly in most European countries, it can be seen that some individuals have a compelling vocation for the monastic life and that it contributes not only to worship and religion but also to society at large. Its vitality was shown most recently by the flood of postulants who came forward to join the monasteries of eastern Europe after the wall came down in 1989 and their lands were returned to them.

CONCLUSION

I shall end by drawing again on the wisdom of Edmund Burke. It is no doubt too easy to succumb to the intoxication of his style. But the way in which he dealt with the issue of monastic secularisations in his *Reflections on the Revolution in France*, published at the end of 1790, in passages thought bizarre in his day and almost unnoticed since, ought to rank as one of the most extraordinary manifestations of his genius. He approached the question with the detachment of someone living in Britain, yet with a rare level of knowledge about French monasticism, and with passionate involvement in the fate of the monasteries, the monks and the nuns.

Before 1789 hardly any English non-Catholic writer had dared to defend monks. Monks, friars and nuns made a good showing in Gothic novels – though one largely unsung by writers on English literature[40] – but as part of the apparatus of fantasy, mystery, antiquarianism and horror that was the staple of such books as *The Castle of Otranto*, *Vathek*, *The Italian*, *The Mysteries of Udolpho* and *The Monk*. Only the last of these works, two of them written before the *Reflections* and three afterwards, betrayed any understanding of the true role of a monk, friar or nun. For Englishmen in general they were objects of derision or contempt; their whole *raison d'être* was seen by most Protestants as worthless.

In the *Reflections on the Revolution in France* Burke began with a few generally acceptable points: the monks have built great libraries, made 'great collections of ancient records, medals and coins . . . and of the specimens of nature'. He entered into the feelings of the expelled and dispossessed regulars who had embarked 'in a course of life . . . upon prospects and provisions held out by the laws, and by all men reputed certain'.[41] But he was mainly concerned to combat the deep prejudices of his adopted country:

the institutions savour of superstition in their very principle . . . This I do not mean to dispute . . . But is superstition the greatest of all possible vices? . . . Superstition is the religion of feeble minds . . . [But] a prudent man [might] think the superstition which builds, to be more tolerable than that which demolishes – that which adorns a country, than that which deforms it – that which endows, than that which plunders – that which leads a man to refuse himself lawful pleasures, than that which snatches from others the scanty subsistence of their self-denial. Such, I think, is very nearly the state of the question between the ancient founders of monkish superstition, and the superstition of the pretended philosophers of the hour.

Burke goes on to confront the issue of monkish idleness:

The monks are lazy. Be it so. Suppose them no otherwise employed than by singing in the choir. They are as usefully employed as those who neither sing nor say. As usefully as those who sing upon the stage. They are as usefully employed as if they worked from dawn to dark in the innumerable servile, degrading, unseemly, unmanly, and often most unwholesome and pestiferous occupations, to which by the social economy so many wretches are inevitably doomed... I should be infinitely more inclined to rescue them from their miserable industry than violently to disturb the tranquil repose of monastic quietude.

One may suspect that he did not really believe that the monks were in principle superstitious and in fact lazy, but conceded – or appeared to concede – these points in order to retain the sympathy of his intolerantly Protestant readers. In comparing the lot of the monks favourably with that of industrial workers he was anticipating, as in another way Chateaubriand was to do in Le génie du christianisme, the romantic Catholicism and Anglicanism, and the Young Toryism, of the 1830s.[42]

He even defended the estates possessed by commendatory abbots, though with perverse irony and without addressing the fundamental objection to their existence, that they siphoned off for the benefit of others income intended for the maintenance of monks or nuns:

Can any philosophic spoiler undertake to demonstrate the positive or comparative evil of having a certain, and that too a large, portion of landed property, passing in succession through persons whose title to it is, always in theory, and often in fact, an eminent degree of piety, morals and learning; a property, which..., on the score of merit, gives to the noblest families renovation and support, to the lowest the means of dignity and elevation...?... it does not seem to me of material injury to any commonwealth, that there should exist some estates that have a chance of being acquired by other means than the previous acquisition of money.

But what, finally, is most striking about Burke's case against the spoilers and 'confiscators' is that it is in relation to the monasteries of France – not, as is usually assumed, in regard to more general issues or to English politics – that he makes his classic defence of reform rather than revolution, and reform instead of reaction. 'There is something else than the mere alternative of absolute destruction, or unreformed existence.' 'A good patriot, and a true politician, always considers how he shall make the most of the existing materials of his country.' 'Had you no way of using the men but by converting monks into pensioners? Had you no way of turning the revenue to account, but through the improvident resource of a spendthrift sale?... Your politicians do not understand their trade; and therefore they sell their tools.' It was in the course of this discussion of monastic suppressions that Burke declared: 'A disposition to preserve, and an ability to improve, taken together, would be my standard of a statesman.'[43]

CONCLUSION

Implausible though it may seem, it was the despotic, impetuous Joseph II who had followed – rather reluctantly, it must be admitted – this conservative policy, which has stood the test of time in Austria to the present day. Granted that the problem in France was greater – greater because there were more and less effective monasteries there than in the Monarchy, and because the French state was bankrupt – a halfway house could surely have been found. One could hardly wish that all the prince-abbeys of Germany had survived, but it was not necessary to bring down all German monasteries and many universities in their wake. The case of Italy would have been especially difficult, since the number of monasteries there was so enormous. They could not all have been allowed to survive, but the reactions to repeated attempts to abolish them showed that the institution enjoyed vast support among Italians and needed reform rather than abolition.

It would not have been conceivable to preserve for much longer the monastic order as it stood in 1750 or 1789. Much had to go, most of the land and most of the privileges, many of the houses and many of their inmates, no doubt a good proportion of the buildings and treasures too. But, if monasteries had become too prosperous, they were too ruthlessly plundered. Rather than destroy monastic institutions completely, it would surely have been preferable everywhere, and ought to have been feasible, to find some compromise solution to the problem, perhaps that arrived at by Joseph II – or that which preserved some elements of medieval monasticism in the colleges of Oxford and Cambridge. The story of the nineteenth and twentieth centuries demonstrated that monasteries continued to answer the needs of many individuals and to serve a wide range of social purposes. To this degree at least, the lazy monks, and still more the useless nuns, have confounded their enemies – whether philosophic spoilers, revolutionary vandals or power-hungry rulers.

NOTES

INTRODUCTION

1. J. McManners (ed.), *The Oxford Illustrated History of Christianity* (Oxford, 1990), pp. 259, 280, 289, 293, 296, 587–8, 663.
2. C.H. Lawrence, *Medieval Monasticism: Forms of Religious Life in Western Europe in the Middle Ages* (2nd edn, London, 1989), p. 288.
3. I arrive at these figures as follows: *Austrian Monarchy*, 1780: 2,000 houses: about 30,000 monks and 15,000 nuns, the latter heavily concentrated in Lombardy and Belgium (see chs. 2 and 8) (these totals of course overlap with the figures for Italy and Poland below); *France*, 1765: 3,000 male houses with 30,000 inmates; 1789: 55,000 nuns (?5,000 houses?) (see ch. 3); *Germany*, 1803: c. 600 houses and at least 10,000 regulars (see ch. 2); *Italy*, 1650: 6,000 male monasteries with 70,000 monks; various local figures for nuns which, extrapolated, suggest an absolute minimum of 3,000 houses with 40,000 inmates; the figure for nuns may well have been much higher, and there is good reason to think overall numbers had risen by 1750 (see ch. 5); *Poland*, 1773: 884 male houses using the Latin rite with 14,500 inmates and 152 nunneries with about 3,000 inmates (plus 144 Basilian communities using the Greek rite, with 1,225 members) (see works cited in n. 2, p. 321); *Portugal*, 1822: c. 400 houses for males and c. 150 for females, with perhaps 7,000 monks and 6,000 nuns, a total of c. 20,000 around 1750 (see ch. 4); *Spain*, 1788: 2,000 male houses with 60,000 inmates; 1,000 female with 30,000 (see ch. 4); *Switzerland*, 1761: c. 120 houses, with 1,634 monks and 711 nuns (see ch. 10). 'Inmates' is a deliberately evasive word: in many cases it is impossible to tell whether the figures refer only to professed monks and nuns or include novices and/or lay brothers and sisters and perhaps even servants. Whatever their precise significance, the figures give a good impression of the scale of the monastic presence and of the variations between countries. To arrive at the figure for 1750, the Jesuits have to be added to the numbers post-1773. See O. Chadwick, *The Popes and European Revolution* (Oxford, 1981), pp. 211–13, for some of these figures and some others.

4   J. Schweder, *Kloster Schöntal* (Lauda-Königshofen, n.d.), p. 13.
5   A. Young, *Travels in France during the Years 1787, 1788 & 1789*, ed. C. Maxwell (Cambridge, 1929), p. 81.
6   G. Chittolini and G. Miccoli (eds.), *La chiesa e il potere politico dal medioevo all'età contemporanea* (Turin, 1986), p. 273.
7   See pp. 5, 32–3.
8   D. Higgs, 'The Portuguese Church' in W.J. Callahan and D. Higgs (eds.), *Church and Society in Catholic Europe of the Eighteenth Century* (Cambridge, 1979), p. 54, gives a total of fifty, of which thirty-two were for men and eighteen for women. Unfortunately, despite the calibre of its contributors, the absence of any source references in this book inevitably reduces its authority. Cf. the map of the city reproduced from B.M. Caeiro, *Os conventos de Lisboa* (Lisbon, 1989), pp. 15–17, which indicates forty-six *conventos*, and p. 12, where we are told that in the area of present-day Greater Lisbon there were seventy monasteries. I am most grateful to Dr Jon Parry who obtained for me a copy of this and other publications on Portuguese monasteries.
9   A. Babeau, *Paris en 1789* (Paris, n.d.), pp. 252, 260. It is astonishingly difficult to get these figures right. The precise date, the area covered and the definition of a monastery vary from estimate to estimate. Babeau says there were 154 nunneries, but others give lower estimates. His figures for male houses must refer to the 1750s, before the Jesuits were suppressed and the work of the *commission des réguliers* bore fruit. B. Plongeron, *Les réguliers de Paris devant le serment constitutionnel* (Paris, 1964), recognises thirty-seven monasteries in the Paris of 1789, but he does not include houses of recent Orders with simple vows, and he does not deal with nunneries. The most recent authority on Paris, *Atlas de la révolution française*, ed. S. Bonin and C. Langlois (Paris, 1987–), vol. IX: *Religion*, p. 78, gives a total figure of 132 for 1789. For Naples see pp. 129, 134.
10 Cf. E. Weis, 'Die Säkularisation der bayerischen Klöster 1802/03', *Sitzungsberichte der bayerischen Akademie der Wissenschaften, philosophisch-historische Klasse* (1983), heft 6, p. 21 and n. For Naples see P. Villani, *La vendita dei beni dello stato nel regno di Napoli, 1806–1815* (Milan, 1964).
11 Weis, 'Säkularisation'; P.G.M. Dickson, *Finance and Government under Maria Theresia, 1740–1780* (2 vols., Oxford, 1987), esp. vol. I, ch. 4, and pp. 444–6, and 'Joseph II's reshaping of the Austrian Church', HJ, 36 (1993), pp. 89–114.
12 For France C. Langlois and T. Tackett, 'A l'épreuve de la Révolution', in F. Lebrun (ed.), *Histoire des catholiques en France* (2nd edn, Paris, 1980), pp. 241–4.
13 See J. Jenkins and P. James, *From Acorn to Oak Tree: The Growth of the National Trust, 1895–1994* (London, 1994), p. xii.
14 See, e.g., P. Goubert, *The Ancien Régime: French Society, 1600–1750* (London, 1973), esp. pp. 122–6.
15 The next few paragraphs are derived from too great a variety of sources to list here (see the general works listed in the bibliography) but with particular help from Chadwick, *Popes and Revolution*, McManners's *Church and Society in Eighteenth-Century France* (2 vols., Oxford, 1998) and Chittolini and Miccoli, *La chiesa e il potere politico*.
16 This subject has been inadequately studied in most countries. One exception is D. Stutzer, *Klöster als Arbeitgeber um 1800: Die bayerischen Klöster als Unternehmenseinheiten und ihre Sozialsysteme zur Zeit der Säkularisation 1803* (Göttingen, 1986).

17 On the Austrian Estates H. Stradal, 'Die Prälatenkurie der österreichischen Landstände', *Anciens pays et assemblées d'états*, 53 (1970), pp. 117–80; for the Monarchy Dickson, *Finance and Government*, esp. vol. 1, pp. 299–305; for the Reich H. Kiesel and P. Münch, *Gesellschaft und Literatur im 18. Jahrhundert* (Munich, 1977), pp. 203–4; for a comparison between the Monarchy and the Reich V. Press, 'The system of Estates in the Austrian hereditary lands and in the Holy Roman Empire: a comparison', in R.J.W. Evans and T.V. Thomas (eds.), *Crown, Church and Estates: Central European Politics in the Sixteenth and Seventeenth Centuries* (London, 1991), pp. 1–22; for France J.F. Bosher, *The French Revolution* (London, 1989), pp. 88–90.

18 See ch. 2.

19 M. Defourneaux, *La vie quotidienne en Espagne au siècle d'or* (Paris, 1964), pp. 125–6. A recent treatment, with many references to other literature, is S. Evangelisti, 'Wives, widows, and brides of Christ: marriage and the convent in the historiography of early modern Italy', *HJ*, 43 (2000), pp. 233–47.

20 This point is made, e.g., in O. Fantozzi Micali's preface to A. Pincelli, *Monasteri e conventi del territorio aretino* (Florence, 2000), pp. 8–10.

21 M.H. Seymour, *A Pilgrimage to Rome* (3rd edn, London, 1848), pp. 154–60, and ch. 5 as a whole.

22 M. Bánhegyi, *The Community Table: The Baroque Dining Hall of the Abbey of Pannonhalma* (Pannonhalma, n.d.), pp. 72–3, 75. Some such figures are found elsewhere, e.g. in John Donne's *Ignatius his Conclave* (J. Hayward (ed.), *Complete Poetry and Selected Prose* (London, 1936), p. 362).

23 See esp. ch. 6.

24 See chs. 8, 9 and 10.

25 See ch. 6.

26 See ch. 8.

27 See chs 8, 9 and 10.

28 For France see chs. 3, 6, 7, 9 and 10; for Germany chs. 2 and 10; for Italy chs. 5, 8 and 10; for Spain and Portugal chs. 4 and 10; for Switzerland chs. 2 and 10; for the Austrian Monarchy including Belgium and Hungary chs. 2, 8 and 10. The main sections on Belgium are on pp. 210–24, 271–4. Hungary is discussed on pp. 205–10. On Poland see the works cited in nn. 2 and 13 on pp. 321–2.

29 See for the Belgian revolt against Joseph II, ch. 8.

30 The best account, astonishingly, is in a great book by an English architectural historian: J. Evans, *Monastic Architecture in France from the Renaissance to the Revolution* (Cambridge, 1964).

31 See chs. 2 and 8.

32 The phrase is G. Penco's in G. Farnedi and G. Spinelli (eds.), *Settecento monastico italiano* (Cesena, 1990), p. 17.

33 On Elton, see the symposium on his work in *TRHS*, 6th series, 7 (1997), esp. the article 'Religion' by C. Haigh – on the Pilgrimage of Grace, pp. 295–6. Among the vast literature on the English Civil War see J.S. Morrill, 'The religious context of the English Civil War', *TRHS*, 5th series, 34 (1984). For the French Revolution two striking pieces of revisionism are D.K. Van Kley, *The Religious Origins of the French Revolution* (New Haven and London, 1996), and T.C.W. Blanning, 'The role of religion in European counter-revolution, 1789–1815', in D. Beales and G. Best (eds.), *History, Society and the Churches* (Cambridge, 1985), pp. 195–214.

34 I.A.A. Thompson and B. Yun Casalilla (eds.), *The Castilian Crisis of the Seventeenth Century* (Cambridge, 1994).

35 Unfortunately the wealth of the Church of England has not been seriously studied, but P. Chaunu's claim that 'even the Anglican Church is richer in property and revenues than the Gallican Church', for which no evidence is given, seems simply preposterous (P. Chaunu, M. Foisil and F. de Noirfontaine, *Le basculement religieux de Paris au XVIIIe siècle* (Paris, 1998), p. 71).

36 By C.M.N. Eire in *From Madrid to Purgatory: The Art and Craft of Dying in Sixteenth-Century Spain* (Cambridge, 1995), p. 521. Cf. his remarks on the Weber thesis on p. 531.

37 H. Hasquin, *Histoire de la laïcité: principalement en Belgique et en France* (Brussels, 1981).

38 C. Hermann, *L'église d'Espagne sous le patronage royal (1476–1834)* (Madrid, 1988), p. 12.

39 E. Le Roy Ladurie, *The Ancien Regime: A History of France 1660–1774* (Oxford, 1991); F. Furet, *Revolutionary France, 1770–1880* (London, 1989), mentions monasteries only on p. 82; see Furet and M. Ozouf, *A Critical Dictionary of the French Revolution* (London, 1989), articles on the Civil Constitution of the Clergy and on dechristianisation.

40 See Lebrun, *Histoire des catholiques en France*, esp. the 'Orientations bibliographiques'. For this paragraph cf. B. Dompnier, *Enquête au pays des frères des anges: les Capucins de la province de Lyon aux XVIIe et XVIIIe siècles* (St-Etienne, 1993), esp. pp. 9–12.

41 The major exception here is Bernard Plongeron, on whose work I shall draw heavily in relation to the French Revolution.

42 A.G. Dickens, *The Counter Reformation* (London, 1968), pp. 99–100.

43 This case was persuasively argued by J. Bossy, 'The Counter-Reformation and the people of Catholic Europe', *Past and Present*, 47 (1970), pp. 51–70. Cf. R. P.-C. Hsia, *The World of Catholic Renewal, 1540–1770* (Cambridge, 1998), esp. pp. 23–4.

44 See, e.g., D. Knowles, *From Pachomius to Ignatius* (Oxford, 1966), though cf. his 'Jean Mabillon' in *The Historian and Character* (Cambridge, 1963), pp. 213–39.

45 E.g., as well as Evans, *Monastic Architecture*; J. Bourke, *Baroque Churches of Central Europe* (2nd edn, London, 1962); J. Lees-Milne, *Baroque in Spain and Portugal* (London, 1960); S. Sitwell, *Monks, Nuns and Monasteries* (London, 1965); and the works listed in n. 1, p. 323.

46 J.C.D. Clark, *English Society 1688–1832* (Cambridge, 1985); A.J. Mayer, *The Persistence of the Ancien Regime* (London, 1981).

47 Cf. E. Duffy, *Challoner and his Church: A Catholic Bishop in Georgian England* (London, 1981); G. Scott, *Gothic Rage Undone* (Bath, 1992); J.K. McNamara, *Sisters in Arms: Catholic Nuns through Two Millennia* (London, 1996), pp. 462–4.

48 *The Diary of John Evelyn*, ed. E.S. de Beer (6 vols., Oxford, 1955), vol. IV, pp. 269–70, 27 Jan. 1682. The diary for the years of James II's reign is packed with evidence of hostility to the Jesuits.

49 In the recent *History of Magdalene College, Cambridge, 1428–1998* by P. Cunich, D. Hoyle, E. Duffy and R. Hyam (Cambridge, 1994) Cunich argues (pp. 31–4) for greater continuity than previously accepted between the Benedictine house and the College.

50 E. Gibbon, *Memoirs of my Life*, ed. G.A. Bonnard (London, 1966), pp. 51–2.

51 J. McManners, *French Ecclesiastical Society under the Ancien Régime: A Study of Angers in the Eighteenth Century* (Manchester, 1960), and his *Church and Society*.

52 E.g. T.C.W. Blanning, *Reform and Revolution in Mainz, 1743–1803* (Cambridge, 1974) and *Joseph II* (London, 1994); Dickson's works listed in n. 11 above; R.J.W. Evans, *The Making of the Habsburg Monarchy, 1550–1700: An Interpretation* (Oxford, 1979).

53 McNamara was published in 1996, Rapley in 1990 and Hufton in 1992.

54 E.g. *Welt des Barock* (2 vols., Linz, 1986) for St Florian; *900 Jahre Benediktiner in Melk* (Melk, 1989)
55 J. Kirmeier and M. Treml (eds.), *Glanz und Ende der alten Klöster* (Munich, 1991). I am most grateful to Professor Blanning and Professor H. Schulze for obtaining a copy of this book for me.
56 M. Rosa (ed.), *Clero e società nell'Italia moderna* (Rome, 1992), and *Clero e società nell'Italia contemporanea* (Rome, 1992). The quotation is from pp. 7–8 of the *contemporanea* volume.
57 Hermann, *L'église d'Espagne*, p. 10.
58 E.g. J. Van Remoortere, *Le Guide Ippa des Abbayes en Belgique* (Brussels, 1995); B. Peugniez, *Routier des abbayes cisterciennes de France* (Strasbourg, 1994); R. Bosi, *Monasteri italiani* (Bologna, 1990); C. Romanò, *Guida ai conventi in Italia* (Milan, 1990), and *Abteien und Klöster in Europa* (Augsburg, 1997).
59 E. Catta, *La vie d'un monastère sous l'ancien régime: La Visitation Sainte-Marie de Nantes (1630–1792)* (Paris, 1954), p. 368n.
60 See pp. 99–101.
61 *Sacrosanctum consilium Tridentinum* (Venice, 1740), p. 214: Sessio XXV, Caput XXII.
62 The meaning of *Stift* is disputed. Cf. W. Luger, *Stifte in Oberösterreich* (Linz, 1969), pp. 7–9; J. Angerer, *Stifte und Klöster in Bayern, Österreich und der Schweiz* (Pattloch, 1987), ch. 8; Evans, *Making of the Habsburg Monarchy*, pp. 181–6.
63 One of the greatest authorities in the field, M. Heimbucher, entitled his work *Die Orden und Kongregationen der katholischen Kirche* (2 vols., Paderborn, 1933–4), but a directory called *Männerorden in der Bundesrepublik Deutschland*, ed. L. Holtz (Cologne, 1984), published under the auspices of an assembly of German *Ordensobern* (monastic superiors), includes congregations, societies, etc.
64 McManners, *Church and society*, vol. 1, p. 647; and see the whole of ch. 21.
65 Bosher, *The French Revolution*, p. 57. Cf. R. Shackleton, *The 'Encyclopédie' and the Clerks* (Oxford, 1970).
66 I have found the following particularly useful here: Heimbucher's great work, cited in n. 63; Knowles, *From Pachomius to Ignatius*; L. Moulin, *Le monde vivant des religieux* (Paris, 1964); O. de La Brosse, A.-M. Henry and P. Rouillard (ed.), *Dictionnaire de la foi chrétienne*, vol. II (Paris, 1968); articles on particular Orders in *DIP*; H. Chadwick, 'The Ascetic Ideal in the History of the Church', in W.J. Sheils (ed.), *Monks, Hermits and the Ascetic Tradition* (Oxford, 1985) (Studies in Church History, vol. 22), pp. 1–24. I am grateful to Olivier marquis de Trazegnies for bringing the work of Moulin to my attention.
67 For some account of the Capuchins and other Franciscan branches see pp. 106–8.
68 E.g. C.N.L. Brooke, 'Monk and canon: some patterns in the religious life of the twelfth century', in Sheils, *Monks, Hermits and the Ascetic Tradition*, pp. 109–30.

1 THE COUNTER-REFORMATION AND THE MONASTERIES

1 Dickens, *Counter Reformation*, p. 183. However, Hsia's recent book, *World of Catholic Renewal*, treats the process of Catholic Reformation as continuing until after the mid-eighteenth century. It also discusses the usage of 'Counter-Reformation', pointing out (pp. 1–2) that it was invented in the eighteenth century to refer to the Catholic recovery in Germany between 1555 and 1648.

Another recent work illuminating this issue is M.R. Forster, *Catholic Revival in the Age of the Baroque: Religious Identity in Southwest Germany, 1550–1750* (Cambridge, 2001).

2 See Evans, *Making of the Habsburg Monarchy*, pp. 283–7, for Hungary. For Poland J. Kłoczowski, 'The Polish Church', in Callahan and Higgs, *Church and Society*; also Kłoczowski's *Dzieje chrzescijanstwa polskiego*, vol. II (Paris, 1991), which Dr R. Butterwick kindly lent me.

3 D. Stievermann, 'Politik und Konfession im 18, Jahrhundert', *Zeitschrift für historische Forschung*, 18 (1991), 177–99. It is difficult to reconcile these facts with bland accounts like that in J.G. Gagliardo, *Germany under the Old Regime, 1600–1790* (London, 1991), esp. pp. 83–5.

4 Cf. W.R. Ward, *The Protestant Evangelical Awakening* (Cambridge, 1992).

5 The classic treatment is P. Hazard, *La crise de la conscience européenne, 1680–1715* (Paris, 1935), transl. as *The European Mind* (London, 1953). P. Gay, *The Enlightenment: An Interpretation* (2 vols., 1967–70), is the best modern discussion of the movement as essentially anti-religious; the most fundamental critique of this approach remains E. Cassirer, *The Philosophy of the Enlightenment* (Princeton, 1951), which originally appeared in German in 1932 and concentrates in dealing with religion on the relationships between Enlightenment and Protestantism. For literature on 'Catholic Enlightenment' see n. 57, p. 327.

6 E.g. P. Boutry et al., *Histoire de la France religieuse*, vol. III: *Du roi Très Chrétien à la laïcité républicaine, XVIIIe–XIXe siècle* (Paris, 1991), p. 221, for Provence; R. Schlögl, *Glaube und Religion in der Säkularisierung* (Munich, 1995), pp. 237–8, for the Rhineland; for Upper Austria M. Pammer, *Glaubensabfall und Wahre Andacht: Barockreligiosität, Reformkatholizismus und Laizismus in Oberösterreich 1700–1820* (Vienna, 1994), esp. pp. 151–2.

7 E.g. J. Quéniart, *Culture et société urbaines dans la France de l'Ouest au XVIIIe siècle* (Paris, 1978): percentage fall from 44 to 30, but nearly fourfold increase of titles.

8 R. Chartier, *The Cultural Uses of Print in Early Modern France* (Princeton, 1987), esp. p. 193. Cf., on Austria and Bohemia, R.J.W. Evans, 'Über die Ursprünge der Aufklärung in den habsburgischen Ländern', *Das achtzehnte Jahrhundert und Österreich*, 2 (1985), esp. pp. 29–30.

9 Dominique Julia in Joutard, *Du roi Très Chrétien*, pp. 195–7; F. Furet and M. Ozouf, *A Critical Dictionary of the French Revolution* (London, 1989), p. 22. See also Schlögl, *Glaube und Religion*.

10 See esp. L. Châtellier, *The Religion of the Poor: Rural Missions in Europe and the Formation of Modern Catholicism, c. 1500–c. 1800* (Cambridge, 1997).

11 Perhaps the most compelling of the now numerous studies on this theme, and one of the few available in English, is L. Châtellier, *The Europe of the Devout: The Catholic Reformation and the Formation of a New Society* (Cambridge, 1989). Among others of special interest are C.F. Black, *Italian Confraternities in the Sixteenth Century* (Cambridge, 1989); M. Agulhon, *Pénitents et franc-maçons de l'ancienne Provence* (Paris, 1968); G. Tüskés and E. Knapp, 'Bruderschaften in Ungarn im 17. und 18. Jahrhundert', *Bayerisches Jahrbuch für Volkskunde* (1992), 1–23; R. Rusconi, 'Confraternite, compagnie e devozioni', in Chittolini and Miccoli, *La chiesa e il potere politico*, pp. 467–506. On the numbers involved, roughly a million are said to have been enrolled in the *Assistenza Germanica* of the Jesuit Marian congregations: 'Compagnia di Gesú', DIP, vol. II, col. 1273. Even if that is an exaggeration, extrapolation of the figures scattered through Châtellier and other sources justifies the word 'millions'.

12 J. Wodka, *Kirche in Österreich* (Vienna, 1959), pp. 272–3; S. Dressler, 'Wallfahrte als Ausdruck barocker Frömmigkeit', in K. Gutkas (ed.), *Prinz Eugen und das barocke Österreich* (Salzburg,

1985), esp. p. 377. Cf. Châtellier, *Europe of the Devout*, esp. pp. 153–5 and L.A. Veit and L. Lenhart, *Kirche und Volksfrömmigkeit im Zeitalter des Barock* (Freiburg, 1956), esp. pp. 66–7, 174–80.

13 E.g. Langlois and Tackett, 'A l'épreuve de la Révolution', esp. pp. 265–6; Hermann, *l'église d'Espagne*, p. 25; X. Toscani, 'Il reclutamento del clero (secoli XVI–XIX)', in Chittolini and Miccoli, *La chiesa e il potere politico*, pp. 573–628. The figures in S. Litak, 'La paroisse du XVIe au XVIIIe siècle', in M. Rechowicz (ed.), *Poland's Millennium of Catholicism (Le millénaire du catholicisme en Pologne)* (Lublin, 1969), pp. 110–13, and in Kłoczowski's article in Callahan and Higgs, *Church and society*, suggest that the same was true of Poland.

14 For Poland see the sources cited in the previous note. Kłoczowski's figures are: in 1700 674 male and 111 female houses; in 1772–3 884 and 152. F.L. Hervay, 'Ungheria', in DIP, vol. IX, cols. 1535–8, where the figures given are: 1700, 130; 1780, 221; but the Jesuits' houses had grown from 21 in 1700 to 50 in 1773, when they were suppressed, and so the total number of monasteries just before that must have been c. 250.

15 See, e.g., pp. 87–8, 131.

16 Cf. Hsia, *World of Catholic Renewal*, introduction.

17 B. Harvey, *Living and Dying in England, 1100–1540: The Monastic Experience* (Oxford, 1993), p. 210.

18 Cf. n. 66, p. 320, and H. Holzapfel, *Handbuch der Geschichte des Franziskanerordens* (Freiburg, 1909).

19 See e.g. Bossy, 'The Counter-Reformation and the people of Catholic Europe'.

20 *Sacrosanctum consilium Tridentinum* (Venice, 1740), pp. 202–11 (Sessio XXV, cap. I–XVIII).

21 I am grateful to Dr Mary Laven for bringing the importance of this measure to my attention. See Hsia, *World of Catholic Renewal*, pp. 33–41.

22 J. Bergin, *Cardinal de La Rochefoucauld: Leadership and Reform in the French Church* (London, 1987); J.H. Elliott, *Richelieu and Olivares* (Cambridge, 1984).

23 See the excellent study by G. Boaga, *La soppressione innocenziana dei piccoli conventi in Italia* (Rome, 1971).

24 On Philip I.A.A. Thompson and B. Yun Casalilla (eds.), *The Castilian Crisis of the Seventeenth Century* (Cambridge, 1994), pp. 260–1; on Louis see pp. 35, 104; on noble complaints F.L. Carsten, *Princes and Parliaments in Germany* (Oxford, 1959), p. 420.

25 For France P. de la Gorce, *Histoire religieuse de la Révolution française* (5 vols., Paris, 1905–23), vol. I, p. 18. See pp. 104–6.

26 See, e.g., V. Press in R.J.W. Evans and T.V. Thomas (eds.), *Crown, Church and Estates: Central European Politics in the Sixteenth and Seventeenth Centuries* (London, 1991), pp. 1–22. On Bavaria Carsten, *Princes and Parliaments*, p. 386.

27 See Dickson, *Finance and government*, vol. II, ch. 10.

28 Chadwick, *Popes and Revolution*, pp. 322–3.

29 Ibid. pp. 64–6, 160–5. Cf. G. Martina, *La chiesa nell'età dell' assolutismo, del liberalismo, del totalitarismo* (7th edn, 4 vols., Brescia, 1988–9), vol. II, pp. 43–5.

30 Cf. Evans, *Making of the Habsburg Monarchy*, p. 135; Dickens, *Counter Reformation*, p. 149.

31 Boaga, *La soppressione innocenziana*.

32 On the very difficult question of Jansenism, its meaning and influence, see for example Chadwick, *Popes and Revolution*, esp. pp. 279–84, 393–5; Martina, *La chiesa nell' età dell'assolutismo*,

vol.II, pp. 147–85; W. Doyle, *Jansenism* (Basingstoke, 2000); McManners, *Church and Society*, vol. II, chs. 35–41.

33 A. Vecchi, 'L'itinerario spirituale del Muratori', in *L.A. Muratori e la cultura contemporanea* (Florence, 1975), esp. pp. 181–4; C. Donati, 'Dalla "regolata devozione" al "Giuseppinismo" nell'Italia del Settecento', in M. Rosa (ed.), *Cattolicesimo e lumi nel Settecento italiano* (Rome, 1981), pp. 77–98; A. Kraus, 'L.A. Muratori und Bayern', in *La Fortuna di L.A. Muratori* (Florence, 1975), pp. 165–6.

34 See pp. 65, 68–73, 80–1, 88–91.

35 See ch. 6.

36 On the impact of Febronius see L. von Pastor, *History of the Popes* (English transl., 40 vols., 1891–1953), vol. XXXVIII; Chadwick, *Popes and Revolution*, pp. 408–10.

37 Cf. *The Memoirs of Chateaubriand*, transl. R. Baldick (Harmondsworth, 1965), p. 369.

2 THE GREAT MONASTERIES OF THE GERMAN CATHOLIC LANDS

1 On the architectural development in general: G. Bazin, *The Baroque: Principles, Styles, Modes, Themes* (London, 1968), esp. pp. 293–5; A. Blunt (ed.), *Baroque and Rococo: Architecture and Decoration* (London, 1978), esp. Part IV by A. Laing, 'Central and eastern Europe'; E. Hempel, *Baroque Art and Architecture in Central Europe* (Harmondsworth, 1965); T. da C. Kaufmann, *Court, Cloister and City: The Art and Culture of Central Europe, 1450–1800* (London, 1995); Bourke, *Baroque Churches of Central Europe*; N. Lieb, *Barockkirchen zwischen Donau und Alpen* (6th edn, Munich, 1992); H.-R. Hitchcock, *Rococo Architecture in Southern Germany* (London, 1968); W. Braunfels, *Monasteries of Western Europe: The Architecture of the Orders* (London, 1972), esp. ch. 10.

2 For the role of the new Orders Evans, *Making of the Habsburg Monarchy*, pp. 124–33.

3 Cf. Hsia, *World of Catholic Renewal*, esp. pp. 160–4, 198–200.

4 One conspicuous exception is Cologne, where many Romanesque churches received only minimal Baroque decoration and where the Gothic cathedral was simply left as a torso from the early sixteenth until the nineteenth century. Cf. Braunfels, *Monasteries*, pp. 178–9.

5 E.g. Gagliardo, *Germany under the Old Regime*, pp. 90–3.

6 Cf. on the Vienna building boom W. Pircher, *Verwüstung und Verschwendung* (Vienna, 1984); on south Germany H. Zückert, *Die sozialen Grundlagen der Barockkultur in Süddeutschland* (Stuttgart, 1988). See pp. 77–8.

7 E.g. abbot Kobolt of Weingarten (R. Schmidt, *Weingarten* (Königstein, 1989), p. 2) and abbot Bürgi of St Peter's in the Black Forest in 1722 (H.-O. Mühleisen (ed.), *Die Vermächtnis der Abtei: 900 Jahre St. Peter auf dem Schwarzwald* (Karlsruhe, 1993), p. 363).

8 For the general conditions favouring monastic building in the Austrian Monarchy see e.g. Evans, *Making of the Habsburg Monarchy*, pp. 180–6; R. Feuchtmüller and E. Kovács, *Welt des Barock* (Linz, 1986); H. Knittler, 'Zum ökonomischen Hintergrund und Beziehungsgeflecht des neuzeitlichen Klosterbaus', in E. Vavra (ed.), *Die Suche nach der verlorenen Paradies: Europäische Kultur in Spiegel der Klöster* (St Pölten, 2000), pp. 93–102. I am very grateful to Mag. E. Fattinger for sending me a copy of this last book.

9 I have relied mainly on *900 Jahre Melk*; F. Würml, *Melk* (Vienna, 1977); and R.N. Freeman, *The Practice of Music at Melk Abbey: Based on the Documents, 1681–1826* (Vienna, 1989) [Sitzungsberichte der österreichische Akademie der Wissenschaften, phil.-hist. Kl., vol. 548].

10 For Tables 1 and 2 and the whole paragraph see H. Knittler, 'Zwischen Stabilität und Veränderung: Ein Beitrag zur Melker Wirtschaftsgeschichte in der frühen Neuzeit', in *900 Jahre Melk*, esp. pp. 481–3, and Dickson, *Finance and Government*, vol. 1, pp. 96–8.

11 B. Ellegast, 'Die Reformation' and 'Prägungen klösterlicher Kultur durch Gegenreformation und Barock', in *900 Jahre Melk*, esp. pp. 356–9; Würml, *Melk*, pp. 34–5.

12 E. Bruckmüller, 'Die öffentliche Funktion des Stiftes', in *900 Jahre Melk*, pp. 373–5.

13 Ibid. pp. 177, 182; Würml, *Melk*, p. 36.

14 For this paragraph see Bruckmüller, 'Die öffentliche Funktion des Stiftes', pp. 375–8; Dickson, *Finance and Government*, vol. 1, esp. pp. 297–304.

15 H. Stradal, 'Die Prälatenkurie der österreichischen Landstände', *Anciens pays et assemblées d'états*, 53 (1970), p. 173n; *850 Jahre Praemonstratenser Chorherrenstift Wilten* (2nd edn, Wilten, 1989), pp. 43–4.

16 Freeman, *Practice of Music*, p. 29; *900 Jahre Melk*, esp. pp. 382–4, and see also p. 359; Würml, *Melk*, p. 71.

17 On Göttweig see p. 55, and P.G. Tropper, 'Das Stift [Göttweig] von der Gegen-Reformation bis zur Zeit Joseph II.', *Geschichte des Stiftes Göttweig* (Studien und Mitteilungen zur Geschichte des Benediktiner-Ordens, 94 (1983), pp. 290–327.

18 G. Flossman and P. W. Kowarik, 'Die Pfarren des Stiftes Melk', in *900 Jahre Melk*, esp. pp. 382–4; see also p. 359.

19 See my article 'Joseph II and the monasteries of Austria and Hungary', in N. Aston (ed.), *Religious Change in Europe, 1650–1914: Essays for John McManners* (Oxford, 1997), pp. 161–84.

20 See Freeman, *Practice of Music* passim.

21 See pp. 54, 63–6, 114, 118–19.

22 See various articles in *900 Jahre Melk*, esp. B. Euler and W.G. Rizzi, 'Zur Bau- und Ausstattunggeschichte der Melker Stiftskirche', pp. 440–52; Würml, *Melk*, pp. 66–82.

23 Bazin, *Baroque*, pp. 42–3.

24 The timetable derives essentially from Freeman, *Practice of Music*, p. 150; I have made additions on the basis of Ellegast, in *900 Jahre Melk*, pp. 120–1, but some of his timings are slightly different, as was the timetable at Göttweig: Tropper, 'Das Stift [Göttweig] von der Gegen-Reformation bis Zur Zeit Joseph II.', pp. 330–1. Much of the material for the next section comes from Freeman's exhaustive work, esp. ch. 3.

25 All this material on wine comes from the excellent recent book of R. Malli, *Der Schatz im Keller: Zur Weinwirtschaft der Waldviertler Klöster* (Horn, 2001), esp. pp. 198–205, 241–4, 262.

26 On music and theatre at Melk see Freeman, *Practice of Music*, esp. ch. 4.

27 On Melk scholarship J. and M. Niederkorn-Bruck, 'Hochbarocke Geschichtsschreibung im Stift Melk', in *900 Jahre Melk*, pp. 399–403. On monastic libraries and their size, G. Heilingsetzer, 'Aufklärung und barocke Tradition: Formen und Stufen der Aufklüng bei den Benediktinern und Augustiner-Chorherren im bayerisch-oberösterreichischen Raum', *Das achtzehnte Jahrhundert und Österreich*, 2 (1985), pp. 35–6. The exceptionally beautiful library at Altenburg has much wall space between its elegant book cabinets.

28 *900 Jahre Melk*, p. 107.

29 See *850 Jahre Wilten*, esp. p. 37; H. Parigger, 'Leben im Kloster', in Kirmeier and Treml, *Glanz und Ende der alten Klöster*, pp. 207–8. The inventories of Hungarian monasteries dissolved by

Joseph II, some of which I saw through the courtesy of Dr Márta Velladics, list many coffee machines owned by individual monks.

30. See F. Matsche, *Die Kunst im Dienst der Staatsidee Kaiser Karls VI.* (2 vols., Berlin, 1981); F. Röhrig, *Stift Klosterneuburg* (3rd edn, Munich, 1967); Lees-Milne, *Baroque in Spain and Portugal*, esp. pp. 181–9. See p. 123.

31. See e.g. G.M. Lechner (ed.), *900 Jahre Stift Göttweig* (Bad Vöslau, 1983).

32. Dickson, *Finance and Government*, vol. I, p. 96, gives this high figure. Knittler's in 'Zum ökonomischen Hintergrund', is just over 44,000 florins. For this and the next paragraph see O. Wutzel (ed.), *1200 Jahre Kremsmünster* (Linz, 1977).

33. There is a valuable account in H. Sturmberger, 'Studien zur Geschichte der Aufklärung des 18. Jahrhunderts in Kremsmünster', *MIÖG*, 53 (1939), pp. 423–80. Cf. for this and many other abbeys Heilingsetzer, 'Aufklärung und barocke Tradition', pp. 36–9.

34. On the concept of 'Catholic Enlightenment', which has attracted a very large literature: the pioneering article (1909) of S. Merkle, 'Die katholische Beurteilung des Aufklärungszeitalters', reprinted in his *Ausgewählte Reden und Aufsätze*, ed. T. Freudenberger (Würzburg, 1965), pp. 361–43; Chadwick, *Popes and Revolution*, esp. pp. 406–7; T.C.W. Blanning, 'The Enlightenment in Catholic Germany', in R. Porter and M. Teich (eds.), *The Enlightenment in National Context* (Cambridge, 1981), pp. 118–26, and E. Wangermann's chapter, 'Reform Catholicism and political radicalism in the Austrian Enlightenment', in the same volume, pp. 127–40; Blanning, *Reform and Revolution in Mainz*; E. Winter, *Der Josefinismus: Die Geschichte des österreichischen Reformkatholizismus* (2nd edn, Berlin, 1962). On St Florian C. Wagner, *Saint Florian* (Vienna, 1986), on Seitenstetten K. Brunner (ed.), *Seitenstetten: Kunst und Mönchtum an der Wiege Österreichs* (Vienna, 1988). So far as I know, there is no equivalent work on the Schottenstift. See additional works cited in nn. 53 and 57 below.

35. F. and R. Malecek, *Strahov Praha* (Prague, ?1993). For Tepl (and to some extent Strahov) see A.K. Huber, 'Das Stift Tepl im Aufklärungszeitalter', *Analecta premonstratensia*, a succession of articles in vols. 26–30 (1950–4), esp. the first in vol. 26, pp. 41–66.

36. See P.C. Hartmann, 'Bevölkerungszahlen und Konfessionsverhältnisse des Heiligen Römischen Reiches Deutscher Nation und der Reichskreise am Ende des 18. Jahrhunderts', *Zeitschrift für historische Forschung* (1996), pp. 345–69. Anyone dealing with German eighteenth-century population statistics has to wrestle with the complications that Belgium, Austria and Bohemia counted as part of the *Reich* and Silesia technically did not. For the *Reich* Hartmann arrives at figures of 15 million Catholics and over 10 million Protestants.

37. See Châtellier, *The Religion of the Poor*; C. Jahn, *Klosteraufhebungen und Klosterpolitik in Bayern unter Kurfürst Karl Theodor, 1778–1784* (Munich, 1994).

38. See in English esp. J.G. Gagliardo, *Reich and Nation: The Holy Roman Empire as Idea and Reality, 1763–1806* (London, 1980); Blanning, *Reform and Revolution in Mainz*. In German, the standard work is now K.O. von Aretin, *Das alte Reich, 1648–1806* (3 vols., Stuttgart, 1988–98), esp. vol. III on 1745–1806.

39. On the position of German ecclesiastical states in general see L. Hüttl, 'Geistlicher Fürst und geistliche Fürstentümer im Barock und Rokoko', *ZBL*, 37 (1974), pp. 1–48. Though this article is almost entirely concerned with the prince-bishoprics, much of it applies equally to the prince-abbacies.

40 There is a useful list of the representatives at the Diet of 1792 in H. Kiesel and P. Münch, *Gesellschaft und Literatur im 18. Jahrhundert* (Munich, 1977), pp. 203–4. A very valuable contemporary survey is A.F. Busching, *A New System of Geography* (6 vols., London, 1762), esp. vol. IV.

41 G. Benecke, 'The German Reichskirche', in Callahan and Higgs, *Church and Society*, p. 80. The population figure is roughly confirmed by Hartmann, *Zeitschrift für historische Forschung* (1996), pp. 348–9.

42 E. Sturm, *Die Bau- und Kunstdenkmale der Stadt Fulda* (Fulda, 1984), p. 50.

43 J. Duft, A. Gössi and W. Vogler, *Die Abtei St Gallen* (St Gall, 1986), esp. pp. 54–7; Busching, *New System of Geography*, vol. III, pp. 743–52. Cf. Salem (see Ill. 40). On the Toggenburg war see two articles by G. Nattrass in *British Library Journal*, 19 (1993), and 25 (1999).

44 On the nature of these states see S. Merkle, 'Die Bedeutung der geistlichen Staaten im alten deutschen Reich', originally published in 1930, in his *Ausgewählte Reden und Aufsätze*, pp. 469–87; Hüttl, 'Geistlicher fürst und geistliche fürstentümer im Barock und Rokoko', pp. 3–46. However, very little is said in these pieces about monastic as opposed to episcopal states. The most interesting recent contribution that I know on monastic states is to be found in Zückert, *Die sozialen Grundlagen*.

45 P. Blickle, 'Das Fürststift Kempten: ein typischer Kleinstaat in der Frühneuzeit', in V. Dotterweich et al. (eds.), *Geschichte der Stadt Kempten* (Kempten, 1989), pp. 184–202. See also M. Erzberger, *Die Säkularisation in Württemberg von 1802–1810* (Stuttgart, 1902), esp. p. 65, on its size and income; M. Winkle and A. Kiechle-Oberhofer, *Stadtführer Kempten* (n.d., Kempten); H.-G. Richardi and A.A. Haase, *Burgen, Schlösser und Klöster in Bayern* (Erlangen, 1993), pp. 98–9.

46 This widespread though far from universal perception is discussed e.g. in Blanning, *Reform and Revolution in Mainz*; P. Wende, *Die geistlichen Staaten und ihre Auflösung im Urteil der zeitgenössischen Publizistik* (Lübeck, 1966); and F. Quarthal, 'Unterm Krummstab ist's gut leben: Prälaten, Mönche und Bauern im Zeitalter des Barock', in P. Blickle (ed.), *Politische Kultur in Oberschwaben* (Tübingen, 1993), pp. 269–86.

47 M. Spindler (ed.), *Handbuch der bayerischen Geschichte*, vol. III/2 (Munich, 1972), p. 1158.

48 On the witchcraft case W. Behringer, *Witchcraft Persecutions in Bavaria* (Cambridge, 1997), pp. 352–4. I am grateful for the help of Dr Ulinka Rublack on this point.

49 J. Brümmer, *Kunst und Herrschaftsanspruch: Abt Benedikt Knittel (1650–1732) und sein Wirken im Zisterzienserkloster Schöntal* (Sigmaringen, 1994); Erzberg, *Säkularisation*, pp. 225–6.

50 See in general A. Kolb, *Ottobeuren: Schicksal einer schwäbischen Reichsabtei* (Kempten, 1986); J. Beer, *Ottobeuren* (Königstein, 1989); Braunfels, *Monasteries*, pp. 214–18, 246–8.

51 Braunfels, *Monasteries*, p. 248 (translation modified). Cf. Zückert, *Die sozialen Grundlagen*, pp. 260–1. Rather lower figures for area and population in Erzberger, *Säkularisation*, p. 65.

52 Kolb, *Ottobeuren*, p. 143.

53 On the University of Salzburg, e.g., Wodka, *Kirche in Österreich*, pp. 281–4; R. Haaß, *Die geistige Haltung der katholischen Universitäten Deutschlands im 18. Jahrhundert* (Freiburg, 1952), pp. 160–5.

54 According to Braunfels, *Monasteries*, p. 214, it had 125 square miles of territory. *Germania benedictina*, ed. F. Quarthal (5 vols., Augsburg, 1975), gives the population figure of 11,000.

55 G. Spahr, *Die Basilika Weingarten: Ein Barockjuwel in Oberschwaben* (Sigmaringen, 1974); Schmidt, *Weingarten*. That the figure given for the cost of the church was so much less than Ottobeuren's is presumably explained by the fact that the Gabler organ and some of the decoration is not

included. It may also be that Ottobeuren budgeted for the materials that came from its own resources, and Weingarten did not. According to Braunfels, *Monasteries*, p. 214, Weingarten's income was 97,000 florins a year in 1792.

56 On the pilgrimage Spahr, *Die Basilika Weingarten*, pp. 162–9. On the organ ibid. pp. 153–9; F. Jacob, *Die grosse Orgel der Basilika zu Weingarten* (Berne, 1986), esp. pp. 20–31. The special effects are rivalled at the Cistercian abbey of Oliva in Poland.

57 E. Hegel, *Die katholische Kirche Deutschlands unter dem Einfluß der Aufklärung des 18. Jhdts* (Opladen, 1975); Haaß, *Die geistige Haltung*, pp. 160–2. See also Blanning, 'The Enlightenment in Catholic Germany', pp. 118–26; Wodka, *Kirche in Österreich*, pp. 290–2; Behringer, *Witchcraft Persecutions*; D. Sorkin, 'Reform Catholicism and religious Enlightenment', AHY, 30 (1999), pp. 187–219.

58 Cf. e.g. Schlögl, *Glaube und Religion*.

59 C. Norberg-Schulz, *Balthasar Neumann: Abteikirche Neresheim* (Tübingen, 1993), p. 17.

60 On Gerbert and St Blasien H. Heidegger and H. Ott (eds.), *St. Blasien: 200 Jahre Kloster- und Pfarrkirche* (Munich, 1983); C. Römer (ed.), *Das tausendjährige St. Blasien* (2 vols., Karlsruhe, 1983).

61 D. Beales, *Joseph II*, vol. I: *In the Shadow of Maria Theresa, 1741–1780* (Cambridge, 1987), p. 477.

62 See pp. 94–6. Historians, whether of architecture or the French Revolution, rarely mention the monastic purpose of Ste-Geneviève. Cf. D. Irwin, *Neoclassicism* (London, 1997).

63 Braunfels, *Monasteries*, p. 220.

64 Quotations from the English edition of H. Brommer, *St. Blasien/Schwarzwald* (Munich, 1989), p. 24; contemporary comment on the organ from Römer, *Das tausendjährige St. Blasien*, vol. I, p. 94. G. Bazin, *Paläste des Glaubens* (2 vols., Augsburg, 1997), vol. II, pp. 202–7, sees Ixnard and St Blasien as the death-knell of German Rococo, inspiring the chilly architecture of Wiblingen, Buchau and Salem.

65 F. Nicolai, *Unter Bayern und Schwaben: Meine Reise im deutschen Süden 1781*, ed. U. Schlemmer (Berlin, 1989), ch. 9, presents Nicolai's account of St Blasien in his eight volumes of travels, published from 1783 to 1787.

66 E.g. Parigger, 'Leben im Kloster', pp. 207–8.

67 G. W. Zapf, *Reisen in einige Klöster Schwabens, durch den Schwarzwald und in die Schweiz im Jahr 1786* (Erlangen, 1786).

68 J.N. Hauntinger, *Reise durch Schwaben und Bayern im Jahre 1784*, ed. G. Spaur (Weißenhorn, 1964).

69 On Felbiger and his work, in English, J.V.H. Melton, *Absolutism and the Eighteenth-Century Origins of Compulsory Schooling in Prussia and Austria* (Cambridge, 1988).

70 Kirmeier and Treml, *Glanz und Ende der alten Klöster*, p. 32.

71 Blanning, *Reform and Revolution in Mainz*, pp. 133, 166–7; Jahn, *Klosteraufhebungen und Klosterpolitik*.

72 See Wende, *Die geistlichen Staaten*, and I. Böhm, 'Literarische Wegbereiter der Säkularisation', *Studien und Mitteilungen zur Geschichte des Benediktiner-Ordens*, 94 (1983), pp. 518–37.

73 See E. Siegfried (ed.), *Kloster Lamspringe* (2nd edn, Göttingen, 1963).

74 Downside abbey MS 205.VII.D. I wish to acknowledge the help and kindness I received at Downside, especially from the Librarian, Dom Philip Jebb.

75 Downside abbey MS 386.VII.D, 'An account of the contest between the abbot of Lambspring and the president of the English Benedictine Congregation', 1801–3.

76 Downside abbey MS 418.VII.D, Liber Conciliorum 1715–1802.

77 P. Morsbach, *St. Emmeram zu Regensburg* (Munich, 1993). According to H. Schwarzmaier (ed.), *Handbuch der baden-württembergischen Geschichte*, vol. III (Stuttgart, 1992), p. 566, six abbeys (presumably in Baden-Württemberg) acquired this status after 1750.

78 Cf. Zückert, *Die sozialen Grundlagen*, passim, and also Forster, *Catholic Revival*, pp. 79–83, 232–3.

79 See Dickson, *Finance and Government*, vol. I, pp. 64–5; E. Krausen, 'Die Herkunft der bayerischen Prälaten des 17. und 18. Jahrhunderts', ZBL, 27 (1964), pp. 259–85.

80 Châtellier, *Europe of the Devout*, pp. 199–201.

81 H. Diemer, *Oberammergau and its Passion Play* (Munich, 1900), though gushing, is not uncritical historically.

82 See e.g. Lieb, *Barockkirchen*, pp. 116–37; Blunt, *Baroque and Rococo*, pp. 216–17, 254, 256, 265, 269–70.

83 Cf. Forster, *Catholic Revival*, esp. ch. 4.

84 The point is strongly made, e.g., for Italy by C. Donati, 'Dalla "regolata devozione" al "Giuseppinismo" nell'Italia del Settecento', in M. Rosa (ed.), *Cattolicesimo e lumi nel Settecento italiano* (Rome, 1981), pp. 77–98.

85 Forster, *Catholic Revival*, pp. 166–7.

86 Cf. Heilingsetzer, 'Aufklärung und barocke Tradition', pp. 34–9.

87 Haß, *Die geistige Haltung*, esp. ch. 3; Hegel, *Die katholische Kirche Deutschlands*; Sorkin, 'Reform Catholicism and Religious Enlightenment'.

88 See e.g. G.J. Buelow (ed.), *The Late Baroque Era: From the 1680s to 1740* (London, 1993), pp. 309–12, 319–20.

89 O.E. Deutsch (ed.), *Mozart: A Documentary Biography* (2nd edn, London, 1966), p. 219.

90 See the works on St Blasien cited in n. 60 above; Hauntinger, *Reise*, pp. 128–9. Cf. C. Schott, *Armenfürsorge, Bettelwesen und Vagantenbekämpfung in der Reichsabtei Salem* (Baden, 1978).

91 The quotation and comment come from K. Schreiner's excellent article, 'Mönchtum im Zeitalter des Barock', in G. von Knorre (ed.), *Barock in Baden-Württemberg* (exhibition catalogue and articles) (2 vols, Karlsruhe, 1981), vol. II, p. 358.

92 Dickson, *Finance and Government*, vol. I, p. 446.

93 K.J. Benz, 'Zu den kulturpolitischen Hintergründen der Säkularisation von 1803', *Saeculum*, 26 (1975), pp. 372–3 and the notes to 373 and 376. Benz says (373n) that no overall figures exist but quotes (376n) for 'Westphalia' 228 monasteries with 3,802 inmates and (it seems, additionally) 30 mendicant houses with 1,237 (!) inmates. For Bavaria he cites (373) 183 houses, not including Kollegiatsstifte; for Württemberg 89 and, given to Prussia by way of compensation, 117, but with no figures for inmates. No indication is given whether any were nunneries. Presumably there is overlap between Westphalia and compensation for Prussia. In consequence 10,000 seems a modest estimate for the number of monks (? and nuns). Benz also contributed the section on German secularizations in DIP, giving confusingly different figures: in Baden 105 houses of which 68 were nunneries, in Cologne 42 houses of which 32 were nunneries, and more than 50 nunneries in addition to the 183 in Bavaria.

94 R. Büttner, *Die Säkularisation der Kölner Geistlichen Institutionen* (Cologne, 1971), pp. 400, 410; for Austria Dickson, 'Joseph II's reshaping of the Austrian Church', and my article in Aston, *Religious Change*; for Bavaria see Weis, 'Säkularisation'.

3 FRANCE

1. Evans, *Monastic Architecture*. See esp. pp. xi–xii. Cf. Bazin, *Paläste des Glaubens*, vol. I, p. 148.
2. McManners, *Church and Society*.
3. Plongeron, *Les réguliers de Paris*, esp. pp. 60–72.
4. L. Lecestre, *Abbayes, prieurés et couvents d'hommes en France: liste générale d'après les papiers de la Commission des Réguliers en 1768* (Paris, 1902).
5. The excellent discussion by Julia in Boutry et al., *Du roi Très Chrétien*, pp. 183–90, insists on the 1730s as the peak, but the information he gives seems to support the more usual stress on the 1740s. The totals of nuns are especially uncertain: see O.H. Hufton, *Women and the Limits of Citizenship in the French Revolution* (London, 1992). For comparisons with other countries see pp. 2–3, 121, 125, 130, ch. 8, p. 316.
6. P. Lavedan, *French Architecture* (Harmondsworth, 1956), p. 96.
7. A. Babeau, *Paris en 1789* (Paris, n.d.), p. 253; McManners, *Church and Society*, vol. I, pp. 491, 493; J. Taralon, *La France des abbayes* (Paris, 1978), esp. p. 188. These figures must include the commendatory abbot's or abbess's large revenues, which were generally spent outside the monastery. See pp. 104–6.
8. See pp. 42–4, 55. I have used the conversion rate of 2.6 florins = 1 livre.
9. McManners, *Church and Society*, vol. I, pp. 97–9, 116–17.
10. Ibid. vol. I, pp. 97, 122–40, 325–7. Cf. P. Goubert, *The Ancien Régime: French Society, 1600–1750* (London, 1973), esp. pp. 122–6. On the Premonstratensians X. Lavagne d'Ortigue, 'La vocation prémontrée à l'époque des lumières', J. de Viguerie (ed.), in *La vocation religieuse et sacerdotale en France, XVII–XIX siècles* (Angers, 1979), p. 52.
11. McManners, *Church and Society*, vol. I, p. 99.
12. Ibid. p. 583.
13. Ibid. pp. 50, 509.
14. E. Burke, *Reflections on the Revolution in France* [1790] (Everyman edn, London, 1910), p. 188.
15. See, e.g., F. Rapp (ed.), *Histoire du diocèse de Strasbourg* (Paris, 1982), pp. 141–3, 158–63.
16. See, e.g., M. Ultee, *The Abbey of St. Germain des Prés in the Seventeenth Century* (London, 1981), pp. 3–6.
17. R. Venture, *L'abbaye de Montmajour: Le temps retrouvé* (Barbentane, 1995), pp. 69–75.
18. R. Knox, *Enthusiasm* (London, 1950), chs. IX and X; McManners, *Church and Society*, vol. II, pp. 391–4; Boutry, *Du roi Très Chrétien*, pp. 20–1; L. Perey, *Histoire d'une grande dame au XVIIIe siècle: la Princesse Hélène de Ligne* (17th edn, Paris, 1892), pp. 158–63.
19. The story is brilliantly told in Chateaubriand's *Vie de Rancé* [1844], ed. G. Condominas (Paris, 1991).
20. See, for a detailed study of this cult in one country, G. Tüskés and E. Knapp, 'Der Kult der Katakombenheiligen in Ungarn', *Ungarn-Jahrbuch*, 19 (1991), pp. 67–88. I am grateful to the authors for supplying me with a copy of this fascinating piece.
21. This paragraph is largely based on D. Knowles, *The Historian and Character and Other Essays* (Cambridge, 1963), 'Jean Mabillon', pp. 213–39.
22. Viguerie, *La vocation religieuse*, p. 56, and Plongeron, *Les réguliers de Paris*, esp. pp. 66–72.
23. Lavagne d'Ortigue in Viguerie, *La vocation religieuse*, p. 56.
24. Evans, *Monastic Architecture*, pp. 33–4.

25 Cf. P. Dubuisson, Brantôme (Rennes, 1995), and Evans, Monastic Architecture, p. 19.
26 Bazin, Paläste des Glaubens, vol. I, pp. 170–4.
27 Ultee, St. Germain, pp. 87–8.
28 E. Martin (ed.), J.B. Kléber architecte, 1784–1792 (Colmar, 1986).
29 McManners, Church and Society, vol. I, ch. 15, while entitled 'The great chapters', has some references to monastic music, e.g. pp. 459, 461, 466, 468.
30 I would support this generalisation, rather precariously, by the chronological distribution of Joan Evans's photographs, which suggest a slow and steady increase between 1600 and 1790, though there were difficult periods like the Fronde and (perhaps) the later wars of Louis XIV.
31 Bazin, Paläste des Glaubens, vol. I, p. 146.
32 McManners, Church and Society, vol. I, pp. 13–14, 524–5.
33 On Laugier W. Hermann, Laugier and Eighteenth Century French Theory (London, 1962). Laugier ceased to be a Jesuit soon after publishing his Essay.
34 See on the Panthéon and other early manifestations of neo-classicism in church architecture Bazin, Paläste des Glaubens, vol. I, pp. 174–8, and W. Kalnein and M. Levey, Art and Architecture of the Eighteenth Century in France (Harmondsworth, 1972), esp. pp. 300–1, 317–23.
35 Hermann, Laugier and Eighteenth Century French Theory.
36 Cf. Kalnein in Art and Architecture of the Eighteenth Century in France, p. 344, on 'Romantic Classicism', which he accepts as the equivalent of 'Revolutionary Architecture' while adding: 'it must be emphasized that the great ideas behind Revolutionary Architecture arose almost without exception under Louis XVI; the Revolution itself made no contribution to them.' There's logic for you.
37 Lavedan, French Architecture, p. 224.
38 Bosher, The French Revolution, pp. 89–90.
39 Ultee, St. Germain, ch. 11.
40 McManners, Church and Society, vol. II, p. 120; P. and M.-L. Biver, Abbayes, monastères et couvents de Paris des origines à la fin du XVIIIe siècle (Paris, 1970), pp. 136–8.
41 Biver, Abbayes, monastères et couvents de Paris, pp. 134–5; Bazin, Paläste des Glaubens, vol. I, pp. 162–3.
42 McManners, Church and Society, vol. I, pp. 537–8.
43 Ibid. p. 505.
44 Lavagne d'Ortigue in Viguerie, La vocation religieuse, pp. 55–6.
45 See O. Hufton, The Prospect before Her (London, 1995), esp. pp. 366–96.
46 Perey, Histoire d'une grande dame, p. 15. This book is the basis of this whole section. The next two paragraphs depend on the Appendix, pp. 455–63.
47 Ibid. pp. 146–50. Cf. McNamara, Sisters in Arms, p. 537.
48 McManners, Church and Society, vol. I, p. 47; Bazin, Paläste des Glaubens, vol. I, p. 158.
49 Bazin, Paläste des Glaubens, vol. I, pp. 159, 161. Among many sources on these salons I have found useful E.H.F. Mills (ed.), Mlle de Lespinasse: Love Letters to and from the Comte de Guibert (London, 1929).
50 See L.S. Greenbaum, Talleyrand, Statesman-Priest: The Agent-General of the Clergy and the Church of France at the End of the Old Regime (Washington, DC, 1970), esp. ch. 11.

51 Cf. H.M. Scott, 'The rise of the first minister in eighteenth-century Europe', in T.C.W. Blanning and D.N. Cannadine (ed.), *History and Biography* (Cambridge, 1996), esp. pp. 43–4.
52 See, e.g., Ladurie, *The Ancien Regime*, pp. 383–6; Greenbaum, *Talleyrand*, pp. 83–4.
53 McManners, *Church and Society*, vol. I, p. 476.
54 Ibid. pp. 477–8.
55 The classic account is W. Doyle, *Venality* (Oxford, 1996).
56 Evans, *Monastic Architecture*, p. 29. J. Bergin, *Cardinal de La Rochefoucauld: Leadership and Reform in the French Church* (London, 1987), pp. 140–1, is especially informative on the pernicious side-effects of the system. For Burke's defence of it see p. 314.
57 J.M. Hayden, *France and the Estates-General of 1614* (Cambridge, 1974), pp. 88–94.
58 Greenbaum, *Talleyrand*, pp. 28–9.
59 C.M. Northeast, *The Parisian Jesuits and the Enlightenment, 1700–1762* (Oxford, 1991), p. 18. I am grateful to Professor T.C.W. Blanning for the very extended loan of this work.
60 See Evans, *Monastic Architecture*, ch. VII, for the whole paragraph, and for the Cordeliers, pp. 114–17; Biver, *Abbayes, monastères et couvents de Paris*, pp. 267–86. On the Franciscans in general, Holzapfel, *Handbuch der Geschichte des Franziskanerordens*.
61 Cf. G. and M. Duchet-Suchaux, *Les ordres religieux: guide historique* (Paris, 1993), pp. 70–1. For numbers of Capuchin monks I have leaned on Dompnier, *Enquête au pays des frères des anges*, ch. 7, whose careful enquiry into the defective statistics of the province of Lyon casts doubt on the reliability of the global figures to be found in other works. See also his pp. 54–61 on the life of Capuchins.
62 See Evans, *Monastic Architecture*, ch. VIII, esp. p. 128; McManners, *Church and Society*, vol. II, ch. 42.
63 Châtellier, *Europe of the Devout*, is essentially a study of these congregations.
64 L.W.B. Brockliss, *French Higher Education in the Seventeenth and Eighteenth Centuries: A Cultural History* (Oxford, 1987), esp. concluding chapter.
65 Northeast, *Parisian Jesuits*, esp. ch. 1.
66 T. Besterman, *Voltaire* (London, 1969), p. 43.
67 Cf. A.M. Wilson, *Diderot* (Oxford, 1972), esp. pp. 152–5, and Northeast, *Parisian Jesuits*, esp. pp. 52–4.
68 Lebrun, *Histoire des catholiques en France*, esp. pp. 133–4, 179, 186–8.
69 Ibid. pp. 166–71.
70 See p. 31.
71 E. Rapley, *The Dévotes: Women and Church in Seventeenth-Century France* (London, 1990), McManners, *Church and Society*, vol. I, pp. 538–42; C. Ferrazzi, *Autobiography of an Aspiring Saint* (London, 1996); and E. Catta, *La Visitation Sainte-Marie de Nantes (1630–1792)* (Paris, 1954).
72 McManners, *Church and Society*, vol. I, pp. 558–70; Duchet-Suchaux, *Les ordres religieux*, pp. 144–6; Hufton, *Women and the Limits of Citizenship*, ch. II.
73 McManners, *Church and Society*, vol. I, p. 545.
74 Ibid. vol. I, pp. 472–3, 545–50. But see n. 9, p. 317.
75 For Voltaire's view, J. McManners, 'Voltaire and the monks', in W.J. Sheils (ed.), *Monks, Hermits and the Ascetic Tradition* (Oxford, 1985) (Studies in Church History, vol. 22), p. 326.
76 See ch. 9 and Conclusion.

4 SPAIN AND PORTUGAL

1. R. Tombs, *France, 1814–1914* (Harlow, 1996).
2. Cf. Bazin, *Paläste des Glaubens*, where Spain and Portugal receive short shrift partly because of the arbitrary exclusion of mendicant and later Orders; C. Norberg-Schulz, *Late Baroque and Rococo Architecture* (London, 1986) offers a contemptible half-page, p. 174. Blunt, *Baroque and Rococo*, is somewhat fuller but includes Latin American with Iberian architecture. More satisfactory is R. Toman (ed.), *Baroque: Architecture, Sculpture, Painting* (Cologne, 1998), and, in its way, Lees-Milne, *Baroque in Spain and Portugal*.
3. On general aspects of early modern Spanish history I have chiefly used J. Lynch, *Spain under the Habsburgs* (2nd edn, London, 1981), and J.H. Elliott, *Imperial Spain, 1469–1716* (London, 1963); on Portugal, A.H. de Oliveira Marques, *History of Portugal* (2 vols., London, 1972). Dr Peter Linehan has been most generous in giving me advice on Spanish church history and putting me in touch with some of its leading practitioners.
4. For Iberian church history, in addition to the works mentioned in n. 3, R. García-Villoslada (ed.), *Historia de la Iglesia en España* (5 vols., Madrid, 1978–80), vol. IV; O. Chadwick, *The Reformation* (Harmondsworth, 1964); Callahan, 'The Spanish Church', and Higgs, 'The Portuguese Church', in Callahan and Higgs, *Church and Society*.
5. There is a fine general book on the history of the old Orders in Spain: A. Linage Conde, *El monacato en España e Hispanoamerica* (Salamanca, 1977). I owe my knowledge of this book and many valuable indications about Spanish monastic history to Professor Antonio García y García of Salamanca.
6. P.N. Palacio, *Monasterios de España*, vol. I (5th edn, Madrid, 1988), pp. 16–17.
7. A.G. Sanz & M.L. Sánchez Hernández, *The Convents of Las Descalzas Reales and La Encarnación (Two Cloistered Convents in Madrid)* (Madrid, 1999).
8. García-Villoslada, *Historia*, vol. IV, pp. 33–4.
9. Ibid. pp. 21–2.
10. See Palacio, *Monasterios*, under the relevant monasteries; Linage Conde, *El monacato en España*, pp. 268–9; for the Hieronymites, pp. 425–71. The Premonstratensians never had many houses in Spain and were eventually subsumed into the Hieronymites.
11. See Hsia, *World of Catholic Renewal*, p. 53, and Eire, *From Madrid to Purgatory*.
12. E.g. Hermann, *L'église d'Espagne*, esp. pp. 23–4.
13. In addition to the works already cited by Linage Conde, García-Villoslada and Marques see J.L. Espinel, *San Esteban de Salamanca: historia y Guía* (2nd edn, Salamanca, 1995); A.A.B Andrade (ed.), *Dicionário de história da Igreja em Portugal* (Lisbon, vol. I, 1979, vol. II, 1983), esp. distribution maps for Augustinian (vol. I, p. 74) and Benedictine (vol. II, p. 320) houses. I have not been able to find later volumes of this work.
14. Figures from García-Villoslada, *Historia*, vol. IV, p. 21; R. Guerra de la Vega, *Iglesias y Conventos del Antiguo Madrid* (Madrid, 1966) (my calculation). Higher figures are often given, e.g. for Seville, where A.L. López Martínez, *La economía de las órdenes religiosas en el antiguo régimen* (Seville, 1992), p. 36, cites seventy and Callahan in Callahan and Higgs, *Church and Society*, p. 37, eighty-four.
15. Callahan in Callahan and Higgs, *Church and Society*, p. 44.
16. See the works cited in n. 2.
17. Linage Conde, *El monacato en España*, p. 389.

18 On the Escorial Palacio, *Monasterios*, pp. 104–35; Braunfels, *Monasteries*, pp. 196–200; Bazin, *Paläste des Glaubens*, vol. I, pp. 98–110; Toman, *Baroque*, pp. 80–91; M.J. Noone, *Music and Musicians in the Escorial Liturgy under the Habsburgs, 1563–1700* (Woodbridge, 1998).

19 W. Beckford, *The History of the Caliph Vathek; and European Travels* (London, 1891), pp. 440–1. On the whole paragraph see Eire, *From Madrid to Purgatory*.

20 Martínez, *La economía de las órdenes religiosas*, p. 36.

21 García-Villoslada, *Historia*, vol. IV, pp. 18–19, 55, 71. Writers in this volume refer to the figures of J. Saez Marin, *Datos sobre la Iglesia española contemporanea, 1768–1868* (Madrid, 1975), without making it clear why the latter are distinctly lower.

22 Martínez, *La economía de las órdenes religiosas*, esp. pp. 44, 110.

23 R. Herr, *The Eighteenth Century Revolution in Spain* (Princeton, 1958), p. 108.

24 J. Townshend, *A Journey through Spain in the years 1786 and 1787* (3 vols., London, 1791), esp. vol. I, p. 378; vol. II, pp. 84, 225.

25 Lees-Milne, *Baroque in Spain and Portugal*, p. 141.

26 Conde, *El monacato de España*, pp. 225–9.

27 Marques, *History of Portugal*, vol. I, pp. 285–7, 398–9; but the statistical basis of these claims is flimsy (see below and n. 34).

28 Marques, *History of Portugal*, vol. I, pp. 389–94; D. Alden, *The Making of an Enterprise: The Society of Jesus in Portugal, Its Empire, and Beyond, 1540–1750* (Stanford, 1996), ch. 23.

29 Bazin, *Paläste des Glaubens*, vol. I, pp. 89–109; Lees-Milne, *Baroque in Spain and Portugal*, pp. 179–89; L.F. da Gama, *Palácio nacional de Mafra* (Lisbon, 1992). B. Borngässer in Toman, *Baroque*, pp. 113, 116, declares that John V died in 1755 instead of 1750 and that the palace of Mafra was never inhabited, which is nonsense. I am grateful to Dr Jon Parry for obtaining a copy of Gama for me.

30 Quoted in K. Maxwell, *Pombal: Paradox of the Enlightenment* (Cambridge, 1995), p. 17.

31 Marques, *History of Portugal*, vol. I, pp. 401–2.

32 See pp. 150, 153.

33 Higgs, in Callahan and Higgs, *Church and Society*, pp. 54–5. Cf. S.J. Miller, *Portugal and Rome c. 1748–1830: An Aspect of Catholic Enlightenment* (Rome, 1978), p. 257. The total population of Portugal is estimated at approximately 2,500,000 in 1750.

34 Marques, *History of Portugal*, vol. I, pp. 398–9; Andrade, *Dicionário*, vol. I, p. 104; Gama, *Mafra*, p. 20.

35 Andrade, *Dicionário*, vol. II, p. 702, and the very important article of F. de Sousa, 'O rendimento das ordens religiosas nos finais do antigo regime', *Revista de História Económica e Social*, 7 (1981), pp. 1–28, which demonstrates the unreliability of standard estimates and also shows that monastic incomes in general rose between 1750 and the 1820s.

36 F. de Almeida, *História da Igreja em Portugal*, vol. III (new edn, Lisbon, 1970), pp. 138–9.

5 ITALY

1 A. de Montesquieu (ed.), *Voyages de Montesquieu* (2 vols., Paris, 1894), vol. I, pp. 153–4.

2 R. Rusconi, 'Gli Ordini religiosi maschili', in Rosa, *Clero e società nell'Italia moderna*, p. 239n. On eighteenth-century Italy generally Chadwick, *Popes and Revolution*; D. Carpanetto and

G. Ricuperati, *Italy in the Age of Reason, 1685–1789* (London, 1987); F. Venturi's vast *Settecento riformatore* (5 vols. (7 tomes), Turin, 1965–90).

3   See Boaga, *La soppressione innocenziana*, esp. table on p. 150 and pp. 48–9.

4   Ibid. p. 152; G. Fragnito in Rosa, *Clero e società nell'Italia moderna*, p. 140. On eighteenth-century Italian monasticism generally, as well as Rosa's collection, his article 'The Italian Churches', in Callahan and Higgs, *Church and Society*; C. Donati, 'La chiesa di Roma tra antico regime e riforme settecentesche', in Chittolini and Miccoli, *La chiesa e il potere politico*, p. 757; G. Penco, 'Aspetti e caratteri del monachesimo nel Settecento italiano', in Farnedi and Spinelli, *Settecento monastico italiano*, pp. 13–33. For population figures Carpanetto and Ricuperati, *Italy in the Age of Reason*, ch. 1.

5   Scolopi is the usual Italian name, Piarists the German usage. See M. Rosa, 'Spiritualità mistica e insegnamento popolare', in G. de Rosa, T. Gregory and A. Vauchez, *Storia dell'Italia religiosa*, vol. II: *L'età moderna* (Rome and Bari, 1994), pp. 287–302.

6   Chadwick, *Popes and Revolution*, esp. pp. 65–6, 231–2.

7   Rosa, *Clero e società nell'Italia moderna*, p. 126n; F. Strazzullo, *Edilizia e urbanistica a Napoli dal '500 al '700* (2nd edn, Naples, 1995), p. 313.

8   Chittolini and Miccoli, *La chiesa e il potere politico*, p. 421. In Florence 'between 1500 and 1799, 46 per cent of the women in a sample of twenty-one patrician families entered the convent': Evangelisti, 'Wives, widows, and brides of Christ: Marriage and the convent in the historiography of early modern Italy', *HJ* (2000), pp. 241–2 and n.

9   Figures for Rome and Naples brought together from Chittolini and Miccoli, *La chiesa e il potere politico*, pp. 577–86; Chadwick, *Popes and Revolution*, pp. 212–13; Strazzullo, *Edilizia*, p. 313; H. Gross, *Rome in the Age of Enlightenment* (Cambridge, 1990), pp. 67–70.

10 G. Cozzi, M. Knapton and G. Scarabello, *La repubblica di Venezia nell'età moderna* (Turin, 1992), p. 635; C. Zaghi, *L'Italia giacobina* (Turin, 1989), p. 20.

11 Zaghi, *L'Italia giacobina*, pp. 20–1; Villani, *La vendita dei beni dello Stato nel regno di Napoli*, p. 37; E. Stumpo, 'Il consolidamento della grande proprietà ecclesiastica', in Chittolini and Miccoli, *La chiesa e il potere politico*, esp. pp. 271–82, 288–9. T. Fanfani, 'Chiese e monasteri del territorio in età moderna', in G. Borelli (ed.), *Chiese e monasteri nel territorio veronese* (Verona, 1981), pp. 239–46, argues that in these Venetian lands monastic property amounted to only 3 per cent of the total, having declined in real value.

12 Chadwick, *Popes and Revolution*, p. 99.

13 Fragnito in Rosa, *Clero e società nell'Italia moderna*, pp. 125–6.

14 Rosa in Callahan and Higgs, *Church and Society*, p. 67; p. 7 above.

15 Donati, 'La chiesa di Roma tra antico regime e riforme settecentesche', p. 758.

16 For this paragraph Rosa, *Clero e società nell'Italia moderna*, esp. Fragnito's chapter. A. Torre's fascinating article, 'Politics cloaked in worship: state, church and local power in Piedmont 1570–1770', *Past and Present*, 134 (1992), pp. 42–92, while it is full of interesting examples of the tension between parishes and religious associations of various kinds, leaves one bemused by its determination to consider them almost exclusively in relation to state power and the influence of local elites and by its astounding failure even to mention monasteries.

17 M. Rosa, 'La Chiesa meridionale nell'età della Controriforma', in Chittolini and Miccoli, *La chiesa e il potere politico*.

18 C. Cattaneo, *Notizie naturali e civili su la Lombardia* (2 vols., Milan, 1844), vol. I, p. xci.

19 Cf. L. Sebastiani, 'I monasteri milanesi nel periodo teresiano', in A. de Maddalena, E. Rotelli and G. Barbarisi (eds.), *Economia, istituzioni, cultura in Lombardia nell'età di Maria Teresa* (3 vols., Milan, 1982–), vol. I, pp. 205–19. On Italian nunneries more generally, G. Zarri, 'Monasteri femminili e città (secoli XV–XVIII)', in Chittolini and Miccoli, *La chiesa e il potere politico*, pp. 359–434.

20 M. Laven, 'Sex and celibacy in early modern Venice', HJ, 44 (2001), pp. 865–88, quotation from p. 873.

21 J. Rosselli, *Singers of Italian Opera: The History of a Profession* (Cambridge, 1992), esp. pp. 94–7.

22 See G.P. Carosi, *I monasteri di Subiaco* (Subiaco 1987), esp. pp. 171–3.

23 Cf. Pincelli, *Monasteri e conventi*, esp. pp. 8–14.

24 See p. 31.

25 Strazzullo, *Edilizia*, pp. 201–4.

26 On the scale and inconvenience of monastic building see ibid. On Santa Chiara Bazin, *Paläste des Glaubens*, vol. I, pp. 62–4.

27 There are hints on these lines in the collection *Arte e religione nella Firenze de' Medici* (Florence, 1980), the product of a conference organised under the auspices of the Basilica S. Croce. See Carosi, *Monasteri di Subiaco*, pp. 127–45.

28 Carosi, *Monasteri di Subiaco*, pp. 175–6.

29 In general and on Lecce and Catania Bazin, *Paläste des Glaubens*, vol. I, pp. 1–68, and Blunt, *Baroque and Rococo*, esp. pp. 70–2, 89–90, 103–6. On Superga H. Domke, in H. Schindler (ed.), *Europäische Barockklöster* (Munich, 1972), pp. 58–84; Goethe, *Italian Journey* (Harmondsworth, 1970), pp. 278–81.

30 I owe knowledge of this remarkable man to Dr J.L. Fuchs, to whom the late Dr R.C. Smail introduced me, who gave me a copy of his article 'An encyclopaedist among the minori conventuali: the policy and educational reforms of Vincenzo Coronelli', *Journal of Religious History*, 14 (1986), pp. 152–66.

31 On Martini see H.E. Poole (ed.), *Music, Men, and Manners in France and Italy 1770* (London, 1969), an edition of Burney's Tour.

32 See the entry for Bianchi in the *Dizionario biografico degli italiani*, ed. A.M. Ghisalberti et al. (58 vols. to date, Rome, 1960–), vol. X, pp. 132–9, and G. Orlandi, 'Monaci e massoneria nel settecento italiano', in F.G.B. Trolese (ed.), *Il monachesimo italiano dalle riforme illuministiche all'unità nazionale (1768–1870)* (Cesena, 1992), pp. 564–6. On Italian monastic learning generally, M. Mazzucotelli, 'Monaci scienziati a docenti universitari', in the same volume, pp. 531–54.

33 X. Toscani, in Chittolini and Miccoli, *La chiesa e il potere politico*, p. 592.

6 THE SUPPRESSION OF THE JESUITS

1 Cf. pp. 36–8, 68–9, 72–3, 80–1, 181–3.

2 See p. 154.

3 Cf. pp. 123–4.

4 See pp. 94–6.

5 Cf. Schlögl, *Glaube und Religion*; L. Châtellier (ed.), *Religions en transition dans la seconde moitié du dix-huitième siècle* (Oxford, 2000). See ch. 2.

6 A.M. Wilson, *Diderot* (Oxford, 1972), esp. ch. 6; T. Besterman, *Voltaire* (London, 1969), esp. chs. 20, 22; pp. 103–4.
7 Viguerie, *La vocation religieuse*; Boutry et al., *Du roi Très Chrétien*, pp. 183–90; and see pp. 91, 107–8, 128.
8 M. Vovelle, *Piété baroque et déchristianisation en Provence au XVIIIᵉ siècle: les attituds devant la mort d'après les clauses des testaments* (Paris, 1973); Schlögl, *Glaube und Religion*; Pammer, *Glaubensabfall und Wahre Andacht*.
9 See, e.g., Blanning, *Reform and Revolution in Mainz*; H.M. Scott (ed.), *Enlightened Absolutism: Reform and Reformers in Later Eighteenth-Century Europe* (Basingstoke and London, 1990).
10 R. Shackleton, *Montesquieu* (Oxford, 1961), chs. XVII–XVIII; M. Cottret, *Jansénismes et lumières* (Paris, 1998), pp. 51–72; E.H. Balázs, *Hungary and the Habsburgs, 1765–1800* (Budapest, 1997), p. 134.
11 J. Lough, *The Contributors to the Encyclopédie* (London, 1973); R. Shackleton, *The 'Encyclopédie' and the Clerks* (Oxford, 1970). One of the contributors to the four-volume supplement was Dom Nicolas Casbois, prior successively of the abbeys of Beaulieu (Argonne) and St-Symphorien, Metz, who wrote on scientific instruments (Lough, *Contributors*, p. 106).
12 On the general story of the *Encyclopédie* see Lough, *Contributors*; Wilson, *Diderot*; R. Darnton, *The Business of Enlightenment* (Cambridge, Mass., 1968).
13 R. Mauzi and S. Menant, *Littérature française: le XVIIIᵉ siècle*, vol. II: 1750–88 (Paris, 1977), p. 243. Cf. Cottret, *Jansénismes et lumières*, pp. 83–6.
14 For this paragraph in general see, in addition to Mauzi and Menant, *Littérature française*, Besterman, *Voltaire*, chs. 32–4; Cottret, *Jansénismes et lumières*, ch. 3.
15 See, e.g., Blanning's books, *Reform and Revolution in Mainz*; *The French Revolution in Germany* (Oxford, 1983); *Joseph II*.
16 See pp. 36–8, 68–9, 72–3, 80–1, 181–3. Cf. Cottret, *Jansénismes et lumières*, p. 111: 'Nous envisageons généralement le siècle des Lumières comme une conquête progressive... Ce schéma rassurant ne correspond pas à la chronologie des relations entre monde des Lumières et jansénistes.'
17 See G. Vidan, *Rudjer Boskovic* (Zagreb, 1983), a rare book which I am grateful to have been given.
18 Probably the best account in English is to be found in Pastor, *History of the Popes*, vols. XXXVI and XXXVII. See also the admirable survey in Chadwick, *Popes and Revolution*, ch. 5. A very good short account by a liberal modern Jesuit is to be found in Martina, *La chiesa nell' età dell' assolutismo*.
19 See Châtellier, *Europe of the Devout*, esp. pp. 70–88, 181–3, 190–4.
20 See for one instance Beales, *Joseph II*, vol. I, pp. 449–50.
21 Cf. Chadwick, *Popes and Revolution*; O. Hufton, 'The widow's mite and other strategies: funding the Catholic Reformation', *TRHS*, 6th series, 8 (1998), pp. 117–37; and Cottret, *Jansénismes et lumières*, pp. 123–32.
22 See, e.g., D. Van Kley, *The Jansenists and the Expulsion of the Jesuits from France, 1757–1765* (London, 1975), pp. 70–1; G. Klingenstein, *Staatsverwaltung und kirchliche Autorität im 18. Jahrhundert: Das Problem der Zensur in der theresianischen Reform* (Vienna, 1970), pp. 106–7.
23 Carpanetto and Ricuperati, *Italy in the Age of Reason*, p. 93.
24 Cf. Martina, *La chiesa nell'età dell'assolutismo*, pp. 223–4.
25 On the Portuguese story in general see pp. 122–5. For the Portuguese suppression Marques, *History of Portugal*, esp. vol. I, ch. 8. The best account of Pombal's ecclesiastical policies is in

26 D. Alden, *The Making of an Enterprise: The Society of Jesus in Portugal, Its Empire and Beyond, 1540–1750* (Stanford, 1996), p. 605.
27 Pastor, *History of the Popes*, vol. XXXVI, p. 4.
28 For this paragraph see Oliveira Marques, *History of Portugal*, vol. I, esp. pp. 359–68; C.R. Boxer, *The Portuguese Seaborne Empire, 1415–1825* (Harmondsworth, 1973), ch. 7; and Maxwell, *Pombal*, esp. ch. 2. The disputed lands are now divided between Argentina, Uruguay and Paraguay.
29 As well as Maxwell, *Pombal*, pp. 3–10 see the essays on Pombal and Freemasonry and on Pombal in Austria in M.H. Carvalho dos Santos (ed.), *Pombal revisitado* (2 vols., Lisbon, 1984), esp. vol. I, pp. 63–4, 415–37. I share the doubts of M.A.R. Correia Afonso dos Santos, expressed in the latter article, that Pombal's specific policies owed much to his Austrian experience. See my comments on Maria Theresa's ecclesiastical policies, pp. 183–92.
30 Maxwell, *Pombal*, p. 53.
31 For this and subsequent paragraphs on the Portuguese suppression see Maxwell, *Pombal*, ch. 4; Miller, *Portugal and Rome*, chs. 3 and 4; Pastor, *History of the Popes*, vol. XXXVI, pp. 1–23; Chadwick, *Popes and Revolution*, pp. 347–53.
32 R. Macaulay, *They Went to Portugal* (London, 1946), pp. 203–6, 271.
33 For this point Miller, *Portugal and Rome*, pp. 44–6.
34 For this quotation, and on the importance of Pombal's publicity campaign, see Venturi, *Settecento riformatore*, vol. II, ch. 1, esp. p. 12n.
35 See DIP, vol. II, cols. 134–6. In 1777 they were subsumed into the Maltese Order.
36 Miller, *Portugal and Rome*, pp. 259–70. Pombal took over much of Gerbert's *Principia theologiae canonicae*.
37 B.M. Caeiro, *OS conventos de Lisboa* (Lisbon, 1989), passim. M.A.L.P. da T. Ferreira, *Mosteira de Santa Maria de Alcobaça* (2nd edn, Lisbon, 1987), p. 22. I am grateful to Dr Jon Parry for supplying me with a copy of this guidebook.
38 W. Beckford, *The History of the Caliph Vathek; and European Travels* (London, 1891), pp. 358–61.
39 There is only one grudging (and inaccurate) reference to the Portuguese case in the otherwise admirable Cottret, *Jansénismes et lumières*. McManners, *Church and Society*, vol. II, ch. 43, valuable though it is, is scarcely more ready to consider Portugal's influence. Chaunu et al., *Le basculement religieux de Paris au XVIIIe siècle*, ignores it.
40 Van Kley, *Jansenists and the Expulsion of the Jesuits*, p. 87.
41 This account of the suppression in France is chiefly based on Van Kley, ibid., and his more recent *Religious Origins of the French Revolution*, esp. ch. 3; McManners, *Church and Society*; Pastor, *History of the Popes*, vol. XXXVI, ch. 8; Cottret, *Jansénisme et lumières*, esp. ch. 4.
42 The king's edict did not apply to the 'new' provinces of France, Alsace for example, from which Jesuits were not expelled until the following year.
43 Pastor, *History of the Popes*, vol. XXXVI, p. 295n.
44 On this point, as well as the sources previously cited, F. Diaz, *Filosofia e politica nel settecento francese* (Turin, 1962), pp. 228–47.
45 See A. Mestre, 'La actitud religiosa de los catolicas ilustrados', in A. Guimerá (ed.), *El reformismo borbónico* (Madrid, 1996), esp. pp. 149–50, on the tiny group influenced by deism.

46 Generally on Spain and the Enlightenment, Herr, *Eighteenth Century Revolution*, esp. pp. 15–17, 37–43, 63; García-Villoslava, *Historia*, vol. IV, passim; J. Sarrailh, *L'Espagne éclairée de la seconde moitié du XVIIIe siècle* (Paris, 1954); C.C. Noel's chapter in Scott, *Enlightened Absolutism*.

47 R. Guerra, *La corte española del siglo XVIII* (2nd edn, Madrid, 1998), p. 15.

48 See Pastor, *History of the Popes*, vol. XXXV; the documents printed in García-Villoslava, *Historia*, vol. IV, pp. 797–808; Hermann, *L'église d'Espagne*, esp. pp. 12–13.

49 García-Villoslava, *Historia*, vol. IV, passim; Hermann, *L'église d'Espagne*, pp. 221–52.

50 See D.A. Brading, *Church and State in Bourbon Mexico* (Cambridge, 1994), ch. 6. I am most grateful to Professor Brading for illuminating conversations on this and related themes.

51 On Charles III generally, Lynch, *Bourbon Spain*; Noel in Scott, *Enlightened Absolutism*; Guerra, *La corte española*; H. Pietschmann's essay in W.L. Bernecker, C.C. Seidel and P. Hoser (ed.), *Die spanischen Könige* (Munich, 1997). I am most grateful to Dr Seidel for giving me a copy of the latter. On the ecclesiastical affairs of the early part of the reign Venturi, *Settecento riformatore*, vol. II, ch. 3.

52 Brading, *Church and State in Bourbon Mexico*, ch. 1.

53 Guerra, *Iglesias y Conventos del Antiguo Madrid*, pp. 104–9.

54 Herr, *Eighteenth Century Revolution*, pp. 18–19. Venturi, *Settecento riformatore*, vol. II, contains much on the influence of Campomanes's writing outside Spain.

55 See for this section T. Egido & I. Pinmedo, *Las causas 'gravissimas' y secretas de la expulsión de los Jesuitas por Carlos III* (Madrid, 1994), esp. ch. 1.

56 See esp. T. Egido's chapter on the expulsion in García-Villoslada, *Historia*, vol. IV; and J.A. Ferrer Benimeli's bibliographical article in Guimerá, *El reformismo borbónico*; R. Herr, *Rural Change and Royal Finances in Spain at the End of the Old Regime* (London, 1989), p. 44.

57 García-Villoslada, *Historia*, vol. IV, pp. 203–5; Hermann, *L'église d'Espagne*, p. 317; cf. C. de Castro, 'Campomanes y el clero regular', in G. Anes et al., *Carlos III y la Ilustración* (3 vols., Madrid, 1989), vol. I, pp. 467–85. Cf. p. 151.

58 J.A. Ferrer Benimeli, 'Carlos III y la extinción de los jesuitas', in Anes et al., *Carlos III y la Ilustración*, vol. I, pp. 239–59.

59 A. von Arneth, *Geschichte Maria Theresias* (10 vols., Vienna, 1863–79), vol. IX, pp. 35–40, 90–1, 550–1.

60 On the Catholic Powers' alliances, Burkhardt, *Abschied vom Religionskrieg: Der siebenjährige Krieg und die päpstliche Diplomatie* (Tübingen, 1985). On the conclave, Chadwick, *Popes and Revolution*, pp. 270–2.

61 Arneth, *Geschichte Maria Theresias*, vol. IX, pp. 91–2, 564–5; A. von Arneth and M.A. Geffroy, *Marie-Antoinette: Correspondance secrète entre Marie-Thérèse et le Cte de Mercy-Argenteau* (3 vols., 2nd edn, Paris, 1874–5), vol. I, pp. 5–6. See also Pastor, *History of the Popes*, vol. XXXVIII, esp. pp. 257–60.

62 Arneth, *Geschichte Maria Theresias*, vol. IX, pp. 118–19.

63 See Klingenstein, *Staatsverwaltung und kirchliche Autorität*. For Jesuits' work on vernacular languages and non-German cultures see, e.g., H. Marczali, *Hungary in the Eighteenth Century* (Cambridge, 1910), esp. pp. 272–7; Evans, *Making of the Habsburg Monarchy*, esp. pp. 253–5, 422–7; P. Shore, *The Eagle and the Cross* (St Louis, 2002), esp. pp. 24–6, 87–9. I' am very grateful to Dr G. Tüskés for reminding me of this aspect of their achievement and to Dr Shore for sending me a copy of his book.

64 For this paragraph, as well as Klingenstein's book, P. Hersche, *Der Spätjansenismus in Österreich* (Vienna, 1977); R. de Maio, 'Maria Teresa e i Gesuiti', *Rivista storica italiana*, 94 (1982), 435–54; A. Fournier, 'Gerard van Swieten als Censor', in his *Historische Studien und Skizzen* (Prague, 1885), pp. 113–19, 79–80.

65 For the *Letters of Joseph II* see my 'The false Joseph II', HJ, 18 (1975), pp. 467–95. Among those who quote at least one of these letters are Pastor, *History of the Popes*, vol. XXXVIII, p. 257, and F. Maaß, *Der Josephinismus* (5 vols., Vienna, 1951–61), vol. I, p. 97n.

66 On Aranda's reputation as a *philosophe* see Egido's chapter in García-Villoslada, *Historia*, vol. IV, esp. pp. 748–52.

67 Beales, *Joseph II*, vol. I, pp. 44, 46, 64, 205, 258, 318, 461–2. On the banning of Busenbaum Klingenstein, *Staatsverwaltung und kirchliche Autorität*, pp. 106–7.

68 R. Khevenhüller-Metsch and H. Schlitter, *Aus der Zeit Maria Theresias* (8 vols., Vienna, 1907–72), vol. VII, pp. 453–6.

69 Beales, *Joseph II*, vol. I, pp. 205–7.

70 F.A.J. Szabo, *Kaunitz and Enlightened Absolutism, 1753–1780* (Cambridge, 1994), pp. 241–7.

71 Maaß, *Josephinismus*, esp. vol. II, pp. 24–31, with the accompanying documents. H. Haberzettl, *Die Stellung der Exjesuiten in Politik and Kulturleben Österreichs zu Ende des 18. Jahrhunderts* (Vienna, 1973).

72 Quoted in Châtellier, *Religions en transition*, p. 41.

73 See C. de Castro, 'Campomanes'; Aranda's fulmination quoted by T. Egido in García-Villoslada, *Historia*, vol. IV, p. 790; and, for Kaunitz, pp. 185–92.

74 Sonnenfels in *Deutsches Museum 1782: Sonnenfels gesammelte Schriften* (8 vols., Vienna, 1783–7), vol. VIII, p. 329.

75 See Chadwick, *Popes and Revolution*, pp. 385–90; F. Hoffmann, *Friedrich II von Preussen und die Aufhebung der Gesellschaft Jesu* (Rome, 1969); DIP, 'Soppressioni', cols. 1831–3.

7 FRANCE: THE *COMMISSION DES RÉGULIERS*

1 Cf. Chaunu et al., *Le basculement religieux de Paris au XVIIIe siècle*, pp. 370–3.

2 D. Julia in Boutry, *Du roi Très Chrétien*, pp. 47–8; McManners, *Church and Society*, vol. I, pp. 522–6; B. Plongeron, *La vie quotidienne du clergé français au XVIIIe siècle*, (Paris, 1974), pp. 198–202; R. Chartier, M.M. Compère and D. Julia, *L'éducation en France du XVIe au XVIIIe siècle* (Paris, 1976), pp. 186–7. For the case of Vienne, R. Bony on education in R. Lauxerrois (ed.), *Vienne à la veille de la Révolution* (exhibition material, Vienne, 1989). The number of Jesuit colleges given in the sources varies, partly because some calculations exclude the less wide-ranging establishments in favour of the 105 major institutions.

3 McManners, *Church and society*, vol. I, pp. 572–3.

4 P. Chevallier, *Loménie de Brienne et l'Ordre monastique (1766–1789)* (2 vols., Paris, 1959–60), vol. I, p. 263. For the *commission des réguliers* in general Chevallier's is by far the most important study, but it is necessary to look also at earlier works which his account does not entirely supersede: J.M. Prat, *Essai historique sur la destruction des ordres religieux en France au dix-huitième siècle* (Paris, 1845); S. Lemaire, *La commission des réguliers, 1766–1780* (Paris, 1926).

5 This account of the pamphlet debate is a summary of the summary made by Prat, *Essai historique*, pp. 164–78.
6 For this and the views of the bishops Chevallier, *Loménie de Brienne*, vol. I, bk I, ch. I.
7 Ibid. vol. I, bk I, ch. 2.
8 These two quotations come from ibid. vol. II, p. 141.
9 For the monks' views ibid, esp. vol. I, bk I, chs. 3 and 4.
10 Ibid, vol. I, bk I, ch. 5
11 Ibid. vol. I, pp. 42–3.
12 Edict in Lemaire, *La commission des réguliers*, pp. 224–40.
13 McManners, *Church and Society*, vol. II, p. 614.
14 Plongeron, *La vie quotidienne*, pp. 159–60.
15 *Memoirs of Chateaubriand*, trans. Baldick, p. 62–3.
16 458 is the figure usually given, but Lemaire, *La commission des réguliers*, p. 248, says 428. Lecestre, *Abbayes, prieurés*, p. xi, gives the figure of 509 monks in the 101 houses of the suppressed Orders, i.e. five per house, but I have found no figure for the total number of monks in the 357 other suppressed houses. If their average number of inmates was also five, then there were 1,785 in total. Added to the 509, this makes 2,294. Plongeron's figure, *La vie quotidienne*, p. 158, of 509 monks for 458 houses is clearly a mistake.
17 Prat, *Essai historique*, p. xxxiv.
18 Plongeron, *Les réguliers de Paris*, pp. 66–7, has shown that the figures of the abbé Sicard, used by Lemaire, *La commission des réguliers*, pp. 213–15, and others, exaggerated the decline.
19 Plongeron, *Les réguliers de Paris*, pp. 68–72. Cf. his *La vie quotidienne*, pp. 162–7.
20 E.g. by Lemaire.
21 Edict in Prat, *Essai historique*, pp. xvi–xxvii.
22 Chevallier, *Loménie de Brienne*, vol. II, pp. 55–7.
23 Ibid. vol. I, bk III, ch. 3.

8 THE AUSTRIAN MONARCHY: THE JOSEPHIST SOLUTION

1 Parts of this chapter have much in common with my article 'Joseph II and the monasteries of Austria and Hungary', in N. Aston (ed.), *Religious Change in Europe, 1650–1914: Essays for John McManners* (Oxford, 1997), pp. 161–84, but I have modified many points in the light of my and others' recent research. The third section on Belgium is new. Professor Peter Dickson's works (see n. 4) are fundamental to this chapter, and its evolution has been made possible by his unstinting help and encouragement.
2 See my article 'Joseph II. und der Josephinismus', in H. Reinalter and H. Klueting (eds.), *Der aufgeklärte Absolutismus im europäischen Vergleich* (Vienna, 2002), pp. 35–53, for a discussion of the origins and meaning of the term.
3 For this population estimate see Dickson, *Finance and Government*, vol. I, ch. 2.
4 This and the following paragraphs lean heavily on ibid., esp. vol. I, chs. 4, 11, and pp. 103, 446, and his 'Joseph II's reshaping of the Austrian Church'.
5 These figures too mainly derive from Dickson's writings. If they appear to differ in some respects from his, it is because, first, I am including the enormous tallies for Belgium and Lombardy

and, secondly, I have sometimes brought together different sets of his figures, e.g. in working out the proportion of regulars to the population in Bohemia I have set the figure given in his *Finance and Government*, vol. I, p. 33, for the total population of the Bohemian lands – almost 4,000,000 – against the number of regulars (5,162) given for Bohemia, Moravia and Silesia on p. 95 of his article.

My figures for Lombardy come from F. Valsecchi, *L'assolutismo illuminato in Austria e Lombardia* (2 vols., 1934), vol. II, pp. 181n, 227n. His figures are for 1771, i.e. after the fall of the Jesuits: 9,557 secular priests, 5,304 monks and friars, 7,151 nuns. For Belgium I obtained from the royal archives in Brussels, through the good offices of Dr M. Isabella, an 'Etat approximatif du Personnel du Clergé tant Regulier que Seculier de la cidevant Belgique', from the Bouteville MSS (see n. 103, p. 348) and said *not* to include the houses suppressed in 1783–4. This produces (as compared with Dickson's figure of 392 *before* these suppressions (*Finance and Government*, vol. I, p. 72)) the very high total of 456 houses, 5,200 male and 4,400 female regulars, including lay brothers and sisters. Maybe it includes the houses that before the French occupation were in the prince-bishopric of Liège.

6   This is the thesis of Evans, *Making of the Habsburg Monarchy*.
7   See Beales, *Joseph II*, vol. I, pp. 465–73. Prof. G. Klingenstein's attempt to modify this picture in her article 'Modes of religious tolerance and intolerance in eighteenth-century Austria', *AHY* 24 (1993), pp. 1–16, is largely unsuccessful. The statement that 'Joseph's legislation . . . only summarized the fundamental changes that had already expanded denominational rights and liberties' (p. 15) is breath-taking. His laws permitted the establishment of Protestant and Orthodox churches and schools in the large parts of the Monarchy where such things had previously been absolutely forbidden.
8   See above, ch. 6.
9   For discussion of the influence (or lack of influence) of the French Enlightenment on Germany and Austria see the first chapter of Blanning, *Reform and Revolution in Mainz*; Porter and Teich, *The Enlightenment in National Context*; Cassirer, *The Philosophy of the Enlightenment*. See n. 50, p. 343.
10 See G. Klaniczay, 'Decline of witches and rise of vampires', *Ethnologia Europaea*, 17 (1987), pp. 165–80. Cf. E.M. Kern, 'An end to witch trials in Austria: reconsidering the Enlightened state', *AHY*, 30 (1999), pp. 159–95.
11 Cf. E. Wangermann, *The Austrian Achievement, 1700–1800* (London, 1973), esp. pp. 130–55; L. Bodi, *Tauwetter in Wien: Zur Prosa der österreichischen Aufklärung, 1781–1795* (Frankfurt, 1977); W. Heindl, *Gehorsame Rebellen: Bürokratie und Beamte in Österreich, 1780 bis 1848* (Vienna, 1990); Blanning, *Joseph II*.
12 Cf. Marczali, *Hungary in the Eighteenth Century*; Balázs, *Hungary and the Habsburgs*.
13 D.F. McKay, *Prince Eugene of Savoy* (London, 1977).
14 Recent important work that justifies this belief includes articles by J. Roegiers: 'Die Bestrebungen zur Ausbildung einer belgischen Kirche und ihre Analoge zum österreichischen (Theresianischen) Kirchensystem', in E. Kovács (ed.), *Katholische Aufklärung und Josephinismus* (Vienna, 1979), pp. 75–92; 'De jansenistische achtergronden van P.F. de Neny's streven naar een Belgische Kerk', *Bijdragen en Mededelingen met Betrekking tot de Geschiedenis der Nederlanden*, 91 (1976), pp. 429–54; 'Un Janséniste devant la Révolution: les avatars de Josse Leplat de 1787 à

15 Cf. Winter, *Josefinismus*; F. Hennings, *Und sitzet zur linken Hand* (Vienna, 1961), pp. 134–40, 331–3, 337–9.
16 See my *Joseph II*, vol. I, pp. 33, 66; Hersche, *Der Spätjansenismus in Österreich*.
17 As well as Hersche's invaluable book, there is a most useful pioneering article by F. Wehrl, 'Der "Neue Geist": Eine Untersuchung der Geistesrichtungen des Klerus in Wien von 1750–1790', *MÖSA*, 20 (1967), pp. 36–114. A valuable recent contribution, of which the author kindly sent me a copy, is W.R. Ward, 'Late Jansenism and the Habsburgs', in J.E. Bradley and D.K. Van Kley (eds.), *Religion and Politics in Enlightenment Europe* (Notre Dame, 2001), pp. 154–86.
18 Ellegast in *900 Jahre Melk*, p. 361. On Eybel see pp. 202–3.
19 N.C. Wolf, 'Am Beispiel Melk: Veränderungen der Autorfunktion der oberdeutschen Literatur des 18. Jahrhunderts', *Das achtzehnte Jahrhundert und Österreich*, 10 (1995), esp. pp. 149–51 and 151n.
20 *Österreich zur Zeit Kaiser Josephs II* (Melk, 1980), p. 592.
21 See pp. 56–8, on Kremsmünster, Tepl and Strahov.
22 Cf. Pammer, *Glaubensabfall und Wahre Andacht*, esp. pp. 151–2, 173, 194, 203.
23 J. Kallbrunner (ed.), *Kaiserin Maria Theresias politisches Testament* (Vienna, 1952), has the best text of the testament. A. Ritter von Arneth, 'Zwei Denkschriften der Kaiserin Maria Theresias', *Archiv für österreichische Geschichte*, 47 (1871), pp. 267–354, is more accessible. On the dates of the two versions see Dickson, *Finance and Government*, vol. II, p. 3n. On the constitutional reform F. Walter, *Die theresianische Staatsreform von 1749* (Vienna, 1958).
24 Kallbrunner, *Kaiserin Maria Theresias politisches Testament*, p. 38.
25 See Maaß, *Josephinismus*, vol. I, pp. 5–9, and *Der Frühjosephinismus* (Vienna, 1969); Wangermann, *The Austrian Achievement*, pp. 74–88.
26 C. von Hock and I. Bidermann, *Der österreichischer Staatsrath* (Vienna, 1879), pp. 397–8.
27 See my *Joseph II*, vol. I, esp. pp. 55–6.
28 The memorandum is printed in full in A. Ritter von Arneth (ed.), *Maria Theresia und Joseph II. Ihre Correspondenz* (3 vols., Vienna, 1867–8), vol. III, pp. 335–61.
29 Printed in full in A. Beer (ed.), 'Denkschriften des Fürsten Wenzel Kaunitz-Rietberg', *Archiv für österreichische Geschichte*, 48 (1872). See esp. pp. 107–9.
30 Maaß makes one back-handed reference to it in his article 'Vorbereitung und Anfänge des Josephinismus im amtlichen Schriftwechsel des Staatskanzlers ... mit ... Firmian, 1763 bis 1770', *MÖSA*, 1 (1948), p. 301. Dickson, 'Joseph II's reshaping of the Austrian Church', p. 97n.
31 On the mortmain legislation the remarkable survey by Carlo Montagnini, *Dell'antica legislazione italiana sulle mani morte*, written in 1770 and published in *Miscellanea di storia italiana*, 19 (1880) by L. Montagnini. On its ineffectiveness Venturi, *Settecento riformatore*, vol. II, pp. 140–2. For Joseph's permissions see HHSA, Rep. DD, Abt. A, Depeschen, vols. LV–LVII, 1779–85.
32 S. Dixon, *The Modernisation of Russia, 1676–1825* (Cambridge, 1999), pp. 67–70.
33 See pp. 151, 167, 171–5.
34 This is the great theme of much of Venturi's *Settecento riformatore*, vols. I and II. Cf. Carpanetto and Ricuperati, *Italy in the Age of Reason*, ch. 18.
35 For Beccaria's life and work see not only Venturi's work but also *Edizione nazionale delle opere di Cesare Beccaria* ed. L. Firpo (10 vols., Milan, 1984–); for Pietro Verri see Venturi again, and

C. Capra (ed.), *Pietro Verri e il suo tempo* (2 vols., Milan, 1999). I owe a special debt of gratitude to Professor Capra for sending me these and other relevant volumes.

36 See my *Joseph II*, pp. 445–50; Maaß, *Josephinismus*, vol. I.

37 As well as Venturi, *Settecento riformatore*, his *Illuministi italiani*, vol. III (Milan, 1958), pp. 563–600.

38 Venturi, *Settecento riformatore*, vol. II, pp. 116–17 and N. Till, *Mozart and the Enlightenment* (London, 1992), pp. 67–71.

39 Chadwick, *Popes and Revolution*, ch. 5. On Malta F. Ciappara, *The Roman Inquisition in Enlightened Malta* (Malta, 2000), pp. 92–6. Dr Ciappara generously sent me a copy of this book.

40 G. Schnürer, *Katholische Kirche und Kultur im 18. Jahrhundert* (Paderborn, 1941), pp. 62–3. This passage avowedly rests on V. Radonic, *Die Klosterreform in Venedig* (Sibenik, 1935), a work to which unfortunately I have not managed to obtain access.

41 See the article 'Soppressioni' in DIP; Venturi, *Settecento riformatore*, vol. II, ch. 6; G. Cozzi, M. Knapton and G. Scarabello, *La repubblica di Venezia nell'età moderna* (Turin, 1992), p. 636; G. Tabacco, *Andrea Tron (1712–1785) e la crisi dell'aristocrazia senatoria a Venezia* (Trieste, 1957); P. Vismara Chiappa, 'Il monachesimo nella politica ecclesiastica teresiano-giuseppina', in Trolese, *Il monachesimo italiano*. On Tuscany see pp. 224–5.

42 C. Capra in D. Sella and C. Capra, *Il ducato di Milano dal 1535 al 1796* (Storia d'Italia, ed. G. Galasso, vol. XI, Turin, 1984), p. 398 (19 Nov. 1768).

43 Ibid. pp. 398–400, 497 for the whole paragraph. For Galicia H. Glassl, *Das österreichische Einrichtungswerk in Galizien (1772–1790)* (Wiesbaden, 1975), pp. 135–40.

44 Beales, *Joseph II*, vol. I, pp. 456–9. See Melton, *Absolutism*.

45 Maaß, *Josefinismus*, vol. II, pp. 139–41.

46 See Beales, *Joseph II*, vol. I, pp. 450–2, and the sources there cited.

47 In 1781 Joseph took pleasure in reminding his cousin, the archbishop-elector of Trier, of the writings of Febronius, his suffragan (see G. Mohnike, 'Briefwechsel zwischen Kaiser Joseph dem Zweiten und Clemens Wenzeslaus, Churfürsten von Trier', *Zeitschrift für historische Theologie*, 4 (1834), pp. 241–90).

48 Quoted by Professor Carlo Capra, who has given me much help on these matters, in Sella and Capra, *Il ducato di Milano*, p. 493: Joseph to the pope, 15 Aug. 1782.

49 Cf. G. de Schepper, *La réorganisation des paroisses et la suppression des couvents dans les Pays-Bas autrichiens sous le règne de Joseph II* (Louvain, 1942), pp. 118–19; G. Winner, *Die Klosteraufhebungen in Niederösterreich und Wien* (Vienna, 1967), ch. IV.

50 These contrasts make it even more unlikely that Joseph was influenced by a memorandum on monastic suppressions supposedly given to him by Brienne during his visit to France in 1777. See H. Wagner, 'Die Reise Josephs II. nach Frankreich 1777 und die Reformen in Österreich', in *Österreich und Europa: Festgabe für Hugo Hantsch* (Graz, 1965), p. 226. The male Orders suppressed were the Carthusians, Camaldolese and Eremites, and the female Carmelites, Poor Clares and Capuchins.

51 For this and the previous paragraph Hock and Bidermann, *Staatsrath*, pp. 295–6.

52 Joseph to Kressel, 22 July 1782: H. Schlitter (ed.), *Pius VI. und Josef II.* (FRA, vol. XLVII/2, Vienna, 1894), pp. 147–8. Schlitter prints the draft instruction for the Ecclesiastical Commission on pp. 41–6.

53 Hock and Bidermann, *Staatsrath*, pp. 405–6, dates this to 1785, but the catalogue *Josefinische Pfarrgründungen* (see below, n. 62), p. 82, says 1783.
54 The instruction is in *Sammlung der kaiserlichen-königlichen Landesfürstlichen Gesetze und Verordnungen in Publico-Ecclesiasticis vom Jahre 1782 bis 1783* (Vienna, 1784), pp. 109–13.
55 Hock and Bidermann, *Staatsrath*, p. 415.
56 Dickson, 'Joseph II's reshaping of the Austrian Church', pp. 107–10.
57 See e.g. E. Kovács, *Ultramontanismus und Staatskirchentum im theresianisch-josephinischen Staat* (Vienna, 1975). Dr Kovács generously gave me a copy of this book.
58 Dickson, 'Joseph II's reshaping of the Austrian Church', pp. 100–5. These doubts about the official statistics have been strengthened by the careful investigations of the Hungarian suppressions by M. Velladics, 'A II. József korabeli szerzetesrendi abolício statisztikája (1782–1847)', *Századok* (1999), pp. 1259–78. See pp. 208–10.
59 Dickson, 'Joseph II's reshaping of the Austrian Church', p. 105. These figures exclude Belgium and Lombardy, but very few if any new parishes were created there.
60 Hock and Bidermann, *Staatsrath*, pp. 487–95.
61 Dickson, 'Joseph II's reshaping of the Austrian Church', esp. p. 100.
62 Cf. J. Weißensteiner in Historisches Museum der Stadt Wien, *Josephinische Pfarrgründungen in Wien* (Vienna, 1985), pp. 56–7 and the whole volume.
63 For this and the next two paragraphs see L. Raber, *Die österreichischen Franziskaner im Josefinismus* (Maria Enzersdorf, ?1983). The book does not deal with other branches of the Franciscan family, e.g. the Recollects or the Capuchins.
64 Garampi's despatch of 8 Mar. 1783 (ASVNV, vol. 182, 1783). I should like to acknowledge the generous help I received from the Rev. Professor Owen Chadwick in obtaining access to this archive, and from Mgr C. Burns in using it.
65 J. Kellner (ed.), *Pfarre Sankt Lorenz am Schottenfeld 1786–1796* (St Pölten, 1986); H. Peichl, 'Die Schottenabtei in der Neuzeit', in F. Krones (ed.), *800 Jahre Schottenabtei* (Vienna, 1960), pp. 56–7. For Melk see Ellegast in *900 Jahre Melk*, pp. 362–4; for Geras J. Ambrósy & A.J. Pfiffig, *Stift Geras und seine Kunstschätze* (St Pölten, 1989), p. 34.
66 See e.g. the accounts in Winner, *Klosteraufhebungen*, and R. Hittmair, *Der josefinische Klostersturm im Land ob der Enns* (Freiburg im Breisgau, 1907); *900 Jahre Benediktiner in Melk*, p. 121.
67 ASVNV, vols. 179–84, 197A, 199–200. H. Schlitter in *Die Reise des Papstes Pius VI. nach Wien* and *Pius VI. und Josef II.* (FRA, vol. XLVII, Vienna, 1892, 1894) uses these files and gives extensive extracts from them, but it seems clear that many of the most confidential documents were not available to him. G. Soranzo, *Peregrinus apostolicus* (Milan, 1937), is rather fuller on the papal side. E. Kovács, *Der Pabst in Teutschland* (Munich, 1983), relies on these two works. T. Vanyó, *A bécsi pápai követség levéltárának iratai Magyarországról, 1611–1786* (Budapest, 1986), is largely confined to references to specifically Hungarian affairs. I am grateful to Professor István Tóth for the reference to Vanyó's book. Father Umberto Dell'Orto, with whom I had valuable conversations in Rome, generously sent me a copy of his very important study, *La Nunziatura a Vienna di Giuseppe Garampi, 1776–1785* (Collectanea Archivi Vaticani, Vatican City, 1995). D. Vanysacker, *Cardinal Giuseppe Garampi (1725–1792): An Enlightened Ultramontane* (Brussels, 1995), contains much interesting material, but the author seems not to have seen the most secret despatches written by his subject.

68 ASVNV, vol. 180, Garampi's despatches of 20 July and 18 Nov. 1781. Crucial portions are printed in my article 'Nuncio Garampi proposes to excommunicate Joseph II, 1781', in J. Kalmár (ed.), *Miscellanea fontium historiae europaeae (Essays in honour of Éva H. Balázs)* (Budapest, 1997), pp. 252–7. My title exaggerates. Garampi did suggest to Rome that Joseph be excommunicated but his own proposed action would not have constituted excommunication. I am grateful to Professor Elisabeth Garms-Cornides for her comments.

69 E.g. E. Wangermann, *From Joseph II to the Jacobin Trials* (2nd edn, Oxford, 1969), pp. 6, 8, 10, 50; and Bodi, *Tauwetter in Wien*, p. 228.

70 ASVNV, vol. 182, despatch of 5 May 1783, section on 'Kroesel'. Dickson, 'Joseph II's reshaping of the Austrian Church', p. 110 and nn. 41, 42, exposes the change of plan and the confusion it has caused historians such as P. von Mitrofanov in his *Joseph II* (2 vols., Vienna, 1910). Leopold's view is to be found in his vast memorandum on his visit to Vienna in 1784 in HHSA, Familienarchiv, Sammelbände 16.

71 See p. 167. He was writing early in 1782.

72 The first edition was in Latin: *Joannis Physiophili Specimen Monachologiae methodo Linnaeana* (Augsburg, 1783).

73 See Bodi, *Tauwetter in Wien*, pp. 53, 125. Hittmair, *Der josefinische Klostersturm*, is very informative about Eybel's activities in Upper Austria, and M. Brandl, *Der Kanonist Joseph Valentin Eybel (1741–1805): Sein Beitrag zur Aufklärung in Österreich* (Steyr, 1976), about his writings.

74 E.g. Caprara's despatch of 3 Aug. 1786 (ASVNV, vol. 199). Dickson, 'Joseph II's reshaping of the Austrian Church', p. 97n.

75 Hittmair, *Der josefinische Klostersturm*, pp. 253–4.

76 Hock and Bidermann, *Staatsrath*, p. 407; F. and R. Malecek, *Strahov Praha*, p. 114. I owe the latter reference to Dr L.C. Van Dijck.

77 For supplying me with material about the case of Lilienfeld I am very grateful to Mag. Elisabeth Fattinger. On the change of emphasis towards suppressing richer monasteries see Hock and Bidermann, *Staatsrath*, pp. 404–9.

78 G. Winner, 'Die Verbauung der Wiener Klostergärten in josefinischer Zeit', *Jahrbuch des Vereins für Geschichte der Stadt Wien*, 12 (1955–6), pp. 145–52.

79 See my *Joseph II*, vol. I, pp. 484–7, and my article 'Was Joseph II an Enlightened despot', *Austrian Studies*, 2 (1991), pp. 1–20.

80 My main published sources on the Hungarian church are Dickson, *Finance and Government*, vol. I, esp. ch. 4, and 'Joseph II's reshaping of the Austrian Church'; Marczali, *Hungary in the Eighteenth Century*, esp. ch. IV; B.K. Király, 'The Hungarian church', in Callahan and Higgs, *Church and Society*; and L. Csóka, *Geschichte des benediktinischen Mönchtums in Ungarn* (Studia Hungarica, Munich, 1980), esp. pp. 312–64. B. Dercsényi, G. Hegyi, E. Marosi and J. Török, *Catholic Churches in Hungary* (Budapest, 1992), provides an invaluable list and photographic record of the major buildings and useful historical surveys, though its emphasis is on parish rather than monastic churches.

For sources in the Hungarian National Archives see n. 85 below – my comments on uneven provision derive from file C.107 of the Ecclesiastical Commission, reinforced by the graphic evidence in the remarkable articles of G. Tüskés and E. Knapp, esp. 'Österreichisch-ungarische interethnische Verbindungen im Spiegel des barockzeitlichen Wallfahrtswesens',

Bayerisches Jahrbuch für Volkskunde (1990), pp. 1–42, and 'Bruderschaften in Ungarn im 17. und 18. Jahrhundert', ibid. (1992), pp. 1–23.

Many Hungarian scholars have helped me to understand better the differences between the Hungarian and Austrian churches. I should particularly like to thank here Professor D. Kosáry, Professor L. Péter, Dr E. Tüskés and Dr M. Velladics.

81 Marczali, Hungary in the Eighteenth Century, p. 271.
82 From Finance and government, vol. 1, pp. 35 and 39, and 'Joseph II's reshaping of the Austrian Church', p. 98.
83 On the three new bishoprics established in 1776 see J. Tomko, Die Errichtung der Diözesen Zips, Neusohl and Rosenau (1776) und das königliche Patronatsrecht in Ungarn (Vienna, 1968), a reference I owe to Professor R.J.W. Evans. Two more were established in the following year at Székesfehérvár and Szombathely, and in addition two Uniate sees (D. Kosáry, Culture and Society in Eighteenth-Century Hungary (Budapest, 1987), p. 82).
84 Kosáry, Culture and Society, esp. pp. 107–12; Marczali, Hungary in the Eighteenth Century, pp. 283–5.
85 The following remarks are based partly on research in the Hungarian National Archives on the collections of Joseph's Normalia (A 58) and the papers of the Ecclesiastical Commission (C 70–107). Professor Éva Balázs made my work there possible, and I was greatly assisted by Dr Éva Hoós and Dr Márta Velladics, who unselfishly abstracted material for me and directed me to appropriate files. I owe special thanks too to the staff of the National Archives, who gave me help far beyond the call of duty.
86 Velladics, 'A II. József korabeli szerzetesrendi abolícío statisztikája'. Her article, which she very kindly sent me, corrects in significant ways the important article of P. Bán, 'Új adatok a szerzetsrendek II. József korabeli megszüntetéséról', Baranya, 3 (1990–1), pp. 61–71, and my own and Professor Dickson's work. Bán's article, however, remains particularly valuable on monastic wealth.
87 I owe this point also to Dr Velladics.
88 Velladics, 'A II. József korapeli szerzetesrendi abolícío statisztikája', p. 1277.
89 I am most grateful to Dr István Szijártó for passing on to me some of the conclusions of his thesis on 'Estates and their institutions in eighteenth-century Hungary' ('Rendiség és rendi intézmények a 18. századi Magyarországon'). It appears that the abbot of Pannonhalma, the provost of Zagreb as head of the monastery of Vrana and the abbot of Luc were normally the only monastic representatives.
90 Cf. Csóka, Geschichte des benediktinischen Mönchtums in Ungarn, pp. 348–52, 262. The Tables in C.107 (see n. 80 above) give only tiny figures for monks acting as parish clergy in Hungary before 1786 (cf. Dickson, 'Joseph II's reshaping of the Austrian Church', p. 101 n. 30, for figures for other provinces). On the number of monks of Pannonhalma working in parishes and the problem posed by the hill see the abbey archives ('Pannonhalmi iratok a világi veretés i dején 1786–1802', fasc. 87 nr 2, 'Documenta Sacrum Montem Pannoniae concernantia de tempore oppressionis').
91 Bán, 'Új adatok a szerzetsrendek II. Jósef korabeli megszüntetéserol', p. 68.
92 Dickson, 'Joseph II's reshaping of the Austrian Church', p. 105. Even though it seems to follow from Dr Velladics's work that this figure must include some monks working in parishes, the

point would remain valid that the increase was proportionally much greater in Hungary than in other provinces.

93 For the 'pastoral letter' see, e.g. my article 'Was Joseph II an Enlightened despot?', esp. pp. 12–13. On the redistribution of revenues Dickson, *Finance and Government*, vol. II, esp. pp. 111–12.

94 See my *Joseph II*, vol. I, pp. 97–101.

95 For eighteenth-century Belgium H. Pirenne, *Histoire de Belgique*, vol. v (Brussels, 1920), remains valuable though, like most of the literature in French, it gives only limited credit to Flemish sources and activities. H. Hasquin (ed.), *La Belgique autrichienne* (Brussels, 1987), is a more up-to-date and balanced French-language collection. W.W. Davis, *Joseph II: An Imperial Reformer for the Austrian Netherlands* (The Hague, 1974), offers a generally reliable account in English of Joseph's reign in Belgium. A useful though superficial summary can be found in E.H. Kossmann, *The Low Countries, 1780–1940* (Oxford, 1978), pp. 51–64. An especially important revisionist article is J. Craeybeckx, 'The Brabant revolution: a conservative revolt in a backward country?', *Acta Historiae Neerlandica*, 4 (1970), pp. 49–83.

96 For a summary of the position of the Estates in the various provinces see J. Gilissen, *Le régime représentatif avant 1790 en Belgique* (Brussels, 1952), pp. 65–8. A useful recent work dealing with the Austrian administration of Belgium, a copy of which Mag. Elisabeth Fattinger very kindly gave me, is R. Zedinger, *Die Verwaltung der Osterreichischen Niederlande in Wien (1794–1795): Studien zu den Zentralisierungstendenzen des Wiener Hofes im Staatswerdungsprozeß der Habsburgermonarchie* (Vienna, 2000). See also H. Coppens, *Het Institutioneel Kader van de Centrale Overheidsfinanciën in de Spaanse en Oostenrijkse Nederlanden tijdens het late ancien régime (c. 1680–1788)* (Brussels, 1993), pp. 112–13. Professor Coppens very generously sent me copies both of this book and of the companion volume cited in n. 99 below. E. de Moreau, *L'église en Belgique des origines au début du XXe siècle* (Brussels, 1944) says (p. 202) that there were thirteen abbots in the First Estate of Brabant, six in Hainaut, eight in Namur and five in Luxembourg. S. Tassier, *Les démocrates belges de 1789* (originally published 1930, 2nd edn, Brussels, 1989), lists most of these (pp. 36–7) and adds two each for Tournai and Flanders.

97 As well as the general works on Belgium cited in n. 94 see D. McKay and H.M. Scott, *The Rise of the Great Powers, 1648–1815* (London, 1983), esp. pp. 64–5, 122–3.

98 See, e.g., Dickson, *Finance and Government*, vol. I, p. 30, vol. II, esp. pp. 102–4, 289–90; A. Cosemans, *De bevolking van Brabant in de XVIIe en XVIIIe Eeuw* (Brussels, 1939); H. van Houtte, *Histoire économique de la Belgique à la fin de l'Ancien Régime* (Ghent, 1920). E. Stols on travellers' reactions to Belgium in Hasquin, *La Belgique autrichienne*, pp. 514–22, emphasises the impression made by its numerous towns.

99 See Dickson, *Finance and Government*, vol. II, pp. 102–4, 289–90, and H. Coppens, *Basisstatistieken voor de reconstructie van de centrale staatsrekening der Spanse en Oostenrijkse Nederlanden ca. 1680–1788* (Brussels, 1993). The reports of Kaunitz and his assistants in HHSA, Belgien, Vorträge, fasz. 11 (1777–81) contain several discussions of secret transfers of Belgian funds to Vienna, most strikingly for the purpose of securing archduke Maximilian's election to the coadjutorship of the archbishop-elector of Cologne in 1780.

100 Pirenne, *Histoire de Belgique*, vol. v, p. 214, writes of 'the extinction of Jansenism', but even his own evidence casts doubt on this assertion. Cf. Hasquin on 'Le joséphisme et ses racines' in *La Belgique autrichienne*, pp. 201–38, and Roegiers's work cited above, n. 14.

101 On Charles of Lorraine see the splendid catalogue of the Europalia exhibition of 1987, *Charles-Alexandre de Lorraine*, ed. C. Lemaire 2 (vols., Brussels, 1987). See E. Stols's article, 'Regards étrangers sur les Pays-Bas autrichiens', in *La Belgique autrichienne*, pp. 505–32.

102 See e.g. Cosemans, *De bevolking van Brabant*, pp. 211–19. Cf. Schepper, *La réorganisation des paroisses*, esp. pp. 60–1, 73–5, 110–14. Schepper's book is really, despite its title, the best book on Belgian monasteries under Joseph II.

103 Dickson, *Finance and Government*, vol. I, p. 30. Belgian historians seem remarkably cagey about numbers of regulars but Moreau, *L'église de Belgique*, p. 201, gives the following figures, said to be 'statistiques autrichiennes contrôlées par Bouteville [the Directory's deputy in 1796]': 110 abbayes, 275 couvents, 15 béguinages, 29 hôpitaux, 21 couvents de sœurs hospitalières; 3,400 curés, 3,400 vicars, 800 regular canons and canonesses, 2,800 religieux d'abbayes, 6,700 religieux dans les couvents. However, the 'Etat approximatif' that I obtained from the archives, which certainly looks like the work of Bouteville (see n. 5 above), has this table:

Statistics of Belgian regular clergy under Joseph II

Number of Houses		Number of monks and nuns	Brothers and sisters
57	Abbeys and priories for men	1,400	100
59	Abbeys and priories for women	1,000	300
160	Men's *couvents*	3,000	700
180	Women's *couvents*	2,500	500
456	[Total]	7,900	1,600

This works out at 5,200 male regulars, incl. brothers, and 4,300 female, incl. sisters.

104 I follow the cautious estimates of P. Verhaegen, *La Belgique sous la domination française* (2nd edn, Brussels, 1935), vol. II, pp. 507–9.

105 Tassier, *Les démocrates belges*, pp. 40, 49.

106 Archives générales du royaume, Brussels, Conseil privé, période autrichienne, Requêtes à Joseph II, 1346B: an isolated piece written in capitals to conceal the petitioner's identity. One of the relatively few pamphlets defending Joseph's policies, perhaps inspired by the government, is *Tableau de l'administration de S.M. l'Empereur Joseph II pendant l'année 1782 avec des réflexions du patriote Bruxelois* (Cologne, 1783). I read this in the library of the Austrian Studies Centre at the University of Minnesota. I should like to thank Professor Stanford E. Lehmberg for making it possible for me to work there.

107 This and the next quotation come from a neglected book, L. Delplace, *Joseph II et la révolution brabançonne* (Bruges, 1891), pp. 34–5. The author, a Jesuit, is certainly no friend to Joseph II, but the work is none the less scholarly and contains a valuable list of 397 relevant pamphlets published between 1782 and 1791.

108 Neither E. Poumon, *Abbayes de Belgique* (Brussels, 1954), pp. 16–17, nor even Delplace, *Joseph II*, ch. III, makes greater claims than this for the Belgian monasteries of the 1780s. Cf. Bazin, *Paläste des Glaubens*, vol. II, esp. pp. 212–20.

109 The four volumes of the journal are in the library of the University of Ghent. It cannot be excluded that Malingié may have reviewed and modified the text in later years but in general it carries conviction as a strictly contemporary record. So far as I know, only a small portion has been published (see E. Varenbergh, 'Les commencements de la révolution brabançonne, par un moine de l'abbaye de Saint-Pierre', *Messager des sciences historiques*, 50 (1876), pp. 327–56, 457–83 etc.).

110 D. Berten, *Recueil des anciennes coutumes de la Belgique . . .: Flandre. Quartier de Gand*, Tome X (Brussels, 1905), p. xxxii. E. de Busscher, *L'abbaye de Saint Pierre à Gand* (Ghent, 1869), p. 26, credits the abbot with a marquisate and two further titles of count.

111 The phrase is 'tous les traits tragiques que le Jubilaire a fait pendant sa vie'.

112 On Joseph's visit generally see E. Hubert, *Le voyage de l'empereur Joseph II dans le Pays-Bas (31 mai 1787–27 juillet 1781)* (Brussels, 1900). On the proceedings in Ghent, Malingié, 'Journal' (see n. 109) vol. I, pp. 109–25.

113 The authority is J. Laenen, *Etude sur la suppression des couvents par l'empereur Joseph II dans les Pays-Bas autrichiens et plus spécialement dans le Brabant (1783–1794)* (Antwerp, 1905). Admirable though this book is, it sows confusion by failing to deal with the admittedly abortive suppression programme after 1786. Cf. Schepper, *La réorganisation des paroisses*.

114 Malingié, 'Journal', vol. I, pp. 167–8.

115 Beales, 'Was Joseph II an Enlightened despot', p. 9.

116 The point is repeatedly made in Laenen, *Etude sur la suppression des couvents*, and Schepper, *La réorganisation des paroisses*, that abbeys with seats in the Estates were left alone.

117 R. Gits, 'L'établissement de la commission ecclésiastique et de la commission des fondations pieuses (1785–1787)', *Analectes . . . pour servir à l'histoire ecclésiastique de la Belgique*, 38 (1911), pp. 67–90, has important details e.g. on Joseph's shift away from appointing the liberal Belgian nobleman, Cornet des Grez, to this commission.

118 Malingié, 'Journal', vol. I, pp. 195–end.

119 *A Review of the Affairs of the Austrian Netherlands in the Year 1787* (London, 1788), pp. 42–3. For a serious modern discussion see Kovács, *Ultramontanismus und Staatskirchentum*.

120 Cf. on the latter point E. Hubert, 'Les Princes-Evèques de Liège et les édits de Joseph II en matière ecclésiastique', *Bulletin de la Commission Royale d'Histoire*, 87 (1923), esp. pp. 143–4, 166–8.

121 Malingié, 'Journal', vol. II, p. 513, 1 Mar. 1789.

122 Schepper, *La réorganisation des paroisses*, pp. 236–49, has much good material on this phase.

123 Poumon, *Abbayes de Belgique*, p. 75.

124 Schepper, *La réorganisation des paroisses*, esp. pp. 250–60.

125 There is a large literature on 'the Brabant revolution', among which the best book in English is J.L. Polasky, *Revolution in Brussels, 1787–1793* (Brussels, Hanover, N.H., and London 1987). This is not, however, an adequate account. Like almost all modern studies it obviously prefers the 'democrats' to the 'statists'. And it does not deal with Flanders or the other provinces.

126 There is an interesting biography of Verlooy by L. Van Den Broeck, *J.B.C. Verlooy* (Antwerp, 1980).

127 On Hermans and his abbey see L.C. Van Dijck, 'Abt Godfried Hermans van Tongerlo en de Brabantse Omwenteling', in H. de Kok (ed.), *Turnhout den eersten troost der staten* (Turnhout, 1989), p. 298. The whole article is invaluable, and I am very grateful to Dr Van Dijck for his help

and kindness during a visit to the archives of the abbey of Tongerlo. See also *Monasticon Belge*, tome VIII, vol. I, ed. U. Berlière et al. (Maredsous, 1992), pp. 354–7; W. van Spilbeeck, *De Abdij van Tongerloo* (Geel, 1888), esp. pp. 561–8. Dr Guy Dejongh most generously sent me a copy of his invaluable thesis, 'Goederen en beheer van de abdij van Tongerlo in de achttiende eeuw', University of Leuven, 1991.

128 On Tongerlo and the Bollandists H. Lamy, 'L'œuvre des bollandistes à l'abbaye de Tongerloo', *Analecta Premonstratensia*, 2 and 3 (1926–7) (in four parts), esp. 2, pp. 382–3.

129 The quotation comes from a MS of Vonck's printed in H. Schlitter (ed.), *Geheime Correspondenz Josefs II. mit seinem Minister in der österreichischen Nederlanden . . . Trauttmansdorff* (Vienna, 1902), p. 701. The collection is an immensely valuable source which has escaped the attention of many of the students of this subject. Vonck himself says that the abbot of St Bernard gave him 10,000 florins, but such a payment appears in the Tongerlo records.

130 See Varenbergh, 'Les commencements de la révolution brabançonne'.

131 Busscher, *L'abbaye de Saint Pierre à Gand*, p. 110.

132 See the works listed in n. 127, esp. Spilbeeck, *Tongerloo*, p. 576. See also Abbey of Tongerlo, Belgium, papers relating to the Belgian uprising of 1789–90, boxes 113, 114.

133 Mitrofanov, *Joseph II*, esp. vol. II, pp. 754–5.

134 ASVNV, vol. 200, Caprara's despatch of 22 Feb. 1790.

135 The standard biography of Leopold is A. Wandruszka, *Leopold II.* (2 vols., Munich, 1963–5), but it is rather general on church matters. F. Scaduto, *Stato e chiesa sotto Leopoldo I granduca di Toscana* (Leghorn, 1885), a book Prof. Dickson introduced me to, is much more informative. Pincelli, *Monasteri e conventi*, pp. 15–19, is also helpful. In English E. Cochrane, *Florence in the Forgotten Centuries, 1527–1800* (Chicago, 1973), book VI. On the reaction see G. Turi, *'Viva Maria': la reazione alle riforme leopoldine (1790–1799)* (Florence, 1969).

136 Leopold to Marie Christine, 25 Jan. 1790 in A. Wolf (ed.), *Leopold II. und Marie Christine* (Vienna, 1867), pp. 80–7.

137 See, e.g., Polasky, *Revolution in Brussels*, pp. 179–82.

138 Perey, *Histoire d'une grande dame*, pp. 471–81.

139 Laenen, *La suppression des couvents*, p. 422.

140 Francis did authorise a few individual suppressions in Austria: see the excellent article by P. Tropper, 'Schicksale der Büchersammlungen niederösterreichischer Klöster nach der Aufhebung durch Joseph II. und Franz (II.) I.', *MIÖG* 91 (1983), pp. 95–150.

141 Maaß, *Josefinismus*, vol. IV, esp. pp. 3–13, 51; J.L.E. Graf von Barth-Barthenstein, *Das Ganze des österreichischen politischen Administration* (4 vols., Vienna, 1838–43), vol. II, p. 133; Dickson, 'Joseph II's reshaping of the Austrian Church', p. 114.

142 *500 Jahre Franziskaner der österreichischen Ordens-Provinz* (Vienna, 1951), p. 189.

143 Laenen, *La suppression des couvents*, p. 399; guide to King's College Chapel, Cambridge.

144 See Tropper, 'Schicksale der Büchersammlungen', and Velladics's recent articles, of which she kindly gave me copies: 'Szerzetesrendi abolíció magyarországon (1782–1790)', *Levéltári közleménye*, 1 (2000), pp. 33–52, and 'A szerzetes rendházak felszámolása II. József Korában', *Egyháztörténeti Szemle*, 2 (2001), pp. 3–42. In the latter article is printed the government instruction of 1786 on how to deal with the money and valuables of suppressed monasteries (in German, pp. 24–42).

9 THE REVOLUTION IN FRANCE

1. The literature bearing on this subject is of course vast. Among the basic studies are W. Doyle, *The Oxford History of the French Revolution* (Oxford, 1989); S. Schama, *Citizens* (London, 1989); T. Tackett, *Becoming a Revolutionary: The Deputies of the French National Assembly and the Emergence of a Revolutionary Culture (1780–1790)* (Princeton, 1996); Chadwick, *Popes and Revolution*; P. de la Gorce, *Histoire religieuse de la Révolution française* (5 vols., Paris, 1905–23); J. McManners, *The French Revolution and the Church* (London, 1969); Boutry et al., *Du roi Très Chrétien*, esp. pp. 73–108; N. Aston, *Religion and Revolution in France, 1780–1804* (Basingstoke, 2000).

2. On French Flanders and St-Vaast, L. Detrez, *La Flandre religieuse sous la Révolution (1789–1801)*, vol. I (Lille, 1928) [no more published]; H. van Zeller, *Downside By and Large* (London, 1954), esp. pp. 15–16; J.M. Thompson, *Robespierre* (2 vols., Oxford, 1935), vol. I, esp. pp. 4–7, 42; Bazin, *Paläste des Glaubens*, vol. I, esp. p. 175.

3. See pp. 176–7. Cf. Plongeron, *Les réguliers de Paris*, esp. the conclusion.

4. G. Michaux, 'Une nouvelle conception de la vie monastique en France', in Châtellier, *Religions en transition*, esp. pp. 67–72.

5. Ibid. p. 65; J.B. l'Ecuy, *Rede von dem Nutzen den die Geistlichen, besonders Stiften und Abteyen, dem Staate und der Gelehrsamkeit geleistet haben, und noch leisten*, in *Neueste Sammlung jener Schriften, die von einigen Jahren her über verschiedene wichtigen Gegenstände zur Steuer der Wahrheit im Drucke erschienen sind* (Augsburg, 1784), quote from p. 29; Plongeron, *Les réguliers de Paris*, pp. 129, 117–18.

6. See pp. 110–11.

7. M. Crosland (ed.), *Memoirs of Madame de La Tour du Pin* (London, 1985), pp. 26–7.

8. See McManners, *Church and Society*, esp. (on toleration) vol. II, ch. 47.

9. Quoted in Doyle, *Oxford History*, p. 54.

10. Lemaire, *La commission des réguliers*, p. 16.

11. K.M. Baker, *Inventing the French Revolution* (Cambridge, 1990), pp. 75–6; McManners, *Church and Society*, vol. I, esp. p. 600; Plongeron, *Les réguliers de Paris*, pp. 150–70.

12. R. Chartier, 'Urban reading practices', in his *Cultural Uses of Print*, esp. pp. 189–98.

13. A. Sicard, *Le clergé de France pendant la Révolution* (3 vols., Paris, 1912–27), vol. I, p. 277n.

14. This article was by the Chevalier de Jaucourt, who wrote a quarter of the entire work. (On Jaucourt see J. Lough, *The Encyclopédie in Eighteenth-Century England and Other Studies* (Newcastle-upon-Tyne, 1970), pp. 25–70.) It echoes Voltaire's *Essai sur les mœurs* (see McManners in W.J. Sheils (ed.), *Monks, Hermits and the Ascetic Tradition* (Oxford, 1985) (Studies in Church History, vol. 22), p. 341).

15. On the role of public opinion, e.g., Doyle, *Oxford History*, esp. pp. 56–7; McManners, *Church and Society*, vol. II, pp. 671–2.

16. [S.N.H. Linguet,] *Essai philosophique sur le monachisme* (Paris, 1775).

17. *Histoire philosophique du monachisme, ou exposition abrégée de ce que l'on trouve de plus singulier & de plus curieux dans l'Institution, la Règle, l'Établissement & la Vie des Moines de tous les Cultes, & de tous les Pays* (2 vols., London, 1788), vol. I, pp. i, v, x–xiv, vol. II, pp. 286–92, 301–9. I am most grateful to Mr J. Robertshaw for directing me to a copy of this rare work, and to Dr C.J. Wright for enabling me to see it and for telling me that it was reissued in 1789, apparently unchanged, under the title *Nécessité de supprimer et d'éteindre les ordres religieux en France, prouvée par l'histoire philosophique du monachisme* (2 vols., London, 1789).

18 R. Darnton, *The Forbidden Best-Sellers of Revolutionary France* (London, 1996), esp. ch. 3 and the translation he gives of *Thérèse philosophe*.

19 There is some discussion of the monastic and religious element in Arnaud's later work in R.L. Dawson, *Baculard d'Arnaud: Life and Prose Fiction* (Banbury, 1976), e.g. pp. 356–60. I owe this reference to the kindness of Dr Mark Ledbury.

20 Doyle, *Oxford History*, p. 85. See n. 1 for the general works I am chiefly relying on in this account of the Revolution.

21 The most recent studies include G. Shapiro and J. Markoff, *Revolutionary Demands: A Content Analysis of the Cahiers de doléances of 1789* (Stanford, 1998); McManners, *Church and Society*, vol. II, ch. 50; R. Chartier, 'From words to texts: the *Cahiers de doléances* of 1789', in his *Cultural Uses of Print*; G.V. Taylor, 'Les cahiers de 1789: aspects révolutionnaires et non révolutionnaires', *Annales* (1973), pp. 1495–514. T. Tackett, *Religion, Revolution, and Regional Culture in Eighteenth-Century France* (Princeton, 1986), though mainly concerned with the Civil Constitution, is helpful here too.

22 For this and the previous paragraph, in addition to the works already cited, A. Denys-Buirette, *Les questions religieuses dans les cahiers de 1789* (Paris, 1919) has proved especially useful.

23 Shapiro and Markoff, *Revolutionary Demands*, p. 381.

24 These figures are from Denys-Buirette, *Les questions religieuses*, p. 349. Cf. G. Shapiro, 'Les demandes les plus répandues dans les cahiers de doléances', in M. Vovelle (ed.), *L'image de la révolution française* (4 vols., Paris, 1990), vol. I, p. 9.

25 F. Roudaut (ed.), *Les cahiers de doléances de la sénéchaussée de Lesneven* (Brest, 1990), p. 23 and n.

26 Denys-Buirette, *Les questions religieuses*, pp. 349–53 and 353n.

27 A. Aulard, *La révolution française et les congrégations* (Paris, 1903), p. 12.

28 C. Bonnet, 'Les pillages d'abbayes dans le Nord et leur signification (1789–1793)' in S. Bernard-Griffiths, M.-C. Chemin and J. Ehrard (eds.), *Révolution française et 'vandalisme revolutionnaire'* (Paris, 1992), pp. 169–73.

29 This and the previous quotation from Plongeron, *Les réguliers de Paris*, p. 77.

30 Cf. Sicard, *Le clergé de France*, esp. ch. III.

31 Evans, *Monastic Architecture*, p. 145 and n. Tackett, *Becoming a Revolutionary*, p. 24n, accepts this figure but adds 'eleven regular curés'. I have not been able to identify these.

32 F.-L. Bruel (ed.), *Un siècle d'histoire de France par l'estampe, 1770–1871* (3 vols., Paris 1909–21), vol. II, p. 17; Schama, *Citizens*, pp. 569–72. On Gerle Plongeron, *Les réguliers de Paris*, pp. 292–3.

33 Plongeron, *Les réguliers de Paris*, p. 134; A. Sorel, *Le couvent des Carmes et le séminaire de Saint-Sulpice pendant la Terreur* (Paris, 1863), pp. 19–21.

34 See Bruel, *Un siècle d'histoire de France*.

35 La Gorce, *Histoire religieuse*, vol. I, p. 121.

36 Sicard, *Le clergé de France*, vol. I, pp. 89, 183–4, 184n, 189.

37 These matters are interestingly discussed in F. Aftalion, *The French Revolution: An Economic Interpretation* (Cambridge, 1990), esp. section 3.

38 AP, 1ère série, vol. IX (1877), pp. 139–68.

39 Ibid. p. 197.

40 Plongeron, *Les réguliers de Paris*, p. 147.

41 AP, vol. IX, p. 233.

42 Ibid. pp. 398–404.
43 Ibid. pp. 424–31.
44 Ibid. p. 433.
45 Ibid. pp. 431–4, quotation from p. 433.
46 Ibid. p. 597.
47 Ibid. pp. 604 (Lebrun), 606 (vicomte de Mirabeau).
48 Ibid. pp. 615–25, quotation from 625.
49 Ibid. pp. 637–9.
50 Ibid., p. 649.
51 Detrez, Flandre, p. 15.
52 AP, vol. IX, pp. 718–21.
53 Aulard, La révolution française et les congrégations, p. 63.
54 Tackett, Becoming a Revolutionary, p. 204.
55 According to C. Maire, 'L'église et la nation: du dépôt de la vérité au dépôt des lois: la trajectoire janséniste au XVIIIe siècle', Annales (1991), pp. 1177–1205, Treilhard, like Lanjuinais, another member of the committee, was much influenced by Jansenism.
56 Aulard, La révolution française et les congrégations, pp. 65–117.
57 See L.G. Mitchell's introduction to The Writings and Speeches of Edmund Burke, vol. VIII: The French Revolution, 1790–1794 (Oxford, 1989).
58 I am most grateful to Dr Ian Harris for having brought this remark to my attention. It is admittedly lord Holland's recollection from more than forty years later, but it rings true: it is just like Windham, but in any case such a comment would hardly have been invented by Holland in 1835. It is to be found, slightly misquoted, in L.G. Mitchell, Holland House (London, 1980), p. 161. The original, Dr Harris tells me, is in the Grey MSS at Durham (GRE/B34/349A), Holland to Grey, 19 Jan. [1835].
59 Plongeron, Les réguliers de Paris, pp. 62–4, 308–11.
60 La Gorce, Histoire religieuse, vol. I, p. 173. Sicard, Le clergé de France, vol. I, gives a full account of the inventory, the behaviour of the monks and the immediate results. Cf. the brilliant brief treatment of McManners, French Revolution, esp. pp. 31–7.
61 Hufton, Women and the Limits of Citizenship, pp. 55–7, 164. Her source makes clear how difficult it is to get at reliable overall figures: C. Langlois and T.J.A. Le Goff, 'Les vaincus de la Révolution: Jalons pour une sociologie des prêtres mariés', in Voies nouvelles pour l'histoire de la révolution française, Colloque Albert Mathiez-Georges Lefebvre (Paris, 1978), pp. 281–312. The statistics rest on the petitions of married clergy to cardinal Caprara asking for indulgence after the concordat of 1802, 5,500 in total. Many will have died by then, others will have felt no need to petition.
62 Doyle, Oxford History, p. 138; Aston, Religion and Revolution, pp. 246–7.
63 D.M.G. Sutherland, France 1789–1815: Revolution and Counter-Revolution (London, 1985), esp. p. 109.
64 For France in general Sicard, Le clergé de France; La Gorce, Histoire religieuse, vol. I, p. 166. For the riots at Montauban see e.g. Boutry et al., Du roi Très Chrétien, p. 87; and for the incident at Toulouse J.C. Meyer, 'La presse et la religion à Toulouse (1789–1801)', in Vovelle, L'image, vol. I, pp. 147–8.
65 For the assignats Aftalion, French Revolution, esp. ch. 4.

66 La Gorce, *Histoire religieuse*, vol. I, p. 186.
67 Plongeron, *Les réguliers de Paris*, p. 387.
68 The Civil Constitution is printed e.g. in F.-A. Hélie, *Les constitutions de la France* (Paris, 1879), pp. 125–33, followed by a republican appraisal from the editor.
69 Plongeron, *Les réguliers de Paris*, p. 292.
70 For the regulars ibid. For the whole issue of the Constitution and the oath Tackett, *Reason, Revolution and Regional Culture*.
71 Pastor, *History of the Popes*, vol. XL, has a good account. The quotation is from p. 179n.
72 Sutherland, *France, 1789–1815*, p. 155.
73 Aston, *Religion and Revolution*, pp. 117–18.
74 For this section L. Réau, *Histoire du vandalisme*, ed. M. Fleury and G.-M. Leproux (Paris, 1994), esp. ch. IV.
75 E. Pommier, 'Discours iconoclaste, discours culturel, discours national, 1790–1794', in Bernard-Griffiths et al., *Vandalisme*, pp. 299–313.
76 See Hufton, *Women and the Limits of Citizenship*, esp. ch. 2. On p. 75 it is stated that the congregations were abolished in September 1793, but my understanding is that this had happened a year earlier (see above).
77 Sutherland, *France, 1789–1815*, p. 151; Plongeron, *Les réguliers de Paris*, pp. 332–3; E. Kennedy, *A Cultural History of the French Revolution* (London, 1989), ch. VI.
78 McManners, *French Revolution*, p. 108; Lebrun, *Histoire des catholiques en France*, p. 284.
79 For this paragraph see Réau, *Histoire du vandalisme*; Bazin, *Paläste des Glaubens*, vol. I; Evans, *Monastic architecture*.
80 See Aston, *Religion and Revolution*, ch. 11; Hufton, *Women and the Limits of Citizenship*, esp. ch. 3.
81 McManners, *French Revolution*, p. 142.
82 See the discussions of the concordat in Chadwick, *Popes and Revolution*; McManners, *French Revolution*.
83 Chateaubriand, *Le génie du christianisme* (2 vols., Paris, 1996), vol. II, pp. 117–21.
84 G. Bruun, *Europe and the French Imperium, 1799–1814* (London, 1938), p. 146, based on the excellent and little-used book by A. Aulard, *Napoléon Ier et le monopole universitaire* (Paris, 1911), which is in fact a history of education under the Empire. See esp. pp. 54–61, ch. VI.
85 C.A. Naselli, *La soppressione napoleonica delle corporazioni religiose* (Rome, 1986), pp. 10–14, summarises the position. See Napoleon's letter permitting a Trappist monastery printed on pp. 216–17.
86 Boutry et al., *Du Roi très chrétien*, p. 136.

10 THE IMPACT OF THE REVOLUTION OUTSIDE FRANCE

1 Réau, *Histoire du vandalisme*, pp. 471–2.
2 Schama, *Citizens*, pp. 585–6, 686–90; T.C.W. Blanning, *Origins of the French Revolutionary Wars* (London, 1986), ch. 5, and *The French Revolutionary Wars 1787–1802* (London, 1996), chs. 2 and 3.
3 L. de Lanzac de Laborie, *La domination française en Belgique* (2 vols., 1895), vol. I, p. 73; Schepper, *La réorganisation des paroisses*, p. 268.
4 See Beales, *Joseph II*, p. 6 and n.

5   See Blanning, *French Revolution in Germany*, esp. chs. 3 and 5.
6   This section depends heavily on Blanning's seminal works: *Reform and Revolution in Mainz*, esp. chs. 7 and 8; *French Revolution in Germany* and *French Revolutionary Wars*; H. Kob, 'Johann Matthias Konz,' *Hémecht*, 50 (1998), pp. 333–56.
7   On Belgium under French rule Chadwick, *Popes and Revolution*, pp. 476–80; Kossman, *Low Countries*, pp. 67–81; Lanzac de Laborie, *La domination française*, vol. I, esp. pp. 71–86, 199–217, 237–54 (quotation from p. 202: the central commissar of forests to the municipal commissar of Bastogne, 3 Dec. 1798). For later divisions H. Hasquin, *Histoire de la laïcité: principalement en Belgique et en France* (Brussels, 1981).
8   See pp. 223–6.
9   B. Cignitti and L. Caronti, *L'abbazia nullius sublacense* (Rome, 1956), pp. 135–6, 171–3, 189. See above, pp. 134, 261.
10 Naselli, *La soppressione napoleonica*, pp. 27–8. The book gives an invaluable account of the legislation of the various governments as well as of the views and actions of Napoleon.
11 Chadwick, *Popes and Revolution*, p. 454. The whole section on Napoleonic Italy in this book is invaluable.
12 On the religious element in Neapolitan and other reactions to French rule see T.C.W. Blanning's spirited 'The role of religion in European counter-revolution 1789–1815', in Beales and Best, *History, Society and the Churches*. A subtle account of the Neapolitan counter-revolution is given in J.A. Davis, '1799: The "Santafede" and the crisis of the "ancien régime" in southern Italy', in J.A. Davis and P.A. Ginsborg, *Society and Politics in the Age of the Risorgimento* (Cambridge, 1991), pp. 1–25. More recently, J. Robertson has given an admirable account of intellectuals' role in the Neapolitan revolution in 'Enlightenment and Revolution: Naples 1799', *Transactions of the Royal Historical Society*, 6th series, 10 (2000), pp. 17–44, but with singularly little reference to the Church.
13 Naselli, *La soppressione napoleonica*, pp. 147–54.
14 Chadwick, *Popes and Revolution*, pp. 508–26, C. Zaghi, *L'Italia di Napoleone* (Turin, 1989) – see esp. pp. 346–9 on the numerous revolts against Napoleonic rule. On Lombardy M. Roberti, *Milano capitale napoleonica* (3 vols., Milan, 1946), esp. vol. I, pp. 442–31, 473–500; on Rome R.T. Ridley, *The Eagle and the Spade: The Archaeology of Rome during the Napoleonic era, 1809–14* (Cambridge, 1992), pp. 5–6, 65, 143, 255 and passim; on Naples Villani, *La vendita dei beni dello stato nel regno di Napoli*, esp. pp. 18–24 and App. I. Much information on the fate of Benedictine and related Orders in Trolese, *Il monachesimo italiano*, and on the province of Arezzo in Pincelli, *Monasteri e conventi*, esp. pp. 19–21.
15 H. Wicki, *Staat, Kirche, Religiosität: der Kanton Luzern zwischen barocker Tradition und Aufklärung* (Stuttgart, 1990), p. 539. On Switzerland generally, J. Steinberg, *Why Switzerland?* (2nd edn, Cambridge, 1996), esp. chs. 2 and 6; DIP, vol. IX, 'Svizzera'; L. Vischer, L. Schenker and R. Dellsperger (eds.), *Ökumenische Kirchengeschichte der Schweiz* (Basel, 1994). The DIP says there were 118 Swiss religious houses in 1789 (1,634 monks, 711 nuns); the *Kirchengeschichte* says 133 in 1798.
16 E. Gibbon, *Memoirs of My Life*, ed. G.A. Bonnard (London, 1966), p. 80.
17 W. Coxe, *Travels in Switzerland* (2 vols., London, 1789), vol. I, pp. 47–51. See Schindler, *Barockklöster*, pp. 85–116; Bazin, *Paläste des Glaubens*, vol. II, pp. 148–54.

18 On St Gall and Vorster, J. Duft, A. Gössi and W. Vogler, *Die Abtei St Gallen* (St Gall, 1986); W. Vogler, *Die Fürstabtei St. Gallen und die französische Revolution* (St Gall, 1990); A. Meier, *Abt Pankras Vorster und die Aufhebung der Fürstabtei St. Gallen* (Freiburg, Schweiz, 1954); Vorster's MS diary in the library of St Gall.
19 Coxe, *Travels in Switzerland*, vol. I, pp. 258–9.
20 Herr, *Eighteenth Century Revolution*, chs. 9–11, and his *Rural Change and Royal Finances*, esp. pp. 93–7, 133, 149–53.
21 Marques, *History of Portugal*, vol. I, pp. 427–30.
22 García-Villoslada, *Historia*, vol. V, pp. 7–11.
23 Ibid. pp. 16–24.
24 Ibid. pp. 52–6, 71–3.
25 Marques, *History of Portugal*, vol. I, pp. 429–30, vol. II, pp. 23–4.
26 Blanning, *French Revolution in Germany*, p. 229. This work is invaluable for the whole of the 1790s.
27 See ch. 2.
28 Cf. Blanning, *French Revolution in Germany*, pp. 225–6.
29 See Wende, *Die geistlichen Staaten*.
30 Quoted from H. von Lang, *Aus dem bösen alten Zeit* (2 vols., Stuttgart, 1910), by Wende, *Die geistlichen Staaten*, p. 54. See pp. 48–50 of Wende on Rastatt and Lunéville.
31 For this and the whole section on Bavaria see Weis's magisterial 'Säkularisation'; Kirmeier and Treml, *Glanz und Ende der alten Klöster*; Aretin, *Das Alte Reich*, vol. III, chs. 6 and 7. On the diplomacy of France and other Powers see P.W. Schroeder, *The Transformation of European Politics, 1763–1848* (Oxford, 1994), esp. pp. 166–72, 187–90, 210–40.
32 The process in and around Cologne is described in great detail by Büttner, *Säkularisation*. For the actual enactments see pp. 61–4.
33 In addition to Weis, 'Säkularisation'; Benz, *Saeculum* (1975), p. 371; W. Brandmüller (ed.), *Handbuch der bayerischen Kirchengeschichte*, vol. III (St Ottilien, 1991), pp. 16–30. I thank Dr Ferdinand Kramer for supplying me with a copy of the last-named piece.
34 The document is printed in E. Walder (ed.), *Das Ende des Alten Reiches* (2nd edn, Berne, 1962), pp. 15–62.
35 I do not know of better figures than those in Benz, 'Zu den kulturpolitischen Hintergründen', p. 373, and Erzberger's in *Säkularisation*, esp. pp. 4, 63–5. See, more generally, on later German suppressions H. Schmid in *Baden und Württemberg in Zeitalter Napoleons* (2 vols., Stuttgart, 1987), vol. II, pp. 135–55, and J.J. Menzel, 'Die Säkularisationen in Schlesien 1810', in J. Köhler (ed.), *Säkularisationen in Ostmitteleuropa* (Cologne, 1984), pp. 85–102.
36 A.M. Scheglmann, *Geschichte der Säkularisation in rechtsrheinischen Bayern* (3 vols., Regensburg, 1903–8, unfinished), vol. I, ch. 1 and passim.
37 For an able recent discussion of this school see T.J. Hochstrasser, *Natural Law Theories in the Early Enlightenment* (Cambridge, 2000).
38 This paragraph is partly directed against Benz's statement ('Zu den kulturpolitischen Hintergründen', p. 373): 'Zu den außerklösterlichen Ursachen zählt nicht die französische Revolution. Sie ist weniger als Ursache anzusprechen, wohl eher als Anlaß.'
39 See esp. Weis, 'Säkularisation', pp. 51–6; Kirmeier and Treml, *Glanz und Ende der alten Klöster*, ch. XI.

CONCLUSION

1 W. Cobbett, *History of the Protestant Reformation in England and Ireland* (2 vols., London, 1829), vol. 1, p. 59.
2 *Itinéraire, ou Voyages de M. l'Abbé Defeller en diverses parties de l'Europe* (2 vols., Liège, 1820), vol. 1, p. 558.
3 See J. Rosselli, *Singers of Italian Opera* (Cambridge, 1992).
4 K. Baedeker, *Italy: A Handbook for Travellers. 3rd Part: Southern Italy and Sicily* (10th edn, London, 1890), p. 258.
5 On music at St Peter's, Salzburg, see P. Eder and G. Walterskirchen, *Das Benediktinerstift S. Peter in Salzburg zur Zeit Mozarts* (Salzburg, 1991).
6 J. McManners, *French Ecclesiastical Society under the Ancien Régime: A Study of Angers in the Eighteenth Century* (Manchester, 1960), p. 92.
7 See pp. 73, 232–3.
8 *Itinéraire . . . Defeller*, vol. 1, p. 313.
9 Beales, *Joseph II*, p. 464.
10 Many aspects of this great change are treated brilliantly in J. McManners, *Death and the Enlightenment* (Oxford, 1981). See esp. pp. 36–8, 68–74, ch. 6, pp. 182–3.
11 Spiegel, minister of the elector-archbishop of Cologne, quoted in H. Klueting (ed.), *Katholische Aufklärung – Aufklärung in katholischen Deutschland* (Hamburg, 1993), p. 8. The elector, Max Franz, did not agree.
12 DIP, 'Soppressioni'; Kłoczowski, *Dzieje chrzescijanstwa polskiego*; Rechowicz, *Poland's Millennium*, pp. 136–40.
13 Henry James, *A Little Tour in France*, ed. L. Edel (London, 1985), p. 193.
14 P. Dupont et al., *Patrimoine public et révolution française* (Toulouse, 1989), p. 92.
15 Weis, 'Säkularisation', p. 48.
16 P. Notario, *La vendita dei beni nazionali in Piemonte nel periodo napoleonico (1800–1814)* (Turin, 1980), esp. ch. 5. For similar studies relating to other parts of Italy see the bibliographical essay, p. 369.
17 Weis, 'Säkularisation', pp. 51–4; *Handbuch der bayerischen Kirchengeschichte*, vol. III, pp. 1–84.
18 Aftalion, *French Revolution*, pp. 186–7.
19 H. Hasquin, *Une mutation: le 'Pays de Charleroi' aux XVIIe et XVIIIe siècles* (Brussels, 1971), makes no reference to monasteries, but cf. A. d'Haenens (ed.), *Abbayes de Belgique* (Brussels, 1973), esp. pp. 326–7 on Orval; Craeybeckx, 'The Brabant revolution'.
20 Cf. R. Sédillot, *Le coût de la révolution française* (Paris, 1987).
21 T.C.W. Blanning, *The Culture of Power and the Power of Culture: Old Regime Europe 1660–1789* (Oxford, 2001), pp. 112–13.
22 Sédillot, *Le coût de la révolution*, p. 93. His figures for 1789 are less optimistic than Blanning's, presumably because they relate to the whole of France.
23 M. Clark, *Modern Italy, 1871–1982* (London, 1984), pp. 34–7, has figures for the years immediately after unification which may be presumed to reflect long-term trends.
24 O. Biba, 'Die Wiener Kirchenmusik um 1783', *Jahrbuch für österreichische Kulturgeschichte*, 1, pt 2 (1971), pp. 7–79.
25 K. Rehberger, 'Ein Beitrag zur Vorgeschichte der "Historikerschule" des Stiftes St. Florian im 19. Jahrhundert', *Mitteilungen des oberösterreichischen Landesarchivs*, 10 (1971), pp. 210–50; V. Bibl,

Die niederösterreichischen Stände im Vormärz (Vienna, 1911), pp. 192–4; Bruckmüller in *900 Jahre Melk*, p. 378; *850 Jahre Wilten*, pp. 46, 74–8.

26 V. Orel, *Mendel* (Oxford, 1984).
27 See, e.g., M. Auer, *Anton Bruckner, Sein Leben und Werk* (Vienna, 1932).
28 I gratefully acknowledge the permission of Her Majesty Queen Elizabeth II to use this material. I am indebted to Lady de Bellaigue for finding these references for me in the Royal Archives at Windsor.
29 I. Kershaw, *Hitler*, vol. 1 (1889–1936) (Harmondsworth, 1998), p. 14.
30 E. Rotter in *900 Jahre Melk*, pp. 486–7; brief references in most histories of particular Austrian houses.
31 *900 Jahre Melk*, p. 378.
32 J.C. Freyherr von Aretin (ed.), *Beyträge zur Geschichte und Literatur, vorzüglich aus den Schätzen der Münchner National-und Hofbibliothek* (8 vols., Munich, 1803–7), vol. 1, pp. 98–9.
33 Scheglmann, *Säkularisation*, vol. 1, p. 263.
34 Stutzer, *Klöster als Arbeitgeber um 1800*, and *Die Säkularisation 1803* (2nd edn, Munich, 1978).
35 K.O. von Aretin in E. Aerts and F. Crouzet (eds.), *Economic Effects of the French Revolutionary and Napoleonic Wars* (Leuven, 1990), pp. 48–55. Similar views are expressed by Menzel in Köhler, *Säkularisationen*, about the Silesian experience.
36 Lebrun, *Histoire des catholiques*, pp. 311–18; and see above, pp. 264–5.
37 Ibid., ch. v.
38 Stendhal, *Scarlet and Black* (London, 1953), p. 391.
39 Lebrun, *Histoire des catholiques*, pp. 395–6.
40 I would like to acknowledge help given to me on this point by Professor R. Baldick, Professor A. Downie and Dr James Raven.
41 This quotation is from his fuller statement, 'Case of the suffering clergy of France, Refugees in British Dominions (supposed to have been drawn up by Mr Burke, and distributed in September 1792)', *Annual Register 1792*, vol. II, p. 125. I do not know why this piece is not included in the new collected edition of Burke's works.
42 Cf. R.J. Smith, *The Gothic Bequest: Medieval Institutions in British Thought, 1688–1863* (Cambridge, 1987).
43 The quotations from the *Reflections* come from pp. 153–9 of the Everyman edition.

BIBLIOGRAPHICAL ESSAY

To produce a full bibliography of the subject of this book would be a vast undertaking, since relevant documents are to be found not only in countless monastic archives but also in most public repositories, and there is a huge secondary literature, including thousands of books and articles on individual Orders and houses. This essay is intended both to indicate the works that I have found particularly useful in writing this book and to guide further reading, especially in English.

ARCHIVES

This book is not primarily based on unpublished materials, but I have used the following:

Archivio segreto vaticano, Rome: the reports of Garampi and Caprara, papal nuncios in Vienna, for 1780–90 (Nunziatura di Vienna, 179–84 (Garampi), Garampi's index 197A, 199–200 (Caprara), also 100, 160); and some files from the papers of the Congregazione dei Vescovi e Regolari.

Mágyarországos levéltár (Hungarian National Archives, Budapest): Joseph's Normalia (A 58) and the papers of the Ecclesiastical Commission (C 70–107).

Haus-, Hof- und Staatsarchiv, Vienna: for this book the most relevant of the large number of files I have studied in other contexts are Belgien, Rep. DD, Abt. A. Depeschen, vols. LV–LVII, 1779–85, Vorträge, fasz. 11 (1777–81), and Leopold II's vast 'Relazione' on his visit to Vienna in 1784 (Familienarchiv, Sammelbände 16).

Archives générales du royaume, Brussels: 'Requêtes à Joseph II', 1781 (Conseil privé, période autrichienne, A 124, 1343–51); 'Etat approximatif du Personnel du Clergé tant Regulier que Seculier de la cidevant Belgique' (papiers Bouteville, 1796).

Downside Abbey, Bath: papers relating to Lamspringe abbey, near Hildesheim.

Abbey of Pannonhalma, Hungary: 'papers concerning the time of oppression, 1786–1802'.

Stift St Florian, near Linz: papers concerning the years 1785–8 and the proposed suppression of the monastery under Joseph II.

Abbey of St Gall, Switzerland: diary of Abbot Pankraz Vorster.

Abbey of Tongerlo, Belgium: papers relating to the Belgian uprising of 1789–90, boxes 113 and 114/1.

Library of University of Ghent, Belgium: 'Journal' of Malingié, 4 vols., 1779–91.

SECONDARY LITERATURE

GENERAL (COVERING MORE THAN ONE COUNTRY)

Two authoritative and manageable surveys of eighteenth-century Europe are W. Doyle, *The Old European Order, 1660–1800* (Oxford, 1978), and T.C.W. Blanning (ed.), *The Eighteenth Century* (Oxford, 2000).

Classic accounts of the Roman Catholic Church in Europe in the eighteenth century are: vols. XIX and XX of A. Fliche and V. Martin (eds.), *Histoire de l'église* (24 vols., Paris, 1934–64); H. Jedin, *History of the Church* (English translation, 10 vols., London, 1965–84), vols. VI and VII; and L. von Pastor, *History of the Popes* (English translation, 40 vols., 1891–1953), esp. vols. XXXIII–XL. Two briefer but very effective studies are G. Schnürer, *Katholische Kirche und Kultur im 18. Jahrhundert* (Paderborn, 1941), and G. Martina, *La chiesa nell'età dell'assolutismo, del liberalismo, del totalitarismo* (4 vols., 7th edn, 1988–9), vols. II and III (with invaluable bibliographies to each chapter). E.E.Y. Hales, *Revolution and Papacy, 1769–1846* (London, 1960), offers a short introductory treatment. None of these works, however, gives adequate space to monks and nuns other than Jesuits. The general survey which is most enlightening about the regulars, and by far the most valuable overall account in English, is O. Chadwick, *The Popes and European Revolution* (Oxford, 1981), which takes the story down to 1830 and includes a most useful bibliography. (It largely omits France because that country was to be covered by J. McManners in another volume in the series (see under 'France').) There is a distinguished collection of essays on the main countries ed. W.J. Callahan and D. Higgs, *Church and Society in Catholic Europe of the Eighteenth Century* (Cambridge, 1979). I do not know of a general documentary collection devoted to monasticism, but for papal decrees see D.C. Mirbt (ed.), *Quellen zur Geschichte des Papsttums* (2nd edn, Tübingen, 1901).

For recent approaches to the Counter-Reformation or Catholic Reformation, superseding older studies such as A.G. Dickens, *The Counter Reformation* (London, 1968), see J. Bossy, 'The Counter-Reformation and the people of Catholic Europe', *Past and Present*, 47 (1970); L. Châtellier, *The Europe of the Devout: The Catholic Reformation and the Formation of a New Society* (Cambridge, 1989), and *The Religion of the Poor: Rural Missions in Europe and the Formation of Modern Catholicism, c. 1500–c. 1800* (Cambridge, 1997); L. Châtellier (ed.), *Religions en transition dans la seconde moitié du dix-huitième siècle* (Oxford, 2000); J. Delumeau, *Catholicism between Luther and Voltaire* (London, 1977); R.P.-C. Hsia, *The World of Catholic Renewal, 1540–1770* (Cambridge, 1998); and W.R. Ward, *Christianity under the Ancien Régime, 1648–1789* (Cambridge, 1999), a book that also embraces Protestantism.

Among works of reference the *Dizionario dell'Istituto dei Maestri Perfetti*, ed. G. Pelliccia and G. Rocca (9 vols. so far, Rome, 1974–), has the best coverage, with excellent articles on individual countries, e.g. 'Ungheria'; on Orders, e.g. 'Compagnia di Gesú'; and esp. on 'Soppressioni'.

Among other Catholic works of reference the best in English is *The New Catholic Encyclopaedia* (18 vols., New York, 1967–89). *The Oxford Dictionary of the Christian Church*, ed. F.L. Cross and E.A. Livingstone (3rd edn, Oxford, 1997), while useful, is not strong on Counter-Reformation Catholicism.

Books on monasticism that pay any attention to the period after the Reformation are few and far between, but M. Heimbucher's *Die Orden und Kongregationen der katholischen Kirche* (2 vols., Paderborn, 1933–4) is an authoritative *catalogue raisonné*, G. and M. Duchet-Suchaux, *Les ordres religieux: guide historique* (Paris, 1993) a handy dictionary, and L. Moulin, *Le monde vivant des religieux* (Paris, 1964) a stimulating essay. J. Angerer, *Stifte und Klöster in Bayern, Österreich und der Schweiz* (Pattloch, 1987), and E. Vavra (ed.), *Die Suche nach der verlorenen Paradies: Europäische Kultur im Spiegel der Klöster* (St Pölten, 2000), while concentrating on the monasteries of the German lands, have wider significance.

Works on art and architecture are numerous, and often helpful in a general way as well as on their specialism. Four that concentrate on monasteries are G. Bazin, *Paläste des Glaubens* (2 vols., Augsburg, 1997); W. Braunfels, *Monasteries of Western Europe: The Architecture of the Orders* (London, 1972); H. Schindler (ed.), *Europäische Barockklöster* (Munich, 1972); and S. Sitwell, *Monks, Nuns and Monasteries* (London, 1965). But many others discuss monasteries as part of general artistic history, e.g. G. Bazin, *The Baroque: Principles, Styles, Modes, Themes* (London, 1968); A. Blunt (ed.), *Baroque and Rococo: Architecture and Decoration* (London, 1978); J. Bourke, *Baroque Churches of Central Europe* (2nd edn, London, 1962); E. Hempel, *Baroque Art and Architecture in Central Europe* (Harmondsworth, 1965); T. da C. Kaufmann, *Court, Cloister and City: The Art and Culture of Central Europe, 1450–1800* (London, 1995); R. Middleton and D. Watkin, *Neoclassical and 19th Century Architecture* (2 vols., London, 1980); C. Norberg-Schulz, *Late Baroque and Rococo Architecture* (London, 1986); N. Pevsner, *An Outline of European Architecture* (Harmondsworth, 1943 and many subsequent editions); and R. Toman (ed.), *Baroque: Architecture, Sculpture, Painting* (Cologne, 1998).

On music see G.J. Buelow (ed.), *The Late Baroque Era: From the 1680s to 1740* (London, 1993), and N. Zaslaw (ed.), *The Classical Era* (London, 1989).

For the Enlightenment generally the best short survey is D. Outram, *The Enlightenment* (Cambridge, 1995). P. Gay's classic study, *The Enlightenment: An Interpretation* (2 vols., London, 1967–70), identifies the movement with paganism, an approach to which E. Cassirer, *The Philosophy of the Enlightenment* (Princeton, 1951) is still the most powerful antidote. R. Porter and M. Teich (eds.), *The Enlightenment in National Context* (Cambridge, 1981), has chapters on every major European country. F. Venturi, *Settecento riformatore* (5 vols. (7 tomes), Turin, 1965–90), although largely based on Italian sources, illuminates aspects of the history and thought of almost every European country in the second half of the eighteenth century. Two volumes (III and IV (tome 1)) have been translated by R. Burr Litchfield as *The End of the Old Regime in Europe, 1768–1776* (Princeton, 1989) and *The End of the Old Regime in Europe, 1776–1789*, vol. I (Princeton, 1991), but probably the most useful volume for this book, vol. II, *La chiesa e la repubblica dentro i loro limiti, 1758–1774* (Turin, 1976), has yet to be translated. On enlightened absolutism or despotism the best survey in English is H.M. Scott (ed.), *Enlightened Absolutism: Reform and Reformers in Later Eighteenth-Century Europe* (Basingstoke and London, 1990); in German, H. Reinalter and H. Klueting (eds.), *Der aufgeklärte Absolutismus in europäischen Vergleich* (Vienna, 2002).

The concept 'Catholic Enlightenment' remains controversial, equally unacceptable to many anticlerical laymen and to the present pope, but it is hard to see how students of eighteenth-century Catholicism can doubt its validity. Some prefer the more or less interchangeable term, 'Reform Catholicism', and discussion of these tendencies inevitably involves Jansenism as well. Most of the best work on these related themes concerns particular countries and will be listed under them, but Chadwick, *Popes and Revolution*, and Ward, *Christianity under the Ancien Régime* use these notions and provide the best accounts in English of the relevant developments across Catholic Europe. Martina's discussion in *La chiesa nell'età dell'assolutismo* is masterly. Among the other rare attempts to consider these themes generally are B. Plongeron's essay 'Was ist Katholische Aufklärung?', in E. Kovács (ed.), *Katholische Aufklärung und Josephinismus* (Vienna, 1979), pp. 11–56, and vol. VI of *Miscellanea historiae ecclesiasticae* (Brussels, 1987), a collection of conference papers under the title 'Les courants chrétiens de l'Aufklärung en Europe de la fin du XVIIe siècle jusque vers 1830', and W. Doyle, *Jansenism* (Basingstoke, 2000).

Work on the early years of the French Revolution necessarily focuses on France and will be listed under that heading. The Revolution's massive impact on Catholicism across the Continent between 1792 and 1814 has received almost no comparative treatment outside the general works already mentioned (Fliche and Martin, Jedin, Martina, Chadwick), G. Bruun, *Europe and the French Imperium, 1799–1814* (originally publ. 1938, London, 1963) and M. Broers, *Europe under Napoleon, 1799–1815* (London, 1996). See also P. Schroeder, *The Transformation of European Politics, 1763–1848* (Oxford, 1994) on Napoleon's policies. T.C.W. Blanning's writings are unique in relating the political, military and diplomatic aspects of the Revolution to its religious impact. Cf. his *The French Revolutionary Wars, 1787–1802* (London, 1996), *The French Revolution in Germany* (Oxford, 1983), and 'The role of religion in European counter-revolution, 1789–1815', in D. Beales and G. Best (eds.), *History, Society and the Churches* (Cambridge, 1985), pp. 195–214, a genuinely comparative study. E. Aerts and F. Crouzet (eds.), *Economic Effects of the French Revolutionary and Napoleonic Wars* (Leuven, 1990), contains challenging pieces.

INDIVIDUAL ORDERS

Most of the great Orders publish at least one scholarly periodical which carries many historical articles, e.g. *Analecta Augustiniana*; *Analecta Cisterciensia*; *Analecta Premonstratensia*; *Archivum Fratrum Predicatorum*; *Archivum Historicum Societatis Jesu*; *Bulletin d'Histoire Bénédictine*; *Etudes franciscaines*.

The Jesuits, especially their fall, have been extensively studied. As well as in the works already listed by Pastor (very lengthy sections), Chadwick, Martina and Venturi (*Settecento riformatore*, vol. II), there are a number of general histories in English, e.g. J.C.H. Aveling, *The Jesuits* (London, 1981). B. Duhr's works are important, esp. *Geschichte der Jesuiten in den Ländern deutscher Zunge*, vol. IV (Munich, 1928).

I have found particularly useful H. Holzapfel, *Handbuch der Geschichte des Franziskanerordens* (Freiburg, 1909); M.A. Pobladura, *Historia Generalis ordinis fratrum minorum cappuccinorum* (4 vols., Rome, 1938–51); P. Schmitz, *Histoire de l'Ordre de Saint-Benoît* (7 vols., Maredsous, 1942–56), vol. IV. The best introductory book on nuns is J.K. McNamara, *Sisters in Arms: Catholic Nuns through Two Millennia* (London, 1996).

BIBLIOGRAPHICAL ESSAY

INDIVIDUAL COUNTRIES

GERMANY

Germany is especially well served. Good general histories are J.G. Gagliardo, *Germany under the Old Regime, 1600–1790* (London, 1991), and J.J. Sheehan, *German History, 1770–1866* (Oxford, 1989). The work of Freiherr K.O. von Aretin on the *Reich* is fundamental, esp. *Das Alte Reich, 1648–1806* (3 vols., Stuttgart, 1988–98). Two books with a special bearing on the Estates and therefore on the background to the position of the monasteries are F.L. Carsten, *Princes and Parliaments in Germany* (Oxford, 1959), and J.G. Gagliardo, *Reich and Nation: The Holy Roman Empire as Idea and Reality, 1763–1806* (London, 1980). The *Handbuch der bayerischen Geschichte*, ed. M. Spindler, vol. III/2 (Munich, 1972), and the *Handbuch der baden-württembergischen Geschichte*, ed. H. Schwarzmeier, vol. II (Stuttgart, 1992) and vol. III (Stuttgart, 1995), have sections on individual monasteries. *Germania benedictina*, ed. F. Quarthal (5 vols., Augsburg, 1975) is a basic source.

From the vast literature on religious tendencies in Catholic Germany the following stand out: H. Klueting (ed.), *Katholische Aufklärung – Aufklärung in katholischen Deutschland* (Hamburg, 1993); L.A. Veit and L. Lenhart, *Kirche und Volksfrömmigkeit im Zeitalter des Barock* (Freiburg, 1956); R. Schlögl, *Glaube und Religion in der Säkularisierung* (Munich, 1995); and M.R. Forster, *Catholic Revival in the Age of the Baroque: Religious Identity in Southwest Germany, 1550–1750* (Cambridge, 2001). The articles by T.C.W. Blanning on Catholic Germany and E. Wangermann on Austria in Porter and Teich (eds.), *The Enlightenment in National Context*, are exceptionally vauable, as is Blanning's *Reform and Revolution in Mainz, 1743–1803* (Cambridge, 1974). On the German Enlightenment W.H. Bruford, *Germany in the Eighteenth Century: The Social Background of the Literary Revival* (Cambridge, 1935), remains impressive. On the economic basis of monastic building and power, much can be learned from H. Zückert, *Die sozialen Grundlagen der Barokkultur in Süddeutschland* (Stuttgart, 1988). Some of the major monasteries of south Germany have been the subject of impressive commemorative volumes, e.g. H. Heidegger and H. Ott (eds.), *St. Blasien: 200 Jahre Kloster- und Pfarrkirche* (Munich, 1983); R. Schneider (ed.), *Salem: 850 Jahre Abtei und Schloss* (Constance, 1984); G. Spaur, *Die Basilika Weingarten* (Sigmaringen, 1974). C. Schott, *Armenfürsorge, Bettelwesen und Vagantenbekämpfung in der Reichsabtei Salem* (Baden, 1978), is a rare work on a monastery's provision of social security, aspects of which are treated more generally in D. Stutzer, *Klöster als Arbeitgeber um 1800: Die bayerischen Klöster als Unternehmenseinheiten und ihre Sozialsysteme zur Zeit der Säkularisation 1803* (Göttingen, 1986). The travel accounts of J.N. Hauntinger, *Reise durch Schwaben und Bayern im Jahre 1784*, ed. G. Spahr (Weißenhorn, 1964), F. Nicolai, *Unter Bayern und Schwaben: Meine Reise im deutschen Süden 1781*, ed. U. Schlemmer (Berlin, 1989), and G.W. Zapf, *Reisen in einige Klöster Schwabens, durch den Schwarzwald und in die Schweiz im Jahr 1781* (Erlangen, 1786), have great value.

On the revolutionary and Napoleonic period, see Blanning, *The French Revolution and Germany*; D. Stutzer, *Die Säkularisation 1803* (2nd edn, Munich, 1978); J. Köhler (ed.), *Säkularisationen in Ostmitteleuropa* (Cologne, 1984); the important articles by K.J. Benz, 'Zu den kulturpolitischen Hintergründen der Säkularisation von 1803', *Saeculum*, 26 (1975), and E. Weis, 'Die Säkularisation der bayerischen Klöster 1802/03', *Sitzungsberichte der bayerischen Akademie der Wissenschaften, philosophisch-historische Klasse* (1983), heft 6; P. Wende, *Die geistlichen*

Staaten und ihre Auflösung im Urteil der zeitgenössischen Publizistik (Lübeck, 1966); R. Büttner, *Die Säkularisation der Kölner Geistlichen Institutionen* (Cologne, 1971); the older works of M. Erzberger, *Die Säkularisation in Württemberg von 1802–1810* (Stuttgart, 1902), and A.M. Scheglmann, *Geschichte der Säkularisation in rechtsrheinischen Bayern* (3 vols., Regensburg, 1903–8); and the excellent exhibition catalogue, *Glanz und Ende der alten Klöster*, ed. J. Kirmeier and M. Treml (Munich, 1991).

On art and architecture, as well as the more general surveys already mentioned, H.-R. Hitchcock, *Rococo Architecture in Southern Germany* (London, 1968), N. Lieb, *Barockkirchen zwischen Donau und Alpen* (6th edn, Munich, 1992), G. von Knorre (ed.), *Barock in Baden-Württemberg* (2 vols., Karlsruhe, 1981), and H.-G. Richardi and A.A. Haase, *Burgen, Schlösser und Klöster in Bayern* (Erlangen, 1993).

SWITZERLAND

J. Steinberg, *Why Switzerland?* (2nd edn, Cambridge, 1996), is a provocative introduction. On church history a scholarly collection in many volumes, *Helvetia sacra*, details the history of ecclesiastical institutions. For a general church history L. Vischer, L. Schenker and R. Dellsperger (eds.), *Ökumenische Kirchengeschichte der Schweiz* (Basel, 1994), is lively (and also available in French). The article 'Svizzera' in vol. IX of the *Dizionario dei maestri perfetti* is excellent on monasteries. The history of Catholic Switzerland is closely involved with that of southern Germany (including Vorarlberg, now in Austria) and with northern Italy. Many dioceses, esp. Constance, straddled political boundaries. Hence many of the books on south Germany (e.g. Forster, *Catholic Revival*) include something about Switzerland. Angerer, *Stifte und Klöster*, Bazin, *Paläste des Glaubens*, vol. II, and Bourke, *Baroque Churches of Central Europe*, have sections on the major Swiss monasteries. On Einsiedeln see also Schindler, *Barockklöster*, pp. 85–116; and on St Gall J. Duft, A. Gössi and W. Vogler, *Die Abtei St Gall* (St Gall, 1986); W. Vogler, *Die Fürstabtei St. Gallen und die französische Revolution* (St Gall, 1990); *Abt Pankraz Vorster und die Aufhebung der Fürstabtei St. Gallen* (Freiburg, Schwyz, 1954). On Lucerne H. Wicki, *Staat, Kirche, Religiosität: Der Kanton Luzern zwischen barocker Tradition und Aufklärung* (Stuttgart, 1990), p. 539. U. Im Hof, *The Enlightenment* (Oxford, 1994), gives Switzerland its due.

THE AUSTRIAN MONARCHY

The best general history of the Austrian Monarchy of this period in English is C.W. Ingrao, *The Habsburg Monarchy, 1618–1815* (Cambridge, 1994). A brilliant treatment, deploying unique linguistic capacity and giving due place to monasteries, is R.J.W. Evans, *The Making of the Habsburg Monarchy, 1550–1700: An Interpretation* (Oxford, 1979), which throws much light also on the eighteenth century. P.G.M. Dickson's magisterial *Finance and Government under Maria Theresia, 1740–1780* (2 vols., Oxford, 1987) contains important information and insights on the Church and on monasteries, supplemented by his major article, 'Joseph II's reshaping of the Austrian Church, *Historical Journal*, 36 (1993), pp. 89–114. J. Wodka, *Kirche in Österreich* (Vienna, 1959), is a useful general history of the Austrian Church. Much has been written on religious developments leading up to and including Josephism. Some of the best works in the field are, in English,

R.A. Kann, *A Study in Austrian Intellectual History: From Late Baroque to Romanticism* (New York, 1960), C.H. O'Brien, 'Ideas of religious toleration at the time of Joseph II: a study of the Enlightenment among Catholics in Austria', *Transactions of the American Philosophical Society*, vol. 59, pt 7 (1969), E. Wangermann, *The Austrian Achievement, 1700–1800* (London, 1973), and F.A.J. Szabo, *Kaunitz and Enlightened Absolutism, 1753–1780* (Cambridge, 1994); and in German G. Klingenstein, *Staatsverwaltung und kirchliche Autorität im 18. Jahrhundert: Das Problem der Zensur in der theresianischen Reform* (Vienna, 1970); P. Hersche, *Der Spätjansenismus in Österreich* (Vienna, 1977); R. Pammer, *Glaubensabfall und Wahre Andacht: Barockreligiosität, Reformkatholizismus und Laizismus in Oberösterreich 1700–1820* (Vienna, 1994), and the three classic works on Josephism: F. Valjavec, *Der Josephinismus: Zur geistigen Entwicklung Österreichs im achtzehnten und neunzehnten Jahrhundert* (2nd edn, Munich, 1945), by a historian of thought who places his theme in a wider context, F. Maaß, *Der Josephinismus* (5 vols., Vienna, 1951–61, documents with introductions), by a hard Jesuit; and E. Winter, *Der Josefinismus: Die Geschichte des österreichischen Reformkatholizismus* (2nd edn, Berlin, 1962), influenced by Marxist historiography. Scholarly biographies of Joseph II, necessarily discussing his legislation, are P. von Mitrofanov, *Joseph II* (2 vols., Vienna, 1910); D. Beales, *Joseph II, vol. 1: In the Shadow of Maria Theresa, 1741–1780* (Cambridge, 1987); and T.C.W. Blanning, *Joseph II* (London, 1994). C. von Hock and I. Bidermann, *Der österreichische Staatsrath* (Vienna, 1879), concentrates on the reign of Joseph II and reveals much about the debates in the *Staatsrat* from material now lost. Works of special value on related themes are: J.V.H. Melton, *Absolutism and the Eighteenth-Century Origins of Compulsory Schooling in Prussia and Austria* (Cambridge, 1988); L. Bodi, *Tauwetter in Wien: Zur Prosa der österreichischen Aufklärung, 1781–1795* (Frankfurt, 1977); E. Kovács, *Katholische Aufklärung und Josephinismus* (Vienna, 1979). A large number of pamphlets was published in the 1780s about Joseph's religious policies, which have been much studied, especially by Bodi and Wangermann. The most important for this book is I. von Born's *Monachologie* (1783).

Specifically concerned with the monasteries and their suppression are G. Winner, *Die Klosteraufhebungen in Niederösterreich und Wien* (Vienna, 1967); R. Hittmair, *Der josefinische Klostersturm im Land ob der Enns* (Freiburg im Breisgau, 1907); A. Wolf, *Die Aufhebung der Klöster in Innerösterreich, 1782–1790* (Vienna, 1871); and L. Raber, *Die österreichischen Franziskaner im Josefinismus* (Maria Enzersdorf, ?1983). Of the many volumes on individual monasteries I have found especially useful E. Bruckmüller, B. Ellegast and others, *900 Jahre Benediktiner in Melk* (Melk, 1989), and R.N. Freeman, *The Practice of Music at Melk Abbey: Based on the Documents, 1681–1826* (Vienna, 1989); on St Florian *Welt des Barock* (2 vols., Linz, 1986).

On art B. Grimschitz et al., *Barock in Österreich* (Vienna, 1962), F. Röhrig, *Alte Stifte in Österreich* (2 vols., Vienna, 1966) and on one particularly important and interesting aspect, wine production and consumption, the excellent work of R. Malli, *Der Schatz im Keller: Zur Weinwirtschaft der Waldviertler Klöster* (Horn, 2001).

Within the Monarchy, V.-L. Tapié, *The Rise and Fall of the Habsburg Monarchy* (London, 1971), is especially well informed on **Bohemia**; and see O.J. Blazicek, *Baroque Art in Bohemia* (Feltham, 1968), and F. and R. Malecek, *Strahov Praha* (Prague, ?1993).

On **Hungary** C.A. Macartney, author of *The Habsburg Empire, 1790–1918* (London, 1968), was particularly knowledgeable, and he included a chapter on Joseph II, but what he had to say about monasteries was mostly wrong. É.H. Balázs, the doyenne of Hungarian historians of the eighteenth-century, has published in English *Hungary and the Habsburgs, 1765–1800* (Budapest, 1997), and the doyen, D. Kosáry, *Culture and Society in Eighteenth-Century Hungary* (Budapest, 1987). H. Marczali, *Hungary in the Eighteenth Century*, transl. A.B. Yolland (Cambridge, 1910), remains useful as the first and introductory volume of a classic three-volume work on Hungary under Joseph II, of which the remaining volumes were never translated: *Magyarország története II. József korában* (Budapest, 1884–5). B.K. Király's chapter in Callahan and Higgs, *Church and Society*, is useful, as is L. Csóka, *Geschichte des benediktinischen Mönchtums in Ungarn* (Munich, 1980), and M. Bánhegyi, *The Community Table: The Baroque Dining Hall of the Abbey of Pannonhalma* (Pannonhalma, n.d.). Important work has appeared on brotherhoods from G. Tüskés and E. Knapp, e.g. 'Bruderschaften in Ungarn im 17. und 18. Jahrhundert', *Bayerisches Jahrbuch für Volkskunde* (1992), pp. 1–23. On the dissolution of monasteries by Joseph II P. Bán, 'Új adatok a szerzetsrendek II. József korabeli megszüntetéséröl', *Baranya*, 3 (1990–1), pp. 61–71, and M. Velladics, 'A II. József korabeli szerzetesrendi abolício statisztikája (1782–1847)', *Századok* (1999), pp. 1259–78.

For **Galicia** there is H. Glassl, *Das österreichische Einrichtungswerk in Galizien (1772–1790)* (Wiesbaden, 1975).

There is no satisfactory general history of **Belgium** in English before the period covered by E.H. Kossmann, *The Low Countries, 1780–1940* (Oxford, 1978). H. Pirenne, *Histoire de Belgique*, vol. V (Brussels, 1920), needs to be supplemented by H. Hasquin (ed.), *La Belgique autrichienne* (Brussels, 1987), and W.W. Davis, *Joseph II: An Imperial Reformer for the Austrian Netherlands* (The Hague, 1974). For the Church E. de Moreau, *L'église en Belgique des origines au début du XXe siècle* (Brussels, 1944), and on monasteries A. d'Haenens (ed.), *Abbayes de Belgique* (Brussels, 1973), contains valuable material. On Joseph's policies towards the monasteries J. Laenen, *Etude sur la suppression des couvents par l'empereur Joseph II dans les Pays-Bas autrichiens et plus spécialement dans le Brabant (1783–1794)* (Antwerp, 1905), and the excellent G. de Schepper, *La réorganisation des paroisses et la suppression des couvents dans les Pays-Bas autrichiens sous le règne de Joseph II* (Louvain, 1942). For the 'Brabant revolution': L. Delplace, *Joseph II et la révolution brabançonne* (Bruges, 1891); S. Tassier, *Les démocrates belges de 1789* (originally published 1930, 2nd edn, Brussels, 1989); J.L. Polasky, *Revolution in Brussels, 1787–1793* (Brussels, Hanover, N.H., and London, 1987); J. Craeybeckx, 'The Brabant revolution: a conservative revolt in a backward country?', *Acta Historiae Neerlandica*, 4 (1970), pp. 49–83. The MS diary of Malingié, monk of St Peter's Ghent, in the University Library of Ghent, is highly informative. On monastic architecture, Bazin, *Paläste des Glaubens*, vol. II.

For the period of French occupation, L. de Lanzac de Laborie, *La domination française en Belgique* (2 vols., Paris, 1895); P. Verhaegen, *La Belgique sous la domination française, 1792–1814* (5 vols., Brussels, 1923–9).

For **Lombardy** and **Tuscany** see the general works listed under Italy below and, specifically for Lombardy, D. Sella and C. Capra, *Il ducato di Milano dal 1535 al 1796* (Storia d'Italia, ed. G. Galasso, vol. XI, Turin, 1984); F. Valsecchi, *L'assolutismo illuminato in Austria e in Lombardia* (2 vols., Bologna, 1931–4). For Tuscany F. Scaduto, *Stato e chiesa sotto Leopoldo I granduca di Toscana* (Leghorn, 1885); A. Pincelli, *Monasteri e conventi del territorio aretino* (Florence, 2000). For the reaction in Tuscany, G. Turi, *'Viva Maria' la reazione alle riforme leopoldine (1790–1799)* (Florence, 1969).

BIBLIOGRAPHICAL ESSAY

FRANCE

Useful works of reference are L. Le Grand, *Les sources de l'histoire religieuse de la Révolution aux Archives Nationales* (Paris, 1914), and L. Bély, *Dictionnaire de l'Ancien Régime* (Paris, 1996). The standard general histories of early modern France, written by professors at her secular universities, virtually ignore monasteries, if not the church as a whole. A lively example is E. Le Roy Ladurie, *The Ancien Regime: A History of France 1660–1774* (Oxford, 1991). Among recent French contributions to religious and ecclesiastical history – 'the new religious history' – four that make a serious attempt to discuss, in their context, the role and development of monasteries are: M. Vovelle, *Piété baroque et déchristianisation en Provence au XVIIIe siècle: les attitudes devant la mort d'après les clauses des testaments* (Paris, 1973); F. Lebrun (ed.), *Histoire des catholiques en France* (2nd edn, Paris, 1980), containing C. Langlois's and T. Tackett's splendid chapter called 'A l'épreuve de la Révolution'; P. Boutry et al., *Histoire de la France religieuse*, vol. III: *Du roi Très Chrétien à la laïcité républicaine, XVIIIe–XIXe siècle* (Paris, 1991); and L. Châtellier (ed.), *Religions en transition dans la seconde moitié du dix-huitième siècle* (Oxford, 2000). Impressive treatments of related issues include R. Chartier, *The Cultural Uses of Print in Early Modern France* (Princeton, 1987); F. Lebrun, M. Venard and J. Queniart, *Histoire générale de l'enseignement et de l'éducation en France*, vol. II (Paris, 1981); R. Darnton, *The Forbidden Best-Sellers of Pre-Revolutionary France* (London, 1996); L.W.B. Brockliss, *French Higher Education in the Seventeenth and Eighteenth Centuries: A Cultural History* (Oxford, 1987).

J. McManners, *Church and Society in Eighteenth-Century France* (2 vols., Oxford, 1998), a learned and loving account of the French Church of the *ancien régime*, is unlikely ever to be superseded and ought to transform the historiography of the period. It does not, however, stray beyond the outbreak of the Revolution. See also McManners' *French Ecclesiastical Society under the Ancien Regime: A Study of Angers in the Eighteenth Century* (Manchester, 1960), and N. Aston, *Religion and Revolution in France, 1780–1804* (Basingstoke, 2000). On Jansenism and the expulsion of the Jesuits, as well as McManners, Pastor and Boutry, see Doyle, *Jansenism*; D.K. Van Kley's two books, *The Jansenists and the Expulsion of the Jesuits from France, 1757–1765* (London, 1975), and *The Religious Origins of the French Revolution* (New Haven and London, 1996); M. Cottret, *Jansénismes et lumières* (Paris, 1998); and P. Chaunu, M. Foisil and F. de Noirfontaine, *Le basculement religieux de Paris au XVIIIe siècle* (Paris, 1998).

On the monasteries themselves, J. Evans, *Monastic Architecture in France from the Renaissance to the Revolution* (Cambridge, 1964), contains a unique photographic record and a most useful introduction to the history of the main Orders. J. Taralon, *La France des abbayes* (Paris, 1978), is an accessible survey. Especially interesting are J. de Viguerie (ed.), *La vocation religieuse et sacerdotale en France, XVII – XIX siècles* (Angers, 1979); on the Capuchins, B. Dompnier, *Enquête au pays des frères des anges: les Capucins de la province de Lyon aux XVIIe et XVIIIe siècles* (St-Etienne, 1993); on nuns E. Rapley, *The Dévotes: Women and Church in Seventeenth-Century France* (London, 1990). For the *commission des réguliers* the invaluable P. Chevallier, *Loménie de Brienne et l'ordre monastique (1766–1789)* (2 vols., Paris, 1959–60) does not wholly supersede S. Lemaire, *La commission des réguliers, 1766–1780* (Paris, 1926), or even J.M. Prat, *Essai historique sur la destruction des ordres religieux en France au dix-huitième siècle* (Paris, 1845). Two statistical surveys rely on the papers of the commission: M. Peigné-Delacourt, *Tableau des abbayes et des monastères d'hommes en France* (Arras, 1875) (with some information on nunneries) and L. Lecestre, *Abbayes, prieurés et couvents* d'hommes en France: liste générale d'après les papiers de la Commission des Réguliers en 1768 (Paris, 1902).

Articles in the *Encyclopédie* are of course illuminating about attitudes to monks and nuns, as are [S.N.H. Linguet,] *Essai philosophique sur le monachisme* (Paris, 1775), and the anonymous *Histoire philosophique du monachisme* (2 vols., London, 1788).

For the Revolution G. Lefebvre, *The French Revolution: From its Origins to 1793* (London, 1962), has a broader approach than many French writings. But the masterpieces of both Burke, *Reflections on the French Revolution* (1790), and Tocqueville, *The Ancien Regime* (1859), are of enduring importance, especially in relation to religion and the Church. W. Doyle, *The Oxford History of the French Revolution* (Oxford, 1989) provides the best introduction to the subject, which, like S. Schama, *Citizens* (London, 1989), pays more attention to the Church and to monks and nuns than do most modern writers on France. Other valuable accounts with different emphases have been given by J.F. Bosher, *The French Revolution* (London, 1989), and D.M.G. Sutherland, *France, 1789–1815: Revolution and Counter-Revolution* (London, 1985). T. Tackett, *Becoming a Revolutionary: The Deputies of the French National Assembly and the Emergence of a Revolutionary Culture (1789–1790)* (Princeton, 1996), explains the radicalisation of the Revolution most effectively, and A. Aftalion, *The French Revolution: An Economic Interpretation* (Cambridge, 1990), clarifies the financial issues. The published debates and *procès-verbaux* of the successive assemblies are splendid sources, as is the welter of pamphlets and caricatures. On religious aspects the grand old works of S. Sicard, *Le clergé de France pendant la Révolution* (3 vols., Paris, 1912–27), and P. de La Gorce, *Histoire religieuse de la Révolution française* (5 vols., Paris, 1905–23), remain invaluable, like A. Denys-Buirette, *Les questions religieuses dans les cahiers de 1789* (Paris, 1919). J. McManners, *The French Revolution and the Church* (London, 1969), is an incomparable short study. L. Detrez, *La Flandre religieuse sous la Révolution (1789–1801)*, vol. I (Lille, 1928 [no more published]) is impressive. O.H. Hufton, *Women and the Limits of Citizenship in the French Revolution* (London, 1992), opens up a major theme.

The suppression of the monasteries as such has attracted relatively little work, but A. Aulard's *La révolution française et les congrégations* (Paris, 1903) is an essential compendium of documents, Sicard gives vivid details of the process, and an excellent study by B. Plongeron, *Les réguliers de Paris devant le serment constitutionnel* (Paris, 1964), shows what could be done for France as a whole. A. Sorel, *Le couvent des Carmes et le séminaire de Saint-Sulpice pendant la Terreur* (Paris, 1863), describes a famous case. L. Réau, *Histoire du vandalisme*, ed. M. Fleury and G.-M. Leproux (Paris, 1994), chronicles, somewhat indiscriminately, the depredations of the revolutionaries. Broader condemnation is to be found in R. Sédillot, *Le coût de la révolution française* (Paris, 1987). Chateaubriand's *Memoirs*, transl. R. Baldick (Harmondsworth, 1965), and his *Le génie du christianisme* (Paris, 1802) remain fundamental sources.

ITALY

Venturi's *Settecento riformatore* is a treasure-house of information and insights about Italian thought, always in relation to that of other countries and often illuminating political, religious and even economic development on the way. Some of his essays were published in S.J. Woolf (ed.), *Italy and the Enlightenment* (London, 1972). His collection of texts, *Illuministi italiani* (7 vols., Milan, 1958–) is immensely valuable. A.C. Jemolo, *Il Giansenismo in Italia prima della Rivoluzione* (Bari, 1928), remains fundamental.

D. Carpanetto and G. Ricuperati, *Italy in the Age of Reason, 1685–1789* (London, 1987), is the best general survey in English. H.M. Acton, *The Bourbons of Naples, 1734–1825* (London, 1956), is useful. On the Italian Church Chadwick, *Popes and Revolution*; M. Rosa (ed.), *Clero e società nell'Italia moderna* (Rome, 1992), and, mostly too late for this book, *Clero e società nell'Italia contemporanea* (Rome, 1992); G. Chittolini and G. Miccoli (eds.), *La chiesa e il potere politico dal medioevo all'età contemporanea* (Turin, 1986); G. de Rosa, T. Gregory and A. Vauchez, *Storia dell'Italia religiosa*, vol. II: *L'età moderna* (Rome and Bari, 1994); and Rosa's article in Callahan and Higgs, *Church and Society*. On monasticism, as well as the works just mentioned, there is a growing series called *Italia benedettina*, published at Cesena; L. Penco, *Storia del monachesimo in Italia nell'epoca moderna* (Rome, 1968), G. Boaga, *La soppressione innocenziana dei piccoli conventi in Italia* (Rome, 1971); G. Farnedi and G. Spinelli (eds.), *Settecento monastico italiano* (Cesena, 1990); F.G.B. Trolese (ed.), *Il monachesimo italiano dalle riforme illuministiche all'unità nazionale (1768–1870)* (Cesena, 1992). In English M. Laven, 'Sex and celibacy in early modern Venice', H J, 44 (2001), pp. 865–88. On art and architecture Bazin, *Paläste des Glaubens*, vol. I; R. Wittkower, *Art and Architecture in Italy, 1600–1750* (Harmondsworth, 1958). On music C. Burney, *Music, Men, and Manners, in France and Italy 1770*, ed. H.E. Poole (London, 1969), and J. Rosselli, *Singers of Italian Opera: The History of a Profession* (Cambridge, 1992).

For the revolutionary period C. Zaghi, *L'Italia di Napoleone* (Turin, 1989); C. Naselli, *La soppressione napoleonica delle corporazioni religiose* (Rome, 1986); R. De Felice, *La vendita dei beni nazionali nella Repubblica romana del 1798–99* (Rome, 1966); P. Notario, *La vendita dei beni nazionali in Piemonte nel periodo napoleonico (1800–1814)* (Turin, 1980); P. Villani, *La vendita dei beni dello stato nel regno di Napoli, 1806–1815* (Milan, 1964).

[See also books listed above under 'Lombardy' and 'Tuscany'.]

POLAND

In English there is J. Lukowski, *The Partitions of Poland* (Harlow, 1999) and J. Kłoczowski's 'The Polish Church', in Callahan and Higgs, *Church and Society*, which can be amplified from his historical atlas, *Dzieje chrzescijaństwa polskiego*, vol. II (Paris, 1991). There is also, mostly in French, M. Rechowicz (ed.), *Poland's Millennium of Catholicism* (*Le millénaire du catholicisme en Pologne*) (Lublin, 1969), and a number of relevant articles in *Miscellanea historiae ecclesiasticae*, 6 (1987).

PORTUGAL

Again, there is a chapter (by Higgs) in Callahan and Higgs, *Church and Society*, collection. A.H. de Oliveira Marques, *History of Portugal* (2 vols., London, 1972), is the best general history available in English. The standard history of the Church is F. de Almeida, *História da Igreja em Portugal*, of which vol. III (new edn, Lisbon, 1970) is the relevant part. The *Dicionário de história da Igreja em Portugal*, ed. A.A.B. de Andrade (Lisbon, apparently only 2 vols. so far, 1979–83) promises well. On Pombal K. Maxwell, *Pombal: Paradox of the Enlightenment* (Cambridge, 1995), and M.H. Carvalho dos Santos (ed.), *Pombal revisitado* (2 vols., Lisbon, 1984); on the expulsion of the Jesuits J. Caeiro, *Historia da expulsão da Companhia de Jesus da provincia de Portugal* (Lisbon, 1991); and on church reform more generally S.J. Miller, *Portugal and Rome c. 1748–1830: An Aspect of Catholic Enlightenment* (Rome, 1978). For architecture, Bazin, *Paläste des Glaubens*, vol. I; J. Lees-Milne, *Baroque in Spain and Portugal* (London, 1960); L.F. da Gama, *Palácio nacional de Mafra* (Lisbon, 1992). For the statistics of monasteries, monks and nuns the least insecure data are to be found in F. de Sousa, 'O rendimento das ordens religiosas nos finais do antigo regime', *Revista de História Económica e Social*, 7 (1981), pp. 1–28.

SPAIN

For a general history of early modern Spain see J.H. Elliott, *Imperial Spain, 1469–1716* (London, 1963); J. Lynch, *Spain under the Habsburgs* (2nd edn, London, 1981), and *Bourbon Spain, 1700–1808* (London, 1989). To these should be added, on the Spanish Enlightenment, R. Herr, *The Eighteenth Century Revolution in Spain* (Princeton, 1958), his *Rural Change and Royal Finances in Spain at the End of the Old Regime* (London, 1989) and J. Sarrailh, *L'Espagne éclairéé de la seconde moitié du XVIIIe siècle*. On church history the essential work is R. García-Villoslada (ed.), *Historia de la Iglesia en España* (5 vols., Madrid, 1978–80), vols. IV and V. Chadwick, *Popes and Revolution*, and Callahan's article in Callahan and Higgs, *Church and society*, are helpful. The history of the old Orders is treated in A. Linage Conde, *El monacato en España e Hispanoamerica* (Salamanca, 1977). Other valuable books are: for Spanish baroque piety C.M.N. Eire, *From Madrid to Purgatory: The Art and Craft of Dying in Sixteenth-Century Spain* (Cambridge, 1995); on royal power over the Church C. Hermann, *L'église d'Espagne sous le patronage royal (1476–1834* (Madrid, 1988); for statistics of monks and nuns M. Saéz Marín, *Datos sobre la Iglesia española contemporanea, 1768–1868* (Madrid, 1975); for monastic revenues A.L. López Martínez, *La economía de las órdenes religiosas en el antiguo régimen* (Seville, 1992); for Charles III's policies A. Guimerá (ed.), *El reformismo borbónico* (Madrid, 1996), and *Carlos III y la Ilustrácion* (2 vols., 1988–90); and for 'disentailment' R. Herr, *Rural Change and Royal Finances in Spain at the End of the Old Regime* (London, 1989).

On architecture, apart from Bazin's, Blunt's and Tomar's general books, there are two volumes on *Monasterios de España* (vol. I by P.N. Palacio, 5th edn, Madrid, 1988; vol. II by W. Rincón García, Madrid, 1998); also Lees-Milne, *Baroque in Spain and Portugal*, and R. Guerra de la Vega, *Iglesias y Conventos del Antiguo Madrid* (Madrid, 1996).

INDEX

Aa, the, Jesuit brotherhood, 148
Abbaye-aux-Bois *see* Paris
abbé, definition, 19
'abbé', article by Voltaire, 236
abbess(es), 5, 21, 33–4, 59, 86, 99, 240
abbeys, definition, 18
abbot(s), 5
   authority challenged, 174, 182, 233
   in Belgium, 210, 211, 219, 221–3, 297
   commendatory, 33, 89, 104–6, 174, 204, 219, 250, 253, 314
   definition, 18–19
   elections, 33–4, 104
   as enlightened rulers, 81
   in France, 107
   grand state, 235, 236, 238
   of humble origin, 78, 293
   imperial, ch. 2; 59
   of Melk, 45–6
   power of, 74–6, 174, 294
   see also Estates, generals, monasteries, monks
Acta sanctorum, 90, 221
Afflighem, Belgian abbey, 213
Africa, north, 115, 116, 150
Aftalion, Florin, historian, 304
afterlife, 120
agriculture, monastic, 87–8, 96, 213
   see also landownership, wine

Albert, prince, of Saxe-Teschen, 216, 219, 226
Albrechtsberger, Johann Georg, 51–2
Alcobaça, Cistercian monastery, Portugal, 124, 153, Ill. 20
Alembert, Jean d', *philosophe*, 103, 145, 156, 167, 177
Allgemeine deutsche Bibliothek, 71
Allio, Donato Felice d', 54
Alps, the, 112
Alsace, 87, 93
altars, 40, 78
Altbayern, 74
Altenburg, Benedictine monastery, Lower Austria, 15
America, 116
ancien régime, nature of, 13
Angelico, Fra, 135, 294
Angers, 14
Anjou, 86
Apology for Womankind, 182
appel comme d'abus, 171
Aquinas, St Thomas, 80
Aragon, 112
Aranda, count of, 159, 164, 167
Aranjuez, 159
archangels, 120
archbishop(s) *see* bishop(s)

371

INDEX

architecture and buildings, 4, 56
    church, beauty of, 268
    French Revolution and, 70–1, 84–5, 264, 265–7
    neo-classical, 70–1, 95
    survival of monastic, 294
    see also Baroque, and under individual countries
Aretin, Freiherr J.C. von, 308
Aretin, Freiherr K.O. von, 309
aristocracy *see* nobility
Arles, 89
armies
    of France, revolutionary, 272, 274
    monastic, 59
Arnaud, Baculard d', 111, 238
Arnauld, Angélique, 89, 104
Arrábidas, Portuguese Order, 122
Arras, abbey of St Vaast, 87, 232, 307
Artois, 87, 232, 235
Asam brothers, 294
assassination
    attempts, 151, 154
    Jesuits alleged to approve, 148, 155, 160
Assembly of Notables in France (1787), 239
assignats, 259, 304–5
Assisi, 126, 294
Augsburg, 72
Augustine, St, 21, 35, 36
Augustinian Orders, 4, 12, 21, 29, 35, 46, 72, 87, 88, 115, 159, 163, 164
Augustinus, 35
Augustus, king of Poland and elector of Saxony, 27
Austria (the Austrian duchies/modern republic), 8–9, 14–15, 16, 18, 22–3, 30, 33, 39–57, 195, 197
    dioceses, 45
    historians, 181
    Lower, 42, 82, 180
    monasteries, 39–57, 58, 74, 84, 87, 179, 180, 181, 226, 227, 307
    Upper, 51, 66, 78, 183, 202
Austrian Empire (after 1804), 8
Austrian Monarchy, ch. 8; 2, 27, 34, 58, 73, 78–81, 82, 127
    alliance with France, 162
    area, 179
    Babenberg rulers of, 42, 54
    central provinces, 180, 185, 226
    compared with France, 169
    constituent parts, 179
    and Counter-Reformation, ch. 2; 181
    education reform, 190, 225, 226
    and Jesuit suppression, 161–6
    monasteries, monks and nuns, numbers of, 86, 130, 180, 185, 316; in nineteenth century, 226; rebuilding and Baroquisation, ch. 2; 181–2; reform, ch. 8, compared with France, 169; suppressions, ch. 8; 8, 161–6; consequences, 306, number, 194–7; surviving, 226, 228, 306, 307
    population, 180
    rulers' power over the Church, 7
    Turkish war (1787–91), 225
    variations between provinces, 180, 184
    and Weingarten, 66
    see also Belgium, Bohemia, Galicia, Hungary, Jesuits, Josephism, Lombardy
Austrian Netherlands *see* Belgium
Austrian Succession, War of the (1740–8), 103–4, 144, 181
Aveiro, duke of, 151
Averbode, Premonstratensian abbey in Belgium, 293
Avignon, 162, 270, 271

Bacon, Francis, 156
Balkans, 18, 54
ballets, 52, 98
balloon ascents, 73, 215
Barnave, 255
Barry, Mme du, 101
Baroque, 13, 143
    criticised, 69, 95, 294
    decline of, 69, 70–3, 143, 181
    fine examples of monastic, 294
    French, 39, 93, 94–6
    German and Austrian, 39–41, 49–68, 76–9, 181–2
    Italian, 39, 60
    and popular culture, 76–9, 81
    Spanish and Portuguese, 118, 122, 123
Basel, Treaty of (1795), 280, 284
Basilian monasteries, 316
Batthyány, count Joseph, cardinal archbishop of Esztergom, 209

INDEX

Baudeau, *abbé*, 295
Bavaria, 3, 7, 14–15, 28, 33, 45, 51, 58, 66, 74, 79, 80, 284, 285–6
 Academy, 80, 106
 exchange proposal, 217
 and Jesuits, 162
 monastic wealth, 82, 289
 suppressions, 58, 285, 286, 289–90; state's gains from, 289, 290; views on, 308–10
Bayle, Pierre, 28
Bazin, Germain, 49–68, 94
Béarn, 87
Beaumont, Christophe de, archbishop of Paris, 153–4
Bec, abbey, Normandy, 92, 105, 251, Ill. 15(a) and (b)
Beccaria, marchese Cesare, 187
Beckford, William, 120, 153
 Vathek, 313
Bédos, dom, 94, Ill. 9
Beer, Michael, architect, 60
beer, production by monasteries, 4, 50–1, 213, 218
Beethoven, Ludwig van, 52, 272
Belém, Portuguese monastery, 115
Belgium, 8–9, 30, 35, 90, 179–80, 204, 217, 260, 277, 283, 316
 clergy, numbers in relation to population, 212
 comparison with France, 231
 constitutions, 210, 211
 and Enlightenment, 212
 and Francis II, 226
 French invasions, 226
 French rule, 226, 231; comparison with Germany, 289
 inaugurations: Joseph II, 213, 216; Leopold II, 226; Francis II, 226
 and Jansenism, 181, 212
 and Joseph II's policies, 143, 219–21, 222
 and Leopold II, 225–6, 260
 monasteries, monks and nuns: criticised, 213; defended by bishops, 213, by Estates of Hainaut, 213; landholding, 213; lifestyle, 213; numbers, 212, 231, 348, in relation to population, 180; popular support for, 226; suppressions by Joseph II, 216, reversed, 226; suppressions by French, 226; wealth, 213
 population, 212
 Revolution in, 219–25
 and treaties, 211
 United Republic
 and the Vienna government, 211, 212
 wealth, 212
 see also Brabant, Flanders, Hainaut, Luxembourg
bells, 96, 153, 183–4, 215, 264, 273, 309
Benedict, St, 126, 237
Benedict XIII, pope 1724–30, 7
Benedict XIV, pope 1740–58, 36–7, 129, 148, 151, 155
Benedictine Order(s), Benedictines, 4, 7, 12, 14–15, 19–21, 29–30, 37, 46, 49, 63, 74–82, 88, 89, 115, 126, 159
 and brotherhoods, 78
 Cluniac branch, 86
 English congregation, 76
 Exempt, Order of, 174–5
 history, 90
 in Hungary, 207, 208
 learning and scholarship, 89–91; *see also* Maurists
 under Napoleon, 268
 Portuguese reform, 122
 in Spain, 156, 159
 in towns, 134
Benediktbeuren abbey, 14–15
Benevento, 162
Bentley, Thomas, 87
Berlin, 71, 312
Bernard, St, 90
Bessel, Gottfried, abbot of Göttweig, 55
Bianchi, Isidoro, 139
Bible, 35, 36, 52, 68, 113, 163
Birnau abbey, 78–9
bishop(s), archbishop(s), 5, 7, 21, 30, 31, 33
 aristocratic, 78, 97, 104
 as commendatory abbots, 104, 105
 in Estates, 96, 209
 and French education, 169
 and French Revolution, 241, 259, 264
 and Jansenists, 153–4
 and monasteries, monks and nuns, 89, 97, 109, 170, 172–5, 182, 213
 prince-, 58, 78, 284
 seminaries, 31, 132, 194
Blanchard, 215

373

Blanning, T.C.W., historian, 14
Blickle, Peter, historian, 60–2
Boaga, G., historian, 128
Bohemia, 30, 33, 39, 57, 181, 203
　ratio of regulars to population, 180
Boisgelin, archbishop of Aix, 253
Bolland, Jean, 90
Bollandists, 221
Bologna, Concordat of (1516), 103
　and monasteries, 131
Bonaparte *see* Napoleon
Bondorf, duchy of, 69
Bonneval abbey, 251
Bordeaux, abbey of Ste-Croix, 94
Born, Ignaz von, 202
　Monachologia, 202
Bosher, J.F., historian, 19
Boskovic, Rudjer, Jesuit scientist, 147, 295
Bourbon dynasty, Spanish, 114, 157, 208
Bouteville, French minister in Belgium, 272–3
Brabant, duchy of, 210
　Council of, 210, 219, 221
　　Estates of, 210, 217, 219, 220, 221, 222, 223, 225, 226
　　　revolutions: little (1787), 219; major (1789), 215, 226
Brandenburg, 59
Brantôme, Maurist abbey, 92
Brazil, 122, 149, 150, 151, 281
Brest, 241
Brewer, Bede, 76
Brienne, archbishop and cardinal Loménie de, 103–6, 170, 173, 177, 193, 239, 246
Britain, 9, 12, 113, 221, 257, 264, 271, 281
　British monasteries abroad, 74
Brittany, 156
brotherhoods, 28, 30, 78, 80, 88, 108, 114, 155, 179, 183, 197, Ill. 28
Brothers of the Christian Schools, Christian Brothers, 109, 111, 268
Broutier, Premonstratensian monk, property, 91
Bruckner, Anton, 307
Brussels, 11, 112, 219, 225, 272
　Coudenberg monastery, 220, 221, Ill. 14
bureaucracy, Austrian, 181
Burke, Edmund, 257
　as prophet, 256
　on French monasticism, 256, 257, 313–15
　Reflections on the Revolution in France, 13, 88, 219, 256–7
Burney, Dr Charles, historian of music, 69, 139
Busenbaum, Hermann, Jesuit canonist, 148, 165
Byzantine monasteries, 131

Caen, abbeys of, 92, 234, 294
Caffè, Il, 139, 187
cahiers de doléance, 240, 264
　attitudes to monasteries in those of the clergy, 240–1; of the nobility, 242; of the Third Estate, 241–2; overall, 242
　reliability as evidence, 240
Cahors, 242
Calais, 87
Calas, Jean, 146
Calasanz, José, 128
calendar, Christian, replaced by revolutionary, 264–5, 282
Calonne, French minister, 239
Calvin, Calvinism, 10, 73, 181, 199
Camaldoli, 134, 136, 276
　Order of, 139
Cambre, La, Cistercian nunnery, Belgium, 213
Cambridge, colleges, 13–14, 91, 296, 315
Campoformio, Treaty of (1797), 284
Campomanes, Pedro de, 159–60, 167
canonesses, 101
　of Ste-Waudru, Mons, 226
canons, 17, 21, 22, 78, 226
cantatas, 52
Caprara, Cardinal Giovanni Battista, papal nuncio in Vienna, 201, 202
Capuchins, 7, 21, 29, 31, 37, 39, 94, 107–8, 280, 296
　characteristics, 107
　numbers, 108, 147, 236
　'poverty' criticised, 187
　reluctant to leave cloister, 258
　some support revolutionary governments, 275
　vocations, 144
cardinals, 7, 34
card-playing, 133
care of the sick, 5, 21, 22, 28, 107, 111, 263, 264, 268
Carlone, Antonio, 55

INDEX

Carmelites, 122
    monks, 247, 281
    nuns, 16; discalced, 110, 120
carnival, 133, 182
Cartesianism, 156, 170
Carthusians, 19–21, 86, 88, 115, 177, 192, 193, 236, 246, 292, Ill. 1
Casoyo, abbot of, 281
Cassino, Monte, Benedictine abbey of, 126, 134, 136
Castile, 10, 112, 114
Catalonia, 280
Catania, Benedictine house of, 138, 294
catechism, 69, 191
cathedrals, 114
Catherine II, empress of Russia, 138, 165, 168, 187, 215
    retains Jesuits, 168
    suppresses monasteries, 186
'Catholic Enlightenment' 'Catholic Reform', 36–7, 57, 58 (Germany), 146–7, 156–7 (Spain), 167, 232–3 (France), 237
'Catholic Reformation', 29, 113
    see also Counter-Reformation
Cattaneo, Carlo, 132
Cela, abbot of, 281
celibacy, vow of, 11, 31, 73, 171, 179, 203, 264, 296
censorship, 28, 39, 52, 163–4, 181
Chadwick, Owen, historian, 14, 126
Champagne, 88
Chancelade, 88
Chantal, Jeanne de, 110
chaplaincies, Joseph II's, 195
chaplains, 131
    see also nobility
Chaplin, Maurus, monk of Lambspring, 75–6
chapter, monastic, 21, 64–5, 76, 279, 284
charity, dispensed by monasteries, 5, 6, 16, 77, 81, 96, 122, 213, 276, 296
Charles V, emperor, 115, 119
Charles VI, emperor 1711–40, 46, 54, 181, 184, 205
Charles II, king of Spain 1665–1700, 157
Charles III, king of the Two Sicilies 1734–59, 135, 157–8; king of Spain 1759–88, 158, 161–6, 282

charterhouses, 19–21, 47, 86, 97, 118, 136
Chartres, bishop of, 247
chastity, vow of, 5, 6, 17, 31, 238
Chateaubriand, vicomte de, 38, 176
    Génie du christianisme (1802), 267–8
Châtelet, duc du, 247
Châtillon, Carmelite nunnery of, 16
Chelsea Hospital, 13
China, 148
Choiseul, Mgr, archbishop of Cambrai, 174
Choiseul, duc de, French minister, 154, 162, 164, 171
choral services, 19, 30, 200
Christianity
    abandoned in France, 264–5
    banned, 265
'Christians, New' in Portugal, 113, 123, 152
Christina, queen of Sweden, 27–8
chronograms, 63
Church, 'constitutional', 113, 265
    see also Civil Constitution of the Clergy
Church, Roman Catholic
    authority, 145
    monasticism: held inessential to, 267; declared essential to, 276
    ownership of land, 3, 10–11, 144, 189, 228
Church of England, 13, 129, 312, 319
Churrigueresque, version of Baroque style, 118, 119
Cistercian Order, 2, 4, 19–21, 29–30, 35, 46, 62, 79, 84, 86, 89, 115, 236
Cîteaux, abbey of, 32, 86, 92, 100
Civil Constitution of the Clergy (1790), 167, 228, 256–7, 259
    clergy reactions to, 260–1, 263
    condemned by pope, 274; oath to, 260
Civil War, English, 10
Clairvaux
    abbey of, 92, 100, 267
    abbot of, 89
Clark, J.C.D., historian, 13
class as historical factor, 10, 303
Clement IX, pope, 129
Clement XI, pope 1700–21, 35, 148
Clement XIII, pope 1758–69, 127, 161, 162
Clement XIV, pope 1769–74, 7, 8, 147, 162, 190

375

clergy, as an order, 304
  regular: agreed to be too numerous, 131; compared with secular, 80, 114, 165, 186, 238; definition, 17–23; numbers in relation to population, 180; *see also* monasteries, monks, nuns and under individual countries
  secular: appointed to parishes by monasteries, 46–7, 132; compared with regular, 80, 114, 165, 186, 238; contributors to the *Encyclopédie*, 145; definition, 17; desire to increase numbers, 175, 295–6; as government ministers, 132; hostility to Jesuits, 163; improvement in education, 174; numbers: in relation to population, 29, 78, 80, 180, in relation to regulars, 3, 35, 36–7, 86, 128–30, 180, increased by Joseph II, 194, 195, 210
  see also under individual countries
Clermont, bishop of, 255
cloister
  meanings, 18
  of Santa Chiara, Naples, 135, Plate 7
Cluny
  abbey of, 32, 86, 92, 265–7, Ill. 37 (a) and (b)
  commendatory abbot of, 171
  Order of, 171, 175, 236, 250
Cobbett, William, 292
Coimbra, University of, 152
Colbert, French minister, 105
colleges, 17–18, 30, 115, 183, 235
  see also Cambridge, Oxford
Collinson, Patrick, historian, 1
Cologne
  archbishop-elector, 59
  city, 82, 225, 323
  electorate, 283–6
Columbus, Christopher, 116
comedies, German, 52
commendatory abbots, *commende*
  in Austrian Monarchy, 182
  in France, 104–6, 115, 132, 232, 234, 235
commission des réguliers, ch. 7; 8, 11, 85–6, 192, 292, 297
  established (1766), 170–1, 185
  evidence to, 172–5
  membership, 171, 177
  monks unrepresented, 171
  pope excluded, 171
  resulting edicts: (1768), 175; (1773), 177; aim to save monasticism, 172; compared with Josephism, 169, 185; impact abroad, 186; implementation, 175, 232, 235, 258; number of suppressions, 176
  sets off a public debate, 171–2, 177, 187
Committee of Public Safety, 264–5, 280
'compensation through secularisation' in Germany, 284
Compiègne, 16
Compton, James, monk of Lambspring, 75
concordat
  French, of 1801, 265–7, 268, 274, 285
  Italian, of 1802, 275
Condé, Louis de Bourbon, commendatory abbot, 105
Condillac, *philosophe*, 19
confessional boxes, 40
confessors, 39, 96
  monks as, 99, 108, 114, 132, 149, 163–4, 172, 193
confraternities *see* brotherhoods
congregations
  Benedictine, of St-Maur *see* Maurists
  of Bishops and Regulars (papal), 34
  of Christian Doctrine *see* Doctrinaires
  meanings, 19
  of monasteries, 21, 31, 44, 89
  secular, in France, mostly female, 111, 262, 263
congrue, the (standard payment to French vicars), 87
conscription, military, 293
conservatories (mostly female), 134, 183, 194, 225, 226
Constance, Lake, 78
'Continental System' of Napoleon, 281
convent, definition, 18
Convention, French revolutionary assembly (1792), 264
conversions to Roman Catholicism, 27–8, 181
conversos, Spanish converts, 113
Copsey, Pitt, monk of Lambspring, 75
Cordeliers (Observant Franciscans in France), 101, 107, 236
Corneille, Pierre, 99
Coronelli, Vincenzo, 139
corporal punishment, 99
Corsica, 276

Coulmiers, M. de, abbot of Abbecourt, 254
Counter-Reformation, ch. 1
   and Austrian Monarchy, 181–3
   and Belgium, 212
   and France, 88
   and Germany, 39, 41, 62, 74
   and Hungary, 205
   and Italy, 127, 136
   and Jesuits, 147
   and monasteries, ch. 1; 12 46, 238, 295
   new Orders of, 22, 31–2
   and Portugal, 122
   and Spain, 113, 157
Coxe, archdeacon, 278, 280
Cowley, prior of St Edmund's, 75
Crimean War, 111
Crimes and Punishments (Dei delitti e delle pene), 187
Croatia, 179, 205
Cross, Stations of the, 34
crusades, 113
Czech republic, 179

Damiens, Robert, 154
dancing, 56, 98, 215
Danube, river, 42
Darmes, Edmund, monk of Lambspring, 75
Dauberval, dancer, 98
David, painter, 246, Ill. 34
deathbeds
   attending, 193; considered useful by Joseph II, 193
death penalty, 187
dechristianization, 12
Declaration of the Rights of Man, 207
Deffand, marquise du, 103
deism, 181
Délica, Capuchin guerrilla leader, 281
democrats, Belgian, 221
Département du Nord, 245
De re diplomatica, 90
Descartes, René, 108, 156
design, study of, 170
despotism/absolutism
   abbots accused of, 81
   enlightened, planned for Hungary by Joseph II, 210

   justified by Pufendorf's writings, 288
   Portuguese, 123
   principal motive for suppression of Jesuits, 166; and for German secularisation, 289, 308
Dickens, A.G., historian, 27
Dickson, P.G.M., historian, 14, 180, 185, 195, 207
Diderot, Denis, 19, 103, 145, 147
   La religieuse, 99, 101
Dientzenhofer, Johann Leonhard, architect, 62
Dietmayr, Berthold, abbot of Melk, 46, 47–9
Dillingen, Jesuit university of, 167
Dillon, archbishop of Narbonne, 234
dioceses
   geography of, 31
   in Austria, 45, 179
Directory, French, 272
Doctrinaires, 109–10, 169–70, 262, 263
dogma, Catholic, decay of belief in, 234
Dominican Orders, Dominicans, 6, 7, 21, 115, 116, 159
   anti-Jesuit, 163
   anti-revolutionary, 281
   bishops, 116
   missions, 116
   numbers, 128, 236
   in parishes, 132
   pro-revolutionary, 247, 275
   urban, 134
Douai, English houses at, 232
Downside abbey, 74, 312
dowries, 5–6, 98, 110, 132
dress of monks and nuns, 2, 172, 182, 273
Dubois, cardinal, 103
Dumouriez, general, 271–2
Durham, 48
Dutch Republic, 113, 212, 217, 219, 221, 271, 274

earthquakes
   Lisbon (1755), 117, 150
   S. Italian and Sicilian (1693), 138
eastern Europe, 27, 227
Ecclesiastical Commission (1782), Joseph II's, for central lands, 193; for Hungary, 193
   achievements, 194–5, 197, 208

ecclesiastical states of the Empire, 59
   abolished, 286–90
   attitude of their inhabitants, 60–2, 77
   compensation issue, 284–6
   discussion of, 283
   monastic principalities small-scale, 284
education
   in Austrian Monarchy, 165, 184, 190, (nineteenth century), 226
   in diocesan seminaries, 72–3, 109, 179
   in France, 169, 262, 268
   in *Normalschulen*, 72
   orders devoted to, 109–10
   in Portugal, 151, 152
   role of regulars in, 5, 7, 8, 16, 28, 46, 52, 69
   teaching girls, 110–11
   training novices, 46
   see also Doctrinaires, Jesuits, Lazarists, Oratorians, Piarists, Sulpicians
Edward VII, king of England 1901–10, 307
Egle, Markus, abbot of Wilten, 45
Einsiedeln, Benedictine abbey of, Switzerland, 277–8, 280, Ill. 38
electors
   ecclesiastical, 37, 59
   secular, 59
Elliott, Sir John, historian, 32
Elton, Sir Geoffrey, historian, 10
émigrés, 262
   clergy, 265
   more seculars than regulars, 265
emperor
   monasteries keep suite for him, 45, 48
   powers, 185
Empire, Holy Roman, 5, 127
   appeals to imperial courts, 62
   betrayed by Francis II, 284–5
   history and structure, 58–60
   partitioned without compunction, 284
   poses special problems to France, 283
   princes of, 78
   princesses, 86
   see also Germany, imperial abbeys, *reichsunmittelbar*, Westphalia
enclosure
   for nuns tightened (1566), 31
   for monks in France (1773), 177

enclosure of common land, 77
encyclopaedia, first alphabetical, 138
Encyclopédie, French (1751–65), 19, 95, 108, 144, 145, 146, 153–4
   article 'Foundations', 236
   banned, 145, 236
   clergy contributors, 145
   and Jesuits, 145
   prospectus (1750), 145
   sale and influence, 145
Engelberg, Swiss Benedictine monastery, 280
England, 4, 7, 10
   abbots in medieval House of Lords, 296
   education, 296
   held up as model to France, 237, 255
   historical tradition, 12–14
   monasteries in, 268, 312
   monks from, in Germany, 74
   travellers from, 87, 278, 280
Enlightenment, the
   beginnings, 28
   Catholic, 58, 146–7, 156, 181
   and Catholicism, 28, 111, 144
   and Christianity, 28
   gains support, 143, 144–6
   in Germany, 287
   in Italy, 187
   and Jesuits, 112–18, 149
   limits of its appeal, 146
   and monasteries, 37, 68, 70–3, 80, 89–90, 95, 117, 172, 236, 237–8, 295, 297
   popular hostility to, 146
   and Portugal, 123, 149
   and Spain, 156–7
Ephémérides du citoyen, 88
Escorial, the, near Madrid, 48, 54, 94, 114, 115, 118–19, 122, 159, Ill. 17
Estany, Louis Parent d', 97
Estates, First, 5, 18, 33
   in Austria, 45–6, 55, 183
   in Bavaria, 74
   in France, 19, 96, 106
   in Italy, 132
   in Portugal, 123
   see also Brabant, Hainaut

INDEX

Estates-General, French
of 1614, 106
of 1789; calls for, 239
becomes National Assembly, 242, 243
clergy in, 241
novel composition, 242
see also cahiers de doléance, National Assembly
Ettal, Benedictine abbey, 78
Eudistes, 109, 263
Eugene of Savoy, prince, 136, 181
Evans, Joan, historian, 84–5
Evans, R.J.W., historian, 14
Eybel, Professor of Jurisprudence at Vienna, 182, 202–3

factories, monastically run, 87, 153
family strategies and monasteries, 97, 132, 189, 190, 294, 297
fasting, 50, 56, 107, 153, 172
Fathers of the Holy Spirit, 268
Febronius, pseudonym of Hontheim, author of *The State of the Church*, 37, 182, 192, 233
Feijoo, Benito, Spanish Benedictine monk, 156, 157
Felbiger, Ignaz, abbot or provost of the Premonstratensian house at Sagan, 72, 191, 305
Feller, F.X., 219, 293, 296
Ferdinand, king of Aragon, 112
Ferdinand VI, king of Spain (1746–59), 156, 157
'feudalism' and abbeys, 77, 87, 245, 247, 279, 282, 307
fire-brigades, 107
Firmian, count Karl, governor of Lombardy, 187, 189
Fischer, J.M., architect, 65
Fisher, Mr, President at Lambspring, 75
fishponds, 55, Ill. 5
Flanders, 75, 87, 210, 222, 232, 254
Flemish language, 221, 223
Fleury, cardinal, 103, 144
Florence, 2, 129
Dominican house of S. Marco, 135
Fontenelle, 28
Fontevraud, royal nunnery, 86, 92
Forest, Black, 69–72

France, chs. 3, 7, 9, 10; 2, 3, 8, 13, 19, 22, 27, 28–9, 30, 33, 34, 35–6, 52, 113, 115, 127, 135, 180
academies, 106
Assembly of Notables (1787), 239
Austrian alliance, 162
bankrupt, 239
Baroque, 39, 95–6
Church, and royal power, 103–6, 157, 170, 171; lands, 87; wealth, 319
colonies, 153, 154
commission des réguliers, ch. 7
comparison with Austrian Monarchy, 179 80, 231, 256, 348
comparison with Belgium, 232, 253–4
edict of 1768 on monasteries, 175; of 1773, 177
foreign policy, 221, 232
historians, 11–12, 95, 124, 239
monasteries: architecture, 92–6; loss of fervour and credibility, 235; mixed experience in eighteenth century, 91, 176, 232, 235, 252; numbers, 125, 130, 180, 236; present-day condition of buildings, 84; tithes, 87; wealth, 69, 85, 86, 173
Orders, new, of nuns, 233
peculiarity, 112, 117, 231
regional variations, 87, 173, 242
secular clergy, 132, 265
see also commission des réguliers, Estates-General, French Revolution
and suppression of Jesuits, 149–56, 158, 160, 162, 180; Portuguese influence, 154, 155–6
Francis, St, 126
Francis (Stephen) I, emperor 1745–65, 127, 181
Francis II, emperor 1792–1835, 226, 233, 271, 284–5
Franciscan Orders, Franciscans, 4, 7, 29, 30, 34, 116, 126, 293
in Austria, 195, 197
characteristics, 106–8, 134–5
divisions, 107
in France, 107
in Hungary, 207
in Italy, 128, 134
Observant, 114, 195, 197
in Portugal, 122

379

INDEX

Franciscan Orders, Franciscans (cont.)
    in Spain, 158, 281
    Third Order, 158, 159
    unreformed, 12, 21, 22, 107
    working in parishes, 132, 196, 197
    see also Capuchins, Minims, poverty, Recollects
François de Sales, St, 22, 110
Franconia, 79
Franz, Father, SJ, 165
Frederick II (the Great), king of Prussia (1740–86), 72, 144, 146, 191, 284
Freeman, Robert, historian, 50
Freemasons, 11, 150, 181, 183, 190
French language, 56, 127
French Revolution, chs. 9, 10; 8–9, 11, 36, 97, 117, 155
    and architecture, 70–1, 94, 95–6, 264, 265
    armies, 231, 272
    attraction to Vonckists, 221
    church policy, 227–8, 231, 238, 251, 254, 259, 265; leads to civil war, 262
    compared with Belgian, 242
    denounced by Burke, 256–7
    denounced by pope, 261
    governments during, 85, 178
    impact outside France, ch. 10
    impact in Belgium, 271, 272–4
    impact in Germany, 270, 271–2, 274, 282–3, 284–6, 287, 289, 290
    impact in Italy, 274, 275
    impact in Portugal, 187, 281
    impact in Spain, 270, 280, 281
    land sales, 259, 267
    monastic policy, 227, 231, 250, 262, 263, 270, 272; compared with Joseph II's, 227, 228, 231, 348; opposition to, 258
    religious policy, failure of, 267
    'second', 263
    suppressions, balance-sheet of, 304–5
    tradition, 84–5, 117
    wars, 75, 264
friars see Augustinian Orders, Dominican Orders, Franciscan Orders
Friedberg, Karl Müller von, 279
Fronde, 32
Fulda, 59, 285
Furet, François, historian, 11

Gabler, Joseph, organ builder, 66–8
Galicia, province of Poland, then (1772) of Austrian Monarchy, 168, 180, 190
    monasteries, 190
Galicia, province of Spain, 281
Galileo, 129
Galli-Bibiena, architect and stage-designer, 49
Gallican Articles, Gallicanism, 155, 178, 242
gambling, 133
Garampi, cardinal, papal nuncio in Vienna 1773–85, 197, 201–2
Gaudin, denounces monasticism, 262
Gemeinde, 77
General Assembly of Clergy of France, 103, 106, 170, 176, 239, 251, 297
generals and superiors of Orders, 5, 21, 192–3, 216
Genoa, republic of, 127
Geoffrin, Mme, 103, Ill. 16
geography, teaching of, 56
George III, king of England 1760–1820, 215, 279
George V, king of England 1910–36, 307
Geras, Premonstratensian abbey, Austria, 51, 200
Gerbert, Martin, abbot of St Blasien, 69–72, 80, 90, 132, 152, 294
Gerle, Dom, Carthusian, 246, 258–9, 260
German language, 52, 56, 182
Germany, 112, 127
    Catholic, ch. 2; 2, 5, 8, 13, 27, 50, 84, 88, 113, 179, 297
    monasteries, monks and nuns: Baroque rebuilding, 30, 37, 38, 39–41, 58–82, 94, 117, 118, 135; independence of, 4, 104; lands of, 82; numbers of, 81, 130, 316, 328; scholars, 90; suppressions, 8, 14–15, 286–90
    population, 40, 58, 59, 325
    rulers and Church, 103, 162, 166
    see also Bavaria, Empire, French Revolution, imperial abbeys, *reichsunmittelbar*
Gesamtkunstwerk, 49
Ghent, Benedictine abbey of St Peter, 213, 214, 218, 222
    bishop Lobkowitz of, 215–16
    Carthusian house, 216
    see also Malingié, Seiger
Gibbon, Edward, 13, 90, 277
Gidding, Little, 13

INDEX

giunta economale, Lombardy, 111
Gleichförmigkeit, 204, 208
Gloucester, duke of, 215
Goethe, J.W. von, 138
Gothic, 12, 40, 54, 92, 95, 118, 119, 267
　novels, 313
Göttweig abbey, 46, 51, 55, Plate 4
Gouffre, Marseilles merchant, 154
Gouttes, abbé, 252
Granada, 112, 116, 118, 294, Plate 9
Grasse, Dominican house of, 175
Greco, El, 120
Greek architecture, 95
Grenoble, 170
Gross, Hanns, historian, 130
Guadelupe, Marian sanctuary in Spain, 115
Gugger, abbot of St Gall, 73
Guiana, penal colony, 263
Guignes, Mlle de, 100

Habsburg dynasty
　archduchesses, 114, 120
　Austrian, 27, 33, 44, 69, 127, 205, 211
　Spanish, 157
Hagenauer, Dominikus, abbot of St Peter's Salzburg, 81
Hainaut
　Estates of, 213
　inauguration of Francis II, 226
Hantsch, Hugo, monk of Melk and historian, 307
Harsnep, monk of Lambspring, 76
Hatzfeld, count, 184
Hauntinger, monk of St Gall, 72–3
Hautefort family, 100
Hautvillers abbey, Champagne, 88
Hawkins, Sir John, musical historian, 69
Haydn, Franz Josef, 52
Haydn, Michael, 295
Heatley, Maurus, abbot of Lambspring, 75
Hédouin, Premonstratensian monk, 233
Heiligenkreuz, Cistercian abbey of, Lower Austria, 294
Helvetic republic, 279
Helvétius, 237
　De l'esprit, 146

Henry IV, king of France 1598–1610, 108
Henry VIII, king of England 1509–47, 10, 33, 227, 236, 305
Hercules, symbolism of, 49–68
heresy, in Spain and Portugal, 113, 123
Hermann, Christian, historian, 11, 15
Hermans, Godfrid, abbot of Premonstratensian house of Tongerlo, 221–3
hermits, 134
Herrmann, Wolfgang, art historian, 95
Hervier, Augustinian monk, 233
Hieronymites, Iberian Order, 115, 118
Hildebrandt, Lucas, architect, 55, 294
Hildesheim, bishopric, 74, 76
historians, historiography of monasteries, 9–14, 15–16, 17, 52, 56, 89–90
Histoire de Dom B., 238
Hitler, Adolf, 307
Hoffmann, abbot Caspar, of Melk, 44
holidays for monks and nuns, 54
Höller, Jesuit confessor, 165
Hontheim, suffragan bishop of Trier, 37, 220
　see also Febronius
hospitality, monasteries' duty of, 48, 77, 293
hospitals, 21, 22, 111, 115, 117, 134, 183, 190
　Chelsea, 13
hours, canonical *see* 'offices'
Hufton, Olwen, historian, 14–15
Huguenots, 35, 92
Hungary, 7, 8, 41, 51, 205–20
　Church, wealth of, comparison with Lower Austria, 205–10
　constituent provinces, 205
　constitution, 211, 217
　Counter-Reformation in, 27, 205
　Jews in, 208
　Joseph II's reforms, 193, 204, 207, 210; many rescinded, 223
　Maria Theresa and, 183, 191, 204–7
　modern, 179, 205
　monasteries, monks and nuns, numbers, 180, 208, 209, 210, 226; rebuilding, 205; represented in Diet, 209; revival in nineteenth century, 226; suppressions, 208
　Orthodox in, 205, 208
　parish provision, 205, 210
　population, 205

381

INDEX

Hungary (cont.)
    Protestants in, 181, 205, 208
    toleration, religious, importance of, 208
hunting, 63

Idomeneo, and vows, 187
Imola, bishop of, later pope Pius VII, 311
imperial abbeys, 59–77, 82, 87
incomes, personal, of monks and nuns, 30, 54, 91, 177
Indians, S. American, 149
industrialisation, 305, 314
infallibility, papal, 34, 145
infâme, the, 146
Innocent X, pope, 32, 34, 127, 128–9, 190
Innsbruck, 45
Inquisition
    Portuguese, 113, 123, 151
    Roman, 129, 139
    Spanish, 113, 118, 156, 157, 161, 281
    Venetian, 189
Ireland, 74, 168, 312
    northern, 4
Isabella, queen of Castile, 112, 116
Isla, José Francisco de, Jesuit polemicist, 157
Italy, ch. 5; 2, 3, 6, 8, 13, 15, 28, 29, 33, 34, 54, 69, 86, 90, 113, 128–30, 179, 189
    Baroque, 39, 118, 127, 136
    conservatories, 183
    Counter-Reformation, 127
    and Enlightenment, 156
    and French Revolution, 231, 274–6, 277
    monasteries, monks and nuns: common characteristics, 127–39; comparison with other countries, 130, 132; numbers, 126, 128, 129–30, 139, 316; music, 69, 134; regional variations, 127, 128; suppressions by revolutionary governments, 275, 276, 277; in Lombardy, 189; in Venice, 189, 190; wealth, 130, 131
    political divisions, 126
    see also Enlightenment, Lombardy, Naples, papal state(s), pope(s), Tuscany, Venice
Ixnard, P.M., architect, 70, 95

Jacobins, 247
James II of England and VII of Scotland, king, 13, 27, 106
James, Henry, 302
Jansen, Cornelius, 35
Jansenism, Jansenists, 35–6, 89, 146, 147, 149, 153, 156, 158, 174, 201, 250
    in Belgium, 181, 212
    Joseph II and, 237
    Maria Theresa and, 163, 181
Jemappes, battle of, 271–2
Jephtha and vows, 187
Jesuits, Jesuit Order, Company or Society of Jesus, 1, 11, 18, 27, 28, 31, 34, 39, 40, 57, 58, 60, 80, 85, 88, 95–6, 115, 296, 316
    calibre, 143
    characteristics, 147
    as confessors, 39, 147, 148, 149, 165, 184
    and Enlightenment, 9
    ex-Jesuits, 75, 165, 166, 221; pensions, 151, 155, 167
    learning, 90, 147, 295
    numbers, 108, 147, 159, 160, 169, 180
    and *philosophes*, 108–9
    and plays, 52, 78
    reasons for their unpopularity, 148, 155, 159, 160
    as parish priests, 166
    and scholastic theology, 56, 80, 148, 156
    suppression (1773), ch. 6: complexity of story, 147; in Austrian Monarchy, 161–6; in France, 153–6, 158, 178, 187; in Germany, 166; in Italy, 187; in Latin America, 149; Portugal, 149–53; significance, 147, 166, 167, 187, 207; in Spain, 156, 157–8, 159, 282; summarised, 298; educational role largely filled by other Orders, 109–10, 129, 151, 152, 160, 169–70
    as teachers, 39, 108, 147, 165, 190
    and *Unigenitus*, 35–6, 148
    University of Salzburg opposed to, 65
    wealth, 148, 151
    see also brotherhoods, censorship, missions, Paris (Sorbonne), universities
Jews, 113, 152, 179, 181, 235, 259
Jiménes, cardinal, 113
John V, king of Portugal 1706–50, 54, 123, 143, 149

382

INDEX

John of the Cross, St, 120
Joseph II, emperor 1765–90, sole ruler of the
    Austrian Monarchy 1780–90, ch. 8; 8, 16, 57,
    58, 73, 81, 254, 297
  attitude to Jesuits and their suppression, 161–6
  and Austria, 192–4, 204, 228
  and Beethoven, 272
  and Belgium, 210–22, 224, 284
  despotism, 210
  and Hungary, 205–9, 210, 226
  idea of education, 185
  and Josephism, 58, 169, 179
  memorandum of 1765, 185–6
  policies on monastic reform, 185, 190, 191,
    192–3, 195, 196, 199–200, 203, 204, 216, 217,
    227, 228, 308
  religious attitudes in general, 192, 200, 203;
    toleration, 208
  suppressions, 74, 193–5, 196–7, 202, 208, 216,
    224
  zeal for statistics, 180
Joseph I, king of Portugal 1750–77, 143, 149, 150,
    154
Joseph (Bonaparte), king of Spain, 281
Josephism, meaning, 179
Joubert, general, 275
journalism, monastic, 88, 109, 219
Joyeuse Entrée, 210, 217, 219, 221

Kalmus, Henry, monk of Lambspring, 75
Kampmiller, Jesuit confessor of Maria Theresa, 164
Kant, Immanuel, 80
Kappel, pilgrimage church, 78
Karl Eugen, duke of Württemberg, 73
Kaunitz, Wenzel Anton von, count, from 1764
    prince, Austrian chief minister, 164, 166, 167
  and Belgium, 210, 212
  on education, 191
  on monasteries, 185, 191
  reforms in Lombardy, 186, 189; suppressions,
    190
Kempten
  Benedictine abbey of, 60, 62, 66, 77
  city, 60–2
Kléber, Jean-Baptiste, architect and general, 93
Kley, Dale Van, historian, 154

Klosterneuburg, 51, 54, 143, Ill. 4
Knittel, Benedict, abbot of Cistercian monastery of
    Schöntal, 62, 68
Knowles, David, Benedictine monk and historian,
    12, 19, 90
Koloman, St, 48
Kremsmünster, Benedictine abbey of, Upper
    Austria, 55–7, 87, Ills. 5, 6
Kressel, Freiherr von, 193, 201

Labrousse, Suzanne, 260
La Chalotais, Louis-René de, 156
Ladurie, E. Le Roy, historian, 11–12
La Flèche, Jesuit college, 108
La Gorce, Pierre de la, historian, 258
Lalande, *Miserere*, 101
La Marck, comte de, defended monasteries in
    National Assembly, 253–4
Lambach abbey, Upper Austria, 79, 307
Lambspring, Benedictine abbey, north Germany,
    74–6
landownership, monastic, generally, 10–11, 87, 171
  sales, 273
Langheim, Cistercian abbey, 79
languages, living, taught, 170
Languedoc, Estates of, 234
Laon, abbey of St Martin, 97
Larive, French actor, 98
La Rochefoucauld, archbishop of Rouen, 171
La Rochefoucauld, cardinal de, 32
Latin, 52, 73, 170, 182
La Tour du Pin, Mme de, 234
La Trappe, Cistercian abbey of, 89, 90
Laugier, Marc-Antoine, architectural theorist, 95,
    295
La Valette, Jesuit, 154, 155, 171
Laven, Mary, historian, 133–4
Lawrence, C.H., historian, 1
lay brothers and sisters, 4, 19, 85, 98, 134, 316
lay men and women, 12, 28, 78
  asserting their claims against the clergy, 81, 145,
    169, 173, 184, 190
  as monastic officials, 44
  as purchasers of church land, 304, 305
Lazarists, 109, 263, 268
laziness of monks, 171, 276, 313

learning and scholarship, monastic, 5, 7, 14, 16, 46, 52, 96, 171, 174, 235
    abbot Gerbert, 69–72
    abbot Knittel, 62
    abbot Mendel, 307
    in Austria and Germany, ch. 2; 80
    historical, 89–90, 138
    at Kremsmünster, 56
    mathematical, 56
    scientific, 56–7, 138–9
    in Spain, 116
Lecce, S. Italy, 129–30, 138
Lecestre, Léon, historian, 85
Lees-Milne, James, art historian, 122
Legislative Assembly, French (1791–2), 262, 263
Leibniz, G.W., 28
Leo X, pope, 199
Leopold II, grand duke of Tuscany 1765–90, emperor and ruler of the Austrian Monarchy 1790–2, 161, 164, 196–202
    monastic policies: in the Monarchy, 226; in Tuscany, 224, 225
    numbers of Tuscan monasteries, monks and nuns, 225
    reaction to his Tuscan reforms, 225
    as ruler of the Austrian Monarchy, 225, 226
Le Paige, Louis-Adrien, 147
Lepanto, battle of (1571), 115
Leronge, Dom, agricultural writer, 88
Le Sage, Hervé-Julien, Premonstratensian monk, 97
Lessing, G.E., vi
Letters of Joseph II, largely false compilation, 164
Lewis, 'Monk', author of *The Monk* (1796), 313
Liberal Catholicism, nineteenth-century, in Belgium, 274
libraries, monastic, 48–50, 52, 57, 73, 89–90, 99, 107, 118, 138, 203, 214, 227–8, 308
Liège, prince-bishopric of, 75, 210
    revolution in (1789), 221
Ligne
    Charles, prince de, 98, 226
    Charles-Joseph, prince de, 98
    Louis, prince de, 223
Liguori, St Alfonso de', 34, 132
Lilienfeld, Cistercian monastery, Lower Austria, 203, 226

Linguet, Simon, 237
Linz, new bishopric founded, 203
Lioncy, Marseilles merchant, 154, 155
Lisbon, 3, 116, 117, 150, 317
    earthquake (1755), 117; rebuilding, 123, 150, 153
Lissoir, Premonstratensian monk, translates Febronius, 233
Lithuania, 98
liturgy
    experience of, 131
    new style, 92, 136
    reforms of, 144, 179, 200
Locke, John, philosopher, 28
Loire valley, 108
Lombardy, 127, 132, 179, 316
    invaded by Napoleon and ruled by France, 274–5
    numbers of clergy, monasteries, monks and nuns, 179, 180
    reform, esp. of monasteries, 186, 187, 189, 190, 274
London, 6–7, 11–12, 95, 150, 307
Lorraine, 86, 87
    Charles, prince of, governor of Belgium, 212, 220
Louis XIII, king of France 1610–43, 32
Louis XIV, king of France 1643–1715, 32, 35, 59, 93, 103, 105, 148, 232, 245
Louis XV, king of France 1715–74, 8, 70, 89, 94–5, 97, 101, 144, 153–4, 155, 171
Louis XVI, king of France 1774–92, executed 1793, 103–4, 107, 162, 177, 256
    and Civil Constitution, 260
    policy from 1786, 239–40, 243–4, 251, 261, 262
Louvain, Leuven, Belgian university and town, 11, 35, 212, 213, 218, 219, 223
Loyola, Ignatius, founder of the Society of Jesus, 11, 34
Lucca, republic of, 130
Lucerne, Switzerland, 277, 280
Ludwig, J.F., architect of Mafra, 123
Lunéville, Treaty of 1801, 284, 285
Lure, abbey of, Alsace, 94
Luther, Martin, 1, 30, 35, 73, 199
Lutheranism, 181
Luxembourg, 179–80
    attempt to found bishopric, 220

INDEX

Maass, Ferdinand, historian, 185
Mabillon, Jean, Maurist monk and historian, 89, 295
McCarthy, pet monkey, 105
Machiavelli, Niccoló, 73
McManners, John, historian, 14, 85, 104, 111, 295
McNamara, J.A.K., historian, 14–15, 99
Madrid, 117, 120, 159
    Dominican church, 156
    Franciscan church rebuilt, 158, Ill. 26
    nunnery of Las Descalzas Reales, 120, Ill. 18
    Treaty of (1750), 149
Mafra, palace-monastery of, 54, 68, 118, 119, 124, 143, 153, Ill. 19
Mainz
    archbishop-elector of, 46, 59, 62, 74, 271, 285
    electorate, 271–2, 283
Malines, Mechelen, archbishop of, 213
Malagrida, Jesuit, 151
Malingié, Emilien, monk of St Peter's, Ghent, 213–22, 224
Malta, 188
Mannerism, 119
manual work in monasteries, 16, 19, 72, Ill. 20
Marczali, Henrik, historian, 207
Maria Theresa, empress, ruler of the Austrian Monarchy 1740–80, 45, 54, 56, 69, 143, 150, 199
    and Hungary, 204–7, 210, 213, 215, 218
    and Jansenism, 163, 181
    and Jesuits, 162, 163, 166, 168, 181, 184
    and Josephism, 179, 201
    'political testament', 183, 185, 192, 193, 205, 207
    reforms, 169, 183–4, 189, 190, 191, 298
    religious intolerance, 118–19, 196
Mariazell, pilgrimage site, 29
Marie Antoinette, queen of France, 162
Marie Christine, sister of Joseph II, 216, 219, 225, 226
Marienbad, 58, 307
Marillac, Louis, 110
Marmontel, *philosophe*, 103
Marmoutier, abbey, 105
Maroilles, Benedictine abbey, 245
Marolle, abbé, 100
Martini, G.B., musical historian, 69, 139, 294
Martinique, island of, French colony, 154

Marx, Karl, Marxism, 10
Masevaux, nunnery of, Alsace, 94
Massalska, Helen, 98–101, 223, 226
Masses, for the souls of the dead endowed, 11, 28, 31, 73, 94–6, 115, 131, 144, 153, 182
    other, 51, 81 (Mozart's in C minor)
    suppressed, 265
    utility of, 176
Mauerbach, Carthusian abbey, Austria, 192–204
Maulbronn abbey, 294
Maurists, Benedictine Congregation of St-Maur, 12, 19, 69, 73, 89–91, 174, 177, 235, 236, 252, 295
Maury, abbé, 251
Max Joseph IV, elector of Bavaria 1799–1825, 285, 286
Mayer, Arno, historian, 13
Mednyansky, Mrs (née Birkbeck), xv
Melk, Benedictine abbey of, Lower Austria, 22, 41–56, 294, Frontispiece, Plate 3, Ill. 2
    changing attitudes within after 1750, 182–3
    life in, 49–54
    music in, 51–2
    number of monks, esp. in parishes, 46, 200, Fig. 1
    rebuilding, 47–9, 65; motives, 48
    in the twenty-first century, 308
    wealth, 42–3, 87, Tables 1 and 2
Melkerhof, the, Vienna, 45, 47
Mémoires de Trévoux, Jesuit periodical, 109
Mendel, Gregor, 307
mendicant Orders, mendicancy, 4, 6, 7, 17, 21, 22, 126, 135, 172, 293
    campaign against begging, 189
    dangers and discomforts of begging, 174
    in France, 107; bishops applaud, 172–3; others attack, 237
    in Germany and Austria, 82; Joseph II on, 195
    in Hungary, 207, 208
    see also Capuchins, Dominicans, Franciscans, Minims, missions, poverty, Recollects and under individual countries
Menzenschwand, 80
Mersch, Jean van der, general, 222
Mesmerism, 233
Metz, 88
Mexico, 157

Michaux, Gérard, historian, 233
Middle Ages, 1–2, 69, 84, 92, 112, 115, 295
Migazzi, count, archbishop of Vienna, 163, 198
Milan
   city of, 139, 187
   duchy of *see* Lombardy
Minims, 107
miracles, 89, 145, 277
missions, 5, 21, 22, 116, 173
   Catholic monks to Britain, 13, 75
   jesuit, 58, 108, 116, 154, 181
   mendicant, 113, 173, 181, 205
   rural, 129
Modena, 36, 130, 139, 188
modernization, 305
Molé, François-René, actor, 98
Molière, 213
monasteries and monasticism, European Catholic
   abandoned by papacy, 267
   advances in eighteenth century, 76, 84, 87, 128–30
   benefits to Catholic rulers, 33
   criticisms of, 30–1, 37, 68, 81, 89, 108, 143, 144, 173, 247
   debts, 174
   decline in eighteenth century, perceived, ch. 7; 14, 143, 144, 147, 170, 171, 172, 173, 174
   definition, 17–18
   discipline, 75, 171, 172, 182–3
   economic impact of, 108, 113, 122
   and education, 190, 292
   exemptions from control by bishops and state, 3, 33, 54, 69, 104, 144, 170, 172, 189, 292
   extra-territorial character
   as hotels, 4, 215, 293
   importance of, 1–7, 9, 291
   independence within Empire, 58–73, 76–82
   infrastructure, 309
   internal disputes, 171
   landownership, 3–4, 5, 8, 41, 82, 87, 121, 267, 292, 305, 309, 310
   loans to farmers, 309
   loans to governments, 33, 293
   numbers of, 2, 5, 29, 37, 291–2, 316; *see also* under individual countries
   obstructing civic improvement, 107, 111, 135
   as patrons of the arts, 4, 293, 294, 295
   proposals to abolish all, 187
   purchasers of their land, 303
   rationale, 1, 5–6, 15–16, 30–2, 235, 292
   rebuilding, 8, 92–6, 105, 172, 181
   reform, chs. 6, 7; 22, 31, 32
   revival in nineteenth century, 311
   seminaries, 191, 194
   suppressions *see under* individual countries and Orders
   in towns, 3, 116, 172, 180
   wealth, 3–4, 5, 12, 29, 41, 55, 62, 82, 84, 86, 87, 88, 116, 130, 173, 213
   see also architecture, Estates, imperial abbeys, libraries, monks, nuns, parish(es), 'regular clerics', wills, under individual countries, Orders and abbeys
monasteries, Orthodox, 18, 180
monks
   and academies, 106
   as bishops, 106
   bled, 51
   British, 168
   choke Italian roads, 126
   complaints against abbots, 174, 182
   conditions of life, 91–4, 172
   demands for reduction, 35, 171, 172, 295–6
   diaries, 74
   duties outside monasteries, 96
   gluttony and bibulousness, 50–1, 81, 92, 172, Ill. 13
   Irish, 168
   jubilee feast, 215
   laxity, 172, 182–3, 235
   as lechers, 238
   neglected by historians, 11–12
   number per house, 87, 94, 110, 113
   numbers, 2, 29, 85, 91, 117, 128–9, 176, 212, 268; in relation to nuns, 3, 121, 129–30, 135; in relation to population, 2, 86, 121, 128, 129–30, 212, 277; in relation to secular clergy ch. 3; 3, 35, 87, 106, 128–30, 174, 186, 212, 295–6, 310
   as parish clergy, 46–7, 79, 157 (Mexico), 172, 191, 214, 227, 297
   as popes, 7

INDEX

rendered less necessary by improvement of seculars, 174
see also abbot(s), mendicant Orders, monasteries, Orders, parish(es), 'regular clerics', vocations
Mons, 226
    abbey of Ste-Waudru, 226
Montauban, riots in, 258
Montecassino *see* Cassino
Monte Oliveto Maggiore, abbey of, 134
Montespan, Mme de, 105
Montesquieu, 126, 144, 237
    De l'esprit des lois (1748), 144, 156
Montgelas, count, Bavarian minister, 286
Montmajour abbey, 89, 302
Monumenta Germaniae Historica, 69
Morellet, 19
mortmain, 29, 33, 159, 160, 171, 186, 189
Moser, C.F. von, 284
Mozart, Wolfgang Amadeus, 52, 81
Müller, Ignaz, provost of Augustinian monastery of St Dorothea, Vienna, 164
Munggenast, Joseph, architect, 48
Munich, 308
Münster, 285
Muratori, Lodovico Antonio (1672–1750), historian and theologian, 36–7, 68, 69, 90, 138, 146, 181, 287
museums, monastic, 56–7, 73, 97, 138
music, 4, 5, 16, 81, 182
    in French houses, 91, 98, 101
    history of, 51, 69–70
    impact of suppressions, 306
    in Italian houses, 134
    Melk establishment, 51–2, 182
Muslims and their rulers, 112–13, 115, 181

Nantes, Edict of (1598); revocation of (1685), 27
Naples
    city of, 3, 34, 134, 135; Carthusian house of S. Martino, 136, Ill. 22; numbers of monks, nuns and clergy, 129; nunnery of Santa Chiara, 135, 292, Plate 8
    kingdom of, 127, 129–30, 157; Charles III's reforms, 157, 274; and Jesuits, 155, 161, 162; foreign policy, 162; French rule, 276; monasteries, suppressed, 276, 289

    see also Charles III, Italy, Two Sicilies, kingdom of the
Napoleon (Bonaparte), French emperor 1804–14, 1815, 8, 9, 45, 117
    concordats with pope, 275
    and Germany, 286–90
    and Italy, 274–5, 277
    and monasteries, monks and nuns, 268, 275–6
    and Portugal, 281
    his regime, 38, 39–41, 265–7, 268
    and Spain, 281
National Assembly, French (1789–91), 8, 257
    abolishes vows, 223
    atmosphere, 245
    early programme supported by monks, 246
    formed, 243
    monks in, 246
    proceedings, 245, 247–9, 250–1, 252, 253–4, 255, 256–7, 258–9, 260
National Guard, French, 244
National Trust, 4
natural law school, 287
Nazi period, 227
Necker, Jacques, French minister, 107, 237, 239, 243, 249
Neerwinden, battle of, 271
Nemours, Dupont de, 250
neo-classicism, 70–1, 95–6, 143, 158, 232
Neresheim, Benedictine abbey of, 65, 68–9, 72–3, 80, 81
Ness, Rupert, abbot of Ottobeuren, 64, 65, 68
Netherlands
    Austrian *see* Belgium
    The *see* Dutch Republic
Newman, cardinal John Henry, 98
Newton, Sir Isaac, 28, 109, 156
Nice, 271
Nicolai, Friedrich, 71–2, 81
Nightingale, Florence, 111
Nîmes, 95, 242, 258
nobility, noble(s), 6–7, 13, 28, 30, 32, 33, 46, 181, 182
    abbots, 104–6, 178
    abolished in France, 261
    bishops, 78, 97
    integration with monasteries in France, 103, 168, 178

387

nobility, noble(s) (*cont.*)
  monasteries for, 60
  monks and nuns from, 74, 78, 98; *see also* family strategies
non-jurors, French, persecution of, 255, 262, 263, 264
Noot, Henri van der, 219, 221, 222
Normalschule, 72
Normandy, 89
Noverre, Jean-Georges, ballet director, 98
novices, 75, 155, 193, 316
nuncio, papal, role in Vienna, 201
nunneries, 74
  aristocratic, 117
  buildings, 21, 92, 94, 132, 135–8
  criticism of, 81, 258
  definition, 18
  enclosure, 14–15, 31, 110, 117, 132, 135
  in France, ch. 3; 255, 258
  Joseph II and, 190, 194, 205
  lands, 6
  laxity, 133
  life in grand, 98–101
  numbers, 2, 82, 86, 129, 225
  in Rome, 276
  in Spain, 117
  and towns, 135
  in Tuscany, 225
  uneven distribution, 297
  for widows, 101
  see also family strategies, monasteries, nuns, suppressions
nuns, 4
  Carmelite, 16, 120
  controlling parishes, 132
  Council of Trent and, 31
  definition, 17–18, 22
  demands for reduction, 35, 36–7, 258
  in France, 265
  and French Revolution, 258, 294
  and Jansenism, 89
  in Italy, 129, Ill. 21
  loss of fervour, 213
  new Orders of, 106, 109, 110, 111, 292; admired by *philosophes*, 238
  numbers, 2, 29, 91; per house, 87; in relation to monks, 3, 86, 180; population, 2, 86, 129, 130

  opportunities, 14–15, 98
  relations with monks, 133–4, 258
  revival in nineteenth century, 269, 273
  in Spain, 117, 126–7, 281
  study of, 14
  vocations, 5–6, 14–15, 98, 99
  see also family strategies, monasteries, nunneries, suppressions
oaths, 187
  to Civil Constitution, 260, 262
  Joseph II's, 216, 217
  to the Republic, 273
  see also vows
obedience, vow of, 5, 17, 22, 147
Oberammergau, 78
'offices', monastic, 19, 22, 172
Old Catholics, 36
old Orders, 2, 4, 18–21, 22–3, 29–30, 31–2
  in Austria and Hungary, compared, 207
  and Catholic Reform, 37, 88
  and Enlightenment, 80
  in France, 86, 88, 113, 114–17, 171, 258; numbers, 91, 171
  in the German lands, ch. 2
  in Italy, 159
  and Jesuits, 147, 165
  lifestyle, 172
  see also Orders, monastic
opera, 134
Oratorians, 109–10, 134, 149, 151, 169–70, 262, 263
oratorio, 134
Orders, monastic, contemplative, 20, 184, 192–3, 208, 226, 343
  definition, 17–18
  disputes between, 36, 37, 171
  educational, 109–10
  founded in eighteenth century, 34
  international character, 5
  military, 5, 21, 115
  number and variety, 2, 17–18, 22
  small, general criticism of, 174
  spontaneous growth, 34
  without full vows, 109, 110
  see also old Orders, and under individual countries and Orders

INDEX

Orléans, Louis, duke of, 97
orphanages, 134, 190
Orpheus and Eurydice, 99
Orthodox, Greek, 181, 199
Orval, Cistercian monastery in Luxembourg, 219, 220
Osma, Fra Joaquin de, 158
Ottobeuren, Benedictine monastery in Franconia, 63–6, 73, 78, Ills. 7, 8
    and peasants, 77
    rebuilding, 64, 68
Oviedo, University of, 156
Oxford, University of, 6, 85, 315
    colleges, 13–14, 17–18
Ozouf, Mona, historian, 12

Paderborn, bishopric of, 76
painting, taught, 98
palace-monastery, Spanish background, 114, 119
    see also Escorial, Klosterneuburg, Mafra
Palacio, Pedro, art historian, 114
Palatinate, the, 59
Pammer, Michael, historian, 183
Pannonhalma, Benedictine abbey in Hungary, 7, 207, 209, 226, Ill. 30
papacy *see* pope(s)
papal state(s), 2, 60, 126–7, 274, 275, 276
    monasteries, monks and nuns, 128, 131
Papini, count, 165
Paraguay, 149
Paris, 3, 6, 9, 86, 89, 96, 97, 98, 105, 317
    archbishop of, 173, 177, 249
    cahiers of, 242
    conservatoire, 306
    and the French Revolution, 244, 245, 263, 264
    monasteries, monks and nuns of, 175, 257, 259, 260–1, 265; Abbaye-aux-Bois, Cistercian nunnery, 89, 98–101; Cordeliers, 107; Jesuit college of Louis-le-Grand, 108–9, 232, 295; Panthéon *see* Ste-Geneviève; St-Germain-des-Prés, abbey of, 14, 86, 89–90, 92, 93, 96, 105, 267; St-Lazare, abbey, 244, 245, 255, 265, Ill. 33; St-Martin-des-Champs, abbey of, 245, 250–1; St-Nicolas-des-Champs, abbey of, 105; St-Sulpice, church of, 93, 95; Ste-Geneviève, abbey of, 70, 86, 92, 94, 95, 143, 158, 265, 294, Plate 1; Sorbonne, the, 11, 146; *see also parlements*
parish(es)
    Council of Trent and, 12
    Counter-Reformation and, 30, 31
    creation of new, by Joseph II, ch. 8
    geography of, 3, 31, 78, 80
    ideal of the *bon curé*, 132, 205
    Jansenists and, 35
    monks working in, chs. 2; 5, 8, 21, 79, 87, 96, 107, 115, 157, 161, 213
    secular clergy in, 4, 12, 114, 131
parlements
    French, 210
    of Paris, 97, 153, 165, 171
Parma, duchy of, 93, 127, 188
partition, of Poland, 284
    policy of in Germany, 284
Passionists, founded in eighteenth century, 129
Pauer, Thomas, abbot of Melk, 182
Paul I, tsar of Russia, 113, 168, 215
peasants, 3, 4, 40, 60, 244, 280
    abbeys' disputes with, 77
    taxation of, 77
Péligry, Christian, 302
pensions for monks, 8, 89, 193, 255, 286
Pergen, count, 190
Pergolesi, G.B., composer, 134
Pérignon, Dom Pierre, 88
Périgord, 88
Pétion, 255
Pez, Bernhard, and Hieronymus, monks of Melk and historians, 52
pharmacies, 134
Philip II, king of Spain 1556–98, 32, 48, 117, 118
Philip III, king of Spain 1598–1621, 114
Philippi, ballet teacher, 98
philosophes, 73, 81, 104, 170, 180, 212
    and *cahiers*, 242
    and Jesuits, 108–9, 153, 167
    and monks, 237–8
    in National Assembly, 250
    and new female Orders, 111, 139
Philosophic History of Monasticism, anonymous (1788), 237
physiocrats, 88
Piarists, educational Order, 128, 191, 207

389

INDEX

picture galleries, monastic, 57–9, 118
Piedmont, 127
piety
   Baroque and Counter-Reformation, 40
   move to a more individual, 91, 143, 149, 181–3
Pilati, Carlantonio, *Di una riforma d'Italia* (1767), 187
Pilgrimage of Grace (1536), 10
pilgrimages and processions, 28–9, 54, 62, 63, 66, 78–9, 88, 96, 131, 183, 278, 282
Pius V, pope 1565–72, 31, 132, 135
Pius VI, pope 1775–99, 45, 167, 199, 260, 261, 274
plainsong, 15
Plateresque style, 119
Plongeron, Bernard, 175, 257
plunder, 277, 281, 289, 290
pocket-money *see* incomes, personal
Pointner, Benno, abbot, on Joseph II's reforms, 199
Poland, 2, 8, 27, 46, 98, 168, 179, 190, 284, 290, 301
   numbers of monasteries, monks and nuns, 316, 322
   see also Galicia
Polling, Bavarian monastery, 74, 167
Pombal, marquis, 150, 152, 153, 158, 163
   as publicist, 151, 154, 186
   enlists papal support, 150, 154, 155
Poor Law, English, 292
poor relief, 81, 172, 179
pope(s)
   authority weakened, 144, 161, 162, 181, 186, 189; enhanced after 1815, 312
   condemns Rousseau's writings, 146
   and France, 155, 170–1, 177, 259, 260, 261, 270; Civil Constitution, 259, 260, 261; concordats, 103, 275
   and Jesuits, 22, 89, 148, 150, 154, 155, 160, 167, 168
   and Joseph II, 190, 199, 201, 228
   and monasteries, 5, 7, 18, 32, 33, 34–5, 36–7, 228, 276
   monk popes, 132
   and nuns, 110
   and sales of church land, 265–7, 268, 285
   and Spain (1753), 118–19, 157
   suppresses Order of St Anthony, 152
popular culture, religion, 12, 28, 78–80, 81
population, 2, 10
   emphasis on, 150, 171
   monasticism held to check growth, 237
   rural, 135
Porée, Father, Jesuit, 109
Port-Royal-des-Champs, nunnery of, 35, 89
Portugal, ch. 4; 2, 8, 127
   architecture, 112, 119
   Baroque, 122
   campaign against Jesuits, 37, 149–53
   compared with Spain, 112, 122, 125
   monastic reform, 122
   numbers of monasteries, monks and nuns, 122, 124, 149, 180, 316
poverty, vow of, 5, 6, 30, 91, 107, 171, 177, 202
Pozzuolo, 134
Pracher, Beda, monk of Neresheim, 72, 73
Prandtauer, Jakob, architect, 48
praying to saints, 31, 182
preaching, 5, 40, 52, 96, 107, 108, 114, 132, 153, 172, 213
Premonstratensian Order of canons, 4, 21, 29, 46, 51, 52, 57–8, 79, 86, 87, 97, 208 (Hungary)
Prémontré abbey, 32, 86, 92, 95, Ill. 14
Prémy, nunnery, sacked 1789, 245
Prévost, abbé, Benedictine and Jesuit, novelist, 91, 295
prior, prioress, 21, 33
prisons, monastic, 99, 189, 191
privilege, ecclesiastical, assailed by aristocracy, 247–9
probabilism, evasive theology associated with Jesuits, 35, 160, 163
profession, 23, 69, 99–101
   age of, 31, 172, 175, 176, 185, 189, 191, 282
'property, spirit of', 172, 177
Protestantism, Protestants, 1, 10–11, 12, 33, 35, 41, 43, 46, 59, 62, 68, 73, 74, 78
   in Austrian Monarchy, 181, 191
   example of Protestant countries, 191, 258; have fewer clergy, 296
   in France, 86, 91; in National Assembly, 250–62
   in Germany, 284, 310
   rulers tolerate Jesuits, 168
   in Spain and Portugal, 113
   in Switzerland, 277, 278
   toleration of, 72–3, 146, 152, 179, 181, 234–5
Provence, 30

provost, head of house, 21
Prunières, Mgr de, bishop of Grasse, 175–6
Prussia, 76, 167, 168, 221, 225
    profits from suppressions, 290
Pufendorf, Samuel, 287
public feeling, opinion, 167, 181, 237, 238, 247
    monks as publicists, 296
    reading public, 155–6
purgatory, 31
'purity of blood', 113
Pyrenees, the, 112

Quarenghi, Giacomo, architect, 138, 294
Quesnel, Jansenist writer, 35

Raber, Ludwig, historian, 195, 197
Racine, Jean, 99
Rákóczi revolt, 205
Rancé, Armand-Jean de, 89, 90, 104
Rapley, Elizabeth, historian, 14–15, 110
Rastatt, Treaty of (1798), 284, 285
Rastignac, Mlle de, 23, 100
Ravenna, 95, 131, 294
Raynal, abbé Guillaume, *philosophe*, 19, 237
Reason and the Supreme Being, cult of, 231, 265
Recollects, 107, 149, 236
Reconquista in Spain and Portugal, 112
recreation for monks and nuns, 54
Redemptorists, 34, 129, 132
Réflexions morales, 35
Reformation, Protestant, 1, 2, 12, 13, 29, 34, 40, 46, 59, 62, 64, 84, 136, 201, 231, 291
    see also Protestants
refractory priests *see* non-jurors
Regensburg, St Emmeram, 76
    rebuilt, 76–9
    St Jakob, 287
Regent of France, 97, 99
'regular clerics', 22
Reichenbach, convention of (1790), 225
Reichsdeputationshauptschluss (1803), 286–90, 309
Reichstag, 59, 286
reichsunmittelbar, abbeys possessing or seeking this
    status, 59, 76–8
    advantages, 76–8
    definition, 59
    status abolished, 286

relics of saints, 40, 89–90, 145
    of archangel Gabriel, 120
    of Holy Blood, 66
    at Einsiedeln, 278
    of Ste-Geneviève, 95, 96
    of Ste-Waudru, 226
religion and modern historians, 9–16
'religio' meaning an Order, 19
'religious' meaning 'regular', 19
Religious Fund
    Maria Theresa's, 194
    Joseph II's, for parishes and pensions, 194, 202, 203, 227
Remiremont, nunnery of, 86, 97, 101
Renaissance, the, 49, 118, 119, 135
rents, Melk's, 43, 44
republics
    French, 95
    Helvetic, 279
    Parthenopean, 275
Restoration, the (1815), 85, 268, 282, 311
Revolution of 1848, 307
Rhine, river, 112
    declared France's 'natural frontier', 188, 271
    left bank under French occupation, 282–3
Rhineland, 59, 271–2
Richardson, Samuel, novelist, 91
Richelieu, cardinal, 32, 88
riding, 56
Rienda, Fra, Andalucian guerrilla leader, 281
road-building, 69
Robert, Hubert, painter, 103–6, Ill. 16
Robespierre, Maximilien, 232, 307
robot (forced labour), 44
Rococo, 39, 58, 95, 143, 158
Roederer, Pierre, 255, 276
Rohan, cardinal de, 232
Romanesque, 40
Romania, 179, 205
Romanticism, 209, 267
Rome, city of, 69, 276
    catacombs, 90
    early basilicas, 95
    numbers of clergy, 129
    St Peter's, 86, 95
    see also Italy, papal state(s), pope(s), Vatican

INDEX

rooms
- heated, 48–50, 52–4, 65
- individual, for monks, 30, 52, 54, 91–4, 172, Ill. 3(a) and (b)

Rosa, Mario, historian, 15
Rottmayr, Johann Michael, 54
Rouen, archbishop of, 171
- St-Ouen, 87

Rousseau, Jean-Jacques, 73, 145, 146, 156, 182, 234, 237, 265
Royal Society of London, 106, 147, 150
Rubens, 294
Ruffo, cardinal, 275
rules, monastic, 17, 18, 31, 76
- Augustinian, 21
- Carthusian, 118
- criticised, 174, 182
- observance of, 3, 35, 50, 72, 174–5, 182
- of St Benedict, 12, 19, 41, 100

Russia, 13, 18, 168, 187, 268, 301

Sacred Heart, veneration of the, 129
Sagan, Premonstratensian monastery in Silesia, 72
St Anthony, regular canons of, suppressed, 152, 161
St Bernard, abbey of, Belgium, 222
St Blasien, Benedictine abbey of, Germany, 69–72, 81, 294
- parish priests, 80
- rebuilding after fire of 1768, 70–1, 73, 95, 158, Ills. 10, 11

St-Denis, royal abbey, 96–7, 264, 265–7
St Florian, Augustinian house, Upper Austria, 57, 203, 307, Plate 2
St Gall, Benedictine abbey, Switzerland, 59, 62, 72–3, 74, 277–80, 294, Plate 7
- and French Revolution, 279, 280

St Pölten, bishopric of, Austria, 195
St-Quentin, renamed, 264
St-Ruf, canons of, ask to be secularised, 174
Ste-Geneviève, Order of (Génovefains), 236
Salamanca, 116
- Dominican monastery of San Esteban, 116
- University of, 116

Salem, Cistercian abbey of, Ill. 40
sale of offices, 105
Salle, Jean-Baptiste de la, 109
Salzburg, prince-archbishopric, 27, 148
- St Peter's Benedictine monastery, 14–15, 65, 81, 284–5, 295
- University of, 65–6, 68

San Manuel, abbot of, 281
Saraiva, cardinal, 125
Sardinia, kingdom of, 127, 136, 148–51, 271
- island of, 127

satirical prints for sale in Vienna, 197, Ill. 28
Savoy, duchy of, 113, 127, 187
Saxony, 59
Schäftlarn abbey, 51
Scheglmann, A.M., historian, 293, 308
Scheldt, river, 211, 214, 217, 271
Schönborn, Lothar Franz von, 46
Schönbrunn palace, near Vienna, 54
Schöntal, Cistercian abbey of, 2, 62, 63, 74
schools, monastic, 47, 56, 66
schoolteachers, 111, 170
Schussenried abbey, library, 73, 79
Schwarzach abbey, 77
science, natural, 129, 138–9, 145, 170
Scolopi *see* Piarists
Scotland, 312
scuole pie, 128
secular congregations, mainly female, 262, 263, 268, 276
secularisation of German ecclesiastical states, 283–6
Seiger, abbot of St Peter's, Ghent, 214, 215
Seine, river, 86
self-flagellation, 107
seminaries
- episcopal, 47, 109, 132, 157
- general (Joseph II's), 194, 195, 201
- monastic, 46, 115

Sens, 242
September massacres (1792), 256, 264
Serbia, 179, 205
serfs, 6, 60, 87
Serro, Giovanni, architect, 60
servants in monasteries, 4, 7, 19, 69–72, 309, 316
Seven Years War, 75, 154, 239
Seville, 116, 117
- kingdom of, 121–2

Seymour, Rev. Hobart, 6
Shaftesbury, 3rd earl of, writer, 28
shooting parties, 58, 63, 307

Sicily, 8, 127, 270, 276, 294
silence, observation of, 89, 90, 182
Silesia, 72, 168
Sisters of Charity, 110–11
    numbers, 111
    of Wisdom, 241, 263, 264
skiing, 84
slaves, 150
Slovakia, 179, 205
Slovenia, 179
Sonderweg of German history, 112
Sonnenfels, baron, cameralist, 167, 202
Soto, Domingo de, physical scientist, 116
Soufflot, Jacques-Germain, architect, 95, 294, Plate 1
Spain, ch. 4; 2, 6–7, 8, 11, 29, 34, 48, 54, 127, 128
    Baroque, 118
    compared with Italy, 126, 127
    compared with Portugal, 112, 122
    and Enlightenment, 156
    and the French Revolution, which a few monks support, 280, but many fight against, 281
    intensity of religion, 119–20, 121
    and Jesuits, in Latin America, 148, 149, 156, 157; expulsion, 159, 160; works for suppression by pope, 162
    liberals and republicans post-1811, 117, 282
    numbers of houses, monks and nuns, 86, 87, 117, 121, 161, 316; special importance thereof, 114–17; suppressions, 281; wealth thereof, 161
    royal power over Church, 103, 118–19
Spanish Succession, the, War of, 136, 211
spas, monastically run, 87, 307
Squillace, minister in Spain, 159
Staatsrat, Austrian, 184, 193, 195
Stadler, Maximilian, Melk musician, 182
Stadl Paura, pilgrimage church, Upper Austria, 78
Stams, Cistercian monastery, Tyrol, 84, 307, Plate 6
state, role of the, chs. 6–10; 22, 31, 32–4, 35, 153
    triumph of the territorial state, 288
Stations of the Cross, devotion, 34
Steingaden, monastery, 79
Steinhausen, pilgrimage church, 78
Stendhal, novelist, *Le rouge et le noir* (1830), 311
Stift, meaning, 18, 55
Strahov, Premonstratensian monastery, Prague, 57, 203, Ill. 29

Strasbourg, 94
Strozzi, Bernardo, Capuchin Genoese painter, 294
Stutzer, Dietmar, historian, 309
Subiaco, Italian abbey, 126, 134, 135, 136, Ill. 24
Sulpicians, 109, 263
Superga, monastery and votive church near Turin, 136, 294, Ill. 25
superstition, Burke on, 313
suppressions of monasteries
    Austrian Monarchy, chs. 6, 8
    Bavaria, differing views on, 308, 309, 310
    Belgium, chs. 8, 10
    France, chs. 6, 7, 9
    French Revolution and, chs. 9, 10
    general, 8–9
    Germany, chs. 2, 6, 10
    importance, discussed: artistic, 302; economic, 305; educational, 305; general, 302; musical, 306
    Italy, chs. 5, 10
    Jesuits, ch. 6
    land transfer resulting, significance of, 303, 304–5
    Portugal, ch. 4
    Spain, chs. 4, 10
    Switzerland, 277–80
    variety of the processes and experiences of suppressions, 299–300, 310
Swabia, 66, 72
Sweden, 57, 60
Swieten, Gerard van, 150, 163
Switzerland, 2, 8, 18, 39, 59, 66, 72, 297
    and French Revolution, 277–80
    numbers of monasteries, 277
symphonies, 51

Taisnières, 245
Talleyrand, bishop of Autun, 251, 261, 285
Tanucci, Bernardo, minister of Naples, 155, 157–8
Távora, marquis of, 151
Tawney, R.H., historian, 10
taxation of monasteries in France, 103–4, 144, 186
Te Deums, 245, 249
Tegernsee abbey, 74
Tepl, Premonstratensian abbey in Bohemia, 57, 307
Teresa of Avila, St, 120

393

Terror, French revolutionary
  anti-Catholic, 264
  anti-Christian, 264–5
Teutonic Knights, 21
theatre(s), monastic, 49, 51, 52, 78, 98, 133
Thérèse philosophe, 238
Third Estate in Estates-General, 241–2, 243
Thirty Years War, 27–8, 40, 57, 64, 74
Thumb, Peter, architect, 73
Tiepolo, painter, 294
Tintoretto, painter, 294
tithe, 4, 41, 43, 44–87, 121, 158, 242, 245, 247–9, 282
Toggenburg, 278
Toledo, 113, 117
toleration, religious, 56, 72–3, 144, 152, 161, 179, 282
Tombs, Robert, historian, 112
Tongerlo, Belgian Premonstratensian abbey, 221–3
Torton, banker, 99
torture, 187
Toulouse, 146, 258–9, 302
Tournai, 75
Tournon, Camille de, 276
towns, monasteries and, 3, 107, 116, 134–5, 172, 173, 175
Townsend, Rev. Joseph, 122
Transylvania, 181, 205
Trappists, 89, 90, 235, 268
Trauttmansdorff, count, abbot of Tepl, 57
Trauttmansdorff, count, minister in Belgium, 223
travel for monks and nuns, 54
Treilhard, M., 254
Tremblaye, dom Guillaume de la, architect, 92, 294
Trent, Council of, 12, 17–18, 22, 29, 30–1, 33, 34, 37, 110, 113, 115, 132, 157, 185, 295
  prince-bishopric of, 187
Trier, 37, 59
  diocese, 220
  elector, 165
  electorate, 283
Trinitarian Order, 21, 194
Trinity College, Dublin, 6
Trives, abbot of, 281
Tron, Andrea, 189
Turgot, baron, 103, 236
Turin, 136

Turks, 40, 41, 43–5, 47, 194, 201, 207, 221, 225
Turnhout, battle of, 222
Tuscany, 127, 134, 161, 189
  conservatories, 225
  Leopold II's rule, 224–5; reaction, 274
  numbers of houses, monks and nuns, 225
Two Sicilies, kingdom of the, 8
  monks in, 128
Tyrol, Estates of, 45
  monks of, 275
  south, 50

Ukraine, 179, 205
Unigenitus, papal bull, 108, 163, 170
Unitarians in Transylvania, 181
Universities
  Austrian, 163–4, 165
  Belgian, 11
  Catholic, 11
  English, 7
  German, 309
  Spanish, 114, 116
Urals, the, 112
Ursulines, 110, 111
usefulness, criterion of, for monasteries, 174, 176, 184, 185–6, 190, 192, 193, 196, 233

Valdeorras, abbot of, 281
Valladolid, 117
Vallombrosa, 134, 268
Valmy, battle of, 271
vandalism, French revolutionary, 208, 264, 265–7, 270, 277, 294, 302
Vatican, 197
Velladics, Márta, historian, 208
Verdelais, Celestine house, 173
Venice, republic of, 127, 274
  and Jesuits, 148
  and music, 134
  numbers of clergy and monasteries, 129, 189, Ill. 27
  particular houses, 133, 275
  reform of monasticism from 1767, 187, 189–90
  suppressions, 189; significance, 189, 292
Verdun, Premonstratensian house at, 52, 91, Ill. 3
Verlooy, J.B.C., advocate of Flemish language, 221
Versailles, palace of, 95, 119, 234, 243, 251

394

INDEX

Victor Amadeus II, king of Sardinia, 136
Vienna, 42, 45, 150
   archbishop, 163
   Baroque rebuilding, 41, 47
   clergy in, 191, 224
   Congress of (1815), 274, 280
   Franciscan houses, 196
   music, 51, 306
   new parishes created by Joseph II, 195
   Oriental Academy, 163
   Pope's visit to, 199
   St Dorothea's monastery, 164
   St Stephen's cathedral, 52
   Schottenstift, 197, 199
   siege of (1683), 40, 41, 205
   Theresianum, 163, 165
   University, 46, 182
Vienne, Jesuit college, 170
Vierzehnheiligen, pilgrimage church, 79, 294, Plate 5
Villefranche-de-Rouergue, Carthusian monastery, Ill. 1
Vilnius, archbishop of, 7
   Virgin Mary, cult of, 29
Visitandines, 110, 111
Vitoria, Francisco de, lawyer, 116
Vivaldi, Antonio, composer, 134
vocations, 5–6, 7, 16–17, 31, 139, 144, 174, 195, 235, 312
Voltaire, 73, 104, 108–9, 123, 144, 182, 187, 265, 287
   writings, 145, 147, 236
Vonck, Jean-François, 221, 222
Vorster, Pankraz, abbot of St Gall, 276
vows, 5, 8, 16, 17, 18, 31, 73, 100, 192
   attacks on lifelong, 171, 185, 187, 237, 254; abolished by France (1790), 231, 252, 255
   Jesuits', 22, 155
   Joseph II sustains, 203
   simple, 22; abolished by France (1792), 231

Wachau, the, 43, 50
Walckiers, vicomte, 223
Waldsassen, Cistercian monastery, 79
Wales, 4
Walpole, Horace, 18–19
wars, impact of revolutionary, ch. 10; 270, 271–2, 288
Weber, Max, 10
Weingarten, monastery, 62, 66, 77, Ill. 12
Weis, Eberhard, historian, 309
Werkmeister, monk of Neresheim, 73, 296
Westminster abbey, 30
Westphalia, Peace of (1648), 27, 30, 41, 60, 283
Wies, Die, 78–9, Ill. 12
wills, Catholics', 28, 144, 148, 183
Winchester, St Cross, 296
Windham, William, 256
wine crop of monasteries, 4, 43, 51, 77, 87, 88, 89, 129
   consumption, 50–1
witches, 62, 66, 161, 181
Witham, Sister Catherine, 150
Whitefield, George, 150
Wolff, Christian, philosopher, 56
woodland owned by monasteries, 4, 311
World Wars of twentieth century, 118, 227
worship, 5, 19, 21, 22, 35, 46, 72, 94, 172, 186
   timetable, 49–54, 200
Wren, Sir Christopher, 52, 54
Württemberg, 290

Young, Arthur, 2, 88
Yuste, Spanish monastery, 115

Zapf, Georg Wilhelm, 72
Zedler, *Lexikon*, 145
Zückert, Hartmut, historian, 77